中国主要旅游客源国与目的地国概况
(双语版)

A Survey of Major Source and Destination
Countries for Chinese Tourist

主　编　潘　玥　崔　竞

副主编　缪真健

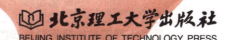

北京理工大学出版社

BEIJING INSTITUTE OF TECHNOLOGY PRESS

内 容 提 要

　　"中国主要旅游客源国与目的地国概况"是旅游管理类专业普遍开设的一门专业必修课程，旨在培养在旅行社、景区、高级酒店等场所从事旅游管理、宾馆服务、翻译导游等涉外旅游相关工作的中高级应用型人才，让学习者较全面地了解世界主要旅游国家，初步掌握接待不同国家、不同阶层境外旅游者的基本原则与方法。全书用中英双语介绍了当今世界 21 个主要旅游国家的地理概览、人文概况及旅游观光等内容。

　　本书选材兼具知识性、趣味性和典型性，顺应了时代的需求，适用性强，可作为高校旅游专业本科生及研究生的双语教材，也可作为英语专业学生及广大英语爱好者的课外读本，还可作为广大旅游从业人员及涉外工作者的参考书。

图书在版编目（CIP）数据

中国主要旅游客源国与目的地国概况：英、汉 / 潘玥，崔竞主编. -- 北京：北京理工大学出版社，2024.10.
ISBN 978-7-5763-4529-2

Ⅰ . F592.6；K91
中国国家版本馆CIP数据核字第2024T45L78号

责任编辑：芈 岚	**文案编辑：**芈 岚
责任校对：刘亚男	**责任印制：**王美丽

出版发行 / 北京理工大学出版社有限责任公司
社　　址 / 北京市丰台区四合庄路 6 号
邮　　编 / 100070
电　　话 / (010) 68914026（教材售后服务热线）
　　　　　　(010) 63726648（课件资源服务热线）
网　　址 / http：//www.bitpress.com.cn

版 印 次 / 2024 年 10 月第 1 版第 1 次印刷
印　　刷 / 河北鑫彩博图印刷有限公司
开　　本 / 787 mm×1092 mm　　1/16
印　　张 / 20.5
字　　数 / 504 千字
定　　价 / 89.00 元

前 言 Preface

党的二十大擘画了全面建成社会主义现代化强国、实现第二个百年奋斗目标的宏伟蓝图。高等教育必须与时俱进，扎根中国、融通中外，为党和国家培养更多高层次国际化人才。面对新形势与新要求，本书编写团队在继承原有校本特色的基础上，深入贯彻落实《习近平新时代中国特色社会主义思想进课程教材指南》文件要求和党的二十大精神，进一步提升教材的思想性、科学性与时代性，全方位贯彻课程素养理念，助推中国式教育现代化，从选题策划到成稿出版，从主题选择到内容编排，均实现了积极的创新和突破。本书具有以下特点。

一、突出"专业＋外语""一精多会""一专多能"复合型人才培养模式

本书采用中英双语编写，符合我国国际旅游业发展的需要，也符合教育部双语教材建设的要求和教学过程的实际需要，学习者在开阔视野、丰富专业知识的同时，还可以提高英语阅读水平。编写双语教材的初衷是需顺应信息化时代经济一体化、金融全球化的趋势，语言文化、旅游、商务等领域的国际合作是大势所趋，培养具有国际视野的复合型专业人才符合当前的社会需求。站在新时代的起点上，编写双语教材，充分发挥教材在育人、育才中的战略性、基础性作用，是培养全面发展的社会主义建设者和接班人的基础和支撑。双语教学在我国起步较晚，目前还存在诸多制约因素。双语教学能否顺利开展，合适的双语教材作为师生开展双语教学的重要载体和媒介尤为关键。购买国外原版教材不仅价格高，给学生造成经济压力，而且在体例、内容上不符合我国教学实际，针对性不强。鉴于此，编者在承担校级双语示范教学基地建设的同时，积极开展双语教材的编写，并在教学实践中对本书不断加以丰富、完善，几经修订后现正式出版，以满足不同类型高校旅游专业开展双语教学的迫切需要。本书共分为六章，体系完整，涵盖人类文化的六大主要方面，内容丰富、实用，可读性强。全书用中英双语介绍了当今世界 21 个主要旅游国家的地理概览、人文概况及旅游观光等内容。全书中英文结合，图文并茂、形式新颖：正文主要是中文，通俗易懂；英文阅读材料中用中文对重要的人名、地名、专业术语等进行注解，免除读者查阅词典的不便，提高阅读效率。通过轻松阅读，读者不仅可以扩充英语词汇量、提高英语阅读水平，同时也可以开阔眼界、丰富专业知识，巩固对中国旅游客源国和目的地国的历史背景、文化知识的掌握，培养用英语介绍相关文化知识的能力。本书选材兼具知识性、趣味性和典型性，顺应时代的需求，适用性强，可作为高校旅游专业本科学生及研究生的双语教材，也可作为英语专业学生及广大英语爱好者的课外读本，还可作为广大旅游从业人员及涉外工作者的参考书。

二、融合课程素养要求，落实立德树人根本任务，促进世界和平与发展，推动构建人类命运共同体

本书全方位、多维度融入党的二十大精神与社会主义核心价值观等关键议题，将价值塑造有机融于话题素材、练习设计、思辨论点、单元任务之中，育人润物无声，能够切实帮助学习者提高国际传播能力，帮助他们讲好中国故事，传播好中国声音，为践行立德树人和服务人才强国战略的使命提供全方位、立体化的解决方案，有效助力广大高校在"新文科"建设、复合型国际人才培养、课程素养建设、外语教学改革等方面开展创新实践，打造具有时代特色的精品课程。2017年1月18日，习近平主席在联合国日内瓦总部发表了题为《共同构建人类命运共同体》的主旨演讲，强调"中国愿同广大成员国、国际组织和机构一道，共同推进构建人类命运共同体的伟大进程"。作为推动世界和平与发展的中国方案，构建人类命运共同体既蕴含着对话协商、共建共享等中国传统智慧，又呈现出和平、发展、合作、共赢等全人类的共同价值观。作为在互联网陪伴下成长起来的一代，当代学生思想多元且开放，能包容不同文化，对不同文化间的交流和互鉴持积极态度。本书在介绍中国主要客源国和目的地国的概况时，增加了拓展阅读素材、案例分析、小组讨论等教学环节，引导学生积极对比中西文化差别，有机融入中国和平合作、开放包容、互利共赢的丝路精神，传递中国追求和平发展、寻求与各国合作共赢、致力于推动构建人类命运共同体的愿景。例如，在了解人类命运共同体的基础之上，本书引入孔子的名言"君子和而不同，小人同而不和"，进一步引导学生掌握应如何待人接物、为人处世；上升到国家层面，则要引导学生进一步明确，国家更应该"和而不同，求同存异"，这才是谋求发展、和平共处的原则，是习近平总书记一直强调的重点，更是中国的外交态度。在这个过程中，学生可以了解、学习并运用我国古代智慧解决当代问题，以此树立文化自信。这一环节也是再一次为学生赋能，引导学生正确理解各种冲突与合作的深层次原因，提高学生的跨文化交际能力，理解不同文化之间的差异，防止陷入偏见和误解，增强文化自信，并且让学生全面了解中国在推动构建人类命运共同体方面做出的巨大努力和取得的重大成就。

三、展现多元文化，促进文明互鉴，推动绿色发展，促进人与自然和谐共生

在纪念孔子诞辰2 565周年的国际学术研讨会上，国家主席习近平指出："不同国家、民族的思想文化各有千秋，只有姹紫嫣红之别，而无高低优劣之分。每个国家、每个民族不分强弱、不分大小，其思想文化都应该得到承认和尊重。"在全球化背景下，各国之间的联系与互动日益紧密。通过对比其他国家的案例与中国自身的实践，我们可以发现许多共同点和差异点，从而引出相关的讨论话题。例如，在介绍国际旅游景点时，适时引入当前的热点话题，如生态环保、文化保护等，展示这些话题如何影响旅游业及其他相关领域的发展。当我们探讨其他国家在生态保护方面的成功案例时，可以与中国自身的绿色发展理念相比较；当我们研究其他国家的文化遗产保护措施时，可以联想到中国的传统文化保护工作。同样，扶贫减贫、全民运动、抗击疫情等方面的经验也可以通过类似的方式引入，帮助学生更好地理解这些主题在中国的具体实践。因此，我们可以自然而然地引出中国传统文化、扶贫减贫、全民运动、抗击疫情、生态环保以及人类命运共同体这六大时代热点话题，引导学生深入思考并理解我国绿色发展理念和生态文明建设的内涵及其取得的一系列显著成就。

四、创新教材形态，学用一体，引领数智化变革

本书提供多种智能化教学及自主学习工具，打通多类型教学资源，打造师生协同评价体系，将数字技术融入教学全过程，助力高等教育教学数智化变革。编者对教材内容、教学平台和数字资源进行了一体化设计，依托超星泛雅学习通平台，通过单元导学、素养讲解微课、拓展阅读、习题库等丰富的教学资源，以及在线交互式课件、智能评阅引擎等全新升级的教学工具，实现纸质教材和数字课程的有机融合，构建线上线下融通的混合式教学流程，驱动教学提质增效。

本书在编写过程中参考了一些出版物和网站资料，出处列于文末，编者在此向原作者的支持和理解表示感谢。

由于编者水平有限，书中难免存在疏漏和不尽如人意之处，恳请广大读者不吝赐教。

编　者

目 录 Contents

国际旅游业的发展概况及中国出入境客源市场

The Development of International Tourist Industry and China's Inbound and Outbound Tourist Market

学习目标

1. 了解国际旅游业发展的现状和基本趋势。

Understand the current status and basic trends of the development of the international tourist industry.

2. 了解我国出入境旅游市场的现状和未来的发展趋势。

Understand the current status and future development trends of China's inbound and outbound tourist market.

3. 掌握世界主要旅游区的划分及概况。

Master the division and overview of the world's major tourist region.

4. 掌握我国主要客源国与目的地国概况。

Master the overview of China's major source and destination countries.

一、国际旅游业的发展概况
The General Introduction to the International Tourist Industry Development

第二次世界大战以后，西方发达国家经历了一个持续、稳定的发展和增长时期。国际环境的相对稳定、科技的高速发展、人们生活和消费观念的改变、交通运输业的发达、人们收入的大幅提高、带薪休假的产生和兴起等因素，使人们对旅游的需求日益高涨，旅游业由此得到了蓬勃发展，在世界范围内形成了社会化的大众旅游热潮，这种大规模群众性旅游活动是世界旅游业进入现代阶段的重要标志。到 21 世纪初，国际旅游已成为世界上最重要

绪论
（英文版）

的经济活动之一，旅游业已成为世界上最大的产业，旅游业的发展不仅给许多国家提供了大量的就业机会，还给它们带来了丰厚的外汇收入。联合国世界旅游组织（UNWTO）数据显示（图 0-1），国际跨境旅游者的数量在 2010—2019 年间总体上呈现不断增长的趋势，2019 年全球旅游总人次（包括国内旅游人次和入境旅游人次）为 123.1 亿；受新冠疫情影响，2020 年是旅游业有记录以来业务最糟糕的一年，与 2019 年相比，国际入境人数下降了 73%，全球旅游人次减少了 4.5 亿，国际旅游收入减少了 9 100 亿美元。2021 年全球旅游人数同比增长 4%，2022 年疫苗接种率上升，再加上由于加强跨境协调和协议而放宽了旅行限制，被压抑的需求得到释放，国际旅游业开始升温并反弹。

现代国际旅游市场在不断向纵深发展，世界六大区域的旅游业呈现发展不平衡的态势；进入 21 世纪，六大旅游区域差异化更加明显，已呈现欧洲、亚太和美洲旅游区三足鼎立的格局。

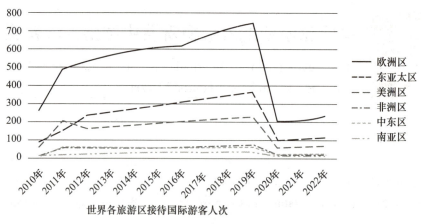

世界各旅游区接待国际游客人次

图 0-1　2010—2022 年国际跨境旅游总人次

1. 欧洲旅游市场 European Tourist Market

欧洲是人类文明的发祥地之一，希腊、罗马文明和基督教文化源远流长，古典时代和中世纪遗留下来的众多古迹都是著名的旅游景点。欧洲现有 45 个国家和地区，在地理上习惯将之分为南欧、北欧、西欧、中欧和东欧。欧洲占世界陆地总面积的 6.8%，人口约为 7.3 亿，约占世界总人口的 11%。居民中大部分属于白种人，语言属于印欧、乌拉尔等五个语系，多信奉天主教、基督教新教和东正教等。欧洲是近代旅游业的发源地，也是世界上国际旅游业最发达的地区。自 20 世纪 50 年代以来，无论是国际旅游接待人次，还是国际旅游收入，欧洲历来居世界各大洲之首。欧洲是世界上最受欢迎的国际旅游目的地，也是世界上最重要的国际旅游客源地。2017 年，欧洲共接待了 6.73 亿入境游客，同比增长 8.6%。2018 年，共接待了 7.10 亿入境游客，同比增长 5.5%。2021—2022 年，受区域内强劲需求和越来越多国家取消旅行限制的推动，欧洲旅游业复苏的进程领先全球。

2. 美洲旅游市场 American Tourist Market

美洲包括 35 个独立国家和十几个地区，以巴拿马运河为界分为北美、南美两大洲。美洲陆地面积约占世界陆地总面积的 28%，人口约为 9.1 亿，约占世界总人口的 13.6%。居民多数为英、法等国移民的后裔，还有印第安人、黑人和混血人种。北美洲主要的通用语言为英语和法语，南美洲巴西的官方语言为葡萄牙语，法属圭亚那为法语，圭亚那为英语，苏里南为荷兰语，其他国家均使用西班牙语。印第安人使用印第安语。居民主要信奉天主教和基督教新教。美洲国际旅游业开始较早，在 20 世纪 80 年代发展尤为迅速。目前，美洲国际旅游业发展水平仅次于欧洲地区和亚洲地区。美洲是世界重要旅游区之一，接待国际游客数量占世界总份额的 20% 以上，国际旅游收入占世界总份额的 30% 左右。美洲的旅游业发展极不平衡，主要集中在北美洲的美国、加拿大和墨西哥等少数几个国家。其中美国是美洲，乃至世界头号旅游大国。虽然之前美洲旅游业受到世界经济衰退、"9·11"事件和反恐战争等因素的影响，发展速度减缓，但 2010 年后，美洲地区的旅游业摆脱了低迷状态，国际入境旅游人数快速增长。漫长的海岸线和广袤的土地，哥伦布探险时期留下的文化遗迹和殖民时期的建筑，吸引着无数的游客。

3. 东亚及太平洋旅游市场 The East Asia and Pacific Tourist Market

东亚及太平洋旅游区（以下简称"东亚太旅游区"）包括东亚（中国、朝鲜、韩国、蒙古国、日本）、东南亚（泰国、马来西亚、新加坡、印度尼西亚、菲律宾、文莱、东帝汶、越南、老挝、柬埔寨、缅甸）和大洋洲（澳大利亚、新西兰以及其他南太平洋岛国和地区）。亚洲约占世界陆地总面积的30%，为世界第一大洲。人口约为40.3亿，约占世界总人口的60.5%。亚洲的种族、民族构成非常复杂，黄种人（又称蒙古利亚人种）为主体种族，占全洲人口的60%以上。其余为白种人、棕色人种及黑人的混合类型。全洲大小民族、种族共有约1 000个，约占世界民族、种族总数的一半。其中，有十几亿人口的汉族，也有人数仅几百的民族或部族。根据语言的近似程度，亚洲的居民分属汉藏语系、南亚语系、阿尔泰语系、马来－波利尼西亚语系、达罗毗荼语系、闪米特－含米特语系、印欧语系等9个语系。亚洲是佛教、伊斯兰教和基督教三大宗教的发源地。大洋洲共有14个独立国家，其他十几个地区为美、英、法等国的属地。大洋洲约占世界陆地总面积的6%，是世界上陆地面积最小的洲。居民中欧洲移民的后裔占70%以上，当地土著居民约占20%，大多数居民通用英语并信奉天主教。随着世界经济贸易的重心向亚太地区转移，加上亚太地区各国政府的重视，地区旅游业发展迅猛，东亚太地区在国际旅游业中的地位越来越重要，已跃居世界第二位。

4. 非洲旅游市场 African Tourist Market

非洲约占世界陆地总面积的20%，人口约为14亿，约占世界总人口的15%。非洲旅游区包括除埃及外的非洲所有国家，居民主要为黑人（占本洲总人口的三分之二），其余为黄种人和白种人。非洲是一个语言种类繁多的大陆，总数在800种以上，占世界语言总数的三分之一左右。它还是世界上民族文化最复杂、最多样化的地区之一。非洲国家都属于发展中国家，大多数国家经济比较落后，加上该地区内民族纷争不断、政局不稳定、自然灾害频繁、传染病流行、社会经济及文化不发达等因素的影响，非洲的旅游业起步较晚。非洲的旅游业主要接待国际旅游者，最大的客源市场是欧洲。非洲旅游业的发展前景十分广阔，奇特风光游、民族风情游、沙漠探险游、珍稀动植物考察游、考古游和海上游都具有较大的吸引力。非洲的现代国际旅游业兴起于20世纪60年代。20世纪70年代后，非洲各国采取了行之有效的措施开发沙漠、雨林及各种特殊的生物资源，总体来看，目前赴非的国际游客数量正呈快速增长之势。旅游业发展较快的国家有摩洛哥、突尼斯、南非等，使非洲的旅游业呈现南强北弱的局面。

5. 南亚旅游市场 South Asia Tourist Market

南亚指亚洲南部地区，介于东南亚与西亚之间，共有7个国家，其中尼泊尔、不丹为内陆国，印度、巴基斯坦、孟加拉国为临海国，斯里兰卡、马尔代夫为岛国。南亚旅游区拥有世界上最高的山脉喜马拉雅山脉，世界上最著名的大平原之一印度大平原，世界上最平坦的高原德干高原。南亚地区人口超过14亿。18世纪后该地区的大多数国家相继沦为西方的殖民地或半殖民地，第二次世界大战后先后取得了独立，民族经济得到不同程度的发展。南亚既是世界四大文明发源地之一，又是佛教、印度教等宗教的发源地。早在公元前3000年左右，恒河流域便出现过一些繁华的城市，而后又相继出现了孔雀王朝、笈多王朝、德里苏丹国和莫卧儿王朝。南亚诸国中，印度、斯里兰卡、尼泊尔都是度假旅行的胜地。印度也是世界三大宗教之一佛教的发源地，旅游资源丰富，是我国居民境外游的首选；斯里兰卡是一个具有悠久文明历史、奇特民俗风情、珍奇动植物和珍贵宝石的热带岛国；位于世界屋脊的尼泊尔是一个仅有3 000万人口的山地之国，独特的地理环境、宜人的气候、神秘的人文气息吸引了来自世界各地的游客。

6. 中东旅游市场 The Middle East Tourist Market

中东是近代西方国家向东方扩张时使用的地理概念，广义的中东泛指欧、亚、非三洲连接的地区，包括伊朗、巴勒斯坦、以色列、叙利亚、伊拉克、约旦、黎巴嫩、也门、沙特阿拉伯、阿拉伯联合酋长国、阿曼、科威特、卡塔尔、巴林、土耳其、塞浦路斯和埃及等国家。中东地区除以色列为犹太人、信奉犹太教，其余国家多为阿拉伯人，信奉伊斯兰教。中东是世界三大宗教——基督教、伊斯兰教和犹太教的发源地，也是穆斯林的圣地。埃及是四大文明古国之一，有世界七大奇观之一的金字塔；土耳其地跨欧亚两洲，扼黑海海峡之咽喉，历史上曾是东罗马帝国和奥斯曼帝国的本土，有丰富、独特的民俗风情和宗教文化古迹。中东地区除旅游业较为发达的土耳其和埃及，其他区域因长期遭受战争和恐怖活动制约，旅游业发展缓慢，是世界国际旅游业发展最不稳定的地区，但近五年来中东接待入境旅游人数保持持续增长的态势。

二、国际旅游业的基本特点 Basic Characteristics of the International Tourist Industry

旅游业对气象灾害、地质灾害、传染性疾病等具有很强的敏感性，同时也易受金融危机、飞机失事、政治动乱等突发事件的影响，抗冲击能力比较弱，受影响过程较长。世界范围内的入境过夜游客数量变化表现出以下特点。

1. 世界各旅游区发展差异显著 Significant Differences in the Development of Tourist Regions in the World

2022 年 3 月 2 日，世界旅游城市联合会（WTCF）与中国社会科学院旅游研究中心在线发布《世界旅游经济趋势报告（2022）》（以下简称《趋势报告》）。报告指出，自 2020 年以来新冠病毒持续变异，全球疫情高位流行。从阿尔法、贝塔、伽马、德尔塔到扩散迅速的奥密克戎，新冠病毒不断变种，疫情不断反复，全球防疫形势十分严峻。到报告发布时为止，全球新冠疫情尚未结束，疫情防控形势依然相当紧迫，全球经济虽处于复苏之中，但经济增长前景仍存在较大不确定性，各国经济复苏步伐也日趋分化。鉴于国际旅行正常化进程缓慢，依赖旅游业的经济体短期增长前景仍然低迷。新冠疫情暴发之前的若干年时间里，全球旅游总体形成欧洲、美洲和亚太地区"三足鼎立"的格局，其中，欧洲和美洲占比略有下降，而亚太地区占比持续上升。自 2020 年以来，尽管全球旅游依然保持"三足鼎立"的态势，但由于不同区域受新冠疫情影响程度有所差别，旅游复苏进程也各不相同，在此背景下，美洲和欧洲在全球占比有所上升，亚太占比有所下降。以旅游总收入相当于 GDP 的比例作为指标来衡量旅游的经济贡献，2021 年五大区域旅游的经济贡献从高到低依次为欧洲、美洲、亚太、中东和非洲。与 2019 年相比，2022 年美洲和欧洲旅游总收入占全球旅游总收入的比重都有所上升，而亚太、中东地区旅游总收入占比有所下降。2022 年，美洲旅游总收入占比 32%，较 2019 年提高 2 个百分点；欧洲旅游总收入占比 31%，较 2019 年提高 1 个百分点；亚太地区旅游总收入占比 33%，较 2019 年下降 2 个百分点；非洲旅游总收入未发生变化；中东旅游总收入占比下降 1 个百分点。从世界六大旅游区接待国际游客的数据可以看到，欧洲旅游区接待国际游客的数量远远高于其他地区，国际旅游业发展极不平衡。亚太、欧洲和美洲三大地区旅游总收入合计占比超过 95%，非洲地区和中东地区合计份额不超过 5%。但从旅游人数和旅游收入对比来看，亚太地区游客的人均旅游消费水平整体较低，远远低于欧洲地区人均旅游消费水平。

2. 全球旅游经济高度集中于 T20 国家 The Global Tourist Economy is Highly Concentrated in Tourist 20 Countries

WTCF 将旅游总收入排名前 20 位的国家和地区称为 T20（Tourist 20 Countries）。总体来看，全球旅游经济 80% 集中于 T20 国家，国内游是 T20 国家的旅游经济支柱（表 0-1），旅游

表 0-1　2012—2022 年旅游总收入排名全球前 20 的国家（T20）

| 排名 | 年份 | | | | | | | | | | |
---	2012	2013	2014	2015	2016	2017	2018	2019	2020	2021	2022
1	美国	美国	美国	美国	美国	美国	美国	美国	美国	美国	美国
2	中国	中国	中国	中国	中国	中国	中国	中国	中国	中国	中国
3	德国	德国	德国	德国	德国	德国	德国	德国	德国	德国	德国
4	日本	英国	英国	英国	英国	日本	日本	日本	法国	墨西哥	意大利
5	英国	日本	日本	日本	日本	英国	英国	英国	英国	意大利	墨西哥
6	法国	法国	法国	印度	印度	印度	印度	印度	意大利	日本	日本
7	意大利	意大利	意大利	法国	法国	法国	法国	法国	墨西哥	英国	英国
8	印度	印度	印度	意大利	意大利	意大利	意大利	意大利	印度	法国	法国
9	墨西哥	墨西哥	墨西哥	墨西哥	墨西哥	墨西哥	墨西哥	墨西哥	日本	印度	印度
10	巴西	西班牙	巴西	西班牙	西班牙	西班牙	西班牙	西班牙	澳大利亚	澳大利亚	西班牙
11	西班牙	巴西	西班牙	巴西	巴西	巴西	巴西	巴西	巴西	西班牙	澳大利亚
12	澳大利亚	澳大利亚	澳大利亚	澳大利亚	澳大利亚	澳大利亚	澳大利亚	澳大利亚	西班牙	巴西	巴西
13	加拿大	加拿大	加拿大	加拿大	加拿大	加拿大	加拿大	加拿大	加拿大	加拿大	加拿大
14	俄罗斯	俄罗斯	俄罗斯	韩国	韩国	泰国	泰国	泰国	奥地利	奥地利	土耳其
15	土耳其	土耳其	韩国	土耳其	土耳其	韩国	韩国	韩国	韩国	土耳其	菲律宾
16	韩国	韩国	土耳其	泰国	菲律宾	土耳其	土耳其	菲律宾	泰国	菲律宾	奥地利
17	泰国	泰国	奥地利	俄罗斯	俄罗斯	菲律宾	菲律宾	土耳其	菲律宾	韩国	俄罗斯
18	瑞士	瑞士	瑞士	瑞士	瑞士	瑞士	俄罗斯	俄罗斯	瑞士	俄罗斯	韩国
19	阿根廷	瑞典	瑞典	奥地利	奥地利	俄罗斯	瑞士	瑞士	土耳其	瑞士	瑞士
20	瑞典	阿根廷	马来西亚	菲律宾		奥地利	奥地利	奥地利	瑞士	泰国	泰国

稳步促进 T20 国家的经济发展。从表 0-1 中可以看出，2012 年以来，美国、中国、德国、日本、英国的旅游总收入一直占据排行榜的前五名。前三名稳定不变，第四、第五名交替轮换。2021 年 T20 国家旅游总收入占全球旅游总收入的比重为 80.2%，比 2020 年提高 11.8 个百分点，比 2019 年提高 1.4 个百分点。2022 年 T20 国家旅游总收入占全球旅游总收入的比重继续抬升至 82.0%。

分析 T20 国家的旅游发展趋势，可将其归为如下四种类型：一是以美国为代表的"低速稳增型"；二是以中国、印度、菲律宾为代表的"减速缓增型"；三是以德国、日本、英国、意大利、巴西等为代表的"正负增长交替型"；四是以法国、墨西哥、澳大利亚、西班牙、加拿大、韩国、土耳其、俄罗斯等为代表的"收入波动型"。

3. 城市面临疫情防控和旅游发展的双重挑战 The City Faces Dual Challenges of Epidemic Prevention and Control and Tourist Development

《趋势报告》指出，2022 年全球旅游业的结构性复苏产生变局，以新兴经济体、亚太板块驱动旅游经济增长的格局已被打破，旅游业更加依赖城市。城市是重要的旅游客源地、集散地和目的地，全球约 80% 的旅游活动通过旅游城市来实现。城市提供了多样化的旅游产品，也需要借助旅游来实现其部分文化、社会和经济目标。快速推进的全球城市化进程、日益多元的城市文化、更加快捷且成本更低的出行方式、更大规模的人口流动等因素促使城市成为热门旅游目的地。新冠疫情暴发以来，城市在全球疫情防控和旅游复苏中发挥着不可替代的重要作用。妥善处理疫情防控和旅游发展之间的关系，成为城市治理能力和治理水平的重要体现。疫情传播的阻断与城市人口的生活方式及城市的运作方式密切相关。城市地区人口密度大且内外部交通便利，使得疫情传播速度快且感染风险大，可以说，城市是疫情防控的第一线。此外，城市对周边地区旅游具有辐射带动作用，旅游城市的疫情防控和旅游复苏情况对周边非城市区域也有直接影响。旅游者（特别是国际旅游者）流动所依赖的机场和车站一般位于城市，其疫情防控情况也直接影响周边地区和外界的连通性。《世界旅游城市发展报告（2021）》（以下简称《发展报告》）显示，2021 年世界旅游产业在全球经济下滑和疫情的双重影响下，恢复比较艰难。在报告所选择的 100 个样本城市中，79 个国际城市接待了入境旅游总人次的 1/3 以上，贡献了入境旅游总收入的 1/5 以上。这些城市主要来自亚太、美洲和欧洲这三个地区，可见，城市格局与旅游经济发展的总体格局高度一致。2021 年 WTCF 发布的排行榜显示，2021 年全球游客人数比 2020 年增加了 4%，但是仅达到 2019 年的 72%。从旅游消费上看，2021 年旅游消费总额达 1.9 万亿美元，比 2020 年增加了 3 000 亿美元，但是仅为疫情前约一半的水平。另外，旅游业的工作岗位仍然没有恢复。疫情前全球旅游业的从业人数达 3.3 亿，截至 2021 年还有 1.2 亿人的工作岗位没有完全恢复，仍在等待之中。值得注意的是，各国国内旅游开始恢复，国际旅游回升比较缓慢。从世界旅游城市发展综合排名及年度变化来看（表 0-2），前 20 名城市的排名变动比较明显。2021 年，巴黎综合排名第一，伦敦排名第二，洛杉矶排名第三，北京排名第七，上海排名第十二。

表 0-2　世界旅游城市发展综合排名及年度变化

城市	2021 年	2020 年	2019 年
巴黎	1	4	2
伦敦	2	3	1
洛杉矶	3	15	21

续表

城市	2021 年	2020 年	2019 年
旧金山	4	25	22
纽约	5	1	3
迈阿密	6	21	30
北京	7	5	5
悉尼	8	19	7
拉斯维加斯	9	42	17
芝加哥	10	24	32
台北	11	21	23
上海	12	8	13
墨尔本	13	17	20
首尔	14	9	6

《发展报告》显示，区域发展呈现新变化，不同类型的城市排位变化非常明显，这是 2021 年世界旅游城市发展的最突出特点之一。疫情前排名靠前的城市，特别是前 10 名的城市基本都是全球的旅游枢纽城市。2021 年的报告显示，除了 12 个洲际中心城市都进入了前 20 名，像拉斯维加斯、夏威夷、布里斯班这些特色城市，都从原来的 30 名至 40 名，进入了前 20 名。2021 年以来，在主要经济体持续宽松的财政货币政策以及全球疫苗生产和接种加速等因素的共同促进下，全球经济活动进一步活跃，增长前景明显改善：一是全球经济复苏动力增强；二是全球货物贸易增长势头更加强劲；三是国际投资回暖较为温和。世界旅游经济也在稳步恢复，城市在疫情背景下所进行的有益探索也推动了旅游业在城市的复苏发展和迭代更新，新冠疫情成为旅游城市思考未来的一个重要契机，促使城市反思和解决痼疾，也加速了产业数字化进程，还提高了决策者和公众对旅游可持续发展重要性的认识。

三、国际旅游业发展的基本趋势 General Trends in the Development of the International Tourist Industry

国际旅游业在第二次世界大战之后得到了快速的发展。进入 21 世纪之后，国际旅游业成为世界上最大的产业，整体上处于积极活跃的状态，旅游者数量达到空前的规模，尽管各个国家的政治、经济情况以及旅游业的发展模式不同，但就整个国际旅游业而言，呈现出以下的发展趋势。

1. 旅游业依然占据世界最大产业的地位 The Tourist Industry Continues to Maintain Its Position as the Largest Industry in the World

旅游业是世界上最大的新兴产业，每年国际旅游业的交易额已超过 3 000 亿美元。旅游业已取代石油工业、汽车工业，成为世界上最大的创汇产业。世界旅游业理事会 WTTC 指出，旅游业是促进经济发展的主要动力，且已成为世界上最大的就业部门，共产生 1.27 亿个工作岗位，约占世界劳动力总数的 6.7%；旅游业是创造高附加值的产业，其增值额已达到 14 490 亿美元；旅游业是各国财政中主要的纳税产业之一，全世界的旅游企业及从业人员的纳税总额高达 3 030 亿美元。旅游业对世界经济的贡献不仅是它巨大的产值和提供的就业岗位，它同时还带动了其他产业的发展，带来一系列的经济效益。

根据 WTCF 与中国社会科学院旅游研究中心共同发布的《趋势报告》，2019—2021 年全球旅游总人次变化如图 0-2 所示。2019 年，全球旅游总人次（包括国内旅游人次和国际旅游人次）为 123.1 亿，较 2018 年增长 4.6%；全球旅游总收入（包括国内旅游收入和国际旅游收入）为 5.8 万亿美元，相当于全球 GDP 的 6.7%。2021 年全球旅游总人次（含国内旅游人次和国际旅游人次，下同）和全球旅游总收入（含国内旅游收入和国际旅游收入，下同）恢复至疫情前的不足 60%。具体而言，2021 年全球旅游总人次和总收入分别恢复至 2019 年的 53.7% 和 55.9%。其中，全球旅游总人次达到 66.0 亿，全球旅游总收入达到 3.3 万亿美元。新冠疫情以来，OTA（在线旅游企业）行业受到很大冲击。2021 年，在疫情防控常态化背景下，越来越多的国家和地区尝试恢复跨境旅行，OTA 行业整体向好且复苏逐步提速。从 Booking、Expedia、携程、同程、艺龙等 OTA 行业代表的财报数据来看，OTA 行业复苏情况存在差异，但总体来看，2021 年营业收入的下滑幅度有所收窄。Booking 集团财报显示，2021 年第三季度总预订额为 237 亿美元，同比增长 77%；住宿预订量为 1.83 亿间，比 2020 年同期增长了 44%。

旅游减贫：延伸产业链带动经济发展

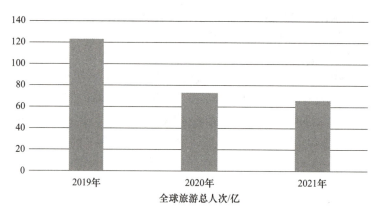

图 0-2　2019—2021 年全球旅游总人次变化

2. 国际旅游区域的重心向东转移的速度加快 The Center of the International Tourist Region Is Shifted to the East，and the Speed Is Accelerating

《趋势报告》指出，产业集中度提升，旅游经济向公共医疗水平高的国家集中，旅游市场向国内和周边集中。在 20 世纪 80 年代以前，欧洲和北美是现代国际旅游业的两大传统市场，几乎垄断了国际旅游市场，接待人数和收入都占世界总数的 90% 左右。20 世纪 80 年代后，亚洲、非洲、拉丁美洲和大洋洲等地区一批新兴旅游市场的崛起，使国际旅游业在世界各个地区的市场份额出现了新的分配组合。到了 21 世纪，亚太地区在国际旅游市场中的份额进一步扩大，欧洲和北美地区在国际旅游市场上的份额进一步缩小，旅游重心由传统市场向新兴市场转移的速度加快。随着发展中国家和地区经济的持续增长和繁荣，这些国家和地区的居民去邻国度假必定会增加，区域性国际旅游将得到极大发展。特别是随着全球经济重心的相应东移，亚太地区逐渐成为国际旅游业的热点区域。近年来，随着国际旅游业重心东移，中国经验、中国市场和中国作用在世界旅游产业格局中的地位更加凸显。在全球疫情防控不同步的背景下，亚太尤其是亚洲地区，特别是中国市场的总体恢复状况较好，成为关注的重点。

3. 国际旅游消费需求向多元化方向发展 International Tourist Consumer Demand Is Developing in A Diversified Direction

国际上传统的旅游方式分为四种，即娱乐型、观光型、疗养型和商务型，大多数旅游活动是各种方式兼而有之。一个国家或地区的旅游方式是由其资源条件、地理位置、市场条件等多方面因素决定的，不同的旅游方式有不同的产品、价格、市场对策等，同时旅游者也有不同的消费要求和消费特点。随着旅游方式向个性化、多样化、自由化、多元化方向发展，观光旅游、度假旅游和商务旅游等已不能满足旅游者的需求，各种内容丰富、新颖、独特的旅游方式和旅游项目应运而生。目前，国际旅游消费需求的基本态势是：从人们出游的组织方式来看，在追求个性化的浪潮下，散客旅游特别是家庭旅游成为全球流行趋势；从旅游动机和目的来看，生态旅游、文化旅游、奖励旅游、探险旅游、科考旅游、潜海旅游，以及其他淡季旅游、美食旅游、体验式旅行、环保式旅行等各种形式的主题旅游，构成了人们外出旅游的主旋律。

酒店多元化
经营

4. 科技创新：新技术引爆新的旅游经济增长点 Scientific and Technological Innovation：New Technologies Create New Growth Points for the Tourist Economy

如今，互联网和科技创新改变了人们的生活，也改变了旅游产业的发展模式。数字化是旅游业面临的最大机遇，在文旅融合的大背景下，科技进步尤其是以大数据、人工智能为代表的新技术主导的文化内容创新，会促进形成很多新的消费热点。5G 与人工智能技术的大规模应用，很可能会在将来使智能机器人成为提供旅游服务的主体，使高品质的 AI、VR 技术进入寻常百姓家，从而改变消费者的消费决策和出游体验。

5. 国际旅游对旅游安全更为重视 International Tourism Pays More Attention to Tourist Safety

旅游经济的健康发展不仅依赖于社会经济和人们收入水平的提高，还取决于安定的国内外政治经济形势、安全的社会治安环境，以及国家或地区之间的友好往来。旅游活动的核心是人员的流动，而人们对各种政治经济形势和社会安全状况非常敏感，因此动荡的局势或不安全的环境必然使旅游者的流向、流量迅速发生变化。由此可见，安全性和可靠性是所有旅游企业应该考虑的首要问题，保证游客的安全是国际旅游的前提。如果旅游目的地存在安全隐患，应该采取有力的防范措施，提供准确的信息，并对不安全地区进行隔离和明示。世界局势的缓和使避免爆发全球性的毁灭战争成为可能，但局部战争和冲突依然时有发生。民族冲突、宗教冲突、国际恐怖主义，随时会对国际旅游业的发展形成局部威胁。在具备闲暇时间和支付能力的条件下，唯一能使旅游者放弃旅游计划的因素就是对安全的顾虑。旅游者考虑的安全因素主要有局部战争和冲突、恐怖主义活动、旅游目的地政局不稳定、传染性疾病流行、恶性交通事故的发生、社会治安状况恶化等。旅游者只有对各方面的安全因素确定无疑后才会启程。因此，各旅游接待国或地区都越来越重视安全因素对旅游市场营销的影响，力求在每一个环节都把好安全关。针对一些不可预测的不安全因素需为游客预先代办保险，一方面可以减轻游客的后顾之忧，另一方面一旦事故发生，可以将其对市场的冲击力降到最低程度。

6. 支付方式将改变国际旅游者的旅行生活 The Payment Method Will Change the Travel Life of International Tourists

在全球电子商务市场中，电子钱包已打破信用卡的主导地位，成为最常用的支付方式，信用卡和借记卡成为第二和第三大支付手段。据英国支付处理商 WorldPay 统计，2018 年，电子钱包支付占总支付方式的 36%，信用卡和借记卡分别占 23% 和 12%。根据 WorldPay 近日发布的《2024 全球支付报告》显示，2023 年电子钱包占全球电子商务消费额的 50%，占全球销售点消费额的 30%。未来，电子钱包仍然是增长最快的支付方式。此外，在全球新兴支付方式中，账户对账户支付（A2A）和先买后付（BNPL）等也表现出了可观的发展潜力，全球支付格局仍处于变动中。从全球来看，移动支付冷热不均，亚太地区的电子支付发展迅速，其中中国的移动支付发展引人瞩目，支付总量居全球第一。支付方式的转变是科技发展的结果，也必将为国际旅游者的旅行带来更多便利。

四、中国国际旅游市场概况 The Overview of Chinese International Tourist Market

中国历史悠久、文化灿烂，旅游资源丰富多彩。改革开放以来，经过 40 余年持续、快速、健康的发展，中国已实现了由旅游资源大国向旅游经济大国的历史性跨越。近年来，我国快速发展的旅游业，不仅成为满足人们美好生活需要的重要源泉，也成为经济增长的重要引擎，在业态创新、旅游扶贫、国际合作等方面为世界旅游发展做出了重要贡献。

1. 中国入境旅游现状 Current Situation of Inbound Tourism in China

从中华人民共和国建立初期到党的十一届三中全会的 20 多年间，由于受国际政治经济环境及国内因素的影响，中国国际旅游业的发展非常缓慢，在有些年份甚至停滞不前。旅游接待工作属于外事活动接待和统战工作的一部分，接待的外国旅游者大部分来自苏联、东欧国家和亚洲的朝鲜、越南和蒙古国等国，还有一些友好国家的人士和爱国的华侨，旅游业对国家的经济贡献微不足道，与世界上许多国家通过发展旅游业来促进经济社会协调发展的现实形成了强烈的反差。20 世纪 90 年代以来，中国旅游业持续发展，在国民经济中所占的比重日益提高，取得了多方面的经济效益、社会效益和生态效益，旅游产业定位日趋明确，国际旅游业保持稳定增长，这一阶段的国际、国内政治经济形势对中国国际旅游业也产生了重要影响。2004 年以来，中国旅游业增长迅猛，入境旅游已成为中国最大的国际服务贸易领域，中国已从旅游资源大国发展成为世界旅游大国。2013 年，我国首次提出建设"新丝绸之路经济带"和"21 世纪海上丝绸之路"的合作倡议，简称"一带一路"倡议，该倡议旨在依靠中国与有关国家既有的双多边机制，借助既有的、行之有效的区域合作平台，借用古代丝绸之路的历史符号，高举和平发展的旗帜，积极发展与沿线国家的经济合作伙伴关系，共同打造政治互信、经济融合、文化包容的利益共同体、命运共同体和责任共同体。自 2013 年提出以来，"一带一路"沿线国家和地区在该倡议的推动下，经济要素有序自由流动、资源高效配置、市场深度融合，有效促进了国家之间的协调联动发展和人员的双边往来，同时也促进了旅游产业的发展。

2016—2020 年我国前十位旅游客源国见表 0-3。

表 0-3　2016—2020 年我国前十位旅游客源国

序号	2016 年	2017 年	2018 年	2019 年	2020 年
1	韩国	缅甸	缅甸	缅甸	缅甸
2	越南	越南	越南	越南	越南
3	日本	韩国	韩国	韩国	韩国
4	缅甸	日本	日本	俄罗斯	俄罗斯
5	美国	俄罗斯	美国	日本	日本
6	俄罗斯	美国	俄罗斯	美国	美国

续表

序号	2016 年	2017 年	2018 年	2019 年	2020 年
7	蒙古国	蒙古国	蒙古国	蒙古国	蒙古国
8	马来西亚	马来西亚	马来西亚	马来西亚	马来西亚
9	菲律宾	菲律宾	菲律宾	菲律宾	菲律宾
10	新加坡	新加坡	新加坡	新加坡	新加坡

从客源市场分布的区域看，中国海外客源市场主体为亚洲市场，其次为欧洲和美洲市场，大洋洲和非洲市场比例较低，但近年来也有增长的势头。以 2019 年为例（图 0-3），入境外国游客人数中（含相邻国家边民旅华人员），亚洲占 75.8%，美洲占 7.7%，欧洲占 13.2%，大洋洲占 1.9%，非洲占 1.4%。

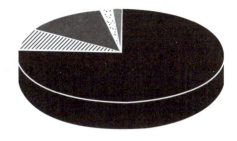

■ 亚洲　◨ 美洲　◫ 欧洲　▨ 大洋洲　■ 非洲

图 0-3　2019 年中国海外客源市场分布

按入境旅游人数排序，我国主要国际客源市场前 20 位国家如下：缅甸、越南、韩国、俄罗斯、日本、美国、蒙古国、马来西亚、菲律宾、新加坡、印度、泰国、加拿大、澳大利亚、印度尼西亚、德国、英国、朝鲜、法国、意大利（其中缅甸、越南、蒙古国、印度、朝鲜含边民旅华人数）。

经过改革开放 40 余年的发展，中国逐步形成了具有自身特色、符合旅游业持续发展需要的海外客源市场组合。从国籍看，20 世纪 80 年代以前，客源国主要是日本、苏联及东欧国家。20 世纪 80 年代以后，随着中国改革开放的不断深入，中国海外客源市场打破了过去狭窄的地域分布格局，客源国数量剧增，遍布世界各大洲，其中日本、美国、俄罗斯、英国、法国、德国、菲律宾、泰国、马来西亚、新加坡成为中国十大稳定的客源市场。进入 21 世纪后，世界政治经济局势进一步发生变化，中国客源市场也发生了较大变化。从旅游目的看，外国旅游者来华旅游的主要目的是观光休闲、参加会议及从事商务活动。2019 年的来华旅游者中，观光休闲占 35.0%，会议商务占 13.0%，探亲访友占 3.0%，服务员工占 14.7%，其他占 34.3%。从性别看，男性旅游者仍是中国海外旅游客源市场的主体。2019 年来华的外国旅游者中，男性占 58.7%，女性占 41.3%。从年龄段上看，具有中高等收入的中青年团体仍是中国海外旅游客源市场的主力军，其中 14 岁以下人数占 3.8%，15 ～ 24 岁占 13.9%，25 ～ 44 岁占 49.3%，45 ～ 64 岁占 28.1%，65 岁以上占 4.9%。从游客的职业构成看，入境游客中商人较多，这也正说明前来从事商贸活动的游客较多，是中国经济快速发展的反映。从入境旅游的季节来看，游客较多集中在 8—11 月，属于旅游旺季，特别是 10 月形成旅游高峰；1、2、12 月游客较少，属于旅游淡季。根据中国旅游研究院发布的《中国入境旅游发展报告 2020》，疫情中断了入境旅游原有的增长态势，对入境游客行为的影响改变了我国入境旅游的客源市场和目的地结构。近距离的周边市场率先得以恢复，受疫情影响较小的、自然资源丰富的目的地更受欢迎。常态化疫情防控背景下，目的地营销推广工作的重心是以"安全"和"健康"为关键词来重塑旅游目的地形象。伴随国内大众旅游市场日趋走向成熟，旅游基础设施不断完善，旅游服务品质持续提升，未来入境旅游高质量发展的基础更加稳固，疫情后入境旅游的恢复和提升势在必行。

2. 中国出境旅游现状 Current Situation of Outbound Tourism in China

中国公民自费出境旅游是中国经济快速发展和改革开放政策的产物，40 多年，来我国出境旅游经历了一个从无到有、稳定增长的市场化发展过程。20 世纪 80 年代中期，中国开始出现出境旅游，其真正的大发展是在 20 世纪 90 年代。刺激中国国内旅游需求最为重要的因素之一是居民可支配收入的增加，另外，还有闲暇时间的增多以及生活和消费方式的转变。我国的出境旅游市场最近十年才形成，总体上出境旅游的客源市场开发力度还不够，发展空间十分广阔。可以预期的是，出境旅游将在中上收入阶层中得到普及，成为一种大众化的消费活动。2019 年，我国的出境旅游市场规模达到 1.55 亿人次，出境旅游消费依然位居世界第一，达 2 770 亿美元。据世界旅游组织统计，中国是世界第一大出境旅游客源国。2001 年中国加入世界贸易组织，为旅游业的发展注入了新的活力，中国现已成为亚洲第一大客源国和全球增长最快的新兴客源输出国。2000—2020 年中国出境旅游发展情况见表 0-4。

表 0-4　2000—2020 年中国出境旅游发展情况一览表

年份	出境人次 / 百万	增长率 /%
2000	10.47	13.43
2001	12.13	15.85
2002	16.60	36.85
2003	20.22	21.81
2004	28.85	42.68
2005	31.03	7.56
2006	34.52	11.25
2007	40.95	18.63
2008	45.84	11.94
2009	47.66	3.97
2010	57.39	20.42
2011	70.25	22.41
2012	83.18	18.41
2013	98.19	18.05
2014	107.28	9.26
2015	116.89	8.96
2016	122.03	4.40
2017	130.51	6.95
2018	149.72	14.72
2019	154.63	3.28
2020	20.33	-86.9

2004 年是中国公民出境旅游增长最快的一年，出境旅游人次达到 2 885 万，较上年增长 42.68%，是中国公民出境旅游目的地数量增加最多的一年。2006—2009 年中国公民出境旅游增长速度放缓，2010 年又达到 20.42% 的增长速度，出境旅游人次达 5 739 万。2013 年我国公民出境旅游创下 9 819 万人次的新高，比上年增长 18.05%。自 2014 年至 2019 年，出境旅游人次从 10 728 万增加到 15 463 万，再创新高。中国不仅是亚洲出境旅游人数最多的国家，

而且是世界出境旅游人均消费最高的国家之一。根据中国旅游研究院统计，2013年中国出境旅游消费在境外已经达到1 287亿美元。早在2012年，中国的出境消费就已经超过了德国和美国，成为世界第一，2013—2019年中国人均出境旅游消费一直保持世界第一。国家外汇管理局数据显示，2019年上半年，中国境外旅行支出1 275亿美元，超五成旅行支出发生在亚洲地区。根据UNWTO统计数据，2019年中国公民出境旅游花费为2 770美元。正是由于中国公民出境旅游人数多、人均花费高，各旅游发达国家争相开发中国旅游市场，同时中国游客在国外的受尊敬程度也与日俱增，出国目的也从观光购物转向享受海外优质的生活环境和服务。出境旅游已成为衡量中国城市家庭和年轻人幸福度的一大标准。中国已连续多年保持世界第一大出境旅游客源国地位。中国银联的数据显示，2019年境外消费前十大客源省市为广东、上海、北京、江苏、浙江、四川、湖北、山东、福建、辽宁，其中8个为东部省市、2个为中西部省市。我国旅游业国际化前景广阔，已连续多年成为世界第一大出境旅游客源国，庞大的出境旅游人数和国际旅游消费量为世界旅游业发展带来巨大红利。在全球旅游格局中，我国旅游市场的体量、分量和质量越发突出，成为影响全球旅游版图和竞争格局的重要力量。近20年高速增长的出境旅游将中国与世界旅游业紧密联系在一起，并成为"一带一路"倡议、亚洲文明对话和人类命运共同体建设的重要组成部分。近年来，我国推进的旅游年、中美旅游峰会、中意文化交流、中俄人文交流等活动促进了文化旅游的交流，中国发起成立的世界旅游联盟、世界旅游城市联合会、世界山地旅游组织等搭建了各国旅游合作的平台。"一带一路"倡议的提出，为我国旅游企业国际化布局开拓了广阔前景。截至2018年年底，我国与"一带一路"沿线国家直飞航线数已经达到接近1 000条；截至2019年4月，已经有51个"一带一路"沿线国家面向我国游客开放便利签证政策，这些都为我国消费者出境旅游提供了便利。"一带一路"沿线是旅游资源的富集区，汇集了80%的世界文化遗产，涉及60多个国家、44亿人口，被视为世界上最具活力和潜力的黄金旅游之路。随着我国与"一带一路"沿线国家旅游合作的持续深入，旅游便利化水平持续提高，我国旅游业沿着"一带一路"实施国际化布局的脚步将越走越快。

第一章
Chapter 1

亚洲旅游区
The Asia Tourist Region

学习目标

1. 熟悉亚洲旅游区主要客源国和目的地国的国情。

Get familiar with the national conditions of major source and destination countries in Asia tourist region.

2. 能根据各国特点开展有针对性的旅游客源开发策划和旅游产品设计。

Be able to carry out targeted tourist source development planning and product design according to the characteristics of various countries.

3. 能根据不同客户的需求，设计出合适的旅游线路。

Be able to design suitable travelling routes according to the client's needs.

4. 掌握日本、韩国、新加坡、泰国、印度尼西亚、印度、阿联酋七个国家主要城市和著名景点的概况，能运用所学理论知识从事实际接待和服务工作。

Master the general situation of major cities and famous scenic spots in Japan, Korea, Singapore, Thailand, Indonesia, India and UAE, and be able to put theoretic knowledge into real practice such as reception and service work.

第一节　亚洲旅游区特征

The General Situation of Asia Tourist Region

　　亚洲旅游区面积约为 4 457 万平方千米，约占世界陆地面积的 1/3，是世界第一大洲。按照地理方位，通常把亚洲旅游区分为东亚、东南亚、南亚、西亚、中亚和北亚六个部分。亚洲人口总数约为 42 亿，约占世界总人口的 60%。亚洲东面是太平洋，北面是北冰洋，南面濒临印度洋，西面以乌拉尔山脉、乌拉尔河、里海、大高加索山脉、黑海、土耳其海峡与欧洲分界，西南面隔亚丁湾、曼德海峡、红海、苏伊士运河与非洲相邻，东北面隔白令海峡与北美洲相望。亚洲共有 48 个国家（地区），是世界七大洲中面积最大、人口最多的一个洲。其绝大部分土地位于东半球和北半球。

亚洲旅游区特征
（英文版）

　　亚洲旅游区是世界旅游资源最丰富的旅游区之一。东亚旅游区是世界上两大高山带和火山带汇合处，地形十分复杂，观光、登山、探险和火山旅游景观众多。东亚旅游区有中国、日本、朝鲜、韩国和蒙古国 5 个国家，人文旅游资源以文物古迹、民俗风情和各种建筑旅游景观为主；东南亚旅游区有越南、柬埔寨、泰国、马来西亚、新加坡、印度尼西亚、缅甸、菲律宾等 11 个国家，该旅游区岛屿和半岛较多，属于亚热带季风气候和热带雨林气候，热带生物旅游资源丰富，形成了世界著名的海滨度假胜地和避寒胜地；南亚旅游区有尼泊尔、印度、巴基斯坦、孟加拉国、斯里兰卡、马尔代夫等 7 个国家，该旅游区气候多属热带季风气候，有丰富的热带季风雨林景观和动植物旅游资源，如印度半岛南端、斯里兰卡岛和马尔代夫群岛，是理想的度假和潜水运动场所；中亚旅游区有哈萨克斯坦、乌兹别克斯坦、吉尔吉斯斯坦等 5 个国家，以温带大陆性气候为主，草原风情游和沙漠探险游是本区旅游的一大特色，中亚还是古丝绸之路必经之地，清真寺、古城遗址、陵墓较多；西亚旅游区有阿富汗、伊拉克、黎巴嫩、阿拉伯联合酋长国（阿联酋）、沙特阿拉伯、土耳其、以色列等 20 个国家和地区，沙漠广布、干谷纵横，有迷人的地中海沿岸风光，是开展徒步探险旅游的理想之地。西亚地区是人类文明的摇篮之一，是三大宗教（伊斯兰教、基督教和犹太教）的发源地，每年都会吸引大批教徒和旅游者，是世界宗教旅游最密集的地区。

本章选取东亚地区的日本、韩国，东南亚地区的新加坡、泰国和印度尼西亚，南亚地区的印度，西亚地区的阿联酋这 7 个富有代表性特色的国家，将主要从国家地理概览、自然资源、民俗风情、主要旅游城市及景点、旅游购物等几个方面展开叙述。

第二节　东亚之旅
Travel in East Asia

樱花之国——日本
The Land of Cherry Blossoms—Japan

导读

中国和日本是一衣带水的邻邦，2 000 多年来，中日两国人民相互学习、相互借鉴，有着割舍不断的历史联系和文化渊源。日本古代就曾派遣唐使学习中国文化，中国唐代高僧鉴真六次东渡扶桑传播文明；日本仿照我国隋唐服饰改造出和服；在语言、佛教、儒学、茶道等方面，日本也深受中国的影响。中华文明促进了日本文化的形成和发展，为日本文化的发展奠定了基础。第二次世界大战后，日本现代旅游业取得了长足发展，特别是 2003 年日本政府实施"观光立国"政策，将旅游业作为其支柱产业之一。日本是中国主要的旅游客源国，也是重要的旅游目的地国之一。

一、地理概览 Geography of Japan

（一）位置 Location

日本位于亚洲东部，南北狭长，四面环海，是一个岛国，西北与俄罗斯、朝鲜、韩国隔海相望，西南与中国隔东海相邻。日本国土面积为37.79万平方千米，主要由四个岛屿组成：本州（面积最大，占国土总面积的60%）、四国（面积最小）、九州和北海道。此外，其他6 800多个小岛，主要位于鹿儿岛和中国台湾之间的太平洋上，围绕海岸线向南延伸。

Japan is located in East Asia, stretching from north to south and surrounded by the sea on all sides, making it an island nation. To the northwest, it faces Russia, Democratic People's Republic of Korea, and South Korea across the sea. To the southwest, it is separated from China by the East China Sea. Japan's land area is 377,900 square kilometers and is primarily made up of four main islands: Honshu (the largest, accounting for 60% of the total land area), Shikoku (the smallest), Kyushu, and Hokkaido. Additionally, there are over 6,800 smaller islands, mostly situated in the Pacific Ocean between Kagoshima and Taiwan, extending southward along the coastline.

漫步北海道，感受世界最浪漫的雪景

（二）地形和气候 The Land and Seasons

日本境内多山，山地约占全国总面积的75%，是世界上罕见的多山之国。富士山是全国的最高峰，海拔3 776米。日本列岛位于环太平洋火山地震带上，火山众多，地震频发，全国有160多座火山，其中50多座是活火山，为世界上有名的地震区。但是火山分布地区景色优美，温泉资源丰富，是日本著名的观光疗养地。

Japan is a mountainous country, with mountains covering approximately 75% of its total area,which makes it a rare mountainous nation in the world. Mount Fuji, standing at 3,776meters above sea level, is the highest peak in the country. The Japanese archipelago is situated on the Pacific Ring of Fire, a region known for its volcanic activity and frequent earthquakes. Within Japan, there are over 160 volcanoes, more than 50 of which are active, contributing to its reputation as a seismically active area. This geological activity, while causing challenges for local residents, also enriches the landscape with stunning views and therapeutic hot springs, transforming the region into a renowned tourist destination.

日本属于温带海洋性气候，四季分明，气候温和、湿润，冬无严寒，夏无酷暑，6月多梅雨，夏秋季多台风。1月平均气温北部–6 ℃，南部16 ℃；7月北部17 ℃，南部28 ℃。年降水量700～3 500毫米，最高达4 000毫米以上。首都东京1月平均气温3 ℃，8月平均气温为25 ℃。

The climate of Japan is predominantly temperate marine with four distinct seasons.Winters are not severely cold, and summers are not scorching hot. June typically experiences more rainfall, while summer and fall see a higher frequency of typhoons. The average temperature ranges from –6 ℃ in the north to 16 ℃ in the south during January, and from 17 ℃ in the north to 28 ℃ in the south during July. Annual precipitation varies from 700 to 3,500 mm, with some areas receiving up to 4,000 mm. the average temperature of The capital city of Tokyo in January is 3 ℃；in August the average temperature is 25 ℃.

（三）自然资源 Natural Resources

日本的水利、森林、渔业资源较为丰富，其他资源较为贫乏。由于水利资源丰富，日本水力发电量约占总发电量的 12%。日本森林面积为 25.21 万平方千米，占国土总面积的 2/3，是世界上森林覆盖率最高的国家之一，但日本国内木材的进口比例达 52%，是世界上进口木材最多的国家。日本近海渔业资源丰富，捕鱼量、渔船与渔民数、水产品消费率常居世界第一，有世界著名的北海道渔场。铁矿石和铜的储量极低，石油、煤炭、天然气极少，约 80% 的资源依赖海外进口，核能开发较早。

Japan is rich in water resources, forest resources and fishery resources, while other resources are relatively scarce. Due to its rich water resources, hydropower accounts for about 12% of Japan's total electricity generation. The forest area in Japan is 252,100 square kilometers, which is two-thirds of its total land area, making it one of the countries with the highest forest coverage in the world. However, 52% of its timber is imported, making Japan the largest importer of timber globally. Japan' offshore fishery resources are rich, with fishing volume, number of fishing boats and fishermen, and seafood consumption rates often ranking first in the world, featuring the renowned Hokkaido fishing grounds. The reserves of iron ore and copper are extremely low, and oil, coal, and natural gas are very scarce, with about 80% of resources relying on imports from abroad. Nuclear energy development began early in Japan.

二、人文概况 Overview of Japanese Humanities

（一）国情认知 Basic Knowledge of National Conditions

日本国名意为"日出之国"。国旗是太阳旗，呈长方形，长宽比例为 3∶2。旗面为白色，正中有一轮红日，白色象征正直和纯洁，红色象征真诚和热忱。日本国歌为《君之代》，国花是樱花，国鸟是绿雉，国技是相扑，国球是棒球。樱花在日本的春天到处可见，日本也因此被誉为"樱花之国"。首都位于东京，主要城市有大阪、神户、京都等。官方语言为日语，货币为日元（JPY）。

Japan is known as "the Land of the Rising Sun". The national flag is known as the Nisshoki, a rectangular flag with a ratio of 3∶2. The flag is white with a red circle in the center, where white symbolizes integrity and purity, and red represents sincerity and enthusiasm. The national anthem of Japan is *Kimigayo*, the national flower is the cherry blossom, the national bird is the green pheasant, the national sport is sumo, and the national ball game is baseball. Japan is known as the "Land of Cherry Blossoms" due to the ubiquity of these flowers throughout the country in the spring. The capital is Tokyo, with major cities including Osaka, Kobe, and Kyoto. The official language is Japanese, and the currency is the yen (JPY).

日本本国人口约 1.25 亿（截至 2022 年），居世界第十位，人口密度世界第一。日本男性平均寿命为 78.07 岁，女性平均寿命为 84.93 岁，是世界上人均寿命最长的国家。日本民族的主体是大和民族，占人口的 99% 以上，少数民族有阿伊努族，旧称虾夷族，生活在北海道地区。日本是个多宗教的国家，主要有神道教、佛教、基督教三大宗教。大多数日本人既信奉神道教，又信奉佛教。

Japan has the world's 10th largest population of approximately 125 million people (2022) and the world's highest population density. Japanese is the country of the longest average life expectancy in the world, with the male's average life expectancy 78.07 years old and female 84.93 years old.The main ethnic group in Japan is the Yamato people, who make up more than 99% of the population, while the Ainu, formerly known as the Ezo, are an ethnic minority group living in the Hokkaido area. Japan is a country of multiple-religions, mainly Shinto, Buddhism and Christianity. Most Japanese believe in both Shinto and Buddhism.

（二）历史简介 History of Japan

4 世纪中叶，大和民族统一日本，建立奴隶制国家——大和国，统治日本长达 300 余年。5 世纪初，大和国达到鼎盛时期，其势力扩及朝鲜半岛南部。公元 645 年通过大化革新，仿照中国唐朝律令制度，建立以天皇为绝对君主的封建中央集权国家体制。12 世纪起，先后经历"镰仓幕府""室町幕府""战国时代""江户幕府"四个时期。1868 年，革新派实行"明治维新"，废除封建割据的幕府体制，重建以天皇为首的中央集权，发展资本主义，逐步走上对外侵略扩张的道路。

In the middle of the 4th century, the Daiwa nation unified Japan and established a slave country, Daiwa, which ruled Japan for more than 300 years. At the beginning of the 5th century, Daiwa reached its peak, and its power expanded to the south of the Korean Peninsula. In 645 AD, the feudal centralized state system with the emperor as the absolute monarch was established by means of great reform and imitating the law and order system of the Tang Dynasty. Since the 12th century, it has experienced four periods: Kamakura shogunate, Murmachi shogunate, Warring States period and Edo shogunate. In 1868, the reformers implemented the "Meiji Restoration", abolished the shogunate system of feudal separatism, rebuilt the centralization headed by the emperor, developed capitalism, and gradually embarked on the road of foreign aggression and expansion.

1894 年，日本发动甲午战争；1904 年，日本挑起日俄战争；1910 年，日本侵吞朝鲜。日本在第二次世界大战中战败，于 1945 年 8 月 15 日宣布无条件投降。战后初期，美军以"同盟国占领军"的名义对日本实行军事占领。1947 年 5 月实施新宪法，由绝对天皇制变为君主立宪的议会内阁制国家，天皇为国家象征，没有实权。20 世纪 60 年代末期，日本跃入世界经济强国之列。

In 1894, Japan provoked the Sino-Japanese War and then the Russo-Japanese War in 1904. In 1910, Japan annexed Korea. Japan was defeated in the Second World War as it announced the unconditional surrender on August 15, 1945. During the initial post-war period, Japan was under the exclusive occupation by the US Army. With the implementation of the new constitution in May 1947, the absolute emperor system was transformed into the parliamentary cabinet system with the emperor as the national symbol. In the late 1960s, Japan's economy leap into the front ranks of the world.

（三）经济状况 The Economy

日本工业和制造业高度发达，工业总产值约占国内生产总值的 40%，是国民经济的主要支柱。汽车、电子、光学、化学、半导体等多个领域位居世界前列，工业机器人产量占世界一半以上。日本的科学研发能力位居世界前列，应用科学、机械和医学等领域尤为突出。日本的服务业规模大，也是世界第一大动漫强国。

Japan's industrial and manufacturing industries are highly developed, with total industrial output accounting for about 40% of GDP, and are the main pillar of the national economy. It ranks among the worlds leaders in a number of fields, including automobiles, electronics, optics, chemistry and semiconductors, and accounts for more than half of the world's production of industrial robots. Japan's scientific R&D capabilities are among the highest in the world, with areas such as applied sciences, machinery and medicine being particularly prominent. Japan has a large service sector and is also the world's number one animation powerhouse.

20 世纪 50 年代起，日本确立了贸易立国的发展方针。尽管地域有限、资源贫乏，日本的经济发展迅猛，20 世纪 60 至 70 年代平均增长率达 7.5%，20 世纪 80 到 90 年代初为 3.2%。随后受泡沫经济和国内政策影响，经济增长速度明显放缓，这段时期被称为"失落的十年"。2000 年，日本政府努力恢复经济增长的举措收效甚微，进一步加剧了全球经济增长速度放缓的局势。2005 年后，日本经济表现出强劲的复苏迹象，国内生产总值增长率达到 2.8%，超过了当时的美国和欧盟。2011 年，日本成为继美国和中国之后的世界第三大经济体，也是世界第四大国有经济实体。

Since 1950s, Japan has established a development policy centered on trade. Despite its limited territory and scarce resources, Japan's economy grew rapidly, with an average growth rate of 7.5% in the 1960s and 1970s, and 3.2% from the 1980s to the early 1990s. Growth slowed down significantly during what the Japanese called "The lost decade", largely because of the property price bubble and domestic policies. Government efforts to revive economic growth met with little success and thus further accelerated the global slowdown in the year 2000. After 2005, Japan showed signs of a strong recovery, with a GDP growth rate of 2.8%, surpassing that of the United States and the European Union at the time. By 2011, Japan was the world's third-largest economy after the United States and China, and the fourth-largest state-owned economy globally.

❓ 讨论题

请大家结合下列照片（图 1-1～图 1-3）说说日本的自然环境和人文概况，分析在日本极简主义盛行的原因以及日本人的世界观。

图 1-1 日本的庭院

图 1-2 日本人的卧室

图 1-3 日本普通家庭的自制午餐

提示：日本的资源稀缺，人们十分注重节约资源、能源，保护环境，爱护动物，与大自然和谐相处。同样，勤俭节约、无私奉献也是中国社会的主流风尚，体现于城乡社会民众的工作劳动和日常生活的衣食住行之中。因此，应引导学生树立"节约光荣，浪费可耻"的价值观，推进节约型校园建设，全面落实立德树人的根本任务。

（四）传统文化 Traditional Culture

日本独特的地理条件和悠久的历史，孕育了别具一格的文化，既有传统的本土文化，又有现代流行文化。传统文化艺术包含茶道、花道、武术、书法等。清酒、寿司、艺伎、温泉是典型的日本传统文化符号；与此同时，新生代文化、动漫文化也闻名于世。日本共有 17 处遗产被联合国教科文组织列入《世界遗产名录》。

Japan's unique geographical conditions and long history have nurtured a distinctive culture that encompasses both traditional indigenous culture and modern pop culture. Traditional cultural arts include tea ceremony, flower arrangement, martial arts, and calligraphy. Sake, sushi, geisha, and hot springs are typical symbols of Japanese traditional culture, while contemporary culture and anime are also renowned worldwide. Seventeen sites in total have been inscribed on the UNESCO World Heritage List.

日本三道——
"茶道、花道、书道"

和服是日本的传统民族服装。公元 8—9 世纪，日本一度盛行"唐风"服装，以后虽有改变并形成日本独特的风格，但仍含有中国古代服装的特色。在婚礼、庆典、传统花道、茶道等隆重社交场合，和服是公认的必穿礼服。男士和服色彩比较单调，偏重黑色，款式较少，腰带较细，装饰品不多。女士和服的款式和花样繁多，是区别年龄和结婚与否的标志。例如，未婚的姑娘穿紧袖外服，已婚妇女穿宽袖外服；梳"岛田"式发型、穿红领衬衣的是姑娘，梳圆发髻、穿素色衬衣的是主妇。

Kimono is the name of Japan's traditional national costume. In the 8th and 9th centuries AD, the "Tang style" of clothing was once prevalent in Japan, and although it has changed since then to form a uniquely Japanese style, it still contains the characteristics of ancient Chinese clothing. The kimono is recognized as a must-have dress for weddings, festivals, traditional flower ceremonies, tea ceremonies, and other grand social occasions. Men's kimonos are more monotonous in color, favoring black, with fewer styles, thinner belts, and fewer accessories. The difference in style and color of women's kimonos is a sign of age and whether they are married or not. For example, an unmarried girl wears a tight-sleeved tunic, while a married woman wears a wide-sleeved tunic; a girl wears a red-collared shirt with a "Shimada" hairstyle, while a housewife wears a round bun and a plain shirt.

能剧，日文中念作"NOU"。"能"是指具有才能或技能。能剧是一种结合了舞蹈、戏剧、音乐和诗歌等的舞台美学表演，是日本最具代表性的传统艺术形式之一，也是世界上现存最古老的专业戏剧之一。能剧的起源可追溯到 8 世纪，之后的发展融入了多种艺术形式，如杂技、歌舞和滑稽戏。日本有专门的国立能乐堂来定期上演能剧。

The Noh Plays of Japan is pronounced "NOU" in Japanese. "Noh" has the meaning of talent or skill. The Noh Plays of Japan is a stage aesthetic performance combining dance, drama, music and poetry. It is one of the most representative traditional art forms in Japan and one of the oldest existing professional dramas in the world. The Noh Plays of Japan can be traced back to the 8th century, and its subsequent development has been integrated into a variety of art forms, such as acrobatics, songs, dance and comics. Japan has a special National Noh Play Hall to perform regularly.

相扑（图 1-4）是一项日本国技，起源于古代招待道教神的演出，至今仍然遵循诸多具有宗教背景的仪式。相扑的基本规则很简单：比赛时，除了脚掌之外的任何部位最先触及地面，或比对手最先出圈的相扑手就为失败。比赛通常只持续几秒，极少数情况下约 1 分钟。横纲

（冠军）是相扑手的最高级别。一旦一个相扑手达到横纲等级，他就不会再失去这一地位，但是当他的成绩开始退步时，人们便期望他引退。许多前相扑手作为日本相扑协会的成员仍然活跃在相扑界。

Sumo wrestling (Figure 1-4) is a national sport in Japan. It originated in ancient times as a performance to entertain the Shinto gods. Many rituals with religious background are still followed today. The basic rules of sumo are very simple: the wrestler who first touches the

图 1-4 日本的相扑手

Figure 1-4　Japanese Sumo Wrestlers

ground with anything besides the soles of his feet, or who leaves the ring before his opponent loses out. The fights usually last only a few seconds, or in rare cases, about a minute. On the top of the sumo wrestlers' hierarchy stand the Yokozuna (grand champion). Once a wrestler reaches the rank of Yokozuna, he cannot lose this status but he will be expected to retire when his results begin to worsen. Many former wrestlers remain active in the sumo world as members of the Japan Sumo Association.

 讨论题

日本相扑选手为何越胖越受欢迎？你们怎么看？

艺伎（图 1-5）是日本特有的一种女性表演艺术工作者，与日本的茶道、书法一样同属于日本传统文化的一部分。艺伎在日语中意为"艺术之人"，就像日本茶道和书法一样。最初的艺伎全部是男性，在妓院和娱乐场所以演奏传统鼓乐、说唱逗乐为生。18 世纪中叶，艺伎渐渐成为女性职业，这一传统也一直沿袭至今。艺伎须通过多年的勤学苦练，才能最终成为通晓琴棋书画，能歌善舞，精通插花、茶道等传统技艺的才女，因此被称为日本古典文化的活化石。

A geisha (Figure 1-5) is a unique type of Japanese female performance artist. Geisha is a symbol of Japan's tradition and culture, alongside practices such as tea ceremony and calligraphy. Geisha is Japanese for "person of art", just like Japanese tea ceremony and calligraphy ceremony. At the very beginning, geisha were all male. They lived in brothels

图 1-5 日本的艺伎

Figure 1-5　Japanese Geisha

and casinos by playing traditional drum music and singing. In the middle of the 18th century, the geisha profession gradually became a female profession, and this tradition has been followed to this day. Only through years of hard study and practice, can those talented women eventually become proficient in piano, chess, calligraphy, painting, singing, dancing, flower arrangement and tea ceremony. Therefore, they are called the living fossil of Japanese classical culture.

日本人的长寿秘诀——饮食文化

讨论题

请登录 CCTV 官网，观看视频"舌尖上的中国"。

分析中日两国饮食文化的相似和不同之处。（Compare and contrast Japanese food culture and Chinese food culture.）

提示：思考美食的多样性以及如何顺应自然的生存之道——"靠山吃山，靠水吃水"。

舌尖上的中国

（五）礼仪禁忌 Social Etiquettes and Taboos

日本人见面多以鞠躬为礼，一般行 30 度或 45 度的鞠躬礼。鞠躬弯腰的深浅表示的含义不同，腰弯得越低，表示越尊敬。鞠躬时，两手自然下垂放在衣裤两侧。表示恭敬时，多以左手搭在右手上，放在身前行鞠躬礼。交换名片时，地位低或年轻的一方先给对方，这种做法被认为是一种礼节。递交名片时，要将名片正对着对方。

Bowing is very common to show etiquette in Japan. Generally, bowing is achieved by 30 degrees or 45 degrees, and different degrees of bowing show different meanings. The lower you bend, the more respect you show. In bowing, hands are naturally put down on both sides of the dress. To show respect, the left hand should rest on the right hand, bowing down with both hands in the front. In business card exchange, the one with lower status or younger age should give the card first, which is considered to be a kind of etiquette. The card should directly face the other when it is handed over.

社交活动中，日本人爱用自谦语，如"请多关照""粗茶淡饭""照顾不周"等。与日本人交谈时，不要边说边指手画脚，别人讲话时切忌插话打断。在交谈中，不要打听日本人的年龄、婚姻状况、工资收入等隐私。对年事高的人不要用"年迈""老人"等字样。

In social activities, Japanese prefer to use humble expressions such as "Nice to meet you" "It's just a homely meal" or "Sorry for the inconvenience, we are not treating you well." When talking with Japanese, try not to gesture too much and be careful not to interrupt when someone else is speaking. It's important not to inquire about private matters such as age, marital status, or salary. Additionally, refrain from using terms like "elderly" or "old" when referring to senior people.

日本人不喜欢紫色，认为紫色是悲伤的色调，最忌讳绿色。日本人忌讳 3 人一起"合影"，认为中间的人被左右两人夹着是不祥的预兆。探望病人时，忌用山茶花及淡黄色、白色的花。日本人忌讳荷花，也不愿接受菊花或有菊花图案的物品，因为它是皇室的标志；喜欢的图案是松、竹、梅、鸭子、乌龟等。通信时，信的折叠、邮票的贴法都要合乎规范，如寄慰问信忌用双层信封，双层被认为是祸不单行；寄给恋人的信件，邮票不能倒着贴，否则意味着分手。

Japanese generally dislike the color purple, associating it with sadness, and they strongly avoid green. Additionally, they are superstitious about taking group photos with three people, believing that the person being sandwiched by the other two in the middle is an omen of misfortune. Japanese also avoid lotus, which means bad luck. When visiting patients, the Japanese don't send camellias or pale yellow, white flowers. Japanese also avoid lotus flowers and are reluctant to accept chrysanthemums or items with chrysanthemum patterns, as the flower is a symbol of the royal family. What Japanese like using as patterns are pine, bamboo, plum, duck and turtle. When it comes to correspondence, the folding of the letter and the placement of the stamp must adhere to proper etiquette. For example, when sending a condolence letter, double-layered envelopes should be avoided, as they symbolize "misfortunes never come singly." Similarly, when sending a letter to a romantic partner, the stamp should never be placed upside down, as this implies a breakup.

日本人在饮食方面的忌讳也很多。一般而言，日本人不吃肥肉和猪内脏；招待客人切忌将饭盛得过满、过多，也不可一勺就盛好一碗；忌讳客人吃饭一碗就够，只吃一碗象征无缘；忌讳用餐过程中整理自己的衣服或抚摸头发，因为这是不卫生和不礼貌的举止；日本人忌把筷子架在碗、碟上面。

Japanese have many dietary taboos. Generally, they avoid eating fatty meats and pork offal. When serving guests, it is important not to overfill the rice bowl or serve too much at once, and it is considered impolite to fill the bowl with just one scoop. It is also frowned upon if a guest eats only one bowl of rice, as this symbolizes a lack of connection. During meals, it is considered unhygienic and rude to adjust your clothing or touch and fix your hair. Additionally, when using chopsticks, it is taboo to rest them across the top of a bowl or plate.

日本有不少言语忌讳，如"9"的发音与"苦"相同、"4"的发音与"死"相同，应尽量避免，医院一般没有号码为 4 和 42 的房间和病床。用户的电话也忌讳用 42，监狱一般也没有 4 号囚室。日本人还忌讳数字 13，许多宾馆没有 13 楼和 13 号房间。

There are many taboos in Japanese language, such as the number 9 has the same pronunciation as "bitter" and 4 has the same pronunciation as "death". They should be avoided as far as possible, so there is no room or bed with number 4 or 42 in a hospital. 42 is also avoided in telephone numbers and there is no number 4 in a prison either. 13 is another taboo number, so there are no floors or rooms of 13 in many hotels.

日本人送礼时，通常送成双成对的礼物，如一对笔、两瓶酒就很受欢迎。但送新婚夫妇红包时，忌讳送 2 万日元或 2 的倍数，日本民间认为"2"这个数字容易导致夫妻感情破裂，一般送 3 万、5 万或 7 万日元。礼品包装纸的颜色也有讲究，黑白色代表丧事，绿色为不祥，也不宜用红色包装纸，最好用花色纸包装礼品。去日本人家中做客，一般不要提出四处看看的请求，特别忌讳男子闯入厨房，上厕所也应征得主人的同意。

When Japanese give gifts, the gifts will usually be in pair, for example, two pens or two bottles of liquor. When giving money to newly wedded couples, never give 20,000 Japanese yen or the amount as multiples of 2, because the Japanese believe 2 will break up the couple's relationship. So generally 30,000 Japanese yen, 50,000 Japanese yen or 70,000 Japanese yen will be given. The color of packaging materials for gift is another thing to pay attention.Black and white stand for something about funeral and green means something unlucky, while red is also not appropriate. Colorful papers are preferred for packaging. When visiting a Japanese home, you should not make a request to look around. Especially, a male is forbidden to break into the kitchen. You should also ask the owner's permission to go to the bathroom.

（六）传统节日 Festivals

1. 樱花节 Cherry Blossom Festival

每年的 3 月 15 日到 4 月 15 日是日本的樱花节。日本的樱花有 30 多个种类、300 多个品种。从江户时期以来，在樱花树下野餐的传统习俗一直在日本

樱花节的由来

普通百姓中十分流行。

The Cherry Blossom Festival is held from March 15 to April 15 every year. There are more than 30 kinds of cherry blossoms in Japan, more than 300 varieties. Since the Edo period, the traditional custom of having a picnic under the cherry tree has been very popular among ordinary Japanese people.

2. 玩偶节 Doll's Festival

3 月 3 日举行的日本玩偶节又被称为"女孩节"，是希望女儿快乐成长的节日。这一天，人们把穿着传统宫廷装束的漂亮木偶和桃花摆在一起，喝糯米酿成的甜酒，为他们年幼的女儿祈祷健康、幸福和兴旺。玩偶节可以追溯到 1 000 多年前的江户时代（1603—1868 年），当时的人们在三月初举行"无病息灾"的祈祷仪式，人们把纸娃娃放在木筏上，并把它们推到河的下游，相信这些娃娃可以驱除邪恶的灵魂或灾难。江户时代之后，这些玩偶被设计成现在玩具的样子。

Doll's Festival is celebrated on March 3, which is also known as the "Girl's Day". In Japan, It is a festival for young girls to pursue happiness and healthy growth. On this day, family display beautiful puppets in traditional costumes and peach flowers together and drink sweet wine made from glutinous rice to pray for health, happiness and prosperity for their young daughter. Doll's Festival can be traced back to the Edo period（1603—1868）more than 1 000 years ago. At that time, people held a prayer ceremony of "no disease and no disaster" at the beginning of March. People put paper dolls on rafts and pushed them to the lower reaches of the river, believing that these dolls can drive away evil or disasters. After the Edo era, these dolls have been designed as what look like current toys.

3. 男孩节（端午节）Boys' Day

每年 5 月 5 日，是日本的男孩节。人们会悬挂鲤鱼旗迎接男孩节，期盼孩子健康成长。为了祝福家中的男孩健康、快乐，这一天日本家家户户都会用纸或布做成色彩鲜艳、形状像鲤鱼的彩带，然后把这些彩带串在竹竿上，和金色的风车绑在一起挂在屋顶上。日本人相信鲤鱼最有精神和活力，希望家中的男孩都像鲤鱼那样，因此这一天又称为"鲤鱼日"。

Japanese Boys' Day falls on every May 5th. People hang carp flags to welcome Boys' Day. The tradition is expected to bring about the healthy growth of children. To bless the health and happiness of the boys in the family, every household in Japan makes colorful ribbons out of paper or cloth, shaped like carp, and then strings these ribbons onto a bamboo pole. They tie them with golden windmills and hang them on the roof. The reason for this is that the Japanese believe carp to be the most energetic creatures, and they hope that the boys in the family will be as strong and resilient as carp. Therefore, this day is also referred to as "Carp Day".

细说日本的
"男孩节"

4. 盂兰盆节 Obon Festival

盂兰盆节是日本民间最大的传统节日，又称"魂祭""佛教万灵会"等，8 月 15 日左右举行，以群体性质的篝火舞蹈仪式为主。传说盂兰盆节时祖先灵魂要回家，所以是纪念祖先、祝福亡灵的日子。日本的祭祖文化是从遣唐使来到中国之后（公元 607 年）开始的，盂兰盆节祭祖习俗也从中国传入了日本。

Obon Festival is the largest traditional folk festival in Japan, also known as "Soul Sacrifice", "Buddhist All Souls Festival" and so on. It is held around August 15. It is mainly a group bonfire dance ceremony. It is said that the ancestors' souls will go home during the festival, so it's a day to remember their ancestors and bless the dead. Japan's ancestor worship culture began after the Japanese envoys visited China (in 607 AD), and the Obon festival customs for honoring ancestors were also introduced to Japan from China.

 小知识

"祭"在日语里面是什么意思?

"祭"在日语里表示"……节",即节日的意思。日本人常说"人生的目的是为祭,祭的形式是狂欢"。前半句体现了祭在日本人眼中的重要性。后半句提到的狂欢,便会使人联想到西方文化中的酒神精神。哲学家尼采认为,酒神精神喻示着情绪的发泄,是抛弃传统束缚回归原始状态的生存体验。日语中的"祭り",往往是指群体的仪式活动,人们熟知的日本三大狂欢节日分别是东京的神田祭、京都的祇园祭和大阪的天神祭。汉语里面"祭"的意思可是大不相同,是表示哀悼的意思。

三、旅游观光 Tourism and Sightseeing

(一)主要旅游城市 Major Tourist Cities

1. 东京 Tokyo

东京是日本首都,是全国政治、经济、文化、交通中心,也是世界特大城市之一。东京面积为 2 190 平方千米,人口数量为 1 385 万(2019 年 1 月)。东京建于 1457 年,古称江户,1868 年明治维新后,明治天皇从京都迁都江户,改称东京。东京是日本最大的工业城市,也是日本的商业、金融中心,还是现代化国际大都市和世界著名旅游城市之一。这座城市既保留了日本传统特色,又兼具浓郁的欧美风情。

Tokyo, as Japan's capital and the political, economic, cultural and transportation center, is one of the largest metropolitan cities in the world. It covers an area of 2 190 square kilometers with a population of 13.85 million (January, 2019). Founded in 1457, Tokyo was known as Edo in ancient times and was renamed Tokyo in 1868 after the Meiji Restoration when Emperor Meiji moved the capital from Kyoto to Edo. Tokyo is Japan's largest industrial city, as well as Japan's commercial and financial center, a modern international metropolis and one of the world's most famous tourist cities. The city retains both traditional Japanese characteristics and a strong European and American flavor.

2. 大阪 Osaka

大阪自古以来就是古都奈良和京都的门户,也是日本商业和贸易发展最早的地区,曾有几代日本天皇在此建都(公元 313—412 年、公元 645—683 年),因此名胜古迹众多。作为历史上的商业中心,大阪一直发挥着引领日本经济的作用。白天和晚上的人口比例达到 100∶141,在日本是最高的,凸显出其作为一个经济中心的地位。

Osaka has been the gateway of the ancient capitals of Nara and Kyoto since ancient times. It is also the area where Japan's commerce and trade developed the earliest. There were several generations of Japanese emperors who established their capital here (313–412 AD, 645–683 AD), so there are many places of interest. As the commercial center in history, Osaka has always played a commanding role for the Japanese economy. The ratio between daytime and nighttime population is 100:141, the highest in Japan, highlighting its status as an economic center.

3. 京都 Kyoto

京都位于东京西南，大阪以东。从东京乘新干线特快车，只需 3 小时即可到京都。作为日本的必游地之一，群山围绕的京都有着众多历史古迹与神奇传说。从 794 年至 1868 年，京都一直是日本的古都，故有"千年古都"之称。市内现尚存 1 877 个寺庙和神社，被定为国宝的文物有 211 件，占全国国家级文物总数的 15%。

Kyoto is located southwest of Tokyo and east of Osaka. It takes just three hours to reach Kyoto from Tokyo by Shinkansen bullet train. As a must-visit destination in Japan, Kyoto is surrounded by mountains and is rich in historical landmarks and enchanting legends. From 794 to 1868, it served as Japan's ancient capital, earning it the nickname "The Thousand-Year Capital". Today, the city is home to 1,877 temples and shrines, with 211 artifacts designated as National Treasures, accounting for 15% of the country's total.

京都的宫殿、园林与建筑皆完好无损，是日本保存得最完好的城市之一，其中包括京都最著名的寺庙——清水寺。古城平安京（京都古称）的设计和建筑风格模仿唐代的洛阳城和长安城，故京都简称"洛"。到京都旅游的最佳时间是春秋两季。每当樱花盛开和秋季来临时，岚山游人如织。岚山山麓的龟山公园内有为纪念周恩来同志而建的"雨中岚山"石碑。

Kyoto's palaces, gardens, and architecture remain perfectly preserved, making it one of the best-preserved cities in Japan. Among its treasures is Kiyomizu-dera, Kyoto's most famous temple. The design and architectural style of the ancient city of Heian-kyo (Kyoto's former name) were modeled after the Tang Dynasty cities of Luoyang and Chang'an, which is why Kyoto is also referred to as "Rakuyo." The best times to visit Kyoto are during spring and autumn. When cherry blossoms are in full bloom or autumn leaves begin to turn, Arashiyama becomes a bustling destination for visitors. At the foot of Arashiyama, in Kameyama Park, stands the "Rainy Arashiyama" poetry monument, dedicated to the memory of Premier Zhou Enlai.

（二）著名旅游景点 Famous Tourist Attractions

1. 富士山 Mount Fuji

如果说樱花是日本的象征，那么富士山（图 1-6）也是如此，两者的结合构成了一幅令人难忘的景象。富士山位于本州岛，是日本最高的山，海拔 3 776 米。富士山是一座活火山，上一次喷发是在 1707—1708 年。富士山有着异常对称的圆锥体山形，每年有几个月被积雪覆盖，周边风景优美。

图 1-6　富士山
Figure 1-6　Mount Fuji

If cherry blossoms symbolize Japan, so does Mount Fuji(Figure1-6), and the combination of the two creates an unforgettable image. Located on Honshu Island, Mount Fuji is Japan's tallest mountain, standing at 3,776 meters. It is an active volcano, with its last eruption occurring between 1707 and 1708. Mount Fuji is renowned for its remarkably symmetrical cone shape, and for several months each year, it is beautifully capped with snow, surrounded by stunning scenery.

2. 浅草寺 Senso Temple

浅草寺（图 1-7）始建于 628 年，是东京最古老的寺庙。浅草寺本堂被称作观音堂，以其主梁的构型优美而闻名，内部分为外阵和内阵。观音堂内阵中央有放置着本尊的宫殿，三面开门，是日本第一大宫殿，也是日本现存的具有"江户风格"的民众游乐之地。

图 1-7　浅草寺
Figure 1-7　Senso Temple

Senso Temple (Figure 1-7), the oldest of its kind in Tokyo, was founded in the year 628. Senso Temple Hondo is referred to as the Goddess of Merey Hall, which is famous for its beautiful architecture of the main beam and is divided into the outer and inner array for its interior.In the central of the inner side of the Goddess of Mercy Hall, there is a Guanyin statue enshrined in the palace, which is open on three sides and is Japan's largest palace. Now it is a popular "Edo style" amusement land in Japan.

3. 银座 Ginza

银座（图 1-8）是东京一个繁华的商业区，相传从前这一带是海，后来德川家康填海造地，这里便成为铸造银币的地方，明治三年（1870 年）更名为"银座"。商业区内有许多国际知名的百货公司、精品店、餐厅和咖啡馆。现在银座被认为是世界上最豪华的购物区之一。

图 1-8　银座
Figure 1-8　Ginza

Ginza (Figure 1-8) is a vibrant commercial district in Tokyo, famously known for its luxurious shopping scene. Historically, this area was once part of the sea until Tokugawa Ieyasu reclaimed it, turning it into a mint for silver coins. In 1870, during the Meiji era, it was officially named "Ginza". Today, the district boasts a plethora of internationally renowned department stores, boutiques, restaurants, and cafes, making it one of the most prestigious shopping areas in the world.

4. 东京塔 Tokyo Tower

东京塔（图 1-9）又名日本东京电视塔，位于东京都港区芝公园西侧。1958 年 12 月建成，于 1968 年 7 月对游客开放。塔高 333 米，占地 2 118 平方米。这座日本最高的独立铁塔上部装有东京 7 个电视台、21 个电视中转台和广播台等的无线电发射天线。

图 1-9　东京塔
Figure 1-9　Tokyo Tower

Tokyo Tower, often referred to as the Tokyo Television Tower (Figure 1-9), is situated on the western edge of Shiba Park in Minato City, Tokyo. Completed in December 1958 and opened to the public in July 1968, the tower stands 333 meters tall and occupies a footprint of 2,118 square meters. As Japan's tallest freestanding tower, its upper section is fitted with radio transmission antennas that support seven Tokyo TV stations, 21 relay stations, and several radio broadcasters. antennas for 7 TV stations, 21 TV relay stations and radio broadcasting stations in Tokyo.

图 1-10　大阪城

Figure 1-10　Osaka Castle

5. 大阪城 Osaka Castle

大阪城（图 1-10）是大阪的著名地标。1583 年，丰臣秀吉花费了两年七个月的时间，由四万民夫建造而成。大阪城分为三部分，四周有护城河。1615 年，原大阪城与丰臣一族毁于战火，后经德川家光增建后才有今天的面貌。现在的大阪城已规划成为公园，作为市民休闲的场所。大阪城为日本三大名城之一。

Osaka Castle (Figure1-10) is Osaka's famous landmark. Originally built in 1583 by Toyotomi Hideyoshi, it took 40,000 workers two years and seven months to complete. The castle is divided into three sections and is surrounded by a protective moat. It was destroyed in war fire in 1615, followed by Tokugawa Iemitsu's reconstruction to achieve the present shape today. Now Osaka City has been renovated into a park for public leisure. It is also recognized as one of Japan's three most famous castles.

6. 唐招提寺 Tōshōdai Temple

唐招提寺（图 1-11）位于奈良市，这座日本佛教律宗建筑由中国唐代高僧鉴真亲手兴建，是日本佛教律宗的总寺院。这座具有中国盛唐建筑风格的建筑物被确定为日本国宝。唐代高僧鉴真（公元 688—763 年）第 6 次东渡日本后，于天平宝字三年（公元 759 年）开始建造，工程大约于公元 770 年完成。寺院大门上红色横额"唐招提寺"是日本孝谦女皇仿王羲之、王献之的字体所书。寺内，松林苍翠，庭院幽静，殿宇重重，有天平时代的讲堂、戒坛，奈良时代（公元 710—789 年）后期的金堂，镰仓时代（公元 1185—1333 年）的鼓楼、礼堂及天平以后的佛像、法器和经卷。御影堂前东面是

图 1-11　唐招提寺

Figure 1-11　Tōshōdai Temple

鉴真墓，院中植有来自中国的松树、桂花、牡丹、芍药、"孙文莲""唐招提寺莲""唐招提寺青莲""舞妃莲""日中友谊莲"和扬州的琼花等名花异卉。

Tōshōdai Temple (Figure 1-11) is located in Nara City. The Japanese Buddhist Legacy Building Complex was built by Jianzhen, a famous monk in the Tang Dynasty of China, and is the main temple of the Japanese Buddhist Legacy. This building with the architectural style of the Chinese prosperous Tang Dynasty was identified as the national treasure of Japan. After Jianzhen (688—763

AD）made his sixth eastward trip to Japan, the construction began in the third year of Tianpingbao（759 AD）and was completed in about 770 AD. The red banner "Tang Zhaoti Temple" on the gate of the temple was written by the Japanese Empress Xiaoqian in imitation of Wang Xizhi and Wang Xianzhi. In the temple, there are green pine forests, quiet courtyards, and numerous halls. There are lecture halls and ordination platform in the Tianping era, golden halls in the late Nara era（710—789 AD）, drum towers and auditoriums in the Kamakura era（1185—1333 AD）, and Buddha statues, magic tools, and scriptures after Tianping. In the east of the front of the Imperial Cinema is the Jianzhen Tomb. In the courtyard, there are famous flowers and different flowers from China, such as pine, osmanthus, peony, peony, "Sun Wenlian" "Tang Zhaoti Temple Lotus" "Tang Zhaoti Temple Qinglian" "Danfei Lotus" "Japan-China Friendship Lotus" and Yangzhou Qionghua.

7. 清水寺 Kiyomizu-dera

清水寺（图 1-12）是一座位于日本京都府京都市东山区的寺院，建于 778 年。清水寺的山号为音羽山，主要供奉千手观音。自平安时代以来，清水寺就经常出现于日本文学作品中。1994 年，清水寺作为古都京都历史遗迹的一部分，被列入《世界遗产名录》。

Kiyomizu-dera (Figure 1-12), founded in 778, is a temple located in Higashiyama-ku, Kyoto Prefecture. Kiyomizu-dera is also called Otowa-san. Kiyomizu-dera is mainly dedicated to the Thousand-

图 1-12　清水寺
Figure 1-12　Kiyomizu-dera

hand Bodhisttva. Since the Heian Period, Kiyomizu-dera has been often seen in Japanese literary works. In 1994, Kiyomizu-dera Temple was inscribed as a UNESCO World Heritage List as part of the Historic Monuments of Ancient Kyoto.

8. 金阁寺 The Temple of the Golden Pavilion

金阁寺（图 1-13）是日本最美丽的建筑之一，与富士山、艺伎并列为外国人对于日本的三大典型印象。该寺于 1397 年以足利义满将军之名所建，专为举办佛教纪念活动所设。金阁寺最高的两层楼全部被金叶包裹，一只金色凤凰矗立屋顶，十分夺目，金阁寺也因此得名。1950 年，金阁寺被一个日本疯和尚付之一炬，后于 1955 年重建。池塘周围的阁亭和花园、是日本最美丽的取景地之一。1994 年被列入《世界遗产名录》。

图 1-13　金阁寺
Figure 1-13　The Temple of the Golden Pavilion

The Temple of the Golden Pavilion (Figure 1-13) is one of the most beautiful buildings in Japan. The Temple, Mount Fuji and Geisha are the three typical impression of Japan in the eyes of foreigners. It was constructed in 1397 for General Ashikaga Yoshimitsu and designed for holding the Buddhist observance. The top two floors are all wrapped in gold leaves and a golden phoenix perches on the rooftop, an eye-catching scene and hence the name. In 1950, the temple was torched by a crazy Japanese monk and was rebuilt in 1955. The pavilions and gardens around the pond are one of the best sites for photograph in Japan. In 1994, it was listed into the World Heritage List.

（三）旅游购物 Shopping

日本清酒：清酒是日本酒文化的代表，是借鉴中国黄酒的酿造方法而发展起来的日本国酒。清酒呈淡黄色或无色，清亮透明，其味甘醇温和，酒精含量为 15%～17%，度数较低。清酒是日本的国粹之一。

Japanese sake:Sake is a representative of Japanese alcohol culture and is developed based on the brewing methods of Chinese yellow wine. It has a light yellow or colorless appearance. It is clear and transparent, and has a mild, sweet flavor with an alcohol content of 15-17%, making it relatively low in strength. Sake is one of Japan's cultural treasures.

玩偶玩具：日本的玩偶玩具小巧精美，有些品牌大家耳熟能详，如和服人偶娃娃、Hello Kitty 系列等。

Toy dolls: Japanese toy dolls are small and exquisite. Some of such brands are highly popular, such as the Kimono Doll, Hello Kitty, etc.

电子产品：日本有许多著名的电子品牌，如东芝、日立、索尼、尼康等。这些品牌的最新款 DV、相机、计算机等产品，有些只能在日本本土才能买到。因为免税，价格相对较低。

Electronic products: Japan has many well-known electronic brands like Toshiba, Hitachi, Sony, Nikon, etc. The latest models for DV, camera, PC of those brands are only available in Japan. Duty-free policy means price is also relatively lower.

护肤品：日本的护肤品价格低，质量上乘，卫生和原料控制严格有保证，是亚洲女性的最爱，特别是近年来人气很旺的药妆。著名的品牌有资生堂、高丝等。

扫码获取：入境须知及海关规定

Skin care products: Japan's skin care products are inexpensive and of high quality, with guarantees of health and material control, making them the most popular among Asian women, particularly the drugstore cosmetics that have emerged in recent years. Famous brands of such products include SHISEIDO, KOSE, and others.

本节习题

1. 某旅游团在日本旅游，游客在欣赏樱花时兴致高涨，其中两人要求与当地导游一起合影，但被导游婉言谢绝了。这是为什么？

2. 某游客去日本一位朋友家做客，游客看见主人没有给自己碗里盛满饭，盛菜的碗碟都很小，心里有点不高兴。请问是主人小气而不让客人吃饱吗？

3. 列举四个日本主要的旅游城市。

4. 简述日本茶道和中国茶道的异同点。

5. 简述唐招提寺与中日两国友好往来的历史渊源。

泡菜之国——韩国
The Land of Kimchi—Korea

导读

　　韩国地理位置优越，自然环境秀美，首尔、釜山、庆州和济州岛是全国著名的四大旅游中心。韩国导游经常把首尔比作北京，釜山相当于上海，济州岛相当于海南。韩国是亚洲经济最发达的国家之一。第二次世界大战后，韩国长期以对美、日外交为主，20世纪 70 年代初开始推行门户开放政策。中国与韩国自 1992 年 8 月建立外交关系以来，两国关系发展迅速。中韩两国不断开展高层往来，增进互信共识，拓展合作领域，在经济上互利合作、不断深化，互为重要贸易伙伴，在文化、教育、科技等领域的交流与合作也日益活跃。通过利用发达的海、陆、空交通优势，韩国采取了一系列发展旅游的措施，吸引着来自世界各国的游客。目前，旅游业已成为韩国经济增长的新亮点。韩国的国际游客主要来自日本和中国，首尔是游客的主要旅游目的地，同时韩国也是中国第一大客源国。

一、地理概览 Geography of Korea

（一）位置 Location

　　韩国（全称大韩民国）位于东亚朝鲜半岛的南部，三面环海，北接朝鲜，西部濒临中国黄海，东边与日本隔海相望。韩国国土面积约为 10.329 万平方千米，占朝鲜半岛总面积的 45%。海域岛屿星罗棋布，其中最大的岛屿是济州岛，还有巨济岛、江华岛、珍岛、南海岛等，海岸线较长，海岸多悬崖绝壁，港湾风光秀丽。s

Republic of Korea is located in the southern part of the Korean Peninsula in East Asia, surrounded by the sea on three sides, bordered by Democratic People's Republic of Korea to the north, facing the Yellow Sea of China to the west, and separated from Japan by the sea to the east. Republic of Korea has a land area of approximately 103, 290 square kilometers, accounting for 45% of the Korean Peninsula's total area. Its waters are dotted with numerous islands, the largest of which is Jeju Island, along with other islands such as Geoje Island, Ganghwa Island, Jindo, and Namhae. The coastline is long, characterized by steep cliffs, and the harbors boast beautiful scenery.

（二）地形和气候 The Land and Seasons

　　韩国地势北高南低、东高西低，山地、丘陵面积较大，名山较多。太白山脉纵贯东海岸，构成半岛南部地形的脊梁。其中，雪岳山、五台山等山势雄伟，以风景优美著称。位于济州岛中心的汉拿山海拔 1 950 米，是韩国的第一高峰，与智异山、金刚山一起被誉为三座神山。平原主要分布于南部和西部，有汉江、湖南、金海和全南平原等。海岸线曲折，形成许多著名的海滨、海岛游览地。

Republic of Korea's terrain is higher in the north and lower in the south, with the east being higher than the west. The country has a significant amount of mountainous and hilly areas, with many renowned mountains. The Taebaek Mountain Range runs along the eastern coast, forming the backbone of the southern peninsula's topography. Mount Seorak and Mount Wutai are among the majestic mountains known for their beautiful scenery. Mount Halla, located in the center of Jeju Island, stands at an elevation of 1,950 meters, making it Republic of Korea's highest peak and is revered as one of the Three Sacred Mountains along with Mount Jiri and Mount Geumgang. Plains are mainly found in the southern and western regions, including the Han River, Honam, Geum River, and Jeonnam plains. The coastline is intricate, creating numerous famous coastal and island tourist destinations.

由于受海洋暖流及东南亚季风的影响，韩国具有海洋性气候和大陆性气候的双重特征。四季分明，春秋短、夏冬长，夏季炎热潮湿，冬季寒冷干燥。年均降水量约为 1 500 毫米，降水由南向北逐步减少，其中 6—8 月雨量较大。各地区之间温差较大，平均温度为 6 ℃～ 16 ℃。全年最热的 8 月平均温度为 19 ℃～ 27 ℃。在韩国可以观赏到分属四季的美景，7—10 月是旅游的黄金季节，8 月是旅游最佳时间。

Due to the influence of ocean currents and the Southeast Asian monsoon, Republic of Korea exhibits a dual climate characteristic of maritime and continental climates. The country experiences distinct four seasons, with short springs and autumns, and long summers and winters. Summers are hot and humid, while winters are cold and dry. The average annual precipitation is around 1,500 mm, with rainfall gradually decreasing from south to north, with higher precipitation levels typically observed from June to August. There are significant temperature variations between regions, with average temperatures ranging from 6 ℃ to 16 ℃ . The hottest month of the year is August, with average temperatures ranging from 19 ℃ to 27 ℃ . Republic of Korea offers picturesque landscapes throughout the four seasons, with the period from July to October being considered the peak tourist season, and August being the optimal time for travel.

（三）自然资源 Natural Resources

韩国矿产资源较少，主要工业原料、燃料均依赖进口；非金属类矿物，如重晶石、云母、萤石和高岭土等，储量很高。韩国物产丰富，人参是当地的重要特产，以盛产"高丽参"闻名世界；森林资源丰富，全国森林覆盖率达 61%；沿海有面积广阔的渔场。

Korea's mineral resources are relatively limited, and the main industrial raw materials and fuels are imported from other countries . However, it is rich in products, with ginseng being an important local specialty; the abundance of "Goryeo ginseng" is known worldwide. Additionally, Korea has rich forest resources, with a forest coverage of 61%, and its coast features extensive fishing grounds.

二、人文概况 Overview of Korean Humanities

（一）国情认知 Basic Knowledge of National Conditions

韩国总人口约 5 162.8 万（2022 年），人口密度约为每平方千米 527.3 人，是世界人口密度最大的国家之一。韩国属于单一民族国家，绝大多数人口为朝鲜族，占全国总人口的 96.25%，只有少数华裔和日裔。官方语言为朝鲜语（或称韩语），但英语也可在旅游区及商业区通用。宗教为佛教、基督新教、天主教。

With a total population of about 51.628 million（2022）and a population density of about 527.3 persons per square kilometer，Korea is one of the most densely populated countries in the world. Republic of Korea is a mono-ethnic country，with the majority of the population being Democratic People's Republic of Korea，accounting for 96.25% of the country's total population，and only a small number of people of Chinese and Japanese descent. The official language is Korean（or Hangul），but English is also widely used in tourist and commercial areas. Its religions are Buddhism，Protestantism and Catholicism.

韩国国旗通称"太极旗"，中间的太极象征宇宙。国徽中央为一朵盛开的木槿花，由一条白色绶带环绕，绶带上有"大韩民国"四个字。木槿花是韩国国花，国鸟为喜鹊。

The national flag of Republic of Korea is commonly known as the"Taegeukgi"，with the central Taegeuk symbolizing the universe. The national emblem features a blooming hibiscus flower at its center，surrounded by a white ribbon that bears the words"Republic of Korea". The hibiscus is the national flower of Republic of Korea，and the national bird is the magpie.

（二）历史简介 History of Korea

根据神话记载，神王檀君在公元前 2333 年建立了高丽王国。随后历史上经历了高句丽、百济和新罗三国鼎立的时代。公元 676 年，新罗统一了三国。公元 918—1392 年进入高丽时代。14 世纪末建立了朝鲜王朝。1910 年朝鲜半岛沦为日本的殖民地。1945 年日本向盟军投降，标志着第二次世界大战的结束，却进一步加剧了外国势力在朝鲜半岛的纷争。北纬三八分界线标志着苏联和美国分别占领朝鲜半岛的北部和南部。1948 年 8 月 15 日，大韩民国成立，李承晚为第一任总统。

According to the mythology，Korea Kingdom was founded by the god-king Tangun in 2333 BC. Subsequently history experienced the three kingdoms of Goguryeo，Baekje and Silla. In 676 AD，Silla unified the three kingdoms. The Goryeo period lasted from 918-1392 AD. The Joseon Dynasty was established in the late 14th century，and the Korean Peninsula was colonized by Japan in 1910. Japan surrendered to the Allied Forces in 1945，signaling the end of World War Ⅱ but further intensifying foreign rivalries in the Korean Peninsula. Division at the 38th parallel north latitude marked the respective occupation of the North and South by Soviet Union and the United States. On August 15，1948，Republic of Korea was established，with Syngman Rhee as the first president.

（三）经济状况 The Economy

韩国是联合国会员国，也是世界贸易组织成员国与 G20 主要国家之一；同时，韩国也是亚太经济合作组织(APEC)、东亚峰会的创始成员国。韩国创造的经济繁荣被称为"汉江奇迹"。钢铁、汽车、造船、电子、纺织等是韩国的支柱产业，其中造船和汽车制造等行业已进入世界前十。三星、现代、SK、LG 和 KT（韩国电信公司）等大企业集团创造的产值在国民经济中所占比重超过 60%，具有十分重要的地位。韩国的经济属于外向型经济，国际贸易在韩国 GDP 中有很大的比重，是世界第七大出口国和进口国。

Republic of Korea is a member of the United Nations，a member of the WTO and one of the major G20 countries.It is also a founding member of APEC and East Asia Summit. The economic prosperity created by Korea has been called the"the miracle on the Han River". Iron and steel，automobiles， shipbuilding, electronics, textiles, etc. are the pillar industries of Korea, of which shipbuilding and automobile manufacturing industries have entered the world's top ten. Large conglomerates such as Samsung, Hyundai, SK, LG and KT (Korea Telecommunications Corporation) play a very important role in Korea's economy, and the output value they create accounts for more than 60% of the national economy. Korea's economy is externally oriented, with international trade accounting for a large portion of Korea's GDP, making it the world's seventh largest exporter and seventh largest importer.

（四）传统文化 Traditional Culture

韩国的饮食以清淡为主，泡菜是韩国的第一美食。烤肉文化是韩国古老的饮食文化。韩国人请客吃饭一般是吃烤肉，就是将牛肉或牛排用佐料卤腌好，放在铁板上烤熟，通常情况下会提供泡菜和包肉用的佐菜。韩服是韩国的传统服装，一般在节日和有特殊意义的日子里穿着。韩国的医美较为发达，整容医生较多，不但明星、演员经常整容，普通人整容也很常见。

Korean cuisine is primarily characterized by its lightness, with kimchi being the country's top delicacy. The culture of grilled meat is an ancient aspect of Korean culinary traditions. When Koreans host a meal, it typically features grilled meat, which involves marinating beef or steak in seasonings and cooking it on an iron plate. It is usually accompanied by kimchi and various side dishes for wrapping the meat. Hanbok is the traditional attire of Korea, typically worn during festivals and on special occasions. The medical beauty industry in Korea is quite advanced, with a high number of plastic surgeons; in addition to celebrity actors frequently undergoing cosmetic procedures, it is also common among ordinary people.

韩国是个具有悠久历史和灿烂文化的国家，在文学、艺术等方面都有自己的特色。韩国的美术主要包括绘画、书法、版画、工艺和装饰等，既继承了民族传统，又吸收了外国美术的特长。韩国人素以喜爱音乐和舞蹈而著称。韩国现代音乐大致可分为"民族音乐"和"西洋音乐"两种，舞蹈以民族舞和宫廷舞为中心，多姿多彩。韩国舞蹈非常重视舞者肩膀、胳膊的韵律。道具有扇、花冠、鼓。韩国的戏剧起源于史前时期的宗教仪式，主要包括假面具、木偶剧、曲艺、唱剧、话剧五类。其中假面具又称"假面舞"，为韩国文化象征，在韩国传统戏剧中占有极为重要的地位。韩国人民十分喜欢运动，尤其爱好参加民间游戏，主要有荡秋千、踩跷跷板、放风筝、踏地神等。韩国民间体育活动包括围棋、象棋、摔跤、跆拳道、滑雪等，种类颇多。

Korea is a country with a long history and splendid culture, and has its own characteristics in literature and art. Korean art mainly includes painting, calligraphy, printmaking, craftsmanship, and decoration, inheriting national traditions and absorbing the specialties of foreign art. Koreans are known for their love of music and dance. Modern Korean music can be broadly categorized into "folk music" and "Western music". Korean dances, centered on folk dances and court dances, are very colorful. Korean dance emphasizes the rhythm of the dancer's shoulders and arms. The props have fans, flower crowns, and drums. Korean drama has its roots in prehistoric religious ceremonies and consists of five main categories: masks, puppet shows, musicals, singing, and dramas. Masks, also known as "Mask Dance", is a symbol of Korean culture and play a very important role in traditional Korean theater. The Korean people are very fond of sports, especially folk games. The main folk games include swinging, teeter-tottering, kite-flying, earth-shaking, etc. There are

韩国假面舞被列入人类非遗名录

many types of folk sports in Korea, including Go, chess, wrestling, Taekwondo, and skiing.

（五）礼仪禁忌 Social Etiquettes and Taboos

韩国受儒家思想影响较深，历来重视礼节，尊老爱幼，互相谦让，对外国游客较为有礼。赴韩应注重礼仪，注意个人形象，在公共场合不要大声喧哗。进入餐厅或韩国人家时要脱鞋，注意鞋袜卫生，不能光脚。未经对方同意不要抽烟。不在大街上吐痰或擤鼻涕等。社会交往中，韩国人见面时的传统礼节是鞠躬，晚辈、下级走路时遇到长辈或上级，应鞠躬、问候，并站在一旁，让其先行，以示敬意。对长辈必用敬语，平辈初次见面也应互致问候。有长辈在场，不能抽烟，不能戴墨镜。政府规定，韩国公民对国旗、国歌、国花必须敬重。电台播放国歌、影剧院放映演出前播放国歌时，观众须起立。

Korea is deeply influenced by Confucianism and has always emphasized etiquette. Koreans have respect for the elderly, love for the young, mutual modesty and courtesy to foreign tourists. Visitors to Korea should pay attention to etiquette and personal image. And do not make a lot of noise in public places. When entering a restaurant or a Korean family, take off your shoes and pay attention to the hygiene of your shoes and socks, and do not go barefoot. Do not smoke without the consent of the other party. Do not spit or blow your nose in the street. The traditional etiquette for meeting Koreans in social interactions is to bow. When a junior or subordinate meets an elder or superior while walking, he or she should bow, say hello, and stand aside to let him or her go first as a sign of respect. Elderly people must use honorific words, and the junior generation should also greet each other for the first time. No smoking or sunglasses in the presence of elders. The government mandates that Korean citizens must honor the national flag, national anthem, and national flower. When the national anthem is played on the radio or before a performance at a theater, the audience is required to stand up.

韩国有比较严格的餐桌礼仪。与长辈一起用餐时，长辈先动筷子后，晚辈才能使用筷子。在餐桌上，以汤匙就食，夹菜时才用筷子，捧碗而食被视为不礼貌的举动。不可以用筷子指指点点或者戳食物，用餐完毕后应将筷子整齐地摆放在桌面上，不能将筷子架在饭碗或其他食器上；吃水果时，应使用牙签。

韩国的餐具

Korea has quite strict dining etiquette. When dining with elders, the younger generation must wait for the elder to begin. At the dining table, a spoon is used for eating, while chopsticks are only used for picking up side dishes. Holding a bowl while eating is considered impolite. It is also inappropriate to point or poke at food with chopsticks. After finishing a meal, chopsticks should be neatly placed on the table; they should not be rested on the rice bowl or other dishes. When eating fruit, toothpicks should be used.

礼物赠送的礼节方面，礼品的贵重与否在很大程度上取决于双方之间的关系。如果你知道对方无法承受相应的回报，就不要送过于昂贵的礼物。应邀到韩国的家庭做客时，一般可以带水果或质量上乘的巧克力或鲜花。数字4是不吉利的，所以礼物数量不应是4的倍数。数字7被认为是幸运数字。礼物应精心包装，使用黄色或粉红色的包装纸，因为它们象征着幸福。不要用绿色、白色或黑色的纸包裹礼物。不要用红色墨水在卡片上签字。

As for gift giving etiquette, the value of the gift depends largely on the relationship between the two parties. It is inconsiderate to give someone an expensive gift if you know that they cannot afford to reciprocate accordingly. Bring fruit or good quality chocolates or flowers if you are invited to a Korean's house. The number 4 is considered unlucky, so gifts should not be given in multiples of 4, but number 7 is considered lucky. Gifts should be wrapped nicely. Alternatively, use yellow or pink paper since they denote happiness. Do not wrap gifts in green, white and black paper. Do not sign a card in red ink.

韩国人接受礼物一般用双手，但不会当着客人的面打开。不宜送外国香烟给韩国人。酒是送韩国男士最好的礼品，但不能送酒给妇女，除非说清楚酒是送给她丈夫的。赠送礼品时应注意，韩国男性多喜欢名牌纺织品、领带、打火机、电动剃须刀等；女性喜欢化妆品、提包、手套、围巾类物品和烹饪调料；孩子则喜欢食品。如果送钱，应放在信封内。

Koreans generally accept gifts with both hands, but do not open them in front of their guests. It is not advisable to give foreign cigarettes to a Korean man. Wine is the best gift for Korean men, but you cannot give wine to a woman unless you make it clear that the wine is for her husband. When giving gifts to Koreans, it should be noted that Korean men tend to like designer textiles, ties, lighters, electric razors, etc.; women like cosmetics, handbags, gloves, scarf-type items, and cooking seasonings; and children like food. If money is given, it should be placed in an envelope.

（六）传统节日 Festivals

1. 独立运动纪念日 Independence Day

1919 年 3 月 1 日，韩国爆发了反对日本殖民统治、争取民族独立的抗日运动，这一运动遭到了当时日本殖民统治者的残酷镇压。为了纪念这一运动，大韩民国临时政府于 1940 年制定《关于国庆日的法律》，将 3 月 1 日定为独立运动纪念日。此后，每年的 3 月 1 日，韩国政府和民间团体都会举行纪念仪式，追悼为国捐躯的烈士。

On March 1, 1919, the anti-Japanese movement against Japanese colonial rule and for national independence broke out in Korea. This movement was brutally suppressed by the Japanese colonial rulers. To commemorate this movement, the Provisional Government of the Republic of Korea enacted *the Law on National Day* in 1940, designating March 1 as the anniversary of the independence movement. Since then, every year on March 1, the Korean Government and civic organizations have held commemorative ceremonies to pay tribute to the martyrs who died in the service of the nation.

2. 佛诞日 Buddha's Birthday

韩国在农历的四月初八纪念释迦牟尼佛的诞辰，称为佛诞日。这一天韩国的各大寺庙会张灯结彩举办庆典及游行等祈福活动，街道上有灯笼点缀，首尔市民会利用假日或周末参加莲花灯笼庆典及游行活动。

In Republic of Korea, the birth of Sakyamuni: known as Buddha's Birthday, is celebrated on the eighth day of the fourth month in the lunar calendar. On this day, major temples across the country are adorned with decorations and host celebrations and parades as part of the festivities. The streets are embellished with lanterns, and citizens of Seoul take the opportunity during the holiday or weekend to enjoy the lotus lantern festivals and parades.

3. 江陵端午祭 Gangneung Danoje Festival

五月初五的江陵端午祭是韩国最著名的文化庆典之一，韩国传统上称

韩国人怎么过端午？

"端午"为"上日"，意为"神的节日"。江陵端午祭也围绕着广泛流传的神话人物展开。所祭祀的神灵包括"大关岭山神""国师城隍"等12位神话人物。在民间，最著名的神话传说是关于"国师城隍"。韩国人在端午并不吃粽子，也没有龙舟比赛，而是男人摔跤，女子用菖蒲汤洗头、荡秋千，全家人会穿上传统的韩国服装聚集在一起吃饭聊天，传统的食品有车轮饼和艾子糕等。现在韩国唯一完整保留端午习俗的是位于东海之滨的江陵。江陵端午祭已被联合国教科文组织正式确定为"人类口头和非物质遗产代表作"。

Gangneung Danoje Festival, held on the fifth day of the fifth month, is one of Republic of Korea's most famous cultural celebrations. Traditionally, Koreans refer to "Dano" as "Sangil", meaning "the day of the gods". The festival revolves around widely circulated mythical figures, with deities including the "Mountain God of Daegwanryeong" and the "National Master City God" among twelve mythological figures honored during the event. The most famous folk legend is about the "National Master City God". During Dano, Koreans do not eat zongzi or participate in dragon boat races; instead, men engage in wrestling, while women wash their hair with mugwort water and swing. Families gather in traditional Korean attire to share meals and conversations, with traditional foods such as wheel cakes and mugwort rice cakes. Today, Gangeung is the only place in Korea that has fully preserved Dano customs. Gangneung Danoje Festival has been officially recognized by UNESCO as a "Masterpiece of the Oral and Intangible Heritage of Humanity".

 思考题

韩国的江陵端午祭和中国的端午节有哪些不同？

4. 显忠日 Hyeonchung Day

每年的6月6日被韩国人称为显忠日。显忠日是纪念为国捐躯的义士，并展现忠诚爱国精神的节日。这一天也是韩国法定的公休日，各机关下半旗，早上10点，全体国民在听到警报声后一起默哀一分钟，为战死的战士们祈福，愿战乱牺牲者们安息。人们还会到国立显忠院、国立墓地、战争纪念馆、独立纪念馆等英灵聚集的地方献花。

June 6 of every year in Korea is known as Hyeonchung Day. Hyeonchung Day is a holiday to commemorate those who died in the service of the nation and to show loyalty and patriotism. On this day, which is also a legal public holiday in Korea, flags are flown at half-mast at all institutions, and at 10:00 a.m., the entire nation joins together to observe a minute's silence after hearing the siren, to pray for the soldiers who died in battle, to wish for the repose of those who sacrificed their lives in war, and to lay flowers at places where the spirits of the heroes gather, such as the National Palace of Hyeonchung, the National Cemetery, the War Memorial Hall, and the Independence Memorial Hall.

5. 辣椒节 The Pepper Festival

韩国人对泡菜的热爱直接决定了他们对红辣椒，特别是干红辣椒和辣椒面的热爱，也决定了他们对辣椒质量的高标准、严要求。虽然早已告别了缺衣少食的年代，但韩国人在冬天储藏大白菜、制作泡菜的习俗却保留了下来。泡菜的味道首先取决于大白菜，然后就是干辣椒。每年的6月16日，在首尔

白菜——韩国人餐桌上的顶梁柱

市中心，人们用各种颜色的辣椒拼出巨大的辣椒造型，迎接即将到来的辣椒节。

Koreans' love of kimchi determines their love of red pepper, expecially dried red peppers and chili noodles, as well as their high standards on the quality of hot pepper. Although the age with lack of food and clothing is long gone, the Koreans preserve the tradition of storage of cabbages and making kimchi during winter. The taste of kimchi depends primarily on the cabbage, then the quality of dried pepper. On June 16, in the downtown of Seoul, people use peppers of a variety of colors to piece together huge pepper modelings to mark the upcoming pepper festival.

6. 开天节 Gaecheonjeol

每年的公历 10 月 3 日是韩国的公假日——开天节，亦称"建国日"。开天节是纪念传说中的韩民族始祖檀君于公元前 2333 年建立古朝鲜的节日，原本定在农历十月初三，但于 1949 年改成公历的 10 月 3 日。在开天节这一天，政府和民间宗教团体都会举行各种隆重的庆典，首尔的祭奠主要是在社稷坛举行。

October 3 is Republic of Korea's public holiday—Gaecheonjeol, also known as "National Foundation Day". Gaecheonjeol is to commemorate the legendary ancestor of the Korean nationality Dan Gun who founded Gojoseon in the year 2333 BC. Originally set on the third day of the tenth lunar month, it was changed to October 3 in the Gregorian Calendar in 1949. On that day, both the government and the civil religious groups will hold grand celebrations, and in Seoul the ceremony is held on Sajikdan.

三、旅游观光 Tourism and Sightseeing

（一）主要旅游城市 Major Tourist Cities

1. 首尔 Seoul

首尔的历史超过 2 000 年，在公元前 18 年由三国时代之一的百济王国建立。当时的百济王国建都于现在的首尔市东南。在朝鲜王朝与大韩帝国时期，首尔一直是韩国的首都。它既是一座现代化的大都市，又是一座历史悠久的文化古城。首尔都市圈有四处联合国教科文组织世界遗产：昌德宫、水原华城、宗庙神殿和朝鲜王朝的皇家陵墓。如今，首尔被认为是全球领先的城市，是世界十强之一的金融和商业中心，有多家跨国集团公司，如三星、LG 和现代。

Seoul's history stretches back over 2,000 years, when it was founded in 18 BC by Backje, one of the Three Kingdoms of Korea, and established its capital in what is now southeastern Seoul. It continued as the capital of Korea under the Joseon Dynasty and the Korean Empire. It is both a modern metropolis and an ancient city with a long history of culture. The Seoul Metropolitan Area contains four UNESCO World Heritage Sites: Changdeok Palace, Hwaseong Fortress, Jongmyo Shrine and the Royal Tombs of the Joseon Dynasty. Seoul is considered to be a leading global city now. It is one of the world's top ten financial and commercial centers, home to major multinational conglomerates such as Samsung, LG and Hyundai.

2. 釜山 Busan

釜山位于首尔东南端 450 千米处，是韩国的第二大城市和第一大港口城市，泛太平洋物流中心，其设施和吞吐能力位居世界前列。釜山的温泉星罗棋布，群山环抱，是一座风景秀丽的海滨城市，同时也是拥有多元文化的国际现代化都市。釜山电影节从 1996 年创办至今，已成为亚洲乃至全球电影商和媒体、明星热衷光顾的电影盛会。

Busan, located 450 kilometers southeast of Seoul, is Republic of Korea's second largest city and the largest port city, and also the logistics center of the Pan-Pacific Ocean. Its facilities and capacity rank in the forefront of the world. The city is dotted with hot springs and surrounded by mountains. It is also a beautiful seaside city and has developed into an international and modern metropolis with cultural pluralism. The Busan International Film Festival was created in 1996 and has become a popular film festival venue for Asian and even global film industry as well as for media and stars.

3. 庆州 Gyeongju

作为新罗王朝的首都，庆州有近千年的历史，是朝鲜半岛历史文化最为悠久和丰富的城市，也是韩国古代文明的摇篮。1979 年，庆州被联合国教科文组织指定为"世界十大历史遗迹"之一。寺院、王陵、王宫、天文台等遗迹遍布全市，有"无围墙博物馆"之称。庆州拥有韩国最大的寺院——佛国寺，其于 1995 年被列为世界文化遗产。

As the capital of the Silla Dynasty for nearly 1,000 years, Gyeongju has the longest and richest history and culture on the Korean Peninsula and is the cradle of Korea's ancient civilization. Gyeongju has many cultural heritages and was inscribed in 1979 by the UNESCO one of the ten World Heritage Sites, with temples, royal tombs, royal palaces, observatories, and other relics scattered throughout the city, and it is also nicknamed as the "City Wall-free Museum". Gyeongju has the largest temple in Korea, Bulguksa Temple, which was designated as a World Heritage Site in 1995.

4. 济州岛 Jeju Island

济州岛，也被称为"神之岛"，是深受亚洲人喜爱的度假胜地。古代建有名为"耽罗国"的独立国家，因此岛上保留着独特的风俗习惯。溶岩洞穴是济州岛的一大奇观。济州岛上有很多火山岩，经常下雨，气候温和，有风多、石头多和女人多的特点，和美国的夏威夷非常相似。游客们可以在济州岛徒步爬汉拿山（韩国最高峰）、在海边看日出日落、看瀑布、骑马，或者躺在海边的沙滩上欣赏美景。济州岛也是很多韩国电视剧的拍摄基地，比如风靡一时的《大长今》等。

Jeju Island, also known as the "Island of the Gods", is a popular vacation escape for Asians. Once built an independent kingdom called the Tamna in ancient time, it has preserved distinguished customs. The lava caves are one of the wonders of Jeju Island. The island's mixture of volcanic rocks, frequent rains, temperate climate and its featured windy weather, numerous stones and many women, makes it very similar to the Hawaian Islands in the United States. The island offers visitors a wide range of activities: hiking on Hallasan (Republic of Korea's highest peak), catching sunrises and sunsets on the beach, viewing majestic waterfalls, riding horses, or just lying comfortably on the sandy beaches. It is also a popular scene to shoot Korean TV series such as *Dae Jang Geum*.

（二）著名旅游景点 Famous Tourist Attractions

1. 景福宫 Gyeongbokgung Palace

景福宫（图 1-14）是首尔规模最大、最古老的宫殿之一，是韩国封建社会后期的政治中心。1592 年"壬辰倭乱"时，宫苑的大部分建筑物被破坏，只有 10 处宫殿保持完整。直到同治七年

图 1-14　景福宫

Figure 1-14　Gyeongbokgung Palace

（1868年），才在高宗的父亲兴宣大院君的主持下重建。景福宫的正殿名为勤政殿，是韩国古代最大的木结构建筑物，雄伟壮丽，是举行正式仪式以及接受百官朝贺的地方。

Gyeongbokgung Palace (Figure 1-14), one of the largest and oldest palaces in Seoul, was the political center of Korea in the late feudal period, and only 10 parts of the palace remained intact after most of the buildings were destroyed during the War in 1592. It was rebuilt in 1868 under the auspices of Heungseon Daewongun, the father of King Gojong. The main hall of Gyeongbokgung Palace, called Geumjeongjeon, was the largest wooden building in ancient Korea, a majestic site where official ceremonies were held and officials paid homage.

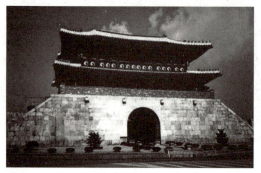

图 1-15　崇礼门
Figure 1-15　Sungnyemum

2. 崇礼门 Sungnyemum

崇礼门（图1-15）位于韩国首都首尔市中区，一般叫作"南大门"。南大门在诸多城门中规模最大，它邻近平民化的南大门市场，是首尔乃至韩国的一个主要地标，是首尔现存历史最悠久的木制建筑。城门中间呈拱形，上端为双层木制城楼，下端为石质门洞，威仪堂堂，傲睨群雄。韩国政府于1962年将崇礼门定为一号国宝。

The Sungnyemun (Figure 1-15) is located in the central district of Seoul, generally called the South Gate. It is the largest one among the gates of Seoul, adjacent to the commoners' Namdaemun market. It is also one of the main landmarks and also the oldest original wooden structure retained in Seoul. With an arch in the center, a double wooden gatehouse at the upper end of the gate, and a stone gateway at the lower end, Chongryeongmun is a majestic gateway that looks down on the rest of the world with pride. The Korean government designated Sungnyemum as Top National Treasure in 1962.

3. 青瓦台 Cheongwadae

图 1-16　青瓦台
Figure 1-16　Cheongwadae

韩国总统官邸，位于首尔钟路区世宗路一号。青瓦台（图1-16）原是高丽王朝的离宫，朝鲜王朝建都汉城（今首尔）后，把它作为景福宫后园，修建了隆武堂、庆农斋和练武场等建筑物，并开辟了一块国王的亲耕地。1927年日本入侵后毁掉五云阁以外的所有建筑，建立了朝鲜总督官邸。1945年日本投降后变为军政长官官邸。大韩民国成立时，它成为总统官邸，改名为景武台。1960年4月尹谱善当选总统入主景武台，为了同美国白宫相对应，给白墙蓝瓦的这群建筑起名为青瓦台，也称"蓝宫"。

The official residence of the President of Republic of Korea, located at 1 Sejong-ro, Jongno-gu, Seoul. Cheongwadae (Figure 1-16) was originally a palace of the Goryeo Dynasty, and after the Joseon Dynasty established its capital in Seoul, it was used as the backyard of Gyeongbokgung Palace, where buildings such as Yongmudang, Gyeongnongjae, and martial arts fields were constructed and a piece of the king's land was cultivated. After the Japanese invasion in 1927, all the buildings other than the Woyungak were destroyed, and the official residence of the Governor General of Joseon was established. It was changed into the official residence of the Chief of the Military Administration after the surrender of the Japanese in 1945. When the Republic of Korea was established, it became the official residence of the president and was renamed Gyeongmudae, and when Yoon Poo-sun was elected president and took over Gyeongmudae in April 1960, the whitewashed and blue-tiled buildings were named Cheongwadae, or the Blue House, in reference to the White House in the United States.

4. 乐天世界 Lotte World

世界上最大的室内主题公园，同美国迪士尼乐园一样被称为世界级的主题公园。乐天世界（图 1-17）位于首尔市中心，其主题公园有惊险的娱乐设施、凉爽的溜冰场、巨大的散心湖、各种表演场、民俗博物馆等集娱乐参观为一体的娱乐场所。除主题公园外，乐天世界还有百货商店、饭店、免税店、大型折扣商场、体育中心等。

图 1-17 乐天世界
Figure 1-17 Lotte World

Lotte World (Figure 1-17) is the largest indoor theme park in the world and is known as a world-class theme park along with Disneyland in the United States. Lotte World is located in the center of Seoul, and its theme park has thrilling amusement facilities, a cool ice skating rink, a huge lagoon, various performance venues, a folklore museum, and other entertainment venues that combine entertainment and visits. In addition to the theme park, Lotte World has department stores, restaurants, duty-free stores, large discount malls, sports centers, and more.

5. 韩国民俗村 The Korea Folk Village

韩国民俗村（图 1-18）位于京畿道首府水原市附近，占地 163 英亩[①]，它将韩国各地的农家民宅、寺院、贵族宅邸及官府等各式建筑聚集于此，再现了朝鲜半岛 500 多年前李朝时期的人文景观和地域风情。村内有 240 座传统的建筑物，有李朝时的衙门、监狱、达官贵族的宅邸、百姓的简陋房屋、店铺作坊、儿童乐园等。民俗村内的店铺和露天集市上的商品大多是当地传统手工制品以及别具风味的食品，有木质雕刻、彩绘纸扇、民族服装、彩色瓷器等。露天场上每日定时都有精彩节目表演，如民俗舞蹈、杂技和乡土鼓乐等，热闹非凡。

图 1-18 韩国民俗村
Figure 1-18 The Korea Folk Village

Located on 163 acres of land near Suwon City, the capital of Gyeonggi Province, the Korean Folk Village (Figure 1-18) recreates the

① 此单位非法定计量单位，1 英亩 =4 046.86 平方米。

humanistic landscape and regional flavor of the Korean Peninsula during the Yi Dynasty more than 500 years ago by bringing together a variety of buildings, such as farm houses, temples, nobleman's mansions, and governmental offices from all over Korea. There are 240 traditional buildings in the village, including the government offices and prisons of the Lee Dynasty, the houses of the nobles, the humble houses of the people, stores and workshops, and a children's playground. Stores and open-air bazaars in the Folk Village offer mostly local traditional handmade products and distinctive foods, such as wooden carvings, painted paper fans, national costumes, and colorful porcelains. The open-air field is bustling with regular daily performances of wonderful programs, such as folk dances, acrobatics and local drums.

图 1-19　龙头山公园

Figure 1-19　Yongdusan Park

6. 龙头山公园 Yongdusan Park

釜山塔所在的龙头山公园（图 1-19）内约有 700 种生长繁茂的植物，是深受釜山市民喜爱的休憩场所。龙头山公园位于貌似出海蛟龙的龙头山上，面积约 6.9 平方千米。釜山塔高 120 米，登上塔顶，可俯视釜山繁华街区与邻近海滨全景。此外，公园内还竖立着朝鲜时代名将李舜臣将军的铜像和 4·19 纪念碑。

Yongdusan Park (Figure 1-19), where Busan Tower is located, is a popular resting place for Busan residents with about 700 kinds of flourishing plants. Yongdusan Park is located on Yongdusan Mountain, which looks like a dragon emerging from the sea, and covers an area of about 6.9 square kilometers. The Busan Tower is 120 m high, and from the top of the tower, you can enjoy a panoramic view of Busan's bustling neighborhoods and the nearby seashore. In addition, a bronze statue of General Yi Sun-sin, a famous general of the Joseon Dynasty, and the 4·19 Memorial Monument are erected in the park.

图 1-20　佛国寺

Figure 1-20　Bulguksa Temple

7. 佛国寺 Bulguksa Temple

佛国寺（图 1-20）坐落在庆州东南 13 千米的吐含山的山腰处，被称为韩国五岳之东岳，海拔 745 米。释迦塔、多宝塔等佛塔体现了新罗时期登峰造极的艺术。寺内诸多的国宝与文化遗产令游客目不暇接。

Bulguksa Temple(Figure1-20) is situated on the slopes of Mount Toham, 13 kilometers southeast of Gyeongju. Known as the eastern peak of Korea's Five Great Mountains, Mount Toham stands at an elevation of 745 meters. The temple's Buddhist pagodas and statues showcase the pinnacle of cultural development during the Silla period. With its abundance of national treasures and cultural heritage, visitors often find that time flies as they explore the site.

8. 城山日出峰 Seongsan Ilchulbong

城山日出峰（图 1-21）是一个耸立在济州岛东端的巨大岩石，海拔 182 米，火山口直径

600 米，深 90 米，是 5 000 多年前海底火山爆发而形成的，号称是世界最大的突出于海岸的火山口。99 块尖石围绕在火山口周围，如同一顶巨大的皇冠，山顶为一片开阔的牧场。2007 年，城山日出峰被列入联合国教科文组织《世界遗产名录》。

图 1-21　城山日出峰
Figure 1-21　Seongsan Ilchulbong

Seongsan Ilchulbong (Figure 1–21) is a massive rock formation standing at the eastern end of Jeju Island. It has a height of 182 meters, a volcanic crater with a diameter of 600 meters, and a depth of 90 meters. Formed by an underwater volcanic eruption over 5 000 years ago, it is renowned as the world's largest volcanic crater protruding from the coastline. Surrounding the crater are 99 sharp rocks resembling a giant crown, with the mountaintop featuring a vast pasture. In 2007, Seongsan Ilchulbong was inscribed on the UNESCO World Heritage List.

9. 汉拿山国家公园 Hallasan National Park

汉拿山国家公园（图 1-22）位于济州岛的中心，海拔 1 950 米，是韩国第一高峰。该山峰自海底延伸，坡度缓和。济州岛就是汉拿山火山喷发后形成的。汉拿山国家公园上生长着亚热带、寒带的 1 800 余种植物与野生昆虫。前来此地的游客可以欣赏春天的花朵、夏天的高山植物、秋天的红叶与冬天的雪景。登山的最佳季节是气候适宜的 5 月和 10 月。

图 1-22　汉拿山国家公园
Figure 1-22　Hallasan National Park

Hallasan National Park (Figure 1–22) is located at the center of Jeju Island, with a height of 1,950 m, the highest peak in Republic of Korea. The mountain extends from submarine mountain range with relatively flat slope. Jeju Island was also formed in the period of Hallasan volcanic eruption. There are more than 1,800 subtropical and frigid species of plants and wild insects. Visitors may come here to enjoy the spring flowers, summer alpine plant, autumn maple leaves and winter snow. The best seasons with moderate climate for hiking are May and October.

（三）旅游购物 Shopping

高丽参：在韩国，高丽参被公认为是能使人元气旺盛的神秘名药，其保健效果居世界之冠。人参分为水参、干参、红参三种，其价格悬殊。除可直接食用根，为方便顾客，商家还为顾客提供参精或粉制品等多种产品。

Ginseng: In Republic of Korea, Ginseng is widely recognized as a precious drug widely believed to make the mysterious strength for humans and to have the top medicinal effects in the world. It can be classified as water ginseng, dried ginseng and red ginseng, and their prices vary greatly. Apart from the direct use of root, ginseng essence or powder products are also available for the convenience of customers.

韩式器皿：韩式器皿有青瓷、白瓷、粉青砂器等，式样、颜色、质地多种多样。除家庭日用品外，可用于装饰的艺术器皿也有很多。一般家用的器皿种类繁多，漆器、木器、玻璃器皿等均物美价廉。

The Korean-style household utensils: Korean-style household utensils include blue, white and pink-green porcelains with different styles, colors and texture. In addition to the household daily necessities, there are many artistic vessels available as well. There are various vessels for family use. Products like lacquer, woodwork and glassware are all of high quality and low price.

济州土产蜂蜜：济州土产蜂蜜品质优良。蜜柑蜜和油菜蜜是从济州产的蜜柑和油菜的花中提取出来的，具有独特的芳香和味道。以此精制的蜂王浆对养生、肠胃疾病相当有效，虽然价格较高，但仍受人们青睐。近来，在土产蜂蜜中加入仙人掌而制成的产品广受游客的喜爱。

The Jeju native honey: The quality of the Jeju native honey is really unique. Mandarin orange honey and rape honey are extracted from the Jeju mandarin and rape flowers with unique aroma and taste. The refined royal jelly is helpful to health and gastrointestinal disease. Many people are interested in this product despite its high price. Recently, this product laced with cactus becomes very popular among visitors.

韩国的化妆品：韩国的化妆品品牌众多，其中人气很高的品牌有雪花秀、Whoo（后）拱辰享系列、赫拉、亦博、兰芝和谜尚等。雪花秀是名副其实的韩国第一化妆品品牌。IOPE 是韩国最大的化妆品公司之———爱茉莉太平洋集团出品的顶级系列化妆品。

Korean cosmetics: There are many cosmetic brands in Korea, and some of the most popular ones are Snowflake, Whoo Hou Gongchen Heung, Hela, IOPE, Laneige, and Missha, etc. Snowflake is the number one cosmetic brand in Korea, and IOPE is one of the top series of cosmetics from Amore Pacific Group, one of the largest cosmetic companies in Korea.

扫码获取：入境须知与海关规定

本节习题

1. 请制作一份韩国旅游宣传册。
2. 请设计一条韩国 5 日游经典线路。
3. 试比较韩国与中国在人文旅游资源方面有什么相似之处。

第三节　东南亚之旅
Travel in Southeast Asia

花园之国——新加坡
The Land of Gardens—Singapore

导读

新加坡是一个发达的资本主义国家，是亚洲重要的金融、服务和航运中心。新加坡十分重视绿化和环境卫生，有花园城市的美称。中国和新加坡于 1990 年 10 月 3 日建立外交关系，建交以来，两国高层交往频繁，尤其是在金融、人文、科技、教育等方面。新加坡政府十分重视旅游业的发展，目前已成为亚洲乃至世界重要的旅游目的地之一。中国赴新加坡旅客人数近年来持续增加，连续多年蝉联新加坡最大入境客源国榜首。中国游客赴新多以休闲娱乐度假和商务活动为主。

一、地理概览 Geography of Singapore

（一）位置 Location

新加坡（全称新加坡共和国，Republic of Singapore）是东南亚的一个岛国，旧称星洲、星岛，别名狮城，由 63 个岛屿组成，海岸线总长 200 余千米，国土面积是 724.4 平方千米，主岛新加坡岛约占全国面积的 91.6%。新加坡坐落在马来半岛南端，北隔柔佛海峡与马来西亚紧邻，南隔新加坡海峡与印度尼西亚的廖内群岛相望。它地处太平洋与印度洋两大洋、亚洲与大洋洲两个旅游区之间的航运要冲，扼马六甲海峡进出口咽喉，是东南亚最繁忙的海陆交通枢纽，享有"东方十字路口"之称。

Singapore, officially known as the Republic of Singapore, is an island nation in Southeast Asia. Formerly called Singapura and Pulau Ujong, it is also known as the Lion City. Comprising 63 islands, Singapore has a total coastline of over 200 kilometers and a land area of 724.4 square kilometers, with the main island of Singapore accounting for approximately 91.6% of the country's total area. Situated at the southern tip of the Malay Peninsula, Singapore is separated by the Johor Strait to the north from Malaysia and faces the Riau Islands of Indonesia across the Singapore Strait to the south. It is situated at a strategic shipping crossroads between the Pacific and Indian Oceans, as well as between the tourist regions of Asia and Oceania, controlling the entrance and exit of the Strait of Malacca. It is the busiest land and sea transportation hub in Southeast Asia and is known as the "Crossroads of the East".

小知识

为什么新加坡又有"狮城"之名？

新加坡的名字来源于梵文 Singapure "信诃补罗"（意为"狮城"），并有着美丽的传说。新加坡古称淡马锡（爪哇语"海市"之意），公元 8 世纪建国，归属印度尼西亚室利佛逝王朝。相传 11 世纪时，室利佛逝王国的王子与谬内岛的公主结为百年之好，在谬内岛住了下来。一天，王子携公主外出打猎，乘船时遇大风浪，在即将翻船时，王子把王冠丢到海里，风浪顿时平静下来。他们便把船划到淡马锡海边。在附近树林里打猎时，他们忽然发现一只头黑胸白、身体红色、行动敏捷的怪兽，随从告诉王子这是一只狮子，王子听了非常高兴，认为这是一个吉祥的地方，便决定留下来。因登岸时首见狮子，后来他就把淡马锡改名为新加坡拉。在马来语中，"新加"是狮子，"坡拉"是城的意思。这便是新加坡和狮城名称的来历。鱼尾狮（图 1–23）现已成为新加坡的代表，鱼尾造型，浮泳于层层海浪间，既代表新加坡从渔港变成商港的特性，也象征着漂洋过海、南来谋生的祖祖辈辈们。

（二）地形和气候 The Land and Seasons

图 1-23 鱼尾狮
Figure 1-23 Merlion

新加坡地势起伏和缓，其西部和中部地区由丘陵地构成，大多数被树林覆盖，东部以及沿海地带都是平原，最高点为武吉知马，海拔 163.63 米。新加坡岛是马来半岛的延续，主岛有时被形容为钻石形，岛上有新加坡河、实里达河（全岛最长的河流，长 14 千米）、加冷河等河流。裕廊岛、德光岛、乌敏岛和圣淘沙是新加坡最大的四座小岛。

Singapore's terrain is gently undulating, with the western and central regions consisting of hilly areas mostly covered by forests. The eastern and coastal areas are plains, with the highest point being Bukit Timah at 163.63 meters above sea level. Singapore Island is an extension of the Malay Peninsula and is sometimes described as diamond-shaped. The island is home to rivers such as the Singapore River, the Seletar River, the longest on the island at 14 kilometers, as well as the Kallang River. Jurong Island, Tekong Island, Ubin Island, and Sentosa are the four largest islands in Singapore.

新加坡地处热带，常年受赤道低压带控制，为赤道多雨气候，无明显四季。常年高温潮湿，雨量充沛，气温年温差和日温差小，平均温度在 23 ℃～35 ℃之间，年平均降雨量约为 2 400 毫米，湿度介于 60%～90% 之间，相对湿度的日变化可以从清晨的 90% 降到午后的 60% 左右。11 月至次年的 1—3 月为雨季，通常午后有雷阵雨，6—9 月吹西南风，气候干燥，4—5 月和 10—11 月是季候风交替月，地面风弱多变、阳光酷热，最高温度可达 35 ℃。

Singapore is located in the tropics and is under the influence of the equatorial low-pressure belt throughout the year, resulting in a tropical rainy climate without distinct seasons. The weather is consistently hot and humid, with abundant rainfall and small annual temperature variations. The average temperature ranges from 23 to 35 degrees Celsius, with an average annual rainfall of about 2 400 mm. The humidity levels range from 60% to 90%, with relative humidity decreasing from around 90% in the early morning to about 60% in the afternoon. The rainy season typically occurs from November to March, with afternoon thunderstorms common. From June to September, there are southwest winds bringing dry weather, while April, May, October, and November are transitional months with variable and weak surface winds, intense sunlight, and temperatures reaching up to 35 degrees Celsius.

（三）自然资源 Natural Resources

新加坡有丰富的水资源和森林资源。新加坡建有 17 个蓄水池为市民储存淡水。新加坡的土地除了用来收集雨水，还发挥着重要的城市"绿肺"功能。为减少对外来水源的依赖，新加坡通过大型蓄水计划，以及海水淡化和循环再利用等技术，使水源供应更加多元化，逐步实现供水自给自足。

Singapore has abundant water and forest resources. There are 17 cisterns to store fresh water for the public. Apart from being used for rainwater harvesting, Singapore's land serves as an important "green lung" for the city. To reduce its dependence on external water sources, Singapore has diversified its water supply through large-scale water storage schemes, as well as technologies such as desalination and recycling, to gradually achieve self-sufficiency in water supply.

新加坡植物繁茂，终年常绿，有茂密的热带雨林、高大的棕榈树、美丽的三叶花、世界上为数不多的大片椰子林、大规模的兰花园和植物园。一年四季皆宜旅游，但5—6月和9—12月为旅游旺季，5月和9月是最佳旅游时间。

Singapore is lush with evergreen plants all year round, with dense tropical rainforest, tall palm trees, beautiful clover, the world's few large coconut forests, large-scale orchid gardens and botanical gardens. It is suitable to travel all the year round, but May to June and September to December are tourist seasons, May and September are the best time for Tourist in a year.

二、人文概况 Overview of Singaporean Humanities

（一）国情认知 Basic Knowledge of National Conditions

新加坡总人口约563.7万（2022年），人口密度每平方千米约7 869人，是世界上人口密度排名第二的国家。新加坡的居民主要是来自马来半岛、中国、印度次大陆和斯里兰卡的移民后裔，主要有三个民族：77%的华人，14%的马来人，8%的印度人和1%的欧亚人（欧亚混血人）以及其他血统的人。大多数原始居民是马来人。新加坡属多宗教国家，主要宗教为佛教、道教、伊斯兰教、基督教和印度教，华人多信奉佛教或道教。

Singapore has a total population of approximately 5.637 million people in 2022, with a population density of around 7,869 people per square kilometer, making it the second most densely populated country in the world. The people of Singapore are mainly descendants of immigrants from the Malay Peninsula, China, the Indian subcontinent, and Sri Lanka. There are three main ethnic groups: 77% Chinese, 14% Malays, 8% Indians, 1% Eurasians, and people of other ancestries. The majority of the indigenous population are Malays. Singapore is a multicultural country with major religions including Buddhism, Taoism, Islam, Christianity, and Hinduism, with many Chinese practicing Buddhism or Taoism.

新加坡有四种官方语言：马来语、汉话、泰米尔语和英语。马来语是国语。英语是商业和管理的主要通行语以及学校的教学语言，被广泛使用和理解。官方所使用的英语源自英国英语（拼写和语法），并受到一些美国英语的影响。当地的英语方言被称为"Singlish"，因其包含了来自各种汉语方言、马来语和印度语的大量词汇和语法。在新加坡的中国人越来越多地使用普通话来代替主要的汉语方言，如粤语、闽南语、客家语等。大多数居民会说多种语言。

There are four official languages in Singapore: Malay, Mandarin, Tamil and English. Malay is the national language. English is the language of business and administration, and is widely spoken and understood. Officially, the English used is derived from British English (spelling and grammar), with some American English influences. The local dialect of English is known formally as "Singlish", having incorporated much vocabulary and grammar from various Chinese dialects, Malay and Indian languages. Mandarin is being increasingly used among the Chinese in place of the main Chinese dialects Cantonese, Hokkien, Hakka. Most residents are multi-lingual.

（二）历史简介 History of Singapore

新加坡古称"淡马锡"，早在 3 世纪就有土著居民，其相关的最早文献记载源自东吴将领康泰所著的《吴时外国传》。8 世纪建国，属室利佛逝王朝。14 世纪，室利佛逝的王子拜里米苏拉建立马六甲苏丹王朝。中世纪的新加坡海运兴盛，成为东南亚国际货物的集散中心。16 世纪起，欧洲殖民者入侵东南亚。1819 年，英国人史丹福·莱福士抵达新加坡，与柔佛苏丹订约，在新加坡设立贸易站，宣布其为自由港，是亚洲第一个自由港。1824 年至第二次世界大战结束沦为英属殖民地，成为英国在远东的转口贸易商埠和在东南亚的主要军事基地。1869 年苏伊士运河开通后，新加坡成为东南亚的商品贸易中心和世界著名的转口港。

Singapore was historically known as " Temasek ". As early as the 3rd century, there were indigenous inhabitants, with the earliest literary reference coming from the work *Records of Foreign Countries During the Wu Period*, written by the Eastern Wu general Kang Tai. The country was founded in the 8th century and was part of the Srivijaya Empire. In the 14th century, a prince of Srivijaya named Parameswara established the Malacca Sultanate. In the Middle Ages, maritime transport rose and became the distribution center of international goods in Southeast Asia. At the beginning of the 16th century, European colonists invaded Southeast Asia. In 1819, the British Stanford Raffles arrived in Singapore, signed a contract with the Sultan of Johor, set up a trading post in Singapore, and declared Singapore a free port, the first free port in Asia. From 1824 to the end of World War Ⅱ, it became a British colony and became a British entrepot trade port in the Far East and a major military base in Southeast Asia. After the opening of the Suez Canal in 1869, Singapore became a commodity trade center in Southeast Asia and a world-famous entrepot.

1942 年新加坡被日本占领，改名为"昭南"。1945 年日本投降后，英国恢复殖民统治。1946 年划为英属殖民地。1959 年实行自治，成为自治邦。1963 年脱离英国管辖，与马来亚、沙巴、沙捞越共同组成马来西亚联邦。1965 年 8 月 9 日在李光耀领导下成立了新加坡共和国，成为一个民主和主权独立的国家。现在的新加坡已成为经济发达的国家。

In 1942, Singapore was occupied by Japan and renamed " Syonan ". After Japan's surrender in 1945, British colonial rule was restored. In 1946, it was designated as a British colony. In 1959, it gained self-governance and became a self-governing state. In 1963, it separated from British jurisdiction and formed the Federation of Malaysia with Malaya, Sabah, and Sarawak. On August 9, 1965, under the leadership of Lee Kuan Yew, the Republic of Singapore was established, becoming a democratic and sovereign independent country. Today, Singapore has become a developed economy.

（三）经济状况 The Economy

新加坡的自然资源匮乏，经济属外贸驱动型，以电子、石油化工、金融、航运、服务业为主，高度依赖美国、日本、欧洲和周边国家市场，外贸总额是国内生产总值的 4 倍。农业在国民经济中所占比例不到 1%，粮食全部靠进口，蔬菜产量仅占 5%。服务业是经济增长的主导产业，包括零售和批发贸易、酒店旅游、交通和电信、金融服务、商业服务等。

Singapore is poor in natural resources and its economy is driven by foreign trade, mainly in electronics, petrochemical, finance, shipping and service industries. Highly dependent on the markets of the United States, Japan, Europe and surrounding countries, the total foreign trade is 4 times of the GDP（gross domestic product）. Agriculture accounts for less than 1% of the national economy，food is all imported，and vegetable production accounts for only 5%. Service industry is the leading industry of economic growth，including retail and wholesale trade，hotel Tourist，transportation and telecommunications，financial services，commercial services，etc.

新加坡是一个发达的资本主义国家，三大经济支柱产业是国际贸易、加工业和旅游业。商业环境较为开放，物价稳定，相比其他发达国家税率较低。海、陆、空交通运输十分活跃，新加坡海港是世界上最繁忙的港口之一，海运十分便利。新加坡樟宜国际机场是世界上最繁忙的航空港之一，成为联系欧洲、美洲、大洋洲的航运中心。旅游业是主要外汇收入来源之一。新加坡是世界上犯罪率最低的国家之一，一直以来都是广受中国游客好评的旅游目的地，也是中国的主要客源国。

Singapore is a developed capitalist country.The three pillars of the economy are international trade，processing industries and Tourist. Singapore has a relatively open business environment，stable prices，and lower tax rates compared to other developed economies. Singapore's sea，land and air transportation is very active. The Singapore seaport is one of the busiest ports in the world，and the sea transportation is very convenient. Singapore Changi International Airport is one of the busiest airports in the world，and becomes the shipping center connecting Europe，America and Oceania. Tourist is one of the main sources of foreign exchange income. Singapore has one of the lowest crime rates in the world，it has always been a popular tourist destination for Chinese tourists，and Singapore is also one of the main source countries of Chinese tourists.

 思考题

　　请学生观看"现代新加坡之父——李光耀精彩访谈"视频并讨论以下问题。

　　1.新加坡为什么能快速崛起？

　　2.你认为什么是"成功人士"？成功人士都有哪些共同特征？

　　提示：Traits of successful people /success is a continuous journey.

现代新加坡之父——李光耀精彩访谈

（四）传统文化 Traditional Culture

新加坡的特色菜是由马来人和在新加坡的华侨，将中国菜与马来菜融合而成的家常菜，称为"娘惹"菜。此外，具有代表性的新加坡食物还有鸡饭、肉骨茶、炒干果条、酿豆腐、云吞面等。这些食物都是早期的中国移民将福建和广东的饮食习惯及风味与当地的风格相结合，才逐渐形成的新加坡特色食物。

"娘惹"菜

Singapore's own specialties are cuisine developed by the Malaysian，Singapore overseas Chinese with mixture of Chinese and Malay food，known as "Nyonya". In addition，representatives of the Singaporean food include Chicken Rice，Bak Kut Teh，Char Kway Teow，Yong Tau Foo，wonton mee，etc. These foods were brought by early Chinese immigrants，incorporated with Fujian and Guangdong style and flavor with local own style, and gradually formed the local own characteristics of food in Singapore.

新加坡地处热带，据说当地人为了排暑去毒，在日常选择食物时偏重麻辣口味。而在各种新加坡传统麻辣口味的料理中，又以辣椒螃蟹和黑胡椒螃蟹最为出名。这两道菜是将肥美的螃蟹连肉带壳加上辣椒或及黑胡椒酱一起拌炒，令人回味无穷。

Singapore is located in the tropics, and it is said that locals tend to favor spicy and hot flavors in their cuisine to combat the heat and humidity. Among the various traditional spicy dishes in Singapore, chili crab and black pepper crab are the most famous. These dishes involve stir-frying succulent crabs with their shells in a sauce made of chili or black pepper, creating a delightful and unforgettable taste.

新加坡——美好之都 or 罚款之都?

新加坡人的国服是一种以胡姬花为图案的服装，在国家庆典或其他隆重的场合穿着。正式场合中，男子一般穿白色长袖衬衫和深色西裤，并打上领带；女子则须穿套装或深色长裙。日常生活中，不同民族的新加坡人穿着打扮往往各具民族特色。华人的日常着装多为长衫、长裤、连衣裙或旗袍；马来人最爱穿"巴汝"、纱笼；锡克人则是男子缠头，女子身披纱丽。在许多公共场所，穿着过于随便，如穿牛仔装、运动装、沙滩装、低胸装、露背装、露脐装的人，往往被禁止入内。

The national dress of Singaporeans, a garment patterned after the hokkien flower, is worn during national celebrations or other solemn occasions. For formal occasions, men generally wear white long-sleeved shirts and dark-colored suit pants with ties, while women are required to wear suits or long dark-colored dresses. In daily life, different ethnic groups tend to dress with their own national characteristics. The Chinese wear long shirts, pants, dresses or cheongsams; the Malays love to wear "Baru" and sarongs; Sikhs wrap their heads around their heads and women wear saris. In many public places, people who dress too casually, such as in jeans, sportswear, beachwear, low-cut, backless, or navel-baring clothing, are often barred from entering.

（五）礼仪禁忌 Social Etiquettes and Taboos

新加坡是一个文明的国度，礼仪是对每个新加坡公民的基本准则。在社交场合，新加坡人与客人相见时，一般行握手礼。男女之间可以握手，但对男子来说，比较恰当的方式是等女士先伸出手来，再去握手。马来人则是先用双手互相接触，再把手收回放到自己胸前。新加坡为了保护环境，在其境内禁止贩卖和食用口香糖，随地吐痰、弃物也是被明令禁止的，否则要被重金罚款。此外，在明令禁烟场所一定要遵守规定。新加坡对留嬉皮士发型的男性管制相当严格，留着长发、穿着牛仔装、脚穿拖鞋的男士，可能会被禁止入境。在与新加坡人进行商务交往时，不要跷二郎腿，把鞋底朝向对方，否则容易导致交易失败。

娘惹装和饰珠鞋

Singapore is a civilized country where etiquette is a fundamental requirement for every citizen. On social occasions, Singaporeans generally shake hands when meeting with each other. It is more appropriate for men to wait for the women to extend their hands first. Malays greet each other by touching hands and then placing their hands back on their chests. To protect the environment, the sale and consumption of chewing gum are prohibited in Singapore. Spitting and littering are also banned, and violators may face heavy fines. Additionally, it is important to follow regulations in designated smoking areas. Singapore has strict regulations regarding men with long hair. Men with long hair who wear jeans and flip-flops may be denied entry into the country. When engaging in business with Singaporeans, avoid crossing your legs and pointing the soles of your shoes toward others, as this could jeopardize the chances of a successful transaction.

谈话中，切忌议论政治得失、种族摩擦、宗教是非和配偶情况等。此外，不能说"恭喜发财"，新加坡华人将"财"理解为"不义之财"或"为富不仁"，说"恭喜发财"会被认为是对别人的侮辱和嘲笑。当地人忌讳乌龟，认为这是一种不祥的动物，有侮辱的含义。新加坡的印度人、马来人忌讳左手传递东西或食物，认为使用左手是一种不礼貌的举止。在新加坡，大年初一不可以扫地，会把好运气都扫走。

Don't talk about political gains and losses, racial friction, religious rights and wrongs, spouse situation, etc. Another taboo in conversation is not to say " congratulations on getting rich". Chinese Singaporeans understand " wealth" as " unjust wealth" or " being rich and unkind". It is considered as an insult and ridicule to others to say congratulations on making a fortune. They taboo tortoises and think that they are an ominous animal with insulting meanings. The Indians and Malays in Singapore taboo passing things or food with the left hand, and think it is impolite to use the left hand. In Singapore, you can't sweep the floor on New Year's Day because it would sweep away all good luck.

（六）传统节日 Festivals

1. 屠妖节 Deepavali Festival（又名万灯节 Festival of Lights）

传说古时候，印度有个凶残的魔王 Narakasura。在他的统治下老百姓生活得十分痛苦，民不聊生。天神 Lord Khrishna 把邪恶的魔王杀掉，为民除害。人们非常高兴，点灯热烈庆祝。从此，人们就将这个日子作为屠妖节，歌颂"邪不能胜正"的精神。屠妖节，又为排灯节、万灯节或印度灯节，也称光明节，一般在 10 月末或 11 月初，这一天是印度历 7 月的第一天，也是新月降临的一日。耆那教、印度教、锡克教和一些佛教信徒庆祝这个节日，"以光明驱走黑暗，以善良战胜邪恶"。瓦腊纳西是庆祝该节日的主要城市。

In ancient times, there was a fierce demon king Narakasura in India. Under his rule, the people suffered greatly and their lives were miserable. The celestial Lord Khrishna killed the evil demon king, ridding the people of harm. People were very happy and lit lights to celebrate it. Since then, people have regarded this day as the Deepavali Festival, praising the spirit of " evil cannot prevail over righteousness". Known as the Festival of Lights, Diwali, or the Hindu Lantern Festival, this festival usually falls at the end of October or beginning of November, marking the first

新加坡屠妖节
庆典

day of the seventh month of the Indian calendar, which is also the day of the new moon. Jainism, Hinduism and Sikhism celebrate the festival of " driving away darkness with light and defeating evil with good". The festival is mainly celebrated in the city of Varanasi.

2. 卫塞节 Vesak Day

卫塞节是庆祝释迦牟尼佛祖诞生、成道、涅槃的节日。除了新加坡，东南亚及南亚很多国家，如泰国、马来西亚、印度尼西亚、斯里兰卡、缅甸、尼泊尔等国的佛教徒，均在这一年一度的重要节日中举行盛大的庆典活动。每年卫塞节的日期根据历法而定，通常是在 5 月的月圆之日。

Vesak Day is the day of birth, enlightenment and nirvana of Sakyamuni. In addition to

Singapore, Buddhists from South East Asian and South Asian countries such as Thailand, Malaysia, Indonesia, Sri Lanka, Myanmar, Nepal, and others, hold grand celebration events during this annual significant festival. According to the official calendar, the annual Vesak Day is usually the day of full moon in May.

三、旅游观光 Tourism and Sightseeing

（一）著名旅游景点 Famous Tourist Attractions

1. 牛车水（又称"唐人街"）Chinatown

新加坡是多民族聚集的国家，各民族之间的文化融会贯通。其中，华人的早期聚集地就是"牛车水"，也称唐人街（图 1-24）。据说当时岛上没有自来水，因此早期的华人居民都以牛车拉水生活。牛车运水的情景在唐人街非常普遍，并且在诸多南方汉语方言中，"车"都有动词"拉水车"之意，华人聚集地的中文名就译为"牛车水"。如今的牛车水是现代购物中心，各色小贩和百年老店在这里毗邻而居。

Singapore is a country with diverse ethnic groups, and the cultures of various ethnic groups are also integrated in Singapore. Among them, the early gathering place of Chinese is " Chinatown" （Figure 1-24）.It is said that there was no running water on the island at that time, so the early Chinese residents all lived with water drawn by cattle carts. The scene of water carried by cattle carts is very common in Chinatown. In many southern Chinese dialects, "cart" has the meaning of the verb " water drawn", thus the area's Chinese name translates to " Ox Cart Water". Today's Chinatown is a modern shopping center where various vendors and century-old shops coexist side by side.

图 1-24　牛车水（唐人街）

Figure 1-24　Chinatown

牛车水范围包括水车路（Kreta Ayer）、直落亚逸（Telok Ayer）、丹戎巴葛（Tanjong Pagar）和武吉巴梳（Bukit Pasoh）四个分区，每个分区都有自己独特的魅力。这里汇聚了很多传统风格的建筑，如斯里马里安曼兴都庙、詹美回教堂、佛牙寺龙华院和博物馆等。如今，这里成了新加坡最大的遗产保护区，历史悠久的寺庙、老字号中药铺与新潮酒吧和生活时尚店铺交错而立，新旧交融并存的独特风味，让海外游客和本地人都流连忘返。要体验新加坡多元的美食文化，可选择牛车水美食街（图 1-25），这条露天餐饮街集结了各种民族备受欢迎的美食，从炒稞条、蚝煎、烤鸭到咖喱饭，各种特色美食应有尽有。

The area of Chinatown includes the Kreta Ayer, Telok Ayer, Tanjong Pagar, and Bukit Pasoh districts, each with its own unique charm. This area is home to many traditional-style buildings, such as the Sri Mariamman Temple, Jamae Mosque, Buddha Tooth Relic Temple, and museums. Today, it has become Singapore's largest heritage conservation area, where historic temples, traditional Chinese medicine shops, and trendy bars and lifestyle stores coexist, creating a unique blend of old and new that captivates both foreign visitors and locals. To experience Singapore's diverse food culture, one can visit the Chinatown Food Street (Figure 1-25), an open-air dining street that offers a variety of popular ethnic cuisines, from fried kway teow, oyster omelettes, and roast duck to curry rice, showcasing the area's culinary diversity.

图 1-25 牛车水美食街
Figure 1-25 Chinatown Food Street

2. 佛牙寺龙华院 Buddha Tooth Relic Temple

佛牙寺龙华院（图 1-26）是位于新加坡唐人街区的一座集佛教寺庙和博物馆于一体的综合建筑，这里既是博物馆，也是朝拜场所。寺院建成于 2002 年 11 月，寺内供奉着佛牙舍利。整座寺庙是根据唐代建筑风格建造的，是唐人街的热门景点，进入寺庙的游客需要着装整洁，不可衣不蔽体。

Buddha Tooth Relic Temple (Figure 1-26) is a Buddhist temple and museum complex located in Singapore's Chinatown district. It serves as both a museum and a place of worship. The temple was established in November, 2002 and houses a relic of the Buddha's tooth. The temple is constructed in the architectural style of the Tang Dynasty and is a popular attraction in Chinatown. Visitors entering the temple are required to be dressed appropriately, with no exposed body parts.

图 1-26 佛牙寺龙华院
Figure 1-26 Buddha Tooth Relic Temple

3. 马里安曼兴都庙 Sri Mariamman Temple

马里安曼兴都庙（图 1-27）是新加坡最古老的兴都庙宇，已有近 200 年历史，前来参拜的信徒络绎不绝。其雄伟的六层印度庙塔让游人无不驻足惊叹，且庙宇内部的装潢同样庄严壮丽。庙宇的守护神神像仅在特殊日子里才会被请出受奉，此外，寺庙内还有许多值得品赏的壁

图 1-27　马里安曼兴都庙
Figure 1-27　Sri Mariamman Temple

图 1-28　詹美回教堂
Figure 1-28　Masjid Jamae

画及供奉杜尔迦、甘尼许和湿婆等兴都神灵的神龛。

Sri Mariamman Temple (Figure 1-27) is the oldest Hindu temple in Singapore, with a history of nearly 200 years, attracting a constant stream of devotees. Its majestic six-tiered gopuram (tower) leaves visitors in awe, and the interior of the temple is equally grand and magnificent. The deity statues within the temple are only unveiled on special days, and there are many exquisite murals and shrines dedicated to Hindu deities such as Durga, Ganesha, and Shiva for visitors to admire.

4. 詹美回教堂 Masjid Jamae

詹美回教堂（图 1-28）是新加坡最早建立的清真寺之一，以奇特的建筑风格闻名，正面看起来像是精细、复杂的宫殿，上面有小门和十字形的窗户。入口是典型的南印度风格，两个祈祷大厅及神殿却是新古典风格，与中国清真寺的建筑风格有很大差别。游客们可以沿着桥南路探索牛车水的多元宗教文化，欣赏詹美回教堂独特的八角形尖塔。

Masjid Jamae (Figure 1-28) is one of the earliest mosques established in Singapore, renowned for its distinctive architectural style. The facade resembles a meticulously crafted palace, with small doors and cross-shaped windows. The entrance is in the typical South Indian style, while the two prayer halls and the sanctuary are in the Neoclassical style, quite different from the architectural style of Chinese mosques. Visitors can explore the multi-religious culture of Chinatown along Pagoda Street and admire the unique octagonal minaret of the mosque.

5. 圣淘沙 Sentosa

"圣淘沙"在马来语里的意思是"和平安宁"。1970 年以前曾是英军的军事基地，现已成为新加坡重要的观光游览区和度假胜地。圣淘沙（图 1-29）距离新加坡本岛南部仅 500 米，由一座堤道跨海大桥与本岛连接起来。圣淘沙延续了新加坡"花园城市"的路线，放眼望去，一片青翠，郁郁葱葱。圣淘沙岛上有西索罗炮台、海底世界、海豚乐园、天空之塔等美丽景点。

图 1-29　圣淘沙
Figure 1-29　Sentosa

"Sentosa" means "peace and tranquility" in Malay. Before 1970, it served as a military base for the British Army, but it has now become an important tourist attraction and resort in Singapore. Sentosa (Figure 1-29) is located just 500 meters south of the main island of Singapore, connected by a causeway bridge. The island continues the "Garden City" theme of Singapore, showcasing lush greenery and vibrant landscapes. Notable attractions on Sentosa Island include Fort Siloso, Underwater World, Dolphin Lagoon, and the Sky Tower.

6. 新加坡环球影城 Universal Studios Singapore

新加坡环球影城（图 1-30）是一个主题公园，位于新加坡圣淘沙岛上，公园共有 24 处景点、7 个主题区，分别是好莱坞、纽约、科幻城市、古埃及、失落的世界、遥远之地和马达加斯加。每个主题都各具特点，重现了电影世界的神奇，为游客开启探险旅程的序幕。

图 1-30　新加坡环球影城
Figure 1-30　Universal Studios Singapore

Universal Studios Singapore (Figure 1-30) is a theme park located on Singapore's Sentosa Island. There are 24 scenic spots and 7 theme areas in the park, including Hollywood, New York, science fiction city, ancient Egypt, the lost world, faraway land and Madagascar. Each theme has its own characteristics, recreating the magic of the movie world and setting the stage for the beginning of an adventure journey for visitors.

7. 新加坡植物园 Singapore Botanic Gardens

新加坡植物园（图 1-31）是一个有着 150 多年历史的热带花园，位于新加坡主要购物区的边缘，是唯一一个被联合国教科文组织列为世界遗产的热带花园，园内有 10 000 多种植物，每年接待约 450 万游客。胡姬花园是植物园的主要景点，有超过 1 000 个兰花品种和 2 000 种杂交兰花。新加坡植物园有一个大约 6 公顷的小型热带雨林，比植物园本身还要古老。

图 1-31　新加坡植物园
Figure 1-31　Singapore Botanic Gardens

The Singapore Botanic Gardens(Figure1-31) is a tropical garden with a history of over 150 years. It is located on the edge of Singapore's main shopping belt and is the only tropical garden designated as a UNESCO World Heritage Site. The garden is home to more than 10,000 plants and attracts approximately 4.5 million visitors each year. The National Orchid Garden is the main attraction within the Botanic Gardens, featuring over 1,000 orchid varieties and 2,000 hybrid orchids. Additionally, there is a small tropical rainforest covering about 6 hectares, which predates the Botanic Gardens themselves.

8. 裕廊飞禽公园 Jurong Bird Park

裕廊飞禽公园（图 1-32）坐落在新加坡西部裕廊山的斜坡上，于 1971 年 1 月 3 日正式开放，占地 20 万平方米，被誉为东南亚最壮观的"鸟类天堂"，是世界上规模最大、珍禽异鸟

图 1-32　裕廊飞禽公园
Figure 1-32　Jurong Bird Park

最多的公园之一。它拥有世界各地超过 600 种不同品种、总数超 7 000 只的飞禽，如天堂鸟、孔雀、鸵鸟、松鸡、美洲秃鹰、白头翁、鸳鸯等。主要景点包括飞禽知识馆、非洲瀑布鸟舍、彩鹦谷、东南亚鸟舍和备受赞誉的非洲湿地，吸引了世界各地成千上万的游览前来参观。游客可以选择搭乘单轨车或以步行方式畅游公园。

Jurong Bird Park (Figure 1-32) is located on the slopes of Jurong Hill in western Singapore and officially opened on January 3, 1971. Spanning an area of 200,000 square meters, it is hailed as the " bird paradise " of Southeast Asia and is one of the world's largest and most diverse bird parks, housing over 600 different species and more than 7 000 birds, including birds of paradise, peacocks, ostriches, pheasants, bald eagles, hornbills, and mandarin ducks. The main attractions include the Bird Discovery Centre, the African Waterfall Aviary, the Lory Loft, the Southeast Asian Birds Aviary, and the acclaimed African Wetlands. Attracting millions of visitors from around the world, the park offers the option of exploring it by monorail or on foot.

图 1-33　新加坡艺术科学博物馆
Figure 1-33　Art Science Museum

9. 新加坡艺术科学博物馆 Art Science Museum

新加坡艺术科学博物馆（图 1-33）位于滨海湾金沙综合度假村内，由世界著名建筑师萨夫迪（Moshe Safdie）执笔设计，总面积达到 4 800 平方米。博物馆的外形好似一朵盛开的莲花，或是一只张开的手，屋顶可以收集雨水和光线，供博物馆日常使用。馆内设有 21 个展厅，用于举办旅行展和展出永久性藏品。新加坡建造艺术科学博物馆的目的不仅是吸引游客，同时也是鼓励人们敢于站在思想前沿，用富有革新性的想法发展新经济。

Art Science Museum (Figure 1-33) in Singapore is located within the Marina Bay Sands resort and was designed by the world-renowned architect Moshe Safdie, covering a total area of 4,800 square meters. The museum's shape resembles a blooming lotus flower or an open hand, with a roof designed to collect rainwater and light for the museum's daily use. Inside, there are 21 galleries used for traveling exhibitions and displaying permanent collections. The purpose of building the Art Science Museum in Singapore is not only to attract tourists but also to encourage people to stand at the forefront of thought and develop new economies with innovative ideas.

10. 小印度 Little India

小印度（图 1-34）位于新加坡以南的实龙岗路一带，是新加坡印度族群的聚集地，充满了印度人

图 1-34　小印度
Figure 1-34　Little India

的生活气息。区内还有一座著名的中国寺庙，名叫释迦牟尼菩提迦耶寺，里面供奉着高为 1.5 米的释迦牟尼像。新加坡的印度籍人都喜欢来此与朋友吃饭或购物。在屠妖节，小印度被装点成金碧辉煌的神话世界。

The Little India (Figure 1-34) is located along Serangoon Road in the southern Singapore. It is a popular gathering place for Indians, serving as an epitome of Indian culture. Indians can be seen everywhere on the streets. There is also a famous Chinese temple in the Little India area called the Sakyamuni Buddha Gaya Temple, which houses a 1.5-meter-high statue of Sakyamuni. Indian workers living in Singapore enjoy dining and shopping here with friends. On the Deepavali Festival, the Little India is decorated as a mythical world like a wonderland.

（二）旅游购物 Shopping

鱼尾狮纪念品：鱼尾狮是新加坡的标志与象征，以鱼尾狮形象制作的水果叉、温度计、闹钟、铅锡盘子、杯子、烟灰缸、名片夹、打火机、钥匙扣、茶叶筒等各种旅游纪念品颇受世界各地游客的青睐。

Merlion souvenirs: Merlion is the icon and symbol of Singapore and souvenirs such as fruit forks, thermometers, alarm clocks, leaded tin plates, mugs, ashtrays, business card holders, lighters, keychains, tea caddies and other souvenirs made in the image of the Fishtail Lion are popular among tourists from all over the world.

肉干：泛指烟熏猪肉干，是许多新加坡人童年时最喜爱的零食之一，同时也是人们走亲访友的必备佳品。"美珍香"是新加坡著名食品品牌，创立于 1933 年，主要经营亚洲风味食物，包括切片肉干、烟熏肉干、猪肉丝等肉制品，名扬海外。

Jerky: It refers to smoked pork jerky, which is one of the favorite snacks of many Singaporeans in their childhood, and is also a must-have for people visiting friends and relatives. The " Bee Cheng Hiang" is a renowned food brand from Singapore, originating in 1933, mainly dealing in Asian-style foods, including sliced meat jerky, smoked meat jerky, pork floss, and other meat products, which are famous overseas.

鳄鱼皮制品：由于从鳄鱼养殖到皮革加工都在新加坡国内进行，因此不仅价格低，而且种类非常丰富，有皮包、鞋子、小饰品等。

Crocodile leather products: Crocodile leather products are made in Singapore from farming to leather processing, which not only makes them affordable but also diverse. These include handbags, shoes, and various small accessories crafted from crocodile leather.

国花镀金标本：新加坡国花镀金标本款式多样，是将新鲜的胡姬花镀金后制成各种别致的首饰，如别针、耳环、垂饰等。

Gold-plated specimens: Gold-plated specimens of Singapore's national flower are available in a variety of styles. Freshly gilded hokkien flowers are made into a variety of chic jewelry such as pins, earrings and pendants.

新加坡司令："新加坡司令"是红遍全世界酒吧的新加坡国家级鸡尾酒。这是一款以石榴汁和金汤尼调制而成的鸡尾酒，口感酸甜。

扫码获取：入境须知及海关规定

Singapore Sling: " The Singapore Sling" is the national cocktail of Singapore, popular in bars around the world. It is a sweet and sour cocktail made with pomegranate juice and gin tonic.

本节习题

1. 新加坡的气候特点和类型有哪些？
2. 新加坡有哪些重要的礼仪和禁忌？
3. 请为国内某旅游团设计一个新加坡 6 日游旅游线路。
4. 列举四种能携带进新加坡境内且无须支付关税的物品。

黄袍佛国——泰国
The Land of the Yellow Robed Buddha—Thailand

导读

　　泰国是一个历史悠久的佛教之国。泰国旅游业发展很快，现已成为泰国经济的重要支柱和外汇收入的重要来源。泰国是我国主要的旅游目的地国和客源国之一，素有"中南半岛上的明珠"之称，被誉为"亚洲最具异国风情的国家"。

　　亚洲游客主要游览泰国曼谷及其附近的历史、自然和文化景点。西方游客不仅游览曼谷及其周边地区，还前往南部的海滩和岛屿。泰国北部是徒步旅行和探险旅行的主要目的地，接待游客最少的地区是东北部的伊桑。泰国的旅游景点包括潜水场所、沙滩、数百个热带岛屿、考古遗址、博物馆、山地部落、植物和鸟类生活园、宫殿、佛教寺庙和一些世界遗产。许多游客都喜欢体验泰式烹饪、佛教和传统泰式按摩。泰国菜因其热衷使用新鲜香草和香料而闻名于世。中泰是友好近邻，自1971年正式建交以来，两国关系保持健康、稳定发展，双方领导人往来频繁，各领域交流合作广泛、深入，两国人民之间有着深厚的友好感情。2012年4月，中泰两国建立全面战略合作伙伴关系。泰国是东盟成员国中第一个与中国建立战略性合作关系的国家。中泰两国在科技、教育、文化、卫生、司法、军事等领域的交流与合作正在稳步发展。

一、地理概览 Geography of Thailand

（一）位置 Location

　　泰国，全称泰王国，位于亚洲东南亚地区中南半岛中部，其北部和东北部与老挝接壤，北部和西北部与缅甸交界，西南部是安达曼海，东部毗邻柬埔寨和泰国湾，南部与马来西亚接壤。

Thailand, officially known as the Kingdom of Thailand, is located in Southeast Asia, in the central part of the Indochinese Peninsula. To the north and northeast, Thailand shares borders with Laos; to the north and northwest, it borders Myanmar; to the southwest, it faces the Andaman Sea; to the east, it is adjacent to Cambodia and the Gulf of Thailand; and to the south, it shares a border with Malaysia.

（二）地形和气候 The Land and Seasons

泰国地势北高南低，山川纵列，平原居中。地形大体分为四部分：西北部山区、东北部高原、西南部的狭长丘陵区、中部的平原区（其中湄南河流域是泰国农耕集中区）。泰国地处热带，绝大部分地区属于热带季风气候，全年气温都比较高。全年月平均气温为 24 ℃～30 ℃。年降水量约 1 000 毫米。泰国全年皆宜旅游。

Thailand's topography is characterized by high elevations in the north and lowlands in the south, with mountains, rivers, and plains in the central region. The terrain is roughly divided into four parts: mountainous areas in the northwest, highlands in the northeast, narrow hills in the southwest, and plains in the center, where the Chao Phraya River Valley is the heart of Thai agriculture. Located in the tropics, the vast majority of Thailand experiences a tropical monsoon climate, with relatively high temperatures throughout the year. The average monthly temperature ranges from 24 ℃ to 30 ℃ . Annual rainfall is approximately 1,000 mm, making Thailand a great place to visit all year round.

（三）自然资源 Natural Resources

森林是泰国最主要的自然资源之一，以热带乔木为主，橡树、樟树、金鸡纳树及柚木都比较珍贵。楠木尤其出名，桂树为国树。20 世纪 60 年代，泰国森林覆盖面积约占全国总面积的 54%，现已锐减到约占全国总面积的 26%。辽阔的海域是泰国海洋渔业的重要基地，每年海产在 200 万吨以上，有鱿鱼、墨鱼、鲳鱼、章鱼、沙丁鱼、对虾、龙虾、海蟹、海参等品种。泰国有丰富的矿产资源，主要有锡矿、钾盐、褐煤、油页岩，还有锌、铜、铝、萤石、石膏、岩盐、钨、铁、锑、铬、重晶石、宝石、石油等。锡的开采已有近千年历史，出口量居世界第三位。钨产量居世界第二位。红宝石、蓝宝石闻名世界。

Forests are one of Thailand's major natural resources, dominated by tropical trees, with oak, camphor, cinchona, and teak being the more valuable. Nanmu is particularly famous, and katsura is the national tree. 54% of the country's area was covered by forests in the 1960s, but this has now been drastically reduced to 26% of the country's area. The vast sea is an important base for Thailand's marine fisheries, with annual seafood production of more than 2 million tons of squid, cuttlefish, pomfret, octopus, sardines, prawns, lobsters, sea crabs, sea cucumbers and other species. Thailand has rich mineral resources, mainly tin ore, potash, lignite, oil shale, as well as zinc, copper, aluminum, fluorite, gypsum, rock salt, tungsten, iron, antimony, chromium, barite, gemstones, petroleum and so on. Tin has been mined for nearly 1,000 years and accounts for the world's third largest export volume. Tungsten production is the second largest in the world. Rubies and sapphires are world famous.

泰国的金柚木行宫

二、人文概况 Overview of Thai Humanities

（一）国情认知 Basic Knowledge of National Conditions

泰国人口约 7 169 万（2022 年），包含泰族、华人、老族、高棉族等 30 多个民族。官方语言是泰语，英语使用也很普遍。泰国以佛教为国教，90% 以上的民众信奉佛教。泰国大约有

14% 的人口是华裔，其中大部分来自中国广东省潮汕地区。泰国的国旗呈长方形，由红色、白色、蓝色 5 个横长方形平行排列构成。泰国的国徽由驮着那莱王的一只大鹏图案构成。那莱王是传说中的守护神，大鹏是传说中降魔除妖的鸟中之王。国歌是《泰王国国歌》，国花是金莲花，国兽是亚洲象。

Thailand has a population of about 71.69 million（2022）and contains more than 30 ethnic groups, including Thai, Chinese, Laotian, and Khmer. The official language is Thai, and English is also commonly spoken. Thailand has Buddhism as the state religion, with over 90% of the population practicing Buddhism. About 14% of Thailand's population is of Chinese descent, most of whom come from the Chaoshan region of Guangdong Province in China. The national flag of Thailand is rectangular in shape, consisting of five horizontal rectangles arranged in parallel in red, white and blue. The national emblem of Thailand consists of a roc bird carrying King Narai. King Narai is the legendary guardian god, and the roc is the king of birds that is said to subdue and remove demons. The national anthem is the *National Anthem of the Kingdom of Thailand*, the national flower is the golden lotus, and the national animal is the Asian elephant.

（二）历史简介 History of Thailand

泰国原名暹罗，大约在 5 000 年前现在泰国所在的地区就有人类居住。公元 6 世纪时，中国南部的部分傣族人南迁至中南半岛，定居于湄公河流域，建立了一些小国家，这就是今天泰国的祖先。1238 年，傣族人建立了一个独立的王朝——素可泰王朝。1350 年，湄南河流域的乌通王在阿瑜陀耶建立了大城王朝。大城王朝历经 33 位君主，历时 417 年。1767 年，大城王朝覆灭，出现了吞武里王朝。15 年后又出现了咖达纳哥王朝，该王朝迁都曼谷，又称"曼谷王朝"。1932 年 6 月，人民党发动政变，改君主专制为君主立宪制，1939 年更名为泰国。

Thailand, formerly known as Siam, has been inhabited by humans for approximately 5,000 years. In the 6th century A.D., some of the Dai people from southern China migrated southward to the Central and Southern Peninsula, settling in the Mekong River Valley and establishing small states that are the ancestors of modern Thailand. In 1238, the Dai people established an independent dynasty known as the Sukhothai Dynasty. In 1350, King U Thong of the Mekong River Valley founded the Ayutthaya Dynasty in Ayutthaya. The Ayutthaya Dynasty lasted for 417 years under 33 monarchs. In 1767, the Ayutthaya Dynasty fell, leading to the emergence of the Thonburi Dynasty, which was followed 15 years later by the Rattanakosin Dynasty, which moved its capital to Bangkok and became known as the Bangkok Dynasty. In June 1932, the People's Party staged a coup d'etat, transforming the monarchy into a constitutional monarchy, and in 1939, the country's name was changed to Thailand.

（三）经济状况 The Economy

泰国原为典型农业国，经济结构单一。泰国土地肥沃，稻米产量占世界总产量的 4%，是世界最大的大米出口国；玉米出口量居世界第五位。经济作物主要有橡胶、木薯、甘蔗、麻类、烟草、柚木棕榈、咖啡、水果、花卉等。近 20 年来，泰国经济结构出现了明显的变化，逐渐向新兴工业国转变，制造业在其国民经济中的比重已日益扩大，而且成为主要出口产业之一，旅游业也保持稳定发展的势头，是外汇收入的重要来源之一。

Thailand was originally a typical agricultural country with a monolithic economic structure. Thailand's land is fertile and rice production accounts for 4% of the world's total, making it the world's largest exporter of rice; corn exports rank fifth in the world. The main cash crops are rubber, cassava, sugar cane, hemp, tobacco, teak palm, coffee, fruits and flowers. Over the past 20 years, Thailand's economic structure has undergone significant changes, gradually transforming itself into a newly industrialized country, with the manufacturing sector accounting for an increasing proportion of its national economy and becoming one of its major export industries, and Tourist maintaining steady momentum and being an important source of foreign exchange earnings.

（四）传统文化 Traditional Culture

泰国文化受到许多国家的影响，包括印度、老挝、缅甸、柬埔寨和中国。其传统文化融合了大量来自印度、中国、柬埔寨和东南亚其他地方的元素。泰国国教上座部佛教对现代泰国人具有重要影响。随着时间的演变，泰国佛教吸收了许多源自印度教、万物有灵论及祭祖的地方信仰等内容。

Thai culture has been shaped by many influences, including India, Laos, Burma, Cambodia and China. Its traditions incorporate a great deal of influence from India, China, Cambodia and the rest of Southeast Asia. Thailand's national religion Theravada Buddhism is important to modern Thai identity. Thai Buddhism has evolved over time to include many regional beliefs originating from Hinduism, Animism as well as ancestor worship.

泰国是一个礼仪之邦，被誉为"微笑的国度"。泰国人见面时通常双手合十于胸前，互致问候，说"萨瓦迪卡"（泰语，意为"您好"），对方则以相同的方式回复。当孩子离开家去学校时，他们应先向父母致意以示尊敬，回家时也一样。这种问候表示尊重和崇敬，类似于印度和尼泊尔的问候方式"合十礼"。普通人不能与僧侣握手。泰国人着装比较讲究，衣服均要熨烫，正式场合和庄重仪式，男士均穿西服，女士穿裙装，忌穿长裤。

Thailand is a country of manners and is known as the "Land of Smiles". When Thai people meet, they usually put their hands together in front of their chest and greet each other by saying "Savadika"(Thai for "hello"), to which the other person replies in the same way. When children leave home to go to school, they should first greet their parents as a sign of respect. The same applies when they return home. This greeting shows respect and reverence and is similar to the Indian and Nepalese greeting. Ordinary people are not allowed to shake hands with monks. Thai people dress more carefully; clothes should be ironed. On formal occasions and at solemn ceremonies, men wear suits, and women wear skirts, avoiding wearing pants.

泰国的舞蹈被誉为世界上最具艺术性的舞蹈之一。泰国以优美、典雅的古典舞蹈和丰富多彩的民间舞蹈著称于世。泰国舞的题材大多取自梵文神话，可分为孔（面部舞）、沙邦（音乐舞）和拉孔（舞蹈剧）三类。

Thai dance is known as one of the most artistic dances in the world. Thailand is famous for its beautiful and elegant classical dances and colorful folk dances. Most of the Thai dances are based on Sanskrit mythology and can be categorized into Kong（facial dance）, Sabang（musical dance）and Rakorn（dance drama）.

泰国是世界上最大的佛教国家，佛处于至高无上的地位。泰国家家供奉佛像，几乎人人身上挂小佛像。几百年来，泰国的风俗习惯、文学、艺术和建筑等各方面都与佛教有着密切关系。在泰国，凡是信奉佛教的男孩子，到了一定年龄，都要一度削发为僧，连王室和贵族也不例外。每天清晨出外托钵、过午不食。大部分青年僧侣是学生。到泰国旅游，处处可见身披黄色袈裟的僧侣，以及富丽堂皇的寺院。因此，泰国又有"黄袍佛国"的美名。佛教为泰国人塑造了道德标准，使之形成了崇尚忍让、安宁和爱好和平的精神风范。

Thailand is the largest Buddhist country in the world, and the Buddha reigns supreme. Every Thai household is dedicated to the Buddha, and almost everyone has a small statue of the Buddha on his or her body. Over the centuries, almost all aspects of custom, literature, art and architecture have been closely related to Buddhism. In Thailand, all Buddhist boys, to a certain age, have to once cut hair as a monk, even the royal family and nobles are no exception. Every day early in the morning they go for alms, and do not eat after lunch. Most young monks are students. Traveling to Thailand, everywhere you see monks wearing yellow robes, as well as magnificent monasteries. As a result, Thailand is often referred to as the "Land of the Yellow Robes". Buddhism has shaped the moral standards of the Thai people, giving rise to a spirit of forbearance, tranquility and love of peace.

泰国是亚洲拥有大象最多的国家，大象在泰国文化中享有很高的地位，是力量与优雅的象征。在泰国，白象被视为象征国运昌盛的国宝。白象生活在皇宫中，被当作神兽受到极佳的待遇。泰式按摩是泰国古代医学文化之一，拥有四千多年历史，是古代泰王招待皇家贵宾的最高礼节。如今，泰式按摩已成为广为人知的天然治疗方法。

Thailand has the largest number of elephants in Asia and elephants enjoy a high status in Thai culture as a symbol of strength and grace. In Thailand, the white elephant is regarded as a national treasure that symbolizes the prosperity of the country. White elephants live in the royal palaces and are treated as sacred animals. Thai massage is one of Thailand's ancient medical cultures, with a history of more than 4,000 years, and was the highest courtesy of the ancient Thai kings to entertain their royal guests. Today, Thai massage is widely known as a natural healing method.

无所不能的泰国大象

（五）礼仪禁忌 Social Etiquettes and Taboos

泰国人认为"头部"象征身体的最高部位，也是最神圣的部位。即使是小孩子的头，也不能随便触摸，甚至要避免在别人头部的上方传递东西，否则在某些情况下可能会惹恼对方。泰国人认为脚底最为低贱，和泰国朋友围坐在一起时，切勿把鞋底翘起对准别人，这是一种侮辱性行为，意即把人踩在脚下，用脚指东西更是失礼，用脚踢门则会被人们视为缺乏教养。切忌用红笔签名，在泰国，死者的名字是被人用红笔写在棺材上的，因此用红笔签名表示此人已死。知识、学问在泰国受到敬重，切勿在找不到凳子时，随意拿本书来坐，这是禁忌。

Thai people consider the "head" to be the highest and most sacred part of the body, both literally and figuratively. The head is believed to house the soul of a person, so it should not be touched, even if it belongs to a small child. This cultural norm extends to avoiding passing objects over someone's head, which can be quite aggravating in certain situations. The feet, on the other hand, are considered the lowest part of the body, and it is impolite to point at someone with your foot. Pointing at objects with your feet is even ruder, and kicking doors is seen as uncouth behavior. Additionally, never sign your name with a red pen; in Thailand, the name of the deceased is written on the coffin with a red pen, and a signature in red ink implies that the person is dead. Knowledge and learning are highly valued in Thailand, and it is considered taboo to take a book and sit on it when you cannot find a stool.

在泰国，到寺庙拜佛或参观时，须衣冠整洁、脱鞋。袒胸露背者及穿短裤、背心者是禁止入内的。游客在进入佛殿前要脱鞋，否则会被视为玷污佛堂。泰国人家里通常没有椅子，大家直接坐在地板上，食物通常也是放到地板上享用。

In Thailand, when worshipping or visiting a temple, one must be fully clothed and take off one's shoes. Bare-chested people and those wearing shorts and vests are prohibited from entering. Visitors are required to take off their shoes before entering a Buddhist temple or they will be seen as defiling the temple. In traditional Thai homes, chairs are rarely used, and people usually sit directly on the floor, where meals are often served and enjoyed as well.

（六）传统节日 Festivals

1. 泰国父亲节 The King's Birthday

12 月 5 日是国王的诞辰，这一天也被称为 "泰国父亲节"。这一天是已故泰王拉玛九世的诞辰，泰国所有的建筑都会装饰上象征君主和国王的标志。

December 5 is the King's Birthday. This public holiday is also known as the Thailand Father's Day. This day is the birthday of the former King Rama Ⅸ. All the buildings of Thailand are covered up with symbols of the monarchy and the king.

2. 水灯节 Loi Krathong

水灯节是一个宗教活动，每年在泰历 12 月的满月之日（公历 11 月的第一个月圆之日）举行。所有的泰国人都会购买或自己做一个 "水灯"。灯是由香蕉叶包裹的泡沫塑料制成的，花和蜡烛放在中间。夜晚来临，泰国人会去河流或池塘放下 "水灯"。

Loi Krathong (Festival of Lights) is a religious event which falls every year on the full moon of December in the traditional Thai Lunar Calendar (first full moon day of November). All Thai people buy or make a "krathong". It is made of styrofoam surrounded by banana leaves, with flowers and a candle in the middle. During the evening, Thai people go to places where there is a river or a pound to launch their "krathong".

3. 宋干节 Songkran Festival

宋干节也叫 "泼水节"，在每年公历的 4 月 13 日到 15 日，代表清除邪恶、不幸和罪恶，开始新的一年。在宋干节期间，人们抬着或用车载着巨大的佛像出游，佛像后面跟着一辆辆花车，车上站着化了妆的 "宋干女神"。在游行队伍经过的道路两旁，善男信女夹道而行，用银钵里盛着的用棕榈树叶浸泡过的、掺有香料的水，泼洒到佛像和 "宋干女神" 身上，祈求新年如意、风调雨顺，然后人们相互洒水，祝愿长辈健康长寿，祝愿亲朋新年好运。未婚的青年男女则用泼水来表示彼此间的爱慕之情。为庆贺新年，泰国人会举行规模盛大的 "赛象大会"，活动包括人象拔河、跳象拾物、象跨人身、大象足球赛、古代象阵表演等。

The Songkran Festival, also known as the "Water Festival", takes place every year from April 13th to 15th. It symbolizes the cleansing of evil, misfortune, and sin, marking the beginning of a new year. During the Songkran Festival, people carry or transport large Buddha statues, followed by flower-covered floats with performers dressed as "Songkran goddesses". Along the parade route, devotees line the streets, pouring water infused with spices, soaked in palm leaves, from silver bowls onto the Buddha statues and the "Songkran goddesses", praying for a prosperous new year and favorable weather. People also splash water on each other, wishing health and longevity for their elders and good fortune for friends and family. Unmarried young men and women use water splashing as a way to express their affection for one another. To celebrate the new year, Thais hold grand events like the "Elephant Roundup", which includes activities such as tug-of-war with elephants, object retrieval games, elephant rides, elephant soccer matches, and ancient elephant parade performances.

三、旅游观光 Tourism and Sightseeing

（一）主要旅游城市 Major Tourist Cities

1. 曼谷 Bangkok

曼谷，泰国首都，在泰语里是"天使之都"的意思，有"佛庙之都"的美誉，是泰国最大、东南亚第二大城市，是泰国的政治、经济、文化和交通中心和世界著名旅游城市。曼谷位于湄南河畔，距泰国湾4千米，离入海口15千米，全市面积为1 568平方千米，人口为800万。市内河道纵横，货运频繁，水上集市贸易十分繁忙，有"东方威尼斯"的美称。曼谷港是泰国和世界著名的稻米输出港。曼谷佛教历史悠久，佛庙林立，有大小佛寺400多座，云集了泰国的佛教精华，被誉为"佛庙之都"，其中玉佛寺、金佛寺、卧佛寺被视为泰国的三大国宝。

Bangkok, the capital of Thailand, means "City of Angels" in Thai and is renowned as the "City of Temples". It is the largest city in Thailand and the second largest city in Southeast Asia, serving as the political, economic, cultural, and transportation hub of Thailand, as well as a world-famous tourist destination. Bangkok is situated on the banks of the Chao Phraya River, 4 kilometers away from the Gulf of Thailand and 15 kilometers from its estuary, covering an area of 1,568 square kilometers with a population of 8 million. The city is crisscrossed with waterways, bustling with cargo transportation and vibrant water markets, earning it the nickname "Venice of the East". Bangkok Port is a renowned export port for rice in Thailand and globally. With a rich Buddhist history, Bangkok is home to over 400 temples of all sizes, showcasing the essence of Thai Buddhism and earning the title of "City of Temples". Among them, the Temple of the Emerald Buddha, the Temple of the Golden Buddha, and the Temple of the Reclining Buddha are considered the three national treasures of Thailand.

曼谷是国际活动中心之一，每年有多达两三百场的国际会议在此举行。曼谷是联合国亚太经社委员会总部所在地，是世界银行、世界卫生组织、国际劳工组织及其他20多个国际机构的区域办事处所在地。曼谷还是世界佛教联谊会（有32个成员国）总部及亚洲理工学院所在地。

Bangkok is one of the centers for international events. Each year, there are up to two to three hundred international conferences held here. The city has the United Nations Economic and Social Commission for Asia and the Pacific headquarters and regional offices of the World Bank, the World Health Organization, International Labor Organization and over 20 other international agencies. The World Buddhist Association (with 32 member states) headquarters and the Asian Institute of Technology are also located in Bangkok.

2. 芭堤雅 Pattaya

芭堤雅曾经是个渔村，最初在越南战争期间成为一个度假地，并逐渐发展为家庭海景度假胜地。来此旅游的外国游客在 2013 年达到 1 020 万人次。

Once as a fishing village, Pattaya first boomed as a holiday resort during the Vietnam War and has developed into a family-orientated seaside destination. The number of foreign tourists in 2013 amounted to 10.2 million.

游客在芭堤雅的游乐活动包括打高尔夫（高尔夫球场 21 个，距芭堤雅 1 小时车程），卡丁车赛车，参观不同的主题公园和动物园，如大象村，那里每天都会展示训练方法和古代礼仪。其他景点包括百万年石林、芭堤雅鳄鱼公园、芭堤雅公园海滩度假村、水上乐园、斯里波恩兰花农场、银湖酒厂、泰国文化芭堤雅剧院（文化表演）、瓶艺术博物馆、信不信由你博物馆和海底世界水族馆。海底世界水族馆是一个世界级的水族馆，它集中展示了大量来自泰国湾的海洋物种，包括鲨鱼和魔鬼鱼。该市也以歌舞表演而闻名，特别是华丽的人妖表演。

Activities in Pattaya include playing golf (21 golf courses within 1 hour drive to Pattaya), kart racing and visiting different theme parks and zoos such as the Elephant Village, where demonstrations of training methods and ancient ceremonial re-enactments are performed daily. Other attractions in Pattaya include The Million Years Stone Park, Pattaya Crocodile Farm, Pattaya Park Beach Resort, Water Park, Siriporn Orchid Farm, Silver Lake Winery, the Thai Alangkarn Theater Pattaya (cultural show), Bottle Art Museum, Ripley's Believe It or Not Museum and Underwater World Pattaya (world-class aquarium), an aquarium where there is a collection of marine species in the Gulf of Thailand including sharks and stingrays. The city is also famous for singing and dancing, especially the magnificent siren shows.

泰国人妖

3. 清迈 Chiang Mai

清迈是泰国北部最大和文化上最重要的城市。它是清迈省首府，兰纳王国（1296—1768 年）的首都，也是 1774 年到 1939 年间清迈王国的附庸国。近年来，清迈已经成为一个日益现代化的城市，每年吸引超过 500 万的游客，其中外国游客达到 140 万～ 200 万人。清迈在政治领域中也有突出贡献。2006 年 5 月，清迈举办了"东盟 +3"（东盟 10 国和中、日、韩 3 国）首脑会议。

Chiang Mai is the largest and most culturally significant city in northern Thailand and the capital of Chiang Mai province. It was a former capital of the Kingdom of Lanna (1296—1768) and the tributary Kingdom of Chiang Mai from 1774 to 1939. In recent years, Chiang Mai has become an increasingly modern city and has been attracting over 5 million visitors each year, of which between 1.4 million and 2 million are foreign tourists. Chiang Mai gained prominence in the political sphere in May 2006, when the Chiang Mai Initiative was announced here at the summit meeting of ASEAN plus Three (10 ASEAN member states plus China, Japan and Republic of Korea).

4. 普吉岛 Phuket

普吉岛是泰国最大的岛屿，面积和新加坡差不多，位于印度洋安达曼海，离泰国首都曼谷南部 867 千米。普吉岛具有得天独厚的宏伟海湾，种满棕榈树的白色沙滩，环绕四周的小岛，好客的人们和美味的海鲜以及令人赏心悦目的跨世纪中葡建筑。这儿会给人们提供许多运动和休闲的机会，还能让游客们欣赏到郁郁葱葱的热带景观。所有的这些都创造出愉快的氛围，为人们带来真正难忘的假期。这儿有最著名的海滩，如巴东、卡塔、卡隆、卡玛拉和奈汉海滩。普吉岛及周边岛屿是出海、潜水和浮潜的理想地，岛上也有游客期望的高尔夫球场及各种体育和娱乐项目。游客还可以乘坐潜艇探索丰富多彩的海底生活。岛上住宿有众多选择，从普通标准间到五星级酒店应有尽有。

Phuket is Thailand's largest island, approximately the size of Singapore. Phuket nestles in Andaman Sea of Indian Ocean, located 867 kilometers south of Bangkok. Phuket is blessed with magnificent coves and bays, powdery and palm-fringed white beaches, smaller surrounding islands, hospitable people and sea food, delightful turn-of-the-century Sino-Portuguese architecture, numerous sporting and leisure opportunities, as well as a lush tropical landscape. All of which combine to create a delightful ambiance for truly memorable holidays. The most famous beaches are Patong Beach, Kata Beach, Karon Beach, Kamala Beach and Nai Harn Beach. Phuket and its islands are ideal for sailing, diving, snorkeling, golfing and all kinds of sports and entertainment you can wish for. You can also take a trip with a submarine to discover the colorful marine lives under the sea. There is plenty of accommodations available ranging from standard bungalows to 5 star hotels.

（二）著名旅游景点 Famous Tourist Attractions

1. 大皇宫 Grand Palace

图 1-35　大皇宫
Figure 1-35　Grand Palace

大皇宫（图 1-35）位于曼谷市中心，是泰国建筑艺术的巨作。这座宫殿自 1782 年以来一直是暹罗（后来的泰国）国王的官邸。1925 年之前，国王、宫廷及皇家政府都坐落在此。已故君主，国王普密蓬·阿杜德（拉玛九世）居住在吉那拉达宫，但大皇宫仍然是官方活动举办地。每年都有数项皇家和国家活动在大皇宫举行。

The Grand Palace (Figure 1-35) is a complex of buildings at the heart of Bangkok. The palace has been the official residence of the Kings of Siam (later Thailand) since 1782. The king, his court and his royal government were based on the grounds of the palace until 1925. The late monarch, King Bhumibol Adulyadej (Rama IX), resided at Kinarada Palace, but the Grand Palace is still used in official events. Several royal and national events are held at the Grand Palace every year.

2. 玉佛寺 Temple of the Emerald Buddha

图 1-36　玉佛寺
Figure 1-36　Temple of the Emerald Buddha

玉佛寺（图 1-36）始建于 1782 年，与卧佛寺、金佛寺并列为"泰国三大国宝"。它位于首都曼谷大皇宫东北角，是大皇宫的组成部分，也是泰国所有寺庙中最崇高的代表。该寺占地 2.1 万平方米，面积为整个大皇宫的 1/4，是泰国最著名的佛寺，也是泰国唯一没有和尚居住的佛寺。

Temple of the Emerald Buddha (Figure 1-36) was founded in 1782 and is well-known, together with Reclining Buddha and Golden Buddha in Thailand, as the three national treasures. Located in the northeast of the Grand Palace, it is part of the Grand Palace, and is also the lofty representative of all the monasteries. The temple covers an area of 21,000 square meters, one fourth of the Grand Palace. It is the most famous temple in Thailand and also the only Thai temple without Buddhist monk residence.

3. 素贴山和素贴寺 Doi Suthep and Wat Phra That Doi Suthep

素贴山上有素贴寺（图1-37），其位于清迈市西7 000米，海拔约1 053米，是最著名的避暑胜地，这里建有泰国国王的避暑行宫——普屏宫。素贴山是清迈市的标志。当地华人称此山为"遇仙山"或"会仙山"，因山上有著名的素贴寺而闻名。山坡上开满五色玫瑰，山顶白云缭绕，风光秀丽。

Doi Suthep has Wat Phra That Doi Suthep (Figure 1-37), located 7 kilometers west of Chiang Mai, and is about 1 053 meters above sea level. It is the most famous summer resort, which was built there as Summer Palace for the king of Thailand—Phu Phing Palace. It is the landmark of the city of Chiang Mai. The local Chinese call it Meeting God Mountain because of the famous temple. The hillside is full of colored rose and provides a view of clouds and other beautiful scenery.

图1-37　素贴寺
Figure 1-37　Wat Phra That Doi Suthep

4. 皮皮岛 Phi Phi Islands

皮皮岛（图1-38）位于普吉岛大岛和马六甲海峡西岸之间。皮皮岛是由两个主要岛屿组成的姐妹岛，1983年被定为泰国国家公园，是炙手可热的度假胜地之一，每年的11月到次年5月都是皮皮岛的最佳旅游季节。这里海水清澈湛蓝，黛翠山岩形态奇特，海滩细沙如银，珊瑚礁生趣盎然，游人可畅游碧波，可潜游海底世界，在鱼群的伴随下，尽情欣赏多彩多姿的珊瑚和各种海洋生物。如今，姐妹岛中较大的大皮皮岛（Phi Phi Don）是泰国最著名的潜水、浮潜、皮划艇和其他海洋娱乐活动的目的地之一。

图1-38　皮皮岛
Figure 1-38　Phi Phi Islands

Phi Phi Islands (Figure 1-38) are located between Phuket Island and the western coast of the Malacca Strait. This pair of sister islands, made up of two main islands, was designated as a Thai national park in 1983. It is one of the most sought-after vacation destinations, with the best time to visit being from November to May each year. The islands are renowned for their crystal-clear turquoise waters, uniquely shaped emerald cliffs, powdery white-sand beaches, and vibrant coral reefs. Visitors can enjoy swimming in the sparkling waters, diving into the underwater world, and exploring the colorful corals and diverse marine life surrounded by schools of fish. Today, Phi Phi Don, the larger of the two islands, has become one of Thailand's most famous destinations for diving, snorkeling, kayaking, and other marine activities.

（三）旅游购物 Shopping

泰国菜混合了五种基本味道：甜、酸、苦、辣、咸。泰国菜中一些常见的食材有大蒜、辣椒、柠檬汁、柠檬草和鱼露。在泰国，大米是主食，特别是名为茉莉香米的水稻品种几乎每餐都有。泰国是世界最大的大米出口国。泰国饮食和柬埔寨、老挝、越南、印度尼西亚等东南亚国家基本相同。泰国菜是以鱼为原料的酸辣菜。因泰国三面环海，海鲜产品丰富，于是海鲜成为泰国菜的一大特色。泰国大米晶莹剔透，蒸熟后有一种特殊的香味，是世界稻米中的珍品。传统料理是除去黏性的米饭淋上掺满香辣作料的调味品。调味品的做法十分考究，一般是根据祖传秘方烹调，堪称一门艺术。泰国人最喜欢的民族风味食品是咖喱饭，它是用大米调以辣椒、椰浆、肉片或鱼片，再配上蔬菜和竹笋烹制的椰浆辣汤做成的。在泰国餐桌上，无论饭菜是否丰富，餐汤都是不能缺少的。泰国的餐汤主要分为三大类：第一类是清淡的肉和菜汤；第二类是稀米汤；第三类是冬阴功汤，被称为"王者之汤"。冬阴功汤的材料包括甘草、胡椒、柠檬、冬葱、鱼露等，再配上各种海鲜，由一个金鼎炭炉奉上，令人回味无穷。比较受欢迎的泰国菜有冬阴功汤、绿咖喱鸡肉、泰式炒面等。

Thai cuisine blends five fundamental tastes: sour, sweet, bitter, spicy, and salty. Some common ingredients used in Thai cooking include garlic, chili, lemon juice, lemongrass, and fish sauce. The staple food in Thailand is rice, particularly jasmine rice, which is included in almost every meal. Thailand is the world's largest exporter of rice. Thai cuisine shares similarities with that of Cambodia, Laos, Vietnam, Indonesia, and other Southeast Asian countries. The main course often features a hot and sour dish made with fish, and because the country is surrounded on three sides by the sea, seafood is a major component of the Thai diet. Thai steamed rice is crystal clear and has a unique flavor, making it one of the top species in the world. Traditional Thai food includes sticky rice served with spicy seasonings. The approach to condiments is very sophisticated, typically based on ancestral secret recipes, and can be regarded as an art form. One of the most popular dishes in Thailand is curry rice, which consists of rice topped with pepper, coconut milk, meat or fish, along with vegetables and bamboo shoots cooked in a spicy coconut milk broth. Regardless of the variety of dishes on the table, soup is always essential. Thai soups are mainly divided into three categories: the first is a light meat and vegetable soup, the second is a thin rice soup, and the third is Tom Yum, often considered the king of soups. The ingredients for Tom Yum include lemongrass, chili, lime, shallots, and fish sauce, complemented by a variety of seafood and served in a golden charcoal oven. Popular dishes include Tom Yum (spicy shrimp soup), Kaeng Khiao Wan (green chicken curry), and Phat Thai (Thai-style fried noodles).

冬阴功汤：冬阴功汤在泰国非常普遍，"冬阴"是酸辣的意思，"功"是虾的意思，冬阴功汤就是酸辣虾汤。现在这道菜也经过了很多改良，汤分为红汤和白汤，可以选择是否加椰浆，虾也可以换成鱼等，但味道不会有太多差异。

Tom Yum Kung: Tom Yum Kung soup is very common in Thailand, "Tom Yum" means hot and sour, and "Kung" means shrimp, meaning hot and sour shrimp soup. Nowadays, this dish has been improved a lot. The soup is divided into red and white, you can choose whether to add coconut milk, shrimp can also be replaced by fish, etc., but the taste will not be too much difference.

青木瓜色拉：青木瓜色拉是泰国人很喜欢的一道开胃小菜，入口酸、甜，随后以辣椒带出青木瓜的鲜腌口感，再搭配生菜与花生颗粒，非常开胃。这道菜有很多种做法，除青木瓜外，黄瓜、笋也可以用同样的方法制作，最特别的是还可以加米线。游客吃的一般是泰式青木瓜色拉，口味略甜，如果喜欢口味重的泰东北式木瓜色拉，可以在色拉里面加腌制的鱼酱和小螃蟹等。

Green papaya salad : Green papaya salad is a very popular appetiser among Thais. It is sour and sweet in the mouth, followed by chilli to bring out the fresh pickled taste of the green papaya, with lettuce and peanut granules for a very appetizing texture. There are many ways to make this dish. Besides green papaya, cucumber, bamboo shoots can also be made in the same way. The most special thing is that you can add rice noodles. Tourists usually eat Thai-style green papaya salad, tasting slightly sweet. If you like heavy taste of the North East Thail-style papaya salad, you can add marinated fish sauce and small crabs and so on.

芒果糯米饭：芒果糯米饭是泰国特色的甜品小吃，将芒果整颗切块装入盘中，另一侧放入淋上椰汁的糯米饭，卖相十分简单。芒果是甜中带一点点的酸，糯米饭是淡淡的甜味。

Mango glutinous rice: Mango glutinous rice is a Thai speciality dessert snack. The whole mango is cut into pieces and put on a plate ; the other side of the glutinous rice is drizzled with coconut milk. The appearance is very simple. The mango is sweet with a little bit of acidity, and the glutinous rice is mildly sweet.

泰丝：近几十年来，因为独到的手工制作工艺、独特的外表和质地，泰丝已成为别具一格的产品，在世界各地广受欢迎。泰丝被用来制作高贵的服饰、手帕、领带、围巾等，广受游客欢迎。

Thai silk: Because of the unique handmade craftsmanship, appearance and texture, Thai silk has in recent years become distinctive in style and popular around the world. Thai silk is used to make sumptuous costumes, handkerchief, necktie and scarf, ete., and is widely popular among tourists.

宝石：泰国是世界珠宝中心，珠宝产业是泰国的第二大产业。曼谷是世界有色宝石之都。红宝石和蓝宝石是本地产的宝石。

Gem: Thailand is a world-renowned center for jewelry, with its jewelry industry ranking as the country's second-largest economic sector. Bangkok, often hailed as the global capital of colored gemstones, is particularly famous for locally mined rubies and sapphires.

漆器：漆器是清迈及泰国北部的特产。这种工艺包括在劈开的竹子和木头上涂漆，然后加上精致的手绘设计，典型的是黑底金线或棕红底黄绿线。游客可以购买漆器碗、盒子、盘子及其他装饰品或纪念品。

Lacquerware: Lacquerware is a specialty of Chiang Mai and northern Thailand. This craft involves applying lacquer to split bamboo and wood, followed by intricate hand-painted designs, typically featuring gold lines on a black background or yellow and green lines on a reddish-brown background. Visitors can purchase lacquerware bowls, boxes, plates, and other decorative items or souvenirs.

扫码获取：入境须知及海关规定

📋 本节习题

1. 泰国有哪些著名的物产？
2. 泰国有哪些名城和名胜古迹？
3. 泰国为什么有"佛教之国"和"大象之邦"的美称？

万岛之国——印度尼西亚
The Thousand Island Country—Indonesia

导读

印度尼西亚位于亚洲东南部，是世界上最大的群岛国家，这里曾经生活着古老的人类——爪哇人。印度尼西亚以"万岛之国"著称于世，岛屿星罗棋布，散落在碧波荡漾的太平洋赤道附近海域上。被联合国教科文组织列为自然遗产与文化遗产的有桑吉兰早期人类化石遗址、苏门答腊热带雨林乌戎库隆国家公园、婆罗浮屠寺庙群、普兰巴南寺庙群、科莫多国家公园和洛伦茨国家公园。作为世界上最大的伊斯兰教国家，印度尼西亚有自己灿烂的文化与独特的民俗。中国与印度尼西亚于 1950 年 4 月 13 日建交。2015 年 4 月 22 日，中国与印度尼西亚发表联合新闻公报，指出双方同意进一步发挥各自优势，在电力、高铁、有色金属、造船、建材等产能领域进行深度合作，实现互利共赢。

一、地理概览 Geography of Indonesia

（一）位置 Location

印度尼西亚位于亚洲东南部，地跨赤道，由太平洋和印度洋之间的 17 508 个岛屿组成，陆地面积约为 190 万平方千米，是世界上最大的群岛国家，也是多火山、多地震的国家。这些岛屿中约有 6 000 个岛屿有人居住，其中最大的岛屿为爪哇岛、苏门答腊岛、加里曼丹岛（与文莱、马来西亚共有）、新几内亚岛（与巴布亚新几内亚共有）和苏拉维西岛。

Indonesia is located in Southeast Asia, spanning across the equator and comprising 17,508 islands between the Pacific and Indian Oceans. It has a land area of approximately 1.9 million square kilometers, making it the largest archipelagic country in the world, as well as one of the most volcanically and seismically active nations. Among these islands, around 6,000 are inhabited, with the largest being Java, Sumatra, Borneo (shared with Brunei and Malaysia), New Guinea (shared with Papua New Guinea), and Sulawesi.

（二）地形和气候 The Land and Seasons

印度尼西亚地形以山地和丘陵为主，间以高原、盆地和平原。伊利安岛上的查亚峰海拔为 5 029 米，为全国最高峰。印度尼西亚海岸线长 54 716 千米。印度尼西亚属于热带雨林气候，平均温度为 25 ℃～ 27 ℃，是有名的"跨越赤道翠绿带"，高山地区气温稍低。全年分为旱、雨两季，旱季从 5 月到 10 月，雨季从 11 月到次年的 4 月。

Indonesia's terrain is predominantly mountainous and hilly, interspersed with plateaus, basins, and plains. The highest peak in the country is Puncak Jaya on Papua Island, which stands at 5,029 meters. Indonesia has a coastline that stretches for 54,716 kilometers. The country experiences a tropical rainforest climate, with average temperatures ranging from 25 ℃ to 27 ℃, earning it the nickname " the

印度尼西亚的
自然灾害

green belt across the equator". The highland areas are slightly cooler. The year is divided into two main seasons: the dry season, which lasts from May to October, and the rainy season, which runs from November to April of the following year.

思考题

1. 火山的成因是什么？火山爆发造成的危害有哪些？
2. 火山爆发有哪些应对措施？
3. 如何开发利用印度尼西亚的火山旅游资源？
4. 哪些国家容易发生火灾？为什么火山喷发对我国"敬而远之"？

答案提示

（三）自然资源 Natural Resources

许多河流流经全国，在一些岛屿上成为十分有用的运输路线。在爪哇岛，河流对于灌溉非常重要。许多岛屿上也点缀着风景秀丽的湖泊。境内生长着 3 万多种植物，其中热带经济作物胡椒、金鸡纳树的产量居世界首位，天然橡胶和椰子产量居世界第二位。印度尼西亚森林覆盖率达 65%，贵重木材有铁力木、檀木、乌木、柚木等。

Many rivers flow throughout the country. They serve as useful transportation routes on certain islands. On Java, rivers are important for irrigation purposes. A number of islands are dotted with scenic lakes. There are more than 30,000 kinds of plants growing in the territory, among which the output of tropical cash crops pepper and cinchona cream accounts for the first in the world, the output of natural rubber and coconut accounts for the second in the world, and the forest coverage rate of Indonesia is 65%. Valuable woods include ferreous wood, sandalwood, ebony, teak, etc.

 小资料

改变历史的金鸡纳树

金鸡纳树帮康熙皇帝治好了疟疾，帮美国人逆转了战局。相信很多小伙伴都看过抗日战争题材的电视剧，救援队冒着枪林弹雨，将阿司匹林和奎宁送往前线，拯救了无数战士的生命。也正因如此，金鸡纳树从古至今一直担负着治病救人的使命。

金鸡纳树的故事

二、人文概况 Overview of Indonesian Humanities

（一）国情认知 Basic Knowledge of National Conditions

印度尼西亚全称印度尼西亚共和国，源于希腊文，意为"水中岛国"，又称千岛之国、火山之国。国旗为长方形，长宽之比为 3 : 2。旗面由上红下白两个相等的长方形组成。红色象征勇敢和正义，白色象征自由、公正和纯洁。印度尼西亚国徽是金色飞鹰，飞鹰象征创造力。鹰的尾巴和翅膀分别有 8 根和 17 根羽毛，象征着印度尼西亚的独立日（8 月 17 日）。飞鹰胸前盾面的黑色横线象征赤道穿过印度尼西亚领土，水牛头象征主权属于人民，榕树象征民族意识，棉桃和稻穗象征丰衣足食及社会必须公正之原则，饰物象征人道主义。黑色小盾和五角星象征宗教信仰，也象征"潘查希拉"——印度尼西亚建国的五项基本原则。神鹰双爪下的白色绶带上用古印度尼西亚文书写着"求同存异"。

The full name of Indonesia is "The Republic of Indonesia". It is derived from the Greek word meaning "island country in the water". It is also known as the Land of a Thousand Islands and the Land of Volcanoes. The flag is rectangular, with a ratio of length to width of 3∶2. The flag consists of two equal rectangles, red on top and white on the bottom. The red colour symbolizes bravery and justice, while the white colour symbolizes freedom, justice and purity. The national emblem of Indonesia is the golden eagle. The eagle symbolizes creativity. The eagle's tail and wings have 8 and 17 feathers respectively, symbolizing Indonesia's Independence Day (August 17). The black channel on the shield on the eagle's chest symbolizes the equator, the buffalo's head symbolizes that sovereignty belongs to the people, the banyan tree symbolizes national consciousness, the cotton peaches and the ears of the rice plant symbolize the principle of food and clothing and the necessity of social justice, and the ornaments symbolize humanism. The black shield and the five-pointed star symbolize religious beliefs and the "Pancasila", the five basic principles on which Indonesia was founded. On the ribbon, the words "Bhinneka Tunggal Ika" (seek common ground while holding back differences) are written in Indonesia.

印度尼西亚人口约 2.62 亿（2022 年），共有 100 多个民族，主要民族有爪哇族、巽他族、马都拉族。印度尼西亚的官方语言为印度尼西亚语，有 200 多种民族语言。主要宗教有伊斯兰教、基督教新教、天主教、印度教、佛教和原始拜物教。印度尼西亚全国约 90% 的人口信奉伊斯兰教，是世界上穆斯林人口最多的国家。货币为印度尼西亚盾。

Indonesia has a population of about 262 million (2022) with a total of more than 100 nationalities. Its main ethnic groups are Java, Sunda and Madurese people. Indonesian is the official language of Indonesia, with over 200 ethnic languages. The main religions are Islam, Protestantism, Catholicism, Hinduism, Buddhism and primitive Fetishism. Across Indonesia, about 90% of the people believe in Islam, and it is the most populous Muslim country in the world. The currency is the Indonesian rupiah.

巴厘岛居民的宗教信仰

（二）历史简介 History of Indonesia

印度尼西亚在 3—7 世纪建立了一些分散的王朝。13 世纪末、14 世纪初，东爪哇出现了强大的信奉印度教的麻喏巴歇封建帝国，对印度尼西亚产生了重要影响。15 世纪先后遭葡萄牙、西班牙和英国入侵。1602 年，荷兰在印度尼西亚建立了具有政府职能的荷兰东印度公司，开始了长达 300 多年的殖民统治。1942 年日本入侵，1945 年日本投降后爆发"八月革命"，8 月 17 日宣告独立，成立印度尼西亚共和国，首任总统是苏加诺，首都为雅加达。

Indonesia established several decentralized kingdoms from the 3rd to the 7th century. In the late 13th and early 14th centuries, a powerful Hindu-Majapahit feudal empire emerged in East Java, which had a significant impact on Indonesia. In 15th century, the country was invaded by the Portuguese, the Spaniards and the Britons. In 1602, the Dutch established the Dutch East India

Company and became the dominant European power, which lasted more than 300 years. Japan invaded Indonesia in 1942 and the revolution of August broke out in 1945 after the surrender of Japan. On August 17, Indonesia declared independence and founded Republic of Indonesia, Sukarno became its first president and Jakarta has been the capital.

（三）经济状况 The Economy

印度尼西亚的经济呈现多样化，私营部门和政府共同发挥着重要作用。该国是东南亚最大的经济实体，也是 20 国集团的主要成员。2011 年，印度尼西亚国内生产总值为 8 457 亿美元。印度尼西亚原以农业为主，20 世纪 60 年代中期以来，工业在国民经济中的地位不断上升，目前已成为该国经济最大的领域，占国内生产总值的 46.4%（2010 年），然后是服务业（37.1%）和农业（16.5%）。然而，从 2010 年开始，服务业雇用人员数量高于其他行业，占劳动力总数的 48.9%，其次是农业（38.3%）和工业（12.8%）。印度尼西亚重视旅游业，旅游业已成为印度尼西亚创汇的主要行业。

Indonesia has a mixed economy in which both the private sector and the government play significant roles. The country is the largest economy in Southeast Asia and a member of the G20 major economies. In 2011, Indonesia's gross domestic product was $845.7 billion. Indonesia used to focus on agriculture. Since the mid 1960s, the position of industry in the national economy has been continuously rising, and now is the economy's largest and accounts for 46.4% of GDP（2010）, this is followed by services（37.1%）and agriculture（16.5%）. However, since 2010, service sector has employed more people than other sectors, accounting 48.9% of the total labor force. This has been followed by agriculture（38.3%）and industry（12.8%）. Indonesia attaches importance to the tourist industry, and tourism has become the main industry for Indonesia to earn foreign exchange.

（四）传统文化 Traditional Culture

印度尼西亚国内有 100 多个民族，每个民族都有其不同的文化，且历经了好几个世纪的发展。这些民族的文化受到印度、阿拉伯国家、中国及欧洲的影响。例如：传统的爪哇和巴厘舞蹈蕴含印度教文化和神话元素，还有皮影戏演出也是如此。印度尼西亚不同地区的纺织品如蜡染、锦缎等，呈现出跨度较大的艺术风格。对印度尼西亚建筑的影响主要来自印度，但来自中国、阿拉伯国家及欧洲建筑的影响也是相当重要的。

Indonesia has about 100 ethnic groups, each with cultural identities developed over centuries, and influenced by Indian, Arabic, Chinese and European sources. Traditional Javanese and Balinese dances, for example, contain aspects of Hindu culture and mythology, as do Wayang Kulit（shadow puppets）performances. Textiles such as batik and brocade are created across Indonesia in styles that vary by region. The most dominant influences on Indonesian architecture have traditionally been Indian; however, Chinese, Arabic and European architectural influences are also significant.

印度尼西亚的皮影戏（哇扬皮影戏）（图 1-39）是一种独特的戏剧形式，常见于印度尼西亚的爪哇岛和巴厘岛。"哇扬"（wayang）为印度尼西亚语"神圣影子"之意，指木偶或皮影戏，今延伸为戏剧之意，是爪哇岛文化中具有代表性的部分。木偶大都根据印度神话《罗摩衍那》和《摩诃婆罗多》制作装扮，用一根细杆从中空的身体穿过，既起到连接头和身子的作用，也是"哇扬"艺人的操纵杆。

Indonesian shadow puppetry (Wayang Kulit) (Figure 1-39) is a unique theatrical form, commonly found on the Indonesian islands of Java and Bali. "Wayang" means "sacred shadow" in Indonesian, which means puppet or shadow play, and now it extends to drama. It is a representative part of Java island culture . Puppets are mostly made and dressed up according to Indian myths *Ramayana* and *Mahabharata*. A thin rod passes through the hollow body, which not only plays the role of connecting the head and body, but also is the joystick of "Wayang" artists.

图 1-39　哇扬皮影戏
Figure 1-39　Wayang Kulit

巴厘岛上有一种重要的表演艺术——甘美兰（图 1-40），这是印度尼西亚历史最悠久的一种民族音乐形式，主要以鼓和锡配上用金属和竹子做成的类似锣的乐器来演奏。许多女孩子很小就进入专门的学校学习这种表演艺术，瞪眼睛是习舞过程中必须掌握的一项技能。

图 1-40　甘美兰传统音乐表演现场
Figure 1-40　Gamelan

There is an important performing art in Bali, Gamelan (Figure 1-40), which is the oldest form of national music in the Republic of Indonesia. This music is mainly played with drums and gongs like instruments made of metal and bamboo. Many girls enter special schools to learn this kind of performing art at a very young age. Widening their eyes is a necessary exercise in the process of learning dance.

（五）礼仪禁忌 Social Etiquettes and Taboos

印度尼西亚人在社交场合与客人见面时，一般习惯以握手为礼。与熟人、朋友相遇时，传统礼节是用右手按住胸口互相问好。印度尼西亚人认为左手是肮脏的，通常在上完厕所后清理时使用，因此不可以用左手给予、接受物品或吃东西。

It is generally customary for Indonesians to greet guests in social situations by shaking hands. When meeting acquaintances and friends, the traditional etiquette is to greet each other with the right hand pressed against the chest. In Indonesia, don't do the following: to give, receive and eat with the left hand. People usually use their left hand to clean up after relieving oneself. That is why they consider the left hand dirty.

与印度尼西亚人谈话或进别人家里时，要摘下墨镜。进入圣地特别是清真寺，一定要脱鞋，参观庙宇或清真寺不能穿短裤、无袖服、背心或裸露的衣服。不要触摸或拍别人的头部。人们认为头部是神圣的，应该得到尊重。印度尼西亚人忌讳在别人面前吐痰。当印度尼西亚人表达厌恶之情或看到恶心的东西时，他们通常会吐痰。

Remove your sunglasses when talking to Indonesians or entering someone's home. Always take off your shoes when entering a holy place, especially a mosque, and avoid wearing shorts, sleeveless clothing, tank tops, or revealing attire when visiting a temple or mosque. Do not touch or pat someone else's head, as the head is considered sacred and should be respected. Avoid spitting in the presence of others; when Indonesians are disgusted or encounter something unpleasant, they often spit.

应邀赴宴时，印度尼西亚人一般不会要求客人带礼物，但客人送鲜花是合乎礼仪的。主人若有馈赠，推却不受是不礼貌的。印度尼西亚人敬蛇如神，但忌讳老鼠和乌龟。当地人不喜欢外国人当众接吻，裸体太阳浴是非法的。爪哇岛流行斗牛，与西班牙斗牛不同的是，西班牙斗牛是人牛相斗，而在这里是两牛相斗。

When invited to a banquet, one is not expected to bring gifts, but it is considered polite for guests to offer flowers. If the host presents a gift, it is impolite for the guest to refuse it. Indonesians hold snakes in high regard but have taboos against rats and turtles. Locals think it is improper to kiss in public, and nude sunbathing is illegal. Bullfighting is popular on Java Island, but unlike Spanish bullfighting, which involves a man fighting a bull, it features two bulls fighting each other.

（六）传统节日 Festivals

1. 建国五基诞生日 Pancasila Day

印度尼西亚立国的基础是建国五项原则（又称"建国五基"），即潘查希拉，此为建立该国基本制度的依据。五项基本原则由印度尼西亚总统苏加诺于 1945 年 6 月 1 日提出，后来这一天被定为"建国五基诞生日"。

The foundation of Indonesia's nation-founding is the five founding principles, namely, the Pancasila, and acts as rationale for its basic system. Proposed by Indonesian President Sukarno on 1 June 1945, the day was later designated as the Birthday of the Five Foundations of the Nation.

2. 开斋节 Eid al-Fitr（拉丁语写法）

这是印度尼西亚最重要的节日。每年伊斯兰教历 9 月，全国的伊斯兰教信徒都要白天斋戒禁食，斋月后第一天便是开斋节。开斋节前夕，伊斯兰教信徒要进行慈善捐赠活动。开斋节法定假日只有 1 天，但实际上一般要放假 3 天以上，有的单位甚至放假 1 周以上。外出工作的人都要赶在开斋节前返回老家与亲人团聚。开斋节前夕是个不眠之夜，各个清真寺整夜念长经，诵经声通过高音喇叭传到四面八方。开斋节当天，家家户户打扫得干干净净，门前挂着用嫩椰叶制作的装饰物。人们都身着盛装，相互拜访。有些组织还会聚会，气氛热烈，一片喜庆景象。

This is the most important festival in Indonesia. During annual September of the Islamic calendar, the Islamists observe the fast of Ramadan, the first day after which is the Eid al-Fitr. On the eve of Eid al-Fitr, the Islamists must conduct charity activities. The legal festival is only one day off, but generally there are three days or more; some organizations or businesses even have more than one week. People working outside have to hurry to return home for family reunion before the festival. Eid al-Fitr's eve is a sleepless night, with reading all night in every mosque, chants spreading all around through loudspeakers. On the Eid day, each and every family clean houses with ornaments made of tender coconut leaves hanging on doors. Dressed in costumes, people visit each other. Some organizations even arrange the gathering in such a warm atmosphere and a festive scene.

印度尼西亚开斋节

三、旅游观光 Tourism and Sightseeing

（一）主要旅游城市 Major Tourist Cities

1. 雅加达 Jakarta

雅加达是印度尼西亚的首都，东南亚第一大城市，是世界著名的海港。它位于爪哇岛西北部沿海，人口为 958 万。雅加达最知名的地标建筑就是印度尼西亚国家纪念塔，高 137 米，为一烛台造型建筑物，内部设有顶楼观景台、纪念博物馆等设施。雅加达历史悠久，早在 14 世纪就已成为初具规模的港口城市。当时叫巽他加拉巴，意思是椰子，当地华人称其为"椰城"。公元 5 世纪，它只是一个小渔村，但现在已成为一个国际多元化大都市。雅加达市区分为旧城区和新城区。北部的老城区靠近海湾，风景独特，历史遗迹众多。大多数建筑都有典型的古典欧洲风格，如前荷兰市政厅。南部的新区非常现代化，是雅加达的政治和金融中心。

Jakarta is the capital of Indonesia, the largest city in Southeast Asia' and a world famous port. Located on the northwest coast of Java Island, it has a population of 9.58 million. The most famous landmark building in Jakarta is the Indonesian National Monument, which is 137 meters high. It is a candlestick shaped building with top floor observation deck, Memorial Museum and other facilities inside. Jakarta has a long history, and became a port city with certain scale as early as in the fourteenth century. At that time, it was called the Sunda Kalapa, which means coconut, and the local overseas Chinese called it " City of Coconut ". It was just a small fishing village back in the 5th century AD, but is now a sprawling international and multicultural metropolis. Jakarta's urban area is divided into an old urban area and a new urban area. The old area in the north is close to the bay, with unique sceneries and many historic sites. Most of the buildings have typical classical European-style architecture such as the former Dutch City Hall. The new area in the south is very modern. It is the political and financial center of Jakarta.

雅加达的旅游名胜众多。在东郊距市中心 26 千米处，有世界著名的印度尼西亚缩影公园，也称为"迷你公园"，也有人称其为"缩景影国"。公园占地 60 公顷，于 1984 年正式开放。全市有清真寺 200 余座，基督教新教及天主教教堂 100 余所，佛教与道教寺院数十座。班芝兰是华人集中地，附近的小南门是华人商业中心区。雅加达以东 10 千米的丹戎不碌是世界著名的海港。这里的寻梦园，也称"幻想公园"，是东南亚最大的游乐园之一。

Jakarta has many tourist attractions. In the eastern suburbs 26 kilometers from the city center, there is a world famous Miniature Park, also known as Mini Park, and some call it the " epitome of the country ". The park covers an area of some 60 hectares, and has officially opened since 1984. The city has more than 200 mosques, over 100 Protestant and Catholic churches, as well as dozens of Buddhist and Taoist temples. Pancoran is the place for overseas Chinese, and nearby the South Gate is the Chinese central business district of Jakarta. Tanjung Priok, 10 kilometers east of Jarkata, is a world famous port. The Dream Garden here, also known as " Fantasy Park", is one of the largest amusement parks in Southeast Asia.

2. 巴厘岛 Bali Island

巴厘岛，行政上称为巴厘省，是印度尼西亚 33 个一级行政区之一。巴厘岛是印度尼西亚著名的旅游区，距印度尼西亚首都雅加达 1 000 千米，与雅加达所在的爪哇岛隔海相望。巴厘岛面积为 5 560 平方千米，人口约 315 万。巴厘岛处于热带地区，气候炎热且潮湿。

Bali, administratively known as the Province of Bali, is one of the 33 first-class administrative regions of Indonesia. Bali Island is a famous tourist district of Indonesia, 1,000 kilometers from the capital Jakarta, and faces across the sea to the Java Island where Jakarta is situated. Bali Island has an area of 5,560 square kilometers, a population of about 3.15 million. Bali Island belongs to tropical area, so the climate is hot and humid.

巴厘岛是一个多山的岛屿，地势东高西低。岛上还有四五座完整的锥形火山峰，其中阿贡火山海拔 3 142 米，是岛上的最高点。巴厘岛风景如画，岛上有许多休眠火山、火山湖、河流、热带雨林和白沙海滩。沙努尔、努沙杜瓦和库塔等处的海滩，是岛上景色最美的海滨浴场，这里的沙细、海水湛蓝且清澈，每年来此游览的各国游客络绎不绝。巴厘岛的居民主要是巴厘人，因为历史上受印度宗教文化的影响，他们大都信奉印度教。全岛有庙宇 12 500 多座，因此，巴厘岛又有"千寺之岛"的美称。巴厘人的古典舞蹈典雅多姿，是为另一种美景，在世界舞蹈艺术中具有独特的地位。其中，狮子舞与剑舞最具代表性。

Bali Island is a mountainous island with mountain range going down from east to west. There are four to five complete conical volcano peaks on the island, including the Mount Agung with an elevation of 3 142 meters, which is the highest point on the island. The island boasts numerous dormant volcanoes, crater lakes, rivers, tropical rain forests and white sand beaches, forming one of Bali Island's most spectacular landscapes. Beaches on Sanur, Nusa Dua and Kuta are the island's most beautiful scenery, featured by fine sand beach and clear blue water. This scenery attracts millions of visitors every year. Residents of Bali Island are mainly local Bali people. Due to historical influence from Indian religion, the island mainly practices Hinduism. Bali Island has more than 12,500 temples, so Bali Island is also known as "Island of Thousand Temples". Bali's elegant classical dance is another pretty scene. The art of dance takes up a unique position in the world cultures. Among them, the lions and the sword dances are the most typical ones.

巴厘岛的雕刻（木雕、石雕）、绘画和手工艺品也以其精湛的技艺、独特的风格闻名遐迩。在岛上处处可见木、石的精美雕像和浮雕，因此，该岛又有"艺术之岛"之誉。巴厘岛的绘画别具一格，大都是用胶和矿物颜料在粗麻布或白帆布上作画，主题取材于田园风光和人们的生活习俗，具有浓郁的地方色彩。因此，巴厘岛素有"诗之岛""东方的希腊"的美称。

Bali Island's carving (wood carving, stone carving), painting and handicrafts are also well-known for its superb artistry and unique style. Everywhere on the island you may be able to see exquisite statues and reliefs in wood or stone carvings, therefore, the island is also called "the Island of Art". Bali's paintings have a style of their own, mostly glue and mineral pigments painted on the coarse linen or white canvas, and their themes are drawn from the pastoral scenery and people's living habits with strong local taste. Therefore, Bali Island is also known as "Poetry Island" or "Oriental Greece".

3. 万隆 Bandung

万隆为西爪哇省首府，位于雅加达东南约 160 千米的被火山群峰包围的高原盆地中，是著名的避暑旅游城市。具有历史意义的万隆会议于 1955 年在万隆市独立大厦举行。万隆是印度尼西亚第三大城市，人口约 240 万。虽接近赤道，但因地势较高，气候凉爽、空气清新，年平均气温为 22.5 ℃，年降水量为 1 988 毫米。万隆景色秀丽、清静幽雅、四季如春，被誉为印度尼西亚最美丽的城市，素有"爪哇的巴黎"之称。万隆的主要旅游景点有皇家玫瑰公园、覆舟火山、万隆温泉、马里巴雅温泉、达哥瀑布和连旺天文台等。

Bandung is the capital of West Java province, located in the highland basin surrounded by volcanic peaks about 160 kilometers southeast of Jakarta, and is a famous summer tourist city. The historic Bandung Conference was held in 1955 at the Independence House in Bandung. Bandung is the third largest city in Indonesia with a population of about 2.4 million. Although it is close to the equator, it has a cool climate and fresh air due to its high terrain, with an average annual temperature of 22.5 ℃ and an annual precipitation of 1,988 mm. With its beautiful scenery, quietness and elegance, and four seasons of spring, Bandung is regarded as the most beautiful city in Indonesia, and is known as the "Paris of Java". The main tourist attractions of Bandung are the Royal Rose Park, the Overboat Volcano, Bandung Hot Springs, Malibaya Hot Springs, Dago Waterfalls, and Lianwang Observatory.

4. 茂物 Bogor

茂物是印度尼西亚历史名城，避暑旅游城市，位于爪哇岛西部一熔岩高原北麓的山间盆地中。由于海拔高又多雷雨，故为优良避暑胜地。由于一年间雷雨日多达 322 天，因而被称为"雷都"。整座城市占地 82 公顷，市内有世界上最大的热带植物园。该园建于 1817 年，园内有 1.3 万种植物，还有世界最大的标本馆，藏有植物标本 50 多万件。

Bogor is a historical city in Indonesia, a summer tourist city, located in a mountainous basin at the northern foot of a lava plateau in western Java. Due to the high altitude and thunderstorms, it is an excellent summer resort. The city is also known as the "Thunder Capital" because it has 322 days of thunderstorms in a year, covering an area of 82 hectares. The city has the world's largest tropical botanical garden. The garden was built in 1817. There are 13,000 kinds of plants in the garden, and there is also the world's largest herbarium in the Tropical Botanical Garden, which has more than 500,000 pieces of plant specimens.

（二）著名旅游景点 Famous Tourist Attractions

1. 雅加达老城区 The Old Town of Jakarta

雅加达老城区（图 1-41），前身是巴达维亚古城，是荷兰殖民统治时期的首都，有很多荷兰人留下的保存完好的建筑。广场中心有一个法塔西拉花园，广场一侧是曾经的荷兰市政厅，现已成为雅加达历史博物馆。即使是当地人也非常喜欢在假期来这里看街头表演，或者在这个怀旧的地方约会和吃饭。

图 1-41　雅加达老城区
Figure 1-41　The Old Town of Jakarta

The Old Town of Jakarta (Figure 1−41), formerly known as Batavia, was the capital during the Dutch colonial era and is home to many well−preserved Dutch colonial−era buildings. At the center of the square is the Fatahillah Garden, and on one side of the square is the former Dutch City Hall, which is now the Jakarta History Museum. Even locals enjoy visiting the area on holidays to watch street performances or to dine and date in this nostalgic setting.

2. 自由广场 Freedom Square

图 1-42 自由广场
Figure 1−42 Freedom Square

自由广场（图 1-42）位于雅加达市中心，也被称为"独立广场"，是人们每年庆祝国庆的地方。独立广场以印度尼西亚人民英雄纪念碑为中心，广场北侧是总统府，西侧有国防部大院和中央博物馆，东侧有甘比尔火车站。广场东南角上有一组根据《摩诃婆罗多》史诗中的故事情节塑造的群马拉车雕塑，十分壮观。纪念碑西侧的公园里还有一个音乐喷泉。

Located in the center of Jakarta, Freedom Square (Figure 1−42), also known as "Independence Square", is where the national day is celebrated annually. At its center stands the monument to Indonesia's people's heroes. On the north side of the square is the Merdeka Palace, the west side houses the Ministry of Defense complex and the Central Museum, and the east side features the Gambir railway station. In the southeast corner of the square, there is a spectacular group of horse−drawn carriage sculptures inspired by the epic tales of the *Mahabharata*. Additionally, there is a musical fountain in the park on the west side of the monument.

3. 伊斯蒂克拉尔清真寺 Istiqlal Mosque

图 1-43 伊斯蒂克拉尔清真寺
Figure 1−43 Istiqlal Mosque

伊斯蒂克拉尔清真寺（图 1-43）是印度尼西亚最大的一座清真寺，也是东南亚最大的一座清真寺，位于雅加达自由广场东北边，建成于 1979 年。印度尼西亚重大的伊斯兰教活动和仪式都在这里举行，印度尼西亚总统及国家政要也常到这里做礼拜。

Istiqlal Mosque (Figure 1−43) is the largest mosque in Indonesia and also the largest one in Southeast Asia. Located in the northeast of Jakarta Freedom Square, it was built in 1979. Major Islamic activities and ceremonies are held here, and Indonesian presidents and dignitaries often worship here.

清真寺的建筑全部用大理石铺设，仅大理石柱就多达 4 400 根。主体建筑是一个白色大圆屋顶覆盖的中央礼拜大厅，圆屋顶的直径达到 45 米，大厅面积达到 1 万平方米，全寺最多可以同时容纳 12 万人做礼拜。

The buildings of the mosque are all paved with marble, and there are 4,400 marble columns alone. The main building is the central worship hall covered with a large white dome, which has a diameter of 45 meters, and the hall has a surface area of 10,000 square meters. The whole temple can accommodate up to 120,000 worshippers at the same time.

4. 雅加达大教堂 Jakarta Cathedral

雅加达大教堂（图1-44）靠近独立广场和伊斯蒂克拉尔清真寺，是雅加达的地标建筑之一，采用的是当时盛行的新哥特式建筑风格，外观十分漂亮，带着欧式建筑的优雅。教堂不是很大，但给人别有情调的感觉，时常还会看到里面在举行婚礼。

As one of Jakarta's landmarks, the Jakarta Cathedral (Figure 1-44) is located near Independence Square and the Istiqlal Mosque. Built in the popular Neo-Gothic architectural style of its time, it boasts a beautiful appearance that shares the elegance of European architecture. Although the church is not very large, it offers a unique atmosphere, and weddings are frequently held there.

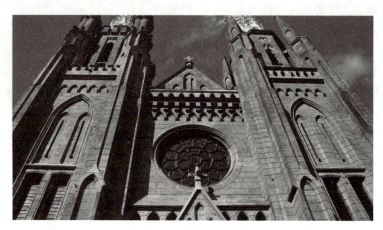

图 1-44　雅加达大教堂
Figure 1-44　Jakarta Cathedral

5. 印度尼西亚国家博物馆 Indonesia National Museum

印度尼西亚国家博物馆（图1-45）是一座欧式的白色建筑，建成于1868年，是印度尼西亚规模最大、收藏品最丰富的博物馆。馆前草坪石墩上立有一座铜大象，为1871年暹罗王拉玛五世来访时所赠，故博物馆又称"大象博物馆"或"象屋"。

Indonesia National Museum (Figure 1-45), built in 1868, is a white European building, which is the largest in size and has the richest collections in Indonesia. There is a copper elephant on the stone pier on the lawn in front of the museum, which was gifted by Rama Ⅴ, King of Siam, when he visited the place in 1871. Therefore, the museum is also called the "Elephant Museum" or "Elephant House".

博物馆中设有金银饰物室、青铜器室、货币室、古物展览室、史前展览室等，其中包括30万年前爪哇猿人头骨化石、三四千年前中国青铜时代的鼎和鬲、中国古代的陶瓷器和古币、爪哇岛上的象首人身佛像、苏门答腊岛独特的房屋模型以及皮影戏、木偶戏道具等。

图 1-45　印度尼西亚国家博物馆
Figure 1-45　Indonesia National Museum

In the museum, there is a gold and silver ornaments room, a bronze room, currency room, antiques exhibition room, and a prehistoric exhibition room, etc. In addition, there is a 300,000 year-old skull fossil of an ancient ape man from Java, a cauldron and an ancient cooking tripod with hollow legs from the Chinese bronze age which was 3,000 or 4,000 years ago, ceramic ware and ancient coins from ancient China, a Buddhist statue of an elephant head and human body, a unique model of Sumatra island, and shadow play and puppet show props.

6. 印度尼西亚缩影公园 Indonesian Miniature Park

印度尼西亚缩影公园（图 1-46）位于雅加达郊区，占地 100 公顷。公园中央是一幅巨大的印度尼西亚群岛模型地图，分为 27 个区，代表印度尼西亚的 27 个省和地区，如中爪哇岛、巴厘岛和雅加达。每个区内有当地传统特色的建筑物，并种植当地特有的植物。游客可以乘小船游览"印度尼西亚各岛"，也可乘空中缆车、小型火车或马车，遍游"全国"，领略印度尼西亚各地的风光特色。公园内有文化表演、庆典、各地美食，特别是在周末和公共假日期间活动较多，游客可以充分体验印度尼

图 1-46　印度尼西亚缩影公园
Figure 1-46　Indonesian Miniature Park

西亚文化。这里还建有博物馆、图书馆、影像中心、少年宫和儿童乐园等。其中最醒目的一座建筑物是金蜗牛全景式电影院，每天定时放映《美丽的印度尼西亚》等全景电影。

The Indonesian Miniature Park (Figure 1-46) is located in the outskirts of Jakarta, and covers an area of 100 hectares. In the center of the park is a model map of the giant Indonesian archipelago, which is divided into 27 districts, representing 27 provinces and regions of Indonesia, such as Central Java, Bali and Jakarta. Each district has its own traditional buildings and plants. Here, you can take a boat tour of the "Indonesian islands", or take an aerial cable car, small trains or carriages to travel around the "whole country", and enjoy the landscape features of Indonesia. There are cultural performances, celebrations and local cuisines in the park, especially during weekends and public holidays. You can fully experience Indonesian culture here. There are also museums, libraries, image centers, children's leisure centers, and children's parks. One of the most striking buildings is the Golden Snail Panoramic Cinema which regularly shows panoramic films like *Beautiful Indonesia* every day.

7. 安佐尔梦幻公园 Ancol Dreamland

安佐尔梦幻公园（图 1-47）是雅加达最大、最著名的娱乐公园，位于雅加达市区北端，紧靠雅加达海湾。园中建有设计新颖的露天电影院、水族馆、海豚表演池、人造波浪大型游泳池等。这里既适合亲子也适合情侣游玩，既有刺激的项目，也有浪漫的摩天轮、人造海浪和海洋馆。

Ancol Dreamland (Figure 1-47), Jakarta's

图 1-47　安佐尔梦幻公园
Figure 1-47　Ancol Dreamland

largest and most famous entertainment park, is located in the northern end of Jakarta, which is close to the Gulf of Jakarta. A newly designed outdoor cinema, aquarium, dolphin performance pool, and artificial swimming pool can be found there. It is suitable for both families and couples. There are exciting activities, a romantic ferris wheel, and an artificial wave pool and aquarium.

8. 茂物植物园 Bogor Botanic Gardens

茂物植物园（图 1-48）位于雅加达以南 56 千米处，毗邻茂物总统府，占地面积 87 公顷，建于 1817 年，是世界最大的热带植物园之一，栽植了从世界各地引入的约 1.6 万种植物。园内有世界最大的植物标本馆，有 50 多万种植物标本。此外，园内有植物研究所，可供世界各地热带植物学家到此研究。

The Bogor Botanic Gardens (Figure 1-48) are located 56 kilometers south of Jakarta, adjacent to the Bogor Presidential Palace. Covering an area of 87 hectares, it was established in 1817 and is one of the largest tropical botanical gardens in the world, featuring approximately 16,000 species of plants introduced from around the globe. The garden also houses the world's largest herbarium, with over 500,000 plant specimens. Additionally, there is a plant research institute within the gardens, providing a venue for tropical botanists from around the world to conduct research.

园内栽培有著名的巨兰"兰花皇后"（又名甘蔗兰），径高 3～5 米，每株可开花 70～80 朵，香气浓郁，为印度尼西亚独有。还有一种腐尸花（图 1-49），每 3 年开一次花，花有一人多高，形状丑陋，傍晚发出恶臭，故而得名。

图 1-48　茂物植物园

Figure 1-48　Bogor Botanic Gardens

图 1-49　腐尸花

Figure 1-49　Corpse Flower

The famous giant orchid, known as the "Orchid Queen" or sugarcane orchid, is cultivated in the park. It reaches a height of 3 to 5 meters, and each plant can produce 70 to 80 blossoms. With its strong fragrance, it is unique to Indonesia. Additionally, there is a type of corpse flower (Figure1-49) that blooms every three years. The flower with an unusual appearance, is taller than a man, and emits an unpleasant odor in the evening.

9. 巴厘岛海滩 Bali Beach

巴厘岛是世界上最受游客欢迎的岛屿目的地之一。巴厘岛的海滩（图 1-50）有很多，每个都各有千秋，从南部棕榈枝环绕的白色沙滩，如库塔、努沙杜瓦和萨努尔海滩，到乌鲁瓦图、巴东、梦幻岛和宾因海滩悬崖守护的"神秘"海岸。巴厘岛海滩还包括北部和西部海岸线上引人注目的黑色沙滩，中间还有尚未开发的海湾。作为冲浪者曾经经常光顾的地方，如今的巴厘岛海滩以一流的酒店和一流的设施欢迎着前来寻找"天堂"的游客。在巴厘岛上，游客可以发现自己最爱的沙滩——武吉半岛南部有一些"秘密"和"隐藏未知"的海滩，正等着游客们前去探索。

Bali has a rich assortment of beaches, each of which is a favourite destination respectively. Bali beaches (Figure 1-50) range from palm-fringed white sand coasts on the island's south such as Kuta, Nusa Dua and Sanur, to the cliff-guarded "hidden" shores of Uluwatu, Padang, Dreamland and Bingin. Bali beaches also comprise striking black sands on the north and western shorelines, with sleepy undisturbed coves in-between. Once the haunt of surfers, Bali's

图 1-50 巴厘岛海滩
Figure 1-50 Bali Beach

beaches now welcome visitors in search of paradise with superb hotels and excellent facilities. You might as well discover your own favourite coast in Bali—there are some "secret" and "hidden" beaches around the southern Bukit peninsula just waiting for you to explore.

 思考题

阅读材料"青山绿水话巴厘"并回答以下问题。

在旅游资源开发的同时，应该如何坚持问题导向，守护大自然赋予人类的绿水青山，打好治污攻坚战？

提示：加强环境保护，让人与自然和谐共生。

青山绿水话巴厘

10. 塔纳罗特海神庙 Tanah Lot Temple

塔纳罗特海神庙（图 1-51）是巴厘岛最具标志性的寺庙之一，位于岩石顶部，周围是不断撞击岩石基底的波浪。白天，在碧海蓝天的映衬下，这座寺庙风景如画；日落时，寺庙的景色最为壮观，成为巴厘岛明信片上的经典照片。塔纳罗特海神庙向海洋守护者致敬，是巴厘岛最重要的海边庙宇之一。陆上点缀着较小的神龛和供游客休闲的设施，如商店、定期举行舞蹈表演的文化公园、供游客享受难忘的日落美景的餐厅。

图 1-51 塔纳罗特海神庙
Figure 1-51 Tanah Lot Temple

Tanah Lot Temple (Figure 1-51) is among the island's most iconic temples, positioned on top of a rock and surrounded by the waves of the open sea that constantly crash against its base. The temple is scenic by day against the blue ocean and sky, but the scene is most dramatic during sunsets with its silhouette creating one of Bali's picture postcard images. Tanah Lot pays homage to the guardian spirits of the sea, and it's also among Bali's key sea temples. The onshore site is dotted with smaller shrines and visitors' leisure facilities, such as shops, a cultural park where regular dance performances are shown regularly, restaurants where you can enjoy a sunset dinner with the memorable view.

图 1-52　布撒基寺
Figure 1-52　Besakih Temple

11. 布撒基寺 Besakih Temple

布撒基寺（图 1-52）是巴厘岛的"母亲庙"，位于巴厘岛最高峰阿贡山的西南坡。布撒基寺是巴厘岛最大的寺庙建筑群，由 18 个独立的圣地组成，每个圣地属于不同的种姓群体。中心建筑群有三座主要寺庙，分别供奉印度教三位一体神灵，即湿婆、梵天和毗湿奴。布撒基寺于 1995 年被提名为世界遗产，但至今仍未被授予。由于每个神社都有自己的周年纪念日，因而每年至少有 70 个仪式或宗教庆典在这里举行。参观寺庙的最佳时间是清晨和傍晚，此时寺庙静谧而雅致。

Besakih Temple (Figure 1-52), the "mother temple" of Bali, sits on the south-western slope of Mount Agung—Bali's tallest peak. Besakih Temple is the largest of all temple complexes in Bali, comprising 18 separate sanctuaries that each belong to different caste groups. They surround a central complex with 3 main temples that are dedicated to the Hindu trinity, namely Shiva, Brahma and Vishnu. Besakih Temple was nominated as a World Heritage Site in 1995, but as yet remains unvested. There are at least 70 ceremonies or religious celebrations held each year here, as each shrine has its own anniversary. The best visiting times are in the early mornings and in the evenings when the temple complex is much quieter and more elegant.

12. 乌布猴林（圣猴森林公园）Ubud Monkey Forest

图 1-53　乌布猴林
Figure 1-53　Ubud Monkey Forest

乌布猴林（圣猴森林公园）（图 1-53）是一个天然森林保护区，是一群灰色长尾猕猴的家园，也是乌布最受游客欢迎的景区之一。遗址保存完好。猴林距离乌布市中心很近，步行即可到达。除了可以在自然保护区观看猴子在林间荡来跳去、在小路中嬉戏玩闹或讨要香蕉，游客们还可以沿着枝繁叶茂的豆蔻林间小道散步。美丽的古刹和覆盖着苔藓的怪异雕像将这里的气氛渲染得古老而神秘。

Ubud Monkey Forest (Figure 1-53) is a natural forest sanctuary that's home to a horde of grey long-tailed macaques. It is one of Ubud's most popular attractions and the site is well-preserved. The forest is within easy walking distance from Ubud's town centre. Besides watching playful monkeys in their natural habitat, swinging through canopies, lazing along pathways or feeding on bananas, you can take cool walks along paved pathways through the leafy nutmeg forest. Beautiful ancient temples with eerie guardian statues covered in moss also call the monkey forest their home.

（三）旅游购物 Shopping

木雕：印度尼西亚的木雕，尤其是巴厘木雕，享誉国内外，到印度尼西亚旅游的外国游客几乎无人不买一两件巴厘木雕留作纪念。巴厘木雕是一种传统工艺品，最初与巴厘人的宗教信仰息息相关。人们把自己崇拜的印度教诸神用石头或木头雕刻出来，供奉在庙宇、庭院、堂室内，后来代代相传，便产生了无数能雕善刻的巧匠。巴厘木雕大都是用质地坚硬、花纹细密的乌木、柚木等木料雕刻而成，其造型千姿百态：有栩栩如生的神鹰、神牛、雄狮、公牛等动物及各种禽鸟，有惟妙惟肖的巴厘渔夫、少女，有民间故事中脍炙人口的传奇人物，也有当代各种抽象艺术形象（图1-54、图1-55）。

图1-54 木雕人偶

Figure 1-54 Wooden Puppets

图1-55 木雕脸谱

Figure 1-55 Wooden Masks

Woodcarving: Indonesian woodcarving, especially Bali woodcarving, is renowned at home and abroad. When traveling to Indonesia, virtually no foreign guests do not buy one or two pieces of wood carving of Bali as a souvenir. Bali woodcarving is a kind of traditional handicraft, which is closely related to people's religious beliefs. People worship their Hindu gods carved from stone or wood, enshrined in the temple, courtyard or indoors hall. With such a practice handed down from generation to generation, it has produced many good carving craftsmen. Most of Bali carvings are crafted from hard wood like ebony and teak with a wide range of shapes. These include condor, cattle, lion, bull and various birds really true to life, and lifelike Bali fishermen, girls and well-known legends in folklore as well as the images of contemporary abstract art (Figure 1-54、Figure 1-55).

巴迪布：巴迪布（图1-56）是一种蜡染印花布，其特点是布上印有多姿多彩的彩色图案，包括几何图形、花鸟图案、对称图案及不对称图案。其色彩一般以黑、红、黄为主，鲜艳明快，也有以蓝、褐、白为主的。这种布不仅深受当地民众的喜爱，而且早已世界闻名。用它制作的长袖男衬衣和布裙已被指定为印度尼西亚的国服，适用于各种正式和非正式场合。游客在选购巴迪布时，要注意其制造工艺，用传统手工绘制印染的巴迪布做工精细，具有较高的艺术价值，但因耗时费力，一般价格较高。而机制的巴迪布由于产量高，价格相对较低，更经济实惠，但艺术价值逊于手工制品。

图1-56 印度尼西亚国服——巴迪布

Figure 1-56 Batiks—The National Costume of Indonesia

Batiks (Figure 1-56): It is a kind of batik printed cloth, which is characterized by the colorful patterns, including various geometric figures and flower motifs, symmetrical patterns and asymmetric patterns. Its color is generally bright such as black, red and yellow, and also featured dark colors like blue, brown and white. This cloth is not only deeply loved by the people of Indonesia, but has long been world-renowned. The long sleeve shirt and sarong produced from this fabric has been set as the Indonesian national dress, suitable for a variety of formal and informal occasions. While purchasing batiks, tourists should pay attention to the manufacturing process. The traditional handicraft dyeing batiks boast fine workmanship and thus the artistic value, but are relatively pricey out of the time-consuming effort. While the machine-made batiks, due to the high yield and lower price, seem more cost-effective but are less than the handmade products in artistic value.

扫码获取：入境须知及海关规定

本节习题

1. 简述印度尼西亚著名旅游区巴厘岛的概况。

2. 请分别以海岛风情、购物旅游、宗教朝拜、旅游观光、历史探索等主题设计三到四条旅游线路，以满足不同文化层次、不同社会背景、不同爱好、不同性别、不同宗教信仰、不同经济收入群体的需求。

第四节　南亚之旅

Travel in South Asia

月亮之国——印度
The Land of the Moon—India

导读

印度是印度共和国（Republic of India）的简称，是南亚面积最大的国家。印度是历史悠久的文明古国之一，具有丰富的文化遗产和旅游资源。印度也是世界三大宗教之一——佛教的发源地。印度是世界上发展最快的国家之一，但也是社会财富分配极度不平衡的发展中国家。目前，印度已经成为软件出口业的霸主，在金融、研究、技术服务等领域也将成为全球重要出口国。印度是金砖成员国之一。印度政府采取各种积极措施吸引国外旅游者，如发展宗教文化旅游、历史文化旅游、海滩旅游和冒险旅游，增建旅馆，提高旅游设施标准等。旅游业作为印度的外汇创收部门发挥着重要的作用，印度的主要客源国是孟加拉国、美国、英国、斯里兰卡、加拿大、澳大利亚、马来西亚、中国、德国、俄罗斯、法国、日本、新加坡等。印度是中国旅游业极具潜力的目的地国和比较重要的客源国，据印度旅游部数据显示，2018年，印度来华旅游达到86.33万人次，增速较快。印度名胜古迹和名山胜水甚多，被联合国教科文组织列为自然与文化遗产的有阿旃陀石窟群、埃洛拉（埃卢鲁）石窟群、阿格拉古堡、泰姬陵、科纳拉克太阳神庙、桑吉佛教古迹、德里的胡马雍陵、德里的顾特卜塔及其古建筑、大吉岭喜马拉雅铁路、卡齐兰加国家公园、盖奥拉德奥国家公园等。

一、地理概览 Geography of India

（一）位置 Location

印度位于南亚次大陆，东北与中国、尼泊尔、不丹、孟加拉国接壤，东部与缅甸为邻，西北与巴基斯坦毗邻，东临孟加拉湾，西濒阿拉伯海，东南部与斯里兰卡隔海相望。面积约298万平方千米，海岸线长5 560千米，为亚、非、欧和大洋洲海上交通枢纽。

India is located in the South Asian subcontinent, bordering China, Nepal, Bhutan, and Bangladesh to the northeast, Myanmar to the east, and Pakistan to the northwest. It is flanked by the Bay of Bengal to the east, the Arabian Sea to the west, and Sri Lanka lies across the sea to the southeast. Covering an area of approximately 2.98 million square kilometers and boasting a coastline of 5,560 kilometers, India serves as a hub for maritime transportation connecting Asia, Africa, Europe, and Oceania.

（二）地形和气候 The Land and Seasons

印度的地势西高东低，沿海有狭窄平原，地形大致可分为四个部分：印度北部为高山区，有喜马拉雅山脉，人烟稀少；中部为平原区，印度河—恒河平原是世界上最大的冲积平原之一，也是世界古代发明的发祥地之一，文物古迹丰富；西部为印度大沙漠；南部为高原区，德尔干高原构成印度半岛的主体。

India's topography is high in the west and low in the east, with narrow plains along the coast, and the terrain can be roughly divided into four parts: the northern part of India is a high mountainous area, with the Himalayas and sparsely populated; the central part is a plain area, and the Indus–Ganges Plain is one of the world's largest alluvial plains, and one of the world's ancient civilizations, with a wealth of cultural relics and ancient monuments; the western part is the Indian Desert; and the southern part is a high plateau, and the Delhi Dry Plateau constitutes the main body of the Indian Peninsula.

印度地处低纬度，大部分地区属热带季风气候，气温因海拔高度不同而异，喜马拉雅山区年均气温12 ℃～14 ℃，东部地区26 ℃～29 ℃。主要河流恒河在境内长2 100千米。

India is situated at a low latitude, with most of the country experiencing a tropical monsoon climate. The temperature varies depending on the altitude: the Himalayan region has an average annual temperature of 12 ℃ –14 ℃, while the eastern region averages 26 ℃ –29 ℃. The main river, the Ganges, runs for 2,100 kilometers within India's borders.

思考题

恒河是印度文明的发源地，同时也是印度人民心中的圣河。在印度人眼中，恒河是神圣而伟大的，是十几亿印度百姓的精神信念所在。每当朝圣时节来临的时候，成千上万的印度教徒蜂拥而至恒河沿岸，去参观寺庙，希望能够以此祈福消灾。甚至还有很多印度教徒一生中最大的梦想就是可以饮用圣水，在恒河沐浴，就连死后也要安葬于恒河当中。请观看视频"生命之河——恒河"并回答问题。

生命之河——恒河

为什么说"人类文明是逐水而生、伴水而居"呢？

提示：人类的所有文明都是伴着河流而生的，如黄河流域、长江流域的中国古代文明，恒河的古印度文明，底格里斯河、幼发拉底河流域的古巴比伦文明，尼罗河流域的古埃及文明。早在两千多年前，我国春秋时期的管子，在他博大精深典籍的第三十九篇——《水地篇》中就生动地阐述了水与生命的关系："地者，万物之本原，诸生之根菀也，……水者，地之血气，如筋脉之通流者也。"

（三）自然资源 Natural Resources

印度矿产资源丰富，有矿藏近 100 种。云母产量世界第一，煤和重晶石产量居世界第三。截至 2021 年年底，印度主要资源可采储量估计为：煤 3 241.28 亿吨，铁矿石 134.6 亿吨，铝土 6.46 亿吨，铬铁矿 9 700 万吨，锰矿石 1.67 亿吨，锌 743 万吨，铜 529.7 万吨，铅 190 万吨，石灰石 756.79 亿吨，磷酸盐 1.42 亿吨，黄金 68 吨，石油 5.87 亿吨，天然气 1 372.64 亿立方米。此外，还有石膏、钻石及钛、钍、铀等。森林 8 090 万平方千米，覆盖率为 24.62%。

India is rich in mineral resources and has nearly 100 mineral deposits. It is the world's largest producer of mica and the third largest producer of coal and barite. By the end of 2021, the recoverable reserves of India's main resources are estimated to be: 324.128 billion tons of coal, 13.46 billion tons of iron ore, 646 million tons of bauxite, 97 million tons of chromite, 167 million tons of manganese ore, 7.43 million tons of zinc, 5.297 million tons of copper, 1.9 million tons of lead, 75.679 billion tons of limestone, 142 million tons of phosphates, 68 tons of gold, oil 587 million tons, and 137,264 million cubic meters of natural gas. In addition, there are gypsum, diamonds and titanium, thorium and uranium. Forests cover 80.9 million square kilometers, with a coverage rate of 24.62 %.

二、人文概况 Overview of Indian Humanities

（一）国情认知 Basic Knowledge of National Conditions

印度总人口为 14.17 亿（2022 年），仅次于中国，位居世界第二。印度有 100 多个民族，其中印度斯坦族人数最多，约占全国总人口的 46.3%；其他人口较多的民族为泰卢固族、马拉提族、泰米尔族、孟加拉族等。官方语言为印地语和英语。印度的国鸟是孔雀。

With a total population of 1,417 million (2022), India ranks second in the world after China.

There are more than 100 ethnic groups in India, of which Hindustani is the largest, accounting for about 46.3% of the country's population; other more populous ethnic groups are Telugu, Marathi, Tamil, Bengali and so on. The official languages are Hindi and English. The national bird of India is the peacock.

印度首都为新德里，印度的国歌为《人民的意志》，是由诗人泰戈尔作词、作曲。印度未正式确定国花，一般认为是荷花。货币为印度卢比。印度是一个民族庞杂、宗教众多、文化各异的国家，绝大多数居民信奉印度教，教徒占总人口的 80.5%。其他宗教有伊斯兰教、基督教、锡克教、佛教、耆那教等。纱丽（又称纱丽服）是印度、孟加拉国、巴基斯坦、尼泊尔、斯里兰卡等国妇女的一种传统服装，是一种用丝绸为主要材料制作而成的衣服。纱丽一般长 5.5 米、宽 1.25 米，两侧有滚边，上面有刺绣。通常围在长及足踝的衬裙上，从腰部围到脚跟成筒裙状，然后将末端下摆披搭在左肩或右肩。

The capital city of India is New Delhi, and the national anthem of India is *The Will of the People*, composed and written by the poet Rabindranath Tagore. India has not officially determined the national flower, generally considered to be the lotus, and the currency is the Indian rupee. India is an ethnically diverse country with many religions and cultures. The vast majority of the population is Hindu, with 80.5% of the total population being Hindu. Other religions include Islam, Christianity, Sikhism, Buddhism and Jainism. The sari (also known as saree) is a traditional garment worn by women in India, Bangladesh, Pakistan, Nepal, Sri Lanka, and other countries. It is primarily made from silk. A typical sari is about 5.5 meters long and 1.25 meters wide, with borders on both sides and embroidery on it. It is usually draped over an ankle−length petticoat, wrapped around the waist to form a skirt, and then the end is draped over the left or right shoulder.

 小贴士

印度为什么又叫"孔雀之国"？

自古以来，印度人就爱孔雀，多见于神殿的建筑物和器皿中。1963 年 1 月，印度政府宣布孔雀为"国鸟"，与神牛和虎等动物一样受到重点保护。在印度民间，有关孔雀的传说和故事很多。传说印度神话中的战神室建陀，也就是大乘佛教的"护法神"，骑着孔雀，拿着弓箭，与魔军战斗。耆那教教祖大雄选择孔雀为坐骑；"天神之王"因陀罗把孔雀封为鸟之王。最有名的是公元前 4 世纪印度历史上曾经出现过的"孔雀王朝"，其第三代帝王阿育王（佛教徒称"安心王"）统治时期是印度历史上最辉煌的时代。

（二）印度历史 History of India

印度是历史悠久的文明古国之一，公元前 2 500 年至公元前 800 年，雅利安人来到印度河流域，创造出前所未有的文明，史称"吠陀时代"。公元前 324 年至公元前 187 年建立的孔雀王朝是印度历史上第一个统一的奴隶制国家，在阿育王统治时期达到全盛，佛教兴盛，并开始向外传播。中世纪时期小国林立，印度教兴起。自 11 世纪起，来自西北方向的穆斯林不断入侵并长期统治印度。1526 年，据称是成吉思汗和帖木儿的后裔巴布尔建立了印度历史上最后一个王朝——莫卧儿王朝。1757 年，印度逐渐沦为英国的殖民地，1849 年英国殖民者侵占全印度。1947 年，英国通过《蒙巴顿方案》，实行印巴分治。8 月 15 日，印度人民在民族英雄甘地的领导下，经过不懈斗争，终于结束了英国在印度长达 190 年的殖民统治，印度获得独立。1950 年 1 月 26 日，印度宣布成立共和国。

India is one of the ancient civilizations with a long history. From 2500 BC to 800 BC, the Aryans came to India and its watersheds, creating an unprecedented civilization known as the "Vedic Period". The Peacock Dynasty, established from 324 BC to 187 BC, was the first united slave state in the history of India, and reached its heyday during the reign of Ashoka. During the reign of King Ashoka, Buddhism flourished and began to spread abroad. The medieval period was characterized by the proliferation of small states and the rise of Hinduism. Since the 11th century, Muslims from the northwest continued to invade and rule India for a long time. 1526, Babur, who claimed to be a descendant of Genghis Khan and Timur, established the Mughal Dynasty, the last dynasty in the history of India. In 1757, India gradually fell into the British colony, and in 1849, the British colonizers invaded all of India. In 1947, Britain adopted the *Mountbatten Plan*, which led to the partition of India and Pakistan, and on August 15, under the leadership of Gandhi, the national hero, the people of India finally ended the 190 years of British colonial rule in India after unremitting struggle and gained the independence of India. India declared the establishment of a republic on January 26, 1950.

（三）经济状况 The Economy

印度是一个农业大国，主要农产品有稻米、小麦、油料等。印度自 20 世纪 60 年代初开始实行绿色革命，解决了国家严重缺粮的问题并实现了粮食的基本自给。印度是世界第一产奶国，也是世界重要的产棉国和产茶国。

India is a large agricultural country, with its main agricultural products being rice, wheat, and oil seeds. In the early 1960s, India began implementing the Green Revolution, which helped the country overcome a severe food shortage and achieve basic self-sufficiency in agriculture. India is the world's largest producer of milk and is also an important producer of cotton and tea.

印度是世界上经济发展最快的国家之一，已经建成较为完整的工业体系，纺织、食品、精密仪器、汽车、医药、钢铁、船舶、电子、航空和空间技术等部门发展迅速，棉制品、珠宝制品、医药及化工制品、皮革、机械及五金制品出口量较大。印度的信息技术产业发展迅速，是世界公认的最大的软件供应国之一。农业及相关服务业是印度最大的经济部门，印度的旅游及服务业也较为发达，在国民经济中占有较大比重。

India is one of the fastest-growing economies in the world, and has built a relatively complete industrial system, with rapid development in sectors such as textiles, foodstuffs, precision instruments, automobiles, pharmaceuticals, iron and steel, ships, electronics, aviation and space technology, and a large volume of exports of cotton products, jewelry products, pharmaceuticals and chemical products, leather, machinery and hardware products. India's information technology

金砖国家

industry is growing rapidly and is recognized as one of the largest software suppliers in the world. Indian agriculture and services are the largest sectors of the economy, and India's tourist and services industries are also relatively well developed and account for a large proportion of the national economy.

（四）传统文化 Traditional Culture

印度是文明古国，待人接物的礼节较多。与友人见面通常双手合掌，表示敬意。合掌时，对长辈宜高，对平辈宜平，对晚辈宜低，分别表示尊敬、对等和关怀。拥抱是常见的礼仪，摸足是行大礼。献花环是印度欢迎客人常见的礼节，尤其是对于远道而来的尊贵客人，主人会献上一个花环，并戴在客人的脖子上。印度人在赞同或同意他人的意见时，是摇头而不是点头。点吉祥痣是印度人欢迎宾客的礼俗，妇女喜欢在眉心点一颗红痣，表示喜庆、吉祥。

India is an ancient civilized nation with numerous customs and etiquettes. When meeting friends, it is very common to put both hands together to show respect. The height at which the hands are held varies: higher for elders to show respect, level for peers to indicate equality, and lower for juniors to express care. Hugging is a common form of greeting, while touching someone's feet is considered a deep gesture of respect. Offering a garland is a traditional way to welcome guests in India, especially for esteemed visitors from afar; the host will place a garland around the guest's neck. In India, people express agreement or approval by shaking their heads rather than nodding. Applying a ceremonial mark, or "tilak," is a customary way to welcome guests. Women often adorn their foreheads with a red dot, symbolizing happiness and good fortune.

印度人把猴子和牛尊为神明，尤其对牛特别崇敬，将牛封为"圣物"，许多印度人认为牛尿可以延年益寿、消除病灾。人们时常可见牛在大街上横冲直撞，随意啃嚼街旁摊位上的水果和蔬菜，摊主不仅不阻拦，反而受宠若惊。一些富人还特意在家门口摆放牛喜爱吃的食物，作为供品。印度教盛行"万物有灵"的自然崇拜，虔诚的印度教徒一生有三大夙愿：到圣城朝拜湿婆神，到恒河洗圣浴、饮圣水，死后葬在恒河。

风靡全球的宝莱坞

Indian people regard monkeys and cattle as god, especially holding cows in special reverence. Cows are considered "holy" and are deeply revered. Many Indians believe that cow urine can prolong life and cure diseases. It is common to see cows roaming freely on the streets, munching on fruits and vegetables from street stalls. Instead of driving them away, stall owners often feel pleased by their presence. Some wealthy individuals even make special offerings of food that cows enjoy in front of their homes. Hinduism, which is prevalent in India, promotes the worship of nature under the belief that "all things have spirit". Devout Hindus have three major wishes in life: to make a pilgrimage to the holy city of Shiva, to bathe in the sacred waters of the Ganges River, and to drink its holy water. After death, they wish to have their ashes scattered in the Ganges River.

（五）礼仪禁忌 Social Etiquettes and Taboos

在印度，切勿抚摸小孩的头，因为印度人认为头部是神圣的。印度居民，尤其是女人皆不喝含酒精的饮料，锡克教信徒不抽烟，伊斯兰教徒不吃猪肉。印度人吃饭大多使用盘子，吃饭时只用右手递接食物，左手被视为不洁，应避免用左手，也不用双手递物品给当地人。受邀吃饭时不必客气推让，在印度人的观念中，吃东西时要大家一起分享，独食是小气而不礼貌的行为，所以印度人邀请他人共餐，绝不是碍于情面假惺惺，而是诚心诚意地邀请，拒人于千里之外的回绝会令当地人不高兴。

In India, it is important not to touch the head of a child, as the head is considered sacred. Indians, especially women, do not drink alcoholic beverages, Sikhs do not smoke, and Muslims do not eat pork. Indians mostly use plates to eat. You are only allowed to use your right hand to receive food. Because they think the left hand is dirty and should be avoided, as well as the use of both hands to pass things to the locals. Invited to eat without having to politely give way, in the Indian concept, to eat together to share, eat alone is petty and impolite behavior, so Indians invite others to share a meal, is never in the way of false sympathy, but a sincere invitation to reject people outside of a thousand miles of rejection will make the locals unhappy.

印度人忌讳数字 1、3、7，总是设法避免这些数字的出现。忌谈个人私事、印度的贫困状况、军费支出等话题。忌讳白色，认为白色表示内心的悲哀，习惯用百合花当作悼念品。忌讳送人百合花作为礼物，忌讳弯月图案，黑色被视为不祥的颜色。忌讳用澡盆给孩子洗澡，印度人认为澡盆水是"死水"。

Indians generally consider the numbers 1, 3, and 7 to be inauspicious and tend to avoid them. It is also advisable to avoid discussing personal matters, topics related to India's poverty, or military spending. White is associated with mourning and symbolizes sorrow, while lilies are traditionally used as funeral flowers, making them an unsuitable gift. Crescent moon patterns are often avoided, and black is regarded as an unlucky color. Additionally, bathing children in a bathtub is considered inappropriate, as the water is believed to be "stagnant" or "lifeless".

首饰是印度人日常生活中的一种不可缺少的装饰品，即使是家境清贫的妇女，也会佩戴金属或塑料首饰。若进入印度教的寺庙，身上不可穿着牛皮制品。皮鞋、皮带、皮包等牛皮制品均不得带入寺庙。印度人进寺庙或厨房前，要先脱鞋，因为他们认为穿鞋进去是不礼貌、不圣洁的行为。

Jewelry is an indispensable adornment in the daily life of Indians. Even women from poor families wear metal or plastic jewelry. If you enter a Hindu temple, you must not wear cowhide products. Leather shoes, belts, leather bags and other cowhide products are not allowed to bring into the temple. Hindus remove their shoes before entering a temple or kitchen because they consider it impolite and unholy to enter with shoes on.

思考题

古印度人创造了光辉灿烂的古代文明，作为最悠久的文明古国之一，印度具有绚丽的多样性文化、丰富的文化遗产和旅游资源。现代人应如何从亚洲的古老文明中汲取智慧？又该如何看待文明与文化的博弈？

（六）传统节日 Festivals

1. 国庆节 National Day

印度国庆节（共和国日）为每年的公历 1 月 26 日。1929 年，印度历史最悠久的政党国大党在其年会上通过决定，规定 1930 年 1 月 26 日为独立节。1947 年 8 月 15 日，印度正式宣布独立后，1 月 26 日被正式定为国庆节。1950 年 1 月 26 日，印度颁布了共和国宪法。此后，每年 1 月 26 日，印度政府都要在总统府前的广场上举行声势浩大的游行。

India's National Day (Republic Day) is celebrated on January 26 every year on the Gregorian calendar. In 1929, the Congress Party, the oldest political party in India, adopted a decision at its annual convention to observe January 26, 1930 as Independence Day. On August 15, 1947, after India's formal declaration of independence, January 26 was officially declared as a national holiday. On January 26, 1950, India promulgated the Republican Constitution. Since then, every year on January 26, the Indian government will hold in the square in front of the Presidential Palace, a powerful parade.

2. 洒红节 Holi

洒红节，也叫"胡里节"或"色彩节"，是印度的传统节日。洒红节源于印度的著名史诗《摩诃婆罗多》，在每年 2、3 月间举行，人们向周围的人泼洒颜料，颜料越多越好，颜色越深越妙。胡里节象征着冬天结束和春天的到来，同时也象征着正义战胜邪恶。现在，胡里节已演变成人们消除误解和怨恨，捐弃前嫌、重归于好的节日。

Holi, also known as the "Festival of Colors", is a traditional Indian festival. It originates from the famous Indian epic the *Mahabharata*, and is celebrated annually in February or March. During Holi, people throw colored powders at each other, with the idea that the more, the better, and the deeper the colors, the more delightful the celebration. Holi symbolizes the end of winter and the arrival of spring, as well as the triumph of good over evil. Today, Holi has evolved into a festival for people to dispel misunderstandings and grievances, letting go of past animosities and reconciling with one another.

打翻的"调色盘"——洒红节

3. 独立日 Independence Day

独立日是印度为庆祝 1947 年摆脱英国殖民统治并成为主权国家而设立的节日，日期定在每年 8 月 15 日。

It is a festival established in India to celebrate India's liberation from British colonial rule in 1947 and its emergence as a sovereign nation, the date of which is set on August 15 every year.

4. 蛇节 The Indian Festival of Snakes

印度的蛇节又叫纳加潘察米节，每年的 8 月 19 日举行。在印度教里，动物的灵性总是与主要的印度教神明紧密联系在一起。毒蛇纳都的神像是湿婆和毗湿奴的标志。每逢节日，农妇们都要献上牛奶、鲜花和朱砂，节日当天不用下田干活，以免惊扰蛇神。

The Indian festival of snakes, also known as Nagar Panchami, is celebrated on August 19 every year. In Hinduism, the spirituality of the animal is always closely associated with the major Hindu gods. The idol of the viper Nadu is a symbol of both Shiva and Vishnu. On the occasion of the festival, peasant women offer milk, flowers and vermilion, and no one works in the fields to avoid disturbing the snake god.

5. 灯节 Festival of Lights

在气候宜人的 10 月至 11 月间庆祝。灯节这一天，全国各地的印度教神庙显得格外热闹，人山人海，熙熙攘攘。妇女们手捧摆满祭品的盘子，缓步朝庙堂走去。祭祀仪式开始时，人们双手合十，闭目祷告。祈祷仪式结束后，祭司在教徒的前额上点白灰、朱砂等，然后赐给信徒们"圣水"，信徒们接在手中，当即饮下或撒在头上，以期未来诸事如意、财运亨通。灯节之夜，家家户户的门口窗前、庭院屋顶都亮着灯，有五光十色的彩色电灯，有绚丽多姿的花灯，有小小的蜡烛，还有别具特色的小油灯。人们认为庆祝灯节能使人的身心得到净化，逢凶化吉。

The Festival of Lights is celebrated during the pleasant climate between October and November.

On this day, Hindu temples across the country are bustling with people. Women walk slowly toward the temples, carrying plates full of offerings. At the beginning of the ritual, participants put their hands together and close their eyes in prayer. After the prayer ceremony, the priest applies white ash and vermilion powder to the foreheads of the worshippers, then gives them "holy water." The devotees receive the water in their hands, immediately drinking it or sprinkling it on their heads, hoping for future prosperity and good fortune. On the night of the Festival of Lights, every house is illuminated with colorful electric lights, vibrant lanterns, small candles, and unique oil lamps at the doorways, windows, courtyards, and rooftops. It is believed that celebrating the Festival of Lights can purify one's body and mind and transform bad luck into good fortune.

三、旅游观光 Tourism and Sightseeing

（一）主要旅游城市 Major Tourist Cities

1. 新德里 New Delhi

新德里位于印度西北部亚穆纳河畔，是一座既具有现代气息又具有古代风貌的花园城市。旧德里城已有 3 400 多年历史，早在公元 1200 年前，印度著名诗篇《摩诃婆罗多》中就有建城的记载。公元 17 世纪，莫卧儿王朝皇帝沙贾汗开始兴建旧德里城，先后有 7 个王朝在此建都，留下了许多历史古迹，如古代的宫殿红堡、库塔布高塔、巨型太阳钟等。新都新德里始建于 1911 年，由英国建筑师埃德温·勒琴斯设计，历经 18 年，1929 年新城才初具规模。通常人们把新、旧德里统称为德里。自 1947 年印度独立后，这里就是全国的政治、经济、文化中心和交通枢纽。

Located on the banks of the Yamuna River in northwestern India, New Delhi is a garden city with both a modern and ancient flavor. The city of Old Delhi has a history of more than 3 400 years. As early as 1200 AD, there were records of city construction in the famous Indian epic, the *Mahabharata*. In the 17th century, the Mughal emperor Shah Jahan began to build the city of Old Delhi. There have been seven dynasties with the city as their capital, leaving many historical monuments, suchas Red Fort, Qutab Ghats, the giant sun clock and so on. The new capital, New Delhi, was built in 1911 and designed by British architect Edwin Lutyens. It took 18 years before the new city took shape in 1929. It is common to refer to New and Old Delhi collectively as Delhi. Since India's independence in 1947, it has been the political, economic and cultural center and transportation hub of the country.

2. 孟买 Mumbai

孟买位于印度西海岸，城市名意为"美丽的海湾"，是印度最大的海港和重要交通枢纽，素有印度"西部门户"之称。孟买是印度的文化中心，也是印度主要的工业和金融中心、最大的棉纺织和贸易中心。孟买是印度印地语影视业（被称为"宝莱坞"）的大本营。由于其众多的商业机会和相对较高的生活水准，孟买吸引了来自印度各地的移民，使该市成为融合了各种社会群体和文化的大杂烩。

Mumbai, located on the western coast of India, means "Beautiful Bay" and is the largest seaport and an important transportation hub in India, often referred to as the "Gateway of the West". Mumbai is a cultural center of India and also serves as a major industrial and financial hub, as well as the largest cotton textile and trade center. It is the headquarters of India's Hindi film industry, known as

"Bollywood". Due to its vast commercial opportunities and relatively high standard of living, Mumbai attracts migrants from all over India, making the city a melting pot of various social groups and cultures.

3. 加尔各答 Calcutta（Kolkata）

加尔各答是印度东部最大的城市，位于恒河下游的支流胡格利河畔，为西孟加拉邦首都，是印度的主要港口和重要的铁路、航空枢纽。1912 年以前曾是英属印度的首府，因此留下了不少历史性建筑，如著名的威廉要塞、维多利亚纪念堂、伊甸花园、印度博物馆、国家图书馆、哥特式建筑圣保罗大教堂等。

Calcutta is the largest city in eastern India, located on the banks of the Hooghly River, a tributary of the lower Ganges, and the capital of the state of West Bengal, as well as a major port and an important railroad and aviation hub in India. Before 1912, it was the capital of British India, and thus has left behind a number of historic buildings, such as the famous Fortress William, the Victoria Memorial, the Garden of Eden, the Indian Museum, the National Library, the Gothic architecture of the St. Paul's Cathedral, etc.

（二）著名旅游景点 Famous Tourist Attractions

1. 泰姬陵 Taj Mahal

泰姬陵（图 1-57）全称为"泰姬·玛哈尔陵"，又译为"泰姬玛哈"，是印度知名度最高的古迹之一，在今印度距新德里 200 多千米外的北方邦的阿格拉城内亚穆纳河右侧。泰姬陵是莫卧儿王朝第五代皇帝沙贾汗为了纪念他已故皇后阿姬曼·芭奴而建立的陵墓，被世人称为世界七大建筑奇迹之一。泰姬陵由殿堂、钟楼、尖塔、水池等构成，全部用纯白色大理石建筑，用玻璃、玛瑙镶嵌，绚丽夺目、美丽无比，有极高的艺术

图 1-57 泰姬陵
Figure 1-57 Taj Mahal

价值，是伊斯兰教建筑中的代表作。来自印度全境和中亚乃至中国的 2 万多名工匠参与了泰姬陵的建造，历时 22 年才完成。1983 年被列入联合国教科文组织《世界遗产名录》。泰姬陵在早中晚所呈现出的面貌各不相同：早上是灿烂的金色，白天的阳光下是耀眼的白色，而在月光下又成了温柔的蓝色。另外，外地游客不要在星期五前往，因为那天只对当地穆斯林开放。

The Taj Mahal（Figure 1-57）, officially known as the "Taj Mahal Mausoleum", is one of the most famous monuments in India, located in Agra, Uttar Pradesh. It is over 200 kilometers from New Delhi, on the right bank of the Yamuna River. The Taj Mahal was built by Shah Jahan, the fifth emperor of the Mughal Dynasty, in memory of his late wife, Mumtaz Mahal. It is regarded as one of the Seven Wonders of the World. The Taj Mahal consists of a mausoleum, a bell tower, minarets, and reflecting pools, all constructed from pure white marble, inlaid with glass and agate, creating a stunningly beautiful and dazzling effect. It holds immense artistic value and is a representative work of Islamic architecture. Over 20,000 artisans from across India, Central Asia, and even China contributed to the construction of the Taj Mahal, which took 22 years to complete. It was inscribed on the UNESCO World Heritage List in 1983. The appearance of the Taj Mahal changes throughout the day; in the morning, it shines with a radiant golden hue, during the day it gleams with a brilliant white under the sun, and at night, it takes on a gentle blue glow in the moonlight. Additionally, visitors are advised not to go on Fridays, as the site is open only to local Muslims on that day.

图 1-58　印度门（印度战士纪念碑）

Figure 1-58　The India Gate（originally called the All Indian Warriors Memorial）

2. 印度门（印度战士纪念碑）The India Gate（originally called the All Indian Warriors Memorial）

印度门（图 1-58）是 1921 年为纪念第一次世界大战中英国和印度阵亡的将士而建的，又称"印度战士纪念碑"，位于拉杰巴特街东端，巍峨耸立在王子公园中心。它的外形与法国巴黎的凯旋门相似，高 48.7 米，宽 21.3 米，全部用红砂石砌成。拱门高 42 米，门上端刻着"印度"的英文字母及修建年代，门洞两壁镌刻着阵亡将士的名字。拱门顶端有一个直径 3.5 米的大油灯，每逢重大节日，油灯在夜间会燃起一米多高的火焰，远远地即可看到。

India Gate(Figure1-58), also known as the "Indian Warriors Memorial", was built in 1921 to honor the British and Indian soldiers who lost their lives in World War Ⅰ. It is located at the eastern end of Rajpath, majestically standing in the center of Princes Park. Its design resembles the Arc de Triomphe in Paris, France, standing 48.7 meters tall and 21.3 meters wide, and it is constructed entirely of red sandstone. The arch itself is 42 meters high, with the word "India" and the year of its construction engraved at the top. The names of the fallen soldiers are inscribed on both walls of the gateway. At the top of the arch is a large oil lamp with a diameter of 3.5 meters. On major holidays, a flame over a meter high is lit at night, visible from a great distance.

图 1-59　胡马雍陵

Figure 1-59　Mausoleum of Humayun

3. 胡马雍陵 Mausoleum of Humayun

胡马雍陵（图 1-59）为莫卧儿王朝第二代帝王胡马雍及其王妃的陵墓，位于印度首都新德里的东南郊、德里东部亚穆纳河畔。建于 1570 年，陵墓主体建筑由红色砂岩构筑，陵体呈方形，四面为门，陵顶呈半圆形。外观宏丽壮观，是伊斯兰教与印度教建筑风格的典型结合，是印度建筑史上的重要分水岭，标志着其从单调的建筑形式进入结构复杂、讲究华丽装饰的建筑新时期。1993 年被列入联合国教科文组织《世界遗产名录》。

Humayun's Tomb is the mausoleum of Humayun（Figure 1-59）, the second emperor of the Mughal Dynasty, and his queen. It is located in the southeastern suburbs of New Delhi, by the banks of the Yamuna River in eastern Delhi. Built in 1570, the main structure of the tomb is made of red sandstone, featuring a square layout with doors on all four sides, and a semi-circular dome on top. Its magnificent appearance is a typical blend of Islamic and Hindu architectural styles and marks an important turning point in Indian architectural history, signifying a shift from monotonous architectural forms to a new era of complex structures with elaborate decorations. It was incribed on the UNESCO World Heritage List in 1993.

4. 埃洛拉石窟群 Ellora Caves

埃洛拉石窟群（图 1-60）位于印度马哈拉施特拉邦的奥兰加巴德市西北 25 ～ 30 千米处，是集佛教、印度教和耆那教三种宗教文化艺术于一体的混合建筑群，1983 年，被列入联合国教科文组织《世界遗产名录》。整座石窟群由佛教、印度教、耆那教三大宗教的石雕艺术组成。其中，佛教石窟有 12 座，印度教石窟有 17 座，耆那教石窟有 5 座。石雕排列在长达两米的陡峭玄武岩壁上，34 座洞穴庙宇一座挨一座，绵延 2 000 多米，散落在萨雅迪利山的斜坡之上，生动、完好地再现了古印度文明。

印度埃洛拉石窟群：全球最匪夷所思的建筑奇迹

The Ellora Caves (Figure 1-60) are located approximately 25 to 30 kilometers northwest of Aurangabad city in the state of Maharashtra, India. They are a complex of mixed religious architectural structures representing Buddhist, Hindu, and Jain religious and cultural art. In 1983, they were inscribed on the UNESCO World Heritage List. The entire cave complex consists of rock-cut sculptures representing the art of Buddhism, Hinduism, and Jainism. There are 12 Buddhist caves, 17 Hindu caves, and 5 Jain caves. The sculptures are carved into steep basalt cliffs, extending over 2 000 meters with 34 cave temples lined up one after another. Scattered on the slopes of the Sahyadri Hills, they vividly and well-preservedly showcase ancient Indian civilization.

5. 维多利亚纪念堂 The Victoria Memorial

维多利亚纪念堂（图 1-61）位于马坦公园东南，是一座融合了文艺复兴时期建筑风格和穆斯林建筑风格的精美的巨大白色大理石宫殿。这座白色宫殿矗立在绿草地上，仿佛一艘荡漾在碧波上的白船，是加尔各答最美丽的地标之一。维多利亚纪念堂完成于 1921 年，分成博物馆和美术馆两部分，内部的展品多达 3 500 件，分列于 25 间展览室，这些展品包括从印度各地收集来的美术品和史书、维多利亚时代的史迹素描和绘画等。

The Victoria Memorial (Figure 1-61) is a fine huge whitemarble palace in the southeast of Matan Park, built in a blend of Renaissance and Muslim styles. Standing on green grass like a white ship on a blue wave, this white palace is one of the most beautiful landmarks of Calcutta. Completed in 1921, the Victoria Memorial Hall is divided into a museum and an art gallery and houses as many as 3,500 exhibits in 25 exhibition rooms, which include art and history books collected from all over India, sketches and paintings of Victorian monuments, etc.

图 1-60　埃洛拉石窟群
Figure 1-60　Ellora Caves

图 1-61　维多利亚纪念堂
Figure1-61　The Victoria Memorial

图 1-62　耆那教寺
Figure 1-62　Jain Temple

6. 耆那教寺 Jain Temple

耆那教寺（图 1-62）位于加尔各答市北部，为该市气势最宏伟的寺庙，奉礼耆那教主，神像坐在银制的莲花上，额头挂着一颗大钻石。寺院有座大庭院，院内有人鱼、希腊神、马其顿士兵、阿拉伯和莫卧儿贵族的雕像。

The Jain Temple (Figure1-62), located in the northern part of Calcutta, is the city's most magnificent temple. It is dedicated to the Jain Tirthankaras, with the deity seated on a silver lotus, adorned with a large diamond on the forehead. The temple features a grand courtyard that houses statues of mermaids, Greek gods, Macedonian soldiers, and Arabian and Mughal nobles.

（三）旅游购物 Shopping

香料：印度是香料大国，在这里你能找到各式各样的香料。咖喱、肉桂、胡椒、八角、柠檬叶、丁香、姜黄、肉豆蔻、番红花、葫芦巴……凡是你能想到的香料，几乎都能在印度的各大市场找到。

Spices: India is a country rich in spices, and you can find an incredible variety here. Curry, cinnamon, pepper, star anise, lemon leaves, cloves, turmeric, nutmeg, saffron, and fenugreek—almost any spice you can imagine is available in nearly every major market across the country.

纱丽：纱丽是印度女性的一种传统服饰，这是一种用丝绸为主要材料制作而成的衣服。上面有刺绣。通常围在长及足踝的衬裙上，从腰部围到脚跟呈筒裙状，然后将末端下摆披搭在左肩或右肩。如果你想购置一件当地特色服饰，纱丽则是一个很好的选择。

Saree: Saree is a traditional dress of Indian women, which is a dress made of silk as the main material. It is embroidered. It is usually worn around an ankle-length petticoat, from the waist to the heel in the shape of a tube skirt, and then the end hem is draped over the left or right shoulder. If you want to acquire a local specialty dress, Saree is an excellent choice.

地毯：印度是世界最大的地毯制造国之一，其中，克什米尔地区的地毯较出名，有毛织与丝织两种，色泽柔和淡雅，布满各种奇特风格的植物花卉图案。

Carpet: India is one of the world's largest carpet manufacturing countries, of which the Kashmir region is more famous for its carpets, wool and silk, soft and light color, covered with a variety of peculiar styles of botanical and floral motifs.

熏香：印度是举世闻名的香料大国，有制作香的悠久历史传统。生产印度香的工厂有很多，品牌也不少。他们大都采取手工制作的方式。印度熏香是给家人朋友的最佳伴手礼之一。

Incense: India is a world-renowned spice country with a long historical tradition of making incense. There are many factories producing Indian incense and many brands. Most of them take a handmade approach. Indian smoked incense is one of the best accompanying gifts for family and friends.

扫码获取：入境须知及海关规定

本节习题

1. 假如你是导游员，接待了一行 26 人的印度旅游团队，主要游客是学者，请问应告知游客在与当地人交往过程中注意哪些礼节？

2. 古代印度在文学、哲学和自然科学等方面对人类文明做出了哪些独创性的贡献？

3. 印度主要旅游城市有哪几个？各有什么特色？

第五节　西亚之旅
Travel in West Asia

石油之国——阿联酋
The Land of Oil—The United Arab Emirates

> **导读**
>
> 阿联酋是石油输出国组织（OPEC）成员国，国家经济以石油生产和石油化工为主，已同 193 个国家建立了外交关系，奉行平衡、多元的外交政策，积极发展同美国、俄罗斯、欧洲国家及中国、日本、韩国等亚洲国家的关系。2021 年 10 月至 2022 年 3 月举办过中东地区首届世界博览会。自中国"一带一路"倡议提出以来，阿联酋积极推进"向东看"的外交战略，其中"向东看"主要指的就是中国。目前，阿联酋是与中国合作程度最深、领域最广、成果最实的中东国家之一。

一、地理概览 Geography of the United Arab Emirates

（一）位置 Location

阿拉伯联合酋长国（简称阿联酋）位于阿拉伯半岛东部，北临波斯湾，西北与卡塔尔为邻，西部和南部与沙特阿拉伯交界，东部和东北部与阿曼毗邻，海岸线长 734 千米，总面积为 83 600 平方千米，是由阿布扎比、迪拜、沙迦、哈伊马角、富查伊拉、乌姆盖万和阿治曼 7 个酋长国组成的联邦国家，首都为阿布扎比。

The United Arab Emirates (UAE), located in the eastern part of the Arabian Peninsula, is bordered by the Persian Gulf to the north, Qatar to the northwest, Saudi Arabia to the west and south, and Oman to the east and northeast. It has a coastline that stretches 734 kilometers and covers a total area of

83,600 square kilometers. The UAE is a federation of seven emirates: Abu Dhabi, Dubai, Sharjah, Ras al-Khaimah, Fujairah, Umm Al-Quwain, and Ajman, with Abu Dhabi serving as its capital.

（二）地形和气候 The Land and Seasons

阿联酋沿海是地势较低的平原，半岛的东北部分属山地，横贯其间的哈杰尔山脉最高峰海拔 2 438 米。此外，阿联酋绝大部分地区是海拔 200 米以上的沙漠和洼地。沙漠占阿联酋总面积的 65%，其中有一些绿洲，以艾因地区的布赖米绿洲面积为最大。

The coastal areas of the United Arab Emirates are characterized by low-lying plains, while the northeastern part of the peninsula is mountainous, with the Hajar Mountains running through it, reaching a peak elevation of 2,438 meters. Additionally, the vast majority of the UAE consists of deserts and lowlands with elevations above 200 meters. Deserts cover 65% of the UAE's total area, with several oases, the largest of which is the Buraimi Oasis in the Ain region.

阿联酋属热带沙漠气候，全年分为两季：5 月至 10 月为热季（夏季），天气炎热潮湿，气温超过 40 ℃，沿海地区白天气温最高达 45 ℃以上，湿度 90% 左右；11 月至次年 4 月为凉季（冬季），气候温和晴朗，有时降雨，气温一般为 15 ℃～ 35 ℃。年平均降雨量约 100 毫米，多集中于 1—2 月份。东部山区则较为凉爽和干燥。

The United Arab Emirates has a tropical desert climate, with two distinct seasons throughout the year. From May to October is the hot season (summer), characterized by hot and humid weather, with temperatures exceeding 40 ℃. In coastal areas, daytime temperatures can reach over 45 ℃, with humidity around 90%. From November to April is the cool season (winter), featuring mild and clear weather, occasional rainfall, and temperatures generally ranging from 15 ℃ to 35 ℃. The annual average rainfall is about 100 mm, mostly occurring in January and February. The eastern mountainous regions are relatively cooler and drier.

（三）自然资源 Natural Resources

阿联酋石油和天然气资源非常丰富。已探明石油储量约为 150 亿吨，天然气储量约为 7.7 万亿立方米，均居世界第六位。阿联酋的海域内水产资源丰富，沿海有珊瑚，盛产珍珠，还有着丰富的渔业资源，已发现鱼类和海洋生物 3 000 多种。椰枣树是阿联酋重要的经济作物，在全国种植超过 4 000 万棵，每年产椰枣上百万吨。

The United Arab Emirates is extremely rich in oil and natural gas resources. Proven oil reserves are approximately 15 billion tons, and natural gas reserves are 7.7 trillion cubic meters, both ranking sixth in the world. The UAE also boasts abundant marine resources, with coral reefs along the coast and a thriving pearl industry, as well as rich fisheries resources, with over 3,000 species of fish and marine life identified. Date palms are an important economic crop in the UAE, with more than 40 million trees nationwide, producing millions of tons of dates annually.

二、人文概况 Overview of the United Arab Emirates' Humanities

（一）国情认知 Basic Knowledge of National Conditions

阿联酋的外籍人口占总人口的 88.5%，主要来自印度、巴基斯坦、菲律宾、埃及、叙利亚、伊朗、巴勒斯坦等国。阿联酋是阿拉伯国家，国教是伊斯兰教，绝大部分居民是穆斯林。

Foreigners account for 88.5% of the total population, mainly from India, Pakistan, the Philippines, Egypt, Syria, Iran and Palestine. The UAE is an Arab country, where Islam is the state religion and the vast majority of residents are Muslims.

阿联酋的国旗呈长方形，长与宽之比为 2：1，由红、绿、白、黑四色组成，这四种颜色代表穆罕默德后代的几个王朝。国徽主体是一只黄白色的隼，爪下的绶带上写着"阿拉伯联合酋长国"。

The flag of the UAE is rectangular in shape, with a ratio of length to width of 2：1, and consists of four colors: red, green, white and black, which represent the dynasties of Mohammad's descendants. The main body of the state microfilm is a yellow and white falcon, with the words "United Arab Emirates" written on a ribbon under its claws.

（二）历史简介 History of the United Arab Emirates

公元 7 世纪时隶属于阿拉伯帝国。自 16 世纪开始，葡萄牙、荷兰、法国等殖民主义者相继入侵。19 世纪初，英国入侵波斯湾地区，并于 1820 年强迫当地 7 个酋长国与其签订《永久休战条约》。此后，各酋长国逐步沦为英国的保护国。1971 年 3 月 1 日，英国宣布同各酋长国签订的条约于年底终止。同年 12 月 2 日，阿拉伯联合酋长国宣告成立，6 个酋长国组成联邦国家。1972 年，哈伊马角酋长国加入联邦。国名简称为"阿联酋"。

It was part of the Arabian Empire in the 7th century AD. From the 16th century onwards, Portuguese, Dutch, French and other colonialists invaded the region, and at the beginning of the 19th century the British invaded the Persian Gulf region and in 1820 forced the seven emirates to sign a *Treaty of Perpetual Truce* with them. On March 1, 1971, the British announced that the treaties with the emirates would be terminated by the end of the year. On December 2 of the same year, the United Arab Emirates was declared a federal state with six emirates, and in 1972, the Emirate of Ras Al-Khaimah joined the federation. The name of the country is abbreviated to "UAE".

（三）经济状况 The Economy

阿联酋的经济以石油化工工业为主。此外，还有液化天然气、炼铝、塑料制品、建筑材料、服装、食品等工业。阿联酋农业不发达，全国可耕地面积为 32 万公顷，已耕地面积为 27 万公顷。主要农产品有椰枣、玉米、蔬菜、柠檬等。粮食依赖进口；渔产品和椰枣可满足国内需求；畜牧业规模很小，主要肉类产品依赖进口。近年来，政府采取鼓励务农的政策，向农民免费提供种子、化肥和无息贷款，并对农产品全部实行包购包销，以确保农民收入，农业得到一定发展。

The United Arab Emirates primarily focuses on the petrochemical industry. Additionally, it has industries in liquefied natural gas, aluminum smelting, plastic products, construction materials, clothing, and food. Agriculture in the UAE is not well-developed, with a total arable land area of 320,000 hectares, of which 270,000 hectares are cultivated. The main agricultural products include dates, corn, vegetables, and lemons. The country relies on imports for grain; however, fish and dates meet domestic demand. The livestock industry is very small, with most meat products being imported. In recent years, the government has implemented policies to encourage farming by providing farmers with free seeds, fertilizers, and interest-free loans, and by guaranteeing the purchase and sale of all agricultural products to ensure farmers' income. As a result, agriculture has seen some development.

珍珠业曾经是阿联酋的支柱产业，一直延续到 1960 年。自从 1966 年在阿联酋发现石油以来，原来的荒芜沙漠一下子变成了富庶的油田，使这个国家在经济上发生了巨大的变化。21 世纪以来，阿联酋发展了民航产业，如阿布扎比王室投资的阿提哈德航空与迪拜王室投资的阿联酋航空，在短期内发展迅速，目前共拥有数百架民航机，并发展了以阿布扎比、迪拜为核心的全球航空转运网络，市场占有率在中东地区居于领先地位。

Before 1960, The UAE's economy was primarily supported by the pearl industry. However, the discovery of oil in 1966 transformed the barren desert into prosperous oil fields, bringing about significant economic change for the country. Since the beginning of the 21st century, the UAE has developed its aviation industry, with Etihad Airways backed by the Abu Dhabi royal family and Emirates Airline supported by the Dubai royal family. Both airlines have experienced rapid growth in a short period and now operate hundreds of commercial aircraft. They have also established a global aviation hub network centered around Abu Dhabi and Dubai, holding a leading market share in the Middle East region.

（四）传统文化 Traditional Culture

阿联酋当地人的传统服饰特点是：男人穿白袍，头戴白头巾；妇女穿黑袍，披黑头巾，将头发遮盖得严严实实，有的还面蒙黑纱。在公共交通工具、部分餐厅等公共场合中，男女的活动场所是分开的。穆斯林每天必须做五次礼拜，即日出前的晨礼、中午的晌礼、下午的晡礼、日落后的昏礼、晚间的宵礼。

Traditional attire in the UAE is characterized by men wearing white robes and white headscarves, while women wear black robes and black headscarves that cover their hair completely, with some even wearing a black veil over their faces. In public spaces such as public transportation and certain restaurants, there are separate areas for men and women. Muslims are required to pray five times a day: the Fajr prayer before sunrise, the Dhuhr prayer at noon, the Asr prayer in the afternoon, the Maghrib prayer just after sunset, and the Isha prayer in the evening.

阿联酋人习惯每日两餐，早餐主要是"弗瓦勒"（一种高粱糊糊）蘸奶油，晚餐为正餐，通常吃阿拉伯饼，配上奶油、蜂蜜等；肉类方面，阿联酋人喜欢牛羊肉。阿联酋人性格粗犷奔放、热情好客，习惯以茶和咖啡待客，格外喜爱甜点、巧克力和椰枣。下班后，当地商人喜欢到咖啡店聚坐。熟人之间的晚宴或者商务晚宴总是在彼此家中进行，与我们国内"在餐厅酒桌上谈生意"的情况不同。应邀至阿联酋商人家做客的往往只有男性，如果关系很熟，并且国籍、习惯相同，主人也可能请客人全家吃饭，但女客一般只在单独的客厅由女主人陪同，不会男女混合入座。

Emiratis are accustomed to two meals a day. Breakfast is mainly "Fwal" (a kind of sorghum paste) dipped in cream. Dinner is the main meal, and they usually eat Arabian cakes, with cream, honey, etc.As for meat, the Emiratis like beef and mutton. The Emiratis are rough and unrestrained, hospitable, used to treating guests with tea and coffee, and particularly fond of desserts, chocolates and dates. After work, local businessmen like to gather in coffee shops. Dinners for acquaintances or business dinners are always held at each other's homes, which is different from the situation of "talking business at the restaurant table" in our country. The guests invited to the UAE businessman's home are often only men. If they are very familiar, and have the same nationality and habits, the host may also invite the whole family of the guest for dinner, but the female guests are generally only in a separate living room accompanied by the hostess. Men and women are not at the same table.

甩发舞（图1-63）是在阿联酋女性中流行的一种民间艺术。表演时，演员们站成一排，脚下无任何动作，只是有节奏地扭动腰肢，晃动颈部，把头发用力甩起来。在一些正式的庆典场合，尤其是阿联酋的婚礼上，一般会安排一群少女表演甩发舞，充分表现年轻女性充满活力的特点。

图1-63　甩发舞
Figure 1-63　Hair Dance

Hair Dance (Figure 1-63) is a folk art form that is particularly popular among women in the UAE. During the performance, the dancers stand in a line, with no movement of their feet. Instead, they rhythmically sway their waists and shake their necks, vigorously tossing their hair. This dance is often performed by a group of young women at formal celebrations, especially at weddings in the UAE, showcasing the vibrant energy of young women.

阿亚拉舞（图1-64）俗称棍舞，是阿联酋一种传统的民间表演艺术形式，已成为阿联酋的一个文化符号。男演员们面对面排成两行，手中挥舞着细长的黑色手杖，配合着口中的"纳巴提亚"唱词（一种流行在海湾地区，以部落俚语演唱的诗歌）；另有几个人击打着长鼓和手鼓，随着音乐节奏，踩着步点，边吟唱边上下翻动着手中的木棍，或是携枪带剑，激发出豪侠之气。阿联酋人会在许多特定的时间和场所，尤其是在国家庆典和一些重要社交场合如婚礼上表演阿亚拉舞，如今这已成为阿联酋地区人们社交活动中的一个重要娱乐形式。

The Ayala Dance(Figure1-64), commonly known as the stick dance, is a traditional folk performance art in the UAE and has become a cultural symbol of the nation. Male performers line up in two rows facing each other, wielding slender black sticks as they chant "Nabatiya" verses—a form of poetry sung in tribal dialects popular in the Gulf region. Accompanied by others playing long drums and hand drums, the dancers move in rhythm with the music, stepping in time as they chant and flip their sticks up and down. Sometimes, they carry rifles or swords, exuding a sense of valor and heroism. The Ayala dance is performed at various specific times and places, especially during national celebrations and significant social events such as weddings. Today, it has become an important form of entertainment in social activities across the UAE.

（五）礼仪禁忌 Social Etiquettes and Taboos

阿联酋是伊斯兰国家，当地每年一次的斋月期间，在日出后和日落前，不许在公共场所和大街上喝水、吸烟、吃东西，当地绝大多数的餐馆和饮品店在这个时期关门停业。女士们要注意穿长袖衣服和长裤，不要太暴露。除在寓所或饭店的客房、酒吧内可以喝酒之外，其他任何公共场所均不许喝酒。在与当地人交往的过程中，与男士谈话不能主动问及其夫人的情况，与妇女交往只能简单问候几句，不能单独或长时间地与她们谈话，更不能因好奇而盯住她们的服饰看，也不要给她们拍照。

The UAE is an Islamic country, and during the annual month of Ramadan, it is prohibited to drink water, smoke, or eat in public places and on the streets from sunrise to sunset. The vast majority of restaurants and beverage shops close during this period. Women should be mindful to wear long-sleeved clothing and long pants, avoiding overly revealing attire. Alcohol consumption is only allowed in private residences or hotel rooms; it is not permitted in any public places. When interacting with locals, men should avoid asking about their wives, and conversations with women should be limited to brief greetings. It is not appropriate to engage in prolonged discussions with them, stare at their clothing out of curiosity, or take their pictures.

图 1-64　阿亚拉舞（棍舞）
Figure 1-64　Ayala Dance (Stick Dance)

阿联酋人喜爱白色、绿色、棕色、深蓝色，禁忌粉红色、黄色、紫色，阿联酋股市大屏上涨股用绿色表示，跌股用红色表示。当地人喜爱羚羊，不喜欢猪和熊猫。与阿联酋人交谈时，切莫提及中东政治、宗教、女权运动、石油政策等问题，不能将十字架、六角形图案的物品送给当地人，忌送酒、毛绒玩具、猪肉制品、美女照片等。不能单独给女主人送礼，也不能送东西给已婚女子。

Emiratis prefer colors like white, green, brown, and deep blue, while they avoid pink, yellow, and purple. In the UAE stock market, rising stocks are indicated in green, while falling stocks are shown in red. Locals have a fondness for antelopes but do not like pigs or pandas. When conversing with Emiratis, it is important to avoid topics such as Middle Eastern politics, religion, feminism, and oil policies. Gifts featuring crosses or hexagonal patterns should not be given to locals, and it is best to steer clear of alcohol, figurines, pork products, and photos of attractive women. Additionally, one should not give gifts directly to female hosts or married women.

阿联酋人爱喝驼奶、红茶、咖啡，在拜访当地人时，主人劝饮的咖啡是必须喝的。用餐时，一般席地而坐，以右手取食物。在他们传统观念中，右手总是干净的，左手是不洁的，吃饭时必须用右手将食物直接送进口里。在待人接物方面，譬如递送东西给他人（端水、递茶），或者接别人递送过来的东西时，必须用右手，否则就是极大的不恭敬。

Emiratis enjoy drinking camel milk, red tea, and coffee. When visiting locals, it is essential to accept and drink the coffee offered by the host. During meals, people typically sit on the floor and use their right hand to take food. In their traditional beliefs, the right hand is always considered clean, while the left hand is deemed unclean, so food must be directly brought to the mouth with the right hand. When it comes to interactions, such as handing something to someone (like water or tea) or accepting items from others, it is crucial to use the right hand; otherwise, it would be considered a great disrespect.

阿联酋国内节假日较多，还有长达一个月的斋月，虽然斋戒月期间仍旧工作，但办事效率比平常低，政府机构及绝大多数的公司都会把下班时间提前到下午 2：30 左右。因此，来阿联酋访问、做生意或办展览要注意避开当地的节假日。

There are many holidays in the UAE and the month-long Ramadan. Although work is still done during Ramadan, it is less efficient than usual, with government agencies and most companies moving their closing time to 2：30 pm. Therefore, when visiting, doing business or organizing exhibitions in the UAE, you should pay attention to avoiding local holidays.

阿拉伯国家之
男女有别

（六）传统节日 Festivals

1. 开斋节 Ed al-Fitr

开斋节是穆斯林斋月结束后，庆祝"斋功"胜利完成的日子。穆斯林在节日当天沐浴更衣，到各清真寺参加会礼，互相祝贺。清真寺也打扫一新，准备鲜美的牛、羊肉汤和油香、糕点、水果等食品，款待聚会的穆斯林。

Ed al-Fitr is the celebration marking the successful completion of Ramadan for Muslims. On this day, Muslims bathe and dress in their finest clothes before attending communal prayers at mosques, where they greet one another with congratulations. Mosques are thoroughly cleaned and prepared, serving delicious dishes such as beef and lamb soup, fried pastries, sweets, and fruits to welcome the gathering of Muslims.

2. 古尔邦节 Eid al-Adha

古尔邦节又称"宰牲节"，在伊斯兰教历 12 月 10 日，即朝觐者在麦加活动的最后一天。穆斯林会沐浴盛装，到各清真寺举行会礼，互相拜会，宰杀牛、羊、骆驼，除自食外，还要互相馈赠，或送给清真寺，以示纪念。

Eid al-Adha, also known as the "Festival of Sacrifice", is celebrated on the 10th day of the 12th month of the Islamic lunar calendar, coinciding with the last day of the Hajj pilgrimage in Mecca. On this day, Muslims bathe and dress in their finest attire before attending communal prayers at mosques, where they greet one another. They sacrifice animals such as cows, sheep, and camels, sharing the meat not only for their own consumption but also as gifts to others or donations to mosques, as a way to commemorate the occasion.

3. 圣纪节 Sacred Ji

圣纪是穆罕默德的诞生日，相传穆罕默德诞生于公元 571 年 4 月 20 日（伊斯兰教历 3 月 12 日）。圣纪节期间，穆斯林到清真寺诵念《古兰经》，讲述穆罕默德的生平事迹，歌颂穆罕默德的高尚品德与丰功伟绩，有的还举行聚餐。

Sacred Ji is Muhammad's birth date. According to legend, Muhammad was

历史人物——
穆罕默德

born on April 20, 571 AD（March 12, Islamic calendar）. During the Sacred Ji, Muslims go to the mosque to recite *the Qur"an*, tell the story of Muhammad's life, and sing praises of Muhammad's noble virtues and great achievements, and some also hold dinners.

4. 登霄节 Festival of Ascension

传说穆罕默德 52 岁时，在伊斯兰教历 7 月 17 日的夜晚，由天使哲布勒伊来陪同，从麦加到耶路撒冷，又从那里"登霄"，遨游七重天，见到了古代先知、天国、火狱等，黎明时返回麦加。从此，耶路撒冷与麦加、麦地那成为伊斯兰教三大圣地。有的穆斯林在登霄节的夜晚举行礼拜、祈祷以示纪念。

Legend has it that when Muhammad was 52 years old, on the night of July 17 of the Islamic calendar, accompanied by the angel Zebulai, he traveled from Mecca to Jerusalem, and from there he " ascended to the night", traveled to the seven heavens, and saw the ancient prophets, the kingdom of heaven, the fire, etc., and returned to Mecca at dawn. Since then, Jerusalem and Mecca, Medina has become the three holy places of Islam. Some Muslims hold services and prayers on the night of the Day of Ascension to mark the occasion.

5. 盖德尔夜 Ghadr Night

盖德尔夜也称"平安之夜"，时间是伊斯兰教历 9 月 27 日。每逢盖德尔夜到来，每个家庭都彻夜灯火通明，制作各种佳美食品，宴请宾朋，整个村庄灯火辉煌、充满生气。穆斯林们于该夜聚在一起礼拜祈祷，诵念《古兰经》，捐赠财物等。很多穆斯林往往彻夜不眠，年长者互相讨论一些关于教义方面的问题，或向儿童们讲述一些《古兰经》中的传说和故事等，因此盖德尔夜也称"坐夜"。

The night of Ghadr, also known as " peaceful night", falls on September 27, Muharram. When the night of Ghadr comes, every family lights up all night long, making all kinds of delicious food and entertaining guests, and the whole village is brightly lit and full of life. Many Muslims gather on this night to worship and pray, recite the *Qur"an*, and donate money and goods. Many Muslims often stay up all night, with the older ones discussing with each other issues of doctrine, or telling children legends and stories from the *Qur"an*, so Ghadr night is also known as "stay up late in the night".

三、旅游观光 Tourism and Sightseeing

（一）主要旅游城市及景点 Major Tourist Cities and Attractions

1. 迪拜 Dubai

迪拜是一个多姿多彩的豪华度假胜地，从"帆船酒店"到空前发展的"棕榈岛""世界岛""迪拜乐园"和"迪拜海滨城"，完备的休闲设施应有尽有，既有景致超群的海滩、五星级的服务、热闹的购物商场和高耸入云的摩天楼，又有传统的集市和古老的独桅帆船。

Dubai is a colorful and luxurious resort with a wide range of leisure facilities, from The Sailboat Hotel, to the unprecedented development of The Palm, World Island, Dubai Land and Dubai Marina, with its superb beaches, five-star services, bustling shopping malls and hidden skyscrapers, to the traditional bazaars and ancient dhows.

像其他中东城市一样，迪拜因石油而富庶，是 21 世纪全球发展最迅速的城市之一。在 20 世纪 50 年代，迪拜只是一个在阿拉伯湾不起眼的海滨小镇，20 世纪 90 年代后有了飞速发展，成为一个国际休闲、购物、商务、会议和展览中心。现代化的建筑、干净的街道、豪华的旅游设施、美丽的海滨、充满神秘的中东风情、友善好客的民众吸引着无数游客前来观光体验。

Like other Middle Eastern cities, Dubai has been enriched by oil and is one of the fastest growing cities in the world this century. From a humble beach town on the Arabian Gulf in the 1950s, Dubai has grown exponentially since the 1990s to become an international center for leisure, shopping, business, conferences and exhibitions. The modern architecture, clean streets, luxurious tourist facilities, beautiful waterfront, mysterious Middle Eastern flavor, and friendly hospitality attract countless tourists to come to visit and experience.

2. 哈利法塔 Burj Khalifa Tower

哈利法塔（图 1-65），原名迪拜塔，又称迪拜大厦或比斯迪拜塔，是世界第一高楼。哈利法塔始建于 2004 年，当地时间 2010 年 1 月 4 日晚，迪拜酋长穆罕默德·本·拉希德·阿勒马克图姆揭开被称为"世界第一高楼"的"迪拜塔"纪念碑上的帷幕，宣告这座建筑正式落成，并将其更名为"哈利法塔"。哈利法塔高 828 米，楼层总计 162 层，造价 15 亿美元，还不包括其内部大型购物中心、湖泊和稍矮的塔楼群的修筑费用。哈利法塔总共使用了 33 万立方米混凝土、6.2 万吨强化钢筋、14.2 万平方米玻璃。为了修建哈利法塔，共调用了大约 4 000 名工人和 100 台起重机，把混凝土垂直泵上逾606 米的地方，打破上海环球金融中心大厦建造时 492 米的纪录。大厦内设有 56 部升降机，速度最高可达 17.4 米 / 秒，另外还有双层的观光升降机，每次最多可载 42 人。

图 1-65　哈利法塔
Figure 1-65　Burj Khalifa Tower

Burj Khalifa Tower (Figure 1-65), formerly known as the Burj Dubai, also known as the Dubai Tower or Bis Dubai Tower, is the world's tallest building. Burj Khalifa was built in 2004, local time on the evening of January 4, 2010, the Ruler of Dubai, Mohammad bin Rashid Al Maktoum, unveiled the monument known as "the world's tallest building" "Burj Dubai" on the curtain, announced that the building was officially inaugurated and renamed "Burj Khalifa Tower". The Burj Khalifa Tower is 828 meters high, with 162 floors and a cost of $1.5 billion, not including the construction costs of the large shopping mall, lake and shorter towers inside, which used a total of 330,000 cubic meters of concrete, 62,000 tons of reinforced steel and 142,000 square meters of glass. To build the Burj Khalifa Tower, some 4,000 workers and 100 cranes were called in to pump the concrete vertically up more than 606 meters, breaking the record of 492 meters set during the construction of the Shanghai World Financial Center tower. The building is equipped with 56 elevators that reach speeds of up to 17.4 meters per second, as well as a double-decker sightseeing elevator that can carry up to 42 people at a time.

3. 棕榈岛 Palm Island

棕榈岛（图 1-66）位于迪拜沿岸，由朱美拉棕榈岛、阿里山棕榈岛、代拉棕榈岛和世界岛四个岛屿群组成。每座岛屿包括三个部分："树干""树冠"和新月形围坝。整座岛屿就是一个巨大的避暑胜地，还是运动、健身和游玩天堂，岛上有 2 400 套海边住房，可以入住5 000 人，还配备了豪华健身房和电影院等设施。

图 1-66　棕榈岛
Figure 1-66　Palm Island

The Palm Islands (Figure 1-66) are located off the coast of Dubai and consist of four island groups: the Palm Jumeirah, the Palm of Alishan, the Palm of Deira and the World Island. Each island consists of three parts : the " trunk ", the " canopy " and the crescent-shaped dam. The whole island is a huge summer resort and a paradise for sports, fitness and fun, with 2,400 beachfront houses for up to 5,000 people. There are also facilities such as a gym and a movie theater.

4. 阿拉伯塔酒店（帆船酒店）Burj Al-Arab

阿拉伯塔酒店（图 1-67），又名帆船酒店，是迪拜的地标性建筑。最初的创意是由阿联酋国防部长、迪拜王储阿勒马克图姆提出的，他梦想给迪拜一个如悉尼歌剧院、埃菲尔铁塔式的地标。经过全世界上百名设计师的奇思妙想，终于缔造出一个梦幻般的建筑，将浓烈的伊斯兰风格和极尽奢华的装饰与高科技手段、建材完美结合。阿联酋帆船酒店是世界上唯一的一座七星级酒店，酒店高 321 米，一共有 56 层，内饰华丽

图 1-67　阿拉伯塔酒店（帆船酒店）
Figure 1-67　Burj Al-Arab

非凡。

The Burj Al-Arab Hotel (Figure 1-67), also known as the Sailboat Hotel, is a landmark in Dubai. The initial idea was put forward by Al Maktoum, the UAE Minister of Defense and Crown Prince of Dubai, who dreamed of giving Dubai a Sydney Opera House and Eiffel Tower-style landmark. After the whimsical ideas of hundreds of designers around the world, a fantastic building was finally created — a perfect combination of strong Islamic style and extremely luxurious decorations with high-tech means and building materials. The Burj Al-Arab is the only seven-star hotel in the world, with a height of 321 meters and 56 floors of magnificent interiors.

5. 阿布扎比 Abu Dhabi

阿布扎比（图 1-68）在阿拉伯语中意为"羚羊之父"。阿布扎比酋长国是阿拉伯联合酋长国最大的酋长国，是阿联酋的首都，面积为 67 340 平方千米，其中包括大约 200 个岛屿，占整个阿联酋国土面积的 80% 以上。石油是阿布扎比酋长国的主要财政收入和经济来源。阿布扎比的石油储量占全国石油储量的 90% 以上。这里有皇宫酒店、阿联酋总统府、阿布扎比卢浮宫、大清真寺、法拉利公园、华纳兄弟主题公园等。

图 1-68　阿布扎比
Figure 1-68　Abu Dhabi

Abu Dhabi (Figure 1-68) means " Father of the Antelope " in Arabic. The Emirate of Abu Dhabi is the

largest emirate in the United Arab Emirates and is the capital of the UAE. It covers an area of 67 340 square kilometers, including about 200 islands, and accounts for more than 80% of the total land area of the UAE. Oil is the main source of revenue and economy of the Emirate of Abu Dhabi. Abu Dhabi accounts for more than 90% of the country's oil. It is home to the Palace Hotel, UAE Presidential Palace, Louvre Abu Dhabi, Grand Mosque, Ferrari Park, Warner Bros. Theme Park and many more.

6. 谢赫扎耶德清真寺 Sheikh Zayed Grand Mosque

谢赫扎耶德清真寺（图1-69）位于阿布扎比，是阿联酋的标志性建筑之一，是阿联酋最大的清真寺，世界第六大清真寺。整个建筑群都用汉白玉筑成，耗资55亿美元，其设计充分体现了伊斯兰风格。主祈祷大厅可容纳超过6 000位朝圣者，整个清真寺可容纳超过1 000名朝圣者同时礼拜。此外，谢赫扎耶德清真寺也是唯一一座允许女性信徒从正门进入的清真寺。

图 1-69　谢赫扎耶德清真寺
Figure 1-69　Sheikh Zayed Grand Mosque

The Sheikh Zayed Grand Mosque（Figure 1-69）is located in Abu Dhabi and is one of the iconic buildings of the United Arab Emirates. It is the largest mosque in the UAE and the sixth-largest mosque in the world. The entire complex is built with white marble and cost 55 billion dollars to construct, with its design fully embodying Islamic architectural style. The main prayer hall can accommodate over 6,000 worshippers, and the entire mosque can host more than 1,000 worshippers at a time. Additionally, the Sheikh Zayed Grand Mosque is the only mosque that allows female worshippers to enter through the main entrance.

该清真寺中有一块世界第一大手工编制地毯，由伊朗艺术家 Ali Khaliqi 设计，由伊朗马什哈德地区的1 200名妇女手工编制而成。整块地毯面积达5 627平方米，材质是来自伊朗和新西兰的顶级羊绒。另外，有一面雕刻了《古兰经》经文的墙壁，整卷圣典的每一个文字都由24 K金镀成，非常奢华。

The mosque contains one of the world's largest hand-woven carpets, designed by Iranian artist Ali Khaliqi and hand-woven by 1,200 women in the Mashhad region of Iran. The entire carpet covers an area of 5,627 square meters and is made of the finest cashmere from Iran and New Zealand. In addition, there is a wall carved with Quranic verses, and every word of the entire holy book is lavishly plated with 24-carat gold.

（二）旅游购物 Shopping

椰枣：阿联酋是全球椰枣生产大国，目前拥有椰枣树4 070万株。阿联酋干旱、酷热和少雨的天气为种植椰枣提供了有利条件。阿拉伯联合酋长国首都阿布扎比街道两旁的树木大部分是椰枣树。椰枣含糖量较高，味道甘甜，含有人体所需的多种维生素。

Dates: The UAE is the world's largest producer of dates, with 40.7 million date palms. The UAE's dry, hot and rainy weather provides favorable conditions for growing dates. Most of the trees lining the streets of Abu Dhabi, the capital of the United Arab Emirates, are date palms. Dates have a high sugar content, a sweet flavor and contain many vitamins that the human body needs.

银铜制品：这些银或铜的制品各式各样，包括阿拉伯样式的匕首、中东样式的茶壶、波斯风情的刀剑等，有些银铜制品上面还镶嵌了绚丽夺目的宝石，看起来会觉得非常高贵和典雅。可以作为礼物送给自己的亲人和好朋友，很是特别且不显俗气。

Silver or copper products: Arab silver and copper items come in a variety of forms, including traditional Arab daggers, Middle Eastern teapots, and Persian-style swords. Some of these silver and copper pieces are adorned with stunning gemstones, giving them an air of sophistication and elegance. They make for unique gifts for loved ones and close friends, offering a special touch that avoids being overly flashy.

香薰：在阿拉伯人的居室中，世代奉行着亘续不断地焚香习俗。檀香木香水还代表着主人对远道而来宾客的衷心欢迎，尤其是女宾光临或出行之际，都会在香味燃放器前稍稍伫立，用罩在衣服外层的斗篷轻轻撩拨烟雾，让香气遍布全身。

Incense: In the Arab's apartment, the custom of burning incense has been practiced for generations. Sandalwood perfume also represents the heartfelt welcome of the host for the guests from far away. Especially when the female guests enter a home or travevers are leaving a home, they will stand in front of the scent burner for a moment, with the cloak coving the outer layer of the clothes gently stirring the smoke, so that the aroma spreads throughout the body.

波斯地毯：波斯地毯在制作上非常考究，制作地毯时既要考虑地毯的美观，也要保证地毯的耐用，因此波斯地毯小有名气。波斯地毯充满着异域的风情，实在不失为装点家居的上等装饰品。在迪拜的任何地方都可以从来自海湾、伊朗、阿富汗及巴基斯坦的商人那里买到地毯。在 Deira Towers 购物商场里有一个地毯市场，价格非常低，而且可以还价。

Persian carpets are known for their meticulous craftsmanship, balancing both aesthetic appeal and durability in their design, which contributes to their esteemed reputation. Rich in exotic charm, Persian carpets are indeed excellent decorative pieces for home interiors. In Dubai, you can find carpets sold by merchants from the Gulf, Iran, Afghanistan, and Pakistan everywhere. There is a carpet market at Deira Towers shopping mall where prices are quite low and negotiable.

扫码获取：入境须知及海关规定

 本节习题

1. 请制作一份阿联酋旅游宣传册。
2. 请设计一条阿联酋 7 日旅游经典线路。

第二章 Chapter 2　欧洲旅游区
The European Tourist Region

学习目标

1. 熟悉欧洲旅游区主要客源国和目的地国的国情。

Get familiar with the national conditions of major tourist source and destination countries in European tourist region.

2. 能根据各国特点开展有针对性的客源开发策划和旅游产品设计。

Be able to carry out targeted tourist source development planning and product design according to the characteristics of various countries.

3. 能根据不同客户的需求，设计出合适的旅游线路。

Be able to design suitable tourist routes according to the client's needs.

4. 掌握英国、法国、俄罗斯、德国、意大利和瑞典六个国家主要城市和著名景点的概况，能运用所学理论知识从事实际接待和服务工作等。

Master the general situation of major cities and famous scenic spots in the UK, France, Russia, Germany, Italy and Sweden, and be able to put theoretic knowledge into real practice such as reception and service work.

第一节　欧洲旅游区特征

The General Situation of European Tourist Region

　　欧洲是西方文化的起源地，全称为欧罗巴洲。相传，"欧罗巴"一词来源于希腊神话中的腓尼基公主欧罗巴的名字。欧洲面积为1 018万平方千米，是世界第六大洲，但人口居世界第三位，仅次于亚洲和非洲。欧洲东以乌拉尔山脉、乌拉尔河，东南以里海、高加索山脉和黑海与亚洲为界，西边、西北隔大西洋、格陵兰海、丹麦海峡与北美洲相望，北接北冰洋，南隔地中海与非洲相望。欧洲共有44个国家和地区，按照地理方位可分为北欧、东欧、中欧、西欧及南欧。北欧旅游区指日德兰半岛、斯堪的纳维亚半岛一带，包括冰岛、丹麦、挪威、瑞典和芬兰5个国家和地区。南欧旅游区指阿尔卑斯以南的巴尔干半岛、亚平宁半岛、伊比利亚半岛和附近岛屿，包括罗马尼亚、保加利亚、塞尔维亚、黑山、克罗地亚、斯洛文尼亚、波斯尼亚和黑塞哥维那、马其顿、阿尔巴尼亚、希腊、意大利、圣马力诺、梵蒂冈、西

欧洲旅游区特征（英文版）

班牙、葡萄牙、安道尔、马耳他 17 个国家和地区。西欧旅游区包括英国、爱尔兰、荷兰、比利时、卢森堡、法国和摩纳哥 7 个国家和地区。中欧旅游区包括波兰、捷克、斯洛伐克、匈牙利、德国、奥地利、瑞士、列支敦士登 8 个国家和地区。东欧旅游区包括爱沙尼亚、拉脱维亚、立陶宛、白俄罗斯、乌克兰、摩尔多瓦和俄罗斯 7 个国家和地区。

欧洲旅游区的地形特点是以平原为主，冰川地貌分布较广，高山峻岭汇集于欧洲南部，海拔 200 米以下的平原约占全区总面积的 60%。欧洲平原西起大西洋沿岸，东至乌拉尔山，绵延数千千米，形成横贯欧洲的大平原。阿尔卑斯山脉横亘欧洲南部，是欧洲最大的山脉。东南部高加索山脉的主峰厄尔布鲁士山海拔 5 642 米，为欧洲最高峰。北部斯堪的纳维亚山脉地势比较平缓，沿途多深入内陆、两岸陡峭的峡湾，其中的阿尔卑斯山是登山、滑雪、探险、避暑、疗养的旅游胜地。欧洲旅游区的河流分布很均匀，水量较充足，欧洲最长的河流是伏尔加河，长 3 692 千米。多瑙河为第二大河，长 2 850 千米。欧洲是一个多小湖群的大洲，湖泊多为冰川作用形成。欧洲旅游区大部分地区地处北温带，气候温和、湿润。西部大西洋沿岸夏季凉爽、冬季温和，是典型的温带海洋性气候。东部因远离海洋，属温带大陆性气候。南部地中海沿岸地区冬季温和多雨，夏季炎热干燥，属地中海气候。夏季往往是欧洲旅游区的最佳旅游季节。

欧洲旅游区经济非常发达，其工业、交通、金融、贸易等在世界上都有重要地位，是世界旅游业最发达的地区。欧洲旅游区是世界上最受欢迎的旅游目的地，其国际游客主要来自欧洲内部各国，约占总人数的 80%，其余游客多来自北美、日本。目前，欧洲已成为中国重要的旅游目的地，欧洲绝大部分国家和地区已对中国公民开放，其中欧盟 27 个国家已经全部成为中国公民出国旅游目的地，一些国家为中国游客入境提供便利条件。在目的地选择方面，传统热门国家人气不减，意大利、法国、英国、德国、西班牙、希腊等国依然领跑，这些目的地也更受"90 后"群体的欢迎，成为他们第一次前往欧洲的目的地选择。而出境游经验较为丰富、有一定经济基础的"80 后"则渐渐倾向于选择新兴国家，其中，爱沙尼亚、保加利亚、克罗地亚、拉脱维亚、斯洛文尼亚等小众目的地热度上升。欧洲的文化是西方社会文化的源头，几乎渗透到世界的每个角落，欧洲人始终为此深感骄傲。同时，深厚的文化底蕴让他们表现得谦虚且彬彬有礼，使整个欧洲都展现出一种含蓄与浪漫。本章重点选取了几个具有代表性的国家：西欧的英国和法国、东欧的俄罗斯、南欧的意大利、中欧的德国及北欧的瑞典，分别从国家概况、民俗风情、主要旅游城市及景点等方面增强学习者对上述典型欧洲国家的认识和了解。

第二节　西欧之旅

Travel in Western Europe

绅士之国——英国
The Land of Gentlemen—The United Kingdom

导读

当你走进英伦的各大都市时，在领略浓浓的历史沉淀之余，扑面而来的是崭新的现代气息，去白金汉宫看一次皇室出行，去伦敦塔感受一番监狱的阴森，去西区品一场戏，去大英博物馆游览一番，会让你了解到这个曾经的"日不落帝国"的昔日辉煌。同时，曼彻斯特英超赛场的人声鼎沸、卡迪夫煤炭港口的万吨吞吐、伦敦金融商业区的高楼林立等则展现着英伦三岛的如今风貌。你也可以在享用了丰盛的英式早餐之后，再尝尝英国的招牌菜——炸鱼和薯条；去境内各具特色的小城镇走一走，宅一家传统的英国小酒吧小酌几杯，感受一下当地的风土人情。英国人杰地灵，是一个诞生过无数风流人物的国家：大文豪、科学家、军事家、政治家，名人不胜枚举。多彩的自然、悠长的历史、多元的文化塑造和影响着英国人的国民性格、人文底蕴与价值观。这里是人们心目中的绅士、淑女之乡，数个世纪的优秀风尚沉淀了英国人温文尔雅的风度、井然有序的传统。英国人没有美国人直率，不如法国人浪漫，缺乏意大利人的奔放，他们保守内敛、讲究传统、重视礼仪，同时也尊重个人自由，思想宽容、温和善良。英国是世界上开展旅游活动较早的国家，是近代旅游业的发源地，是国际旅游业最发达的国家之一，被联合国教科文组织列为自然与文化遗产的有伦敦塔、威斯敏斯特宫、巴斯城、布莱尼姆宫、达勒姆大教堂、爱德华国王城堡、汉德里安防御墙、亨德森岛、皇家种马场公园、方廷斯修道院、巨石阵等。

一、地理概览 Geography of the United Kingdom

（一）位置 Location

英国由大不列颠岛（包括英格兰、苏格兰、威尔士）、爱尔兰岛东北部和一些小岛组成，首都为伦敦。英国坐落于欧洲大陆西北部，被大西洋包围。英国东临北海，西临大西洋，南面是英吉利海峡和多佛尔海峡，与欧洲大陆隔海相望，陆地边界与爱尔兰共和国接壤，国土面积为24.41万平方千米。由于英格兰是全国的重心，经济最发达，政治占优势，人口占绝大多数，因此人们非正式地以"英格兰"来代表整个"联合王国"。

The United Kingdom（the UK）is composed of the island of Great Britain (which includes England, Scotland, and Wales), the northeastern part of the island of Ireland, and several smaller islands, with London as its capital. Located in the northwestern part of the European continent, the UK is surrounded by the Atlantic Ocean. It is bordered by the North Sea to the east, the Atlantic Ocean to the west, and the English Channel and the Strait of Dover to the south, facing the European continent across the sea. It shares a land border with Ireland. The total area is 244,100 square kilometers. Since England is the focal point of the nation, with the most developed economy, political dominance, and the majority of the population, people often informally use "England" to represent the entire "United Kingdom".

思考题

1. 你是如何理解以下这段话的？

When people say England, they sometimes mean the Great Britain, sometimes the United Kingdom, sometimes the British Isles—but never England（*How to be an Alien*, by George Mikes）.

2.案例分析

In 1970, BBC showed a series of programs about the history of the British Empire. Before the series started, they advertised it. The advertisement mentioned "England's history". Within a few hours, BBC had received thousands of angry calls of protest and it was forced to make an apology.

Question 1：Who do you think the angry callers were?

Question 2：Why did BBC apologize?

Tips：

1.People in Scotland, Wales and Northern Ireland consider it insulting and hate hearing Britain being referred to as "England" as it appears to ignore their existence.

2.Many people think that "English" is the same as "British". It is not. Although everyone in the UK has a British citizenship, they have different nationalities.The diverse history of England, Scotland and Wales has led to different culture traditions. The Scots and Welsh have right to feel aggrieved whenever the term "English" is used wrongly, to mean all three.

（二）地形和气候 The Land and Seasons

从地形上看，英国地势由西北向东南逐渐倾斜，北部的苏格兰为山地，到处牛羊成群；南部英格兰原野风光令人陶醉；西部的威尔士以崎岖的山岭和碧绿的河谷而闻名。英国河流、湖泊众多，主要河流有大不列颠岛上的第一长河塞文河和流经牛津、伦敦的泰晤士河。

Geographically, the Great Britain descends gradually from the northwest to the southeast. The northern part in Scotland is highland where flocks of sheep and owes can be seen everywhere. The southern part is England which is plain with the beautiful natural review. And the west part is Wales which is famous for its rugged mountains and green valleys. The UK is full of lakes and rivers. The main rivers are River Seven which is the longest in Great Britain and the Thames which passes through Oxford and London.

英国属海洋性温带阔叶林气候，终年温和湿润、冬暖夏凉，夏天最高温度不超过 32 ℃，冬天平均温度为 4 ℃～6 ℃。英国雨量充沛，四季晴雨常常不定。多雨雾是英国气候的显著特点，雨伞成了英国人外出的必备之物。

The United Kingdom has a temperate maritime broad leaf forest climate, characterized by mild and humid conditions throughout the year. Winters are warm, and summers are cool, with summer temperatures rarely exceeding 32 ℃, and average winter temperatures ranging from 4 ℃ to 6 ℃. The UK experiences abundant rainfall, and the weather can be quite unpredictable across the seasons. The weather in UK is mainly featured with frequent rain and fog,making an umbrella an essential item for anyone venturing outdoors.

 思考题

英国人为何爱谈论气候？

提示：在其他欧洲人看来，英国人最显著的特点是思想保守、沉默寡言。英国人爱谈论天气，因为英国的天气常难以预测，有可能在一天之内经历四季的温度，故见面时常以谈论天气来代替通常的问候。在与英国人交谈时，切忌谈及个人隐私、家庭状况、婚姻状况、年龄、职业、收入、宗教等问题。没有受到邀请不能擅自到别人家里，"英国人的家就是他的城堡"，这句话很好地道出了英国人在家里不愿受人打扰的习惯。

In the European's opinion, the most notable feature of the British is that they would always strive to be calm and void demonstrative words or behaviors. The British love to talk about the weather because of the unpredictable weather. It has been said that one can experience four seasons in the course of a single day. Therefore, when meeting each other, people often use talking about the weather as a substitute for the usual greetings. Don't ask the British about their personal affairs, family, marriage, age, occupation, income and religion. The British don't welcome visitors who are not invited to their home. "An Englishman's home is his castle" means that he or she doesrit want to be disturbed at home.

保守的英国人

（三）自然资源 Natural Resources

英国是欧盟中能源、资源最丰富的国家，也是世界主要的石油和天然气生产国，其主要能源有煤、石油、天然气、核能和水力等。英国开发核能已有几十年的历史，目前供发电的核电站有 14 座。英国重视对新能源及可再生能源的研究开发。英国的非能源资源不丰富，主要工业原料依赖进口。英国的渔业资源比较丰富，农业资源比较缺乏。英国森林面积约占全国土地总面积的 6%，仅能满足英国木材需求量的 15%，其余要依靠进口。

The UK is the country with the richest energy resources in the EU, and it is also a major producer of oil and natural gas in the world. The main energy sources include coal, oil, natural gas, nuclear energy, and hydropower. The UK has a history of developing nuclear energy for decades, and currently there are 14 nuclear power stations for power generation. The UK attaches great importance to the research and development of new and renewable energy sources. The UK is not rich in non energy resources, and its main industrial raw materials rely on imports. The UK is relatively rich in fishery resources, while agricultural resources are relatively scarce. The forest area of the UK accounts for about 6% of the country's land area, which can only meet 15% of the UK's timber demand. The rest depends on imports.

二、人文概况 Overview of British Humanities

（一）国情认知 Basic Knowledge of National Conditions

英国人口约 6 697 万（2022 年），其中英格兰 5 300 万、威尔士 310 万、苏格兰 530 万、北爱尔兰 180 万，英格兰人占了 80% 以上。英国是一个人口稠密的国家，人口密度约为每平方千米 273.65 人，但人口分布极不均匀，80% 以上的人口居住在城市。

The population of the United Kingdom is approximately 66.97 million (2022), with England accounting for 53 million, Wales 3.1 million, Scotland 5.3 million, and Northern Ireland 1.8 million. Over 80% of the population resides in England. The UK is a densely populated country, with a population density of about 273.65 people per square kilometer. However, the population distribution is highly uneven, with more than 80% of the population living in urban areas.

英国主要有四个民族，即英格兰人、苏格兰人、威尔士人、爱尔兰人。这些民族都带有凯尔特人的血统，融合了日耳曼人的成分。官方语言为英语，威尔士北部还使用威尔士语，苏格兰西北高地及北爱尔兰部分地区仍使用盖尔语。居民多信奉基督教新教，主要分为英格兰教会（亦称英国国教、圣公会）和苏格兰教会（亦称长老会）。另有天主教会及伊斯兰教、印度教、锡克教、犹太教和佛教等较大的宗教社团。

There are four main ethnic groups in Britain, namely, the English, Scottish, Welsh, and Irish. These ethnic groups all have Celtic ancestry and incorporate Germanic elements. The official language is English. Welsh is also spoken in northern Wales, while Gaelic is still spoken in parts of the northwest highlands of Scotland and Northern Ireland. Most residents believe in Protestant Christianity, mainly divided into the Church of England (also known as the Anglican Church or Episcopal Church) and the Scottish Church (also known as the Presbyterian Church). There are also larger religious communities such as the Catholic Church and Islam, Hinduism, Sikhism, Judaism, and Buddhism.

英国佬名称的由来

（二）历史简介 History of the United Kingdom

英国历史是一部征服与合并的历史。公元 1 至 5 世纪，大不列颠岛东南部受罗马帝国统治，后盎格鲁、撒克逊、朱特人相继入侵。7 世纪开始形成封建制度。公元 829 年英格兰统一，史称"盎格鲁－撒克逊征服"。1066 年诺曼底公爵威廉渡海征服英格兰，建立诺曼底王朝。1536 年英格兰与威尔士合并。1640 年爆发资产阶级革命，1649 年 5 月 19 日宣布成立共和国。1660 年王朝复辟。1688 年爆发"光荣革命"，确立了君主立宪制。1707 年英格兰与苏格兰合并。1801 年又与爱尔兰合并。18 世纪 60 年代至 19 世纪 30 年代成为世界上第一个完成工业革命的国家。

The history of the United Kingdom is full of conquest and consolidation. From the 1-5 centuries AD, the southeastern part of the island of Great Britain was under the rule of the Roman Empire. The post Anglo, Saxon, and Jute peoples invaded successively. The feudal system began to take shape in the 7th century. England was unified in 829 AD, known as the "Anglo Saxon Era" in history. In 1066, William, Duke of Normandy, crossed the sea to conquer England and established the Normandy dynasty. England and Wales merged in 1536. The bourgeois revolution broke out in 1640, and the founding of the Republic was announced on May 19, 1649. The dynasty was restored in 1660. In 1688, the "Glorious Revolution" occurred, establishing a constitutional monarchy. England merged with Scotland in 1707. In 1801, it merged with Ireland. From the 1760s to the 1830s, it became the first country in the world to complete the industrial revolution.

1914 年，英国占有的殖民地面积比其本土面积大 111 倍，成为第一殖民大国，自称"日不落帝国"。1921 年，爱尔兰南部 26 郡成立"自由邦"，北部 6 郡仍归英国。第一次世界大战后，英国开始衰落，其世界霸权地位逐渐被美国取代。第二次世界大战严重削弱了英国的经济实力。随着 1947 年印度和巴基斯坦相继独立，英国的殖民体系开始瓦解。目前，英国在海外仍有 13 块领地。1973 年 1 月英国加入欧共体（今欧盟），2020 年 1 月退出欧盟。

The colonial area occupied by Britain in 1914 was 111 times larger than that of its native land, making it the first colonial power and calling itself the "The empire on which the sun never sets". In 1921, 26 counties in the south of Ireland were established as a "Free State", while 6 counties in the north still belonged to the United Kingdom. After the First World War, Britain began to decline, and its world hegemony was gradually replaced by the United States. The Second World War severely weakened Britain's economic strength. With the successive independence of India and Pakistan in 1947, the British colonial system began to disintegrate. Currently, the UK still has 13 territories overseas. In January,1973, Britain joined the European Community (now the EU) and withdrew from the EU in January,2020.

英国是一个具有多元文化和开放思想的国家。英国的艺术、音乐、文化和饮食一直受到来自世界各地不同国家的人民及民族习惯的影响，并与许多国家有着悠久且紧密的联系。直到现在，它仍与美国、加拿大、澳大利亚和新西兰等英语国家保持着密切的关系。

The UK is a country with multi-culture and open mind. Its arts, music, culture and food are affected by different people and customs from all over the world, and have a long and close ties with many countries. Until now, it has had a close contact with some English-speaking countries such as the United States, Canada, Australia and New Zealand.

首都为伦敦，国花为玫瑰，国鸟为红胸鸲，货币为英镑。英国实行君主立宪制。国王是世袭的国家元首、立法机关的组成部分、最高司法长官、武装部队总司令和英国国教的世俗领袖。议会是英国最高立法机构，由国王、上院（贵族院）、下院（众议院）组成。每届议会大选后，首相由多数党领袖担任，并由英王任命。

The capital is London, the national flower is rose, the national bird is European Robin, and the currency is Pound Sterling. The United Kingdom follows a constitutional monarchy. The monarch serves as the hereditary head of state, a component of the legislative body, the highest judicial authority, the commander-in-chief of the armed forces, and the secular leader of the Church of England. The Parliament is the highest legislative body in the UK, consisting of the monarch, the House of Lords (House of Peers), and the House of Commons (House of Representatives). Following each parliamentary election, the Prime Minister is appointed by the monarch upon the recommendation of the leader of the majority party.

（三）经济状况 The Economy

英国是发达的资本主义国家，是世界第五大经济体。英国的工业在国民经济中占绝对优势，但在第二次世界大战后，其发展缓慢。主要工业有采矿、冶金、化工、机械、电子、电子仪器、汽车、航空、食品、饮料、烟草、轻纺、造纸、印刷、出版、建筑等。生物制药、航空和国防是英国工业研发的重点，也是英国最具创新力和竞争力的行业。农业生产水平不高，农产品产量可满足国内需求的2/3。英国的交通十分发达，设施完备，为旅游业的发展提供了条件。

Britain is a developed capitalist country and the fifth largest economy in the world. British industry has an absolute advantage in the national economy, but after World War II, British industry developed slowly. The main industries include mining, metallurgy, chemical engineering, machinery, electronics, electronic instruments, automobiles, aviation, food, beverage, tobacco, light textile, paper-making, printing, publishing, construction, etc. Bio-pharmaceuticals, aviation, and defense are the focus of industrial research and development in the UK, and are also the most innovative and competitive industries in the UK. The level of agricultural production is not high, and agricultural products can meet two-thirds of domestic demand. The transportation and facilities in Britain are very developed, providing conditions for the development of tourism.

英国奉行自由贸易，主张开放的多边贸易体系和世界贸易的进一步自由化。与世界 80 多个国家和地区有贸易关系，主要贸易对象是欧盟成员国、美国和日本。主要出口产品包括化妆品及相关产品、化工产品（主要是医药）、食品、烟草、饮料、酒水（威士忌等）、机械设备等。

The United Kingdom adheres to a policy of free trade, advocating for an open multilateral trading system and further liberalization of global trade. It maintains trade relations with over 80 countries and regions worldwide, with its main trading partners being EU member states, the United States, and Japan. The UK's primary exports include cosmetics and related products, chemical products (mainly pharmaceuticals), food, tobacco, beverages , alcoholic drinks (such as whisky), machinery, equipment and so on.

（四）传统文化 Traditional Culture

英国人对音乐会、戏剧、歌剧、舞剧和室内音乐等古典音乐有着浓厚的兴趣。流行音乐、民间音乐和爵士音乐也十分受人欢迎。甲壳虫乐队，又名"披头士"乐队，是流行音乐历史上最伟大、最有影响力、拥有歌迷最多、最成功的乐队，也成为英国文化和英国历史的一个标志，甲壳虫乐队中有成员被英国女王加封晋爵。

The British have a wide interest in classical music such as concerts, dramas, operas, dance dramas, and chamber music. Pop music, folk music, and jazz music are also very popular. The Beatles are the greatest, most influential, most popular, and most successful band in the history of pop music. They have also become a symbol of British culture and history. Some members of the Beatles have been knighted by the Queen of England.

披头士（甲壳虫乐队）

英国的国服是西服。西装源自英国王室的传统服装，它是男士穿着的由同一面料制作的三件套装，包括上衣、背心和裤子。其在造型上延续了男士礼服的基本形式，属于日常服装中的正统装束，使用场合甚为广泛。萨维尔街（Savile Row）位于英国伦敦，是定制西装的发源地，是世界男装的工艺典范。百年来，身着一套萨维尔街的定制西装成为世界各国权贵、富商、明星的身份象征。

The national attire of the United Kingdom is the suit. Originating from the traditional garments of the British royal family, the suit is a three-piece ensemble for men, consisting of a jacket, waistcoat, and trousers made from the same fabric. It maintains the basic form of men's formal wear and is considered a classic attire for everyday occasions, suitable for a wide range of events. Savile Row, located in London, is the birthplace of bespoke tailoring and stands as a benchmark of craftsmanship in men's fashion worldwide. For over a century, wearing a bespoke suit from Savile Row has been a symbol of status among dignitaries, wealthy businessmen, and celebrities across the globe.

西服如何从英国走向世界

英国威士忌历史悠久，在世界上最负盛名。苏格兰高地的特殊水质和严格的酿酒工艺，使那里出产的威士忌被誉为"液体黄金"。英国苏格兰的威士忌、法国的干邑白兰地、中国的茅台酒并称为世界三大名酒。

British whisky has a long history and is the most famous in the world. The special water quality and strict brewing technology of the Scottish highlands make the whiskey produced there known as "liquid gold". Whisky in Scotland, Cognac Brandy in France and Moutai in China are ranked as the world's three most famous liquors.

英国有非常古老且悠久的烟斗文化及制斗历史。在英国，大多数高质量手工制作的烟斗都是由优质的石楠木材制成的，生长多年的石楠根瘤最适合制作烟管。烟斗让男士们爱不释手，不但具有使用价值，还具有极高的艺术价值和收藏价值。著名作家马克·吐温曾表示，如果天堂没有烟斗，他宁愿下地狱。烟斗的魅力可见一斑。

The United Kingdom boasts a long-standing and rich tradition of pipe culture and pipe-making history. In the UK, most high-quality, handcrafted pipes are made from premium briar wood, with briar root burls that have matured over many years being the most suitable for crafting pipes. Smoking pipes are irresistible to men, as they have practical value, but also have high artistic value and collection value. The famous writer Mark Twain once remarked that if heaven had no smoking pipes, he would rather go to hell, highlighting the undeniable allure of pipes.

茶是英国最受欢迎的饮料，红茶传入英国，与一位嗜茶的葡萄牙公主有关。1662 年，葡萄牙公主凯瑟琳（Catherine of Braganza）嫁给英国国王查理二世，她将茶叶作为嫁妆带入英国宫廷，从此，饮茶成为英国上流社会的时尚，凯瑟琳也被人称为"饮茶皇后"。下午茶是一种典型的英国习俗，通常在下午 4 点到 6 点之间进行，喝茶时搭配精致小巧的三明治、司康饼、奶油果酱以及精选的小蛋糕。虽说家中也能享用下午茶，不过，体验下午茶的最佳方式是去精品酒店或咖啡馆。享用下午茶的几个最知名的地方是位于伦敦的凯莱奇酒店、萨伏依酒店或丽兹酒店。

Tea is the most popular beverage in the United Kingdom, and the introduction of black tea to Britain is linked to a tea-loving Portuguese princess. In 1662, Catherine of Braganza married King Charles II of England and brought tea as part of her dowry into the English court. This marked the beginning of tea drinking as a fashionable pastime among the British upper class, and Catherine became known as the "Tea-Drinking Queen." Afternoon tea is a quintessential British tradition, typically enjoyed between 4 p.m. and 6 p.m., accompanied by delicate sandwiches, scones with clotted cream and jam, and a selection of fine cakes. While afternoon tea can be enjoyed at home, the best way to experience it is at a boutique hotel or cafe. Some of the most renowned places to enjoy afternoon tea include Claridge's, The Savoy, and The Ritz in London.

英国人的红茶情结

英国人常自嘲不精于烹调，英国菜相对来说比较简单，口味清淡。英国菜最常见的烹饪技法是水煮和煎炸。最常用的食材是牛羊鱼肉、土豆、培根、鸡蛋、青豆、番茄及一些时令蔬菜。但英式早餐比较丰富，他们创造的炸鱼、薯条和三明治成为现代快餐业的标志，炸鱼、薯条成为英国的国民小吃。英国人进餐时会喝酒，一般喝啤酒，还喜欢喝威士忌等烈性酒，苏格兰的威士忌在世界上久负盛名。下午茶是英国人生活的一部分，每个英国人年均消费的茶叶量在西方各国中居于首位，茶可谓英国的民族饮料。较为知名的英国菜有牛肉腰子派、炸鱼排等。

The British often humorously admit that they are not particularly skilled in cooking, with British cuisine being relatively simple and mildly flavored. The most common cooking methods in British cuisine are boiling and frying. The staple ingredients include beef, lamb, fish, potatoes, bacon, eggs, peas, tomatoes, and some seasonal vegetables. However, the English breakfast is quite hearty, and their creations like fish and chips and sandwiches have become icons of the modern fast-food industry, with fish and chips being a national snack. During meals, Britons often drink alcohol, typically beer, and they also enjoy strong spirits like whisky, with Scotch whisky being renowned worldwide. Afternoon tea is an integral part of British life, and the average annual tea consumption per person in the UK is the highest among Western countries, making tea the national beverage. Some well-known British dishes include steak and kidney pie and fish fillets.

英国是一个非常重视教育的国家，是现代大学的发源地之一，云集了许多古老的世界著名大学，每年都有成千上万的海外留学生赴英留学。著名的高等院校有牛津大学、剑桥大学、帝国理工学院、曼彻斯特大学、爱丁堡大学等。

The United Kingdom places a strong emphasis on education and is one of the birthplaces of the modern university system. It is home to many of the world's oldest and most prestigious universities, attracting thousands of international students each year. Renowned higher education institutions include the University of Oxford, the University of Cambridge, Imperial College London, the University of Manchester, and the University of Edinburgh.

牛津和剑桥

（五）礼仪禁忌 Social Etiquettes and Taboos

长期的王室文化和贵族文化形成了英国人特有的礼仪。保守、矜持、幽默是英国国民的特点。英国人做事有耐心，和蔼，诚实守信。"打扰一下""对不起""谢谢"永远都是使用频率最高的词。无论是在售票处、银行、超市，还是在公交车站，到处都是耐心排队的人。排在队尾的人常被问道："请问你在排队吗？"哪怕在公交车站只有两三人也会排队。不管是在拥挤的电梯里还是在排队队伍中，英国人总是避免相互碰撞，他们常说的一句话是"保持距离"。

The UK etiquette adopts the British royal and aristocratic culture. The national characteristics are conservative, courteous and humorous. The people keep patient, good-tempered, honest and trustworthy as a rule. The terms used most often are "Excuse me" "Sorry" and "Thank you". People get used to queuing no matter where they are: ticket offices, banks, supermarkets or bus stations. The person at the end of the line will be often inquired as "Excuse me, are you waiting in the queue?" Even when there are only two or three persons in the bus station they will queue to get on the bus. People always avoid touching each other whether they are in the crowded lifts or in the lines and always say "Keep your distance".

到英国人家中做客时，不要提前到，最好是晚于约定时间10分钟到达。客人不要送太贵重的礼物，礼物一般是巧克力、红酒、威士忌或鲜花，当然，中国的民族特色工艺品也很受欢迎。不要送有公司标志的礼品。不要送菊花，菊花在欧洲只用于万圣节和葬礼。白色百合在英国象征死亡。

When visiting a British home, it's best not to arrive early; ideally, you should arrive about 10 minutes after the agreed time. Guests should avoid giving overly expensive gifts. Common gifts include chocolates, wine, whisky, or flowers, and traditional Chinese handicrafts are also well-received. Avoid gifts with company logos. Do not give chrysanthemums, as they are associated with Halloween and funerals in Europe. White lilies should also be avoided, as they symbolize death in the UK.

英国人讲究穿戴，特别是参加宴会、集会和出席特定场合时，都要穿正式的服装，如黑色西装，打不带条纹的领带。"头戴黑皮帽，身穿黑色燕尾服，手拿一把折好的雨伞"，这也许是中国人心目中的英国绅士形象。英国的"绅士风度"是对男性礼貌举止、文明教养、尊重女性等一系列行为规范的总称。尊重女性是"绅士风度"的集中体现。"女士优先"贯彻在生活的每一角落。购物时，英国人不喜欢讨价还价，认为这是很丢面子的事情。如果他们认为一件商品的价钱合适，就买下。

The British pay great attention to dressing, especially when attending banquets, gatherings, or specific occasions, where formal clothing such as black suits and plain ties is required. The image of a British gentleman in the minds of many Chinese might be a man wearing a black bowler hat, a black tailcoat, with an umbrella in hand. The British gentleman is a series of codes of conduct of the British male's behavior, courtesy and respect for women. Respect for women is a concentrated expression of the British gentleman. "lady first" is carried out in every corner of life. When it comes to shopping, the British do not like bargaining, thinking it will lose face. If the price is acceptable, they will take it.

 思考题

Do Chinese people bargain?

When people go shopping, especially in street markets or some small stores, they frequently bargain with the seller on every commodity. For one thing, people can gain more discounts from the bargain, which will make the goods they want to buy more cost-effective. For another, some people also can obtain great pleasure and sense of satisfaction from the bargaining process.

 讨论题

英国人对下午茶的热爱几乎可以媲美"跨越生死的爱恋"。请看礼仪专家 William Hanson 传授的英式下午茶官方指南（扫码获取），教你像英国贵族那样优雅地喝下午茶，包括应该如何摆放餐巾和搅拌红茶，先涂果酱还是奶油，餐后又该如何擦嘴。

英国同中国在茶艺及茶文化方面有什么差异？

如何正确享用英式下午茶

（六）传统节日 Festivals

1. 万圣节 Halloween

万圣节是在每年的 11 月 1 日。10 月 31 日是万圣节前夜。英国是万圣节的起源地。公元前 5 世纪，当时居住于爱尔兰的凯尔特人将 10 月 31 日定为夏末，象征一年的结束。凯尔特人因为怕成为鬼魂的目标，便在夜晚熄灭家中的炉火，戴上狰狞、可怕的面具，并打扮成鬼怪模样走到街上巡游，以驱赶鬼怪。渐渐地，它成了孩子们的一个节日，年轻人在这天会举办化装舞会。万圣节前夕，孩子们会提着南瓜灯，装扮成小鬼怪，敲邻居家的门索要糖果，不停地对主人说"trick or treat"，不给吃的就要捣乱，因此这一天孩子们往往收获颇丰。

Halloween is on November 1. October 31 is All Hallow's Eve. The festival originated in the UK. In the 5th century BC, the Celtics living in Ireland set the October 31 as the end of the summer day and the symbol of the end of the year. The Celts, fearing they would become targets for ghosts, would extinguish the fires in their homes at night, wear terrifying masks, and dress up as monsters to walk the streets in a parade to drive away the spirits. Gradually, the festival becomes the kids' favorite. It is also the masquerade festival for young people. On All Hallows' Eve, the children will carry pumpkin lamps, disguise as little ghosts, knock at the doors of neighbors and ask for candy. "Trick or treat" is the word they continue to say to the host. The kids will receive lots of candies.

万圣节的由来

2. 复活节 Easter

据《圣经》记载，耶稣被钉死在十字架上，是为了赎世人的罪，第三天耶稣复活，复活节因此得名。复活节是仅次于圣诞节的重大节日。通常，这个日子是在 3 月 21 日或其后的第一个月圆之后的星期日，一般在 3 月 22 日至 4 月 25 日之间。复活节是最古老、最有意义的基督教节日之一，庆祝耶稣的复活，象征着重生和希望。世界各地的基督徒每年都会举行庆祝活动。除教会的庆典之外，复活节有不少传统习惯。典型的复活节礼物与春天和再生有关系，最经典的要数复活节彩蛋。

According to the *Bible*, Jesus was crucified on the cross in order to redeem sins of the world. On the third day, Jesus was resurrected from the dead. So the festival got its name. Easter is a major holiday after Christmas. Typically, this day is on March 21 or the Sunday after the first full moon day, generally between March 22 and April 25. Easter is one of the oldest and most meaningful Christian holidays. It celebrates the resurrection of Jesus and also symbolize of rebirth and hope. Christians around the world celebrate it every year. In addition to the celebration of the church, Easter has many traditional rituals. Typical Easter gifts have connections with spring and regeneration. The most typical one is the Easter eggs.

三、旅游观光 Tourism and Sightseeing

（一）主要旅游城市 Major Tourist Cities

1. 伦敦 London

伦敦位于英格兰东南部，跨泰晤士河下游两岸，是英国第一大城市及第一大港口，也是欧洲最大的都会区之一、世界三大金融中心之一以及世界十大首都之一，人口为 820 万，面积为 1 577.3 平方千米。伦敦不仅是英国最重要的政治、金融中心，而且是著名的旅游城市。由于历代王朝建都于此，伦敦拥有丰富的历史和文化古迹。泰晤士河两岸风光无限：南岸有水族馆、壮观的伦敦眼、别致的泰特现代美术馆、莎士比亚环球剧院；北岸有著名的国会大厦及沿岸的古建筑群，如大英博物馆。

Located on the banks of the Thames River in the southeast of England, London is the largest city and port in the UK. It is also one of the largest capital cities in Europe and one of the world's three major financial cities. London is also one of the top ten capital cities in the world, with an area of 1,577.3 square kilometers and population of 8.2 million. London is not only the center of politics and finance but also a well-known tourist city. As the capital for all the British dynasties, London is full of historic and cultural relics. Along the both sides of the end of Thames River, there are numerous scenic spots. Along the south bank of Thames, there appear a large aquarium, the giant Eye of London, the elegant Tate Gallery of Modern Art and Shakespeare's Global Theatre. On the north bank, stand the Parliament and historic buildings such as the British Museum.

2. 爱丁堡 Edinburgh

爱丁堡自 11 世纪开始一直是苏格兰首府，是苏格兰政治、文化和金融中心，位于苏格兰南部低地的中心。爱丁堡得名于 7 世纪诺森伯里亚王国的一位名叫爱德温的国王。爱丁堡于 1392 年建成，1437 年成为苏格兰王国的首都。爱丁堡历史悠久、风景秀丽，是英国最美丽的城市之一，素有"北方雅典""欧洲最有气势的城市"之称。中世纪以来，爱丁堡在欧洲文化交流中占有重要地位，是苏格兰的文化、艺术中心。1974 年以来，每年 8 月、9 月，爱丁堡都会举行为期 3 周的国际艺术节，来自世界各国的艺术团体云集于此，成为世界瞩目的一大盛事，参加艺术节的游客数量相当于爱丁堡的人口数。此外，爱丁堡也是苏格兰民俗和文化的展示中心，尤其是方格呢裙与风笛（图 2-1）。游客到访最多的是爱丁堡城堡，它是苏格兰王国最重要的城堡，屹立于市中心的一座死火山上，在此可以俯瞰整个市区，是英国最古老的城堡之一。据说亚瑟王和他的十二骑士的故事就起源于这个地方。1995 年，联合国教科文组织把爱丁堡老城区列入《世界遗产名录》。

Edinburgh has been the capital of Scotland since the 11th century. It is the political, cultural and financial center of Scotland and located in the center of the southern lowlands of Scotland. Edinburgh was named after King Edwin from the Kingdom of Northumbria in the 7th century. Built in 1392, Edinburgh became the capital of the Kingdom of Scotland in 1437. With a long history and charming scenery, Edinburgh is one of the most beautiful cities in the UK, known as the "Athens of the North" and "Europe's most imposing city". Since the Middle Ages, Edinburgh has occupied an important position in the European cultural exchanges and has been the Scottish cultural and arts center. Edinburgh has held the annual International Arts Festival which lasts 3 weeks between August and September since 1974. The art groups from around the world will gather here. The event attracts the world's attention and the number of visitors attracted to Edinburgh for the festival is roughly equal to the resident population of the city. Edinburgh is also the center of Scottish folklore and culture exhibition, especially tartan kilts and bagpipes (Figure 2-1). The most-visited tourist attraction is the Edinburgh Castle, an important fortress of the Kingdom of Scotland. It dominates the top of the extinct volcano of city of Edinburgh of Scotland, overlooking the whole city, and is one of the oldest castles in the UK. It was said it was the place where the story of King Arthur and his twelve knights happened. The Old City of Edinburgh was listed into World Heritage List by UNESCO in 1995.

图 2-1　苏格兰的方格呢裙与风笛
Figure 2-1　Scottish Tartan Kilts and Bagpipes

图 2-2　埃弗顿足球俱乐部和利物浦足球俱乐部
Figure 2-2　Everton Football Club and Liverpool Football Club

3. 利物浦 Liverpool

利物浦是英国仅次于伦敦的第二大港口，位于英格兰西北部，距离伦敦 325 千米。昔日的利物浦是英国著名的制造业中心，今天的利物浦是英国国家旅游局认定的最佳旅游城市，该市最为著名的是音乐（"披头士"乐队的故乡）与足球〔有两支参加英超的球会——埃弗顿足球俱乐部和利物浦足球俱乐部（图 2-2）〕。

Liverpool, located at the northwest of the England, is the second largest port after London in the UK and is 325 kilometers away from London. Liverpool was the famous manufacturing center in the UK and is the best tourist city certified by National Tourist Bureau of UK. It is famous for music（the hometown of the Beatles）and football [There are two Premier League teams in the city, Everton Football Club and Liverpool Football Club (Figure 2-2)].

（二）著名旅游景点 Famous Tourist Attractions

1. 白金汉宫 Buckingham Palace

图 2-3　白金汉宫
Figure 2-3　Buckingham Palace

白金汉宫始建于 1703 年，1762 年英王乔治三世购得此屋，改建成国王的寝宫，并沿用至今。每天上午 11：30 开始，持续 45 分钟的卫兵换岗仪式（图 2-3）是游客必看的节目。

Buckingham Palace（Figure2-3）was originally built in 1703. In 1762, King George Ⅲ purchased the house and rebuilt it as a royal residence,which has been in use ever since. The 45 minutes of daily changing guards,starting from 11:30 am is the must-see for visitors.

2. 伦敦塔 Tower of London

伦敦塔（图2-4、图2-5）是英国伦敦市中心泰晤士河北岸的一座历史悠久的城堡。伦敦塔是由威廉一世为镇压当地人和保卫伦敦城于1087年开始动工兴建的。自12世纪以来，伦敦塔就一直作为王室居所，其主体建筑是白色的塔。城堡还曾作为军械库、财政部、动物园、皇家造币厂、档案室和监狱（专门关押上层阶级囚犯的监狱）。英语里有一句俗语"sent to the Tower"，意思就是"关入监狱"。

The Tower of London (Figure 2-4 and Figure 2-5) is a historic castle on the north bank of the Thames River in central London, England, which was built in 1087 for the suppression of local people and defending the city of London by William Ⅰ. It has been royal household since the 12th century. The main building is the white tower. The castle was also used as an armory, a treasury, a menagerie, the home of the Royal Mint, a public records office and prison (especially upper-classprisoners). Thus the phrase "sent to the Tower" means "put somebody into prison".

图 2-4 伦敦塔
Figure 2-4 Tower of London

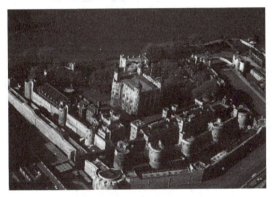

图 2-5 伦敦塔城堡全景
Figure 2-5 The Panoramic View of the Tower of London

伊丽莎白一世在她姐姐玛丽一世统治时曾被关在此处一段时间。伦敦塔最后一次作为监狱使用是在第二次世界大战期间，关押鲁道夫·赫斯。目前，其是一座王室珍宝的展览馆（图2-6）。伦敦塔于1988年被列入《世界遗产名录》。

Elizabeth Ⅰ was imprisoned here for a period during the reign of her sister, Mary I. The Tower of London was last used as a prison during World War Ⅱ, when Rudolf Hess was held there. Today, it serves as an exhibition space for the Crown Jewels (Figure2-6), showcasing the crowns and

图 2-6 珍宝展览馆
Figure 2-6 Home of the Crown Jewels

jewels worn by British royalty during weddings, coronations, and christenings. The Tower of London was listed as a World Cultural Heritage Lite by UNESCO in 1988.

3. 大本钟 Big Ben

大本钟（图2-7）是位于威斯敏斯特宫（又称议会大厦）北面钟楼的昵称，建于1859年，高96米，是当时世界上最高的哥特式建筑。顶部安装了重达13.5吨的当时世界上最大的机

图 2-7　大本钟
Figure 2-7　Big Ben

图 2-8　伦敦塔桥
Figure 2-8　Tower Bridge

械钟，时针和分针的臂长分别为 2.75 米和 4.27 米。大本钟是以当时设计和监造此项工程的本杰明·霍尔爵士的名字命名的。

Big Ben (Figure2-7) is the nickname for the clock tower located on the north side of the Palace of Westminster, also known as the Houses of Parliament. Built in 1859, it stands 96 meters tall and was the tallest Gothic structure in the UK at the time. At the top, it houses what was then the world's largest mechanical clock, weighing 13.5 tons, with hour and minute hands measuring 2.75 meters and 4.27 meters, respectively. The name "Big Ben" is derived from Sir Benjamin Hall, who was responsible for the design and construction of the tower.

4. 伦敦塔桥 Tower Bridge

伦敦塔桥（图 2-8）是伦敦的标志性建筑，建于 1894 年，是维多利亚时代的哥特式建筑，因位于伦敦塔边而得名。伦敦塔桥升起时最为壮观，遇有大船通过或特殊场合时，塔桥桥面会升起，可达 40 米高、60 米宽。伦敦塔桥是体验塔桥、了解塔桥历史和建筑文化以及欣赏泰晤士河风光的最佳地点。

The Tower Bridge (Figure2-8) is the symbol of London. It was built in an iconic landmark in London, constructed in 1894 in Gothic style of Victorian dynasty. The bridge is most spectacular when it lifts, which occurs to allow large ships to pass or during special occasions. When raised, the bridge can reach a height of 40 meters and a width of 60 meters. Tower Bridge is the perfect place to experience the bridge itself, learn about its history and architectural culture, and enjoy the views of the River Thames.

5. 大英博物馆 British Museum

大英博物馆（图 2-9）是英国最大的综合性博物馆，亦是世界上著名的博物馆之一，与纽约大都会艺术博物馆、巴黎卢浮宫和俄罗斯冬宫博物馆并称为世界四大博物馆。大英博物馆建于 1753 年，是世界上历史最悠久、最重要的文化和历史博物馆。大英博物馆拥有古埃及馆、古希腊和罗马馆、古中东馆、版画和素描馆、史前历史和欧洲馆、亚洲馆等。大英博物馆以收藏古罗马遗迹、古希腊雕像和埃及木乃伊而闻名于世，是人类文化遗产的宝库。

The British Museum (Figure 2-9) is the UK's largest comprehensive museum and also one of the famous museums in the world. The British Museum，along with the New York Metropolitan Museum of Art，the Louvre in Paris and Russian Winter Palace，is known as one of the world's top four museums. Established in 1753, it is one of the oldest and most important museums of culture and history in the world. The museum owns the departments of Ancient Egypt, Greece and Rome, the Middle East, Prints and Drawings, Prehistory and Europe, Asia and so on. It is famous for the collection of ancient Roman ruins, the ancient Greek statues and ancient Egyptian mummies. It is a treasure trove of cultural heritage of mankind.

图 2-9　大英博物馆
Figure 2-9　British Museum

6. 威斯敏斯特教堂 Westminster Abbey

威斯敏斯特教堂（图 2-10）位于伦敦西部，意为"西部大教堂"。威斯敏斯特教堂是由 11 世纪号称"笃信者"的英王爱德华建立的。教堂的主要特点是大门处有一对塔楼。教堂自建立以来，一直是英国历代国王或女王举行加冕典礼和王室成员结婚的场所。英国历代国王去世后，大部分葬在这里。威斯敏斯特教堂被称为"荣誉的宝塔尖"。

The Westminster Abbey (Figure 2-10), which means "the big church in the west", is located in the west of London. It was built in the 11th century by King Edwards who was named as "Confessor". Twin towers in the front feature the Church. Since it was established, it has been it has been the place where the kings or queens are crowned or the wedding ceremonies of the royal family are held. Kings of many dynasties were buried here. Westminster Abbey is also regarded as "the spire of the tower of glory".

7. 温莎古堡 Windsor Castle

温莎古堡（图 2-11）是世界上最著名、最古老的城堡之一，位于伦敦市郊 34 千米处的温莎小镇，始建于 1070 年。"不爱江山爱美人"的温莎公爵在此度过浪漫的蜜月。世人皆知的查尔斯王子和戴安娜王妃的婚姻也由此开始。如今，温莎古堡是重要的王室博物馆，收藏了王室的大部分文物和珍宝。古堡的大部分大厅均对外开放。

图 2-10　威斯敏斯特教堂
Figure 2-10　Westminster Abbey

Built in 1070 and located at the Windsor Town, 34 kilometers away from London, the Windsor Castle (Figure 2-11) is one of the largest and oldest castles in the world. Duke Windsor, who loved his wife more than the kingdom, spent his honeymoon here. The well-known marriage

图 2-11　温莎古堡
Figure 2-11　Windsor Castle

图 2-12　杜莎夫人蜡像馆
Figure 2-12　Madame Tussaud's
Wax Museum

between Prince Charles and Princess Diana also initiated here. Now the Castle is also an important royal museum. Most of the collections are royal artifacts and treasures. And most of the castle halls are open to the public.

8. 杜莎夫人蜡像馆 Madame Tussaud's Wax Museum

杜莎夫人蜡像馆（图 2-12）是位于英国伦敦的一间蜡像馆，其在阿姆斯特丹、纽约和拉斯维加斯等地都有分馆，中国的上海分馆也于 2006 年开幕。蜡像馆是由蜡制雕塑家杜莎夫人建立的。杜莎夫人蜡像馆是全世界水平最高的蜡像馆之一，有众多世界名人的蜡像，其中恐怖屋最为出名。

Madame Tussaud's Wax Museum (Figure 2-12) is a wax museum in London, UK. It has branches in Amsterdam, New York and Las Vegas, and its Shanghai branch in China was also opened in 2006. The wax museum was established by Madame Tussaud, a wax sculptor. Madame Tussaud wax museum is one of the highest level wax museums in the world. There are many wax statues of world celebrities, of which the horror house is the most famous.

（三）旅游购物 Shopping

红茶：英国红茶世界闻名。Whittard 是英国的一个经典茶饮品牌，从其诞生之时到现在一直为顾客带来品质最高的红茶，其一丝不苟的态度、对高品质产品的追求和与时俱进的创新精神成就了该品牌在英国茶界的百年好名声。

Black tea: British black tea is world famous. Whittard is a classic British tea brand that has been providing customers with the finest quality teas since its inception. Its meticulous attention to detail, commitment to high-quality products, and innovative spirit have earned Whittard a stellar reputation in the British tea industry for over a century.

羊绒制品：英国羊绒以绒山羊所产的绒毛为质量最好，是用特制的铁梳从山羊身体上抓取的绒毛，称为原绒。洗净的原绒经分梳，去除其中的粗毛、杂毛和皮屑后得到英国羊绒，称为无毛绒。用这些羊绒制成的围巾、服装等产品非常有名。

Cashmere products: British cashmere is renowned for the superior quality of the wool produced by cashmere goats. The raw wool, known as raw cashmere, is collected using special metal combs to gently gather the fibers from the goat's body. After washing, the raw cashmere undergoes a combing process to remove coarse hairs, impurities, and skin flakes, resulting in what is known as de-haired cashmere. Scarves, clothing, and other products made from this cashmere are highly acclaimed.

剑桥纪念品：来到剑桥，你怎么能不带些具有剑桥特色的纪念品回家呢？从印有剑桥大学字样的 T 恤、运动衫，到国王学院教堂模型，甚至还有徐志摩书签，相信无论是送人，还是放在家中作为摆设，都是一份美好的回忆。

Cambridge souvenirs: When you visit Cambridge, how can you resist taking home some souvenirs with Cambridge characteristics? From T-shirts and sweatshirts emblazoned with the University of Cambridge logo to models of King's College Chapel, and even Xu Zhimo bookmarks, these items make for wonderful gifts or cherished mementos to display at home.

泰迪熊：用于儿童玩耍的玩具熊。泰迪熊毛绒玩具历史悠久，深受孩子们的喜爱。近年来，一些泰迪熊变成了昂贵的收藏品。世界上第一个泰迪熊博物馆于 1984 年在英格兰的汉普郡彼得斯菲尔德建立。

扫码获取：入境须知及海关规定

Teddy bears:Teddy bearsare stuffed toy bears specially for children. With a long-standing history, teddy bears have been beloved by children for generations. In recent years, some teddy bears have become valuable collectibles. The world's first teddy bear museum was established in Petersfield, Hampshire, England, in 1984..

本节习题

1. 英国的西方礼仪和绅士风度表现在哪些方面？
2. 英国有哪些著名的城市和名胜古迹？
3. 请结合英国的代表性景点，设计 2 ～ 3 条旅游线路。

浪漫之都——法国
The Romantic Country—France

导读

法兰西民族在人类文明史上创造了令人艳美的成就，在世界文化的长卷上留下了浓墨重彩的一笔。一提到法国，人们就会想起闻名于世的建筑，如埃菲尔铁塔、凯旋门、巴黎圣母院，或精致讲究的美食，如鹅肝、牛排、葡萄酒，又或是蜚声世界的巨匠，如笛卡儿、卢梭、雨果、巴尔扎克……今天的法国不仅是联合国安理会五个常任理事国之一，而且是大西洋公约组织、欧洲联盟等国际组织的成员。法国是世界上经济最发达的国家之一，其工农业发达，尤其是在高铁、航天、核能等领域取得了世界领先的成就。法国也是第一个与中国建交的西方大国，中法两国高层互访日益频繁。法国是世界性旅游大国，也是最早发展旅游业的国家之一，全境有 30 处名胜古迹被联合国教科文组织确定为世界文化和自然遗产。

一、地理概览 Geography of France

（一）位置 Location

法国位于欧洲大陆西部，西临大西洋，西北隔多佛尔海峡、英吉利海峡与英国相望，南濒地中海，东与瑞士相依，东北毗邻比利时、卢森堡和德国，东南与意大利相连，西南与西班牙、安道尔接壤，是连通北欧、南欧、西欧、中欧的重要纽带。法国版图犹如六边形，三边临水，三边靠陆，距离英国的最短距离仅 33 千米，这 33 千米是连接英国和欧洲大陆的最短海道，因而成为国际重要航道。

France is located in the west of the Continental Europe. To the west is the Atlantic Ocean and the northwest is the Strait of Dover and English Channel which separates the UK from France. To its south is the Mediterranean. It connects with Switzerland to the east. It borders Belgium, Luxembourg and Germany to the northeast and Italy to the southeast. It links with Spain and Andorra to the southwest. It is the hub to connect Northern Europe, Southern Europe, Western Europe and Central Europe. The shape of France is like a hexagon. It faces the sea on its three sides and the continent on the other three sides. The narrowest distance of the channel between the UK and France is only 33 kilometers which is the shortest sea route connecting Britain and the European continent so it is the important international channel.

（二）地形和气候 The Land and Seasons

法国地势东南高、西北低。山地集中在东部和南部边境地带，有阿尔卑斯山脉、比利牛斯山脉、汝拉山脉等。南部地中海沿岸平原狭长、风景秀丽，是世界最重要的游览区。法意边境的勃朗峰是欧洲最高峰。地中海上的科西嘉岛是法国最大的岛屿。法国境内河流众多，主要河流有流入大西洋的卢瓦尔河、塞纳河和加龙河，以及流入地中海的罗讷河。

The terrain of France slopes from the southeast to the northwest. The mountains are concentrated in the eastern and the southern border. The main mountain ranges are Alps, Pyrenees Mountains and Jura Mountains. The plain along the Mediterranean is narrow and long but it is so beautiful that it becomes the most important international attraction. Mont Blancon the border between France and Italy is the peak of Europe. Corsica in the Mediterranean is the largest island of France. There are many rivers in France among which the major ones are the Loire, Seine and Garonne which empties into the Atlantic, and the Rhone which flows into the Mediterranean.

法国西部受西风影响较大，冬暖夏凉，年温差较小，终年湿润多雨，云雾多；东部和中部距海较远，属大陆性气候，特点为冬季较冷，年温差较大；南部属亚热带地中海气候，冬季温暖多雨，夏季炎热干燥。

Western France on the Atlantic is influenced by west wind. It is warm in winter and cool in summer. The temperature difference is small with humid, rainy and cloudy days all year round. The climate of the eastern and central France where is far from the sea is continental. It is cold in winter and the temperature throughout the year differs greatly. Southern France belongs to subtropical Mediterranean climate with mild, rainy winters and hot, dry summers.

（三）自然资源 Natural Resources

法国缺少能源，主要矿藏为铁矿，其次为铝矾土和钾盐矿。铁矿储藏量约 10 亿吨，但品位低、开采成本高，煤炭资源几近枯竭，所有铁矿、煤矿均已关闭，所需矿石完全依赖进口。有色金属储量很少，几乎全部依赖进口。能源主要依靠核能，约 78% 的电力靠核能提供。此外，水力和地热资源的开发利用比较充分。森林面积约 1 556.5 万公顷，覆盖率为 28.6%。

France faces a shortage of energy resources. Its primary mineral deposits are iron ore, followed by bauxite and potash. The iron ore reserves are approximately 1 billion tons, but they are of low grade and costly to extract. Coal reserves are nearly depleted, and all iron and coal mines have been shut down, making the country entirely reliant on imports for these ores. Non-ferrous metal reserves are scarce, with almost total dependency on imports. The country's energy needs are primarily met by nuclear power, which provides about 78% of its electricity. In addition, the development and utilization of hydroelectric and geothermal resources are quite advanced. France has a forest area of approximately 15.565 million hectares, with a coverage rate of 28.6%.

二、人文概况 Overview of French Humanities

（一）国情认知 Basic Knowledge of National Conditions

法国全称"法兰西共和国"，人口为 6 797.1 万（2022 年）。法国是以法兰西民族为主体的国家，法兰西人约占全国总人口的 82%，少数民族包括阿尔萨斯人、布列塔尼人、科西嘉人、弗拉芒人、嘉泰隆人和巴斯克人等，还有来自非洲和欧洲的外国移民。法国官方语言和通用语言均为法语，法语是联合国和国际会议的工作语言，使用人数超过 1 亿。法国居民中，64% 的人信奉天主教、3% 的人信奉伊斯兰教、3% 的人信奉基督教新教。

France is known as the "French Republic" and has a population of 67.971 million (2022). France is a predominantly French nation, with the French accounting for about 82% of the total population, and minorities such as Alsatians, Bretons, Corsicans, Flemish, Catalans and Basques, as well as foreign immigrants from Africa and Europe. France's official and lingua franca is French, which is the official language of the United Nations, the working language of international conferences, and is spoken by more than 100 million people. 64% percent of the French population is Catholic, 3% Islamic and 3% Protestant.

法国的国旗呈长方形，旗面由三个相等的竖长方形构成，从左到右分别是蓝色、白色、红色。三色旗曾是法国大革命的象征，代表自由、平等和博爱。国歌是《马赛曲》，国花是鸢尾花。

法国国花的来历

The flag of France is rectangular in shape and consists of three equal vertical rectangles, blue, white and red from left to right. The tricolor flag was once the symbol of the French Revolution, representing liberty, equality and fraternity. The national anthem is *La Marseillaise* and the national flower is iris.

（二）历史简介 History of France

公元前 1500 年到公元前 58 年，凯尔特人来到法国的中央高原及周围地区（即高卢地区）定居，并逐渐成为高卢人。公元前 58 年，恺撒赢得高卢战争胜利。罗马帝国在高卢建省，设立行政中心。罗马人统治高卢达 400 年，并将天主教带入高卢。罗马人在高卢推广拉丁语，并在此基础上形成了法语。

During the years from 1500 BC to 58 BC, the Celtics came to the central highland of France, i.e. Gaul, settled down and gradually became Gauls. Caesar won the Gaul war in 58 BC. The Roman Empire set up a province in Gaul and a political center was established. The Romans dominated the Gaul for 400 years and brought Christianity to the Gaul. French was formed on the base of Latin language the Romans brought to Gaul.

275 年，野蛮人（即日耳曼部落）开始入侵并定居高卢。481—751 年，其中的一个部落——法兰克人建立了墨洛温王朝，将高卢命名为法兰西，定都巴黎。768 年，查理曼大帝建立了加洛林王朝，在他统治期间，法国国土从波罗的海地区延伸到地中海地区，征服了西欧大部分地区，包括法国、德国和意大利。他死后，其孙子把帝国分成三部分，即今天的意大利、法国和德国。1066 年，征服者威廉一世征服英伦三岛，并建立诺曼底王朝，统治英格兰及法国西北部。15 世纪末到 16 世纪初，形成中央集权国家，17 世纪中叶，君主专制制度达到顶峰。最终，1789 年 7 月 14 日，法国爆发大革命，市民攻占巴士底狱。1792 年建立了法兰西第一共和国。

In the year of 275, the Barbarian, named as Germanic tribes, started to invade Gaul and settled down. Among them one of the tribes, Frank, established the Merovingian Dynasty during 481 and 751, and named Gaul as France and made Paris the capital. Charles the Great established Carolingian Dynasty in 768. The territory he conquered covered most parts of Western Europe from the Baltic Sea region to the Mediterranean including France, Germany and Italy. His grandsons divided the empire into three countries after he died, i.e. Italy, France and Germany. In 1066, William Ⅰ the Conqueror conquered England, established the Norman Dynasty and ruled England and Northwest France. In the late 15th and early 16th centuries, a centralized state was formed, and in the middle of the 17th century, the system of absolute monarchy reached its peak. Finally the revolution occurred on July 14, 1789 and the Bastille was taken over. The French First Republic was established in 1792.

1799 年 11 月 9 日，拿破仑·波拿巴发动政变，成为第一执政者。尽管他统治法国的时间不长，却对当时的世界产生了非常大的影响。1848 年爆发"二月革命"，共和党人掌握政权，建立了第二共和国。然后，1852 年，路易·拿破仑建立了法兰西第二帝国。1870 年，法国在普法战争中战败后，法兰西第二帝国解体，第三共和国建立。1871 年 3 月 18 日，巴黎建立了世界上第一个无产阶级政权——巴黎公社。

On November 9, 1799, Napoleon Bonaparte staged a coup and became the first Consul. Though he ruled the country for a very short time, he influenced the world greatly. The February Revolution occurred in 1848, while the bourgeois republican won the power and established the Second Republic. However, Louis Napoleon took the power and established the Second French Empire in 1852. In 1870 French declared war against Prussia. They were defeated in the war so that the Third Republic replaced the Second French Empire. On March 18, 1871, Paris established the world's first proletarian regime—the Paris Commune .

第一次世界大战期间，英法领导的协约国战胜德国并签订了《凡尔赛条约》，法国得到大笔赔款，促进了经济的恢复和发展。第二次世界大战期间，法国遭德国侵略，戴高乐将军在伦敦成立流亡政府领导抵抗运动。1944 年法国解放，1946 年成立第四共和国。1958 年第五共和国成立，戴高乐当选为第五共和国第一任总统。他设计并建立了强大的第五共和国的制度，这一制度能让人们通过投票来选出总统。法国从此开始了现代化的进程并获得了经济的持续发展。

During the First World War, the Allies led by France and the UK defeated Germany. After the *Treaty of Versailles* was signed, France won a huge amount of compensation which promoted the economy recovery and development. During the Second World War, when Germany occupied France, Charles de Gaulle set up a government in exile in London and led the people to fight against Germany. France was liberated in 1944 and the Fourth Republic was set up in 1946. In 1958, the Fifth Republic was established and de Gaulle became the first president. After de Gaulle took the power, he designed and established the strong system of executive power of the Fifth Republic. That is the system allowing people to choose their president by voting. France has begun its modernization since then and has gained continuous development of economy.

高卢雄鸡

（三）经济状况 The Economy

作为第二个完成第一次工业革命的国家，法国在 19 世纪末就已完成了资本的积累，经济实力一直排在世界前列，仅次于美国、中国、日本和德国。法国素有"西欧粮仓"之称，是欧盟最大的农业生产国，也是世界主要的农副产品出口国，粮食产量占全欧洲粮食产量的 1/3，农产品出口仅次于美国，居世界第二位。法国也是世界贸易大国，出口商品主要有机械、汽车、化工产品、钢铁、农产品、食品、服装、化妆品和军火等。法国葡萄酒享誉全球，酒类出口量占世界酒类出口总量的一半。法国时装、法国大餐、法国香水闻名遐迩。法国是个极具魅力的旅游大国，旅游业是法国经济的重要组成部分。风情万种的花都巴黎、美丽迷人的蓝色海岸、阿尔卑斯山的滑雪场等都吸引着来自世界各地的游客。

As the second country to complete the First Industrial Revolution, France had already accumulated capital by the end of the 19th century, maintaining a leading position in global economic strength, ranking just behind the United States, China, Japan, and Germany. France is considered as the "granary of Western Europe". France is the largest agricultural country of European Union and the world major exporting country of farm and subsidiary products. Its grain output makes up one third of that of Europe. And the exporting of agricultural products ranks the second of the world after the United States. France is also a major trading country. The major exporting products are mechanical products, automobiles, chemical products, iron and steel products, agricultural products, foods, garments, perfume and weapons. French wine is well-known in the world. The quantity of wine export is half of the world. France is also famous for its garments, cuisine and perfume. France is one of the largest charismatic tourist countries. The tourist industry is an important part of its economy. Visitors from all over the world are attracted to the exceedingly fascinating and charming city of Paris as well as the beautiful French Riviera and ski resorts in Alps, etc.

（四）传统文化 Traditional Culture

法国人十分注重礼仪、善于交际。对法国人来说，社交是人生的重要内容，没有社交活动的生活是难以想象的。法国人诙谐幽默、天性浪漫，在人际交往中大都热情、善良，爱高谈阔论，好开玩笑，讨厌不爱讲话的人，对愁眉苦脸者更是难以接受。在人际交往中，法国人的礼节主要有握手、拥抱、贴面和吻手。和不认识的人见面时，一般要说"你好"，并加上"女士""小姐""先生"等头衔，熟悉的人才称呼名字。初次见面可以握手，但通常是女士先伸手，年长者对年轻者先伸手，上级对下级先伸手。在交谈中不要询问对方的隐私，如收入、年龄、婚姻及宗教等。

French pay great attention to etiquette and are good at communication. They are characterized with sociability that is very important for their life. It is unbelievable if there is no social life. In interpersonal interactions, French are humorous and romantic. They are warm, kind and talkative. They don't like those who keep silent or always are in low spirits. French people in interpersonal etiquette are mainly taken to shake hands, hug, kiss the check and kiss the hand. When addressing a stranger, you should say "Bonjour"(Hello) and their title or first name if you are friends. The titles are Mademoiselle(Miss), Madame(Ms.) and Monsieur(Mr.). Shaking hands is a popular way to greet somebody, but remember that the lady will give the hand first, and so will the older to the young and the superior to the subordinate. When communicating with someone, it is important not to inquire about their private affairs such as income, age, marriage, religions, etc.

巴黎是时尚的代名词。这里有全世界最负盛名的服饰品牌，因此，法国被称为世界时尚中心。但法国人和其他欧洲人一样，讲究不同场合穿不同的服饰。在选择发型、手袋、帽子、鞋子、手表、眼镜时，都十分强调要与着装协调一致。

Paris is synonymous with fashion. It is home to some of the world's most prestigious clothing brands, which is why France is often called the fashion capital of the world. Like other Europeans, French pay great attention to dressing appropriately for different occasions. When choosing hairstyles, handbags, hats, shoes, watches, and glasses, they place a strong emphasis on ensuring everything is coordinated and harmonious with their outfit.

法国是欧洲的浪漫中心。受传统文化的影响，法国人不仅爱冒险，而且喜欢浪漫，他们渴望自由，纪律性不强。法国人被视为世界上最著名的"自由主义者"。"自由、平等、博爱"不仅被当作国家箴言写入宪法，而且在国徽上明文写出。法国人把生活中所做的每一件事都当作享受来看待，所以生活节奏缓慢。在法国，最先需要学会的就是"等待"和"约会"两个单词。

巴黎时装周

France is the epicenter of romance in Europe. Influenced by traditional culture, French are not only adventurous but also romantic, yearning for freedom and generally lacking in strict discipline. They are regarded as the world's most renowned "liberals". "Liberty, Equality, Fraternity" is not only enshrined in the constitution as the national motto but is also clearly inscribed on the national emblem. French approach everything they do as an opportunity for enjoyment, which results in a slower pace of life. In France, the first words you need to learn are "wait" and "make an appointment".

作为举世皆知的世界三大烹饪王国之一，法国的饮食文化有着悠久的历史和传统。法国菜不仅做起来复杂，强调色、香、形、味，而且吃起来很有讲究，从酒与菜的搭配、餐具和酒具的形状乃至服务员上菜、倒酒的方式都有严格的规定。法国人注重原材料的新鲜和口味的纯正。法国菜选料广泛，但法国人偏好牛肉、海鲜、蔬菜等，特别是蜗牛、松露、蘑菇、龙虾、鹅肝、鱼子酱；在配料方面，酒、橄榄油、鲜奶油及各式香料是他们的最爱。一顿标准法式大餐的上菜顺序为冷盘菜、汤类、主菜和甜品。第一道菜是冷盘菜，一般是沙丁鱼、火腿、奶酪、鹅肝酱和沙拉等，用于开胃。第二道菜是汤类，汤大致为清汤、蔬菜汤、肉汤或海鲜汤，一般要配面包一起食用。第三道菜是主菜；鱼类包括淡海水鱼、贝类及软体动物类；肉类有牛羊肉、家禽等，其中牛排是常见的主菜；常用的烹调方式有烤、煎、铁扒等。享用完主菜后，便到甜品了。法国人爱好甜食是出了名的，蛋糕、冰激凌、馅饼、酥饼、布丁等，种类口味多样。饭前一般要喝度数不高的甜酒，习惯称之为"开胃酒"；吃饭时要喝不带甜味的葡萄酒或玫瑰酒；吃肉时一般喝红葡萄酒；吃海鲜时喝白葡萄酒或玫瑰酒；饭后要喝一点儿带甜味的"消化酒"；每逢宴请还要喝香槟酒，以增加席间欢乐的气氛。法国的葡萄酒、香槟和白兰地享誉全球。

As one of the three countries with famous cuisine, the cuisine culture of France has a long history and tradition. French cuisine is not only complicated in color, smell, shape and taste but also has a strict process on table. They will match wine with the dishes, tableware with wine glass, and even the way for the waiters to serve the dishes or fill up the glass. They pay much attention to the freshness of ingredients and the originality of the taste. The material is various but they prefer beef poultry, seafood and vegetables, especially escargot, truffle (fungus), mushrooms, lobster, foie gras and caviar; and the condiments such as wine, olive oil, fresh cream and various spices. The standard order for French dinner will be cold dish, soup, main course and desserts. First course is cold dish, usually sardines, ham, cheese, foie gras and salad for an appetizer. Second course is soup which can be clear soup, vegetable soup, meat soup, or seafood soup, usually with bread. Third course is the main course including fresh or salty water fish, shellfish or mollusks and meat like beef mutton and poultry. Normally beef is the main course that is usually toasted, grilled or mushed. After the main course it is dessert time. French are famously fond of sweets, with a wide variety of cakes, ice creams, pies, pastries, and puddings available. Before meals, it is customary to drink a low-alcohol sweet wine known as an "aperitif". During meals, non-sweet wines or rose wines are served; red wine is typically paired with meat, while white wine or rose is paired with seafood. After meals, a sweet "digestif" is often enjoyed. During special occasions, champagne is served to enhance the festive atmosphere. French wine, champagne, and brandy are celebrated worldwide.

法国的咖啡文化

（五）礼仪禁忌 Social Etiquettes and Taboos

法国女性在家庭和社会中的地位很高。有这样的说法：在法国家庭中，女人排在第一位，狗排在第二位，孩子排在第三位，男人排在最末位。这句话虽带有调侃的成分，但是能很好地反映女人和狗在法国的地位。法国的男人非常尊重女人，"骑士风度"是法国人引以为豪的传统。无论在何处走路、进屋、入座，都要让女士先行；介绍两人认识时，若职务相等，先介绍女士；同她们握手时，一定要等其先伸手，女士可戴着手套，而男士一定要脱掉手套。

In France, women hold a very high status both in the family and in society. It is often said that in the family hierarchy, the woman comes first, followed by the dog, the child, and finally the man. Although this is meant humorously, it does reflect the perceived status of women and even pets. French men always show respect to women and take pride in their "chivalrous conduct". When walking, entering a building, or taking a seat, ladies go first. When introducing people of equal standing, ladies should be introduced first. During a handshake, ladies should extend their hand first. Women are allowed to wear gloves while shaking hands, but men are expected to take them off.

一般不宜随意送给法国人菊花、玫瑰、水仙花、金盏花等。法国人把每一种花都赋予了一定的含义，所以送花时要格外注意。送花的枝数不能是双数，菊花是表示对死者的哀悼，红玫瑰象征爱情，水仙花表示冷酷无情，金盏花表示悲伤。

　　Chrysanthemum, rose, daffodil and marigolds should not be chosen as gifts for French. The French give meanings to every kind of flowers. People must be careful when they send flowers to French. The number of branches of flowers should not be an even number. Chrysanthemum is for funeral, red rose for love, daffodil means grim and cold-hearted and marigold means sorrow.

　　法国人认为鲜艳的色彩即高贵。他们认为马是勇敢的象征，认为蓝色是宁静和忠诚的标志，粉红色是积极向上的标志。法国人忌讳胡桃色，厌恶墨绿色，忌用黑桃图案，商标上忌用菊花。法国人还视孔雀为恶鸟，并忌讳仙鹤（认为它是愚蠢的象征）、乌龟，而且认为杜鹃花、纸花不吉利。

　　French regard bright colors as nobility. They regard the horse as the symbol of bravery. They think blue color is the symbol of peace and faithfulness and pink is the symbol of positiveness. They don't like walnuts and hate greenish black and spade pattern. Chrysanthemum should not be used as trade marks. Peacocks are regarded as bad birds. They don't like cranes (which are the symbol of foolishness) and turtles. They regard azaleas and paper flowers as unlucky symbols.

　　在人际交往中，法国人对礼物十分看重，对其有特别的讲究。客人宜选择具有艺术品位和纪念意义的物品，不宜选择刀、剑、剪刀、餐具或带有明显广告标志的物品。在接受礼物时，主人若不当着客人的面打开包装，则是一种无礼的表现。如果初次见面就送礼，法国人会认为你不善交际，甚至认为你粗俗。法国人重视情意的表达。例如，在亲友家做客后总要即时写一封措辞美好的感谢信；到远方旅游时不忘给亲朋好友寄张明信片；旅行回来时总要带点小礼物分赠亲友。

　　In social interactions, French place great importance on gifts, but they have specific preferences. Gifts should be artistically tasteful or meaningful which should not be knives, swords, scissors, tableware or articles with commercial marks. It is considered impolite if the host does not open the gift in front of the guest. Gifts are not appropriate at the first meeting. Otherwise you will be regarded as gauche or even vulgar. French will always show their affection. For example, they will write a thank-you letter, and they will send a card to their friends or relatives during their journey and bring some souvenirs to them when they are returning home.

（六）传统节日 Festivals

1. 国庆节 National Day

　　国庆节在 7 月 14 日，是法国最隆重的节日。1789 年 7 月 14 日，巴黎人民攻占了象征封建统治的巴士底狱，推翻了君主政权。1880 年 7 月 14 日被正式确定为法国的国庆日，法国人每年都要隆重纪念这个象征自由和革命的日子。为庆祝国庆节，法国每年都要在香榭丽舍大街上举行大规模的阅兵仪式，总统会发表演讲并颁发奖章，夜间会燃放五彩缤纷的烟花。

　　National Day falls on July 14 and is the most important public holiday. On July 14, 1789, people of Paris occupied Bastille, which was the symbol of feudal reign, and ended the monarchy. July 14 was announced officially as National Day in 1880. French celebrate this important day which means freedom and revolution every year. A series of celebrations will be held in the Avenue des

Champs-Elysees. There will be a review of troops and the French president will deliver a speech and award prizes. In the evening fireworks will be displayed.

2. 诸圣节 All Saints' Day

11 月 1 日是诸圣节，亦称"诸圣瞻礼"，是基督教节日之一。在诸圣节，全国放假一天。法国的民间习惯是在这一天到墓地去祭奠、凭吊已故的亲人，相当于中国的清明节。

November 1st is All Saints' Day, also known as the Feast of All Saints, which is a Christian holiday. It is a public holiday in many countries. In France, it is customary for people to visit cemeteries on this day to pay their respects and commemorate deceased loved ones, similar to the Qingming Festival in China.

三、旅游观光 Tourism and Sightseeing

（一）主要旅游城市 Major Tourist Cities

1. 巴黎 Paris

巴黎是法国的首都，位于法国北部盆地中央，跨塞纳河两岸，故又被称为"塞纳河的女儿"。巴黎是欧洲最大的城市，是时尚流行、文明、艺术和文化的代名词，被称为"世界花都""时装之都""香水之都"。有人曾这样评价巴黎："鲜活的建筑史教科书，生动的法国编年史。"作为欧洲一流的旅游名城、浪漫之都，这座有着 2 000 多年历史的文化名城从 12 世纪起就一直是历代王朝的首都，拥有许多世界闻名的历史名胜与建筑。塞纳河把巴黎一分为二，习惯上称为右岸和左岸。对于巴黎人来说，右岸代表着贸易和商业、国家级文物古迹和高级时装店，左岸则是以知名大学和咖啡馆而闻名。巴黎的主要景点都集中在塞纳河的两岸。巴黎的历史中轴线是一条从市中心笔直向西延伸的直线，东端开始于罗浮宫，然后经过杜伊勒里花园、协和广场、香榭丽舍大街，到达戴高乐广场中央的凯旋门。

Paris, the capital of France, is located in the center of the northern French basin, straddling both banks of the Seine River, which is why it is often referred to as the "Daughter of the Seine". As the largest city in Europe, Paris is synonymous with fashion trends, culture, art, and intellectual pursuits, earning it titles such as the "City of Light", the "Fashion Capital", and the "Perfume Capital". It has been described as a "living textbook of architectural history" and a "vivid chronicle of France". As a premier tourist destination and the romantic capital of Europe, this cultural city with over 2,000 years of history has been the capital of successive dynasties since the 12th century, boasting numerous world-renowned historical landmarks and artistic buildings. Paris is divided into right bank and left bank by Seine. The representatives of right bank are trade and commerce, national monuments and fashion. The left bank, for Parisians, is famous for its well-known universities and cafes. The major attractions of the city are along Seine. The historical principle axis is the line from the city center to the west along which there are lots of historical relics. The important attractions from the starting of the line from the east to the west are the Louvre, Tuileries Garden, Place de La Concorde, the Avenue des Champs-Elysees, and Arc de Triomphe at the Place Charles de Gaulle.

2. 马赛 Marseille

法国南部的尼斯、戛纳、马赛地区被称为"蓝色海岸"。马赛是法国最大的港口和第二大城市，也是仅次于鹿特丹的欧洲第二大港口，位于法国南部地中海利翁湾东岸，是普罗旺斯

图 2-13　马赛港口
Figure 2-13　Marseille Port

的首府，法国南部的行政、经济、文化和交通中心（图 2-13）。著名的《马赛曲》（现为法国国歌）即诞生于此。同时，马赛还是几千年来东方货物进入西方世界的要道，所以马赛城弥漫着混杂的异国气息。马赛是法国最古老的城市之一，建于公元前 6 世纪的古希腊时代，已有 2 600 年的历史。马赛拥有众多的文物古迹，距马赛老港口 3 000 米处有一座 16 世纪建造的要塞——伊夫堡，传说是大仲马《基督山伯爵》一书中主人公被囚禁的地方，每年吸引着成千上万的旅游者来此参观。

Nice, Cannes and Marseille are known as "Côte d'Azur" (Blue Coast) in the southern France. Located along the east bank of the Gulf of Lion of Mediterranean in the south of France, Marseille, the capital of Provence, is the largest port and the second largest city in France, and the second largest port in Europe (after Rotterdam) (Figure 2-13), and the center of politics, economy, culture and transportation in southern France. The well-known song *Le Marseillaise*, now the National Anthem of France, was sung here for the first time. It has been one of the most important cities for the Eastern goods to be imported to the Western countries since several thousand years ago, so the city is mixed with various exotic tastes. Marseille, founded in the 6th century BC by Greek as one of the oldest cities in France, has a history of 2,600 years. Lots of historic relics can be found here. Château d'If, 3 kilometers away from the old port, is an important fortress built in the 16th century which was said to have been the place where the hero in *The Count of Monte Cristo* by Dumas was imprisoned. Thousands of tourists visit here every year.

图 2-14　尼斯海岸
Figure 2-14　Nice Coast or Côte d'Azur

3. 尼斯 Nice

尼斯是位于地中海沿岸的法国南部城市，距巴黎 933 千米，是"蓝色海岸"地区的首府，是法国仅次于巴黎的第二大旅游胜地，也是全欧洲最具魅力的黄金海岸（图 2-14）。尼斯是欧洲的首选度假地。在地理上，尼斯三面环山，一面临海，有着 7 500 米长的海岸线。群山的阻拦，使尼斯免受寒冷的北风侵凌，冬暖夏凉。尼斯以其全年温和的地中海气候、灿烂的阳光、绵延的海滩，以及晒太阳的美女而闻名。尼斯被人称为"世界富豪聚集的中心"。海边的豪华别墅、比比皆是的奢侈品店和艺术气息的交织形成了尼斯独特的富丽堂皇与典雅优美。尼斯狂欢节是法国最有名的节日之一，也是世界最著名、最盛大的狂欢节之一，创办于 1873 年，最精彩的是花车游行、烛光游行和奇装异服表演。

Located on the bank of Mediterranean in the southern France, Nice, the capital of the Côte d'Azur department, 933 kilometers away from Paris, is the second tourist city after Paris in France and also the most attractive golden beach in Europe (Figure 2-14). The city is among the first option for holiday in Europe. Geographically, Nice is open to the sea on one side and surrounded on three sides by mountains so that the cold air from the north can not enter, and the weather here is warm in winter and cool in summer. It has a coastline of 7,500 meters. With the mild Mediterranean climate all year round, Nice is noted for bright sunny days, long beaches and lots of beauties in sunbath and it is referred to as "the world center of the riches". Nice has its unique beauty because the luxury villas along the seashore and the lavish brand shops are mixed with the taste of art. The Carnival de Nice, started in 1873, is one of the most famous festivals in France, and one of the most well-known and biggest carnivals in the world. The most fascinating shows are flower floats parade, candle-lit parade and fancy fashion show.

4. 戛纳 Cannes

戛纳是欧洲有名的旅游胜地和每年戛纳名流的社交集会场所，因逐年举办的戛纳电影节而闻名于世。戛纳位于法国南部地中海沿岸，距尼斯约 26 千米，拥有世界上最洁白、漂亮的海滩。这里气候温和、阳光普照、海水蔚蓝，来自世界各地的游艇汇集于此，主要景点有海滨大道、老城区、建造于 11 世纪的城堡等。戛纳是世界级的影都，著名的戛纳电影节被誉为"电影界的奥运会"。该电影节颁发的金棕榈大奖被公认为电影界的最高荣誉之一。

Cannes is a well-known tourist city in Europe and a venue for the world celebrities to have social gatherings. It is famous for its annual Cannes Film Festival. Located on the coast of Mediterranean in the southern France, Cannes, about 26 kilometers away from Nice, has the clearest and most beautiful beaches in the world. With the mild climate and sunny days, the sea is blue and Cannes is full of yachts from all over the world. The main attractions are seashore avenue, old city, the castle of the 11th century, etc. Cannes is a world-class capital of films. The Cannes Film Festival held in May every year is honored as the "The Olympics of the Movie World". The most prestigious award given out at Cannes is the Palme d'Or, one of the highest honors in the film industry.

（二）著名旅游景点 Famous Tourist Attractions

1. 巴黎圣母院 Notre-Dame de Paris

巴黎圣母院（图 2-15）始建于 1163 年，坐落在塞纳河中间的西岱岛上，被称为"法国最伟大的艺术杰作"，与卢浮宫、埃菲尔铁塔并称为巴黎三大旅游热点。巴黎圣母院以其哥特式的完美建筑、正门的"玫瑰玻璃窗"和悠久的历史而著称。1804 年 12 月 2 日，拿破仑在此举行盛大的加冕仪式。1996 年，百余国特使在此为已故法国总统密特朗举行安魂弥撒。圣母院广场的零起点是法国丈量全国各地里程时所使用的起测点。

图 2-15　巴黎圣母院
Figure 2-15　Notre-Dame de Paris

Notre-Dame de Paris (Figure 2-15) was built in 1163, situated on the island of Sidai, in the middle of the Seine. Regarded as "France's greatest masterpieces of art", Notre-Dame de Paris is one of the top three tourist attractions in Paris. The other two are the Louvre and the Eiffel Tower. It is a piece of Gothic architectural perfection with the typical rose windows above the portal and represents the history of France. Napoleon crowned himself here on December. 2, 1804. Hundreds of special envoys came here to hold Requiem for the late French president Mitterrand mass in 1996. The Notre-Dame de Paris is the zero point from which the nationwide survey on mileage starts.

图 2-16　卢浮宫

Figure 2-16　The Louvre

2. 卢浮宫 The Louvre

卢浮宫（图 2-16）是世界上最大的美术博物馆，位于巴黎市中心塞纳河右岸。卢浮宫始建于 1204 年，是法国最大的王宫建筑之一，展现了法国文艺复兴时期建筑的特点和成就。卢浮宫正门入口处的透明金字塔建筑是美籍华裔建筑师贝聿铭的杰作。馆内收藏了大量 17 世纪及欧洲文艺复兴时期艺术家的作品，总数接近 40 万件。卢浮宫美术博物馆分为 6 大部分：希腊和罗马艺术馆、东方艺术馆、埃及艺术馆、欧洲中世纪艺术馆、文艺复兴时期和现代雕像馆、历代绘画馆。里程碑式的艺术经典都汇集在这里，名画《蒙娜丽莎》及雕塑《爱神维纳斯》《萨莫特拉斯的胜利女神》是著名的宫中三宝。

The Louvre (Figure 2-16) is the largest art museum in the world, located on the right bank of Seine of the centre of Paris. It is one of the largest palace architectures in France, which was built in 1204 and shows the features and achievements of French Renaissance architecture. In front of the entrance, there is a glass pyramid designed by L. M. Pei, the Chinese-American architect master. The museum has a large collection of works nearly 400,000 items during the 17th century and the Renaissance. The Louvre art museum is divided into 6 departments including Museum of Greek and Roman Art, Museum of Oriental Art, Museum of Egyptian Art, Museum of the Middle Ages Art, the Renaissance and modern sculpture and all previous dynasties painting pavilion. It is home to many iconic masterpieces, including the famous painting *Mona Lisa* and the sculptures *Venus de Miloand*, *Winged Victory of Samothrace*, which are known as the museum's three treasures.

图 2-17　协和广场

Figure 2-17　Place de la Concorde

3. 协和广场 Place de la Concorde

协和广场（图 2-17）是位于塞纳河右岸、香榭丽舍大街东端的一个八角形大广场，是法国最著名的广场和世界上最美丽的广场之一。协和广场始建于 1757 年，它的设计者为著名建筑师卡布里埃尔。因广场中心曾有路易十五的骑像而被命名为"路易十五广场"。1763 年法国大革命时期又被改名为"革命广场"。1795 年又将其改称为"协和广场"。协和广场中央矗立着一尊 23 米高、有 3 400 年历史的著名的巨大埃及方尖碑，这是路易·菲利普于 1831 年从埃及卢克索移来的著名文物。

Located on the right bank of the Seine, a large octagonal square at the eastern end of the Avenue des Champs-Elysees, Place de la Concorde (Figure 2-17) is France's most famous square and one of the world's most beautiful squares. The square was built in 1757. Its designer is renowned architect Ange-Jacques Gabriel. There used to be a statue of Louis XV of France in the center of the square, so it was named "Place Louis XV". In 1763, during the French Revolution, the square was called Place de la Revolution. The square was given the current name, Place de la Concorde in 1795. The famous relic in the center is the giant Egyptian obelisk with a height of 23 meters and a history of 3 400 years which was moved from Luxor of Egypt by Louis Philippe in 1831.

4. 香榭丽舍大街 Avenue of Champs-Elysees

香榭丽舍大街（图 2-18）起始于协和广场，终止于凯旋门，全长约 1 800 米，是巴黎最漂亮、最著名的街道。在法文中，"香榭丽舍"是"田园乐土"的意思。香榭丽舍大街齐聚了巴黎最繁华的百货公司、时装店、咖啡馆等。同时，它还是法国许多重大节庆典礼的庆祝中心，如每年 7 月 14 日的国庆阅兵式、新年联欢活动都在这条著名的街道上举行。

图 2-18 香榭丽舍大街
Figure 2-18 Avenue of Champs-Elysees

Starting from the Place de la Concorde to the Arc de Triomphe with a length of 1,800 meters, the Avenue of Champs-Elysees (Figure 2-18) is the most beautiful and famous among the Paris streets. The meaning of Champs-Elysees is "idyllic paradise" in French. The Avenue of Champs-Elysees is bordered by the most prosperous department stores, boutiques, cafes and so on. It is also France's major festivals ceremony center, for example, the National Day military parade on July 14 of each year and the New Year celebrations.

5. 凯旋门 Arc de Triomphe

作为巴黎的三大地标之一，凯旋门（图 2-19）坐落在巴黎市中心戴高乐广场的中央，是法国为纪念拿破仑 1806 年在奥斯特里茨战役中打败俄奥联军而建的。凯旋门建成于 1836 年，高 50 米，宽 45 米，是世界上最大的凯旋门。凯旋门的每一道外墙上都有巨幅浮雕，其中最著名也是最精美的一幅就是右侧石柱上的《马赛曲》浮雕。门前有建于 1920 年的无名战士墓地，墓前火炬常年不灭。

图 2-19 凯旋门
Figure 2-19 Arc de Triomphe

As one of the three landmarks of Paris, located in the center of Place Charles de Gaulle in the heart of Paris, Arc de Triomphe (Figure 2-19) was built to commemorate Napoleon's victory over the Russian and Austrian armies in the Battle of Austerlitz in 1806 and was completed in 1836. The Arc is 50 meters high and 45 meters wide. It is the world's largest triumphal arch. Each exterior wall of the Arc de Triomphe has a huge relief, of which the most famous and the most beautiful one is on the right side of the pillars of *La Marseillaise* relief. The ground of the center is tomb of the unknown soldiers built in 1920, with a torch in front of the grave that burns perpetually.

6. 埃菲尔铁塔 Eiffel Tower

埃菲尔铁塔（图 2-20）位于巴黎市中心塞纳河南岸，是世界上第一座钢铁结构的高塔，

图 2-20　埃菲尔铁塔
Figure 2-20　Eiffel Tower

也是巴黎的最高建筑物和游览中心，被视为巴黎的象征。1889 年，世界万国博览会在法国巴黎举行，同年也是法国大革命改革一百周年的纪念。为纪念这一特殊日子，法国著名建筑师斯塔夫·埃菲尔设计了铁塔，铁塔也由此而得名。塔高 320 米，塔身重达 9 000 吨，分为 3 层。埃菲尔铁塔是巴黎最易识别的标志。

Located on the south bank of Seine in the heart of Paris, Eiffel Tower (Figure 2-20) is the first steel structure of the tower in the world. It is also the highest building in Paris and tourist center. It is regarded as the symbol of Paris. It was built in 1889 in memory of the 100th anniversary of France Revolution and for the Exposition Universal. The designer was engineer Stave Eiffel and it was named after him. The three-story tower is 320 meters high and 9,000 tons in weight. It is the most recognizable symbol of Paris.

图 2-21　凡尔赛宫
Figure 2-21　Palace of Versailles

7. 凡尔赛宫 Palace of Versailles

凡尔赛宫（图 2-21）位于巴黎西南郊的凡尔赛镇，是欧洲最富丽堂皇的皇家宫苑，也是西方古典主义建筑的代表作。它是 17 世纪专制王权的象征，路易十四、路易十五和路易十六三代帝王都曾在这里生活居住。许多举世瞩目的大事也在此发生。1980 年，被联合国教科文组织列入《世界遗产名录》。

Located at the Versailles town in the southwest of Paris, Palace of Versailles (Figure 2-21) is the most magnificent palace in Europe. It is the representative work of western classic architecture. It is the symbol of the king of autocracy in the 17th century. King Louis XIV, XV and XVI had spent their lives here. Many remarkable events had happened here. It was inscribed on the World Heritage List by UNESCO in 1980.

（三）旅游购物 Shopping

时装：高级时装是法国服装的精华，每件时装都犹如一件艺术作品。在巴黎，每年都会举行巴黎春夏时装周和巴黎秋冬时装周。这是世界上最受瞩目的时装盛会，引领着全世界的服装潮流，影响着人们关于流行的观念。著名设计师圣·洛朗、香奈儿和克里斯汀·迪奥并称法国时装界"三圣"。

Fashion: Superior fashion is the essence of French garments, which is just like works of art. Every year in Paris, there will be Paris Fashion Week with Spring/Summer and Autumn/Winter events which are well-known all over the world leading the world's fashion trend and affecting people's idea of fashion. The well-known three designers, Saint Laurent, Chanel and Christian Dior are considered as "Three Saints" of French fashion.

香水：法国香水及化妆品举世闻名。香水、时装和葡萄酒并列为法国三大精品产业，是法国人的骄傲。法国香水是全球女性的挚爱，巴黎商店里琳琅满目的香水大都是由被誉为"香水之都"的格拉斯生产或提供原料的。在法国，香水业与时装业的结合是一种很有意思的文化现象。1925 年，香奈儿公司推出了"香奈儿 5 号"香水，在世界范围内获得了认可，被视为法国香水发展史上的里程碑。至今，各名牌时装公司几乎都保留了自己牌号的香水。

Perfume: Both French perfume and cosmetics are well-known all over the world. Perfume, fashion and wine are listed as the three leading boutique industries, of which French feel proud. French perfume is the women's favorite in the world. In fact, most of the fragrances in Parisian shops are produced or supplied with raw materials from Grasse. Which is known as "the capital of perfume" In France, it is a meaningful cultural phenomenon to combine perfume industry with fashion industry. In 1925, Chanel launched Chanel No. 5 perfume and was accepted all over the world. It was regarded as the milestone of the French perfume history. Up to now all the fashion companies have their own brand repertoires of perfume.

香水之都——
格拉斯

葡萄酒：自从古代英勇无畏的水手把葡萄藤从尼罗河的山谷和克里特岛带到希腊、西西里和意大利南部，再由此传入法国之后，葡萄的种植和酿酒技术便在法国被一代又一代人改良、提升和发扬光大。葡萄酒文化不仅表现了法兰西民族对精致美好生活的追求，而且是法国文明和文化不可分割的一个重要组成部分。波尔多玛格丽红葡萄酒享誉世界，有"法国葡萄酒皇后"的美称。波尔多是公认的世界最大的葡萄酒产地。

Red wine: After the brave sailors brought the grapevine branch from Nile valleys and Crete to Greece, Sicily and southern Italy and then to France, the technology of vines cultivation and wine brewing has been improved, promoted and carried forward in France by generation after generation. The wine culture shows not only the French pursuit of good life but also the integral part of the French civilization and culture. Margery red wine in Bordeaux is known throughout the world and is rated as "the queen of French wine". Bordeaux is recognized as the largest wine producing area in the world.

芝士：法国出产近 400 种芝士，花样繁多、各具风味，是世界上芝士品种最多的国家。法国芝士有牛奶、绵羊奶、山羊奶或混合奶制成的不同品种。法国各地都有地道的芝士产品，其制法历史悠久、源远流长。

Cheese: France produces nearly 400 types of cheese, each with its own unique flavor and variety, making it the country with the most cheese varieties in the world. French cheeses are made from cow's milk, sheep's milk, goat's milk, or a combination of these. Each region of France has its own authentic cheese products, with a long history and a rich tradition of production methods.

扫码获取：入
境须知及海关
规定

本节习题

1. 法国的地形与气候有什么特点？
2. 法国历史上有哪些著名的文学艺术大师？
3. 法国有哪些著名的名胜古迹？
4. 请设计一条 7 日经典法国旅游线路。

第三节　东欧之旅
Travel in Eastern Europe

冰雪之国——俄罗斯
The Land of Ice and Snow—Russia

导读

> 俄罗斯是世界上国土面积最大的国家，其东南与中国接壤，是中国最大的邻国，有历史悠久的克里姆林宫、红场等名胜古迹，拥有彼得大帝、列宁、斯大林等政治家，普希金、柴可夫斯基等文学、作曲家，经历了两次世界大战、冷战、苏联解体之殇，有战斗民族之称。1949 年 10 月 2 日，中国与苏联建交。苏联解体后，1991 年 12 月 27 日，中、俄两国在莫斯科签署《会谈纪要》，解决了两国关系的继承问题。1998 年 11 月，中、俄两国在莫斯科发表了《关于世纪之交的中俄关系的联合声明》，两国间的经贸往来和文化交流日渐频繁，双边关系在历经正常化、建设性伙伴关系、战略伙伴关系、全面战略伙伴关系的层次递升后，目前已进入一个新的发展阶段。

一、地理概览 Geography of Russia

（一）位置 Location

俄罗斯联邦，简称俄罗斯，位于欧洲东部和亚洲大陆北部，其欧洲领土的大部分是东欧平原。俄罗斯与挪威、芬兰、爱沙尼亚、拉脱维亚、立陶宛、波兰、白俄罗斯、乌克兰、格鲁吉亚、阿塞拜疆、哈萨克斯坦、中国、蒙古、朝鲜接壤，与日本、美国、加拿大、格陵兰岛、冰岛、瑞典隔海相望。俄罗斯绵延的海岸线从北冰洋一直延伸到北太平洋，还包括内陆海黑海和里海。俄罗斯是世界上国土面积最大的国家，亦是世界第二大军事强国。

Russia, officially known as the Russian Federation, is a country in Eastern Europe and Northern Asia. Most of Russian territories are in East European Plain. Russia shares borders with Norway, Finland, Estonia, Latvia, Lithuania, Poland, Belarus, Ukraine, Georgia, Azerbaijan, Kazakhstan, China, Mongolia and DPRK. It also has maritime borders with Japan, the United States, Canada, Greenland, Iceland and Sweden. Its extensive coast stretches from the Arctic Ocean to North Pacific Ocean, including the Black Sea and Caspian Sea. Russia is the largest country and the second military power in the world.

（二）地形和气候 The Land and Seasons

俄罗斯的大部分地区为平原，山脉集中在俄罗斯南部和太平洋沿岸，乌拉尔山脉是欧洲和亚洲的分界线。俄罗斯境内的主要河流包括欧洲第一长河——伏尔加河（全长 3 685 千米，是俄罗斯的母亲河）、鄂毕河、叶尼塞河、勒拿河及阿穆尔河（即黑龙江）。主要湖泊有贝加尔湖（世界上最深的淡水湖）等。俄罗斯幅员辽阔，纬度较高，国土跨寒带、亚寒带和温带三个气候带。俄罗斯大部分地区处于北温带和北寒带。气候以大陆性气候为主，冬季严寒漫长。俄罗斯冬季全境几乎都降雪，积雪期和积雪的厚度随纬度增高而增加，冰雪旅游资源丰富。黑海沿岸一带为地中海气候，最大的海滨疗养胜地索契坐落在黑海之滨；西伯利亚地区十分寒冷，奥伊米亚康被称为"北半球的寒极"（在这里记录了有人居住地区的最低温度：-71.2 ℃），对敢于冒险的旅游者有极大的吸引力。

Most area in Russia is plain. In the south and along the Pacific Ocean are some mountain ranges and among which Ural Mountains divide Europe from Asia. The major rivers in Russia include the longest river in Europe—Volga River（3,685 kilometers，the mother river of Russia），Ob River，Yenisei River，Lena River and Amur River（Heilong Jiang in China）. The major lakes include Lake Baikal（the world's deepest fresh water lake）and so on. The enormous territory size of Russia and the high latitude result in the country in three climate zones—Frigid Zone，Sub-frigid Zone and Temperate Zone. Most of its territory is in the North Temperate Zone and North Frigid Zone. Its main climate is dominant by continental climate with a long term of winter. Almost all of Russia's winter is covered with snow，and the snow cover period and thickness increase with increasing dimensions. There are abundant ice and snow tourist resources. The Black Sea coast has a Mediterranean climate，and the largest seaside resort，Sochi，is located on the shores of the Black Sea. The Siberian region is extremely cold，and Oimiakon is known as the "cold pole of the Northern Hemisphere"（It was here that the lowest ever temperature in an inhabited place was recorded：-71.2℃），which has a great attraction to adventurous tourists.

（三）自然资源 Natural Resources

俄罗斯具有丰富的矿产、森林和水力资源，自然资源的自给程度高。在矿产资源中，煤、铁、石油、天然气、有色金属等储量居世界前列。库兹巴斯的煤、库尔斯克的铁、西西伯利亚的秋明油田，都很有名。俄罗斯的森林面积约占其国土面积的1/3，西伯利亚大部分地区、东欧平原北部都有大片的针叶林，是俄罗斯的森林宝库和木材基地。水力资源主要分布在东部地区，特别是东西伯利亚地区。

Russia has abundant mineral，forest，and hydraulic resources，with a high degree of self-sufficiency in natural resources. Among the mineral resources，the reserves of coal，iron，oil，natural gas，nonferrous metals，etc. rank among the top in the world. Kuzbas is famous for its coal，Kursk's iron，and the Qiuming oil field in Western Siberia. The forest area of Russia accounts for about 1/3 of its land area. Most of Siberia and the northern East European Plain are distributed with large areas of coniferous forest，which is Russia's forest treasure house and timber base. Water resources are mainly distributed in the east，especially in Eastern Siberia.

二、人文概况 Overview of Russia's Humanities

（一）国情认知 Basic Knowledge of National Conditions

俄罗斯人口为1.44亿（2022年），首都为莫斯科，官方语言为俄语。俄罗斯有194个民族，其中俄罗斯族占77.7%。主要少数民族为鞑靼、巴什基尔、车臣、楚瓦什、亚美尼亚、乌克兰、达吉斯坦、哈萨克、阿塞拜疆和白俄罗斯等。全国约有 130 种语言，俄语是俄罗斯的官方语言，属于印欧语系，全国 89% 的居民会讲俄语，6.8% 的居民讲阿尔泰语系语言，2.4% 的居民讲高加索语系语言，1.8% 的居民讲乌拉尔语系语言。俄罗斯 55% 的居民信奉宗教，主要宗教为东正教，其次为伊斯兰教。

Russia has a population of 144 million（2022）. The capital is Moscow. The official language is Russian. It has 194 nationalities. 77.7% of the population is Russian and the main minorities are Tatars, Bashkirs, Chechens, Chuvash, Armenians, Ukrainians, Daghestan, Kazalkhs, Azerbaijanis and Belarus. There are approximately 130 languages spoken in the country, with Russian, the official language of Russia, belonging to the Indo-European family of languages, being spoken by 89% of the country's inhabitants, while 6.8% speak Altaic languages, 2.4% Caucasian languages, and 1.8% Uralic languages. Religion is practiced by 55% of the Russian population, with Orthodox Christianity being the main religion, followed by Islam.

俄罗斯的国旗由三个平行且相等的白、蓝、红长方形组成，旗帜中的白色代表寒带一年四季的白雪茫茫；蓝色代表亚寒带，又象征俄罗斯丰富的地下矿藏和森林、水力等自然资源；红色代表温带，也象征俄罗斯的历史悠久和对人类文明做出的贡献。国歌是《俄罗斯，我们神圣的祖国》，沿用的是苏联国歌《牢不可破的联盟》的旋律。国花是向日葵，货币为卢布。

The national flag of Russia consists of three parallel and equal white, blue and red rectangles. The white in the flag represents the year-round snow of the frigid zone; the blue represents the sub-frigid zone, which in turn symbolizes Russia's rich underground mineral deposits and natural resources such as forests and hydropower; and the red represents the temperate zone, which also symbolizes the country's long history and its contribution to human civilization. The national anthem is *Russia，Our Sacred Motherland*, which follows the melody of the former Soviet Union anthem *Unbreakable Union*. The national flower is sunflower and the currency is ruble.

（二）历史简介 History of Russia

俄罗斯是一个古老的国家，其祖先为东斯拉夫人。15 世纪末至 16 世纪初，以莫斯科大公国为中心，逐渐形成多民族的封建国家，1547 年，伊凡四世（伊凡雷帝）改大公称号为沙皇。1721 年，彼得一世（彼得大帝）改国号为俄罗斯帝国。1861 年废除农奴制。19 世纪末、20 世纪初成为军事封建帝国主义国家。1917 年 2 月，资产阶级革命推翻了专制制度。1917 年 11 月 7 日（俄历 10 月 25 日），十月社会主义革命爆发，建立了世界上第一个社会主义国家政权——俄罗斯苏维埃联邦社会主义共和国。1922 年 12 月 30 日，俄罗斯联邦、外高加索联邦、乌克兰、白俄罗斯成立苏维埃社会主义共和国联盟（后扩至 15 个加盟共和国）。1990 年 6 月 12 日，俄罗斯苏维埃联邦社会主义共和国最高苏维埃发表《国家主权宣言》，宣布俄罗斯联邦在其境内拥有"绝对主权"。1991 年 8 月，苏联发生"8·19"事件。1991 年 9 月 6 日，苏联国务委员会通过决议，承认爱沙尼亚、拉脱维亚、立陶宛三个加盟共和国独立。1991 年 12 月 8 日，俄罗斯联邦、白俄罗斯、乌克兰三个加盟共和国的领导人在别洛韦日签署《独立国家联合体协议》，宣布组成"独立国家联合体"。1991 年 12 月 21 日，除波罗的海三国和格鲁吉亚外的苏联 11 个加盟共和国签署《阿拉木图宣言》和《独立国家联合体协议议定书》。1991 年 12 月 26 日，苏联最高苏维埃举行最后一次会议，宣布苏联停止存在。至此，苏联解体，俄罗斯联邦成为完全独立的国家，并成为苏联的唯一继承国。1993 年 12 月 12 日，经过全民投票通过了俄罗斯独立后的第一部宪法，规定国家名称为"俄罗斯联邦"。

Russia is an ancient country. Its ancestors were Eastern Slavs. In the late 15th and early 16th centuries, centered on the Grand Duchy of Moscow, Russia gradually formed a multi-ethnic feudal state. In 1547, Ivan Ⅳ（Ivan the Terrible）changed the title of the Grand Duke to Tsar, and in 1721, Peter Ⅰ（Peter the Great）changed the name of the country to the Russian Empire. In 1861 it abolished the serfdom system, and in the late 19th and early 20th centuries, became a military feudal imperialist state. In February, 1917, the bourgeois revolution overthrew the autocratic system. On November 7, 1917（October 25 on the Russian calendar）, the October Socialist Revolution broke out, and the Russian Soviet Federative Socialist Republic（RSFSR）, the first socialist state power in the world,was established. On December 30, 1922, the Russian Federation, Transcaucasian Federation, Ukraine and Belarus formed the Union of Soviet Socialist Republics（later expanded to 15 Union Republics）. On June 12, 1990, the Supreme Soviet of the Russian Soviet Federative Socialist Republic issued a *Declaration of State Sovereignty,* declaring that the Russian Federation had "absolute sovereignty" over its territory. In August 1991, the Soviet Union experienced the "August 19" incident. On September 6, 1991, the State Council of the USSR adopted a resolution recognizing the independence of the three Union Republics of Estonia, Latvia and Lithuania, and on December 8, 1991, the leaders of the three Union Republics of the Russian Federation, Belarus and Ukraine signed the *Agreement on the Commonwealth of Independent States*（the *Commonwealth of Independent States Agreement*）in Belovezh, declaring the formation of the "Commonwealth of Independent States". On December 21, 1991, the eleven republics of the USSR, with the exception of the three Baltic States and Georgia, signed the *Declaration of Alma-Ata* and the *Protocol to the Agreement on the Commonwealth of Independent States*, and on December 26, 1991, the Supreme Soviet of the USSR held its last session and declared that the USSR had ceased to exist. Thus, the Soviet Union was dissolved and the Russian Federation became a fully independent State and the sole successor to the USSR, and on December 12, 1993, Russia's first post-independence constitution was adopted by referendum, giving the country the name "Russian Federation".

 讨论题

　　2020 年，俄罗斯胜利日红场阅兵彩排时中国人民解放军三军仪仗队高唱《喀秋莎》；2022 年北京冬奥会，在女子冰球小组赛美国队与俄罗斯奥委会代表队的比赛中场期间，现场 DJ 放起了名曲《喀秋莎》。

　　为何《喀秋莎》在中国有较高的知名度和普及度？对于中国人民来说，在上述场合歌唱《喀秋莎》的意义是什么？

喀秋莎

《喀秋莎》的
象征意义

（三）经济状况 The Economy

　　俄罗斯是世界经济大国。苏联时期，它是世界第二经济强国。苏联解体后，俄罗斯从中央计划经济体制向市场经济体制过渡。由于石油价格的上升和卢布的疲软，俄罗斯经济走向好转。2000 年之后，俄罗斯经济在大量出售资源的情况下得以迅速发展。俄罗斯拥有丰富的自然资源，有世界上最大的矿产储量、能源储量和森林资源，其淡水储量占世界总储量的 1/4。目前，俄罗斯经济主要依靠自然资源的出口，其中石油、天然气、金属及木材的出口占到 80%。俄罗斯是世界上最大的天然气输出国和 OPEC（石油输出国组织）以外的最大石油输出国。近年来，俄罗斯的计算机工业、航空业、高科技产业迅速崛起。特别是俄罗斯的国防工业在世界上占有重要的地位，其武器产品出口到全球各地。俄罗斯的核工业和航天业在世界上也占有重要地位。

Russia is a large economy in the world. It ranked the second in the world in Soviet period. After the disintegration of the Soviet Union, the economic policy of Russia turned into the market economic system instead of central planned system. Because of the rising of the oil price and the weakening of the Ruble, Russian economy became better. After 2000, the economy of Russia has increased rapidly based on the selling of large amouns of its resources, because the country has enormous natural resources, such as the largest mineral reserves, energy and forest reserves as well as it has 1/4 fresh water on the earth. Currently, Russian economy depends on the export of natural resources, 80% of which are oil, natural gas, metals and timber. Russia is the largest exporter of nature gas and the largest exporter of oil except the OPEC (Organization of the Petroleum Exporting Countries). In recent years, computer industry, aviation and high-tech industry have developed fast. The national defense industry of Russia occupies special status in the world. Its weapons are exported to many countries and regions in the world. Russian nuclear industry and space industry also enjoy important status in the world.

俄罗斯是一个工农业、交通运输、科学技术都比较发达的国家。俄罗斯工业发达，部门齐全，以机械、钢铁、冶金、石油、天然气、煤炭、森林工业及化工等为主，木材和木材加工业也较发达，但民用工业落后状况尚未得到根本改变。俄罗斯的农业远不如工业发达，但由于土地面积大，农产品产值并不低。农牧业并重，主要农作物有小麦、大麦、燕麦、玉米、水稻和豆类，经济作物以亚麻、向日葵和甜菜为主，畜牧业主要为养牛、养羊、养猪业。

Russia is a relatively developed country in industry, agriculture, transportation and science and technology. Russia has developed industries and complete departments, mainly including machinery, steel, metallurgy, oil, natural gas, coal, forest industry and chemical industry. The wood and wood processing industry is also relatively developed, but the backwardness of civil industry has not been fundamentally changed. Russia's agriculture is far less developed than its industry, but due to its large land area, the output value of agricultural products is not low. Agriculture and animal husbandry are equally important. The main crops are wheat, barley, oats, corn, rice and beans. Cash crops are mainly flax, sunflower and sugar beet. Animal husbandry mainly includes cattle, sheep and pigs.

（四）传统文化 Traditional Culture

伏特加是世界知名的酒精饮料，也是俄罗斯传统的酒类之一，深受俄罗斯大众，尤其是男性的喜爱。在俄罗斯零下几十摄氏度的地方，几乎所有的饮品都会结冰，只有伏特加能保持液态，因此它成为俄罗斯人最喜爱的冬季饮品。大多数俄罗斯男士都能喝酒且酒量不错。

Vodka is a world-renowned alcoholic beverage and one of the traditional alcoholic beverages in Russia, popular among Russians, especially men. In Russia, where temperatures are below-tens of degrees Celsius, almost all beverages freeze, and only Vodka can remain liquid, making it the favorite winter drink for Russians. Most Russian men can drink alcohol and have a good tolerance.

俄罗斯演艺界有三宝：芭蕾、戏剧和马戏。俄罗斯的芭蕾舞艺术在世界上享有很高的声誉，著名芭蕾舞剧目有《天鹅湖》《罗密欧与朱丽叶》《吉赛尔》等。马戏在俄罗斯的表演历史可谓源远流长，从18世纪起，每一位沙皇都有自己专属的皇家马戏表演者，这些表演者以马戏、驯兽为家族事业，世代相传，形成了许多仍然活跃在世界马戏表演舞台上的著名马戏世家。20世纪50年代，俄罗斯政府组建了当时世界规模最大、表演水平最高的马戏表演团体——"俄罗斯国家大马戏"。

Russian performing arts have three treasures: ballet, theater and circus. Russian ballet enjoys a high reputation in the world, with famous ballet productions such as *Swan Lake*, *Romeo and Juliet*, and *Giselle*. Circus in Russia's performance history can be said to have a long history. From the 18th century, each Tsar has his own special department of the Royal Circus performers. These performers take the circus and animal taming for the family business, which are passed down from generation to generation, forming a number of famous circus families who are still active on the stage of the world circus performances. In the 1950s, the Russian government set up the Russian State Circus, which was the largest and most advanced circus organization in the world at that time.

熊被俄罗斯人称为"俄罗斯森林的主人"。俄罗斯人认为熊是他们的守护神。在俄罗斯流传着许多与熊有关的传说，"熊"的形象出现在许多文学作品、地名，甚至是人名中，如俄罗斯前总理梅德韦杰夫的名字（Медведев）就源于"熊"（медведь）这个单词。如今熊已经成为俄罗斯的象征，俄罗斯执政党统一俄罗斯党的标志就是一只正在漫步的北极熊。2014年10月24日，俄罗斯时任总统普京在瓦尔代会议上发表讲话时表示，可以把熊比作俄罗斯的化身，熊是无论如何也不会放弃自己的森林的。俄罗斯的多个城市也把熊作为城市徽章及旗帜上的素材。在中国，对别人说"熊样"是贬义，但是若对俄罗斯朋友说"你像只熊"，他会很高兴。

Bears are known by Russians as the "owner of Russian forest". Russians believe that bears are their guardian gods. There are many legends related to bears circulating in Russia, and the image of "bears" appears in many literary works, place names, and even human names, such as the former Russian Prime Minister Medvedev（Медведев）originating from the "bear"（медведь）. Nowadays, bears have become a symbol of Russia, and the symbol of the ruling party, the United Russia Party, is a wandering polar bear. On October 24, 2014, current Russian President Putin delivered a speech at the Valdai Conference, stating that the bear can be compared to the incarnation of Russia. Bears will never give up on their own forest. Several cities in Russia also use bears as materials for city badges and flags. In China, saying "bear like" to others is derogatory, but if you say "you're like a bear" to a Russian friend, he will be very happy.

"战斗民族"
俄罗斯

套娃（图2-22）是俄罗斯的一种民间木制玩具。它一般由七八个木娃组成，由小到大依次套合在最大的木娃体内。据说在19世纪末，一位侨居日本多年的俄罗斯基督教传教士看到日本的套瓷玩具时受到启发，就用木料削制了世界上第一套套娃。他把这套套娃绘成了俄罗斯农家姑娘的形象，以寄托他的思乡之情。后来，套娃流传到莫斯科，被一位玩具制作高手仿制成现在的套娃。1900年，俄罗斯套娃参加了巴黎万国博览会，受到大家的欢迎并获得了奖章。一时间，莫斯科郊区的很多手工艺作坊都开始生产套娃。不久，这些地区就成了"套娃之

图 2-22　俄罗斯套娃
Figure 2-22　Matryoshka Dolls

乡"。如今，俄罗斯套娃已名扬四海，它也成为俄罗斯的独特标志及人文使者。

Matryoshka dolls (Figure 2-22) are a set of seven to eight wooden dolls of decreasing size placed one inside the other. The first set of Russian matryoshka doll was carved in late 19th century by Russian Christian missionary who was living in Japan for a long time and inspired by the Japanese ceramic dolls. He made the dolls look like the girls in his hometown to comfort his homesickness. Later, the matryoshka doll came back to Moscow, and was copied by a doll craftsman into matryoshka dolls. In 1900, the matryoshka doll participated in the Paris International Exposition, got the popularity and won the medal. Suddenly, many factories in the Moscow suburban began to make the dolls. Then the area became the hometown of Russian matryoshka dolls. Now, the doll is famous all over the world. It is a kind of Russian special symbol as well as the humanity ambassador.

（五）礼仪禁忌 Social Etiquettes and Taboos

俄罗斯人素来以热情、勇敢、耿直而著称于世。俄罗斯人比较注重礼貌。"您好""早安""万事如意""请原谅"等礼貌语经常挂在嘴上，即使是在亲人间也常用。问好的时候，男士要先向女士问好，戴帽子的应把帽子抬一抬，戴有色眼镜的也应把眼镜摘下来。拥抱、亲吻和握手是俄罗斯人的重要礼节。在正式的场合，如国家领导人见面时，为了表示友好和尊敬，俄方领导人会与对方拥抱并握手。俄罗斯人对女性颇为尊敬，在比较正式的场合，男士会弯腰并亲吻女士的右手背，以表示尊重。如果是男女间握手，男士不能先伸手，男士如戴手套应在握手前脱下，女士则不用脱。

Russians are famous for their enthusiasm, braveness and frankness. They pay much attention to their politeness. They greet each other with "Hello" "Good morning" "Wish you all good" "Excuse me", even among the relatives. When people give their greetings, men make greetings to women first. If people wear hats, they should lift the hat a little higher. If people wear color glasses, they should take off them for a while too. Hugging, kissing and hand-shaking are important etiquette in Russia. On a formal occasion, when two national leaders meet, Russian leader hugs and shakes hands with the other leader to show friendliness and respect. Russian people give much respect to women. On the formal occasion, men bend forward to kiss the right hand of women. If men shake hands with women, men should not hand out first. If men wear gloves, they should take off the gloves first and then shake hands while women do not have to take off the gloves.

俄罗斯人有尊重女性的美德，"女士优先"的理念深入人心，凡在公共场所，无论是行走让路，还是乘车让位，男士会特别优待女士。在剧院中，男士要协助女士脱掉大衣，入场时为女士开路并找座位，而且要等女士落座后男士才能入座。男女同行时，男士空手，而让女士拎重物是不允许的；男士要走在女士的左侧，保护女士；男士要陪伴女士过马路。在社交场合，交谈中不要讨论女士的长相、年龄；临别时，男士要帮助女士穿上大衣、拉开门，要让女士先行，不能自己开门拂袖而去。

Russians respect women, and the rule of "ladies first" is practiced everywhere. In public places, on the streets, or on buses, men treat women with special consideration. At the theater, men are supposed to help ladies take off their coats, show the way to the seat and wait until the lady to sit down first. When men and women are walking together, it is not allowed to see a man carry nothing while a woman carries the heavy stuff. While walking, men are supposed to walk at the left side of the women to protect them. When women are crossing the roads, men have to accompany with them. During the conversation, people don't discuss about the appearance of the women and their ages. At the moment of goodbye, men should help women put on coats, open doors and let the women leave first. Men are not allowed to leave first.

俄罗斯人捧出"面包和盐"是向客人表示最热烈的欢迎。俄罗斯人对盐十分崇拜，并将盐视为祭祀用的供品和珍宝。他们认为盐具有驱邪除灾的力量。如果有人不慎打翻了盐罐或是将盐撒在地上，便被认为是家庭不和的预兆。为了摆脱凶兆，他们总习惯将打翻在地上的盐拾起来撒在自己头上。因为在古代俄罗斯，盐要从很远的地方运来，价格高，而用盐腌制的食物可以长时间保存，不易腐烂，由此产生了盐的象征意义：可靠性、持久性、友谊和尊重。

"Bread and salt" is the most warming welcome to the guests. Russians admire the salt and consider salt as sacrifice and treasure. They believe salt has the power of driving away the devil. If someone breaks the salt jar accidentally or spreads the salt on the ground, it is believed a bad sign for family peace. To avoid the bad luck, they usually pick up the salt on the ground and scatter it on the head. Because in the ancient Russia, the salt was transported from far away with high price and the food salted can be kept long time, the symbols of salt are reliability, durability, friendship and respect.

在俄罗斯，被视为"光明"象征的向日葵深受人们的喜爱，是俄罗斯的国花。拜访俄罗斯人时，送给女士的鲜花数量宜为单数。在数字方面，俄罗斯人和其他西方人一样，忌讳13这个数字，因为在基督教的传说中，背叛者犹大正好排第13位。他们也厌恶666这个数字，因为在《圣经》中这是魔鬼的代号。他们常用7这个数字，认为"7"象征幸福和成功。有些新婚夫妇在婚礼后乘坐彩车要经过7座桥才心满意足。

In Russia, the sunflowers are popular for the symbol of "brightness". It is the national flower of Russia. When visiting Russian people, the number of flowers sent to the ladies is better to be singular. When talking about numbers, the Russian people are just like the westerners; they don't like the number 13. Because according to the Christian legend, the betrayer Judah ranked 13. They dislike 666 too, because in the Bible this number is the code for devil. They like to use 7, because they believe this number represents happiness and success. Some newly-married couple would like to go through 7 bridges by car.

（六）传统节日 Festivals

1. 胜利日 Victory Day

1945年5月9日，法西斯德国被迫签署投降书，第二次世界大战彻底结束，此后，每逢5月9日，俄罗斯人都会到烈士陵墓前敬献花圈。

On May 9, 1945, fascist Germany was forced to sign the instrument of surrender, and World War II came to a complete end. Since then, every May 9, Russians have been laying wreaths in front of martyrs' tombs.

2. 谢肉节（送冬节）Maslenitsa

谢肉节又称送冬节，是俄罗斯民间节日中最古老、最热闹的传统节日之一。每年2月底、3月初会举行谢肉节。它有双重含义：民间意义上的送冬节是送走严寒、迎来春暖花开，人们载歌载舞，举行丰富多彩的户外活动；宗教意义上的谢肉节是按东正教教历的规定，先尽情狂欢一周，此后持续七周斋戒，期间禁止杀生、娱乐、吃肉。

Maslenitsa, also known as the Farewell to Winter Festival, is one of the oldest and most vibrant traditional holidays in Russian folklore. It is celebrated annually from late February to early March. The festival has a dual significance: in a folk sense, it symbolizes the farewell to the harsh winter and the welcoming of the warm, blossoming spring, during which people sing, dance, and engage in a variety of colorful outdoor activities. In a religious context, Maslenitsa marks a week of joyful celebrations according to the Eastern Orthodox Church calendar, followed by a seven-week period of Lent during which killing, entertainment, and eating meat are prohibited.

3. 洗礼节 Epiphany

洗礼节在1月19日，这是东正教节日。洗礼原本是基督教的一种入教仪式。圣水祭是洗礼节的一项重要活动。在洗礼节前一天，将水放入教堂，之后进行隆重的祷告仪式。在祈祷后，信徒们用圣水洗去自己的罪恶。此外，有的人还会跳入河中的冰窟窿里洗一洗。洗礼节通常是冬季最冷的时候，因此有"洗礼节严寒"之说。1月18日晚按风俗习惯是占卜日，女孩子们要预卜自己的终身大事。

The Feast of the Epiphany, an Orthodox Christian holiday, is celebrated on January 19th. Baptism originally was a Christian initiation rite. The Holy Water is an important activity in the Epiphany. Before the holiday, water is put into the church, followed by formal praying. After the praying, the disciples use holy water to wash away the evil on their bodies. Besides, some people will jump into the holes in icy river to wash themselves. The Epiphany is usually in the depth of winter. Thus it comes the saying "the holiday is very cold". In the evening of January 18, people practice divination. Especially, the girls will predict their marriages at that night.

4. 俄罗斯宇航节 Russian Cosmonautics Day

1961年4月12日，苏联宇航员加加林乘坐"东方"号飞船进入太空，揭开了人类载人航天历史的第一页，4月12日这一天也成为苏联和俄罗斯的宇航节。

On April 12 1961, Soviet cosmonaut Gagarin went into space on board the Vostok spacecraft, opening the first page in the history of human spaceflight, and the day of April 12 has become Cosmonautics Day in the Soviet Union and Russia.

 讨论题

阅读拓展材料"第一个上太空的宇航员"（扫码获取），试结合苏联宇航员和苏联航天史以及中国神舟五号飞船、神舟十二号飞船的成功发射，讨论中国载人航天精神的基本内涵和"中国梦之航天梦"的含义。

第一个上太空
的宇航员

三、旅游观光 Tourism and Sightseeing

（一）主要旅游城市 Major Tourist Cities

1. 莫斯科 Moscow

莫斯科是俄罗斯首都，政治、经济、文化、科技和交通中心，人口为 1 151 万，是世界特大都市之一和欧洲人口最多的城市。有数个被列入《世界遗产名录》的建筑群，其城市布局以克里姆林宫和红场为中心，呈环形、放射形展开。克里姆林宫是俄罗斯联邦总统的官邸，位于莫斯科中心，是一个防御森严的建筑群，俯瞰着南面的莫斯科河、东面的圣瓦西里大教堂、红场和亚历山大花园。莫斯科还有很多科研机构和近百所高等院校，其中历史最悠久、规模最大的是国立莫斯科大学。

Moscow is the capital of Russia and the center of politics, economy, culture, technology and transportation, with a population of 11.51 million. It is one of the metropolises in the world and the most populous city in Europe. Many architecture clusters in the city are listed in the World Heritage List. With Kremlin and Red Square as the center, the city spreads out in the form of circle. The Kremlin is the official residence of the president of the Russian Federation. It is a fortified complex at the heart of Moscow, overlooking the Moskva River to the south, St. Basil Cathedral and Red Square to the east and Alexander Garden. There are also many scientific research institutions and nearly 100 institutions of higher learning in Moscow, of which Moscow State University has the longest history and the largest scale.

2. 圣彼得堡 Saint Petersburg

圣彼得堡位于俄罗斯西北部、波罗的海沿岸，是列宁格勒州的首府，也是仅次于莫斯科的俄罗斯第二大城市，是世界文化名城之一，也是重要的旅游城市。整座城市由 40 多个岛屿组成，市内水道纵横，700 多座桥梁把各个岛屿连接起来。风光旖旎的圣彼得堡因而有"北方威尼斯"的美誉。因其地处北纬 60°，每年夏天都有"白夜"现象，是世界上少数几个有白夜的城市之一。圣彼得堡始建于 1703 年，至今已有 300 多年的历史，市名源自耶稣的弟子圣徒彼得。1712 年，圣彼得堡成为俄国首都。其后 200 年它始终是俄罗斯帝国的中心。1914 年改称彼得格勒，1924 年列宁逝世后又被命名为列宁格勒，1991 年经市民投票恢复原名。圣彼得堡市中心的建筑多为 18、19 世纪的巴洛克和新古典主义风格。著名的建筑物有彼得保罗要塞、彼得大帝夏宫、斯莫尔尼宫、冬宫、喀山大教堂、伊萨基辅大教堂。俄罗斯的许多著名作家诞生于此，如普希金、莱蒙托夫、高尔基等。著名的音乐大师柴可夫斯基也诞生于此地。圣彼得堡还是花样滑冰的发源地。

Saint Petersburg is located in the northwest of Russia along the coast of Baltic Sea. It is the capital of Leningrad Oblast and the second largest city in Russia, second only to Moscow, one of the world's cultural and tourist cities. The whole city consists of over 40 islands. In the city, channels are everywhere and over 700 bridges connect those islands. The beautiful Saint Petersburg thus enjoys the name of "Venice of the North". Because the city is located at 60° N latitude, it has white nights every summer. It is one of the cities that have sleepless night. The city was built in 1703 and named after Saint Peter. It has a history of 300 years. In 1712, the city was the capital of Russia. Later, it remained being the heart of Russian Empire for 200 years. It was renamed Petrograd in 1914 and

Leningrad in 1924 after the death of Lenin and then back to the name of Saint Petersburg in 1991 based on the votes by the public. The buildings in the central district of the city were constructed in baroque and neoclassicism style of the 18th and 19th century, including Peter and Paul Fortress, Summer Palace of Peter the Great, Smolny Palace, Winter Palace, Kazan Cathedral and Siant Isaac's Cathedral. The city is also the birthplace of many famous authors such as Pushkin, Lermontov and Gorky, etc. The great musician Tchaikovsky was born here too. Saint Petersburg is also the original place of figure skating.

（二）著名旅游景点 Famous Tourist Attractions

1. 红场 Red Square

图 2-23　红场
Figure 2-23　Red Square

红场（图 2-23）是俄罗斯首都莫斯科市中心的著名广场，与克里姆林宫一样是俄罗斯的标志，是俄罗斯历史的见证，也是俄罗斯举行各种大型庆典及阅兵活动的中心地点。红场原名"托尔格"，意为"集市"，1662 年改为"红场"，意为"美丽的广场"。红场的地面很独特，全部由条石铺成。红场上的建筑群是在数百年的时间里逐渐建成的。红场的历史与俄罗斯的历史有着密不可分的联系。红场上的每一座建筑物都与某个重大历史事件有关。著名的建筑物包括：西侧的列宁墓和克里姆林宫的红墙及三座高塔；列宁墓与克里姆林宫之间的 12 块墓碑，包括斯大林等苏联政治家的墓碑；南侧的莫斯科的象征——圣瓦西里大教堂，这座大教堂是伊凡四世下令建造的，约建于 1555 年至 1561 年间，由 9 间礼堂组成，采用了当时流行的穹顶教堂风格；北侧的国家历史博物馆，建于 1873 年，也是莫斯科的标志性建筑，附近还有为纪念第二次世界大战胜利 50 周年而建造的第二次世界大战英雄朱可夫元帅的雕像，以及无名烈士墓；东侧的世界知名十家百货商店之一——古姆商场。红场是俄罗斯举行各种活动的主要场所，也是俄罗斯人举行婚礼的必到之地。

Red Square (Figure 2-23) is a famous square in Moscow. Just like the Kremlin, the Square is another symbol of Russia and the witness of Russian history. It is also the central site for various public ceremonies and parades. The original name of this square is Torg, meaning the marketplace. In 1662, the name was changed into Red Square, meaning beautiful square. The ground of the Red Square is very special and made of lath stone. The architecture groups on the square have been built up for hundreds of years. The history of this square is closely connected with Russian history. Every architecture on the square is linked with certain important historical event as well. The famous buildings include Lenin's Mausoleum, Red Walls of Kremlin and three towers in the west, 12 tombstones between Lenin's Mausoleum and the Kremlin, including the Soviet politicians such as Stalin, and the classic symbol Saint Basil's Cathedral in the south. Ordered by Ivan Ⅳ, Saint Basil's Cathedral was built from 1555 to 1561 which was consisted of nine auditoriums, and adopted the popular arch roof church style at that time. In the north, it is State Historical Museum, which was established in 1873, also a symbol of Moscow. Nearby, there is a hero sculpture of the General Zhukov for celebrating the 50th anniversary of the victory of the World War Ⅱ and anonymous graves. In the east is the Gum Department Store, one of the ten famous department stores in the world. Red Square is the major site for all kinds of activities held by Russian, the wedding included.

2. 圣瓦西里大教堂 Saint Basil's Cathedral

圣瓦西里大教堂是俄罗斯最著名的教堂之一，精美的东正教教堂圣瓦西里大教堂（图2-24）以其形状和颜色各异的九个"洋葱头"而闻名，已成为莫斯科市中心最美丽的景点之一。现在是国家历史博物馆的一部分，里面有美丽的壁画供游客欣赏。

Saint Basil's Cathedral(Figure 2-24) is one of Russia's most famous churches. This exquisite Orthodox cathedral is renowned for its nine "onion heads" in different shapes and colors, and has

图 2-24 圣瓦西里大教堂
Figure 2-24 Saint Basil's Cathedral

become one of the most beautiful scenic spots in the center of Moscow. It's now part of the State Historical Museum and has beautiful murals inside it for tourists to admire.

3. 克里姆林宫 Kremlin

克里姆林宫（图2-25）是莫斯科最有名的观光地，既是政治中心，又是俄罗斯东正教的中心。作为俄罗斯国家的象征，克里姆林宫位于俄罗斯首都的最中心，是世界上最大的建筑群之一，也是历史、文化和艺术古迹的宝库，被联合国教科文组织列入《世界遗产名录》。克里姆林宫始建于1156年，曾为18世纪以前的沙皇皇宫，十月革命胜利后，成为苏联党政领导机关所在地。现为俄罗斯联邦总统府等政府机关所在地。克里姆林宫初为木墙，后屡经扩建，至20世纪40年代成为现在宏大的克里姆林宫。

图 2-25 克里姆林宫
Figure 2-25 Kremlin

克里姆林宫城堡内有精美的教堂、宫殿、钟塔等。在克里姆林宫的中心教堂广场，有圣母升天大教堂、报喜大教堂及天使大教堂，内有帝王墓碑。

Kremlin (Figure 2-25) is the most famous tourist attraction in Moscow, the center of politics and the Orthodox Catholic. As the national representative, Kremlin is located in the center of Russian capital. It is one of the largest architecture groups. It is also the historic, cultural and art treasure, listed by UNESCO as the World Heritage Site. Established in 1156, the Kremlin was Tsar's palace before the 18th century. After the victory of October Revolution, it became the Soviet's headquarters. Now it is the site for government offices including President House. Kremlin started with wooden walls, and later it was rebuilt several times. Till 1940s, it became large Kremlin. Inside Kremlin, there are churches, palaces, clock towers and so on. On the center of Cathedral Square, there is Assumption Cathedral, Cathedral of the Annunciation, and Cathedral of Archangel Michael with

图 2-26　莫斯科国立大学
Figure 2-26　Moscow State University

emperors' graves in.

4. 莫斯科国立大学 Moscow State University

莫斯科国立大学（图 2-26）历史悠久，是俄罗斯的最高教育机构之一，始建于 1755 年。目前，它是世界上最受认可的大学之一，培养了一大批学术精英和诺贝尔奖获得者。20 世纪 50 年代以来，许多优秀的中国学生被派往莫斯科国立大学进行学习交流。因此，莫斯科国立大学与中国结下了不解之缘，学校已成为许多中国游客到莫斯科旅游的必去之地。

As one of the highest educational institutions in Russia, Moscow State University (Figure 2-26) has a long history dating back to its founding in 1755. At present, it's also one of the world's most-recognized universities, and has cultivated a large number of academic elites and Nobel Prize winners. Since the 1950s, many excellent Chinese students have been sent to Moscow State University for study exchanges. As a result, Moscow State University and China have an unbreakable bond, and the school has turned into a must-see location for many Chinese tourists traveling to Moscow.

图 2-27　普希金广场
Figure 2-27　Pushkin Square

5. 普希金广场 Pushkin Square

普希金广场（图 2-27）位于莫斯科市中心。旧称苦行广场，因广场上有古老的苦行修道院而得名，1937 年，为纪念俄国伟大诗人普希金逝世 100 周年，当时的苏联政府把苦行广场改名为"普希金广场"。广场上耸立着 4 米多高的普希金青铜纪念像。广场上有个小花园，广场内有花岗石台阶、红色大理石喷泉、饰灯等，景色优美。

The Pushkin Square (Figure 2-27) is located in the center of Moscow. It was formerly known as Strastnaya Square, named after the ancient Strastnoy Monastery that once stood there. In 1937, to commemorate the 100th anniversary of the death of the great Russian poet Alexander Pushkin, the Soviet government renamed it "Pushkin Square". The square features a bronze statue of Pushkin that stands over four meters tall. There is also a small garden on the square, adorned with granite steps, a red marble fountain, and decorative lights, creating a picturesque setting.

6. 冬宫 Winter Palace

冬宫（图 2-28）坐落在圣彼得堡宫殿广场上，初建于 1754 年至 1762 年，是 18 世纪俄罗斯巴洛克式建筑风格最伟大的作品。1837 年一场大火将其焚毁，1838 年至 1839 年间得以重建。冬宫原为俄国沙皇的皇宫，现为国立博物馆，与巴黎卢浮宫、纽约大都会艺术博物馆、伦敦大英博物馆齐名，是世界四大博物馆之一。

Winter Palace (Figure 2-28) is located at Palace Square in Saint Petersburg. Established in 1754 to 1762, it is the greatest memorial of Russian baroque architecture art in the 18th century. It was destroyed by a fire in 1837 and rebuilt in 1838 to 1839. Winter Palace was originally Tsar's palace. Now it is the national museum, enjoying the fame as the Louvre in Paris, the Metropolitan Museum of Art in New York and British Museum in London. It is one of the largest museums in the world.

图 2-28　冬宫
Figure 2-28　Winter Palace

7. 彼得大帝夏宫 Summer Palace of Peter the Great

彼得大帝夏宫（图 2-29）位于芬兰湾南岸的森林中，距圣彼得堡市约 30 千米，占地近千公顷，是历代俄国沙皇的郊外离宫。18 世纪初，俄国沙皇彼得大帝下令兴建夏宫，其外貌简朴、庄重，内部装饰华贵。如今，夏宫已成为包括 18 世纪和 19 世纪宫殿花园的建筑群，该宫殿以其直通芬兰湾的喷泉阶梯和园林内众多设计巧妙的喷泉而闻名，被誉为"俄罗斯的凡尔赛"。

The Summer Palace of Peter the Great (Figure 2-29) is located in the forests near Gulf of Finland, 30 kilometers away from Saint Petersburg. It occupies

图 2-29　彼得大帝夏宫
Figure 2-29　Summer Palace of Peter the Great

nearly a thousand hectares. It was the Tsars' suburban palace. In the early 18th century, Peter the Great ordered to build up the Summer Palace. Its appearance is simple and solemn but the inside decorations are luxurious. Now, the Summer Palace becomes the architecture complex including palaces built during the 18th and 19th century. The palace is famous for its fountain stairs going directly to the Gulf of Finland and many delicate designed fountains, enjoying the name of "Russian Versailles".

8. 贝加尔湖 Lake Baikal

贝加尔湖（图 2-30）是世界上最深（最深的地方有 1,637 米）、最古老（有 2 500 万年的历史）、蓄水量最大的淡水湖，约占世界地表淡水总量的 1/5。湖中生存着约 600 种植物和 1,200 多种动物，其中 3/4 为贝加尔湖的特有品种。贝加尔湖湖水清澈、群山环抱、风景绮丽，有矿泉 300 多处，被誉为"西伯利亚的蓝眼"。1996 年，该湖被联合国教科文组织列为世界遗产。

Lake Baikal (Figure 2-30) is the deepest (1 637 meters in the deepest place), the oldest

图 2-30　贝加尔湖
Figure 2-30　Lake Baikal

（with a history of 25 million years）and the largest freshwater lake in the world, accounting for about 1/5 of the world's total surface freshwater. There are about 600 kinds of plants and 1,200 kinds of animals in the lake, of which 3/4 are unique to Lake Baikal . Lake Baikal has clear water, surrounded by mountains, beautiful scenery, and more than 300 mineral springs. It is known as the " blue eye of Siberia". In 1996, the lake was listed as a World Heritage Site by UNESCO.

图 2-31　黑海海岸
Figure 2-31　Black Sea Coast of Russia

9. 黑海海岸 Black Sea Coast of Russia

黑海海岸（图 2-31）日照充足，有环境优美的海滨浴场，拥有具有医疗效果的矿泉水、医疗用泥等，是闻名于世的疗养区。位于黑海东岸的索契是俄罗斯疗养胜地，以温暖的海水和具有医疗效果的硫化氖矿泉水著称，一年四季都可接待国内外游客。

Black Sea Coast of Russia (Figure 2-31), a world-renowned sanatorium, has ample sunshine, beautiful seaside bathing areas, medical mineral water and medical mud. Sochi is located on the eastern coast of the Black Sea. It is a Russian sanatorium known for its warm seawater and medical neon sulfide mineral water. It is a popular sea resort for both domestic and foreign tourists all year round.

（三）旅游购物 Shopping

围巾披肩：俄罗斯的气温是非常寒冷的，围巾十分受当地人的欢迎，基本上每一个人都会拥有一条围巾。俄罗斯生产的围巾都是披肩式的，而且是纯羊毛编织的，不仅可以很好地抵御寒冷，还可以作为服装的配饰。

Scarf: Temperatures in Russia can be extremely cold, making scarves a popular accessory among locals. Nearly everyone owns a scarf. Russian-made scarves are typically shawl-style and woven from pure wool, offering excellent protection against the cold while also serving as a stylish addition to one's outfit.

伏特加：伏特加是非常有名的俄罗斯酒，是用谷物和土豆酿造而成的，口感香醇浓郁。伏特加还可以作为鸡尾酒的调制酒基，在世界各地都非常受欢迎。

Vodka: Vodka is a very famous Russian spirit made from grains and potatoes and has a flavorful and rich taste. Vodka can also be used as a base for cocktails and is very popular all over the world.

俄罗斯套娃：俄罗斯套娃非常著名，体现了浓郁的俄罗斯风情，是人们最熟悉的俄罗斯工艺品。套娃一般用木质材料做成，可以用来作为摆饰物件，也可以用来装杂物。

Matryoshka dolls: Matryoshka dolls are very famous, reflecting rich Russian customs, and are the most famous crafts in Russia. Matryoshka dolls are generally made of wood, and can be used as ornamental pieces, but also can be used to load miscellaneous items.

鱼子酱：俄罗斯的鱼子酱被称为黑黄金，通常来自里海或黑海的鲟鱼，鱼子酱里面的微量元素、矿物盐、蛋白质、氨基酸和重组基本脂肪酸可以促进皮肤的新陈代谢，让皮肤更加细腻有光泽。

Caviar: Russian caviar, known as black gold, is usually sourced from sturgeon from the Caspian or Black Seas. The trace elements, mineral salts, proteins, amino acids, and restructured essential fatty acids inside caviar stimulate the skin metabolism and give it a more refined and glowing appearance.

琥珀、蜜蜡、绿松石：琥珀是史前松树脂的化石，形成于 4 000 万～6 000 万年前，世界上没有两块相同的琥珀。琥珀非常适合作为装饰物，非常结实、温暖、美观。蜜蜡和绿松石也是非常好的纪念品。

Amber, Beeswax, Turquoise: Amber is the fossilized prehistoric pine resin, produced between 40 million and 60 million years ago, and there are no two identical pieces of amber in the world. Amber is perfect for decorative purposes, being very strong, warm and beautiful. Beeswax and turquoise are also great souvenirs

扫码获取：入境须知及海关规定

本节习题

1. 俄罗斯绝大部分领土在亚洲，为什么却是一个传统的欧洲国家？
2. 俄罗斯的气候类型和特点是什么？对旅游有什么影响？
3. 俄罗斯人有哪些独特的习俗？
4. 俄罗斯文化对世界有什么突出贡献？

第四节　中欧之旅
Travel in Central Europe

欧洲心脏——德国
The Heart of Europe—Germany

导读

德国是一个富有魅力的世界性旅游大国，其主要客源国是美国、荷兰、英国、瑞典、意大利、法国、日本、瑞士和丹麦等。南部的阿尔卑斯山是欧洲重要的夏季疗养地和冬季运动中心，西南部的黑森林地区是德国著名的旅游区之一，多瑙河沿岸景色秀丽，博登湖是著名的疗养胜地。德国是一个诞生了贝多芬、歌德等众多杰出人物的国度，是一个以强大的汽车制造业而闻名世界的经济体，也是一个以啤酒和香肠为代表性饮食的国家。德国是欧盟最大的经济体，是仅次于美国、中国和日本的全球第四大经济体。"德国制造"体现了对产品质量和创新能力的始终关注，是德国成为全球重要经济体的基础和动力保证。中德两国于 1972 年建立外交关系以来，在政治、经贸、教育等领域开展了广泛的合作与交流。在中国国家主席习近平提出共建"一带一路"倡议后，德国政府在欧洲国家中率先予以积极回应。2013 年以来，依托"一带一路"蓝图，中德两国的合作与交流迎来了新的发展契机。

一、地理概览 Geography of Germany

（一）位置 Location

德国，全称为德意志联邦共和国，位于欧洲的西部和中部，北接丹麦，东连波兰和捷克，南靠奥地利和瑞士，西南接壤法国和卢森堡，西北连荷兰和比利时。从地图上看，德国位于欧洲的心脏地带，是欧洲邻国最多的国家，欧洲的水、陆、空道路都要经过德国，故也被称为"欧洲走廊"。

The Federal Republic of Germany, briefly Germany, is located in the western and the central part of Europe, bordering Denmark to the north, Poland and Czech to the east, Austria and Switzerland to the south, France and Luxembourg to the southwest and Holland and Belgium to the northwest. So Germany is located in the heart of Europe and it is the country with the most European neighbors. All roads by water, land and air pass through Germany. That's why it is known as "European corridor".

（二）地形和气候 The Land and Seasons

德国地势北低南高，北部是平均海拔不到 100 米的平原，中部是东西走向的山地，西南是莱茵河谷区，莱茵河两边的山地为森林和高山牧场，东南是巴伐利亚高原和阿尔卑斯山区，境内最高峰是位于阿尔卑斯山的楚格峰，海拔为 2 962 米。主要河流莱茵河（德国境内长度约 865 千米）、易北河、美因河均向北流淌，唯有多瑙河自西向东注入黑海。德国湖泊星罗棋布，最大的天然湖康斯坦茨湖位于德国、瑞士和奥地利的交界处。

Its terrain is high in the south and low in the north. The elevation of the northern plain is less than 100 meters and the central is the mountainous area ruming from east to west. Its southwest is the Rhine Valley, both sides of which are forested mountains and alpine pasture. Its southeast is Bavarian Highland and Alps mountainous region. Its peak is Zugspitze with 2,962 meters high in Alps. The main rivers are the Rhine (865 kilometers in the territory), the Elbe and the Main flowing to the north, but the Danube flows from west to east into the Black Sea. Germany is dotted with lakes, among which the largest natural lake is Lake Constance, located at the junction of Germany, Switzerland and Austria.

德国的西北部为温带海洋性气候，往南和往东则逐渐过渡为温带大陆性气候。德国 1 月平均气温为 0 ℃，山区为 -10 ℃，夏季平均气温为 20 ℃，适合旅游。

The climate in the northwest is temperate maritime zone, gradually transitioning to the temperate continental climate as it moves to the south and east. The average temperature in january is 0 ℃ in January and -10 ℃ in mountainous region. The average temperature in summer is 20 ℃ and it is suitable for traveling.

（三）自然资源 Natural Resources

德国自然资源贫乏，除硬煤、褐煤和钾盐的储量丰富外，原料供应和能源方面在很大程度上依赖进口，矿物原料（铁矿石、铝土矿、锰、磷酸盐、钨和锡）对国外的依赖特别大。德国拥有少量铁矿和石油，天然气需求量的 1/3 可以由国内满足，2/3 的初级能源需要进口。

Germany is poor in natural resources and, with the exception of abundant reserves of hard coal, lignite and potash, is largely dependent on imports for the supply of raw materials and energy, with mineral raw materials (iron ore, bauxite, manganese, phosphates, tungsten and tin) being particularly dependent on foreign countries. Germany possesses small quantities of iron ore and oil, one third of the demand for natural gas can be met domestically, and two thirds of primary energy needs to be imported.

二、人文概况 Overview of German Humanities

（一）国情认知 Basic Knowledge of National Conditions

德国居民人数为 8 379 万（2022 年），是欧盟人口数量最多的国家，主要是德意志人，还有少数丹麦人、吉卜赛人、索布族人和犹太人，索布族是德国唯一的少数民族。德国的犹太人数量约为 12 万，居中欧第三位。德国是欧洲人口最稠密的国家之一，人口密度为 231 人／平方千米，也是目前世界上出生率最低的国家之一。德国的通用语言为德语，德语属于印欧语系中的日耳曼语族。德国居民多信奉基督教和天主教，其中 30.2% 的人信奉天主教，29.2% 的人信奉基督教新教，1% 的人信奉东正教；此外，还有穆斯林和佛教、犹太教、印度教教徒。德国的国旗呈横长方形，自上而下由黑色、红色、金色 3 个平行且相等的横长方形相连而成。国歌是《德意志之歌》，国花是矢车菊，象征日耳曼民族爱国、乐观、顽强、俭朴的特征。矢车菊也被认为有吉祥之兆。

With 83.79 million inhabitants (2022), Germany is the most populous country in the European Union, with a predominantly German population, as well as a small number of Danes, Gypsies, Sorbs, and Jews, with the Sorbs being the only minority in Germany. Germany has about 0.12 million Jews, the third highest number in Central Europe. Germany is one of the most densely populated countries in Europe, with a population density of 231 people per square kilometers, and also currently has one of the lowest birth rates in the world. German is commonly spoken in Germany and belongs to the Germanic group of the Indo−European language family. Germany's residents are mostly Christians and Catholics, of which 30.2% are Catholics, 29.2% are Protestants, 1% are Orthodox, and there are also Muslims, Buddhists, Jews and Hindus. The national flag of Germany is a horizontal rectangle with three parallel and equal horizontal rectangles in black, red and gold from top to bottom. The national anthem is the " *Deutschlandlied* " (*The Song of Germany*), and the national flower is the cornflower, which symbolizes the Germanic people's patriotism, optimism, tenacity and frugality, and is considered to be an omen of good fortune.

（二）历史简介 History of Germany

尽管真正统一的德国历史要从普鲁士王国成立才开始，但是德意志民族可以追溯到公元前

100年，从斯堪的纳维亚半岛至德国北部逐渐形成的日耳曼部落。在奥古斯都统治德意志地区时期，日耳曼部落开始抵抗罗马帝国的统治。公元5世纪末，克洛维一世建立法兰克王国，日耳曼进入了法兰克时代。公元800年，查理曼大帝统一了欧洲西部的大部分地区。查理曼逝世后，其孙子把法兰克王国分成西、中、东三部分。莱茵河以东的东法兰克王国成了后来的德意志王国的基础。公元919年，萨克森公爵亨利一世在东法兰克王国建立萨克森王朝。公元962年，国王奥托一世加冕为神圣罗马帝国皇帝。1806年，拿破仑入侵德意志地区，神圣罗马帝国破裂，建立莱茵邦联。1871年，法国在普法战争中失败，威廉一世加冕为德意志皇帝，德意志帝国成立，定都柏林。1914年，斐迪南大公被杀后，第一次世界大战爆发，1918年11月，德国革命开始，威廉二世政权被推翻。1919年，建立魏玛共和国。1933年，希特勒上台实行独裁统治。德国于1939年发动第二次世界大战，给世界人民带来深重的灾难。1945年，苏联红军占领柏林，德国战败投降。1949年5月23日，被英、法、美占领的西部建立德意志联邦共和国定都波恩。同年10月7日，被苏联占领的东部成立德意志民主共和国，东柏林为其首都。1990年10月3日，德国实现统一，重新定都柏林。

Though the history of the united Germany started from the establishment of the Kingdom of Prussia, the history of the Germanic tribes which were from Scandinavia and northern part of Germany could be traced back to 100 BC. During the period of Emperor Augustus' reign of German area, the Germanic tribes learned to fight against the Rome. At the end of the fifth century AD, the Kingdom of Franks was established by Clovis I .The Germanic tribes entered the Frankish era. In 800 AD, Charles the Great united the most areas in western Europe. After his death, his three grandsons separated the kingdom into three parts—the west, the middle and the east. The Kingdom of Eastern Franks in eastern Rhine was the basic area of the Germany. In 919 AD, Henry I , Duke of Saxony established the Saxony Dynasty in the Kingdom of Eastern Franks. In 962 AD, the King Otto I was crowned as the emperor of Holy Rome Empire. In 1806, Napoleon invaded the German area and set up the Confederation of the Rhine with the collapse of the Holy Rome Empire. In 1871, France was defeated during the war between Prussia and France, William I was crowned as the emperor of the German Empire, hence German Empire was established and Berlin was the capital. In 1914, the First World War started after the Archduke Ferdinand, was assassinated. In Nov. 1918, the German Revolution began, William II abdicated and Weimar Republic was established in 1919. In 1933, Adolf Hitler came into power and ruled despotically. In 1939, Germany started the Second World War and brought the world disaster. In 1945, the Red Army of the Soviet Union occupied Berlin and Germany surrendered. The Federal Republic of Germany was founded in the area occupied by the Britain, France and United States on May 23, 1949 and Bonn became the capital. On October 7, 1949, the German Democratic Republic was established in the area occupied by the Soviet Union and East Berlin was the capital. On October 3, 1990, Germany was reunited and Berlin became the capital again.

（三）经济状况 The Economy

德国是高度发达的资本主义工业国。德国的经济实力位居欧洲首位，是世界上仅次于美国、中国、日本的第四大经济体。德国的国内生产总值占欧盟的25%，德国经济也因此被称为"欧洲经济的火车头"。其中，汽车工业是德国经济发展的动力，德国是世界第四大汽车生产国，位列中国、美国和日本之后。德国是欧洲货币联盟的创始成员国，欧洲中央银行总部设在法兰克福，同时德国也是西方八国首脑会议的成员国。

Germany is a highly-developed capitalist industrial country. Its economic power is the strongest in Europe and is ranked the fourth after America, China and Japan in the world. The GDP of Germany accounts for 25% of the total amount of European Union. The economy of Germany is called as the locomotive of the train for the European economy. Auto industry is the barometer of German economy. The output is ranked the fourth after China, United States and Japan. Germany is the member of the founders of the European Monetary Union. The headquarters of the European Central Bank is in Frankfurt. Germany is the member of the G8 Summit.

（四）传统文化 Traditional Culture

讲到德国的文化艺术，人们首先想到的是德国的哲学家。德国是许多哲学流派的发源地，如德国唯心论、马克思主义等，代表人物有康德、黑格尔、费尔巴哈、马克思、叔本华、尼采等。德国图书出版量居欧洲第一位。

When people talk about the culture of Germany, they will think about the philosophers. Germany is the source for lots of schools of philosophy such as German Idealism and Marxism. The representatives are Kant, Hegel, Feuerbach, Karl Marx, Schopenhauer, Nietzsche, etc. Germany ranks first in Europe in terms of book publishing volume.

音乐是德国人生活中不可缺少的组成部分。德国也是音乐家的摇篮，诞生了许多著名的世界级音乐家，特别是古典音乐家，主要代表人物是巴赫和贝多芬。其他世界知名的作曲家有亨德尔、瓦格纳、勃拉姆斯等。柏林爱乐乐团更是享誉世界。可以说，德国是名副其实的音乐之乡。

Music is an integral part of German life. Germany is the cradle of many musicians. Lots of world-class musicians, especially the classic musicians were born here, and the main representatives are Bach and Beethoven. Other world famous composers are Handel, Wagner, Brahms, etc. The Berlin Philharmonic Orchestra is known throughout the world. It can be said that Germany is truly a country of music.

音乐巨人——贝多芬

德国有 3 000 多座博物馆，收藏内容十分丰富。每年都会举办各种艺术节、博览会等。德国人喜欢阅读，即使在当今电视及网络普及的年代，德国人仍然保持着爱读书的传统。法兰克福和莱比锡是德国图书出版业中心，德国图书出版量在世界上仅次于美国，排第二位。此外，众多的教堂、宫殿和古堡也是德国重要的文化遗产。

Germany has more than 3,000 museums with rich collections. Each year there are lots of art festivals and fairs. Germans like reading. Even today they still keep the tradition though the TV and Internet are so popular. Frankfurt and Leipzig are centers of German book publishing industry. The quantity of book publishing in Germany is ranked second in the world after the US. In addition, a large number of churches, palaces and castles are important cultural heritages in Germany.

德国菜不像法国菜那样复杂，也不像英国菜那样清淡，它以朴实无华、经济实惠的特点独立于西餐中。德国人餐桌上的主角是肉食，他们最爱吃猪肉，牛肉次之，爱吃猪肉制成的各种香肠。他们制作的香肠有 1 500 种以上，许多种类风行世界，像以地名命名的"黑森林火腿”，可以切得像纸一样薄，味道奇香无比。德国人一般胃口较大，喜食油腻之物。在口味方面，德国人爱吃冷菜和偏甜、偏酸的菜肴，不爱吃辣的和过咸的菜肴。在饮料方面，德国人最爱喝啤酒，也很喜欢咖啡、红茶、矿泉水。

German cuisine is not as intricate as French cuisine nor as mild as British cuisine; it stands out in Western cuisine for its simplicity and affordability. The centerpiece of the German table is meat, with pork being the favorite, followed by beef. Germans particularly enjoy various sausages made from pork. With over 1,500 types of sausages, many have gained international popularity. For example, the "Black Forest ham", named after its region, can be sliced paper-thin and is renowned for its exquisite flavor. Germans generally have hearty appetites and enjoy rich, fatty foods. In terms of taste, they prefer cold dishes and those that are slightly sweet or sour, while spicy and overly salty foods are less favored. When it comes to beverages, Germans love beer the most, but they also enjoy coffee, black tea, and mineral water.

德国人对住房的要求极高，拥有一套单独宅院的住房是普通德国人毕生奋斗的目标。人们平日辛勤工作，积攒钱盖房，为自己和子孙后代营造一处宽敞、体面、舒适的住房被视为人生完美、充实的标志。德国民居样式大致相同：楼房呈正方形，有陡坡状瓦式大屋顶，为了有效利用空间，屋顶会露出几扇窗户。有的住宅没有院墙，有的住宅有半米高象征性的小院墙，给人一种不设防的错觉。住宅内房间布局没有规律，大小房屋交叉错落分布，十分复杂，每间房屋都有固定的用途，凡是带窗户的一般是卧室、客厅、书房、厨房或浴室，密室和储藏室都没有窗户，室内完全靠灯光照明，可能这样更安全。许多家庭每人都有一间小密室，有的还在地下室内建有永久性的钢筋混凝土防空室，里面全部是现代化设施，透气、通水、通电，并备有充足的饮料和食品，以防突发性事件。

Germans have very high requirements for housing, and owning a house in a separate courtyard is the ideal that ordinary Germans strive for all their lives. People work hard on weekdays, and save up money to build a house. Creating a spacious, decent, comfortable housing for themselves and their descendants is regarded as a symbol of a perfect and fulfilling life. German houses are generally similar, with square buildings, steeply pitched tile roofs, and a few windows exposed on the roof for the effective use of space. Some houses do not have a courtyard wall, and some have a half-metre-high symbolic small courtyard wall, giving the illusion of being undefended. There is no regularity in the layout of the rooms in the residence, and the distribution of large and small houses is very complicated. Each house has a fixed purpose. All those with windows are usually bedrooms, living rooms, studies, kitchens or bathrooms. There are no windows in the secret rooms and storerooms, and the interior of these rooms relies entirely on lighting, which is probably safer. Many families have a small secret room for each person, and some have permanent reinforced concrete sheltered rooms in the basement, which are fully modernized, air-permeable, water-permeable, electrically-permeable, and well-stocked with drinks and food in case of emergencies.

（五）礼仪禁忌 Social Etiquettes and Taboos

在德国文化的不断熏陶下，德国人的性格形成了一些共性：有礼貌、守时、勤奋、节俭、整洁、遵纪守法、做事一板一眼。正如谚语所云："一个德国人可以成为哲学家，三个德国人可以组成一个俱乐部。"这些共同的特点使德国人几乎都愿意加入各种非营利性质的俱乐部。

在公共社交场合，德国人往往显得呆板、沉重，拘泥于形式，缺乏幽默感。德国人在工作中一丝不苟，就像一部机器。传统德国妇女的生活往往可以用三个词来描述：下厨、照看孩子、去教堂做礼拜。然而，正如欧洲其他国家一样，这种传统模式在逐渐消失。德国的出生率逐年下降，如今德国相当数量的人信奉独身主义。但是他们仍然喜欢聚会、公共假期、传统节庆等公众活动。德国是欧洲公共假期最多的国家。

Germans have developed common features because of their culture background. They are polite, punctual, diligent, frugal, clean, law-abiding and do everything according to the rules. An old saying goes Like "One German can be a philosopher, and three can organize a club". The common features lead them to join the non-profit clubs. In public, Germans seem to be stiff, formal and humorless. They are strict in their work, just like a machine. The traditional role for women can be concluded in three words: kitchen, kid and church. However, just like the people of other European countries, the tradition is gradually disappearing. The rate of birth is declining every year as more people don't want to get married. But they still love parties, holidays and festivals. Germany is the country which has the most public holidays in Europe.

德意志民族是一个讲究秩序的民族。德国人注重规则和法律。同德国人打交道没有太多的麻烦。多数情况下，他们都比较干脆、直接。他们会直接告诉你什么事能做到，什么事做不到。他们会非常明确地回答问题。

Germans pay great attention to orders. They do everything according to the rules and law. We don't have too much trouble to deal with Germans, in most cases, they are relatively simple and direct. They will reply immediately what they can do or can't do. They will answer unambiguously.

德国人非常注重时间，凡事都喜欢提前预约。德语中有一句话"准时是帝王的礼貌"。德国人非常守时，约定好的时间，无特殊情况绝不轻易变动。应邀到别人家做客或外出拜访朋友时，都会准点，让主人干等或浪费他人时间是不礼貌的。如果有特殊原因无法准时赴约，应向朋友表示歉意，并请求原谅。德国人讲究礼仪，如处处体现女士优先的原则，在日常生活中，"您好""请问""谢谢""再见"等礼貌用语总是不离口。当两人在路上、办公室、宾馆或电梯相遇时，不管认识不认识，都会相互打招呼。在同人交谈时，德国人很注意尊重对方，不过问私事，如不问女性的年龄、不问对方的收入等。

Germans pay great attention to time. They like to make reservations for everything in advance. German word goes like "Just-in-time is the courtesy of the emperor". Germans are very punctual. Appointments could not be easily changed without any special conditions. It should be punctual to pay a visit or to be one's guest. It is impolite to let the host wait or waste others' time. If there are special reasons for the lateness for appointments, making an apology and asking for forgiveness is necessary. Germans pay attention to the etiquette. Lady first is the rule. In daily life, those terms are often used, such as "Hello" "Please" "Thank you" and "Goodbye". When people meet on the way, in the office, the hotel or the lift, they always say hello to each other no matter whether they are familiar or not. They respect each other. They won't mention the personal affairs during the social interaction such as lady's age, salary and so on.

德国人很讲究清洁和整齐。德国人在穿着打扮上的总体风格是庄重、朴素、整洁。在一般情况下，男士大多爱穿西装、夹克，并且喜欢戴呢帽。女士大多爱穿翻领长衫和色彩、图案淡雅的长裙。在日常生活中，德国妇女以淡妆为主。在正式场合，必须穿戴整齐，衣着多为深色。在商务交往中，男士讲究穿三件套西装，女士讲究穿裙式服装。传统的女装常常有配套的帽子，帽子的样式多种多样，有的妇女干脆用鲜花编成花环戴在头上，十分娇艳。德国人较重视发型，男士不宜剃光头；少女的发式多为短发或披肩发，烫发的妇女大多是已婚者。

Germans are very particular about cleanliness and tidiness. Germans dress in the overall style of solemn, simple and neat. In general, most men love to wear suits, jackets, and like to wear tweed hats. Women love to wear long shirts with lapels and long skirts with light colours and patterns. In everyday life, German women mainly wear light make-up. On formal occasions, they must be neatly dressed, mostly in dark colours. In business, men wear 3-piece suits and women wear dresses. Traditional women's clothing often have matching hats of various styles. Some women simply use flowers weave a garland with flowers and wear on the head, which is very delicate and charming. Germans pay more attention to hairstyles, men should not shave their heads; young girls tend to have short or shawl hairstyles, and most of the women with permed hair are married.

德意志民族是一个团结守纪律的民族，在公共场合下礼让老弱妇孺，不会大声喧哗。如果晚上要搞聚会活动，事先要向邻居讲明情况，请求他们的谅解，并尽可能安排在周末而且不要大声喧闹。否则，邻居会投诉甚至报警。

German people are known for being a disciplined and united nation. In public, they are considerate towards the elderly, the weak, women, and children, and they refrain from making loud noises. If one plans to hold a gathering or event in the evening, it is customary to inform the neighbors in advance and seek their understanding, ideally scheduling it for the weekend and keeping the noise to a minimum. Failing to do so might result in annoyed neighbors who could confront you directly or even call the police to intervene.

德国人待人接物严肃拘谨，态度诚恳坦率。应邀去别人家做客时，一般会带礼物。大部分人会带一束鲜花，也有一些男性客人会带瓶葡萄酒、自己写的书或画册等。在参加生日宴会、节日聚会或婚礼时，贺卡更为普遍。德国人不会选择贵重的礼物，而是以实用和有意义为原则。礼物要事先用礼品纸包好，德国人会当着送礼者的面打开包装。德国人用餐有许多规矩：忌讳张开嘴巴咀嚼或身子凑近盘子吃东西，忌讳含着满口食物说话，忌讳只同右面的女士说话，更忌讳吃饭时谈有关世界观或政治的话题。德国人忌讳数字13。每月的13日若和星期五是同一天，则被视为最不吉利。德国人最忌讳的是13个人坐一桌吃饭。

Germans are serious and reserved in their approach to dealing with people, and their attitude is honest and direct. When they are invited to visit somebody's home, normally they will take gifts, most of which are flowers. Some male guests also bring a bottle of wine, a book or picture album they have written. When attending the birthday party, festival party or wedding ceremony, greeting cards are more popular. Germans will not choose the most expensive gifts but useful and significant

默克尔的节俭

gifts. All the gifts in gift wrap should be opened in front of the guests. Germans have lots of rules for dinner. It is a taboo for Germans to open mouth chewing or lean the body closely to the dish, speak while eating, talk only to the woman on the right side. More taboo is discussing the world view or political affairs while eating. It is a taboo for Germans to use the number 13. It will be regarded as the most unlucky if the date is Friday the 13th. The most taboo among Germans is 13 persons have dinner on one table.

（六）传统节日 Festivals

1. 慕尼黑啤酒节 Oktoberfest

慕尼黑盛产啤酒，饮用量为世界第一，因此人们习惯称慕尼黑为"啤酒之都"。慕尼黑啤酒节于每年 9 月末至 10 月的第 1 个周末举行，一般历时 16 天左右。慕尼黑啤酒节是世界规模的民间节日、慕尼黑一年中最盛大的活动，它完整地保留了巴伐利亚的民间风采和习俗。慕尼黑啤酒节起源于 1810 年 10 月 12 日，是为庆贺德国巴伐利亚王国太子路德维希一世和萨克森－希尔登豪森的特蕾西亚公主共结百年之好而举行的一系列庆祝活动。德国的 10 月正值大麦和啤酒花丰收的时节，人们在劳动之余，欢聚在一起饮酒、唱歌、跳舞，表达内心的喜悦之情。今天，人们用华丽的马车运送啤酒，在巨大的啤酒帐篷里开怀畅饮，欣赏巴伐利亚铜管乐队演奏的民歌乐曲和令人陶醉的情歌雅调。人们在啤酒节上品尝美味佳肴的同时，还举行一系列丰富多彩的娱乐活动，如赛马、射击、杂耍、各种游艺活动以及戏剧演出、民族音乐会等。

The output of beer in Munich is very large and the consuming is ranked the first in the world, so Munich is named as "the capital of beer". Oktoberfest is a 16-day festival celebrating beer held annually in Munich, running from late September to the first weekends in October. Oktoberfest is a world-class folk festival, and Munich's biggest events of the year, which retains the integrity of the Bavarian folk style and customs. Oktoberfest was first held on October 12, 1810 in honor of the marriage of Crown Prince Ludwig Ⅰ of Bavaria to Princess Therese von Sachsen-Hildburghausen. October is the season for the harvest of barley and hops in Germany. People gather together, drinking, singing, dancing and expressing the inner joy apart from working. Nowadays, people send the beer by beautiful carriages. People appreciate the folk songs and music from the Bavarian brass band while drinking in the giant tents. While people taste delicious food at the Oktoberfest, lots of activities will be held such as horse racing, shooting, acrobats, various amusements, theatrics, folk song concerts, etc.

2. 科隆狂欢节 Cologne Carnival

科隆狂欢节于每年 11 月 11 日 11 点 11 分开始至第二年复活节前 40 天为止，科隆狂欢节被称为一年中的第五个季节，仅次于巴西狂欢节，是全德国最盛大的节日，有着超过 800 年的历史。从前，人们为了将冬季恶灵驱逐出城，便头戴面具上街游行，现在这一惯例被保留了下来。1823 年 2 月 10 日，科隆狂欢节庆祝委员会在科隆成立，狂欢节就此成为这个城市的一个固定节日。除了由狂欢节庆祝委员会举办的众多活动（包含演讲），狂欢节的活动还包括"女性狂欢节""玫瑰星期一"大游行等。

Cologne Carnival officially begins at 11:11 a.m. on November 11 and lasts until 40 days before Easter the following year. Known as the "fifth season of the year", Cologne Carnival is second only to the Rio Carnival and is the largest festival in all of Germany, boasting a history of over 800 years. In the past, people would wear masks and parade through the streets to drive away the evil spirits of winter, a tradition that has been preserved to this day. On February 10, 1823, Cologne Carnival Festival Committee was established, marking the beginning of the carnival as an independent and organized event. In addition to numerous activities organized by the Festival Committee, including speeches, the carnival also features highlights such as "Women's Carnival Day" and grand "Rose Monday" parade.

三、旅游观光 Tourism and Sightseeing

（一）主要旅游城市 Major Tourist Cities

1. 柏林 Berlin

柏林是德国的首都、全国第一大城市，位于德国东北部。柏林是著名的欧洲古都，始建于1237年。1871年，柏林成为德意志帝国的首都。在第二次世界大战中，柏林损毁严重。第二次世界大战后，柏林被分为东柏林和西柏林。1990年德国统一，柏林墙倒塌，结束了一个城市、两种制度的局面，重新成为德国的首都。柏林是欧洲旅游胜地，古典与现代风格的建筑相互映衬、相得益彰，体现了德意志建筑艺术的特色。这里集中了国家美术馆等多个博物馆，收藏了世界各国珍贵的艺术品，同时也是德国文化最大的对外窗口。

Located in the northeast of Germany, Berlin, the capital of Germany, is the largest city in Germany. Berlin is also a well-known ancient capital in Europe built in 1237. It became the capital of the united German Empire in 1871. It was destroyed seriously in the Second World War. After the war, the city was divided into East Berlin and West Berlin. The reunification of Germany in 1990 and the fall of the Berlin Wall brought an end to one city, two systems and the re-emergence of Berlin as German capital. Berlin is a European tourist attraction, where classical and modern architectural art complement each other, reflecting the characteristics of German architectural art. There is a concentration of several museums, such as the State Gallery, which collect valuable works of art from all over the world, and it is also the largest external window on German culture.

2. 慕尼黑 Munich

慕尼黑位于德国南部，是巴伐利亚的首府，是仅次于柏林、汉堡的德国第三大城市。慕尼黑位于阿尔卑斯山北麓，多瑙河的支流伊萨尔河流经此地，自古以来就是北欧进入中欧、南欧的交通要冲，故有"通向世界的门户""欧洲大转盘"之称。慕尼黑建于1158年，1806年成为巴伐利亚王国的都城。路德维希一世执政时修建了大量古典风格的建筑，使慕尼黑成为欧洲著名的城市。作为历史文化名城，慕尼黑与法国的巴黎、奥地利的维也纳并列为欧洲三大文化中心。此外，这里经常举行各种音乐、戏剧盛会和博览会，慕尼黑也因此成为国际驰名的大都会、全球著名的国际展览和会议中心。旅游收入是这个城市的重要经济来源，以每年10月举办的慕尼黑啤酒节最为著名。

Located in the south of Germany, Munich is the capital of Bavaria and the third largest city in Germany after Berlin and Hamburg. It is located in the north of the Alps, where the Isar River—a tributary of the Danube flows through. Since ancient times, it has been the Nordic transportation hub to Central Europe and Southern Europe. So it is known as the "Gateway to the World" "the European Big Wheel". The city was first built in 1158 and became the capital of Kingdom of Bavaria in 1806. During the period of King Ludwig I, lots of classic buildings were built and Munich became a famous city in Europe. As a historical and cultural city, Munich, Paris and Vienna are considered as the three major European cultural centers. In addition, Munich is a metropolis of international renown and a globally renowned centre for international exhibitions and congresses, thanks to its frequent music and theatre events and fairs. Tourism is an important source of income for the city, which is best known for the Munich Oktoberfest held every October.

3. 法兰克福 Frankfurt

法兰克福位于德国中部的美因河畔，是进入欧洲的交通枢纽、德国商业与制造业的中心，也是德国的金融中心和博览会城市。实行欧元后，欧洲中央银行就设在法兰克福，因此使法兰克福成为世界著名的金融中心。法兰克福机场是全球现代化程度最高的机场之一，是欧洲大陆最大的机场。法兰克福拥有"德国最大的书柜"——德意志图书馆。

Frankfurt is located on both sides of the Main in Germany. It is the gateway to Europe, the center of Germany's business and manufacturing, also the financial center and the trade fair city of Germany. After the introduction of the Euro, the European Central Bank is located in Frankfurt which makes Frankfurt the world's leading financial center. Frankfurt Airport is one of the most modern airports in the world, and the largest airport on the European continent. Frankfurt is home to the Deutsche Bibliothek, "Germany's largest bookcase".

4. 科隆 Cologne

科隆是莱茵河流域的重要城市，是德国第四大城市，位于德国西部。早在公元前50年，科隆就已是罗马帝国的重要殖民地，其名字就是由英文"殖民地"一词演变而来。至今，科隆仍保留着不少罗马帝国时代的历史遗迹。如今的科隆是莱茵区最大的国际商业中心，经常举办各类国际博览会，有"传媒与通信之城"的美誉。科隆有三宝，即香水、狂欢节、教堂，其中最出名的是科隆大教堂。

Located in the west of Germany, Cologne is Germany's fourth largest city with the famous Rhine flowing through the city. As early as 50 BC, Cologne was an important colony of the Roman Empire, whose name is from the word "Colony". Cologne retains many historical monuments of the era of the Roman Empire. Today Cologne is the biggest international business centre of the Rhine region. International fairs of various fields are often held here and Cologne wins the "Media and Communications City" in the world. There are three treasures in Cologne: perfume, carnival and cathedral, of which the most famous is the Cologne Cathedral.

5. 海德堡 Heidelberg

海德堡（图2-32）位于德国的西南部，是德国历史最悠久的古城之一，也是一个兼具文艺浪漫气息与热闹活泼气氛的大学城。海德堡过去曾是科学和艺术的中心，在罗马帝国时期，这里成为边陲。海德堡不仅有其引以为荣的中世纪城堡，还拥有欧洲最古老的教育机构之一——海德堡大学。今天，海德堡仍是德国乃至欧洲的大学科研基地。

图 2-32　海德堡
Figure 2-32　Heidelberg

Located in the southwest of Germany, Heidelberg (Figure 2-32) is one of the Germany's oldest ancient cities and is a romantic and lively university town. Heidelberg used to be the center of science and art. In Roman Empire time, it became borderland village. Heidelberg is not only home to a proud medieval castle, but also to the University of Heidelberg, one of the oldest educational institutions in Europe. Today, Heidelberg is still the university research base in Germany even in the Europe.

（二）著名旅游景点 Famous Tourist Attractions

1. 勃兰登堡门 Brandenburg Gate

图 2-33　勃兰登堡门

Figure 2-33　Brandenburg Gate

勃兰登堡门（图 2-33）位于柏林市中心菩提树大街西端，是柏林城的标志。勃兰登堡门是依据雅典城门造型而建的，是德国古典主义建筑的杰作。勃兰登堡门于 1791 年竣工，门楼上耸立着胜利女神驾驭四马战车的雕塑。在战后东、西德分裂时期，勃兰登堡门内侧筑起柏林墙。1989 年柏林墙被拆后，勃兰登堡门与柏林墙一同成为德国统一的象征。柏林人对勃兰登堡门怀有特殊的感情，称它为"命运之门"。

Brandenburg Gate (Figure 2-33) is located at the western end of Linden strasse in the centre of Berlin and is the symbol of the city. It was erected according to the design of colonnade of Acropolis of Athens in 1791 and is Germany's masterpiece of classical architecture. Atop the gate stands a sculpture of the Goddess of Victory driving a four-horse chariot. During the post-war partition of Germany, the gate was isolated and inaccessible immediately next to the Berlin Wall. After the Berlin Wall was torn down in 1989, Brandenburg Gate and the Berlin Wall are considered the symbol of united Germany. Berliners have a special affection for the Brandenburg Gate, calling it the "Gate of Destiny".

2. 柏林墙遗迹 Ruins of the Berlin Wall

柏林墙的正式名称为"反法西斯防卫墙"。柏林墙是 1961 年 8 月 13 日东德在柏林城建起的城墙，目的是隔离东德和西德，是第二次世界大战以后德国分裂和冷战的标志性建筑。柏林墙于 1989 年被拆毁，为了纪念这段历史，保留了一段长约 1 300 米的柏林墙。墙上绘有来自 21 个国家的艺术家不同风格的作品，也称"东边画廊"（图 2-34）。

图 2-34　柏林墙遗迹

Figure 2-34　Ruins of the Berlin Wall

The Berlin Wall, officially known as the "Anti-Fascist Defence Wall". The Berlin Wall was a barrier constructed by the German Democratic Republic starting on August 13, 1961, that completely cut off (by land) West Berlin from East Berlin. It is the symbol of the Cold War and the separation of Germany. The wall was torn down in 1989 but the 1,300-meter-long wall was kept for commemorating the history. On the wall, there are different paintings by the artists from 21 countries, which also was named "East Art Lounge" (Figure 2-34).

3. 玛利亚广场 Marienplatz

玛利亚广场（图 2-35）是慕尼黑的中心广场，是慕尼黑最繁华的地方。广场的名称来自广场上的"玛利亚"圆柱，设立的目的是颂扬圣母玛利亚。广场中央是圣母玛利亚的雕像，广场北面是哥特式建筑市政厅，其高达 85 米的钟楼上有著名的玩偶报时钟。西北面是有两个绿圆顶钟楼的圣母教堂，它是慕尼黑的象征，为哥特式教堂，钟楼高 99 米，建于 1468 年。

图 2-35 玛利亚广场
Figure 2-35 Marienplatz

Marienplatz (Figure 2-35) is in the center of Munich and Munich's most prosperous areas. The name of Marienplatz comes from the "Maria" column in the square which was set up just to celebrate the Virgin Mary. The sculpture of Mary stands in the center of the plaza. To its north is the Rathaus（City Hall）. It is a Gothic style building with the 85 meters high bell tower. In the bell tower, there is a famous doll bell which strikes the hours. To the northwest is the Frauenkirche, with two green-domed bell towers, which is the symbol of Munich. It is the Gothic cathedral built in 1468 with a 99-meter-high bell tower.

4. 歌德故居 Goethe House

歌德故居（图 2-36）位于法兰克福市中心，大文豪歌德在此出生并度过青年时光。歌德故居虽遭受过第二次世界大战战火的破坏，但经重建后基本保持了原貌，并公开让各界人士参观。歌德在此完成了《浮士德》及《少年维特的烦恼》等著名的作品。

图 2-36 歌德故居
Figure 2-36 Goethe House

Goethe House (Figure 2-36) is located in the center of Frankfurt, in which great writer Goethe was born and spent his youth time here. The original home was destroyed near the end of the Second World War, but it was then restored as closely as possible to its original condition. Today, Goethe House is open to all visitors. It is the place where Goethe completed his *Faust* and *The Sorrows of Young Werther* and other famous works.

5. 科隆大教堂 Cologne Cathedral

科隆大教堂（图 2-37）位于德国科隆市中心的莱茵河畔，是一座典型的欧洲宗教建筑，以轻盈、雅致著称于世，是科隆的象征，也是世界最高的教堂之一。作为最完美的哥特式大教堂，科隆大教堂始建于 1248 年，建造期长达 630 多年。1996 年，科隆大教堂被列入《世界遗产名录》，与巴黎圣母院、梵蒂冈圣彼得大教堂并称为欧洲三大宗教建筑。

图 2-37 科隆大教堂
Figure 2-37 Cologne Cathedral

Located on the banks of the Rhine in the centre of Cologne, Germany, Cologne Cathedral (Figure 2-37) is a typical European religious building. Cologne Cathedral, known for its lightness and elegance in the world, and is also one of the tallest churches in the world. As the most perfect Gothic Cathedral, Cologne Cathedral was first built in 1248 and the construction lasted for more than 630 years. In 1996, Cologne Cathedral was added to the World Heritage List. The Cathedral, the Notre-Dame de Paris and St. Peter's Basilica in Vatican City are regarded as three largest European religious buildings.

图 2-38 海德堡城堡
Figure 2-38 Heidelberg Castle

6. 海德堡城堡 Heidelberg Castle

这座红褐色古城堡是海德堡的标志。海德堡城堡（图 2-38）坐落在内卡尔河畔树木繁茂的王座山（Koenigsstuhl）上，为选帝侯官邸的遗址。城堡主要用红褐色的内卡尔河砂岩筑成，城堡内部结构复杂，包括防御工事、居室和宫殿等。始建于 13 世纪，历时 400 年才完工。17 世纪时城堡曾两度被法国人摧毁，城堡主人选帝侯家族也迁居曼海姆，被遗弃的城堡后来有一部分得以修复重建，至 19 世纪末主体建筑才恢复原貌并得以使用。现在城堡多数的房间开放给游客参观，保存完好的一些大厅仍可举行宴会及艺术表演。未修复的部分仍为残垣断壁，上部某些房间只留有一面外墙。这是一座美丽的大城堡，也是一座满目疮痍的城堡遗址。马克·吐温曾如此形容海德堡城堡："残破而不失王者之气，如同暴风雨中的李尔王。"

This old reddish-brown castle is the symbol of the city of Heidelberg. Heidelberg castle (Figure 2-38) is situated on the heavily wooded Koenigsstuhl by the river Neckar and is the site of the Elector's official residence. The castle is mainly made of reddish-brown sandstone from the river Neckar and has a complex interior consisting of fortifications, apartments and a palace. It was built in the 13th century and took 400 years to complete. The castle was destroyed twice by French in the 17th century, and the owner of the castle, the Marquis de Chantilly, moved to Mannheim. Part of the abandoned castle was later restored and rebuilt, and the main building was restored to its original form and used only at the end of the 19th century. Most of the rooms of the castle are now open to visitors, and some of the well-preserved halls are still used for banquets and artistic performances. The unrestored part of the castle is still in ruins, with only one outer wall remaining in some of the upper rooms. It is a large and beautiful castle, but also the ruins of a castle full of changes. Mark Twain even said: "Heidelberg Castle is as dilapidated and kingly as King Lear in a storm."

7. 无忧宫 German Carefree Palace

无忧宫（图 2-39）位于德国东部勃兰登堡州首府波茨坦市北郊，宫名取自法文的"无忧"（或"莫愁"），无忧宫及周围的园林是普鲁士国王腓特烈二世在 1745—1757 年仿效法国凡尔赛宫建造的建筑。整个园林占地 290 公顷，坐落在一座沙丘上，故有"沙丘上的宫殿"之称。无忧宫全部建筑工程前后延续了约 50 年，为德国建筑艺术的精华。室内多用壁画和明镜装饰，辉煌璀璨。宫殿的东侧是珍藏有 124 幅名画的画廊，多为文艺复兴时期意大利、荷兰画家的名作。在无忧宫的花园内有一座六角凉亭，被称为"中国茶亭"。茶亭是采用了中国传统的伞状圆形屋顶、上盖碧瓦、黄金圆柱落地支撑的建筑结构。亭内桌椅完全仿造东方式样制造，亭前矗立着一只中国式香鼎，据说当年普鲁士国王常在此品茶消遣。

Located on the northern outskirts of Potsdam, the capital of the state of Brandenburg in eastern Germany, the name of the palace is taken from the French word for "carefree" (Figure 2-39), and the palace and its surrounding gardens were built by King Frederick II of Prussia from 1745 to 1757, modelled on the Palace of Versailles in France. The whole garden covers an area of 290 hectares and is situated on a sand dune, which is why it is called "Palace on the Sand Dune". The whole construction project of the carefree palace lasted for about 50 years before and after, which is the essence of German architectural art. The interior is decorated with frescoes and mirrors, which are brilliant. On the east side of the palace, there is a gallery with 124 famous paintings, most of which are masterpieces of Italian and Dutch painters in the Renaissance

图 2-39　无忧宫
Figure 2-39　German Carefree Palace

period. There is a hexagonal pavilion called the "Chinese Tea Pavilion". The pavilion adopts the traditional Chinese architectural structure of a round umbrella-shaped roof covered with green tiles and supported by golden columns on the floor. Inside the pavilion, the tables and chairs are modelled on Oriental styles, and in front of the pavilion stands a Chinese-style incense pot, where the King of Prussia is said to have enjoyed his tea.

（三）旅游购物 Shopping

香肠：德国人喜欢吃肉，尤其喜欢香肠。德国的香肠品种多达 1 500 种。慕尼黑小白肠、纽伦堡指肠非常有名，黑森林火腿销往世界各地。香肠通常与面包搭配，德国面包的质量和数量位居世界前列，但是德国人一般不单独食用面包，而是要抹上一层厚厚的奶油，配上干酪和果酱，加上香肠或火腿一起食用。

Sausage: Germans are fond of meat, particularly sausages. There are as many as 1,500 varieties of sausages in Germany. The Munich Weisswurst and Nuremberg Rostbratwurst are quite famous, and Black Forest ham is exported worldwide. Sausages are typically paired with bread, and Germany is renowned for both the quality and variety of its bread. However, Germans usually don't eat bread on its own; instead, they spread a thick layer of butter on it, add cheese and jam, and enjoy it with sausages or ham.

猪肉：德国比较有特色的菜有巴伐利亚烤猪脚、烤猪肉、醋焖牛肉等。德国猪脚堪称一道享誉世界的名菜，也是德国人的传统美食之一，在巴伐利亚尤其受欢迎，要佐以德国酸菜等进食。德国烤猪脚的特色就在于猪脚皮脆而不干，嚼起来非常有劲，猪肉也饱满入味。在食用德国猪脚的时候，通常还要配上地道的德国啤酒。

Pork: The characteristic German cuisine are Bavaria roasted pork knuckle, roasted pork and vinegar braised beef. Pork knuckle is Germany's well-known dish in the world and is one of the typical dishes of German cuisine that is popular in Bavaria and always eaten with sour cabbage (sauerkraut). The characteristics of roasted pork knuckle are crispy but not dry, very chewy and also flavorful. In Germany, pork knuckle is always accompanied by authentic Germany beer.

啤酒：德国啤酒和葡萄酒以种类繁多而闻名于世。1516 年，巴伐利亚公国的威廉四世大公颁布《纯正啤酒法》，规定德国啤酒只能以大麦芽、啤酒花和水三种原料制作，所以近 500 年来德国啤酒成为纯正啤酒的代名词。今日的德国为世界第二大啤酒生产国，境内共有 1 300

多家啤酒厂，生产的啤酒种类高达 5 000 多种。根据官方统计，每个德国人平均每年喝掉 138 升的啤酒，世界上再也找不到比德国人更热爱啤酒的民族了。

Beer: Both the beer and wine of Germany are famous in the world. In 1516, Grand Duke William Ⅳ of Bavarian Duchy enacted the rule of *Pure Beer Law* in which three kinds of raw materials—barley malt, hops and water can only be used for producing beer, so German beer has become synonymous with a so-called pure beer for nearly 500 years. Today Germany is the world's second largest beer producer. There are 1,300 breweries and more than 5,000 species of beer. According to the official statistics, each German drinks 138 liters of beer a year on average. No one loves beer more than Germans.

德国生产的各款名牌产品，因其品质高、实用性强及耐用性好而获得一致好评，尤其是做工精良的工具、照相机、光学仪器、钟表、钢笔和刀具。此外，德国的木雕制品、皮革制品、宝石也很精美。每年德国商店都会举行两次降价清仓的活动，特别是圣诞节结束后至次年 2 月，以及 6 月末至 7 月。

Germany has been unanimously praised for the brand-name products with quality, practicality and durability, especially the well-made tools, cameras, optical instruments, watches and clocks, pens and knives. In addition woodcarving, leather and jewelry made in Germany are also delicate and beautiful. Every year particularly from the end of Christmas to February as well as from the end of June to July, there are two seasons on sale in Germany.

刀具、厨具：德国的钢材全世界有名，以优质钢材制成的刀具耐用持久、刀刃锋利，双立人就是其中之一。德国生产的锅具有导热性好、油烟少等优点，以菲仕乐和福腾宝最为有名。

Knives and kitchenware: Germany is famous for steel in the world. The knives made of high quality steel are durable and sharp. J. A. Henckels is one of them. The pots made in Germany have good thermal conductivity with less smoke. The most famous pot series are Fissler and WMF.

笔和皮具：持久耐用的德国皮具和钢笔兼具德国严谨的制造工艺与欧洲先进的设计，深受各界推崇。零钱包、皮夹、手袋、旅行袋等各式产品都有品质保证。知名品牌包括爱格纳、金箭、MCM、BREE 等。此外，户外品牌"狼爪"也享誉全球，产品包括防水夹克、背包系列等。设计简洁、书写流畅的百利金及万宝龙的钢笔在各大百货店都可以买到。

Pens and leather: Durable German leather products and pen series are deeply respected with Germany's stringent manufacturing process and advanced design of Europe. All the products are quality guaranteed such as coin purses, wallets, handbags, travel bags and other various styles of adequate products. Famous brands are Aigner, Gold Pfeil, MCM, BREE and so on. In addition, the brand Jack Wolfskin is well worldwide known for its outdoor products, including waterproof jackets, backpack series. Pelikan and Mont Blanc pens with simple designs and easily writing are available in major department stores.

梅森瓷器：德国的梅森市以瓷器著称，以前一直为皇室烧陶瓷。梅森瓷器制作精美、款式多样、风格独特，素有"瓷中白金"之称，可以说是欧洲高级瓷器的代名词。

Meissen porcelain: Meissen, a city of Germany, is known for its porcelain and had supplied ceramic products for the Palace. Meissen porcelain is exquisitely crafted, diverse in design, and uniquely styled, often referred to as " White Gold of

扫码获取：入境须知及海关规定

Porcelain", and can be considered synonymous with high-end European porcelain.

本节习题

1. 假设你是一位中德旅游产品推广人员，需要设计一条中欧工业旅游线路，请结合本章所学内容完成线路设计。

2. 如果你是一名德国导游，正在接待来自美国的旅游团，需要提醒游客注意哪些礼仪和禁忌？

3. 德国音乐名人辈出，有不少与音乐家有关的纪念地适合学习观摩，请你以音乐为研学主题，设计一次研学游活动。

第五节　南欧之旅

Travel in Southern Europe

欧洲花园——意大利
The Garden of Europe—Italy

导读

　　作为一个既古老又年轻的国度，意大利的历史可追溯至古希腊时期，辉煌的罗马帝国在亚平宁的土地上留下了众多的历史遗迹。从罗马帝国开始，到中世纪天主教盛行时期，意大利一直在欧洲占据着经济和文化的中心位置，罗马、佛罗伦萨、威尼斯等著名城市是欧洲乃至世界的文化中心，达·芬奇，米开朗琪罗、贝尼尼等艺术大师辈出，古老的博洛尼亚大学是全世界历史最为悠久的学府，歌剧也是意大利献给世界文艺舞台的艺术瑰宝。由于地理位置优越，意大利在漫长的中世纪一直是东方商品进入欧洲的必经之地，也是古代丝绸之路的终点，早在古代就发挥着东西方经济文化交流的桥梁作用，意大利人马可·波罗和利玛窦更是成为促进中西方相互了解的先驱。意大利的旅游资源十分丰富，是世界遗产最多的国家，拥有艺术、美食、历史、时尚、文化以及美丽的海岸、群山和珍贵的古代遗迹，旅游收入是弥补国家收支逆差的重要来源。据世界旅游组织统计，近年来，中国人赴意大利旅游发展迅猛，意大利也是中国极具潜力的旅游客源国。

一、地理概览 Geography of Italy

（一）位置 Location

　　意大利共和国，简称意大利，地处欧洲南部，包括亚平宁半岛、西西里岛、撒丁岛和其他小岛。北方的阿尔卑斯山区和法国、瑞士、奥地利以及斯洛文尼亚接壤。其国土内还有两个袖珍国家——梵蒂冈和圣马力诺。意大利的地理位置十分重要，最南端几乎接近非洲大陆海岸，与突尼斯、马耳他和阿尔及利亚隔海相望。意大利是欧洲到达非洲和亚洲的南大门。

The Republic of Italy, briefly Italy, is located in the south of Europe, comprising Apennine Peninsula and a number of islands including Sicily and Sardinia and other small islets. To its north is Alps mountainous area and it borders France, Switzerland, Austria and Slovenia. Inside the territory there are two small countries Vatican City State and San Marino. Italy's geographical position is very important, its south point is almost close to the coast of the African continent, and Italy faces Tunisia, Malta and Algeria across the sea. Italy is the south gate of Europe to Africa and Asia.

（二）地形和气候 The Land and Seasons

意大利全境4/5为山丘地带，多火山地震。山地和丘陵约占国土总面积的80%，平原只占20%。境内有阿尔卑斯山脉和亚平宁山脉。亚平宁山脉和阿尔卑斯山脉之间是著名的波河平原。波河平原约占意大利国土面积的1/6，是著名的农业区和天然粮仓。意法边境的勃朗峰海拔4 810米，为欧洲西部第一高峰。亚平宁半岛西侧有著名的维苏威火山，西西里岛的埃特纳火山海拔3 350米，为欧洲最高的活火山。

4/5 of Italy's territory is mountainous and prone to volcanic earthquakes. Mountains and hills account for about 80%, while plains account for about 20%. There are the Alps and Apennines within the territory. Between the Apennines and the Alps it is Po Plain which has an area of the 1/6 of the Italian territory and it is the famous agricultural district and natural barn. Mont Blanc, on the border with France with 4,810 meters above sea level, is the highest mountain in Western Europe. To the west of Apennine Peninsula is the famous Mount Vesuvius. Mount Etna in Sicily is 3,350 meters above the sea level which is the highest active volcano in Europe.

意大利由于地形狭长，境内多山，并且地处地中海腹部，因此南北气候相差较大。总体来说，意大利北部为大陆性气候而南部为典型的地中海气候。北部冬季寒冷、湿润和多雪，而南部沿海地区冬季暖和、夏季干燥。

With narrow terrain and mountainous area, Italy is located in the middle of the Mediterranean. The climate is quite different from the north to the south. Generally speaking, the north belongs to continental climate and the south is typical Mediterranean climate. The north is cold, moist and snowy in winter, while the south is warm in winter and dry in summer.

（三）自然资源 Natural Resources

意大利自然资源贫乏，仅有水力、地热、天然气等能源和大理石、黏土、汞、硫黄以及少量铅、铝、锌和铝矾土等矿产资源。石油和天然气产量只能满足一小部分国内市场需求，75%的能源供给和主要工业原料依赖国外进口。意大利传统、重要的可再生能源为地热和水力，地热发电量为世界第二，仅次于美国，水力发电量为世界第九。意大利一直重视发展太阳能，2011年意大利是世界第一光伏装机容量国（占世界份额的1/4），意大利国内可再生能源供给比例已经达到能源总需求的25%。

Italy is poor in natural resources, with only energy sources such as hydropower, geothermal energy, natural gas, and mineral resources such as marble, clay, mercury, sulfur, as well as small amounts of lead, aluminum, zinc, and bauxite. Oil and natural gas production can only meet a small portion of domestic market demand, with 75% of energy supply and main industrial raw materials relying on foreign imports. Italy's traditional important renewable energy sources are geothermal and hydropower, with geothermal power generation ranking second only to the United States in the world, and hydropower generation ranking ninth in the world. Italy has always attached great importance to the development of solar energy. In 2011, Italy was the world's largest photovoltaic installed capacity country（accounting for one fourth of the world share）, and the domestic renewable energy supply proportion in Italy has reached 25% of the total energy demand.

二、人文概况 Overview of Italian Humanities

（一）国情认知 Basic Knowledge of National Conditions

意大利人口约 5 894 万（2022 年），95% 的居民为意大利人，此外，还有少量法国人、拉丁裔等。意大利的官方语言是意大利语，属于印欧语系罗曼语族。个别地区讲法语和德语。90% 以上的居民信奉天主教。

The population of Italy is about 58.94 million（2022）, 95% of the inhabitants are Italians, in addition to a small number of French, Latins and others. The official language is Italian, which belongs to the Romance group of the Indo-European language family. French and German are spoken in some areas, and over 90% of the population is Catholic.

意大利的国旗为三色旗，由同样宽度的绿、白、红三色长条纵列组成。国徽呈圆形，中心图案是一个带红边的白色五角星，象征意大利共和国；五角星背面是一个大齿轮，象征劳动者；齿轮周围有橄榄枝和橡树枝环绕，象征和平与强盛。底部的红色绶带上用意大利文写着"意大利共和国"。国歌是《马梅利之歌》，国花为雏菊，货币为欧元。

The national flag of Italy is a tricolor flag, consisting of long vertical stripes of green, white and red of the same width. The national emblem is round, the central design is a white five-pointed star with a red border, symbolizing the Italian Republic; on the back of the five-pointed star is a large gear, symbolizing the laborers; the gear is surrounded by olive branches and oak branches, symbolizing peace and strength. The red ribbon at the bottom reads "Italian Republic" in Italian. The national anthem is the *Marmeli Song*, the national flower is daisy, and the currency is the Euro.

（二）历史简介 History of Italy

意大利是古罗马帝国的发源地。公元前的古希腊文明对古罗马影响巨大，促使古罗马从君主制过渡到共和制（公元前 509 年到公元前 27 年）。罗马共和国通过不断扩张，到恺撒时期已经成为横跨非洲、欧洲和亚洲，称霸地中海的超级大国。公元 395 年，罗马帝国分为西罗马帝国和东罗马帝国（拜占庭帝国）。公元 962 年受神圣罗马帝国统治。11 世纪诺曼人入侵意大利南部并建立王国，12—13 世纪时又分裂成许多王国、公国、自治城市和小封建领地。14 世纪意大利成为文艺复兴的发源地。从 16 世纪起，意大利先后被法国、西班牙、奥地利占领，1861 年 3 月建立意大利王国。1870 年，法国在普法战争中失败，撤回在罗马的军队，意大利国王乘机吞并教皇国，意大利最终完成统一，迁都罗马。1922 年，墨索里尼上台执政，开始实行长达 20 余年的法西斯统治。1940 年，意大利向英、法宣战。1943 年，盟军登陆西西里岛，意大利无条件投降。1946 年，意大利共和国正式宣布成立。

Italy was the cradle of Roman Empire. The ancient Rome was affected so deeply by the civilization of ancient Greek that the Roman monarchy was replaced by the Roman Republic（509 BC to 27 BC）. Roman Republic became a superpower which included some part of Africa, part of Asia and part of Europe and dominated the Mediterranean in Caesar period. In 395 AD, Diocletian separated the Empire into two—West Roman Empire and East Roman Empire（Byzantine Empire）. In 962 AD, it was ruled by the Holy Roman Empire. In the 11th century, the Normans invaded southern Italy and established kingdoms. From the 12th to the 13th century, they split into many kingdoms, principalities, autonomous cities, and small feudal territories. In the 14th century, Italy became the birthplace of the Renaissance. From the 16th century, Italy was successively occupied by France, Spain and Austria, and the kingdom of Italy was established in March 1861. In 1870, France was defeated in the war against Prussia and withdrew the army from Rome. The King of Italy took over the papal state, and Italy was unified at last and made Rome as the capital. In 1922, Mussolini took the power and carried out the fascist regime for over twenty years. In 1940, Italy declared the war on Britain and France. In 1943, the allies invaded Sicily and Italy surrendered. The Republic of Italy was founded in 1946.

（三）经济状况 The Economy

意大利是发达资本主义国家，是欧洲的大国之一。第二次世界大战后到 20 世纪 60 年代期间，意大利经济得以迅速发展，从农业国家迅速成为高度工业化国家。但意大利的世界级大公司较少，主要依靠中小企业。中小企业在意大利经济中占有重要地位，近 70% 的国内生产总值由这些企业创造。意大利北部和南部经济发展不平衡。北部人均生产总值高于欧盟平均水平，南部却比欧盟平均水平低。意大利的汽车工业发达，居欧洲第五位，法拉利、菲亚特等品牌的汽车畅销海外。意大利是军火生产大国，是世界上仅次于美、俄、法的第四大军火出口国。意大利的家用电器、服装和鞋类产品在世界上声誉卓著，尤以高级服装著称于世。意大利素有"制鞋王国"之誉，所产皮鞋在很多人眼中是地位和品质的象征。意大利农业发达，是世界三大橄榄油生产国之一。意大利的葡萄和葡萄酒产量位居世界前列，每年都有大量葡萄酒出口法国、德国和美国，出口量居世界首位。意大利的交通运输业相当发达，自古就有"条条大路通罗马"之说。意大利国内自然资源贫乏，原料和能源主要依赖进口，对外贸易是意大利经济的主要支柱，传统产品为其出口创汇的主体。

Italy is a developed capitalist country and one of the great powers in Europe. During the period from the end of the Second World War to the 1960s, Italy's economy develop quickly and became an industrial country instead of the agricultural country. Only a few world-class companies exist in Italy. Most of the companies are medium and small in size. Small and medium-sized companies play an important role in Italian economy, and they create 70% of the GDP. The economy of south and north are uneven in Italy. The average GDP of the north zone is higher than the average of European Union, while the south is lower than that. Italy has a large auto industry which is the 5th largest in the Europe, especially the popular overseas market of Ferrari and Fiat. Italy is a major arms producing country and the fourth largest military arms exporter in the world after the United States, Russia, and France. The electrical household appliances, garments and boots are well-known in the world. The high-class fashion in Italy is particularly renowned in the world. Italy is known as the " Kingdom of Boots", and the boots mode in Italy are the symbol of status and quality in many people's view. Italy is also a developed agricultural country. It is one of the three major countries that manufacture olive oil. The output of grape and wine ranks among the top in the world. Italy exports lots of wine to France, Germany and the United States every year, and the quantity has been ranked first in the world. Italy's transportation industry is quite developed, since ancient times, there has been a saying that "All roads lead to Rome". Italy's domestic natural resources are scarce, and raw materials and energy mainly rely on imports. The foreign trade is the mainstay of the economy and the traditional products are the backbone to earn foreign currency.

（四）传统文化 Traditional Culture

意大利是世界文明古国、文艺复兴运动的发祥地。意大利文化别具特色，在文学、艺术、建筑设计、雕塑、绘画、军事科学、农业技术、地理、医学等许多方面都达到了很高的水平，名人辈出。在罗马帝国时期，意大利的建筑及雕刻达到了顶峰。他们利用火山灰加水拌石子发明了原始的混凝土，从而使高大建筑成为现实，并且留下了许多传世佳作，罗马斗兽场、凯旋门、古罗马遗址、万神庙等都是当时高大建筑的代表。庞贝古城遗址再现了古罗马时期的城市文明。在绘画、雕塑方面，代表人物有文艺复兴三杰——达·芬奇（代表作：《最后的晚餐》《蒙娜丽莎》）、米开朗琪罗（代表作：《大卫》《创世纪》《最后的审判》）和拉斐尔（代表作：《雅典学院》及宗教绘画）。

Italy is the world's ancient civilized country and the birthplace of the Renaissance. Italian culture has its unique characteristics. Its literature, art, architectural design, sculpture, painting, military science, agricultural technology, geography, medicine and many other aspects have reached a very high level with lots of famous persons. During the period of Roman Empire, architecture and the art of carving reached its peak. They invented the ancient concrete by mixing volcanic ash and small stones with water. Therefore giant buildings came to the world and many timeless buildings were left. The representatives of giant buildings at that time are Colosseum, Are de Triomphe, the ancient Roman remains and Pantheon. The ancient city of Pompeii revealed the city civilization of ancient Roman period. The representatives of painting and sculpture are the three outstanding persons of the Renaissance— Leonardo da Vinci(*The Last Supper*; *Mona Lisa*), Michelangelo(*David*, *Genesis*, *The Last Judgment*) and Raphael(*The School of Athens* and his religion paintings).

意大利文化

意大利是西餐的鼻祖。意大利的美食高贵、典雅、味道独特。精美可口的面食、奶酪、火腿和葡萄酒成为世界各国美食家的向往。意大利菜肴注重原料的本色，成品力求保持原汁原味。在烹调过程中喜欢用橄榄油、黑橄榄、帕玛森干酪、香料、西红柿与 Marsala 酒，烹调方法以炒、煎、炸、烩等见长。意大利人喜爱面食，面食往往是第一道菜。面条的做法、吃法很多，面条的形状、颜色、味道各不相同，每种面还配有不同的调料、酱汁。此外，还有意式馄饨、意式饺子等。面包在意大利是非常重要的一种日常食品。意大利面包大致可分为软式（早餐食用）和硬式（正餐食用）两种。另一种传统的意大利食品是冰激凌。17 世纪，意大利就出现了冰激凌。意大利从南到北都适宜种植葡萄，所有地区都盛产葡萄酒。

Italy is the ancestor of Western cuisine. Italian cuisine is noble, elegant with unique taste. Beautiful and delicious pasta, cheese, ham and wine are favored by international gourmets. Italian dishes attach most importance to the nature of the raw material and original taste of finished food. In the process of cooking, olive oil, black olives, Parmesan cheese, spices, tomatoes and Marsala wine are made best use of. The means of cooking are frying, grilling, deep-frying and stewing. Italians like wheaten food which is usually the first course. They cook,and eat noodles in many ways. The shape, color and taste of noodles are various each type comes with different seasonings and sauces. And there are Italian ravioli and dumplings. Bread is the important daily food for Italians. The bread can be classified as soft which is for breakfast and hard which is for the main meal. Historical records show that ice cream first appeared in Italy as early as the 17th century. Italy's climate, from the south to the north, is ideal for growing grapes, making every region a prolific producer of wine.

比萨饼的起源

意大利是崇尚自由的国度，开朗、乐观、热情是意大利人的特点，但他们也比较懒散，工作效率低。意大利人的作息时间通常会延后，也就是晚睡晚起。午餐一般在下午 1 点半左右，晚餐在八九点钟。意大利人不喜欢守时，约会时迟到 15～20 分钟是正常的。在意大利，一年中有很多假期，大都以宗教理由放假。意大利人每日的工作时间不长，大致是上午 9 到 12 点、下午 4 到 6 点，中午休息时间很长。因此不管是旅游、购物还是办事都要特别注意各地点的开放或营业时间，以免有所耽误。

Italy is the land of liberty. Italians are cheerful, optimistic and enthusiastic but also lazy and low efficient. The routine time for Italian is usually delayed. They go to bed late and get up late. The lunch is generally around 1:30 p.m., and dinner at 8 or around 9 o'clock. Italian are not likely to be punctual so that they are always 15 minutes or 20 minutes late for the appointed time. In Italy, there are lots of holidays all year round, mostly for religious reasons. Their daily work time is not long, usually from around 9 am to 12 am and from 4 p.m. to 6 p.m. They have a long lunch time, so you must pay more attention to the time to avoid possible delay for visiting, shopping or for business.

意大利人的家庭观念比较重，完全以家庭为中心。祖母非常受人尊重，每年还会举行"最酷奶奶"评选活动。与其他欧洲国家相比，1/3 的意大利已婚男女每天都会与他们的母亲见面，50% 的已婚男子与他们的母亲住在一个城市，15% 的人甚至与父母住在同一幢公寓。有 70% 的超过 35 岁的独身男子与他们的父母住在一起，1/4 的离婚男子会搬回与母亲同住。无论何时，意大利的亲情纽带都会将家人紧密连在一起。家人们喜欢周末相聚，也经常一起吃饭，团结和亲情是意大利人力量的源泉。

Italians have a strong family notion and their life center is their family. The grandmother is respected so much so that they will elect the coolest grandmother every year. Unlike people in the other European countries, one third of married Italians meet their mothers every day. 50% of the married men live in the same city with their mothers and 15% even stay in the same building. It is so strange that 70% of the single men at the age up to 35 years old live with their parents. One fourth of the divorced men will come back to live with their mothers. The family bond is very tight in Italy, no matter when. They like to stay together at weekends and have dinner together. Solidarity and love for the family is the source of power for Italians.

（五）礼仪禁忌 Social Etiquettes and Taboos

意大利人善于交际和沟通，也喜欢争论和辩论。在日常生活中，见到长者或不太熟悉的人，要称呼他的姓，再加上"先生""夫人""小姐"和荣誉职称。"小姐"和"夫人"这两种称谓切忌混用，如果不清楚该如何称呼对方，可以使用意义较为模糊的"女士"一词。意大利人见面时会握手或招手示意，握手时忌四个人同时交叉握手，这样会形成一个十字架形状，在意大利人眼中十字架是不吉利的象征。

Italians are good at social interaction and communication. They get used to arguing and debating. In daily life, when you see the elderly, or people who you are not familiar with, you should call his surname with "Mr." "Mrs." "Miss" and the honorary title. Both "Miss" and "Mrs." titles should never be mixed. If you do not know how to greet a female, you can use "Madam". Italians shake or wave hands when they meet. But it is considered as bad manners if four people shake hands together with their hands crossing, because in Italy the cross is a symbol of bad luck.

意大利人的肢体语言非常丰富，讲话时同时配有各种肢体动作。有人开玩笑说意大利人不做动作就不会讲话了。如果手势表达不正确，很容易造成双方误会。当他们用大拇指和食指围成圆圈，其余三指向上翘起时，一般表示"好""行"或"一切顺利"，在餐桌礼仪中则表示称赞"好吃极了"或"做得棒极了"；他们用食指顶住脸颊来回转动，意为"好吃""味道鲜美"；竖起食指来回摆动表示"不""不行"；耸肩、摊掌加上摇头，表示"不知道"；五指并拢、手心向下、对着胃部来回转动，表示"饥饿"。

Italians have rich body languages. They always use their body languages to express themselves while speaking. Someone joked that Italians cannot speak if they don't use their body languages. Wrong hand gestures will cause misunderstandings. When they circle with the thumb and forefinger, and the rest raise upward, it means "Good" "OK" or "Everything is going well", and in table etiquette, it indicates praise, such as "Delicious" or "You've done exceptionally well". When they touch the cheek with their index finger and turn it back and forth, it means "Delicious" or "Tasty". When the index finger is up and swings back and forth, they mean "No or You can't do that". When they shrug, show the open palms and shake head, it means "I don't know". When they show their hunger, they close fingers with palms down and move back and forth towards the stomach.

意大利有"服装之乡"的美称。意大利人穿着讲究，上班穿制服，参加宴会或重要活动时穿礼服。意大利人热情好客，但聚餐时往往是AA制，除非有人声明请客。他们喜欢和朋友、家人或亲戚一起进餐，边吃边聊，时间非常长。用餐的时候，不要把刀叉弄得叮当作响。在吃面条时，用叉子将面条卷起来往嘴里送，不可用嘴吸，尤其是在喝汤时，不要发出响声。客人一定不可以将盐撒落在地上，这是对主人极大的不尊敬。早在2 000多年前的罗马帝国时期，盐就被看作是一种珍贵的商品，还曾被用来支付军队士兵的薪饷，主人向客人表示欢迎的方式是敬盐。

Italy is a fashion country. Italians pay particular attention to their dress. They wear uniforms to work, and they dress formally when attending a party or an important event. Italians are warm-hearted and hospitable. They always have dinner together but they will go Dutch except when somebody claims to pay. Italians like to have dinner with family, friends or relatives. It will take a long time to have dinner as they talk with each other while eating. During the dinner, it is a taboo to make noise with the forks and knives. When you eat noodles, you must roll them up with a fork and don't slurp the noodle directly. When you eat soup, never make noise. Never spread the salt on the floor because it is impolite to the host. As early as 2,000 years ago in the Roman Empire, salt was regarded as a precious goods and was even used to pay the salary of soldiers. To send the salt to the guests is to welcome the distinguished guests.

受邀到朋友家做客时可以带一些小礼物，包装要精美，但忌讳送十字架形的礼物。意大利人喜欢鲜花，但送花有不少讲究：菊花是丧葬、扫墓之时用以凭吊故人之花，玫瑰花比较普遍，但红玫瑰只送情人或妻子。送花以单数为宜。意大利人非常在意礼物的包装。收到礼物后，主人会当着客人的面打开礼物，并说一些感谢的话。意大利人忌讳送手帕，因为手帕是用来擦眼泪的。

It is better to take gifts with fine packing when you visit friends, but it is a taboo to send cross-like items as a gift. Italians like flowers but you must be careful to choose proper ones. Chrysanthemum is for funeral or tomb-sweeping. The rose is more popular but the red one is only for lovers or one's wife. The number of the flowers should be singular. Italians care much about the packing of the gift. They will open the present in front of the guests and express gratitude to them. It is rude to send handkerchief as they think it for wiping tear.

（六）传统节日 Festivals

1. 威尼斯狂欢节 Carnival of Venice

威尼斯狂欢节于 2 月复活节前的 40 天举行。威尼斯狂欢节是当今世界上历史最悠久、规模最宏大的狂欢节之一，与巴西嘉年华及法国尼斯嘉年华并列为世界三大嘉年华。威尼斯狂欢节又称威尼斯面具节，这一传统可追溯到 1 700 年前。权贵和穷人可以通过面具融合在一起，面具将社会差异暂时消除，所有的阶级、身份与地位此时都不再有任何意义。威尼斯狂欢节最大的特点是面具，其次是华丽服饰。在狂欢节期间，人们戴着各种面具，穿着传统的服装，到街上游行、表演。现在，每年的狂欢节都会有一个主题。官方的活动中心是圣马可广场。

The Carnival of Venice starts in February, 40 days before Easter. It is one of the oldest and biggest carnivals in the world today, and is regarded as one of the three largest carnivals in the world with Brazilian Carnival and Nice Carnival in France. The carnival is also known as Venetian Mask Festival. It can be traced back to 1,700 years ago. The rich would integrate with the poor with the masks and the class differences would temporarily be eliminated behind the masks. All class, identity and status in this period was no longer meaningful. The biggest feature for the Carnival of Venice is the masks and followed by the gorgeous costumes. People in a variety of masks will wear traditional clothes and march into the street for performances. The Carnival of Venice is officially held in St. Mark's Square with a theme every year.

2. 赛船节 Boat Race Festival

每年 6—9 月，水城威尼斯都要举行七八次划船比赛，这是人们最崇尚的活动之一。其中，以每年 9 月第一个星期日的划船比赛最为隆重，历史也最悠久，被称为"历史性的雷加塔"，即划木桨船比赛。

Every year from June to September, Venice, the city of water, hosts seven or eight rowing competitions, which are among the most revered activities. The most prestigious of these is the race held on the first Sunday of September, known for its long history as the "Historical Regatta", which involves rowing traditional wooden boats.

3. 圣母升天节 Ferragosto

圣母升天节在每年的 8 月 15 日，是意大利的公共假日。它的历史可以追溯到 2 000 多年前的古罗马。当年，为了让人们尽情地享受生活，奥古斯都大帝将该节日定在 8 月 1 日。从 17 世纪末，圣母升天节改为 8 月 15 日。人们要在圣母升天节前后度假，以避免在一年中最热的时候工作，而是尽情地享受生活。

Ferragosto is an Italian public holiday celebrated on August 15. It can be traced back to the ancient Rome 2,000 years ago. In order to enjoy life, Emperor Augusto stipulated August 1 as the holiday. And since the end of the 17th century, the date was changed to August 15. People will have a rest before or after Ferragosto to avoid working in the hottest weather of the year and to enjoy life.

三、旅游观光 Tourism and Sightseeing

（一）主要旅游城市 Major Tourist Cities

1. 罗马 Rome

罗马位于亚平宁半岛中部的台伯河畔，是意大利的首都，也是全国政治、经济、文化和交通中心。"条条大路通罗马"形象地描述了罗马作为地中海地区交通中心的重要性。罗马于公元前 753 年 4 月 21 日建立，著名的"母狼乳婴"故事就是关于罗马古城建立的传说。如今，4 月 21 日被定为罗马建城日，"母狼乳婴"成为罗马的城徽图案。作为古罗马帝国的发源地，罗马有着非常丰富的旅游资源，被称为"永恒之都"。罗马还是一座艺术宝库、文化名城，古城酷似一座巨型的露天历史博物馆。在罗马古城遗址上，矗立着帝国元老院、凯旋门、万神殿和罗马斗兽场等世界闻名的古迹。罗马还有文艺复兴时期的许多精美建筑和艺术精品，以及市中心的天主教圣地梵蒂冈。

Located on the riverside of the Tiber in the middle of Apennine Peninsula, Rome is the capital of Italy, and the political, economic, cultural and transportation center. The old saying "All roads lead to Rome" can describe how important Rome is as a center of transportation in the Mediterranean. Rome was established on April 21 of the year 753 BC. The myth of she-wolf suckling the infant twins recorded the legend of the establishment of the ancient Roman City. Today April 21 is the date of memorial of establishment of Rome and the city emblem is the she-walf suckling the infant twins. As a cradle of the establishtnent of the ancient Roman ancient Roman Empire, there are lots of tourist resources and it is named as "Eternal City". Rome is also an art treasure and cultural city. The old town is a large open museum of history. In the ancient ruins in Rome stand the Imperial Senate, Arc de Triomphe, Pantheon, Colosseum and other famous historic remains. There are many beautiful buildings of the Renaissance and art works as well as holy land Vatican City in the center of the city.

罗马城徽

2. 佛罗伦萨 Florence

佛罗伦萨是托斯卡纳大区和佛罗伦萨省的首府。美第奇家族曾经长期控制佛罗伦萨，并把它经营成欧洲中世纪重要的文化、商业和金融中心。在 1865 年至 1871 年间，佛罗伦萨曾是意大利统一后的首都。佛罗伦萨是一座美丽的文化古城。有人称罗马是意大利的政治首都，米兰是经济首都，佛罗伦萨是文艺首都。佛罗伦萨是文艺复兴的发源地，是世界上文艺复兴时期的艺术作品保存最完整的地区之一，是艺术与建筑的摇篮之一，拥有众多的历史建筑和藏品丰富的博物馆。历史上有许多文化名人在此地诞生、活动，最著名的包括但丁、达·芬奇、米开朗琪罗。整个城市仍保留着文艺复兴时的风貌。佛罗伦萨堪称那个伟大时代留给后人的独一无二的标本，被称为"西方的雅典"。佛罗伦萨旧城区被联合国教科文组织列入《世界遗产名录》。

Florence is the capital city of the region of Tuscany and of the province of Florence. Medici family had controlled the area for a long time and it became the medieval center of culture, commerce and finance in Europe.It was the capital of the united Italy from 1865 to 1871.Florence is a beautiful cultural ancient city.It is said that Rome is the political capital, Milan is the commercial capital and Florence is cultural and art capital. Florence is the birthplace of the Renaissance and one of the world's richest regions in terms of preserved Renaissance art. It is one of the cradles of arts and architecture. There are numerous historic buildings and museums with rich collections. Many cultural celebrities were born or lived here such as Dante, Leonardo da Vinci and Michelangelo. The whole old town still keeps the style of the Renaissance. It is the only specimen left by the Great Age and is named as the "Athens of the West". The old town was listed in the World Heritage List by UNESCO.

3. 威尼斯 Venice

威尼斯是意大利东北部一座著名的旅游和工业城市。作为亚得里亚海上的一颗明珠，威尼斯城四周环海，由亚得里亚海沿岸和威尼斯咸水潟湖上的 118 座岛屿、150 条水道和 400 座桥梁组成。它是闻名于世的水上之城，有"水都""百岛之城"之称。"贡多拉"是威尼斯最具代表性的早期传统的代步小船。威尼斯也是世界著名旅行家马可·波罗的故乡。威尼斯还是一座文化艺术名城，全城有教堂、钟楼、修道院、宫殿、博物馆等艺术及历史名胜 450 多处。文艺复兴时期，威尼斯是继佛罗伦萨和罗马之后的第三个中心。1932 年，威尼斯又创办了世界上第一个电影节——威尼斯国际电影节。作为世界上独一无二的水上城市，威尼斯具有宝贵的历史文化价值，被联合国教科文组织列入《世界遗产名录》。

Located in the northeast of Italy, Venice is a famous tourist and industrial city. As a pearl of Adriatic Sea, Venice, surrounded by the sea, consists of 118 islands, 150 canals and 400 bridges on the Venice Saltwater lagoon or along the Adriatic coast. It is a world-renowned city on water which is known as the "City of Water" and the "City of a Hundred Islands". Gondola is the most representative of traditional small boat for transportation in Venice at the earlier time. Venice is the hometown of Marco Polo, a world famous traveler. Venice is a well-known art and cultural city. There are more than 450 famous historical attractions including cathedrals, bell towers, monasteries, palaces and museums. Venice is the third center after Florence and Rome during the period of Renaissance. Venice International Film festival established in 1932 is the first film festival in the world. As a unique city on water, thanks to its historic and cultural value, it has been listed as World Heritage List by UNESCO.

4. 米兰 Milan

米兰是意大利的第二大城市、伦巴第大区的首府。米兰是意大利最重要的经济中心，有"经济首都"之称，也是艺术家的摇篮和许多天才人物的故乡。米兰以其特有的意大利式工作方式和生活方式而被认为是意大利最重要的城市。自古以来，米兰就是连接地中海与中欧的主要交通枢纽，是意大利的商业及金融中心。米兰工业发达，经济实力雄厚，其工业产值占意大利工业产值的一半以上。米兰是一座现代化的城市，同时也蕴藏着大量珍贵的文化艺术遗产及著名古迹。主要名胜古迹有埃玛努埃莱二世长廊、斯卡拉歌剧院等。

Milan is the second-largest city in Italy and the capital of the Lombardy. It is the country's most important economic center, with a name of "Economic Capital". It is also the cradle of artists and hometown of many talented persons. With a special Italian work and life style, Milan is considered to be the most important city in Italy. Since the ancient time, Milan has been a commercial and financial center and an important transportation center as it connects the Mediterranean with Central Europe. Milan has developed industries and strong economic power. Its industrial output value is more than half of Italian industrial output. Milan is not only a modern city, but also contains a treasure trove of cultural and artistic heritages and famous monuments. Main attractions are Galleria Vittorio Emanuele Ⅱ, La Scala Opera House and so on.

5. 那不勒斯 Naples

那不勒斯（图2-40）是意大利南部的第一大城市，著名的维苏威火山和庞贝古城就在附近。那不勒斯以其丰富的历史、文化、艺术和美食而著称，这里历史悠久、风光美丽、文物众多，一年四季阳光普照，是地中海最著名的风景区之一。比萨饼起源于那不勒斯。音乐在那不勒斯文化中产生了广泛影响，浪漫的吉他和曼陀林均发明于此。那不勒斯音乐对歌剧和民谣的产生和发展做出了巨大贡献。那不勒斯人生性开朗、充满活力，善于歌唱，那不勒斯的民歌传遍世界。那不勒斯因此被人们称颂为"阳光和快乐之城"，被视作意大利的一颗明珠。那不勒斯历史中心还被联合国教科文组织列入《世界遗产名录》。

图 2-40　那不勒斯
Figure 2-40　Naples

Naples (Figure 2-40) is the largest city in southern Italy nearby the famous Mount Vesuvius and Pompeii. Naples is known for its rich history, culture, art and cuisine. Here is one of the most famous scenic sites in Mediterranean with a long history, beautiful scenery, rich cultural relics and year-round sunshine. Pizza originated in Naples. Music is an important component impacting on Naples culture. Romantic guitar and Mandolin were invented here. Naples music also has made great contributions to opera and folk songs. Neapolitans are good at singing with open character and energetic power. Neapolitan folk songs are spread around the world. Therefore, Naples is praised as a "City of Sunshine and Happiness" and it is considered as a peart of Italy. The historic center of Naples is also on the UNESCO World Heritage List.

(二) 著名旅游景点 Famous Tourist Attractions

1. 罗马斗兽场 Colosseum

罗马斗兽场（图2-41）或竞技场，又称弗莱文剧场，是由混凝土和石头建成的圆形剧场，坐落于罗马市中心。作为罗马帝国最大的露天剧场，它被

图 2-41　罗马斗兽场
Figure 2-41　Colosseum

认为是罗马式建筑和工程最伟大的作品之一。罗马斗兽场于公元72年由罗马皇帝斯佩西安在位时开始修建，由他的继任者提图斯在公元80年完成。罗马斗兽场可以容纳50 000名观众，主要用于斗兽和角斗士角斗，如模拟海战、狩猎动物、死刑或重演著名战役和古典神话戏剧。中世纪前期，该建筑不再被用于娱乐。进入21世纪，罗马斗兽场由于地震和盗石只剩下断墙残壁，但它仍是罗马帝国的一个象征，也是罗马最热门的旅游景点之一。

The Colosseum (Figure 2-41) or Coliseum, also known as the Flavian Amphitheatre, is an elliptical amphitheatre in the center of the city of Rome. Built of concrete and stone, it was the largest amphitheatre in the Roman Empire, and is considered one of the greatest works of Roman architecture and engineering. Construction began under the Emperor Vespasian in 72 AD, and was completed in 80 AD under his successor and heir Titus. The Colosseum seated 50,000 spectators, and was used for gladiatorial contests and public spectacles such as mock sea battles, animal hunts, executions, re-enactments of famous battles, and dramas based on classical mythology. The building ceased to be used for entertainment in the early medieval era. Although in the 21st century, it stays partially ruined because of damage caused by devastating earthquakes and stone-robbers, the Colosseum is still an iconic symbol of Roman Empire. It is also one of Rome's most popular tourist attractions.

图 2-42　特拉维许愿池
Figure 2-42　Trevi Fountain

2. 特拉维许愿池 Trevi Fountain

特拉维许愿池（图2-42）位于三条街的交叉口，Trevi 即指此意。罗马有"喷泉之都"的称号，全市拥有壮观的喷泉1 300多个。特拉维喷泉是罗马最大的巴洛克风格喷泉，据说闭着眼睛背对着许愿池投硬币，愿望就会成真。许愿池因电影《罗马假日》而闻名于世。许愿池建于1629年，于1732年重建，最终于1762年完工。它是由18世纪的建筑师尼科拉·萨尔维设计的。许愿池上部那座巴洛克式的群雕以波里公爵的楼房为依托，呈现了海神得胜的景象。海神的上方有一座少女浮雕，传说少女曾为干渴的古罗马士兵指明水源所在地，因此该泉也被称为"少女泉"或"童贞之水"。

Trevi Fountain (Figure 2-42) is located at the intersection of three streets which is the name of Trevi from. Rome has got the reputation of "Fountain City" with more than 1,300 spectacular fountains in the city. Trevi Fountain is the largest Baroque fountain in Rome. It is said that when you make a wish with your back to the fountain and throw a coin into the pond, the dream will come true. It became famous after the movie *Roman Holiday*. The fountain was built in 1629, rebuilt in 1732, and finished in 1762. It was designed by Nicola Salvi, an architect of the 18th century. This group of Baroque sculptures is set the backdrop of the Palazzo Poli, presenting the scene of the victory of Nereus. There is a girl on top of Poseidon emboss. It is said that the girl specified where the water was for thirsty Roman soldiers, so the springs are also known as "Girl Spring" or the "Water of Virgin".

3. 西班牙广场 Piazza di Spagna

西班牙广场（图2-43）位于罗马市中心，300多年以来一直是罗马文化和旅游的中心地带，因在17世纪时曾是西班牙驻梵蒂冈大使馆所在地而得名。自古以来，西班牙广场便是作家、诗人、音乐家、画家聚会的场所。李斯特、拜伦、歌德、安杰里卡·考夫曼、巴尔扎克、司汤达、安德逊及另外一些名人曾在广场附近居住过。1821 年，英国诗人济慈在大台阶靠右边的那间屋子里与世长辞。西班牙广场的主要名胜就是石阶，于 1723 年建成，又名"西班牙之阶"。

图 2-43　西班牙广场
Figure 2-43　Piazza di Spagna

Piazza di Spagna (Figure 2-43) is located at the center of Rome which has been the heart of Roman culture and Tourist for more than 300 years. It was named because of the location of the Spanish Embassy in Vatican City in the 17th century. Since ancient times, it has been the gathering place of writers, poets, musicians and painters. Many famous people such as Liszt, Byron, Goethe, Angelica Kauffman, Balzac, Stendhal, Anderson and others had lived near the piazza. Keats, a poet of the United Kingdom died in the room on the right near the steps in 1821. The piazza's main attraction is stone steps on the hill. The large steps were completed in 1723, with artistic characteristics, and it was named as "Spanish Steps".

4. 威尼斯广场 Piazza Venezia

威尼斯广场（图 2-44）因旁边的威尼斯宫而得名，是罗马最大的广场，也是罗马最热闹的地方。广场上有建于 1935 年的维托里奥·埃玛努埃莱二世的纪念堂、雕塑及无名烈士墓，许多名人故居也分布在广场附近。意大利人称威尼斯广场为"祖国祭坛"，很多外国元首到意大利正式访问时都要到此敬献花圈，意大利总统接见外国元首等重大活动也都在此举行。威尼斯广场是意大利人引以为傲的地方，因其象征着团结和自由。

图 2-44　威尼斯广场
Figure 2-44　Piazza Venezia

Piazza Venezia (Figure 2-44) is named because of the Venice Palace nearby. It is the largest piazza and the most crowded place in Rome. In the piazza, there is the Vittorio Emmanuel II monument built in 1935, sculptures and nameless revolutionary martyr's tombs. There are also many famous houses for the well-known persons around the piazza. Italians call Piazza Venezia as the "Altar of the Motherland" and many heads of foreign countries will come here for wreaths when they officially visit Italy. And it is also the Italian place for the president to hold the important welcome ceremony to the heads of foreign countries. Italians are proud of the place as it is the symbol of unity and independence.

5. 万神殿 Pantheon

万神殿（图 2-45）是迄今唯一保存完整的古罗马帝国时期的遗迹。公元前 27 年至公元前 25 年，为纪念奥古斯都皇帝远征埃及的战功而建造了这座

图 2-45　万神殿
Figure 2-45　Pantheon

神殿。它的历史比罗马斗兽场还要早 100 多年。万神殿的内部为圆形，四面无窗，顶部开有一个直径为 9 米的天窗，是内部唯一的光线来源。殿顶的圆形曲线继续向下延伸，形成一个完整的球体与地面相接。这是建筑史上的奇迹，展现了古罗马建筑师们所掌握的高深的建筑知识和先进的计算方法。意大利实现统一后，万神殿成为国王和一些伟大的意大利艺术家的陵墓，其中最重要的人物有拉斐尔。万神殿被列为国家圣地，与斗兽场和地下墓穴并称为"罗马三大古迹"。

Pantheon (Figure 2-45) is the only intact monument of the ancient Roman Empire. It was built during the years from 27 BC to 25 BC that was 100 years earlier than the construction of the Colosseum, to commemorate the Emperor Augustus, expedition to Egypt. It is round inside with no windows on the walls but a skylight of a diameter of 9 meters on the top, which is the only source for the internal light. The roof curve reaches down, resulting in a complete sphere which meets the ground. This is a miracle in the history of architecture and shows that the ancient Roman architects had deep architectural knowledge and advanced esoteric calculations. After the unification of Italy, the Pantheon became tombs of kings and some great Italian artists, of which the most important person is Raphael. The Pantheon is listed as a national holy site and is one of the " Three Great Monuments of Rome" along with the Colosseum and the Catacombs.

图 2-46　圣母百花大教堂
Figure 2-46　Basilica of Saint Mary of the Flower

6. 圣母百花大教堂 Basilica of Saint Mary of the Flower

圣母百花大教堂（图 2-46）是天主教佛罗伦萨总教区的主教堂，也是佛罗伦萨最著名的建筑物，又称杜奥莫大教堂，是文艺复兴时期第一座伟大的建筑。它始建于 1296 年，为罗马式建筑，外部以白、红、绿三色大理石按几何图案装饰，橘红色巨型圆顶堪称文艺复兴时期的圆顶之最。圣母百花大教堂仅次于梵蒂冈的圣彼得大教堂和伦敦的圣保罗大教堂，是欧洲三大教堂之一。

The Basilica of Saint Mary of the Flower (Figure 2-46) is the mother church of the Roman Catholic Archdiocese of Florence and Florence's most famous building. It was the first great building of the Renaissance known as the Duomo Cathedral. It was set up in 1296, a Roman-style architectural work, with its external wall decorated with white, red and green marble according to geometric patterns. The orange giant dome is the largest in Renaissance domes. It is the third largest church in Europe after St. Peter Basilica in Vatican City and St. Paul's Cathedral in London.

7. 圣马可广场 Piazza San Marco

圣马可广场（图 2-47）包括公爵府，圣马可大教堂，圣马可钟楼，新、旧行政官邸大楼，连接两幢楼的拿破仑翼大楼。初建于 9 世纪的这个

图 2-47　圣马可广场
Figure 2-47　Piazza San Marco

长方形广场长约 170 米，东侧宽约 80 米，西侧宽约 55 米。广场四周都是文艺复兴时期的精美建筑。马可是《马可福音》的作者，威尼斯人将他奉为守护神。相传在 828 年，两个威尼斯商人从埃及的亚历山大城将马可的遗骨偷运到威尼斯，并在同一年为马可兴建教堂，教堂内有马可的陵墓。大教堂前的广场也因此得名"圣马可广场"。1797 年，拿破仑攻占威尼斯后，赞叹圣马可广场是"欧洲最美的客厅""世界上最美的广场"。

Piazza San Marco (Figure 2-47) consists of Duke Palace, St. Mark's Basilica, St. Nork's Clock Tower, new and old official buildings and Napoleonic Wing which connects the two official buildings. The rectangular piazza was built in the 9th century which is 170 meters long, 80 meters wide in the east and 55 meters wide in the west. The surrounding buildings are the elegant buildings of the Renaissance. San Marco was the writer of *Gospel of Mark* and was regarded as patron saint of Venice. It was said that in 828 the remains of San Marco was moved back to Venice secretly by two Venice businessmen from Alexander in Egypt. The basilica was established in the same year to bury the body of San Marco and thus the piazza was named as well as the basilica. In 1797 when Napoleon invaded Venice and lived here, he praised the piazza as " The Most Beautiful Sitting Room in Europe " and "The Most Beautiful Piazza in the World".

8. 圣马可大教堂 St. Mark's Basilica

雄伟壮丽的圣马可大教堂（图 2-48）始建于 829 年，不久便毁于一场大火，重建于 1043 年至 1071 年间。它曾是中世纪欧洲最大的教堂，是威尼斯建筑艺术的经典之作。它融合了东西方的建筑特色：拜占庭式的直线、哥特式的尖拱门、文艺复兴时期的栏杆装饰、伊斯兰式的圆顶。整座教堂的结构又呈现出希腊式的十字形设计，曾有"世界上最美的教堂"之称。圣马可大教堂不仅是一座教堂，而且是一座博物馆，有丰富的艺术收藏品。

图 2-48　圣马可大教堂
Figure 2-48　St. Mark's Basilica

Magnificent St. Mark's Basilica (Figure 2-48) was built in 829, but soon destroyed in a fire, and was reconstructed during the years from 1043 to 1071. It was Europe's largest church in the Middle Ages, and it is the classical work, of Venice architectural art. It combines Eastern and Western architectural features: Byzantine lines, Gothic pointed arches, decorative railings of the Renaissance and the Islamic dome. The entire basilica structure presents a Greece-style cross design and it was once called " The Most Beautiful Church in the World". St. Mark's Basilica is not only a church, but also a museum, a collection of a large number of art works.

9. 里亚托桥 Rialto Bridge

在威尼斯有 400 多座桥，其中从火车站通往市中心的里亚托桥（图 2-49）（又名商业桥）最为有名。里亚托桥全部用白色大理石筑成，是威尼斯的象征。大桥长 48 米，宽 22.9 米，高 7.32 米，建于 1588 年至 1592 年间，由安东尼奥·庞特设计。桥顶有一座浮亭，两侧是出售首饰和纪念品的商店。里亚托桥所在区域是威尼斯最重要的商业区之一，

图 2-49　里亚托桥
Figure 2-49　Rialto Bridge

曾作为欧洲的商业中心达 300 年之久，在世界上的知名度很高。莎士比亚的名剧《威尼斯商人》就是以这里为背景的。

There are more than 400 bridges in Venice, among which Rialto Bridge (Figure 2-49), also the Commercial Bridge, connected the railway station with downtown is the most famous. The bridge, built of white marble, is a symbol of Venice. Designed by Antonio Ponte and built during the years from 1588 to 1592, it was 48 meters long, 22.9 meters wide, and 7.32 meters high. There is a floating pavilion on the bridge with jewelry and souvenir shops on both sides. It is one of Venice's most important business districts and has served as the commercial center of Europe for more than 300 years. It is quite well-known in the world. William Shakespeare's dramatic work, *The Merchant of Venice*, is set here.

图 2-50 米兰大教堂
Figure 2-50 Milan Cathedral

10. 米兰大教堂 Milan Cathedral

米兰大教堂（图 2-50）是位于米兰市中心的一座哥特式大教堂，是全世界最华丽的教堂之一，规模仅次于梵蒂冈的圣彼得大教堂。米兰大教堂始建于 1386 年，1897 年最后完工，历时 5 个世纪，它不仅是米兰的象征，也是米兰的中心。拿破仑曾于 1805 年在米兰大教堂举行加冕仪式。米兰大教堂的整个外观极尽华美，主教堂用白色大理石砌成，是欧洲最大的大理石建筑之一，有"大理石山"之称，被马克·吐温称赞为"大理石之诗"。米兰大教堂也是世界上雕像最多的哥特式教堂，教堂内外墙等处均点缀着圣人、圣女的雕像，共有 6 000 多座，仅教堂外就有 3 159 座之多。教堂顶耸立着 135 个尖塔，每个尖塔上都有精致的人物雕刻。

Milan Cathedral (Figure 2-50), one of the world's most magnificent churches, is a Gothic cathedral in downtown Milan and the second largest after St. Peter's Basilica in Vatican City. Milan Cathedral was founded in 1386 and completed in 1897 which lasted for five centuries. It is not only the symbol of Milan but also the center of Milan. In 1805, Napoleon's coronation ceremony was held in Milan Cathedral. Entire appearance of the cathedral is very gorgeous and decorated with white marbles. It is one of Europe's largest marble buildings and was named as the "Mountain of Marble".

图 2-51 圣玛丽亚感恩教堂
Figure 2-51 Santa Maria delle Grazie

Mark Twain praised it as "Marble of Poetry". Milan Cathedral is a Gothic cathedral with the most statues in the world. There are more than 6,000 Saints and Saintess decorated on the interior and exterior walls of the cathedral and other places. There are 3,159 statues outside the cathedral. On the top stand 135 towers, each with exquisite engravings.

11. 圣玛丽亚感恩教堂 Santa Maria delle Grazie

圣玛丽亚感恩教堂（图 2-51）是米兰的古迹之一，达·芬奇创作的巨画《最后的晚餐》就画在这座教堂旁的修道院餐厅的墙壁上。达·芬奇于 1495 年开始动笔，1498 年才完成。这幅巨画宽 8.8 米，高 4.6 米，画中的人物比真人大一半，画面描绘的是耶稣和 12 个门徒共进晚餐时的情景。第二次世界大战时，市民们用沙袋将教堂的墙保护起来，使这一杰作得以保存。1980 年，圣玛丽亚感恩教堂被联合国教科文组织列入《世界遗产名录》。

Santa Maria delle Grazie (Figure 2-51) is one of the monuments in Milan with Leonardo da Vinci's mural of *The Last Supper* on the wall of the refectory of the convent. Leonardo da Vinci started painting in 1495 and completed in 1498. This mural painting is 8.8 meters wide and 4.6 meters high. The Figures in the painting are 1/2 bigger than real people. The mural depicts the story of Jesus having dinner with his 12 disciples. During the World War II, the citizens protected the wall with sandbags so that this masterpiece could be preserved. In 1980, Santa Maria delle Grazie was inscribed on the UNESCO World Heritage List.

12. 梵蒂冈 Vatican City

梵蒂冈（图 2-52）是世界上最小的主权国家，也是世界上人口最少的国家。梵蒂冈位于意大利首都罗马城西北角的梵蒂冈高地上，面积为 0.44 平方千米，四面都与意大利接壤，是一个"国中国"，同时也是全世界天主教的中心——以教皇为首的教廷所在地。名胜古迹包括圣彼得广场、圣彼得大教堂和梵蒂冈博物馆等。梵蒂冈是伟大的文化瑰宝，城内的建筑如圣彼得大教堂、西斯廷教堂等都是世界建筑史上的经典之作，教堂里收藏了桑德罗·波提切利、贝尼尼、拉斐尔和米开朗琪罗等人的作品。

图 2-52　梵蒂冈
Figure 2-52　Vatican City

梵蒂冈拥有一个馆藏丰富的图书馆以及一个博物馆，专门收藏具有历史、科学与文化价值的艺术品。圣彼得广场可容纳 50 万人。每逢新年、复活节、圣诞节，广场上往往都会聚集约 20 万人。每逢礼拜日，也总有成千上万的人在此聆听教皇在阳台上播送的晨祷词，接受教皇的祝福。1984 年，梵蒂冈被联合国教科文组织列入《世界遗产名录》。

Vatican City (Figure 2-52) is the world's smallest sovereign state with the least population in the world. Located on the Vatican Hill in the northwest corner of Rome, the capital of Italy, Vatican City has an area of 0.44 square kilometers and is bordered by Italy on all sides. As a state within a state, Vatican City is also the center of the Catholic world headed by the Pope of the Holy See in Rome. The cultural sites include St. Peter's Square, St. Peter's Basilica and Vatican Museum. Vatican City itself is a great master art work. The buildings in the city including St. Peter's Basilica and Sistine Chapel are classic works in the history of world architecture, collecting the works of Sandro Botticelli, Bernini, Raphael and Michelangelo. Vatican City also has a library with large collections and a museum dedicated to collections of historical, scientific and cultural works of art. St. Peter's Square can hold more than 500,000 people. There will be more than 200,000 peopce gathering in the square every New Year's Day, Easter and Christmas day. Thousands of people will come here every Sunday morning to listen to the Pope's Matins and receive the Pope's blessing from the balcong. In 1984, Vatican City was added by UNESCO to the list of World Heritage List.

2

图 2-53　比萨斜塔
Figure 2-53　Leaning Tower of Pisa

13. 比萨斜塔 Leaning Tower of Pisa

比萨距离佛罗伦萨约 1 小时车程。比萨斜塔（图 2-53）实际上是比萨大教堂的钟楼，由著名建筑师博南诺·皮萨诺于 1173 年开始主持修建，它位于比萨大教堂的右后方，是比萨城的标志。刚开始修建时，塔高设计为 100 米左右，但动工五六年后，塔身从 3 层开始倾斜，直到完工还在持续倾斜，在其完工前，塔顶已南倾（即塔顶偏离垂直线）3.5 米。比萨斜塔还曾因一个著名的科学试验而世界闻名。比萨斜塔和相邻的大教堂、洗礼堂、墓园对 11 ～ 14 世纪意大利建筑艺术产生了巨大的影响，1987 年被联合国教科文组织列入《世界遗产名录》。

Pisa is about an hour's drive from Florence. The Leaning Tower of Pisa is actually the bell tower of the Pisa Cathedral. It was constructed in 1173 under the direction of the renowned architect Bonanno Pisano. Located at the rear right of the Pisa Cathedral, it is a symbol of the city of Pisa. Initially designed to be around 100 meters tall, the tower began to lean after five or six years of construction, starting from the third floor. The tilt continued even after the tower was completed, with the top leaning 3.5 meters southward from the vertical line before its completion. The Leaning Tower of Pisa also gained worldwide fame due to a famous scientific experiment. In 1987, the Leaning Tower, along with the adjacent cathedral, baptistery, and cemetery, was inscribed on the UNESCO World Heritage List for its significant influence on Italian architectural art from the 11th to the 14th centuries.

图 2-54　庞贝
Figure 2-54　Pompei

14. 庞贝 Pompei

庞贝（图 2-54）是位于意大利那不勒斯海湾维苏威火山下的一座古罗马城市，始建于公元前 8 世纪，公元 79 年因维苏威火山爆发而被掩埋，1748 年被发现。庞贝是如今世界上唯一的一座其构造保留了古罗马时期风貌的城市。庞贝的街道棋盘似的纵横交错，这是传统的古罗马式街道。庞贝为研究者了解古罗马时期的社会生活和文化艺术提供了重要资料。

Pompeii (Figure2-54) is an ancient Roman city located at the foot of Mount Vesuvius in the Bay of Naples, Italy. It was founded in the 8th century BC and was buried by the eruption of Mount Vesuvius in 79 AD, only to be rediscovered in 1748. Pompeii is the only city in the world today that has preserved the architectural layout of the ancient Roman era. Its streets intersect in a grid-like pattern, characteristic of traditional Roman street design. Pompeii provides researchers with invaluable insights into the social life and cultural arts of ancient Rome.

（三）旅游购物 Shopping

威尼斯面具与玻璃：威尼斯的面具文化在欧洲文明中独具一格，在威尼斯的传统文化中也占有重要的地位。18 世纪以前，威尼斯居民的生活离不开面具，人们外出时，不论男女，都要戴上面具、披上斗篷。威尼斯独有的面具为包塔面具。今天，在威尼斯的大街小巷都可以看到各种面具。除此之外，慕拉诺所产的玻璃也是水城的特色。

Venice mask and glass: The mask culture of Venice holds a unique place in European civilization and plays a significant role in Venetian tradition. Before the 18th century, masks were an integral part of daily life for Venetian residents. Whether male or female, people would wear masks and cloaks when going out. Venetian masks are known as "bauta." Today, you can find a variety of masks throughout the streets and alleys of Venice. In addition to masks, Murano glass is also a distinctive feature of this water city.

佛罗伦萨皮制品：在古代，意大利半岛的居民就是闻名遐迩的皮革匠，所以最早的手工制鞋作坊也出现在意大利。历经百年，这种传统的制鞋工艺一直流传至今。如今，意大利有60%的制鞋厂仍然在坚持使用手工或半手工的方式制鞋。佛罗伦萨的皮革品更是声名远扬。

Florence leather products: In ancient times, the residents of Italian Peninsula were famous as leather craftsmen and the earliest handmade shoes workshop also appeared in Italy. For hundreds of years, this traditional shoe-making process has been passed down. Nowadays, 60% of factories still insist on manufacturing shoes by hand or semi-hand. And leather goods in Florence enjoy a widespread reputation.

意大利咖啡：浓咖啡是意式咖啡的精髓，其做法起源于意大利，意大利语意为"特别快"。其特征是利用蒸汽压力，瞬间将咖啡液抽出。所有的牛奶咖啡或花式咖啡都是以浓咖啡为基础制作出来的。喝意大利咖啡时，只需尝一小口，就会迅速被其浓郁的口味和香气折服，这正是意大利咖啡与其他咖啡的不同之处。香味和浓度是衡量意大利咖啡是否好喝的两个尺度。

Italian coffee: Espresso, which means "extremely fast" in Italian, is the essence of the Italian coffee whose practice originated in Italy. Its characteristic is that the use of steam pressure makes the liquid of coffee extract momentarily. All milk coffee or fancy coffee is Espresso-based production. A sip of Italian coffee, people will quickly be humbled by its rich taste and aroma. And this is how Italian coffee differs from the other coffee. Flavor and intensity are two measurements to judge if Italian coffee is good or not.

时装：米兰是世界三大时尚之都之一。意大利设计师的大胆革新和丰富创意使意大利制造的时装能与法国时装分庭抗礼。古驰绝对是意大利的同义词，华伦天奴是高端时尚的代名词，Miu Miu 把尼龙背包设计成为一种风尚，菲拉格慕一直在寻找最理想的鞋型，乔治·阿玛尼是低调美学的王者风范，而范思哲是古典巴洛克的金色风华。

Fashion: Milan is one of the three major fashion capitals in the world. Italian fashion can compete with French fashion because the Italian designers always reform the design and have rich imagination. Gucci is undoubtedly synonymous with Italy, while Valentino is the epitome of high-end fashion. Miu Miu turned nylon backpacks into a trend, Salvatore Ferragamo is always in pursuit of the ideal shoe design, Giorgio Armani embodies the kingly elegance of understated aesthetics, and Versace represents the golden splendor of classical Baroque.

扫码获取：入境须知及海关规定

本节习题

1. 以小组为单位讨论意大利有哪些主题游，请选取一个合适的主题写一篇导游词。
2. 为什么说意大利是文艺复兴的摇篮？
3. 讨论并设计一条意大利5日游经典线路。

第六节　北欧之旅
Travel in Northern Europe

森林王国——瑞典
The Kingdom of Forests—Sweden

导读

　　瑞典王国于 1950 年 5 月 9 日与我国建立大使级的外交关系，是第一个与中国建立外交关系的西方国家。瑞典奉行"和平时期军事不结盟"的政策，在邻近地区、欧洲和世界事务三个层面积极参与国际合作，重视同美国、俄罗斯的关系，以促进人权和参与联合国事务为外交基石，近年来重视发展与亚太国家的关系。瑞典地广人稀，风光秀丽，拥有大面积的"未遭破坏的大自然"，而且经济基础好，旅游基础设施完善，社会安定，政局稳定，这与许多西欧或东欧国家的情况形成强烈对比。瑞典的文化传统、语言文字、风土人情与欧洲大陆国家也有很大差异，十分独特，因此颇受入境旅游者的喜爱。瑞典的旅游业在其日益发展的服务业中发挥着越来越重要的作用。

一、地理概览 Geography of Sweden

（一）位置 Location

　　瑞典，全称瑞典王国，是一个位于斯堪的纳维亚半岛的国家，北欧五国之一，首都是斯德哥尔摩。它西邻挪威，东北与芬兰接壤，西南濒临斯卡格拉克海峡和卡特加特海峡，东边为波罗的海与波的尼亚湾。瑞典与丹麦、德国、波兰、俄罗斯、立陶宛、拉脱维亚和爱沙尼亚隔海相望，海岸线长 2 181 千米，总面积为 45 万平方千米，是北欧面积最大的国家。

　　Sweden, officially known as the Kingdom of Sweden, is a country located on the Scandinavian Peninsula and is one of the five Nordic countries. Its capital is Stockholm. It is bordered by Norway to the west, Finland to the northeast, the Skagerrak Strait and the Kattegat Strait to the southwest, and the Baltic Sea and the Gulf of Bothnia to the east. Sweden faces Denmark, Germany, Poland, Russia, Lithuania, Latvia, and Estonia across the sea. It has a coastline of 2,181 kilometers and a total area of 450,000 square kilometers, making it the largest country in Northern Europe by area.

（二）地形和气候 The Land and Seasons

　　瑞典地势自西北向东南倾斜，北部为诺尔兰高原，全国最高峰凯布讷山海拔 2 117 米，南部及沿海多为平原和丘陵。大部分地区属温带针叶林气候，有约 15% 的土地在北极圈内。

　　The terrain of Sweden slopes from the northwest to the southeast, with the Norrland Plateau in the north. The country's highest peak, Kebnekaise, rises to 2,117 meters above sea level. The southern regions and coastal areas are mostly plains and hills. Most of the country experiences a temperate coniferous forest climate, with about 15% of its land lying within the Arctic Circle.

受大西洋暖流影响，瑞典靠近海洋的大部分地区属温带针叶林气候，最南部属温带阔叶林气候。受北大西洋暖流影响，1 月份瑞典北部的平均气温为 –16 ℃，南部为 –0.7 ℃；7 月北部的平均气温为 14.2 ℃，南部为 17.2 ℃。

Affected by the Atlantic Warm Current, most of Sweden's coastal areas are temperate coniferous forest climate, and the southernmost part is temperate broad-leaved forest climate. Affected by the North Atlantic Warm Current, the average temperature of Sweden in January is –16 ℃ in the north and –0.7 ℃ in the south；14.2 ℃ in the north and 17.2 ℃ in the south in July.

瑞典主要河流有约塔河、达尔河、翁厄曼河。湖泊约 10 万个，可通航河流较少。最大的维纳恩湖面积 5 585 平方千米，居欧洲第三。

极昼极夜现象

The main rivers in Sweden include Yota River, Dar River and Ongman River. There are about 100,000 lakes and a few navigable rivers. The largest Lake Verne covers an area of 5,585 square kilometers, ranking third in Europe.

（三）自然资源 Natural Resources

瑞典有铁矿、森林和水力三大资源。截至 2022 年，瑞典已探明铁矿储量为 40 亿吨，是欧洲最大的铁矿出口国。铀矿储量为 25 万～30 万吨。森林覆盖率为 54%，蓄材 26.4 亿立方米。常年可利用的水力资源有 2 014 万千瓦，已开发其中的 81%。此外，北部和中部地区有硫、铜、铅、锌、砷等矿石，但储量不大。

Sweden is rich in three major resources: iron ore, forests, and hydropower. As of 2022, the proven iron ore reserves stood at 4 billion tons, making Sweden the largest exporter of iron ore in Europe. The uranium reserves are estimated to be between 250,000 and 300,000 tons. Forests cover 54% of the country, with a timber volume of 2.64 billion cubic meters. The country has 20.14 million kilowatts of annually exploitable hydropower resources, of which 81% have been developed. Additionally, the northern and central regions contain minerals such as sulfur, copper, lead, zinc, and arsenic, although the reserves are not large.

二、人文概况 Overview of Swedish Humanities

（一）国情认知 Basic Knowledge of National Conditions

瑞典人口约 1 048.7 万（2022 年），其中绝大多数为瑞典人（日耳曼族后裔），外国移民及其后裔超过 100 万，移民多来自中东、东南欧、非洲等地区。北部萨米族是唯一的少数民族，约 2 万人。主要宗教为基督教路德宗。瑞典民族中，瑞典族占 90%。北部有芬兰族约 3 万人，拉普族近 2 万人。此外，还有丹麦人、挪威人、德意志人、犹太人等。

Sweden has a population of about 10.487 million（2022），with an overwhelming majority of Swedes（of Germanic descent）and more than one million foreign immigrants and their descendants，mostly from the Middle East，Southeastern Europe，Africa and other regions. The Sami nationality in the north is the only ethnic minority，with about 20,000 people. The main religion is Lutheran

Christianity. Among the Swedish nationalities, the Swedish nationality accounts for 90%. There are about 30,000 Finnish people and nearly 20,000 Lapu people in the north. In addition, there are Danes, Norwegians, Germans, Jews, etc.

瑞典人为北欧民族之一，属欧罗巴人种的北欧类型，身材高大、皮肤白皙、金发碧眼。统一的瑞典民族形成于9—11世纪，是由作为主体的斯维尔人和高特人，同其不断吸收的后来迁入的移民及部分拉普人和芬兰人构成的。官方语言为瑞典语，英语也是通用语言。瑞典的国旗底色为蓝色，黄色十字略偏向左侧。瑞典国旗的历史可追溯至16世纪，蓝色、黄色是来自瑞典皇室徽章的颜色。国歌为《你古老的光荣的北国山乡》，国花是铃兰。货币名称为瑞典克朗（SK），1瑞典克朗=100欧尔。

The Swedes are one of the Nordic peoples, belonging to the Nordic subtype of the Europid race. They are typically tall, with fair skin, blonde hair and blue eyes. The unified Swedish nation, formed from the 9th to the 11th century, a mainly composed of the Swedes and Goths, and constantly absorbs the immigrants who later immigrated, as well as some Lapps and Finns. The official language is Swedish, and English is also the common language. The national flag of Sweden has a blue background with a yellow cross slightly to the left, the history of the Swedish flag dates back to the 16th century, and the blue and yellow colors come from the colors of the Swedish royal emblem. The national anthem is *Your Old Glorious Northern Mountain Country*, and the national flower is the lily of the valley and the currency is Swedish Krona (SK), 1 SEK = 100 Eur.

（二）瑞典简史 History of Sweden

11世纪初形成统一的瑞典王国，1157年兼并芬兰，1397年与丹麦、挪威组成卡尔马联盟，受丹麦统治。1523年，脱离卡尔马联盟重获独立。1654—1719年为国力鼎盛时期，被称为"瑞典帝国"，领土包括芬兰、爱沙尼亚、拉脱维亚、立陶宛，以及俄国、波兰和德国的波罗的海沿岸地区。1718年，瑞典对俄国、丹麦和波兰作战失败后逐步走向衰落。1721年，瑞典战败，丧失了波罗的海属地及其军事强国地位。1805年，参加拿破仑战争。1809年，瑞典败于俄国后被迫割让芬兰。1814年从丹麦取得挪威，结成瑞挪联盟。1905年独立。瑞典在两次世界大战中均保持中立且未参战。

At the beginning of the 11th century, a unified Kingdom of Sweden was formed. In 1157, it annexed Finland. In 1397, it formed the Kalma Union with Denmark and Norway and was ruled by Denmark. In 1523, it seceded from the Kalma Union and regained its independence. During the period from 1654 to 1719, the country was in its heyday and was called the "Swedish Empire". Its territory included Finland, Estonia, Latvia, Lithuania and the Baltic coastal areas of Russia, Poland and Germany. In 1718, Sweden gradually declined after losing the war against Russia, Denmark and Poland. In 1721, Sweden was defeated and lost its Baltic dependency and its status as a military power. In 1805, it participated in the Napoleonic War. In 1809, Sweden was forced to cede Finland after losing to Russia. In 1814, it joined the Swiss and Norwegian alliance, gaining Norway from Denmark. In 1905, it became independent. Sweden remained neutral in two world wars.

（三）经济状况 The Economy

瑞典以高工资、高税收、高福利著称。瑞典的农业、工业和服务业非常发达。森林覆盖率为 54% 左右，享有"森林之国""湖泊之国"的美誉。森林、铁矿和水力是瑞典的三大自然资源。瑞典着重发展以出口为导向的工业化经济，工业在国民经济中占有十分重要的地位，82% 的工业品出口到国外。20 世纪 70 年代中期以后，高科技产业发展迅速，交通、通信、医药保健、信息、环保领域在世界上具有较强的竞争力，滚珠轴承、冷冻设备等传统产品在国际市场上都享有很高的声誉。钢铁工业历史悠久，化学工业中以石油化学、石油精炼最为突出，塑料、化纤、药品和化肥等行业也有较大的发展。汽车工业在第二次世界大战后发展迅速，各种卡车、小汽车产量的 1/3 销往美国。能源工业在瑞典经济中居于十分重要的地位，瑞典是一个能源高消费国家，仅电力消耗每人年均就达 1.3 万千瓦时左右。瑞典人民时生活水平多年来名列世界前茅，为典型的福利国家。

Sweden is famous for its high wages, high taxes, and generous welfare system. The country's agriculture, industry, and service sectors are highly developed. The forest coverage rate is about 54%, enjoying the reputation of the "Country of Forests" and the "Country of Lakes". Forest, iron ore and water are Sweden's three natural resources. Sweden focuses on the development of export-oriented industrial economy. Industry plays a very important role in the national economy, and 82% of industrial products are exported abroad. Since the mid-1970s, the high-tech industry has developed rapidly, and the fields of transportation, communications, medicine and health care, information and environmental protection have strong competitiveness in the world. Traditional products such as ball bearings and refrigeration equipment have enjoyed a high reputation in the international market. The iron and steel industry has a long history. The chemical industry, especially petrochemical and petroleum refining, is the most prominent. Plastic, chemical fiber, medicine and fertilizer also have a great development. The automobile industry developed rapidly after the Second World War, with 1/3 of the production of various trucks and cars sold to the United States. The energy industry plays a very important role in the Swedish economy. Sweden is a country with high energy consumption, and only electricity consumption per capita is about 13,000 kilowatt-hours per year. Swedish people's living standards have been among the best in the world for many years, and Sweden is a typical welfare country.

诺贝尔

（四）传统文化 Traditional Culture

瑞典人以西餐为主，口味清淡，通常加入较少的佐料，尽量保持原有风味，不喜欢吃太油腻的食品。以面包和马铃薯为主食，尤其喜欢黑面包，喜欢喝浓汤。瑞典沿海的地理环境适合鲑鱼、鲈鱼等鱼类的生长繁殖。菜肴基本上以鱼为主。瑞典人比较喜欢吃生的和冷的食品，肉片和鱼块都是半熟的。蔬菜和水果的种类较少，而且价格很高，原因是瑞典气候寒冷，不适合植物生长。人们习惯每天吃固定的菜品，就像是学校的固定菜谱一样，从来不觉得枯燥无味。例如，星期一吃牛肉和鲱鱼，星期四吃豌豆汤和薄煎饼。他们还有一种代表性的吃法，即在一张大桌上摆上几十种菜，按自己的喜好取用，这种用餐形式被称为"海盗席"。

The Swedish diet primarily consists of Western cuisine, characterized by mild flavors with minimal seasoning to preserve the original taste of the ingredients. Swedes generally avoid overly greasy foods. Their staple foods include bread and potatoes, with a particular fondness for rye bread, and they enjoy hearty soups. The coastal geography of Sweden provides an abundance of fish such as salmon and perch, making fish a central component of the Swedish diet. Swedes tend to prefer raw and cold foods, with meats and fish often being served semi-cooked. Due to Sweden's cold climate, which is not conducive to plant growth, the variety of vegetables and fruits is limited and they tend to be quite expensive. People in Sweden are accustomed to eating a fixed menu daily, much like a school cafeteria menu, and they never find it boring. For example, they might have beef and herring on Mondays, and pea soup with pancakes on Thursdays. A distinctive dining tradition in Sweden is the "smorgasbord", where a large table is laden with dozens of dishes, allowing individuals to select what they like according to their preferences.

瑞典男子的传统服装是上身穿短上衣和背心，下身穿紧身齐膝或长到踝部的裤子，头上戴高顶礼帽或平顶帽子。少女一般不戴帽子，已婚的妇女则戴式样不一的包头帽。在正式场合，男子一般是西装革履，加上一件长外套；女子穿装饰有各种花色的长裙，有的腰间拴有荷包或小袋，上身常是坎肩和衬衣。瑞典人的服装上镶有各种花边，编结、刺绣、抽纱等工艺广泛应用在服装上，连手套的背部也要刺绣，并镶上皮毛作为缘边。结婚时，新郎、新娘的衣服都要绣上各种花纹。为了绣制婚服，女性要从少女时就在母亲的督促下花费几年时间才能完成。婚礼上，新娘还要戴上王冠式女帽。瑞典人服装的另一个特点是穿木鞋。由于过去生活贫困，而瑞典国内又森林遍布，人们于是就地取材，便形成了穿木鞋的传统。现在人们的生活水平提高了，但穿木鞋的习惯仍然延续了下来。

Traditional Swedish men's attire includes a short jacket and vest on the upper body, with tight-fitting knee-length or ankle-length trousers, and a high top hat or flat cap. Young girls typically do not wear hats, while married women wear various styles of headscarves. In formal settings, men usually wear suits with a long coat, while women don long dresses adorned with various patterns. Some women may have a pouch or small bag tied around the waist, and the upper body is often dressed in a vest and blouse. Clothing is embellished with various lace trims, and techniques like braiding, embroidery, and drawn thread work are widely used, even on the back of gloves, which are often edged with fur. The bride and groom's outfits are intricately embroidered with various patterns. Women spend several years, starting from their youth under their mother's guidance, to complete their wedding attire. During the wedding ceremony, the bride also wears a crown-like headdress. One distinctive feature of traditional Swedish clothing is the use of wooden shoes. Historically, Sweden's vast forests and periods of economic hardship led people to craft wooden shoes from readily available local materials. While living standards have significantly improved over time, the tradition of wearing wooden shoes has endured and remains a part of Swedish culture today.

瑞典人酷爱戴戒指，戒指既是装饰品，也是职业的象征。戒指上有橡树叶图案的，多为中学教师；有刺槐叶图案的，多为木匠；饰有一顶桂冠图案者，可能是擦玻璃工。此外，家族戒指、行业戒指也多以树叶形状为标志。象征职业的戒指戴在食指上，结婚戒指戴在无名指上。

Swedes have a strong affinity for wearing rings, which serve both as adornments and symbols of one's profession. Rings featuring oak leaf designs are typically worn by secondary school teachers; those with acacia leaf patterns are often worn by carpenters; and a ring adorned with a laurel wreath might indicate a window cleaner. Additionally, family rings and trade rings are also marked by leaf-shaped designs. Rings that symbolize a profession are worn on the index finger, while wedding rings are traditionally worn on the ring finger.

瑞典的城市没有围墙，民居的围墙不但低矮，而且中间镂空，有些甚至只是用铁条、木条围成栅栏，与外界形成象征性的分隔。瑞典人没有住在一起的习惯，即使是一家人，也是各有各的房间，家庭成员互不干扰，保留着各自的隐私。瑞典的民居一般是三层楼，一楼是公共空间，有餐厅、厨房、客厅；二楼是个人空间，是家庭各成员的书房和卧室；地下室就是一个大的储藏室。每家一个大院子，院子里面放置一些玩具供孩子玩耍。但是院子并没有高大而严实的围墙，这与中国建筑中的高墙形成了鲜明对比。

Swedish cities are not enclosed by walls, and residential fences are not only low but also often have gaps in them. Some are merely symbolic barriers made of iron or wooden bars. Swedes do not have the habit of living in close quarters; even within a family, each person has his or her own room, ensuring privacy and minimal interference among family members. Typical Swedish homes are three stories high. The first floor serves as a communal area, housing the dining room, kitchen, and living room. The second floor is dedicated to personal spaces, with studies and bedrooms for each family member. The basement is usually a large storage area. Each home typically has a spacious yard with toys for children to play with. However, these yards lack tall, solid walls, which stands in stark contrast to the high walls often found in Chinese architecture.

（五）礼仪禁忌 Social Etiquettes and Taboos

瑞典人文化素质较高，热情好客、纯朴诚实、谈吐文明、行为规矩、重诺守时。瑞典人十分重视环境保护，热爱花、鸟和其他野生动物，热爱大自然。参加体育活动更是瑞典人的喜好。

Swedes are well-educated, warm and hospitable, straightforward and honest. They speak politely, behave properly, and are known for keeping their promises and being punctual. They place great importance on environmental protection, have a love for flowers, birds, and other wildlife, and possess a deep appreciation for nature. Sports activities are also a favorite pastime among Swedes.

瑞典人与宾客见面时一般以握手为礼。与亲朋好友见面时，瑞典人往往会与对方拥抱、贴面，或是向对方脱帽、举手、点头致意。在与客人交谈时，一般会保持1.2米左右的距离，他们不习惯靠得太近。他们喜欢在交谈时直视对方，认为这是尊重对方的表现。在瑞典，情绪激动、动辄疾言厉色是没有涵养的表现，在公众场合抠鼻孔、擤鼻涕也被认为是不道德的行为。

Swedes usually shake hands when meeting guests. When meeting relatives and friends, Swedes tend to hug and cheek-kissing each other, or take off their hats, raise their hands and nod to each other. When talking with guests, they usually keep a distance of about 1.2 meters. They are not used to getting too close. They like to look at each other directly when talking, and think it is a sign of respect for each other. In Sweden, it is a sign of lack of self-restraint to be emotional and quick to speak and bluff. It is also considered immoral to pick your nose and blow your nose in public.

瑞典人普遍爱惜动物和环境。他们对于伤害鸟类、猫、狗，当众吸烟，乱丢废弃物等行为都十分反感。在色彩方面，因为瑞典的国旗颜色是蓝色和黄色，所以这两种颜色被视为国家的代表色，瑞典人忌讳在商品上滥用黄色与蓝色，也不喜欢大红色，认为红色是凶兆的象征。瑞典人忌讳的数字和日期有"13""666""星期五"。另外，与瑞典人聊天时，不宜涉及王室、宗教问题及政治倾向。

Swedes generally cherish animals and the environment. They are particularly averse to harming birds, cats, and dogs, smoking in public, and littering. In terms of colors, because the Swedish flag is blue and yellow, these two colors are considered national symbols. Swedes are cautious about the excessive use of yellow and blue in products, and they also tend to dislike bright red, as it is associated with bad omens. Numbers like "13" and "666," as well as "Friday", are considered unlucky. Additionally, when conversing with Swedes, it's best to avoid topics related to the royal family, religion, and political views.

瑞典是个半禁酒的国家。瑞典的餐馆只准在晚餐时供应少量的酒。人们想在家里喝酒，也要持"购酒特许证"到指定地点去买。酒精含量超过 2.25% 的啤酒只向年满 18 周岁的顾客出售。在瑞典的城乡都设有戒酒医院，社会上对饮酒也有种种限制。如果警察发现醉汉，可以随时拘留。

Sweden is a country that forbids alcohol in large area. Swedish restaurants are only allowed to serve a small amount of wine at dinner. If people want to drink at home, they should also hold a "liquor purchase license" to buy at a designated place. Beer with an alcohol content of more than 2.25% is only sold to customers over the age of 18. In Sweden, both urban and rural areas have alcohol abstinence hospitals, and there are various restrictions on drinking in society. If the police find a drunk, they can detain him at any time.

（六）传统节日 Festivals

1. 五朔节 Maypole

每年 5 月 1 日的前一天晚上，是瑞典人庆祝冬去春来的一个节日。人们称 4 月 30 日的晚上为"沃尔帕吉斯夜"，据说在这个晚上，生命和春天的力量将战胜死亡和冬天。在庆祝节日时，人们都要在晚上点燃篝火。这些篝火是节日庆贺开始的信号，会一直燃烧到天亮。在瑞典南部，人们还在篝火旁举行诗歌和唱歌比赛，优胜者不仅能获得奖品，还能得到当地最漂亮女孩的亲吻。在这个节日里，家家户户都要准备丰盛的餐点，围坐在一起开怀畅饮，共庆春天的来临。入夜后，人们在涂以红色的木桩上缀满色彩斑斓的花朵和一片片绿叶，大家围着象征春天来临的"五月树"跳起欢快的舞蹈。

The night before May lst is a Swedish holiday, celebrating the end of winter and the beginning of spring. People call the night of April 30 "Walpurgis Night", a night when the forces of life and spring are said to triumph over death and winter. The festival is celebrated by lighting bonfires at night. These fires signal the start of the festival celebrations and burn until dawn. In southern Sweden, poetry and singing contests are held around the fires, with the winners receiving not only prizes, but also kisses from the prettiest girls in the area. In this festival, every family prepares a sumptuous meal, sit together and openly drink, to celebrate the arrival of spring. As night falls, people adorn the red-painted wooden poles with colorful flowers and lush green leaves. Everyone dances joyfully around the "Maypole", a symbol of the arrival of spring.

2. 仲夏节 Midsummer Festival

每年的 6 月 24 日是瑞典古老的传统节日——仲夏节。瑞典、芬兰等北欧国家靠近北极，冬季漫长，大部分地区几乎有半年时间不能见到太阳。仲夏节前后，这一地区处于一年中阳光最为充足的时节，仲夏节又是白天最长的一天，几乎没有黑夜。因此，人们在这一天庆祝光明驱除黑暗及万物繁盛日子的到来。篝火晚会是节日的重要内容。按古老传统，篝火要由新婚夫妇点燃。人们身穿民族服装进行各种传统民间手工艺表演，并点燃熊熊篝火，载歌载舞欢度仲夏之夜。如今仲夏节已经成为一个预祝五谷丰登的节日，吸引着广大的人民群众。

Midsummer Festival, an ancient Swedish traditional festival, falls on June 24th every year. Sweden, Finland and other Nordic countries are close to the North Pole and have a long winter. Most areas can't see the sun for almost half a year. Before and after the Midsummer Festival, this area is in the most sunny season of the year, and the Midsummer Festival is the longest day in the year, with almost no night. Therefore, on this day, people celebrate the arrival of the day when light drives out darkness and all things flourish. Bonfire party is an important part of the festival. According to the ancient tradition, the bonfire should be lit by the newlyweds. People wear national costumes to perform various traditional folk handicrafts, light a burning bonfire and celebrate the midsummer night with singing and dancing. Now the Midsummer Festival has become a festival to wish for a good harvest of grain, attracting the masses of the people.

3. 斯德哥尔摩水节 Stockholm Water Festival

斯德哥尔摩水节始于 1991 年，每年 8 月举行，其主题是保护水资源、防止水污染。水节期间的文化娱乐活动丰富多彩，有歌舞、音乐、杂技、戏剧、电影，以及陆地上或水上的体育竞赛和表演等。演出者除了一流艺术家和专业文艺团体，还有业余文艺爱好者。节日期间会举行由瑞典国王主持的皇家音乐会，盛大而隆重，音乐会上由瑞典和外国的一些艺术家演奏或演唱世界名曲、名歌等。市中心的王宫、议会、外交部、国王公园一带是主要的娱乐活动区，到处是临时搭起的大舞台或演出帐篷。活动场地内设有整齐的餐厅、酒馆、咖啡厅和出售手工艺品、旅游纪念品及快餐食品的售货亭。

The Stockholm Water Festival began in 1991 and is held in August every year. Its purpose is to protect water resources and prevent water pollution. Cultural and recreational activities during the Water Festival are rich and colorful, including singing and dancing, music, acrobatics, drama, movies, and sports competitions and performances on land or water. In addition to the first-class artists and professional literary troupes, there are also amateur artists. The Royal Concert hosted by the King of Sweden was grand. At the concert, some Swedish and foreign artists played or sang world famous songs. The palace, parliament, the Ministry of Foreign Affairs and the King's Park are the main entertainment areas in the city center, and there are large temporary stage or performance tents everywhere. There are orderly restaurants, taverns, cafes and kiosks selling handicrafts, tourist souvenirs and fast food in the activity area.

4. 露西娅女神节 Swedish Goddess Lucia Festival

每年的 12 月 13 日是瑞典传统的露西娅女神节。露西娅被瑞典人尊奉为"圣女"，在瑞典有一段关于她的非常美丽、动人的传说。相传露西娅原为罗马帝国的一位官员夫人，约出生于 2 世纪。因笃信基督教而遭仇视，被罗马当局百般迫害，并被刺瞎双眼。她失明之后仍虔诚地向耶稣祈祷，祈祷耶稣给她带来光明。她的行动感动了耶稣，一天夜里，耶稣在梦中告诉她睁开双眼即可重见光明。露西娅睁开双眼，奇迹发生了，她果然重见光明了。消息传开后，人们采取各种方式前来祝贺。大家都称露西娅为"圣女"，把她降临人间的 12 月 13 日定为露西娅女神节，并通过各种各样的形式加以庆祝，久而久之便形成了习惯并相传至今。

December 13 every year is the traditional Swedish Goddess Lucia Festival. Lucia is honored by the Swedes as the " Holy Virgin ". In Sweden has a very beautiful and touching legend. According to legend, Lucia was originally an official wife of the Roman Empire, was born in the 2nd century.

Because of her passion for Christianity, she was hated ard persecuted by the Roman authorities persecution, and was blinded. After she was blinded, she still prayed to Jesus to bring her sight. Her faith moved Jesus, and one night, He appeared to her in a dream, telling her she would see again if she opened her eyes. Lucia opened her eyes, and a miracle occurred—she regained her sight. When the news spread, people came to congratulate her in all kinds of ways. Everyone called Lucia the "Holy Virgin" and designated December 13, the day she came to earth, as the Day of the Goddess Lucia, and celebrated it in a variety of ways, which formed a custom over time and has been passed down to the present day.

三、旅游观光 Tourism and Sightseeing

（一）主要旅游城市 Major Tourist Cities

1. 斯德哥尔摩 Stockholm

斯德哥尔摩在英语里意为"木头岛"。城市始建于公元 13 世纪中叶。那时，当地居民常常遭到海盗侵扰，于是便在梅拉伦湖入海处的一个小岛上用巨木修建了一座城堡，并在水中设置木桩障碍，以便抵御海盗，因此这个岛便得名"木头岛"。

Stockholm means "Wood Island" in English. The city was built in the middle of the 13th century. At that time, the local residents were often harassed by pirates, so people built a castle with huge wood on an island at the entrance of Lake Melaran, and set up wooden pile barriers in the water to resist pirates, so the island was named "Wood Island".

斯德哥尔摩是瑞典的首都及第一大城市，是全国政治、经济、文化中心。全市由大小十四座岛屿和大陆上的乌普兰及南曼兰地区组成，是一个多岛之城。城区水道纵横，在市内古老的中世纪建筑与现代化的高楼大厦之间那密如蛛网的河道里，快艇穿梭往来，不亚于素以水上城市著称的意大利水城威尼斯，因而也被誉为"北方的威尼斯"。

Stockholm is the capital and the largest city of Sweden and the national political, economic and cultural center. The city is composed of 14 islands and the regions of Upland and South Manland on the mainland, so it is a city with many islands. The city is crisscrossed with waterways. Beside the ancient medieval buildings and modern high-rise buildings in the city, speedboats shuttle through the cobweb of waterways as dense as cobwebs, nothing inferior to the Italian water city Venice, so it is also known as "Venice in the North".

目前，斯德哥尔摩市郊已建成坦斯塔、基斯塔、切霍尔姆、林肯贝、布兰德贝根、法斯塔、波契卡、胡斯贝、阿卡拉和霍德林格 10 个卫星城市。它们连同市区在内，被统称为"大斯德哥尔摩"，面积达 2 590 平方千米。服务业是斯德哥尔摩最大的产业，提供了大约 85% 的就业职位。在斯德哥尔摩几乎没有重工业，这使它成为世界上最干净的大都市之一。斯德哥尔摩是阿尔弗雷德·诺贝尔的故乡。从 1901 年开始，在每年 12 月 10 日诺贝尔逝世纪念日这天，斯德哥尔摩音乐厅都会举行隆重仪式，由瑞典国王亲自给诺贝尔奖获得者授奖，并在市政厅举行晚宴。

At present, ten satellite cities have been built in the outskirts of Stockholm, including Tansta, Kista, Cheholm, Lincolmbey, Brandbergen, Fasta, Bochka, Husby, Akara and Hodlinger. Together with the urban area, they are collectively known as "Great Stockholm", covering an area of 2,590 square kilometers. The service industry is the largest industry in Stockholm, providing about 85% of jobs. There is hardly any heavy industry in Stockholm, making it one of the cleanest metropolises in the world. Stockholm is the hometown of Alfred Nobel. Since 1901, on the anniversary of Nobel's death on December 10 every year, the Stockholm Concert Hall held a grand ceremony. The Swedish King personally awarded the Nobel Prize winners and held a dinner at the city hall.

2. 哥德堡 Gothenburg

哥德堡坐落在瑞典的西海岸卡特加特海峡，是瑞典最大的河流——约塔河的出海口，全市人口约 90 万，是一座风光秀丽的海港城。哥德堡港终年不冻，成为瑞典和西欧通航的主要港埠。哥德堡地处哥本哈根、奥斯陆和斯德哥尔摩这三个北欧国家首都的中心，有 450 多条航线通往世界各地，是北欧咽喉要道，方圆 300 千米内是北欧三国的工业最发达地区，是北欧的工业中心。哥德堡是瑞典旅游胜地之一，17 世纪建造的皇家住宅、1699 年建造的旧市政府、18 世纪中叶建造的瑞典东印度公司及 1815 年建造的大教堂等名胜，每年都吸引着数十万国内外观光游客。其他旅游设施有文化、航海、历史等多所博物馆。

Gothenburg is located in the Kattegat Strait on the west coast of Sweden. It is the outlet of the largest river in Sweden—the Yota River. With a population of about 900,000, Gothenburg is a beautiful seaport city. The port of Gothenburg is not frozen all the year round and has become the main port for navigation between Sweden and Western Europe. Gothenburg is located in the center of the three Nordic capitals including Copenhagen, Oslo and Stockholm, and has more than 450 routes to all parts of the world. It is the throat of Nordic countries. Within a radius of 300 kilometers, Gothenburg is the most developed industrial region of the three Nordic countries and the industrial center of Nordic countries. Gothenburg is one of the tourist attractions in Sweden. The Royal Residence built in the 17th century, the old municipal government built in 1699, the Swedish East India Company built in the middle of the 18th century and the cathedral built in 1815 attract hundreds of thousands of domestic and foreign tourists every year. Other tourist facilities include many museums of culture, navigation, history and so on.

（二）著名旅游景点 Famous Tourist Attractions

1. 斯德哥尔摩市政厅 Stockholm City Hall

斯德哥尔摩市政厅（图 2-55）位于瑞典首都斯德哥尔摩市中心的梅拉伦湖畔，是瑞典民族浪漫主义风格最杰出的建筑之一。市政厅建于 1911 年，历时 12 年才完成，是瑞典建筑的代表作。市政厅两边临水，一座巍然矗立着的塔楼与沿水面展开的裙房形成强烈的对比，加之装饰性很强的纵向长条窗，整个建筑犹如一艘航行中的大船，宏伟壮丽。整个建筑的墙壁

图 2-55 斯德哥尔摩市政厅
Figure 2-55 Stockholm City Hall

由 8 800 万块红砖砌成，内有装饰精美的"蓝厅"与"金厅"。被称为"蓝厅"的宴会厅位于一层，是市政厅内最大的宴会厅，可容纳约 1 200 名来宾，每年 1 月 10 日瑞典国王在此宴请诺贝尔奖得主。二层的金色大厅四壁用约 1 800 万块大概一厘米见方的金色马赛克装饰，壁画则展示了斯德哥尔摩的历史，在明亮的灯光映射下，整座大厅金碧辉煌、熠熠生辉。除了有名

的"金厅"和"蓝厅"外，市政厅内还有结婚登记厅。斯德哥尔摩的市民从这里领走的不只有结婚证书，还有这个美丽城市对他们的深情祝福。

Located on the bank of Lake Merallen in the center of Stockholm, the capital of Sweden, the Stockholm City Hall (Figure 2-55) is one of the most outstanding buildings in the Swedish national romantic style. The city hall was built in 1911 and took 12 years to complete. It is the most important work in Swedish architecture. On both sides of the building, facing the water, there is a tower, which forms a strong contrast with the podium spreading along the water. With the highly decorative longitudinal long window, the whole building is like a sailing ship, which is magnificent. The whole building wall is made of 88 million red bricks, and there are beautifully decorated "Blue Hall" and "Gold Hall". The banquet hall, known as the "Blue Hall", is located on the first floor. The "Blue Hall" is the largest banquet hall in the City Hall, which can accommodate about 1,200 guests. The King of Sweden hosts a Nobel Prize winner here on January 10 every year. The four walls of the golden hall on the second floor are decorated with about 18 million pieces of gold square mosaic decotation in one square centimeter. The murals show the history of Stockholm. Under the bright light, the whole hall is resplendent and shining. In addition to the famous "Gold Hall" and "Blue Hall", there is also a marriage registration hall in the city hall. The citizens of Stockholm take not only the marriage certificate, but also this beautiful city's deep feelings and blessings to them.

图 2-56　瑞典皇宫
Figure 2-56　The Swedish Royal Palace

2. 瑞典皇宫 The Swedish Royal Palace

瑞典皇宫（图 2-56）建于公元 17 世纪，是一座方形小城堡，在正门前有两只石狮，两名头戴一尺多高红缨军帽、身穿中世纪军服的卫兵持枪而立。卫兵换岗仪式在平时的中午 12 点举行，周日及节假日举行时间为 13:10。这里是国王办公和举行庆典的地方，也是斯德哥尔摩的主要旅游景点。皇宫对外开放的部分包括皇家寓所、古斯塔夫三世的珍藏博物馆、珍宝馆、三王冠博物馆、皇家兵器馆。在宫内可以欣赏到各种金银珠宝、精致的器皿，以及精美的壁画和浮雕。

The Swedish Royal Palace (Figure2-56), built in the 17th century, is a square-shaped castle. In front of the main entrance stand two stone lions and two guards, each wearing a tall red-plumed military hat and dressed in medieval military uniforms, holding rifles. The changing of the guard ceremony takes place at noon on weekdays and at 1:10 p.m. on Sundays and public holidays. The palace serves as the office and ceremonial venue for the King and is a major tourist attraction in Stockholm. The parts of the palace open to the public include the Royal Apartments, the Gustav Ⅲ Museum of Antiquities, the Treasury, the Tre Kronor Museum, and the Royal Armory. Visitors can admire various gold and silver treasures, exquisite utensils, as well as beautiful murals and reliefs within the palace.

3. 瓦萨沉船博物馆 The Vasa Museum

"瓦萨"号是世界上唯一保存完好的 17 世纪船舶。"瓦萨"号是一艘古战船，奉瑞典国王古斯塔夫二世的旨意于 1625 年开始建造。这艘战船本来设计是单层炮舰，当国王得知瑞典的海上强敌丹麦已拥有双层炮舰，便下令把单层炮舰改造为双层。1628 年 8 月 10 日，斯德哥尔摩海湾风和日丽，一艘旌旗招展、威武壮观的大型战舰在岸上人群的一片欢呼声中扬帆启航。不料刚刚行驶数百米，一阵强风袭来，"瓦萨"号战舰便摇摆着连人带船沉入 30 多米深的海底。333 年后的 1961 年沉船被成功打捞起来，经防腐处理后，沉船船体及船上 2.4 万件文物得到保护，并在沉船遗址附近建立了这座博物馆

图 2-57　瓦萨沉船博物馆
Figure 2-57　The Vasa Museum

（图 2-57），成为全球最引人注目的旅游观光点之一，为人们了解 17 世纪的瑞典提供了一个独特的视角。

Vasa is the only well-preserved 17th century ship in the world. Vasa is an ancient warship, built in 1625 at the behest of King Gustav Ⅱ of Sweden. The warship was originally designed as a single-deck gunship. When the king learned that Denmark, Sweden's powerful maritime enemy, had a double-deck gunship, he ordered the single-deck gunship to be converted into a double-deck gunship. On August 10, 1628, a large warship with flags waving and majestic force set sail in Stockholm Bay on a sunny day, amid the cheers of the crowd on the shore. Unexpectedly, just a few hundred meters away, a strong wand blew, and the warship Vasa swung and sank into the sea more than 30 meters deep. In 1961, 333 years later, the sunken ship was successfully salvaged. After anti-corrosion treatment, the sunken ship hull and 24,000 pieces of cultural relics on the ship were protected. The Vasa museum (Figure 2-57) was built near the sunken ship site, becoming one of the most attractive tourist attractions in the world, providing a unique perspective for people to understand Sweden in the 17th century.

4. 诺贝尔博物馆 The Nobel Museum

诺贝尔博物馆（图 2-58）是由希腊历史学家吉奥戈斯·马库决定兴建的，其在科学、教育、文化等方面具有重大的国际性意义。诺贝尔博物馆专门宣传有关诺贝尔奖、诺贝尔奖得主和阿尔弗雷德·诺贝尔生平的资讯。馆址位于瑞典斯德哥尔摩老城大广场北侧，与瑞典学院和诺贝尔图书馆一样都位于证券交易所大楼内。

图 2-58　诺贝尔博物馆
Figure 2-58　The Nobel Museum

The Nobel Museum (Figure 2-58) was built by the Greek historian Giorgos Marcou. It has great international significance in science, education and culture. The Nobel Museum specially publicizes information about the Nobel Prize, Nobel laureates and Alfred Nobel's life. The museum is located on the north side of the Great Square in Stockholm's Old Town, sharing the Stockholm Stock Exchange Building with the Swedish Academy and the Nobel Library.

图 2-59　阿比斯库国家公园
Figure 2-59　The Abyscu National Park

5. 阿比斯库国家公园 The Abyscu National Park

位于北极圈内的瑞典阿比斯库国家公园（图 2-59）山势不高、森林密布，与同纬度其他地区相比气候温和、风景秀丽。这里是"欧洲最后的土著"萨米人世世代代生活的乐土，这里还是"雪地精灵"——北极狐生活繁衍的栖息地，这里是欧洲著名徒步路线"皇家之路"的起点，吸引着来自世界各地的人们从这里踏上漫漫征途。

The Abyscu National Park (Figure 2-59) in Sweden, located in the Arctic Circle, is not high in mountains and densely forested. Compared with other regions in the same latitude, the climate is mild and the scenery is beautiful. This is the paradise where the Sami people, the "Last Native of Europe", have lived for generations. This is the habitat where the "snow elf" arctic fox lives and thrives. This is the starting point of the famous European hiking route "Royal Road", attracting people from all over the world to embark on a long journey from here.

阿比斯库国家公园浓缩了斯堪的纳维亚山脉的精华景观，四季景色不同：春天是一个滑雪胜地，夏天则可以使徒步的游客尽情享受极昼的快乐，秋天是狩猎和观赏红叶的季节，到了冬天也不荒凉，随着极光划破天际，游客仿佛置身于迷幻世界。

Abyscu National Park condenses the essence of the Scandinavian Mountains. The scenery of the four seasons is different. In spring, it is a ski resort, while in summer it allows hikers to enjoy the joy of the polar day. Autumn is the season for hunting and watching red leaves. In winter, it is not deadly silent. The aurora breaks through the sky, making tourists feel like they were in a psychedelic world.

（三）旅游购物 Shopping

瑞典巧克力：瑞典巧克力非常多，本土老字号 Marabou 巧克力口感好且价格适中，有很多新奇的口味，还会有季节限定款。

Swedish chocolate: Sweden has a lot of chocolate, the local brand Marabou chocolate tastes good and is affordable. There are a lot of novelty flavors and a seasonal limited edition.

达拉彩绘木马：达拉彩绘木马是一种起源于瑞典达拉纳省（Dalarna län）的纯手工打磨与绘制的小木马，被誉为"瑞典的象征"，是当地人馈赠外宾的常备礼品，也是各国游客选购的热门纪念品。

Dalarna Trojan Horse: Dalarna Trojan Horse is a hand-sanded and hand-painted wooden horse originating from Dalarna län, Sweden. Known as the "Symbol of Sweden", it is a common gift for locals to present to foreign guests and is a popular souvenir for tourists from all over the world.

DW 手表：DW 的全称为 Daniel Wellington（丹尼尔·惠灵顿），其设计时尚，深受全球年轻人的追捧。DW 表身轻薄，表带有皮质表带、金属表带和红白蓝条纹尼龙表带可供选择。

DW watches: DW stands for Daniel Wellington, a brand known for its fashionable designs that are highly popular among young people worldwide. DW watches are sleek and lightweight, offering a variety of strap options including leather, metal, and the signature red, white, and blue striped nylon straps.

皮具：瑞典的皮具持久耐用，深受各界推崇。硬币包、钱包、手袋、旅行袋等各种款式的皮具，无论是质地、光泽还是做工，都非常不错。驯鹿皮制品最具本地特色，常见的有钥匙扣、冰箱贴和各类摆件。

Leather goods: Swedish leather goods are durable and well respected. Coin purses, wallets, handbags, travel bags and other styles of leather goods are very good in terms of texture, luster and workmanship. Reindeer leather products are the most distinct local items, commonly including key chains, refrigerator stickers and all kinds of ornaments.

扫码获取：入境须知及海关规定

本节习题

1. 请简述瑞典的地理环境。

2. 与瑞典人交往需要注意哪些礼仪禁忌？

3. 假设你是旅行社的出境部门经理，负责瑞典旅游线路的推广，请设计一条针对中国游客的特色主题旅游线路。

1. 了解美国和加拿大的基本情况，包括两国的自然环境特征、风俗民情、主要旅游城市和景点。

Get familiar with the national conditions of the United States and Canada, including the natural environmental characteristics, and customs of each country, as well as major tourist cities and scenic spots.

2. 能在旅游接待活动中利用所学关于美国和加拿大的旅游景点介绍、习俗禁忌、出入境海关规定等知识，做好服务工作。

Be able to utilize knowledge of tourist attractions, customs and taboos, entry and exit customs regulations of the United States and Canada in Tourist reception activities to provide good service work.

3. 能根据美国和加拿大的特点和游客的不同需求，设计旅游线路、开发旅游产品。

Be able to carry out targeted tourist source development planning and product design according to the characteristics of United States and Canada and customers' needs.

第一节 北美洲旅游区特征

The General Situation of North America Tourist Region

美洲是南美洲和北美洲的合称，又被称为"新大陆"。北美旅游区位于西半球大陆北部，东濒大西洋，西临太平洋，北接北冰洋，南以巴拿马运河同南美旅游区相隔。北美旅游区包括加拿大、美国、墨西哥以及中美洲、西印度群岛上的国家。

北美洲旅游区特征（英文版）

北美旅游区地形呈明显的三个南北向纵列带。西部是高大的科迪勒拉山系，国家公园、大峡谷，山水旅游景观丰富；东部为低缓的山地、高原（包括古老的阿巴拉契亚山地和拉布拉多高原等），自然旅游资源和人文旅游资源兼备；中部是起伏平缓的低高原和平原，自然旅游资源丰富。中美洲和加勒比海地区海岸线漫长曲折，热带海岛多，阳光明媚、碧海银滩、景色迷人，是游泳、日光浴和泛舟的理想之地，是世界上最受欢迎的海滨旅游度假胜地之一。

北美旅游区气候类型多样，拥有热带、寒带和温带的各种气候类型。其大部分地区位于温带，以温带大陆性气候为主，生物旅游资源丰富。南部全年适合旅游。北部现代冰川分布广泛，冰雪旅游景观丰富，是冰雪旅游和探险旅游的最佳去处。北美旅游区的通用语言是英语，最早的居民为印第安人和因纽特人（爱斯基摩人），其余大部分居民是欧洲移民的后裔，以盎格鲁-撒克逊人为最多。北美旅游资源比较丰富，再加上其雄厚的经济基础、完备的旅游基础设施和服务设施，旅游业十分发达。长期以来，无论是接待国际游客数量，还是国际旅游收入，北美旅游区均处在世界前列。美国和加拿大均跻身于全球15大国际旅游接待国、国际旅游收入国及国际旅游消费支出国之列。

第二节　北美洲之旅

Travel in North America

山姆大叔——美国
Uncle Sam—The United States of America

导读

美国是高度发达的现代化国家，其国内生产总值居世界首位，具有世界级规模的现代化市场经济。其工业生产长期保持稳定，信息、生物等高科技产业发展迅速。美国法律制度较为健全，市场体系较为完善，营商环境良好，基础设施发达，在市场容量、科技实力、教育创新、劳动生产率等方面稳居全球领先地位。美国是联合国安理会常任理事国之一，也是北约、世贸组织、亚太经济合作组织等国际组织成员国，其在政治、外交、经济、文化等领域对世界均有较强的影响力。美国重视稳定和同世界上各主要力量的关系，不断加强同欧、日在政治安全上的协调与合作。1972年2月，美国总统理查德·尼克松访华，中美双方发表了《中美联合公报》（即《上海公报》），标志着中美两国20多年相互隔绝状态的结束。1979年1月1日，中美两国正式建立大使级外交关系。1982年8月17日，中美发表《八一七公报》，这一公报联同《上海公报》和《中美建交公报》被称为"中美三个联合公报"。多年来，中美关系虽经历了不少曲折和起伏，但总体上是向前发展的。中美保持着领导人互访和高级官员相互磋商的机制，两国在经贸、科技、文化、教育、军事等多个领域不断开展交流与相互合作。

美国绰号"山姆大叔"的由来

一、地理概览 Geography of the United States

（一）位置 Location

美利坚合众国，简称美国，地处北美洲中部，东临大西洋，西濒太平洋，南靠墨西哥和墨西哥湾，北邻加拿大。国土总面积约为 937 万平方千米，仅次于俄罗斯、加拿大和中国，居世界第四位。美国由 50 个州和华盛顿哥伦比亚特区组成，其中 48 个州位于本土，2 个州在本土以外，即北美西北部的阿拉斯加州和太平洋的夏威夷州。

The United States of America, briefly known as the USA, is located in central North America, bordering the Atlantic Ocean to the east, the Pacific Ocean to the west, Mexico and the Gulf of Mexico to the south, and Canada to the north. The total area of the country is approximately 9.37 million square kilometers, making it the fourth largest country in the world after Russia, Canada, and China. The country consists of 50 states and the District of Columbia, with 48 contiguous states situated on the mainland. The other two states are geographically separated: Alaska is located in the northwest extremity of North America, while Hawaii is an archipelago in the mid−Pacific.

（二）地形和气候 The Land and Seasons

美国地势东西高、中间低，可以分为三个地形区：东部是阿巴拉契亚山脉构成的古老山地及大西洋沿岸平原；西部是科迪勒拉山系构成的高原和山地，包括落基山脉、海岸山脉、内华达山脉、喀斯特岭，以及一系列山间高原、盆地和谷地；中部为大平原。

The United States features a topography that is high in the east and west, with a lower central region, which can be divided into three geographical areas. The eastern region consists of the ancient Appalachian Mountains and the Atlantic Coastal Plain; the western region is characterized by the Cordillera mountain system, which includes the Rocky Mountains, Coast Ranges, Sierra Nevada Mountains, and the Cascade Range, along with a series of inter−mountain plateaus, basins, and valleys; the central region is known as the Great Plains.

美国幅员辽阔、地形复杂，各地气候差异较大，大体可分为五个气候区：东北部为沿海的温带气候区，东南部为亚热带气候区，中央平原为大陆性气候区，西部高原为干燥气候区，太平洋沿岸为海洋性气候区。其中，佛罗里达半岛南端属于热带；阿拉斯加位于北纬 60°～70°，属于北极圈内的寒冷气候；夏威夷位于北回归线以南，属于热带气候。

The United States is vast and geographically diverse, resulting in significant climate variations across the country. It can be broadly divided into five climate zones: the northeastern region has a coastal temperate climate, the southeastern region has a subtropical climate, the central plains experience a continental climate, the western plateau is characterized by an arid climate, and the Pacific coast has a marine climate. The southern tip of the Florida Peninsula falls within the tropical climate zone; Alaska, located between 60 to 70 degrees north latitude, experiences the cold climate typical of the Arctic Circle; and Hawaii, situated south of the Tropic of Cancer, also has a tropical climate.

美国亚利桑那州大峡谷

（三）自然资源 Natural Resources

美国自然资源丰富，煤、石油、天然气、铁矿石、钾盐、磷酸盐、硫黄等矿物储量均居世界前列。其他矿物还包括铜、铅、钼、铀、铝矾土、金、汞、镍、碳酸钾、银、钨、锌、铝、铋等。战略矿物资源钛、锰、钴、铬等主要靠进口。

The United States is rich in natural resources, with reserves of coal, oil, natural gas, iron ore, potash, phosphates, and sulfur ranking among the highest in the world. Other minerals include copper, lead, molybdenum, uranium, bauxite, gold, mercury, nickel, potassium carbonate, silver, tungsten, zinc, aluminum, and bismuth. Strategic mineral resources such as titanium, manganese, cobalt, and chromium are primarily imported.

美国森林面积达 310 万平方千米，全球排名第四，森林主要分布在西北部太平洋沿岸、东北部和东南部。水资源总量仅次于中国、俄罗斯，居世界第三位，主要分布于哥伦比亚河、科罗拉多河和田纳西河。全国耕地面积约 19 745 万公顷，人均耕地面积约 0.7 公顷，均居世界前列。美国拥有发展工农业生产所需要的丰富资源和有利自然条件。美国旅游资源丰富，各地的旅游景观各具特色，国家公园分布广泛，全年中适宜旅游的时间较长。

The forest area in the United States covers 3.1 million square kilometers, ranking fourth in the world. It is mainly distributed along the Pacific coast in the northwest, northeast, and southeast. The United States ranks third in the world after China and Russia in terms of water resources, mainly distributed in the Columbia River, Colorado River, and Tennessee River. Approximately 197.45 million hectares of arable land are cultivated nationwide, with a per capita arable land of 0.7 hectares, ranking among the top in the world. The United States has abundant resources and favorable natural conditions which are necessary for the development of industrial and agricultural production. The United States is rich in tourist resources, with distinctive tourist landscapes and extensive distribution of national parks. The suitable time for traveling throughout the year is relatively long.

二、人文概况 Overview of American Humanities

（一）国情认知 Basic Knowledge of National Conditions

美国的居住人口约为 3.33 亿左右 (2022 年)，居世界第三位。美国人基本上都是移民或是移民的后裔。印第安人、因纽特人和夏威夷人是最早居住在美国本土的土著人。美国人口中，白人占 64%，拉丁裔占 16.3%，黑人占 12.6%，亚裔占 4.7%。美国华裔如今已成为亚裔人群中占比最高的族群。美国没有法定的官方语言，英语是事实上的国家语言。由于地理的阻隔、时间的流逝，美、英两国语言已产生了很大的差异，演变出了具有美国特色的美式英语。除了英语，使用人口数量超过 100 万的语言还包括西班牙语、法语和汉语。

As of 2022, the United States has a population of approximately 333 million, making it the third most populous country in the world. Most Americans are either immigrants or descendants of immigrants. Native Americans, Inuits, and Hawaiians were the earliest indigenous peoples to inhabit the land. Among the population, 64% are White, 16.3% are Hispanic or Latino, 12.6% are Black or African American, and 4.7% are Asian. Chinese Americans have become the largest group within the Asian population. The United States does not have an official language by law, but English is the de facto national language. Due to geographical separation and the passage of time, American and British English have diverged significantly, resulting in the distinct variety known as American English. Besides English, languages spoken by more than one million people include Spanish, French, and Chinese.

美国的国旗为长方形星条旗，主体由 13 道红色、白色相间的横条组成，旗面左上角为蓝色长方形，分 9 排横列着 50 颗白色五角星。美国的国歌为《星光灿烂的旗帜》，国花是玫瑰花，国鸟是白头海雕。51.3% 的居民信奉基督教新教，23.9% 信奉天主教，1.7% 信奉犹太教，此外，还有东正教、佛教、伊斯兰教和印度教等。

The flag of the United States is the rectangular Stars and Stripes, the main body of which consists of 13 horizontal stripes of red and white, with a blue rectangle in the upper left corner of the flag. 50 white-pointed stars arranged horizontally are divided into nine rows on the blue rectangle. The national anthem of the United States is *The Star-Spangled Banner*, the national flower is rose, and the national bird is the white-headed sea eagle. 51.3 percent of the United States inhabitants are Protestant Christians, 23.9 percent are Catholics, 1.7 percent are Jews, and there are also Eastern Orthodox Christians, Buddhists, Muslims and Hindus.

（二）历史简介 History of the United States

在哥伦布发现美洲大陆以前，北美洲生活着印第安人和因纽特人。15 世纪末期，新大陆的发现引起了欧洲殖民国家的关注，大批殖民者蜂拥而至。1775 年，美国爆发了反对殖民统治的独立战争。1776 年，13 个殖民地从大英帝国脱离出来，在发表《独立宣言》、发动独立战争的那一年，他们成立了世界上第一个立宪制的民主联邦共和国——美利坚合众国。

Before discovered by Columbus, the North American continent was inhabited by American Indians and Inuits. At the end of the 15th century, the discovery of the new continent drew the attentions from the European colonial countries and a large number of colonists flocked here. In 1775, the War of Independence against colonial rule broke out in the United States. In 1776, the 13 colonies split from Great Britain and formed the United States, the world's first constitutional and democratic federal republic, after issuing the *Declaration of Independence* and the Independence War in the same year.

1783 年，根据《巴黎条约》，美利坚合众国的地位得到承认。19 世纪中期，在各州权力划分和奴隶制扩张的问题上，南北方出现了明显的分歧。北方各州反对农奴制，但南方各州认为为了南方农业发展的需要必须保持并扩张奴隶制，并且要求扩大农奴区域。1861 年，争论达到关键时期，南方七个州从联邦中分离出去，成立美国南部联邦，引发了国内战争。战争期间，亚伯拉罕·林肯发表《解放黑人奴隶宣言》，要求反叛的各州解放所有的奴隶，但是直到 1865 年战争结束后奴隶才获得真正的解放。

The nation of the United States of America was recognized following the *Treaty of Paris* in 1783. In the mid-19th century, a major disagreement occurred in the US over the issue of division of states' powers and the expansion of slavery. The northern states opposed to slavery, while the southern states saw it as necessary for the continued success of southern agriculture and wanted it expanded to the territories. The dispute reached a crisis point in 1861, when seven southern states seceded from the Union and formed the Confederate States of America, leading to the Civil War（1861）. During the war, Abraham Lincoln issued the *Emancipation Proclamation*, mandating the freedom of all slaves in states in rebellion, though full emancipation of slaves did not take place until after the end of the war in 1865.

1898 年，美西战争爆发，美国最终取胜，标志着美国正式步入帝国主义强国行列并开始对外扩张。第一次世界大战的胜利使美国获利丰厚，而第二次世界大战的胜利则奠定了美国世界第一强国的地位。20 世纪末，随着苏联解体及冷战结束，美国国力更是空前强大。自 1870 年以来，美国国民经济总量就高居全球第一。如今的美国是联合国安理会五个常任理事国之一，其在全球的政治、经济、军事、娱乐等众多领域的庞大影响力更是其他国家所无法匹敌的。

In 1898, America won the war against Spain, growing into one of the powerful imperialist countries, and embarked on foreign expansion. America benefited a lot from the victory of World War Ⅰ, and the victory in the World War Ⅱ secured its status as the most powerful country in the world. At the end of the 20th century, with the ending of Cold War and disintegration of the Soviet Union, the national power of America rose to an unprecedented level. Since 1870, the national economy of America has topped the world. Nowadays, America is one of the five permanent members of the United Nations Security Council and its powerful influences in such areas as politics, economy, military and entertainment are unparalleled by any other countries.

（三）经济状况 The Economy

美国是一个经济高度发达的国家，国民生产总值和对外贸易额常年居世界前列。美国工业以技术先进、门类齐全、生产实力雄厚而著称，其中汽车工业和建筑业是美国经济的两大支柱产业。美国在计算机技术、电子电信、生物工程、化学及航空航天等高技术领域的实力居世界首位。美国的服务业发达，金融、保险、航运和商业服务业在国民经济中所占比重较大，全国 3/4 的劳动力从事服务业。纽约是美国最大的城市及金融中心，同时也是世界级的金融、航运服务中心。美国农业高度发达，机械化程度高，粮食产量约占世界的 1/5，是世界上规模较大的农产品出口国。美国旅游业发达，拥有完整、便捷的交通运输网络，旅游基础设施完备。

The United States is a highly developed country with GDP and value of the foreign trade ranking first in the world for a long time. The industry is known for its developed technology, complete ranges of products and huge powerful production strength. The auto and building industries are two mainstay industries of American economy. The United States has advanced technology and ranks first in high-tech sectors such as computer technology, electronics and telecommunications, bioengineering, chemistry, and aerospace. America has vigorous service industry, the services like finance, insurance, shipping and commercial services accounting for a large proportion of the national economy. Three quarters of the labor force in the country is engaged in the service industry. New York is the largest city and financial center in the United States, as well as the world's largest financial and shipping service center. The agriculture of the United States is highly developed, with a high degree of mechanization, accounting for about 1/5 of the world's grain production, and is the world's largest exporter of agricultural products. The tourist industry in the United States is developed, with a complete and convenient transportation network and complete tourist infrastructure.

（四）传统文化 Traditional Culture

美国是个移民国家，各种移民文化的相互交融是美国文化的最大特色。不断涌入的人口促成了新文化与传统文化的完美融合，因而美国通常被称为"大熔炉"。多元文化遍及美国社会，其中欧洲文化对美国文化的影响最为深刻。早期的移民把欧洲文化带到美国，并且很快就在美国各地传播开来。独特的社会文化催生了具有美国独有特色的文学，并成为世界文学的主流之一。早在建国初期，美国就孕育产生了许多杰出的作家。多位美国作家曾经获得诺贝尔文学奖，如剧作家尤金·欧尼尔，小说家索尔·贝娄、赛珍珠、福克纳、海明威等。

The United States is a nation of immigrants, and the biggest cultural feature of American culture is the fusion of immigrant cultures. The inpouring population created a perfect blend of cultures and traditions, which is normally referred to as the "Melting Pot". American society is diverse culturally, while the European culture influenced the American culture most significantly. The early immigrants brought European culture to the United States. And these cultures spread and the special social culture developed the literature with unique American feature which has grown into one of the mainstreams of world literature which also has unique American features. As early as the beginning of the nation, many outstanding writers sprung up. Several Americans have been awarded Nobel Prize in Literature, such as the playwriter Eugene O'Neill, and writers like Saul Bellow, Pearl S. Buck, William Faulkner, Ernest Hemingway and so on.

许多生活在美国的人，无论是土生土长的美国人，还是漂洋过海来到美国的外国移民，都有一个梦，即通过自己的努力，改变自己的社会地位，实现自己的人生梦想，这就是人们常津津乐道的"美国梦"。300 年前，当英格兰移民乘坐着"五月花"号横穿大西洋来到马里兰，寻找一块清教徒能居住的"净土"时，"美国梦"便开始悄然萌芽。自 1776 年以来，世世代代的美国人都深信不疑，只要经过努力不懈的奋斗便能获得更好的生活，而非依赖特定的社会阶级和他人的援助。"美国梦"包含几个要素：美国提供了人人都能成功的机会；成功取决于自己的才能和努力，而不是家世和背景；人人都拥有平等的权利；人人都有信仰的自由。"美国梦"是美国文化精神的缩影，是个人至高无上的各种价值的实现和实际利益的满足。但是近年来，随着美国经济的持续疲软和社会问题的集中显现，很多人心中的"美国梦"正在破碎。

Many people living in the United States, whether native Americans, or immigrants who came to the United States across the ocean, have a dream, that is, through their own efforts, to change their social status and to achieve their dreams in life, which is often talked about as the "American Dream". 300 years ago, when the English immigrants took the "Mayflower" ship across the Atlantic Ocean to Maryland, looking for a piece of the Puritans can live, "American Dream" began to germinate quietly. Since 1776, generations of Americans have been convinced that a better life can be achieved through hard work and perseverance, rather than dependence on a particular social class and the assistance of others. The "American Dream" consists of several ideas: the United States provides opportunities for everyone to succeed; success depends on one's talent and hard work, not on one's family or background; all people have equal rights; and all people have the freedom to believe. The "American Dream" is the epitome of the American culture and spirit, the realization of various individual values and the satisfaction of practical interests of the individual. However, in recent years, with the continued weakness of the U.S. economy and the emergence of social problems, the "American Dream" in the hearts of many people is being shattered.

❓ 思考题

请观看选自中国日报网的一段视频——"中国梦的内涵"。习近平总书记对于"中国梦"的阐释表明，实现中华民族的伟大复兴，就是中华民族近代以来最伟大的梦想。此后，"中国梦"成为一个人尽皆知的流行热词。

请思考："美国梦"的本质是什么？"美国梦"与"中国梦"的区别在哪里？

"中国梦"的
内涵

（五）礼仪禁忌 Social Etiquettes and Taboos

美国人大多性格热情、开朗大方、易于接近，人际交往上随性自由。美国人酷爱闲聊，话题包罗万象，体育、天气、工作或过去经历等都可以成为聊天话题，但是不会与陌生人谈论宗教、政治或个人生活等隐私话题。在美国社会中，一切行为都是以个人为中心，个人利益是神圣不可侵犯的。这种准则渗透于社会生活的各个方面。在人们的日常交谈中，忌谈有关年龄、婚姻状况、收入、宗教信仰、服饰价格等非常冒昧和失礼的问题。

Americans are generally warm, outgoing, generous, and approachable, with a casual and free-spirited approach to social interactions. They love to engage in small talk, covering a wide range of topics such as sports, weather, work, or past experiences. However, they typically avoid discussing religion, politics, or personal matters with strangers. In American society, everything is centered around the individual, and personal interests are considered sacred and inviolable. This principle permeates all aspects of social life. In everyday conversations, it is considered impolite and intrusive to discuss topics such as age, marital status, income, religious beliefs, or the cost of clothing

美国人会经常使用肢体语言：耸肩而面带不高兴的表情表示惊讶；耸肩而面带笑容表示肯定；食指和中指构成"V"形，表示"胜利、加油"；拇指和食指构成"6"形，表示"对，同意，很好"的意思；把手搭在他人的肩膀上，表示肯定与鼓励；手掌朝上，手指来回运动，表示招呼人过来，手掌朝下则表示和动物打招呼。

Americans use body language frequently. When they feel surprised they will shrug their shoulders with a sad look. And they shrug their shoulders with a smile to express approval. They only extend their index and middle fingers to form the shape of "V" to show victory and encouragement. They curve the thumb and index finger to form the shape of "6" to show agreement. They pat on your shoulders to show affirmation or encouragement. When they turn their palms upward and move fingers back and forth, it is a sign to ask someone to come over. If they turn their palms downward, it is used for animals.

"残疾人优先、女士优先、老人优先、儿童优先"是美国人的习惯，因为弱势群体理应得到健康人士的关照。美国人很珍惜时间，浪费他人的时间等同于侵犯他们的个人权利。如果要登门拜访，必须先打电话预约。

"Priority for people with disabilities, women, the elderly, and children" is a common practice in the United States, as it is believed that vulnerable groups deserve the care and consideration of those who are able-bodied. Americans highly value their time, and wasting someone else's time is seen as an infringement on their personal rights. If you plan to visit someone at their home, it is essential to call ahead and make an appointment.

案例分析

美国所有公共停车场必须按照规定设立一定数量的残疾人停车位，而且这些车位往往设置在最方便的地方，宽敞且设有醒目的"蓝色轮椅"标志，只有持残疾人车牌的人方能在此泊车。黄小姐参加了美国自驾游，在逛超市的时候看到有很多预留的残疾人车位，于是把车停到了残疾人专用车位上，结果仅仅几分钟后就接到了电话，警察开出500美元的高额罚单。对此黄小姐十分懊恼，觉得美国人小题大做。请问：该罚单是否合理？

美国人讨厌蝙蝠，认为它是吸血鬼和凶神的象征，忌讳数字"13""星期五"等；忌讳询问女性的婚姻状态、年龄及服饰价格等私事；忌讳黑色，认为黑色是肃穆的象征，是丧葬用的颜色；特别忌讳向他人赠送带有公司标志的便宜礼物，因为这有做广告的嫌疑。在美国，千万不要把黑人称作"Negro"，可以使用"Black people"来称呼他们，因为 Negro 主要是指从非洲贩卖到美国为奴的黑人。

Americans hate bats, considering it as a vampire and the symbol of the evil god. They don't like the unlucky numbers such as "13" "Friday", etc. It is a taboo to ask women about personal matters such as marital status, age, or clothing prices. Black is a taboo for Americans, because it is regarded as a symbol of solemnity and a color used for funerals. And Americans avoid giving inexpensive gifts with company logos that look like advertising. In the United States, it is impolite to call the black people Negro. Negroes are mainly black people who were trafficked from Africa to the U.S. to work as slaves.

讨论题

你如何看待美国的人权问题？

（六）传统节日 Festivals

1. 独立日 Independence Day

独立日是美国的主要法定节日之一，是为了纪念 1776 年 7 月 4 日在费城第二次大陆会议正式通过的《独立宣言》而设立的。《独立宣言》是美国历史上的重要文献，宣告了美国的诞生，之后每年的 7 月 4 日就是美国的国庆日。在这一天，美国会举办各种活动，其中最重要的就是敲响位于费城的自由钟。其他的庆祝活动包括花车游行、节日游行等。

Independence Day, one of the major federal holidays in the United States, commemorating the adoption of the Declaration of Independence on July 4, 1776, by the Second Continental Congress in Philadelphia. The *Declaration of Independence* is a great literature which has historic significance. On the national day of the United States, a variety of activities will be held nationwide, the most important of which is striking the Liberty Bell in Philadelphia. Other celebrations include floats parades, festive parades, etc.

2. 林肯纪念日 Lincoln Memorial Day

亚伯拉罕·林肯是美国南北战争的领导者，为废除奴隶制立下了不朽功勋。其诞辰日 2 月 12 日现为美国除南部外的 26 个州的法定纪念日。

Abraham Lincoln was the leader of the American Civil War and made immortal contributions to the abolition of slavery. His birthday, February 12, is now a statutory anniversary in 26 states except the southern states of the United States.

3. 母亲节 Mother's Day

这一节日的倡导者是费城的一位女教师安娜·扎维德。在 5 月的第二个星期日，美国各地的母亲都会收到儿女们送来的节日贺卡、鲜花和礼物。

The advocate of this festival is Anna Zavid, a female teacher from Philadelphia. On the second

Sunday of May, mothers in the United States will receive holiday greeting cards, flowers, and gifts from their children.

4. 圣诞节 Christmas Day

每年的 12 月 25 日是圣诞节，是美国最大、最热闹的节日。圣诞节原是基督教徒为庆祝耶稣诞辰而定的节日，现已不再只是宗教节日，而成为了政府规定的公众假期。人们在圣诞节要互赠礼品，互相祝贺。圣诞节的庆祝活动从 12 月 24 日夜间开始，半夜时分达到最高潮，这一夜就被称为"平安夜"，平安夜是一年中最热闹的夜晚，相当于中国春节的除夕夜。

December 25 is the largest and busiest holiday in the United States every year. Originally a holiday was set by Christians to celebrate the birth of Jesus. Now, it is no longer just a religious program, and also a government mandated public holiday. People should give each other gifts and congratulate each other on Christmas Day. The celebration of Christmas Day starts on the night of December 24 and reaches its peak in the middle of the night. This night is called "Christmas Eve", it is the busiest night of the year, just like Chinese New Year's Eve.

5. 感恩节 Thanksgiving Day

感恩节在每年 11 月的最后一个星期四，它的由来可以追溯到美国历史的起源。1620 年，著名的"五月花"号轮船满载不堪忍受英国国内宗教迫害的清教徒到达北美洲。一些心地善良的印第安人帮助了这些饥寒交迫的清教徒。按照宗教传统习俗，这些移民选定了特别的一天来感谢上帝，他们还邀请印第安人共同庆祝，以此来感谢印第安人的帮助。美国独立后，感恩节成为全国性的节日。在这一天，家庭成员团聚一堂，吃着传统风味的火鸡大餐，城乡市镇到处都会举行化装游行、戏剧表演和体育比赛等。

圣诞节的由来

Thanksgiving Day falls on the last Thursday of November every year. The origin of the festival can be traced back to the beginning of American history. In 1620, the well-known "Mayflower" arrived in North America carrying puritans who suffered from religious prosecutions. Some kind-hearted Indians helped them when they were in hunger and cold. According to religious traditions, those immigrants designated a special day to express their gratitude to God, and invited the Indians over to celebrate together to thank for their help. After the independence of America, Thanksgiving Day became a national holiday. During the festival, family members get together, enjoying the turkey prepared in the traditional way. In the towns and cities, other activities are held such as costume parade, theatre performances and sports games, etc.

三、旅游观光 Tourism and Sightseeing

（一）主要旅游城市 Major Tourist Cities

1. 华盛顿哥伦比亚特区 Washington，D.C.

华盛顿哥伦比亚特区（Washington, D.C.）英文全称为 Washington District of Columbia，缩写为 WDC，简称为华盛顿，是美利坚合众国的首都。华盛顿位于马里兰州和弗吉尼亚州之间，是美国的政治中心，是大多数美国联邦政府机关与各国驻美国大使馆的所在地，也是世界银行、国际货币基金组织、美洲国家组织等国际组织总部的所在地，还拥有为数众多的博物馆与文化史迹。

Washington District of Columbia（Washington，D.C.）abbreviated as WDC，short for

Washington, is the capital of the United States of America. Washington, D.C., located between Maryland and Virginia, is the political center of the United States, home to most U.S. federal government agencies and embassies, the headquarters of the World Bank, the International Monetary Fund, the Organization of American States and other international organizations, as well as numerous museums and cultural and historical sites.

2. 纽约 New York

纽约，别称大苹果、哥谭镇、不夜城、帝国之城等，是美国最大的城市及最大的海港，也是世界经济中心之一。纽约市占据五个行政区：曼哈顿、布鲁克林、布朗克斯、皇后区和史坦顿岛。这座城市以其文化、娱乐、餐饮、时尚、艺术、体育、金融等闻名于世。纽约拥有超过 18 000 家餐厅、150 家世界级博物馆和 10 000 多家各类零售商店。纽约与伦敦、巴黎、莫斯科并称为世界四大国际大都会。纽约的旅游景点主要有自由女神像、帝国大厦、时代广场、中央公园、联合国总部大楼、百老汇、华尔街、大都会博物馆等。

New York is also nicknamed the Big Apple, Gotham, the City that Never Sleeps and the Empire City, etc. It is the biggest city and port in the United States, as well as one of the economic centers in the world. It occupies five boroughs : Manhattan, Brooklyn, the Bronx, Queens and Staten Island. The city is known internationally for its culture, entertainment, dining, fashion, art, sports, finance and more. New York offers more than 18,000 restaurants, 150 world-class museums, and more than 10,000 retail shops of every variety. New York, together with London, Paris, Moscow are called the world's four major international metropolises. The main tourist attractions of New York are the Statue of Liberty, the Empire State Building, Times Square, Central Park, United Nations Headquarters, Broadway, Wall Street, the Metropolitan Museum of Art, etc.

3. 费城 Philadelphia

费城是美国历史名城。17 世纪初为瑞典人移居地。1682 年由英国教谊会派移民始建城市。1701 年设市，到 18 世纪中叶，费城已发展为英国美洲殖民地中最大的城市。1774—1775 年两次大陆会议在此召开并通过了《独立宣言》；1787 年在此举行制宪会议，诞生了第一部联邦宪法。19 世纪以来，费城的铁路和港口经济发展很快。制造业也逐渐兴起，1860 年时其产值已提升至占全国总量的 30%。现仍为美国经济、交通、文化中心之一。费城的著名旅游景点有艺术博物馆、自由钟、独立大厅、宾夕法尼亚大学等。

Philadelphia is a historic city in the U.S. It was settled by Swedes in the early 17th century, and was founded in 1682 by settlers sent by the Fellowship of England. It was incorporated as a city in 1701, and by the middle of the 18th century had grown into the largest city in the British colonies in America. *The Declaration of Independence* was adopted by the two Continental Congresses held here from 1774 to 1775, and the first *Federal Constitution* was adopted by the Constitutional Convention held here in 1787. Since the 19th century, Philadelphia's railroad and port economy has grown rapidly. Manufacturing was also on the rise, with output increasing to 30% of the nation's value in 1860. Philadelphia is still one of the major economic, transportation and cultural centers in the United States. Famous tourist attractions in Philadelphia include the Museum of Art, the Liberty Bell, Independence Hall, and the University of Pennsylvania.

4. 芝加哥 Chicago

芝加哥位于美国密歇根湖的南部，是美国第三大城市，也是世界国际金融中心之一。芝加哥地处北美大陆的中心地带，是美国最大的商业中心区和最大的期货市场之一，也是美国黑人、犹太人聚居的城市。芝加哥市内保存着早期传统的西欧古建筑，同时也有壮观巍峨的现代高楼大厦，被誉为"摩天大楼的故乡"。

Chicago is located on the southern shores of Lake Michigan and is the thirdlargest city in the United States, as well as one of the world's major international financial centers. Situated in the heart of the North American continent, Chicago boasts the largest commercial district in the U.S. and one of the biggest futures markets. It is home to significant African American and Jewish communities. The city preserves early traditional Western European architecture while also featuring impressive modern skyscrapers, earning it the nickname "The Home of the Skyscraper".

5. 洛杉矶 Los Angeles

洛杉矶位于美国加利福尼亚州西南部，是加州第一大城市。洛杉矶是西班牙语的音译，意为"天使之城"。洛杉矶陆地面积为 1 214.9 平方千米，是美国人口第二多的城市，仅次于纽约。洛杉矶是世界工商业、国际贸易、科教、文化、娱乐和体育中心之一，拥有美国西部最大的海港，也是美国石油化工、海洋、航天工业和电子业的最大基地之一。洛杉矶拥有许多世界知名的高等学府，包括加州理工学院、加州大学洛杉矶分校、南加州大学、佩珀代因大学等。在娱乐方面，好莱坞、加州迪士尼乐园、环球影城等都位于洛杉矶，使洛杉矶成为一座举世闻名的"电影城"和"旅游城"。

Los Angeles, located in the southwestern state of Californo and is the largest city in California. Los Angeles is a Spanish transliteration, meaning "City of Angels". Los Angeles has a land area of 1,214.9 square kilometers and is the second most populous city in the United States, second only to New York. Los Angeles is one of the world's centers of commerce and industry, international trade, science and education, culture, entertainment and sports. It has the largest seaport in the western United States and is one of the largest bases for the petrochemical, marine, aerospace and electronics industries in the United States. Los Angeles has many world-renowned institutions of higher education. The Greater Los Angeles region's famous institutions of higher education, include the California Institute of Technology (Caltech), the University of California at Los Angeles (UCLA), the University of Southern California (USC), Pepperdine University and so on. In terms of entertainment, Hollywood, California Disneyland, Universal Studios and so on are all located in Los Angeles, making Los Angeles a world-famous "Movie City" and "Tourist City".

6. 旧金山 San Francisco

旧金山是美国加利福尼亚州太平洋沿岸港口城市，是世界著名旅游胜地、加州人口第四多的城市。旧金山靠近世界著名高新技术产业区硅谷，是世界最重要的高新技术研发基地和美国西部最重要的金融中心，也是联合国的诞生地（1945 年《联合国宪章》在此签署）。旧金山属亚热带地中海气候，拥有享誉世界的旧金山湾区、金门大桥和渔人码头，气候冬暖夏凉、阳光充足，靠近众多美国国家公园（如约塞米蒂国家公园）和加州葡萄酒产地纳帕谷，被誉为"最受美国人欢迎的城市"。旧金山唐人街位于市中心联合广场以北，东与金融区为邻，西接高级住宅区，占地 40 多个街区，是亚洲以外最大的华人聚居区。

San Francisco is a port city on the Pacific coast of California, a world-famous tourist destination and the fourth largest city in California in terms of population. San Francisco is close to Silicon Valley, the world's leading high-tech industrial zone, it is the world's most important high-tech research and development base and the most important financial center in the western United States, as well as the birthplace of the United Nations（*United Nations Charter uas signed here* 1945）. San Francisco has a subtropical Mediterranean climate, with the world-famous San Francisco Bay Area, Golden Gate Bridge and Fisherman's Wharf. The climate here is warm in winter and cool in summer, with plenty of sunshine. And it is close to many U.S. national parks（such as Yosemite National Park）and the Napa Valley, the wine production area of California, and has been known as "The Most Popular City in the U.S.". San Francisco's Chinatown is located in the heart of the city, north of Union Square, adjacent to the financial district to the east and the high-class residential district to the west, and covers more than 40 blocks, making it the largest Chinese community outside of Asia.

（二）著名旅游景点 Famous Tourist Attractions

1. 国会大厦 The United States Capitol

图 3-1　国会大厦
Figure 3-1　The United States Capitol

国会大厦（图 3-1）是美国国会的办公大楼，坐落在一处高约 30 米的高地上，故名"国会山"。美国人把它看作最高点和权力的象征。国会大厦于 1793 年 9 月 18 日由美国总统乔治·华盛顿亲自奠基，1800 年投入使用。1814 年美国第二次独立战争期间被英国人焚烧，部分建筑被毁。后来增建了参众两院会议室、圆形屋顶和圆形大厅，并经过多次改建和扩建。国会大厦东侧的国会图书馆是世界上最大的图书馆之一。

The Capitol is the office building of the U.S. Congress (Figure 3-1), situated on a plateau about 30 meters high, hence the name "Capitol Hill". To Americans, it is seen as the pinnacle and symbol of power. President George Washington personally laid its cornerstone on September 18, 1793, and it was put into use in 1800. The British set fire to the building in 1814, partially destroying it. Later, the House and Senate chambers, the dome, and the rotunda were added, along with numerous renovations and expansions. On the east side of the Capitol is the Library of Congress, one of the largest libraries in the world.

图 3-2　国会图书馆
Figure 3-2　The Library of Congress

2. 国会图书馆 The Library of Congress

国会图书馆（图 3-2）位于国会大厦以东的一个街区，拥有约 1 亿件藏品，包括 2 600 万本书、3 600 万份手稿和地图、照片、乐谱及乐器。国会图书馆是美国四个官方国家图书馆之一，是历史悠久的联邦文化机构。它已成为世界上最大的知识宝库，是美国知识和民主的重要象征，在美国文化中占有重要地位。其内部结构主要由三部分组成：托马斯·杰斐逊大楼、约翰·亚当斯大楼和詹姆斯·麦迪逊大楼。

Located in one block east of the Capitol, the Library of Congress (Figure 3-2) has a collection of approximately 100 million items, including 26 million books, 36 million manuscripts and maps, photographs, sheet music, and musical instruments. The Library of Congress is one of the four official national libraries in the United States and a historic federal cultural institution. It has become the world's largest repository of knowledge, which is an important symbol of American knowledge and democracy, and holds an important status in American culture. The interior structure consists of three main parts: the Thomas Jefferson Building, the John Adams Building and the James Madison Building.

图 3-3 白宫
Figure 3-3 White House

3. 白宫 White House

白宫（图 3-3）是美国总统府所在地，位于华盛顿西北宾夕法尼亚大道 1600 号。因外墙为白色砂砾石，故名"白宫"。白宫共占地 7.3 万多平方米，由主楼和东、西两翼三部分组成。白宫的国家宴会厅、东大厅等部分在规定时间内向全世界开放，成为游客观光的热点，它是世界上唯一定期向公众开放的国家元首官邸。

The White House(Figure 3-3), the official residence of the U.S. President, is located at 1600 Pennsylvania Avenue NW in Washington, D.C. Its name comes from its white sandstone exterior. Covering over 73,000 square meters, the White House consists of the main building and the East and West Wings. Portions like the State Dining Room and the East Room are open to the public at designated times, making it a popular tourist attraction. It is the only official residence of a head of state that regularly opens its doors to the public.

4. 林肯纪念堂 Lincoln Memorial

林肯纪念堂（图 3-4）是为纪念亚伯拉罕·林肯而建造的，被视为美国的永恒雕像和华盛顿的象征。这里也是象征和平的著名之地，马丁·路德·金在这里发表了"我有一个梦想"的演讲。纪念堂是一座由白色花岗岩和大理石制成的古希腊寺庙式建筑。纪念堂外廊周围有 36 根高大的石柱，象征着林肯在世时的美国 36 个州。馆内正中是 8.53 米高的林肯坐像，神态庄严。

图 3-4 林肯纪念堂
Figure 3-4 Lincoln Memorial

The Lincoln Memorial (Figure 3-4) is a pure white ancient Greek temple-style building built in memory of Abraham Lincoln and is regarded as an eternal statue of the United States and a symbol of Washington. It is also a well-known place for the pursuit of peace, where Martin Luther King Jr. delivered his "I Have a Dream" speech. The Memorial Hall of Architectural Art is an ancient Greek temple-style memorial hall made of white granite and marble. There are 36 tall stone pillars around the outer corridor of the memorial hall, symbolizing the 36 states of the United States when Lincoln was alive. In the center of the Memorial is the 8.53-meter-high seated statue of Abraham Lincoln in a solemn manner.

图 3-5　帝国大厦

Figure 3-5　The Empire State Building

图 3-6　自由女神像

Figure 3-6　Statue of Liberty

5. 帝国大厦 The Empire State Building

帝国大厦（图 3-5）和自由女神像一起被称为纽约的标志。帝国大厦共 102 层，高 443 米，是大萧条时期仅用 410 天时间建造的石灰石经典建筑，因此被认为是美国经济复苏的象征。在第 86 层和第 102 层上有展望台，天气晴朗时，可以眺望周围 100 千米以内的景色。

The Empire State Building (Figure 3-5), along with the Statue of Liberty, is considered an iconic symbol of New York. Standing at 443 meters tall with 102 floors, this limestone classic was constructed in just 410 days during the Great Depression, making it a symbol of America's economic recovery. Observation decks on the 86th and 102nd floors offer stunning views, allowing visitors to see up to 100 kilometers away on a clear day.

6. 自由女神像 Statue of Liberty

自由女神像（图 3-6）是法国在 1876 年赠送给美国独立 100 周年纪念的礼物，坐落于美国纽约州纽约市附近的自由岛，是美国重要的观光景点。自由女神像重 45 万磅[①]，高 46 米，底座高 45 米，正式名称是"照耀世界的自由女神"。整座铜像以 120 吨钢铁为骨架，80 吨铜片为外皮，30 万只铆钉装配固定在支架上，总重量达 225 吨。铜像内部的钢铁支架是由建筑师约维雷勃杜克和以建造巴黎埃菲尔铁塔闻名于世的法国工程师埃菲尔设计制作的。自由女神像右手高举火炬，左手捧着《独立宣言》，象征着美国人民争取自由的崇高理想。1984 年，自由女神像被联合国教科文组织列入《世界遗产名录》。

The Statue of Liberty (Figure 3-6), a gift from France to the United States of America for the 100th anniversary of its independence in 1876, is located on Liberty Island near New York City, New York State, USA, and is an important tourist attraction in the United States. The Statue of Liberty weighs 450,000 pounds, is 46 meters tall with a 45-meter-high base, and is officially known as "Liberty Enlightening the World". The entire bronze statue used 120 tons of steel for the skeleton, 80 tons of copper sheet for the outer skin, and 300,000 rivets for assembling and fixing the bracket. The total weight of the statue is 225 tons. The internal steel support of the statue was designed and produced by the architect Jovi Rebduke and the French engineer Eiffel, who is famous for building the Eiffel Tower in Paris. The Statue of Liberty, holding a torch in its right hand and the *Declaration of Independence* in its left hand, symbolizes the noble ideals of the American people in their struggle for freedom, and was inscribed on

---

　　① 　此单位非法定计量单位，1 磅 =0.4536 千克。

UNESCO's World Heritage List in 1984.

7. 独立厅 Independence Hall

独立厅（图 3-7）建于 1732—1756 年，是美国著名的历史古迹。这是一幢两层的老红砖建筑，白色门窗，白色尖塔，主屋和塔楼之间镶嵌着一个钟，该景点最初是殖民时期的宾夕法尼亚州议会大厦。

Independence Hall (Figure 3-7) is a famous historical monument in the United States. It was built from 1732 to 1756. It is a two-story old red brick building with white doors and windows, a white minaret, and a bell inlaid between the main house and the tower. The attraction was originally the Pennsylvania State Capitol during colonial times.

图 3-7 独立厅
Figure 3-7 Independence Hall

8. 自由钟 Liberty Bell

自由钟（图 3-8）是费城的象征，是美国自由精神的象征，也是美国人的骄傲。自由钟在美国历史上占有非常重要的地位，是来费城必看的景点。钟最初被放置在独立宫大楼的钟楼上，后来因为钟体破裂，被陈列在独立厅草坪外的纪念馆里。走近自由钟，可以清楚地看到钟体上的裂缝。钟面上刻着《圣经》中的名言"向世界上所有人宣告自由"。自由钟对面还有一个透明的圆筒捐款箱，里面装着来自世界各地游客捐赠的硬币。

图 3-8 自由钟
Figure 3-8 Liberty Bell

Liberty Bell (Figure 3-8) is a symbol of the city of Philadelphia, a symbol of the American spirit of freedom, and the pride of Americans. The Liberty Bell occupies a very important status in American history. The Liberty Bell is a must-see attraction in Philadelphia. The bell was originally placed on the bell tower of the Independence Palace building. Later, because the bell body cracked, it was displayed in the memorial hall outside the lawn of the Independence Hall. Approaching the Liberty Bell, you can clearly see the crack on the bell body. The famous saying from the *Bible* is engraved on the bell face " Declare freedom to all people in the world ". There is also a transparent cylinder donation box opposite the Liberty Bell, which contains coins donated by tourists from all over the world.

9. 好莱坞 Hollywood

好莱坞（图 3-9）位于美国西海岸加利福尼亚州洛杉矶市西北部郊外，依山傍水，景色宜人。好莱坞不仅是全球时尚的发源地，也是全球音乐、电影产业的中心地带，拥有着世界顶级的娱乐产业和奢侈品牌，引领并代表着全球时尚的至高水平。20 世纪福克斯、哥伦比亚电影公司、环球公司、华纳兄弟电影公司等电影业巨头都汇集在好莱坞。

Hollywood (Figure 3-9) is located on the west coast of the United States in the northwestern suburbs of the city of Los Angeles, California. By the mountains and the water, the scenery is pleasant.

图 3-9　好莱坞
Figure 3-9　Hollywood

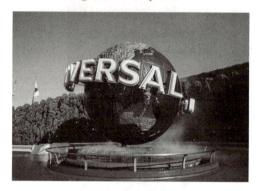

图 3-10　环球影城
Figure 3-10　Universal Studios

图 3-11　迪士尼乐园
Figure 3-11　Disneyland

Hollywood is not only the birthplace of global fashion, but also the center of the global music and film industry, with the world's top entertainment industry and luxury brands, leading and representing the highest level of global fashion. 20th Century Fox, Columbia Pictures, Universal, Warner Bros. Pictures, and other film giants are gathered in Hollywood.

10. 环球影城 Universal Studios

好莱坞环球影城（图 3-10）位于洛杉矶市区西北郊。20 世纪初，电影制片商在此发现了理想的拍片自然环境，使这一块土地逐渐成为世界闻名的影城。1908 年，好莱坞在此拍出了最早的故事片之一《基督山伯爵》。在环球影城，你可以参观电影的制作，解开特技镜头之谜，回顾经典影片中的精彩片段。踏入影城，会让你流连忘返。

Universal Studios Hollywood (Figure 3-10) is located in the northwestern suburbs of downtown Los Angeles. It became a world-renowned film studio in the early 1900s when film producers found an ideal natural environment for filming, and in 1908 Hollywood produced one of the earliest feature films *The Monte Cristo*. At Universal Studios, you can tour the making of the film, solve the mystery of the stunt shots, and review highlights from classic films. Stepping into the Studios will keep you coming back for more.

11. 迪士尼乐园 Disneyland

迪士尼乐园（图 3-11）是世界上最大的综合游乐场，园内设有冒险乐园、动物王国、拓荒者之地、米奇卡通城、未来王国等八个主题公园，以其丰富的想象力设计出人间幻境来招揽游客，号称是"全世界最快乐的地方"。

Disneyland (Figure 3-11) is the world's largest integrated amusement park with eight theme parks, including Adventure land, Animal Kingdom, Pathfinder land, Mickey's Toontown, and Future Kingdom, etc. It is known as "The Happiest Place in the World" because of its imaginative design of the world's fantasy land to attract visitors.

（三）旅游购物 Shopping

鲁本三明治：将用粗盐腌过的牛肉切成薄片，放在烧烤架上烤到吱吱冒油，然后趁热摆上美式瑞士奶酪，浇上酸甜的千岛酱，最后配上德国泡菜，夹在两片烤得香脆的黑麦面包之间食用。

Reuben sandwich: Thinly sliced, coarsely salted beef is grilled on the grill until it sizzles, then topped with American Swiss cheese, sweet and sour Thousand Island dressing, and finished with sauerkraut between two slices of crispy and toasted rye bread.

法黑塔（一种墨西哥式铁板烤肉）：最常见的吃法是将肉烤好后切成细条放在铁板上，用的肉可以是猪肉、鸡肉、牛肉或虾，再搭配些墨西哥蔬菜，如洋葱、青椒之类。美式吃法往往还会搭配一些生菜丝，在生菜丝上浇点酸奶油、牛油果酱、墨西哥酸辣椒，还有碎奶酪块。吃法也很简单，可以用墨西哥饼皮把蔬菜和肉卷着吃。

Fajitas (Mexican barbecue meat): The most common way to enjoy this dish is by grilling the meat, slicing it into thin strips, and placing it on a hot plate. The meat can be pork, chicken, beef, or shrimp. It's typically served with Mexican vegetables like onions and bell peppers. The American style often includes a heap of shredded lettuce topped with sour cream, guacamole, pickled jalapenos, and cheese crumbles. It's easy to eat too; you'll be given a stack of tortillas so you can wrap the vegetables and meat for a delicious bite.

纯正加州牛奶：加州是美国乳品生产第一州。得益于充沛的阳光、温和的气候以及现代化的牧场管理，生活在加州的奶牛被称为"快乐奶牛"。只有快乐的奶牛才能产出优质且安全的牛奶，从而用来制作多种美味的乳制品。加州生产超过250个不同品种的奶酪，如蒙特利杰克、切达、马苏里拉等传统美式奶酪，以及布里、蓝奶酪、卡蒙尔等特殊风味奶酪。除此之外，加州还出产其他多种特色乳制品，包括冰激凌、酸奶等。所有加州生产的乳制品包装上都印有"Real California Cheese"（纯正加州奶酪）或"Real California Milk"（纯正加州牛奶）的标记，以表明产品100%产自加州且安全优质。

Pure California milk: California is the number one dairy producing state in the United States. Thanks to its abundant sunshine, mild climate and modern farm management, cows in California are known as "happy cows". Only happy cows produce high quality and safe milk that is used to make a wide variety of delicious dairy products. California produces more than 250 different varieties of cheese, including traditional American cheeses such as Monterey Jack, Cheddar, and Mozzarella, as well as specialty cheeses such as Brie, Blue Cheese, and Camembert. In addition, California also produces a variety of other specialty dairy products including ice cream, yogurt, and more. All California dairy products are labeled "Real California Cheese" or "Real California Milk" to ensure that they are 100% California produced.

美国花旗参：美国花旗参的品质好，药用价值高。这里的花旗参产自没有污染的土地，所以其味道很甘香。用它来煮汤、冲茶都是很好的选择。

American Ginseng: American ginseng is of exceptional quality and high medicinal value. The ginseng, grown in unpolluted soil, has a sweet flavor and can be used for making soup or tea.

美国巧克力：很多世界有名的巧克力品牌都来自美国，所以在美国买些巧克力作为伴手礼，或是带回去给自家家人吃是非常好的选择。在美国，买巧克力非常方便，机场就有很多，当地的超市也有。另外，要是想更好地感受巧克力文化，还可以去宾夕法尼亚州的好时巧克力世界。

Chocolate: Many of the world's most famous chocolate brands are made in America. Therefore, it's a good choice to buy some chocolate in the United States, either as a souvenir or grfts to your family. It is very convenient to buy chocolate, at

扫码获取：入境须知及海关规定

the airport and local supermarkets. In addition, if you want to better experience the chocolate culture, you can go to Hershey's Chocolate World in Pennsylvania.

本节习题

1. 以小组为单位，制作一份美国旅游宣传册。
2. 请设计一个美国 6 日旅游线路图。
3. 为什么美国能成为世界上旅游业最发达的国家？

枫叶之国——加拿大
The Land of the Maple Leaves—Canada

导读

加拿大是全球最发达的经济体之一，制造业、高科技产业、服务业发达，资源工业、初级制造业和农业是国民经济的主要支柱，国内经济持续稳定增长。加拿大是联合国（UN）、国际货币基金组织（IMF）、世界银行（WBG）、世贸组织（WTO）、七国集团（G7）、20 国集团（G20）和亚太经合组织（APEC）成员国。加拿大把维护世界和平与国家安全、促进经济发展、在全球范围内推动民主和尊重人权、宣传加拿大文化价值观作为对外政策的重中之重。加拿大作为英联邦成员国，十分注重与美国的战略同盟关系，同时也积极发展与欧盟、亚太和拉丁美洲各国的关系，致力于同亚太国家建立起更加紧密的伙伴关系。1970 年 10 月 13 日，中加两国建交。中加两国人民的友谊源远流长。孙中山先生曾三次到过加拿大的温哥华。伟大的国际主义战士白求恩大夫为中国人民的解放事业贡献了自己的宝贵生命。加拿大旅游资源丰富，全国有 20 多个国家公园、50 多个国家历史公园和历史古迹，主要旅游城市有温哥华、渥太华、多伦多、蒙特利尔、魁北克城等。

一、地理概览 Geography of Canada

（一）地理位置 Location

加拿大位于北美洲北半部，东临大西洋，西濒太平洋，西北部与美国阿拉斯加州为邻，南与美国接壤，北靠北冰洋。加拿大国土面积约为 998.5 万平方千米，整体面积仅次于俄罗斯，居世界第二位，其中陆地面积为 909.4 万平方千米，淡水覆盖面积为 89.1 万平方千米。加拿大海岸线曲折漫长，再加上沿海岛屿，总长约为 24.4 万千米，是世界上海岸线最长的国家。

Canada is located in the northern half of North America, bordering the Atlantic Ocean to the east and the Pacific Ocean to the west, with the U.S. state of Alaska neighboring to the northwest, the United States bordering to the south, and the Arctic Ocean to the north. Canada has a land area of about 9,985,000 square kilometers, the second largest overall area in the world after Russia, with a land area of 9,094,000 square kilometers and a freshwater coverage of 891,000 square kilometers. Canada's coastline is long and winding, and with the coastal islands, the total length of the coastline is about 244,000 kilometers, making it the longest coastline in the world.

（二）地形气候 The Land and Seasons

加拿大地形复杂，地势中间低、东西高。西部是科迪勒拉山系，是加拿大地势最高的地区，有许多海拔 4 000 米以上的高峰，包括落基山脉、海岸山脉，最高峰洛根峰海拔 5 951 米；东部是古老的拉布拉多高原；中部是广阔的平原，约占全国面积的一半；东南部多为低山和丘陵。

Canada's topography is complex, with the terrain low in the center and high in the east and west. In the west is the Cordillera mountain system, the highest terrain in Canada. There are many peaks above 4,000 meters, including the Rocky Mountains, the Coastal Range, the highest peak Logan Peak of 5,951 meters above the sea level; in the east is the ancient Labrador Plateau; in the middle is a vast plain, accounting for about half of the country's surface area; the southeastern part of the country is mostly low mountains and hills.

加拿大
落基山脉

加拿大国土辽阔，各地气温差异较大。加拿大的冬季比较漫长，1 月全国 2/3 地区的平均气温在 –18 ℃左右。加拿大北部地区地处高纬度，冬季寒冷漫长，人迹罕至，一年仅两三个月气温在 0 ℃以上。南部气候温和，四季分明。西海岸由于受太平洋暖湿气流的影响，夏季凉爽干燥，冬季温和潮湿。秋季是加拿大最漂亮的季节，漫山遍野的枫叶使加拿大有了"枫叶之国"的美誉。

The vast expanse of territory of the country reasonably results in a spectrum of temperature. The winter in Canada is redatively long, and two thirds of the country features an average temperature of around – 18 degrees Celsius in January. The northern regions of Canada are located at high latitudes, with long, cold winters and sparse human presence. There are temperatures above 0 ℃ for only two or three months a year. South Canada presents a mild climate with clear-cut four seasons. As a result of warm and wet currents coming from the Pacific Ocean to its west coasts, summer here is normally cool and dry, while winter is mild and humid.Autumn is the most beautiful season in Canada, with the hills and fields covered in maple leaves, earning the country its nickname "The Land of Maple Leaves".

加拿大为什么
又叫枫叶
之国？

（三）自然资源 Natural Resources

加拿大境内矿藏丰富。石棉、镍、锌、白银的产量居世界之首；铜、石膏、钾碱、硫黄的产量居世界第二位；钴、铬、钼、铂、铋、钍、钾盐等矿物储量均居世界前列。已开发生产的有石油、天然气、铜、铁、镍、锌、石棉、黄金、白银、铀、铂等 60 余种。加拿大是世界上除美国、俄罗斯外最大的产矿国之一。加拿大森林资源丰富，森林覆盖面积为 440 万平方千米，约占全国总面积的 44%，仅次于俄罗斯和巴西，居世界第三位。

Canada is rich in mineral deposits. The production of asbestos, nickel, zinc and silver occupies the first place in the world; the production of copper, gypsum, potash and sulphur occupies the second place in the world; and the reserves of cobalt, chromium, molybdenum, platinum, bismuth, thorium, potash and other minerals rank among the world's top. It has developed and produced more than 60 kinds, including oil, natural gas, copper, iron, nickel, zinc, asbestos, gold, silver, uranium, platinum and so on. Canada is one of the largest mineral-producing countries in the world except the United States and Russia. Canada is rich in forest resources, with a forested area of 4.4 million square kilometers, accounting for about 44% of the country's total area, after Russia and Brazil, ranking third in the world.

二、人文概况 Overview of Canadian Humanities

（一）国情认知 Basic Knowledge of National Conditions

加拿大人口约 3 893 万（2022 年），是世界上人口密度较小的国家。大部分的加拿大人居住在加、美边界地带。在加拿大，越到北方人口越稀少。加拿大是移民国家，居民主要为英、法等欧洲国家的后裔。其中，英裔居民占总人口的 42%，法裔居民占 27%，土著居民为印第安人和因纽特人，约占总人口的 3%，其余为亚洲、拉丁美洲、非洲移民的后裔。近年来亚洲移民大量涌入加拿大，来自中国的华人达 80 万人，集中居住在安大略省的多伦多（40 万人）、魁北克省的蒙特利尔（15 万人）、不列颠哥伦比亚省的温哥华（25 万人）。英语和法语同为加拿大的官方语言。信奉天主教的居民占总人口的 47.3%，信奉基督教的居民占 41.2%。枫树是加拿大国树，枫叶是加拿大国花，遍布加拿大全国的枫树中以糖枫和黑枫最为著名，三月枫糖节是加拿大的重要节日。国歌为《哦! 加拿大》，货币为加元。

Canada has a population of approximately 38.93 million (as of 2022), making it one of the countries with a lower population density globally. Most Canadians live near the Canada-U.S. border, with population density decreasing as you move northward. As a nation of immigrants, Canada's residents are primarily of European descent, with 42% being of English descent and 27% of French descent. Indigenous peoples, including the First Nations and Inuit, make up about 3% of the population, while the rest are of Asian, Latin American, and African descent. In recent years, there has been a significant influx of Asian immigrants, with around 800,000 Chinese from mainland China, Taiwan region, and Hong Kong SAR residing in Canada. They are primarily concentrated in Toronto, Ontario (400,000), Montreal, Quebec (150,000), and Vancouver, British Columbia (250,000). Both English and French are official languages. Residents who adhere to Catholicism account for 47.3%, while those following Christianity make up 41.2%. The maple tree is Canada's national tree, and the maple leaf is its national emblem. Among the various types of maple trees across Canada, the sugar maple and black maple are the most renowned. The Maple Syrup Festival in March is an important Canadian celebration. The national anthem is *Oh!Canada* and the currency is the Canadian dollar.

（二）历史简介 History of Canada

加拿大这个名字来源于印第安语。加拿大的历史是一部移民史，印第安人和因纽特人是加拿大最早的居民。从 16 世纪起，加拿大沦为法、英殖民地。1756—1763 年，英、法在加拿大爆发"七年战争"，法国战败，将殖民地割让给英国。1848 年英属北美殖民地成立了自治政府。1867 年，英国议会通过《不列颠北美法案》，将加拿大省、新不伦瑞克省和新斯科舍省合并为一个联邦。由此，该联邦成为英国最早的一个自治领，称加拿大自治领。此后的 1870 年至 1949 年，其他省也陆续加入联邦。1926 年英国承认加拿大的"平等地位"，加拿大始获独立外交权。1931 年，加拿大成为英联邦成员国，其议会也获得了同英议会平等的立法权。1982 年 3 月，英国通过《加拿大宪法法案》，加拿大从此获得了立法和修宪的全部权力，但仍为英联邦成员国。

The name of Canada is derived from the Indian language. The history of Canada is a history of immigration, with the Indians and Inuit being the earliest inhabitants of Canada. From the 16th century onwards, Canada was colonized by the French and the British. From 1756 to 1763, the Seven Years' War broke out between the British and the French in Canada, in which the French lost the war and ceded the colony to the British. In 1848, the British North American colonies set up a self-government. In 1867, the British Parliament passed the *British North America Act*, which merged the provinces of Canada, New Brunswick and Nova Scotia into a federation and became one of the earliest self-governing territories of Britain, called the Dominion of Canada. From 1870 to 1949, other provinces joined the federation, and in 1926 the British recognized Canada's "equal status" and Canada gained diplomatic independence. In 1931, Canada became a member of the British Commonwealth, and its Parliament gained equal legislative power with the British Parliament. *Canadian Constitution Act* was passed in March 1982, Canada has since gained the full power to legislate and amend the constitution, but it is still a member of the British Commonwealth.

（三）经济状况 The Economy

加拿大是世界上最富有的国家之一，是世界第八大经济体。加拿大是典型的以服务型经济为主的国家，经济增长率居世界七大工业国的第二位，仅次于日本。劳动生产率排名世界第二，仅次于美国，是世界上经济最发达、最稳定的国家之一，其福利制度非常完善。加拿大资源丰富，国民经济严重依赖资源型产业，森林业、采矿业、能源业、农业及渔业是加拿大传统的重要经济支柱。加拿大以贸易立国，其最大的贸易伙伴是美国，经济上受美国影响较大，对外资、外贸依赖程度很高。加拿大的旅游业也十分发达，在世界旅游收入最高的国家中排在第九位。此外，加拿大是全球最重要的教育枢纽之一，教育也是加拿大最重要的经济产业之一，每年吸引了不少来自世界各地的留学生，这不仅为国家带来了丰厚的外汇，而且为这个属于知识型经济体系的国家吸纳了不少人才。

Canada is one of the world's most wealthy nations with its economy ranking 8th in the world. Secondly to Japan, Canada ranks the second among G7 in terms of economic growth which is grounded firmly in the pillar industries of service. Canada ranks second only to the U.S. in terms of labor productivity, Canada is one of the most advanced and stable economies with sophisticated welfare provisions. Due to its rich natural resources, the country relies heavily on resource industries with forestry, mining, energy, farming and fishery as its traditional pillars. Rooted in trading, the country is greatly influenced by the U.S., its largest trading partner, and relies enormously on foreign investment and international trade. It also has a well-developed tourist industry and ranks the ninth in terms of tourist revenues. Furthermore, Canada is one of the most important educational hubs in the world, and the education industry is also one of Canada's most significant economic industries, attracting many international students from all over the world each year. This not only brings substantial foreign exchange to the country but also absorbs a great deal of talents for this knowledge-based economic system nation.

（四）传统文化 Traditional Culture

加拿大是一个名副其实的移民国家，移民占全国人口的 99%。作为一个多民族人民的移民国家，加拿大各民族人民宽容待人、和睦相处。加拿大人热情好客、待人诚恳、平易近人、风趣幽默。加拿大人往往温和又耐心，工作和生活节奏较慢，常是"一天只做一件事"。加拿大人充分肯定自我价值，认为每个人都应该追随自己的内心，并对自己的行为负责。"我才不在乎呢"是加拿大人的口头禅。

Canada is truly a nation of immigrants, with immigrants making up 99% of the population. As a multicultural immigrant country, the various ethnic groups in Canada coexist harmoniously and treat each other with tolerance. Canadians are known for being warm, hospitable, sincere, approachable, and having a good sense of humor. They are often gentle and patient, embodying a relaxed and casual demeanor. The pace of work and life is relatively slow, with a common saying being " one thing at a time ". Canadians place great emphasis on self-worth, believing that each individual is solely responsible for their own successes and failures, without needing to worry about others' opinions, focusing instead on their own feelings. "I don't care" is a common expression among Canadians.

加拿大地广人稀，森林资源丰富，住房多为全木结构。加拿大人在非正式场合的穿着比较随意，不拘于形式，夹克衫、圆领衫、便装裤到处可见，牛仔裤和运动鞋是最常见的搭配。但是在正式场合（如办公室、教堂、表演现场、宴会等），加拿大人穿着很讲究，男子一般穿西装，女子穿西装裙。加拿大女子的服装不太讲究面料，但是讲究款式新颖、颜色协调、穿着舒适方便。

Canada is vast with a sparse population and abundant forest resources, which results in many homes being constructed entirely of wood. In informal settings, Canadians dress quite casually and without much emphasis on formality. Jackets, crew-neck shirts, and casual pants are commonly seen, with jeans and sneakers being the most typical combination. However, in formal settings such as offices, churches, performances, and banquets, Canadians are particular about their attire. Men usually wear suits, while women opt for skirt suits. Canadian women's clothing doesn't focus heavily on fabric but rather on innovative styles, coordinated colors, and comfort with elegance.

加拿大人的饮食习惯接近于美国，饮食以肉类、蔬菜为主，以面食、米饭为辅。加拿大人喜欢牛肉、鸡肉、鱼和野味，喜欢西红柿、土豆、菜花、洋葱和黄瓜等蔬菜。加拿大人口味比较清淡，偏爱甜味和酸味，讲究食物的营养价值，一般不用辛辣的调味品，也不喜欢太咸。烹调方式主要有煎、烤、炸等，喜欢酥脆食物。加拿大人习惯在用餐后喝咖啡、吃水果，他们喜欢荔枝、香蕉、苹果、梨等水果，也喜欢松子、葡萄干、花生等干果。加拿大人喜欢饮酒，喜爱白兰地、香槟、啤酒、威士忌、葡萄酒、蜂蜜酒等，也喜欢中国的红茶。加拿大人比较喜欢中餐，尤其是江苏菜和上海菜。

Canadians' eating habits are quite similar to those in the United States, with a diet primarily consisting of meat and vegetables, supplemented by pasta and rice. They enjoy beef, chicken, fish, and game meats, as well as vegetables like tomatoes, potatoes, cauliflower, onions, and cucumbers. Canadians tend to prefer mild flavors, with a fondness for sweet and sour tastes, and they emphasize the nutritional value of their dishes. They generally avoid spicy seasonings and overly salty foods. Common cooking methods include pan-frying, grilling, and deep-frying, and they have a preference for crispy foods. After meals, Canadians typically enjoy drinking coffee and eating fruits. They like fruits such as lychees, bananas, apples, and pears, as well as nuts and dried fruits like pine nuts, raisins, and peanuts. Canadians also enjoy drinking alcohol, favoring beverages like brandy, champagne, beer, whiskey, wine, mead, and they also appreciate Chinese black tea. Additionally, Canadians have a particular liking for Chinese cuisine, especially dishes from Jiangsu and Shanghai.

 思考题

加拿大文化为什么又叫"马赛克"文化？与美国的"熔炉"文化相比，有什么不同之处？

（五）礼仪禁忌 Social Etiquettes and Taboos

加拿大人性格坦诚，平易近人，时间观念极强，有准时赴约的良好习惯。按照他们的礼貌习惯，若因故不能按时赴约，则要事先打个电话通知对方。与加拿大人交谈时，切忌用手指点，交谈距离应远近适宜，交谈内容不要涉及个人生活、收入、花销、女性体重等隐私问题。避免将加拿大与美国做比较。

Canadians are frank, approachable, have a strong sense of time, and have a good habit of being on time for appointments. According to their polite habits, if for any reason you can't make the appointment on time, you have to make a phone call to inform the other party in advance. When talking with Canadians, you should avoid pointing with your finger and pay attention to the distance, and the conversation should not involve private life, income, expenditure, women's weight and other private issues. Comparison between Canada and the United States should be avoided.

应邀到加拿大人家中做客，最好带上一些如糖果、巧克力之类的小礼物送给主人，但记住不能将白色的百合花作为礼物送人。在加拿大看来，白色的百合花表示死亡，人们只在葬礼上使用。加拿大人大多信奉天主教或基督教（新教），他们特别忌讳"13"和"星期五"，无论做什么事，他们总是力图避开上述数字和日期。接待时须注意不能安排单数的席次，尤须避免安排13个席次。饮食上，他们忌食虾酱、鱼露、腐乳和臭豆腐等有怪味、腥味的食物，以及各种动物的内脏和脚爪。此外，他们一般也不爱吃辣味菜肴。每年6至8月，加拿大人大多选择度假，因此开展商务活动宜避开这段时间。此外，当地节假日期间也应避免前往，特别是圣诞节和复活节前后两周均不宜前往。

When invited to a Canadian's home, it is a good idea to bring small gifts such as candies and chocolates to your hosts, but remember not to give white lilies as gifts. To them, white lilies signify death and people use them at funerals. Most Canadians are either Catholic or Protestant, and they are particularly wary of "13" and "Friday", and will always try to avoid these numbers and dates whatever they do. While recepting others, it must be careful not to arrange an odd number of seats, especially to avoid arranging 13 seats. They avoid eating shrimp paste, fish sauce, fermented bean curd and stinky tofu and other strange, fishy food, as well as a variety of animal offal and claws. In addition, they are generally not fond of spicy dishes. From June to August each year, most Canadians choose to be on vacation, business activities should be avoided during this time. In addition, business activities should also be avoided during local holidays, especially two weeks before and after Christmas and Easter.

白求恩——
一个英雄的
成长

 **知识拓展**

观看在线资源纪录片"白求恩——一个英雄的成长"。

讨论题

总结该影片展现了加拿大共产党员、国际著名外科医生诺尔曼·白求恩哪些平凡的生活经历和伟大精神。

提示：如伟大的国际主义献身精神。

思考题

白求恩的感人事迹，体现了哪些职业精神？如何将个人的价值追求与职业选择相结合？如何在职业中将专业技能与家国情怀有机融合？

提示：如屠呦呦的职业精神、奉献精神等。

（六）传统节日 Festivals

1. 魁北克冬季狂欢节 The Quebec Winter Carnival

魁北克冬季狂欢节是魁北克省居民最盛大的节日，规模浩大，内容丰富多彩，具有浓郁的法兰西色彩，一般在每年2月举行，为期10天。节前要用冰块筑成一座五层高的"雪之城堡"；节日期间会举行冰雕比赛、划船比赛、越野滑雪比赛、轮胎滑雪比赛、大型滑车比赛、狗拉雪橇比赛、冰上赛马等各种体育活动。魁北克冬季狂欢节已成为魁北克市第三大产业，被公认为全世界最大的冬季狂欢节之一。

The Quebec Winter Carnival, a ten-day February tradition featuring French style, is the most magnificent annual event with various activities celebrated by citizens in the Quebec Province. Before the festival, people need to build a five-storey high "snow castle" with ice. There are a variety of games like ice sculptures, canoe races, cross-country skiing, inner-tube skiing, snow-boarding, dog-sled races, horse races on ice and other sports events are held during the festival. The Winter Carnival is now the third largest industry of the Quebec City and is listed among the world's top winter carnival.

2. 枫糖节 The Maple Syrup Festival

每年3月底至4月初是加拿大特有的传统民间节日——枫糖节。人们在节日里欢歌曼舞，品尝枫糖糕和太妃糖。在加拿大的枫树品种中，最著名的一种叫糖枫，它的树叶含糖量达3.5%，可熬制枫糖浆。

The Maple Syrup Festival is held from the end of March to the beginning of April, a unique Canadian festival when people sing and dance and taste maple cake and toffee. Among the many maples in Canada, the most famous is sugar maple, and the sugar content of the leaves is 3.5%, for making maple syrup.

3. 加拿大郁金香节 Canadian Tulip Festival

5 月的最后两周是首都渥太华的盛大节日——郁金香节。这个节日源于第二次世界大战期间，荷兰皇室来到加拿大避难，受到加拿大人的热心帮助。战争结束后，荷兰赠予加拿大 10 万株郁金香，以表达感激之情。此后，荷兰皇室每年都会向加拿大赠送 1 万株郁金香。1953 年 5 月，首届加拿大郁金香节在首都渥太华举办。如今，加拿大郁金香节已成为世界上最大的郁金香节，并为渥太华赢得了"北美郁金香之都"的称号。节日期间会举行各种彩车游行，人们还会选出一位美丽的"皇后"。人群尾随"皇后"的花车，以乐队为前导徐徐前行。

The last two weeks of May are Canadion Tulip Festival, a grand festival in the capital city of Ottawa. The Canadian Tulip Festival is a symbol of peace during the Second World War when the Royal Dutch Family received enthusiastic aid in Canada for refuge. After the war, Holland sent 100,000 tulips to Canada in gratitude and from then on the Royal Dutch Family sends 10,000 tulips to Ottawa each year. The first Canadian Tulip Festival was held in the capital of Ottawa in May, 1953. Today, the Canadian Tulip Festivals is the largest Tulip Festival in the world and has won the crown of "North America Capital of Tulips" for Ottawa. Various parades of floats are held during the festival. A beautiful "queen" is also chosen, and the crowd follows her float, led by a marching band, as it slowly moves forward.

4. 淘金节 Gold Rush Celebrations

在加拿大阿尔伯塔省，人们每年会从 8 月底起连续 10 天举行淘金庆祝活动，以纪念祖先们的奋斗精神。人们身着淘金时代的服装上街游行，在埃德蒙顿广场举行各种文艺演出，夜晚则燃放烟火。

The people of Alberta, Canada, hold gold rush celebrations for 10 consecutive days from the end of August every year to commemorate the fighting spirit of their ancestors. People parade through the streets dressed in gold-rushing costumes, hold various theatrical performances in Edmonton Square, and set off fireworks at night.

 思考题

请阅读材料"曲棍球：加拿大的全民运动"，思考中国的体育精神内涵以及如何打造健康中国。

曲棍球：加拿大的全民运动

三、旅游观光 Tourism and Sightseeing

（一）主要旅游城市 Major Tourist Cities

1. 多伦多 Toronto

多伦多是加拿大安大略省的省会，是加拿大第一大城市及金融中心，世界著名的国际大都市。"多伦多"在印第安语中是"汇聚之地"的意思。1996 年，联合国正式确认多伦多是世界上最有多元文化特色的城市之一，此处也是加拿大的华裔居民最集中的地区之一。多伦多的标志性建筑有市政厅和高达 553 米的加拿大国家电视塔，其占据世界第一高塔的位置长达 34

年，也是多伦多的标志、加拿大的象征，现为世界第六高塔。从多伦多开车 1 小时便可到达位于美、加边境的尼亚加拉瀑布，以位于加拿大境内的"马蹄瀑布"气势最为宏大、最为惊险，是世界著名的奇观。

Toronto, " land of gathering" in Indian language, is the capital of Ontario Province, Canada's largest city and its financial center. In 1996, the United Nations officially recognized Toronto one of the most multicultural cities in the world. Toronto is one of the Canadian regions with the densest Chinese concentrations. Landmarks in Toronto are City Hall and the Canadian National Tower (CN Tower) of 553 meters high, and CN Tower world's is Toronto's landmark and Canada's symbol. Now No.6 among world's skyscrapers, CN Tower stood highest of the world's high-rise for 34 years. Within one-hour drive from Toronto is the Niagara Falls bordering Canada and the US. The Horseshoe Falls in Canada, the most massive and thrilling of falls, is a world wonder.

2. 渥太华 Ottawa

渥太华是加拿大的首都，原是一个经营木材和皮毛的小镇，现已成为全国政治与文化中心。在渥太华，人们可以感受到英国和法国两种不同的文化交织在一起，几乎一半的居民都是双语者。渥太华是世界上最寒冷的首都之一，每年约有 8 个月夜晚温度在 0 ℃以下，最低气温可以达到 -39 ℃，有"严寒之都"之称。正因为其气候寒冷、冬季漫长，渥太华的冰上运动非常发达，特别是冰球运动，加拿大素有"冰球王国"之称，渥太华则是"冰球之城"。当年荷兰皇室为感谢加拿大政府而赠送的 10 万株郁金香，每到春天就开满全城，因此渥太华又被称为"郁金香城"。

Ottawa is the capital of Canada, originally a small town dealing in lumber and furs, now it has become the political and cultural center of the country. In Ottawa, people can feel a blend of English and French cultures; almost half of the residents are bilingual. Ottawa is one of the coldest capitals in the world, with nighttime temperatures falling below 0 ℃ for about eight months each year. The lowest temperatures can reach as low as -39 ℃, earning it the nickname " The Extreme Cold Capital". A cold climate and a long winter, therefore, attribute to advanced ice sports, especially ice hockey. Whilst Canada is nicknamed " Kingdom of Ice Hockey", and Ottawa is the " City of Ice Hockey". Ottawa is also known as the " City of Tulips", for 100,000 tulip plants were once bestowed by the Royal Dutch Family in gratitude to the Canadian government, and tulips spread all over the capital in full blossom when spring comes.

3. 温哥华 Vancouver

温哥华是加拿大西海岸的第一大城市及工业中心。温哥华的名称源自到此探险的英国航海家乔治·温哥华，起初就是一个渔业和锯木业较发达的小镇。温哥华三面环山，西面面向太平洋，终年气候温和、湿润，环境宜人，是加拿大著名的旅游胜地。温哥华的气候与加拿大其他地区不同，因靠近太平洋而十分温和，夏季温度在 20 ℃左右，而冬季也很少低于 0 ℃，气候四季宜人，连续多年被选为世界上最适合人类居住的城市之一。温哥华的旅游景点众多，包括北美最大的城市公园——史丹利公园，北美洲最大的滑雪场——威斯勒滑雪场。温哥华也是华人聚集地之一，是北美第二大"中国城"，汉语是第二大语言。温哥华也是北美继洛杉矶和纽约后第三大影视制作中心，更有"北方好莱坞"之称。

Vancouver is the largest city and industrial center on the west coast of Canada. The name Vancouver comes from the British explorer George Vancouver, who visited the area. Initially, it was a small fishing and lumber town. Vancouver is surrounded by mountains on three sides and bordered by the sea to the west. It enjoys a mild and humid climate year-round, making it a popular tourist destination in Canada. The climate in Vancouver is different from that in other regions in Canada; due to its proximity to the Pacific Ocean, it is very mild, with the summer temperature around 20 ℃ and the winter temperature rarely dropping below 0 ℃. The city has been consistently ranked among the most livable cities in the world for several years. Vancouver boasts numerous attractions, including Stanley Park, the largest urban park in North America, and Whistler, the largest ski resort in North America. It is also one of the major hubs for the Chinese community, and the second-largest Chinatown in North America,with Chinese being the second most spoken language. Furthermore, Vancouver is the third-largest film production center in North America, following Los Angeles and New York, and is often referred to as "Hollywood North".

4. 蒙特利尔 Montreal

蒙特利尔位于渥太华河和圣劳伦斯河交汇处，是加拿大第二大城市，也是加拿大历史最悠久的城市。蒙特利尔居民 70% 以上是法国后裔，因此这里充满了浓厚的法国色彩，是加拿大最具欧洲风格的城市，有"北美巴黎"或"小巴黎"之称。作为北美的浪漫之都，蒙特利尔以法式建筑为主，有"尖塔之城"的美誉。蒙特利尔老城是一座魅力无穷的 18 世纪城市，到处可见马车及咖啡馆。蒙特利尔圣母大教堂和美术馆以及闻名加拿大的地下城是必游景点，而著名的国际爵士乐节、国际焰火节等更是吸引了世界各地的游客。蒙特利尔被联合国评定为最适合人类居住的城市之一。

Sitting where Ottawa River converges with St. Lawrence River, Montreal is the second largest city in Canada. Montreal has the longest history among Canadian cities. Over 70% of its citizens being French Canadians, the city features rich French culture and is the most European city in Canada, known as "Paris in North America" or "Little Paris". As a romantic city of North America, Montreal features dominant French architecture and is acclaimed as the "City of Towers". The old town of Montreal is an 18th-century city with great charm which wagons and coffee houses evenrywhere. Notre-Dame Basilica in Montreal, Art Gallery and the household Underground City are must-sees. Besides, and events like the International Jazz Festival and Montreal Fireworks Festival attract visitors from all over the world. Montreal is recognized by the United Nations as one of the most livable cities for human habitation.

（二）著名旅游景点 Famous Tourist Attractions

1. 国家电视塔 CN Tower

加拿大国家电视塔（图 3-12）位于安大略湖畔，塔高 553 米，是世界上最高的建筑之一。它的名字"CN"代表加拿大国家铁路公司，该公司建造了这座塔。1995 年，加拿大国家电视塔被美国土木工程师协会列为"世界七大工程奇迹"之一。塔内拥有多部观光电梯，只需 58 秒即可到达最高层，透过观景台的大玻璃窗，可以看到多伦多市和美丽的安大略湖全景。电视塔还设有餐厅、纪念品商店、小型电影院和儿童游乐场等场所。塔楼周围环绕着花园和游泳池。到了晚上，不断变化的彩色灯光使电视塔成为多伦多的一道绚烂风景。

图 3-12　加拿大国家电视塔
Figure 3-12　CN Tower

The CN Tower (Figure 3–12) is located on the shore of Lake Ontario, with a tower height of 553 meters, which is one of the tallest buildings in the world. "CN" refers to the Canadian National Railway Company, which built the tower, and in 1995 it was listed as one of the "Seven Engineering Wonders of the World" by the American Society of Civil Engineers. The tower has a number of scenic elevators that take only 58 seconds to reach the top. Through the large glass windows, you can see the panoramic view of Toronto city and the beautiful Lake Ontario. The CN Tower has restaurants, souvenir shops, a small cinema and a children's playground. The tower is surrounded by gardens and pools. At night, the constantly changing colored lights make the CN Tower a beautiful sight in Toronto.

图 3–13　卡萨洛马城堡
Figure 3–13　Casa Loma Castle

2. 卡萨洛马城堡 Casa Loma Castle

卡萨洛马城堡（图 3–13）建于 1911 年，最初是著名金融家亨利·佩拉特爵士的私人豪宅。这座中世纪风格的城堡耗资 350 万美元，耗时 3 年建成。它由装饰华丽的套房、800 英尺①的隧道、古老的塔楼、马厩和 5 英亩②的花园组成。城堡一楼为大厅，二楼为卧室和套房，三楼为女王步枪博物馆，此外，还有地下酒窖、室外花园和高塔。

Casa Loma Castle (Figure 3–13) was built in 1911 as the private mansion of the famous financier Sir Henry Pellatt. This medieval-style castle cost $3.5 million and took 3 years to build. It consists of ornately decorated suites, a 800-foot tunnel, ancient towers, stables and a 5 acres of garden. Floor distribution: The first floor of the castle is the hall, the second floor is the bedroom and suite, the third floor is the Queen's Rifle Museum. In addition to the underground wine cellar, there is an outdoor garden and a high tower.

图 3–14　多伦多市政厅
Figure3–14　Toronto City Hall

3. 多伦多市政厅 Toronto City Hall

多伦多市政厅（图 3–14）包括建于 1965 年的新市政厅及 1899 年揭幕的旧市政厅。新市政厅由芬兰设计师 Viljo Revell 设计。高矮不同的两栋建筑呈弧形，中间包围着市议会大楼，从天空俯瞰像一只眼睛，因此有"天眼"之称。新奇的造型也让市政厅成为电影中的常客，最著名的当数《生化危机》。晚上会有声光表演，广场上的游泳池夏天是喷泉，冬天是溜冰场。

Toronto City Hall (Figure 3–14) consists of the New City Hall, built in 1965, and the Old City Hall, unveiled in 1899. The New City Hall was designed by Finnish designer Viljo Revell. The two buildings of different heights, are curved and surround the City Council building in the center, while the view from the sky resembles an eye, hence it got the name "Eye in the Sky". The novelty of the shape has also made City Hall a regular feature in movies, most notably *Resident Evil*. In the evenings

---

① 此单位非法定计量单位，1 英尺 =0.304 8 米。

② 此单位非法定计量单位，1 英亩 =4 046.86 平方米。

there are sound and light shows, and the plaza's swimming pool serves as a fountain in the summer and an ice rink in the winter.

4. 国会山 Parliament Hill

国会山（图 3-15）是位于安大略省渥太华市中心的一片王室领地，其哥特式复兴建筑群是加拿大议会的所在地，包含了许多具有国家象征意义的建筑元素。每年夏季举行的卫兵换岗仪式和灯光秀为这个加拿大著名的地标又增添了几分历史沧桑感和新的活力。永不熄灭的百年圣火、永久开放的广场、高耸入云的和平塔和栩栩如生的雕塑，以及向公众开放的国会大厦，这些特色景点无时无刻不在吸引着来自世界各地的游客。

图 3-15　国会山
Figure 3-15　Parliament Hill

Parliament Hill (Figure 3-15) is a royal estate located in the heart of downtown Ottawa, Ontario. Its Gothic Revival building complex is home to the Parliament of Canada and encompasses many national symbolic elements. The ceremony of changing guards and the light show that take place every day in summer add a sense of historical vicissitudes and an up-to-date vitality to this very famous landmark in Canada. The eternal Centennial Flame, the ever-accessible square, the towering Peace Tower, the lifelike sculptures, and the Parliament Buildings open to the public continuously draw visitors from around the world

5. 里多运河 Rideau Canal

古老的里多运河（图 3-16）建于 1826—1832 年，全长 202 千米，其中的 7.8 千米穿过渥太华市中心。里多运河是加拿大首都文化积淀的重要贡献者，已被列入联合国教科文组织《世界遗产名录》。夏季，人们可以沿着运河划独木舟，欣赏美丽的城市景观；在冬季，穿上溜冰鞋，就可以滑行在世界上最大的户外溜冰场。

The ancient Rideau Canal (Figure 3-16) was built from 1826 to 1832, with a total length of 202 kilometers, of which 7.8 kilometers passed through the city center of Ottawa. The Rideau Canal is an important contributor to the cultural heritage the capital of Canada, and is on the UNESCO World Heritage List. In summer, you can canoe along the canals and enjoy the beautiful city views; in winter, you can put on ice skates and enjoy the world's largest outdoor ice skating rink.

图 3-16　里多运河
Figure 3-16　Rideau Canal

6. 温哥华唐人街 Vancouver's Chinatown

温哥华唐人街（图 3-17）大约有一百年的历史，是北美洲第二大华人社区，仅次于美国圣弗朗西斯科（旧金山）的唐人街。这里不仅能买到

图 3-17　温哥华唐人街
Figure 3-17　Vancouver's Chinatown

新鲜蔬果、杂货和海鲜，还能品尝到地道的中国菜肴。千禧门是温哥华唐人街的象征和入口。整条街上的房屋灯柱都以红色为主，上面写着汉字的拱门给人一种置身于中国古代的错觉。每年春节，舞龙舞狮的表演都会吸引大量当地居民，十分热闹。

Vancouver's Chinatown (Figure 3-17), with a history of about 100 years, is the second largest Chinese community in North America after San Francisco's Chinatown in the U.S. It sells fresh fruits and vegetables, groceries, seafood, etc., and you can also taste authentic Chinese cuisine. The Millennium Gate is the symbol and entrance of Vancouver's Chinatown. The lampposts of the houses on the entire street are mainly red, and the arches with Chinese characters written on them give people the illusion of being in ancient China. Every Spring Festival, the performance of dragon and lion dance attracts a large number of local residents and the scene is very lively.

图 3-18　皇家山
Figure 3-18　Mount Royal

7. 皇家山 Mount Royal

皇家山（图 3-18）是加拿大蒙特利尔的最高峰，位于市中心北侧，由三座连绵的山峰组成。皇家山最高海拔为 233 米，是蒙特利尔名称的出处。皇家山于 1876 年由设计纽约中央公园的著名设计师弗雷德里克·劳·奥姆斯特德（Frederick Law Olmsted）设计修建，山区部分被开辟成为皇家山公园。整个园区占地 101 公顷，不仅保留了皇家山独特的自然风貌，而且是蒙特利尔最大的公园之一，也是城市中心的一片

绿洲。公园的点睛之笔在于可从山上的不同角度遍览城区的迷人风光。

Mount Royal (Figure 3-18) is the highest peak in Montreal, Canada, located on the north side of downtown and composed of three continuous mountains. Although Mount Royal reaches only 233 meters above the sea level, Montreal was named after it. Designed in 1876 by the renowned designer Frederick Law Olmsted, who also designed New York's Central Park, the mountain area was developed into Mount Royal Park. Covering an area of 101 hectares, the park not only preserves the unique natural landscape of Mount Royal, but also serves as one of the largest parks in Montreal, becoming a major oasis in the city center. The highlight of the park lies in that people can enjoy the charming views of the city from different angles on the mountain.

图 3-19　蒙特利尔地下城
Figure 3-19　Montreal Underground City

8. 蒙特利尔地下城 Montreal Underground City

蒙特利尔地下城（图 3-19）始建于 1962 年。起初它只是一个地下商场，后期逐渐发展成一个巨大的商场。整个地下城与 2 个公交总站、10 个地铁站、1 200 个写字楼、2 000 家商店、2 家百货公司、200 家餐厅、40 家银行、30 家电影院、3 个家庭展览中心、1 座教堂，以及奥林匹克公园、蒙特利尔大学、魁北克大学蒙特城校区相连相通。

The Montreal Underground City (Figure 3-19) was established in 1962. Initially, it was just an underground shopping center, but later it gradually developed into a huge consumer shopping center. The entire underground city is connected to 2 bus terminals, 10 subway stations, 1 200 office buildings, 2 000 stores, 2 department stores, 200 restaurants, 40 banks, 30 cinemas, 3 family exhibition centers, a church, the Olympic Park, Montreal University, Quebec University Mont City campus and so on.

9. 蒙特利尔圣母大教堂 Notre-Dame Basilica of Montreal

蒙特利尔圣母大教堂（图 3-20）是北美最大的教堂。它建于 1829 年，位于蒙特利尔市旧城区的中心地带，在达尔姆广场对面，是蒙特利尔市的象征。圣母大教堂的正面矗立着两座高耸雄伟的塔楼，西塔上有一口北美古老的巨钟，外形像极了哥特式风格的城堡。走近教堂，正面有三个高耸的拱门，每个拱门都有一尊雕像，中间的一尊是被星星环绕的圣母雕像。教堂正门两侧是高 70 米的双塔，整个教堂的外观非常宏伟、庄严。

图 3-20　蒙特利尔圣母大教堂
Figure 3-20　Notre-Dame Basilica of Montreal

The Notre-Dame Basilica of Montreal （Figure3-20）is the largest church in North America. Built in 1829, it is located in the heart of Old Montreal, opposite Place d'Armes, and serves as a symbol of the city. The facade of the basilica features two towering spires, with the western tower housing a North America's old bells on the western tower resembling a Gothic-style castle. As approaching the basilica, three tall arches stand on the front, each adorned with a statue, and the central statue depicting the Virgin Mary is surrounded by stars. Flanking the main entrance are twin towers that rise 70 meters high, giving the entire basilica a magnificent and solemn appearance.

10. 蒙特利尔市政厅 Montreal City Hall

蒙特利尔市政厅（图 3-21）位于蒙特利尔老城区雅克卡迪亚广场北侧，建于 1878 年。原建筑由 Henri-Maurice Perrault 和 Alexander Cowper Hutchison 设计，采用当时流行的"法兰西第二帝国风格"，是巴洛克和法国建筑元素的组合，也被称为巴洛克复兴建筑。1922 年，大部分原始建筑被大火烧毁。建筑师路易斯·帕兰特奉命重建。重建的建筑采用了当时先进的钢结构设计。为了保留其原有的风格，还以法国旅游市政厅作为蓝本。重建设计中加入了属于当时主流的新装饰主义风格，还修改了原有的

图 3-21　蒙特利尔市政厅
Figure 3-21　Montreal City Hall

石板屋顶材料，改用铜屋顶。该建筑于 1984 年被选入加拿大标志性历史建筑名单。

On the north side of Place Jacques Cadia in Old Montreal is the City Hall of Montreal (Figure 3-21). The building was built in 1878. The original building was designed by Henri-Maurice Perrault and Alexander Cowper Hutchison, using the popular "French Second Empire style" at that time. It is an eclectic mix of Baroque and French architectural elements, also known as Baroque Revival architecture. In 1922, most of the original building was destroyed by fire. The architect Louis Parant was ordered to rebuild it. The reconstructed building structure adopted the advanced steel structure design at that time. In order to ensure the original style, it was modeled after the French Tour City Hall. The design added the mainstream neo-decorist style at that time, and also modified the original slate roofing material and used a copper roof instead. The building was selected into the List of Iconic Historic Buildings in Canada in 1984.

图3-22　爱德华王子岛
Figure 3-22　Prince Edward Island

11. 爱德华王子岛 Prince Edward Island

爱德华王子岛（图3-22）南北长约255千米，东西宽6.4～54千米，有"圣劳伦斯湾公园"之称，是加拿大最小的省份。该岛北岸多沙滩，形成了众多的天然海滨浴场。著名景点有拖鞋兰车道、爱德华王子岛国家公园、安妮的绿色小屋等，令人流连忘返，久久不能忘怀。爱德华王子岛不仅农业、渔业和旅游业等老牌行业在加拿大名列前茅，而且近些年还拓展了航天和生物科学等新领域。顺着圣劳伦斯海湾，从西边的小镇法兰西河起，往东60千米就是爱德华王子岛国家公园，其宽度从几百到几千米不等。公园内遍布高耸的沙丘，海滩上的砂岩赤壁使公园的海滩更加动人。海滩是整个公园最大的特色：由于土壤中含有大量的氧化铁，所以地面呈红褐色，土质肥沃。奇特的海岸景观和生长着众多奇花异草的湿地森林让人赏心悦目，很多加拿大人选择来这里度蜜月。

Prince Edward Island (Figure 3-22), stretching about 255 kilometers north to south and 6.4 to 54 kilometers east to west, is known as the "Park of the St. Lawrence Bay" and is the smallest province in Canada. The northern coast of the island is characterized by sandy beaches, forming numerous natural seaside resorts. Famous attractions include the Confederation Trail, Prince Edward Island National Park, Anne's Green Gable, and more, all of which leave visitors enchanted and unforgettable. Prince Edward Island not only excels in traditional industries such as agriculture, fisheries, and Tourist in Canada, but in recent years has also expanded into new sectors like aerospace and biosciences. Following the St. Lawrence Bay, starting from the western town of French River and stretching east for sixty kilometers, with widths ranging from hundreds to thousands of meters, lies the Prince Edward Island National Park. The park is dotted with towering sand dunes, and the red sandstone cliffs on the beaches add to the park's allure, making the beaches a major highlight. Due to the high iron oxide content in the soil, the ground appears reddish-brown and is fertile. The unique coastal landscapes and wetland forests teeming with exotic flora make a visually pleasing experience, attracting many Canadians for honeymoon getaways.

（三）旅游购物 Shopping

枫糖浆：美丽迷人的枫树，除极具观赏价值，还是加拿大重要的经济来源之一。早在1600年前后，已有"印第安糖浆"的记载。由于含糖量高，糖枫树被用来提取汁液加工糖浆。目前，全世界70%的枫糖制品集中在魁北克。这种从树龄40年以上的糖枫中所采集的汁液非常珍贵，平均40升的枫树浆只能提炼出1升的枫糖浆。

Maple syrup: The beautiful and enchanting maple tree is not only admired for its beauty but also serves as one of Canada's important economic resources. As early as around 1600, there were records of "Indian syrup". Today, 70% of the world's maple syrup products are concentrated in Quebec. The sap collected from sugar maples that are over 40 years old is extremely precious, with an average of 40 liters of sap required to produce just 1 liter of maple syrup. It is known for its benefits in soothing the lungs and improving digestion. There are many other maple products, such as maple butter, maple jelly, maple jam, and maple cotton candy, making it one of Canada's most famous specialties.

冰酒：冰酒是加拿大独特且稀有的特产，举世闻名，乃葡萄酒中的极品，享有"加拿大国酒"的美誉。真正的冰酒不仅要用优质的且出汁率极低的葡萄品种和非常严格的酿造工艺来制作，其品质的好坏还取决于天气因素和恰当的时机。冰酒最初于1794年诞生在德国的弗兰克尼，但加拿大尼亚加拉半岛的气候更适合于冰酒的生产。经过200多年的发展，冰酒已经成为酒中极品。加拿大冰酒在国际上一直享有很高的声誉。加拿大安大略省的尼亚加拉地区是目前世界上最著名的冰酒产区。

Ice wine: Ice wine is a unique and rare Canadian specialty, renowned worldwide as the pinnacle of wines, often referred to as the "National Wine of Canada". True ice wine requires not only high-quality grape varieties and a very strict winemaking process but also depends heavily on weather conditions and timing, with a very low juice yield. Ice wine was first created in 1794 in Franconia, Germany. Due to the climate of Canada's Niagara Peninsula being particularly suited for ice wine production, it has developed over more than 200 years into a premium wine. Canadian ice wine has consistently enjoyed a high reputation internationally. The Niagara region in Ontario, Canada, is currently the most famous ice wine-producing area in the world.

三文鱼（鲑鱼）：加拿大首屈一指、闻名全球的水产品就是三文鱼（也叫鲑鱼）。加拿大的特产鲑鱼可在土产店的鱼品柜买到，如多伦多的金山等超市。加拿大的海岸线长，海产品很多，其中三文鱼被誉为深海鱼中的"冰海之皇"。三文鱼的食法多样、千变万化，烤、煎、煮、烟熏或腌制都各具特色。其他海产品，如贝类及鲍鱼的熏制品以及昆布等也值得推荐。

Salmon: Canada's most renowned seafood globally is salmon, also known as the "King of the Ice Sea." This Canadian specialty can be found in the fish sections of local stores, such as supermarkets like T&T in Toronto, though winter is considered the off-season. With its extensive coastline, Canada offers a wealth of seafood, and salmon stands out as a major player among deep-sea fish. There are countless ways to prepare salmon, including grilling, pan-frying, boiling, smoking, or curing, each with its unique flavor. Other recommended seafood products include smoked shellfish, abalone, and kelp.

扫码获取：入境须知及海关规定

本节习题

1. 简述为什么加拿大是枫叶之国。

2. 某游客去加拿大一位朋友家做客，带了白色的百合花作为礼物，主人见状十分不高兴，请问原因是什么？

3. 加拿大有哪些著名的旅游资源？

4. 请概况总结多伦多城市文化的独特性。

第四章
Chapter 4

南美洲旅游区
The South America Tourist Region

学习目标

1.了解巴西和阿根廷的基本情况，包括各国的自然环境特征、风俗民情、主要旅游城市和景点。

Get familiar with the national conditions of Brazil and Argentina, including the natural environmental characteristics, and customs of each country, as well as major tourist cities and scenic spots.

2.能在旅游接待活动中利用所学的巴西、阿根廷旅游景点介绍、习俗禁忌、出入境海关规定等知识，做好服务工作。

Be able to utilize knowledge of tourist attractions, customs and taboos, entry and exit customs regulations, etc. of Brazil and Argentina in Tourist reception activities to provide good service work.

3.能根据巴西、阿根廷两国的各自特点和游客的不同需求，设计旅游线路、开发旅游产品。

Be able to carry out targeted tourist source development planning and product design according to the characteristics of various countries and customers' needs.

第一节　南美洲旅游区特征

The General Situation of South America Tourist Region

南美洲旅游区位于西半球美洲大陆南部，东临大西洋，西濒太平洋，北临加勒比海，南隔德雷克海峡与南极洲相望，北部与北美洲旅游区以巴拿马运河为界。总面积为1 784万平方千米。南美洲旅游区地形可分为三个南北向纵列带：西部为狭长的安第斯山，中部为广阔平坦的平原低地，东部为波状起伏的高原。其中，平原约占全洲面积的60%，海拔3 000米以下的高原、丘陵和山地约占全洲面积的33%，海拔3 000米以上的高原和山地约占全洲面积的7%。全洲平均海拔为600米。

南美洲旅游区特征（英文版）

南美洲是世界上火山较多、地震频繁且多强烈地震的一个洲，以太平洋沿岸地区为甚。

若以科迪勒拉山系的安第斯山为分水岭，则南美洲的东、西部分属于大西洋水系和太平洋水系。南美洲旅游区的大部分地区属于热带雨林气候和热带草原气候。南美洲旅游区总人口约4.34亿（2019年）。人口密度地区分布不均衡，西北部和东南沿海一带人口稠密，且人口高度集中在少数大城市。民族成分复杂，有印第安人、白人、黑人及各种不同族群的混血儿，其中以印欧混血儿为最多。语言也比较多样化，印第安人用印第安语，巴西的官方语言为葡萄牙语，其他国家均以西班牙语为官方语言。居民绝大多数信奉天主教，少数信奉基督教。

　　南美洲旅游区是世界古代文明的发祥地之一，这里孕育了灿烂的古印第安文明，曾经创造了玛雅文化、托尔特克文明和阿兹特克文明等光辉、灿烂的古文明，留下了许多规模宏大的石结构古建筑，如神庙、金字塔、祭坛、宫殿、卫城、广场等，虽然其中一些仅剩废墟，但依然具有较高的历史研究价值。该地区的文化和生活方式以及艺术、宗教、建筑等受西班牙、葡萄牙、法国、意大利等国移民的影响较大，经过长期发展，形成了独具特色且多姿多彩的旅游资源，为地区旅游业的发展奠定了坚实的基础。南美洲旅游区最主要的旅游类型是海滨度假旅游，其中以巴西最为典型。由于足球世界杯、奥运会，等全球性赛事提升了公众对南美洲的关注度，再加上智利、厄瓜多尔、阿根廷等南美洲国家先后对中国出台签证利好政策，中国游客赴南美洲旅游人数不断增加。中国游客较偏爱的目的地是巴西、阿根廷、智利和玻利维亚。

第二节　南美洲之旅

Travel in South America

足球王国——巴西
The Kingdom of Football—Brazil

4

导读

　　巴西是一个多姿多彩的多民族国家，以节日众多闻名于世，素有"旅游王国"的称号。在这块神奇的土地上，除了观赏足球、桑巴舞以及各种各样的表演节目，还可以去参观巴西三大特色城市，即巴西利亚、圣保罗、里约热内卢。巴西北部有被称为"地球之肺"的亚马孙热带雨林，南部有气势恢宏的伊瓜苏大瀑布，中西部的大沼泽地是野生动物的天堂，漫长的海岸线上分布着大量风景绚丽的海滩。旅游业是巴西近年来发展较快的行业之一，游客多数来自拉丁美洲、欧洲、美国、加拿大和日本。巴西奉行独立自主、不干涉内政、尊重主权与领土完整、和平解决争端以及友好共处的对外政策，认为外交应为巩固民主制度和促进经济发展服务，赞同世界多极化，要求建立"不含任何形式霸权主义的民主化的国际关系"。1974年8月15日中巴两国建交。建交以来，中巴在政治、经贸、科技、文化等领域的友好合作关系全面发展。中巴联合研制的地球资源卫星项目成为南南高科技合作的典范。

一、地理概览 Geography of Brazil

（一）位置 Location

巴西位于南美洲东南部，是南美洲国土面积最大的国家。北邻法属圭亚那、苏里南、圭亚那、委内瑞拉和哥伦比亚，西邻秘鲁、玻利维亚，南接巴拉圭、阿根廷和乌拉圭，东濒大西洋。巴西国土面积为 851.49 万平方千米，居世界第五位。

Brazil is located in the southeastern part of South America and is the largest country on the continent. It shares its northern borders with French Guiana, Suriname, Guyana, Venezuela, and Colombia; its western borders with Peru and Bolivia; and its southern borders with Paraguay, Argentina, and Uruguay. To the east, it is bordered by the Atlantic Ocean. Brazil covers an area of 8.5149 million square kilometers, making it the fifth-largest country in the world.

（二）地形和气候 The Land and Seasons

全境地形分为亚马孙平原、巴拉圭盆地、圭亚那高原和巴西高原。其中，平原面积约占全国总面积的 1/3。主要河流为亚马孙河，横贯巴西西北部，是世界上流域面积最广和河口年平均流量最大的河流，全长 6 751 千米，在巴西境内的长度为 3 000 多千米。主要湖泊有帕图斯渴湖、米林湖等。内布利纳峰海拔为 3 014 米，为巴西最高峰。主要岛屿有马拉卡岛、罗卡斯岛和费尔南多迪诺罗尼亚岛。国土面积的 80% 位于热带雨林地区，最南端属亚热带气候。北部亚马孙平原属赤道气候，年平均气温为 27 ℃～ 29 ℃。中部高原属热带草原气候，分旱、雨季。南部地区平均气温为 16 ℃～ 19 ℃。

The terrain is divided into the Amazon Plain, the Paraguay Basin, the Guiana Highlands, and the Brazilian Plateau. The plains account for about one-third of the country's total area. The main rivers include the Amazon River, which crosses the northwest and is the river with the largest drainage area and highest average annual flow in the world, spanning 6,751 kilometers in total length, with over 3,000 kilometers within Brazilian territory. Major lakes include Lake Paranoá and Lake Mirim. The Neblina Peak, at 3,014 meters above sea level, is the highest peak in Brazil. Main islands include Maracá Island, Rocas Island, and Fernando de Noronha Island. 80% of the country's land is located in tropical rainforest regions, with the southernmost part having a subtropical climate. The northern Amazon Plain experiences an equatorial climate with average annual temperatures ranging from 27 ℃ –29 ℃ . The central plateau has a tropical savanna climate with distinct dry and rainy seasons. The southern region has average temperatures of 16 ℃ –19 ℃ .

（三）自然资源 Natural Resources

巴西矿产、森林、土地和水资源丰富。已探明铁矿砂储量为 333 亿吨，占世界总储量的 9.8%，居世界第五位；年产量 3.7 亿吨，居世界第二位；出口量也位居世界前列。还有其他 29 种矿物的储量也十分丰富，其中，镍储量占世界总储量的 98%，锰、铝矾土、铅、锡等多种金属储量也各占世界总储量的 10% 以上。已探明的铌矿储量为 410 万吨，占全球总储量的 97%。此外，还有较丰富的铬矿、黄金矿和石棉矿。煤矿探明储量 101 亿吨，但品位很低。2007 年以来，巴西在东南沿海相继发现大油气田，预计石油储量将超过 500 亿桶，有望进入世界十大石油国之列。2012 年，巴西生产原油 7.21 亿桶。巴西国内的森林覆盖率为 60.7%，木材储量为 658 亿立方米。水资源丰富，拥有世界 18% 的淡水，人均淡水拥有量达 29 000 立方米。

Brazil is rich in minerals, forests, land and water resources. Proven reserves of iron ore amount to 33.3 billion tons, accounting for 9.8% of the world's total reserves, ranking fifth in the world, the annual output of 370 million tons ranks second in the world, and the volume of exports ranks among the world's tops. Brazil is rich in 29 kinds of mineral reserves, with nickel reserves amounting to 98% of the world's total reserves, and manganese, bauxite, lead, tin and other metal reserves accounting for more than 10% of the world's total reserves. Niobium ore reserves have been proven 4.1 million tons, accounting for 97% of global resoives. There are also rich chromite, gold and asbestos mines. Coal mine reserves amout to 10.1 billion tons, but the grade is very low. Since 2007, the successive discovery of large oil and gas fields in the southeast coast of Brazil, and oil reserves were expected to be more than 50 billion barrels. It would be expected to enter the world's top ten oil countries. In 2012, the production of crude oil was 721 million barrels. Forest cover is 60.7%, with timber reserves of 65.8 billion cubic meters. Water resources are abundant, with 18 percent of the world's fresh water and 29,000 cubic meters of fresh water per capita.

二、人文概况 Overview of Brazilian Humanities

（一）国情认知 Basic Knowledge of National Conditions

巴西全国总人口约 2.15 亿（2022 年），居拉丁美洲首位。东南部地区是巴西人口最多的地区，约占巴西人口总数的 42%。该地区拥有巴西 3 个人口最多的州。由于巴西历史上曾为葡萄牙的殖民地，因此其官方语言为葡萄牙语。巴西是一个移民国家，移民来自世界各地，因而集中了东西方多种宗教信仰。巴西的各种宗教中，天主教是信奉人数最多的宗教，约 64.6% 的居民信奉天主教，22.2% 的居民信奉基督教福音教派。巴西的国旗呈长方形，旗的底色为绿色，中央为黄色菱形，菱形中央是深蓝色圆形天球仪，其上有一条白色绶带，绶带上面书以葡萄牙文"秩序与进步"。绿色和黄色是巴西的国色，绿色象征森林，黄色象征矿藏和资源。国歌为《听，伊皮兰加的呼声》，国花为毛蟹爪兰，是亚马孙热带雨林中的一种附生植物，体色鲜绿，茎多分枝，常成簇悬垂，一根枝条由若干节组成，数节连贯似蟹爪，因而得名。巴西曾经将此花馈赠给中国，丰富了中国的兰花品种。

Brazil has a total national population of approximately 215 million (2022), ranking the highest in Latin America. The Southeastern region is the most populous region in Brazil, accounting for approximately 42% of the country's total population. The region is home to three of Brazil's most populous states. As Brazil was historically colonized by Portugal, its official language is Portuguese. Brazil is a country of immigrants from all over the world, which has resulted in a concentration of Eastern and Western religious beliefs. Among the various religions in Brazil, Catholicism is the largest, with about 64.6% of the population practicing Catholicism and 22.2% practicing Evangelical Christianity. The national flag of Brazil is rectangular in shape, with a green background and a yellow lozenge in the center, in the center of which is a dark blue circular celestial globe, surmounted by a white ribbon with the words " Order and Progress " in Portuguese. Green and yellow are the national colors of Brazil, with green symbolizing forests and yellow symbolizing minerals and resources. The national anthem is *Listen, the Cry of Ipiranga*. The national flower is the orchid for the hairy crabapple (Phyllostachys edulis), a kind of epiphyte in the Amazon rainforest, the body color is bright green, and the stem is more branched, often in clusters overhanging. A branch consists of a number of sections, a number of sections coherent like a crab's claw, and thus the name. Brazil once gave this flower to China, enriching the Chinese orchid treasures.

（二）历史简介 History of Brazil

古代巴西为印第安人居住地。1500 年 4 月 22 日，葡萄牙航海家佩德罗·卡布拉尔到达巴西。16 世纪巴西沦为葡萄牙殖民地。1807 年拿破仑入侵葡萄牙，葡萄牙王室逃到巴西后，巴西实际上成了葡萄牙的帝国中心。1821 年葡萄牙王室迁回里斯本，王子佩德罗留在巴西任摄政王。1822 年 9 月 7 日获得独立，建立巴西帝国。1888 年 5 月废除奴隶制度。1889 年推翻帝制建立巴西合众国。1960 年将首都由里约热内卢迁往巴西利亚。1964 年 3 月 31 日，巴西右翼军人发动政变上台，实行独裁统治，1967 年改国名为巴西联邦共和国。1985 年军政府还政于民。1989 年 11 月 15 日，巴西举行了近 30 年来第一次全民直接选举总统，费尔南多当选总统。

Ancient Brazil was inhabited by Indians. On April 22, 1500, Portuguese navigator Pedro Cabral arrived in Brazil. It became a Portuguese colony in the 16th century. After Napoleon's invasion of Portugal in 1807, the Portuguese royal family fled to Brazil, which became the center of Portugal's empire. In 1821, the Portuguese royal family moved back to Lisbon, and Prince Pedro stayed in Brazil to serve as the regent. On September 7, 1822, the country gained independence and established the Brazilian Empire. Abolished slavery in May, 1888, the imperial system was overthrown and the United States of Brazil established in 1889. The capital moved from Rio de Janeiro to Brasilia in 1960. On March 31, 1964, right-wing military forces in Brazil staged a coup, establishing a dictatorship, and in 1967, the country's name was changed to the Federative Republic of Brazil. In 1985, the military government returned power to civilians. On November 15, 1989, Brazil held its first direct universal presidential election in nearly 30 years, and Fernando was elected as the president.

（三）经济状况 The Economy

巴西拥有拉丁美洲最为完善的产业体系，经济实力居拉丁美洲首位、世界第八位。巴西工业体系较为完善，主要工业部门有钢铁、汽车、造船、石油、水泥、化工、冶金、电力、纺织、建筑等。核电、通信、电子、飞机制造、军工等产业已跨入世界先进国家的行列。巴西的农牧业发达，是世界蔗糖、咖啡、柑橘、玉米、鸡肉、牛肉、烟草、大豆的主要生产国。巴西还是世界第一大咖啡生产国和出口国，素有"咖啡王国"之称。

Brazil has the most complete industrial system in Latin America, and its economic strength ranks first in Latin America and eighth in the world. Brazil's industrial system is relatively complete, and the main industrial sectors include iron and steel, automobiles, shipbuilding, petroleum, cement, chemical industry, metallurgy, electric power, textile, construction and so on. Nuclear power, communications, electronics, aircraft manufacturing, military and other industries have crossed into the ranks of the world's advanced countries. Brazil's agriculture and animal husbandry are developed, and it is the world's leading producer of sugar, coffee, citrus, corn, chicken, beef, tobacco and soybeans. Brazil is also the world's largest coffee producer and exporter, known as the "Kingdom of Coffee".

（四）传统文化 Traditional Culture

巴西文化中既有土著印第安人的淳朴，又有非洲人的热情，还有欧洲人的庄重。然而，它又不是欧洲文化、非洲文化或印第安文化的简单翻版，它是一种开放性的文化，在对多种文化进行兼收并蓄的过程中，逐步形成了自己独特的文化。巴西的音乐以优美、多样而著称，舞蹈颇具特色，韵律最迷人的当属桑巴，桑巴舞被称为巴西的"国舞"。足球是巴西人最热爱的体育项目，当地小孩通常上午上课，下午去体育场踢足球。巴西拥有众多高水平的职业足球俱乐部，前首都里约热内卢的马拉卡纳足球场堪称世界上最大的足球场，可容纳20多万名观众，成为"足球王国"巴西的象征。

Brazilian culture is characterized by the simplicity of the indigenous Indians, the warmth of the Africans, and the solemnity of the Europeans. However, it is not a simple replica of European, African or Indian cultures; it is an open culture, which has gradually formed its own unique culture in the process of absorbing and incorporating various cultures. Brazilian music is famous for its beauty and variety, and the most typical and charming rhythm of music and dance is the samba, which is called the "national dance" of Brazil. Soccer is the most popular sport among Brazilians, and local children usually attend classes in the morning and play soccer in the stadium in the afternoon. Brazil has many high-level professional soccer clubs, and the Maracana Stadium in Rio de Janeiro, the former capital of Brazil, is the largest soccer stadium in the world, with a capacity of more than 200 000 spectators, and has become a symbol of the "Kingdom of Soccer".

 思考题

阅读拓展材料"巴西为什么被称为'足球王国'"。

思考：巴西为什么能位列世界足球强国？

巴西为什么被称为"足球王国"

巴西人大多性情直率，在人际交往中活泼好动、幽默风趣、爱开玩笑。与客人见面和分手时都行握手礼，亲朋好友见面常热烈拥抱，妇女之间相见时行贴面礼。男人平时喜欢穿短裤和衬衫，在社交场合则穿西服；女人喜欢穿色彩艳丽的裙装。巴西人平常主要吃欧式西餐。因为畜牧业发达，巴西人所吃食物之中肉类所占比重较大，喜欢饮咖啡、红茶和葡萄酒。巴西人很讲公德，注意维护社会秩序，在商场、影院、车站排队时遵守纪律。巴西的大街上严禁倒垃圾，也不允许在禁烟处吸烟。巴西人具有尊敬老人的传统美德。到巴西人家中做客，如果双方互赠礼品，则都应将对方的礼品当面打开，赞美一番并向赠礼人致谢。巴西的法律注重对妇女的保护，一旦夫妻离异，男人需按时付给女人生活费和未成年子女的教育费。如果男方富有，女方还可要求分割财产。

Most Brazilians are straightforward and lively in their interpersonal interactions, with a good sense of humor and a love of jokes. When meeting and parting with guests, they perform a handshake, and when meeting friends and relatives, they often embrace each other warmly. When women meet each other, they do the face-to-face salute. Men usually like to wear shorts and shirts, but in social occasions, they wear suits; women like to wear colorful dresses. Brazilians usually eat mainly European-style Western food. Because of the developed animal husbandry, Brazilians eat a larger proportion of meat in the food, like to drink coffee, black tea and wine. Brazilians are public-spirited, pay attention to maintaining social order, and observe discipline when standing in line at shopping malls, theaters, and stations. It is strictly forbidden to dump garbage in the street or smoke in no-smoking places. Brazilians have the traditional virtue of respecting the elderly. When visiting a Brazilian's home, if both parties give gifts to each other, they should open them in person, praise them and thank the giver. In Brazil, women are legally protected, and once a couple divorces, the man is required to pay the woman's living expenses and the education of her minor children on time. If the man was wealthy, the woman could also claim a share of the property.

巴西烤肉

（五）礼仪禁忌 Social Etiquettes and Taboos

巴西人忌讳棕黄色、紫色和深咖色。他们认为棕黄色表示绝望，紫色表示哀伤，深咖色会招来不幸。送礼时还应注意不要赠送手帕或刀具，因为这两样东西会引起争吵或带来不快。巴西人忌讳数字"13"，认为它是不祥之数，会给人带来厄运或灾难，每年的8月13日是巴西传统的禁忌日。在巴西忌讳"OK"的手势，这会被认为是非常不文明的动作。巴西人忌吃奇形怪状的水产品和用两栖动物制作的菜品，也不喜欢吃用牛油制作的点心。在与巴西人交谈时，应回避政治、宗教及其他有争议的话题，一般不要向别人打听工资收入等情况，对女性则不问年龄和婚姻状况。

In Brazil, people avoid brownish-yellow, purple, and dark brown colors due to their negative connotations. Brownish-yellow is associated with despair, purple is seen as a color of mourning, and dark brown is believed to bring misfortune. When giving gifts, it's important not to give handkerchiefs or knives, as these are believed to provoke arguments or bring displeasure. The number "13" is considered unlucky in Brazil, thought to bring misfortune or disaster, and August 13 is traditionally seen as a day of taboo. The "OK" hand gesture is also considered very rude in Brazil. Brazilians tend to avoid eating oddly shaped seafood and dishes made with amphibians, and they also dislike pastries made with lard. When conversing with Brazilians, it's best to steer clear of topics like politics, religion, and other controversial subjects. It's generally inappropriate to inquire about someone's salary or income, and it's considered impolite to ask women about their age or marital status.

（六）传统节日 Festivals

1. 海神节 Neptune's Day

每年的1月1日是海神节。这是一个辞旧迎新、供敬海神、祈祷保佑家人来年平安的节日，至今已有200多年的历史。

January 1 is Neptune's Day. This is a festival that has been celebrated for over 200 years to welcome the old and the new, to honor the god of the sea, and to pray for the safety of family members in the coming year.

2. 圣灵节 Feast of the Holy Spirit

圣灵节是起源于葡萄牙的一个民间节日，1819 年首次在巴西举行庆祝活动。圣灵节每年 6 月初开始，历时 10 天。

Feast of the Holy Spirit is in Early June. A folk festival of Portuguese origin, was first celebrated in Brazil in 1819, which begins in early June and lasts 10 days.

3. 敬牛节 Toast to the Cow Festival

敬牛节是在 6 月下旬，是巴西东北部的传统节日。庆祝活动以游行演出为主，节目的内容丰富多彩，大多是通过牛的遭遇来抒发对当今社会的爱与恨，体现出人们敬牛、爱牛的风俗。

Toast to the Cow Festival is in late June. It is a traditional festival in northeastern Brazil. Celebration is the parade as the main form of performance, and the festival's program content is rich and colorful, mostly through the cattle encounter to express the love and hate of today's society, to express people's respect for cattle and the custom of loving cattle.

4. 狂欢节 Carnival

狂欢节起源于中世纪的欧洲，在信奉天主教的国家，如意大利、西班牙、法国、葡萄牙等最为盛行。狂欢节是由葡萄牙人传入巴西的，因吸收了黑人的音乐和舞蹈而成为闻名遐迩的巴西特有的传统节日，在每年的 2 月中旬或下旬举行。正式节期为四旬斋的前 3 天，因为教会禁止在大斋期内食肉和娱乐，人们就在进入大斋期之前欢歌狂舞数天，以图过瘾尽兴。如今巴西的狂欢节已经成为世界性的节日，被称为"世界上最伟大的表演"。

Carnival originated in medieval Europe and is most popular in Catholic countries such as Italy, Spain, France, and Portugal. The Brazilian Carnival was introduced by the Portuguese and has incorporated African music and dance, becoming a unique and renowned traditional festival in Brazil. It is held annually in mid or late February. The official celebration lasts for the three days preceding Lent, as the church prohibits meat consumption and festivities during Lent. People indulge in singing and dancing for days before the fasting period begins to fully enjoy themselves. Today, Brazil's Carnival has become a global event, often referred to as "The Greatest Show on Earth"..

三、旅游观光 Tourism and Sightseeing

（一）主要旅游城市 Major Tourist Cities

带你去看巴西各地的狂欢节

1. 巴西利亚 Brasilia

巴西利亚是巴西首都，全国政治、经济、文化和交通中心。巴西利亚以其独特的建筑而闻名于世。其总体建设计划由建筑大师卢西奥·科斯塔完成。在灯火通明的夜晚从空中俯视，巴西利亚宛如一架驶向东方的巨型飞机。整座城市沿垂直的两轴铺开：沿机翼向南北延伸的公路轴和沿机身向东西延伸的纪念碑轴。机头是三权广场，机身是政府机构所在地，机翼则是现代化的立体公路。三权广场左侧是总统府，右侧是联邦最高法院。广场对面是国会参议院、众议院，两院会议大厅的建筑外观如同两只大碗，众议院的碗口朝上，象征"民主""广开言路"；参议院的碗口朝下，象征"集中民意"。国会的两座 28 层大楼之间有通道相连，呈"H"形，为葡萄牙语"人"的首字母。三权广场上的议会大厦、联邦最高法院、总统府和外交部水晶宫等是巴西利亚的标志性建筑。其他文化设施有国家剧院、巴西博物馆、历史研究所、大学图书馆和广播电视台等，还有很多电影院和体育场所等，巴西利亚是最年轻的人类文化遗产，融汇了世界古今建筑艺术的精华，有"世界建筑巴西利亚博览会"之称。1987 年联合国教科文组织将巴西利亚列入《世界遗产名录》。

Brasilia is the capital of Brazil and the political, economic, cultural and transportation center of the country. Brasilia is famous for its unique architecture. Its whole building plan was completed by architect Lucio Costa. When viewed from the sky on a brightly lit night, Brasilia looks like a giant airplane heading east. The entire city is laid out along two vertical axes: the highway axis, which runs north-south towards the wings, and the monumental axis, which runs east-west along the fuselage. In the nose is the Square of the Three Powers, in the fuselage is the location of the government, and in the wings are the modern three-dimensional highways. To the left of the Square of the Three Powers, is the Presidential Palace and to the right is the Federal Supreme Court. Across the plaza is the Senate and the House of Representatives, the two chambers of the building appearance of the meeting hall as two large bowls, the House of Representatives of the bowl up, symbolizing the "democracy" and "wide-open speech"; the Senate's bowel is upside down, symbolizing the "concentration of public opinion". The two 28-storey buildings of the National Assembly are connected by a passageway, in the shape of "H", which is the initial letter of the Portuguese word "human". The Parliament Building, the Federal Supreme Court, the Presidential Palace and the Water Palace of the Ministry of Foreign Affairs in the Square of the Three Powers are among the landmarks of Brasilia. Other cultural facilities include the National Theater, the Brazilian Museum, the Historical Institute, the University Library and the Radio and Television Station. There are also many movie theaters and sports venues. Brasilia is one of the youngest cultural heritages of mankind, and has been recognized as the "Brasilia Expo of World Architecture" because it is the best example of ancient and modern architecture in the world, and was inscribed on the UNESCO World Heritage List in 1987.

2. 里约热内卢 Rio de Janeiro

里约热内卢是巴西第二大城市、著名的海港城市、里约热内卢州首府，位于瓜纳巴拉湾西岸，濒临大西洋。城市面积 1 171 平方千米，人口约 534 万。里约热内卢始建于 1565 年，1822—1960 年为巴西首都，是巴西经济最发达的城市之一，也是巴西重要的交通枢纽和文化中心。1960 年首都迁往巴西利亚后仍然保留了相当多的联邦政府机构、社会团体、公司总部等，许多军政知名人士也寓居于此。因为在政治上仍有相当大的影响，故有巴西"第二首都"的美誉。里约热内卢是巴西最大的商业中心，同时也是南美洲最大的金融中心，许多大企业、银行和跨国组织在此设立办事机构。经济比较发达，文化教育事业也比较发达，拥有许多高等学府，以及著名图书馆、博物馆、科研机构和全国最大的电视台。里约热内卢依山傍海，山丘起伏，丛林繁茂。港湾腹宽口窄，群山环抱，以面包山和驼峰山最为著名。

Rio de Janeiro is the second largest city in Brazil, a famous seaport city and the capital of the state of Rio de Janeiro, located on the west coast of Guanabara Bay, bordering the Atlantic Ocean. It has an area of 1,171 square kilometers and a population of about 5.34 million. Rio de Janeiro was founded in 1565, for the capital of Brazil from 1822 to 1960. It is one of the most developed cities for the Brazilian economy, and also an important transportation hub and cultural center of Brazil. In 1960, after the capital moved to Brasilia, it still retained a considerable number of federal government agencies, social groups, company headquarters, etc. Many military and political celebrities also live here. Rio de Janeiro is known as the "Second Capital" of Brazil because of its political influence. Rio de Janeiro is the largest commercial center in Brazil, and it is also the largest financial center in South America, where many large enterprises, banks and multinational organizations have set up offices. The economy is more developed, culture and education are also more developed, with many institutions of higher education, as well as famous libraries, museums, scientific research institutions and the country's largest television station. Rio de Janeiro is surrounded by mountains and sea, with rolling hills and lush jungles. The harbor has a wide body and a narrow entrance, surrounded by mountains, which are famous for Bread Mountain and Humpback Mountain.

3. 伊瓜苏 Iguassu

伊瓜苏市位于巴西、巴拉圭、阿根廷三国交界的巴拉那河与伊瓜苏河汇合处。"伊瓜苏"在印第安瓜拉尼语中意为"大水"。伊瓜苏市是巴西主要的旅游中心，年均接待游客约700万人次，当地居民主要从事商业和旅游业。著名的伊瓜苏瀑布距市区28千米。

The city of Iguassu is located at the confluence of the Paraná Rive and the Iguassu River on the border among Brazil, Paraguay and Argentina. The word "Iguassu" means "a large amount of water" in the Indian Guarani language. The city of Iguassu is a major tourist center in Brazil, receiving an average of 7 million visitors annually, and the local residents are mainly engaged in commerce and tourism. The famous Iguassu Falls are 28 kilometers from the city.

4. 萨尔瓦多市 Salvador

萨尔瓦多市位于巴伊亚州，东临大西洋，是葡萄牙人在巴西最早建立的首府城市。城市建成于1549年，1763年之前是葡萄牙殖民当局的贸易、防卫机构以及首府所在地，主要分为上城及下城两大区。萨尔瓦多是巴西文化的发源地，保留着浓厚的巴伊亚文化色彩，1985年被列入《世界遗产名录》。

The city of Salvador, located in the state of Bahia and facing the Atlantic Ocean, is the earliest capital city established by the Portuguese in Brazil. Founded in 1549, Salvador was the location of trade, defense, and capital of the Portuguese colony until 1763, and is divided into two main districts, Upper and Lower. Salvador is the cultural birthplace of Brazil and retains a strong Bahian culture, which was inscribed on the World Heritage List in 1985.

（二）著名旅游景点 Famous Tourist Attractions

1. 巴西利亚电视塔 Brasilia TV Tower

巴西利亚电视塔（图4-1）是巴西最高的建筑，高225米。铁塔瞭望台位于75米处，可容纳150人，游电视塔的游客可免费乘电梯登台。每逢周末铁塔周围有手工艺品市场。

The Brasilia TV Tower (Figure 4-1) is the tallest building in Brazil, standing at a height of 225 meters. The tower's observation deck is located at 75 meters of the tower and has a capacity of 150 people, and visitors to the tower can take the elevator to the top free of charge. On weekends, there is a handicraft market

图 4-1　巴西利亚电视塔
Figure 4-1　Brasilia TV Tower

around the tower.

2. 三权广场 Square of the Three Powers

三权广场（图4-2）位于巴西首都巴西利亚，是一座露天广场，也是巴西的标志性建筑之一。三权广场代表着行使国家三种权力的机构，即总统府、国会、联邦最高法院，被称为巴西的神经中枢。广场周围环绕着众议院、参议院、国家大法院、总统府、外交部、国家民族独立纪念馆、劳动者纪念碑等众多建筑。三权广场的建筑设计构思大胆，线条优美。

图 4-2　三权广场
Figure 4-2　Square of the Three Powers

Located in Brasilia, the capital of Brazil, the Square of Three Powers (Figure 4-2) is an open-air square and one of the country's iconic landmarks. The Square of Three Powers represents the three powers of the state, namely the Presidency, the Congress, and the Federal Supreme Court, and is known as the nerve center of Brazil. The square is surrounded by the Chamber of Deputies, the Senate, the National Court of Justice, the Presidential Palace, the Ministry of Foreign Affairs, the National Monument of National Independence, the Monument to the Workers, and many other buildings. The architectural Square of the Squere of the Three Powers is bold in conception and graceful in its lines.

3. 耶稣山（又称科尔科瓦多山）Mount Jesus (also known as Mount Corcovado)

耶稣山（图4-3）位于巴西里约热内卢的国家公园内，高710米。山顶塑有一座巨大耶稣像，塑成于1931年，是为纪念巴西独立运动100周年而建。耶稣像是法国赠送的，其头和手在法国制造，通过海运送至里约热内卢，全部工程历时5年。耶稣站立着，两手向旁边平伸，从远方看就像一个巨型十字架。耶稣像在里约热内卢市的每个角落都可以看到。耶稣山是里约热内卢的象征之一。

图 4-3　耶稣山
Figure 4-3　Mount Jesus

Mount Jesus (Figure 4-3) is located in a national park in Rio de Janeiro, Brazil, at a height of 710 meters. At the top of the mountain there is a statue of Jesus, that was built in 1931 to commemorate the 100th anniversary of the Brazilian Independence Movement. The statue was a gift from France, its head and hands were made in France and shipped by sea to Rio de Janeiro, and the whole project took five years. Jesus stands with his arms outstretched flat to the side, resembling a giant cross when viewed from a distance. The Jesus statue can be seen in every corner of the city of Rio de Janeiro, and the Mount Jesus in Rio de Janeiro, Brazil is one of the symbols of Rio de Janeiro.

4. 伊瓜苏瀑布 Iguassu Falls

伊瓜苏瀑布是南美洲最大的瀑布，也是世界著名的大瀑布之一，位于巴西和阿根廷的边境，距伊瓜苏河和巴拉那河的汇合点约23千米。"伊瓜苏"在瓜拉尼语中是"大水"的意思。伊瓜苏瀑布（图4-4）形成于1.2亿年前，1542年被西班牙殖民者阿尔阿·努内斯·德·瓦卡发现。瀑布呈马蹄形，宽约4千米，为尼亚加拉瀑布的4倍。浪花飞溅形成150米高的雾幕，彩虹辉映，蔚为奇观。瀑布地区植被丰富多样，瀑布倾泻处长有珍贵的河苔草科水生植物，森林中栖息着许多珍禽异兽，可称得上是一座超大的热带植物博物馆。巴西和阿根廷两国均在瀑布周围设有国家公园，旅游服务设施完备。大瀑布虽有3/4在阿根廷境内，但从巴西一侧看去更为壮观。伊瓜苏瀑布每年接待游客200多万人次，是著名的旅游胜地。1984年，伊瓜苏瀑布被联合国教科文组织列入《世界遗产名录》。1986年，巴西伊瓜苏国家公园被联合国教科文组织作为自然遗产列入《世界遗产名录》。

图 4-4　伊瓜苏瀑布
Figure 4-4　Iguassu Falls

Iguassu Falls (Figure 4-4) is the largest waterfall in South America and one of the most famous waterfalls in the world. Located on the border between Brazil and Argentina, about 23 kilometers from the confluence of the Iguassu River and the Paraná River, "Iguassu" means "a large amount of water" in Guarani. The Iguassu Falls were formed 120 million years ago, and were discovered in 1542 by the Spanish colonizer Ala Nunes de Vaca. It has a horseshoe shape and is about 4 kilometers wide, four times the size of Niagara Falls. The splashing of the waves creates a 150-meter-high fog. There is rich and diverse vegetation in waterfalls area, the precious river moss grass aquatic plants growing from the place of waterfalls pouring, and many rare birds and animals inhabiting in the forest so the falls area can be called a tropical plant museum. Both Brazil and Argentina have national parks around Shambu, with complete tourist services. Three-fourths of the Falls are in the territory of Argentina, but the view from the Brazilian side is even more spectacular. Iguassu Falls receives over two million visitors annually, becoming a famous tourist destination. In 1984, Iguassu Falls was inscribed on the UNESCO World Heritage List, and in 1986, Iguassu National Park was inscribed on the UNESCO World Heritage List as a natural heritage site.

5. 伊泰普水电站 Itaipu Hydroelectric Power Plant

伊泰普水电站（图4-5）位于巴西与巴拉圭之间的界河巴拉那河上，距离伊瓜苏市北12千米处，是世界第二大水电站，由巴西与巴拉圭共建，发电机组和发电量由两国均分。伊泰普在印第安语中意为"会唱歌的石头"。自1991年起，伊泰普水电站每年的发电收益约为23亿美元。

Located on the Paraná River, the border between Brazil and Paraguay, 12 kilometers north of the city of Iguassu, Itaipu Hydroelectric Power Plant (Figure 4-5) is the second largest hydroelectric

图 4-5　伊泰普水电站
Figure 4-5　Itaipu Hydroelectric Power Plant

power plant in the world, and was built by Brazil and Paraguay, with the generating units and power generated divided equally between the two countries. Itaipu means "singing stone" in the Indian language. Since 1991, the Itaipu Hydroelectric Power Plant has generated approximately $2.3 billion per year.

（三）旅游购物 Shopping

巴西咖啡：巴西是世界上最大的咖啡生产国和出口国，其生产的咖啡以质优、味浓而驰名全球。咖啡原产于非洲的埃塞俄比亚，1727 年传入巴西。20 世纪初，巴西的咖啡产量占世界总产量的 75% 以上，从而赢得了"咖啡王国"的美称。在巴西，无论在城市还是乡村，各式各样的咖啡屋随处可见。人们几乎随时随地都可以喝到浓郁芳香的热咖啡。

Brazilian coffee: Brazil is the world's largest producer and exporter of coffee, and its coffee is famous for its high quality and strong flavor. Coffee is native to Ethiopia in Africa and was introduced to Brazil in 1727, and at the beginning of the 20th century, Brazil's coffee production accounted for more than 75% of the world's total production, thus earning it the nickname of the "Kingdom of Coffee". Coffee houses of all kinds can be found everywhere in Brazil, both in the cities and in the countryside. People can get a cup of rich, aromatic hot coffee almost anywhere, anytime.

瓜拉那：瓜拉那是亚马孙地区特产的一种野莓，是巴西最知名且很早就有历史记载的雨林药用植物之一，内含天然绿色咖啡因、维生素，以及丰富的生物碱、单宁酸、蛋白质等。所制成的饮料风味独特，是一种健康饮料。1907 年，巴西开始用瓜拉那制作饮料，之后很快流行起来。1940 年以后，瓜拉那逐步成为巴西的象征。由于其浓烈的热带地域特色风味，瓜拉那被广泛用于食品、饮料和制药工业，在消费者中很受欢迎。它被誉为巴西的"国饮"，并在 2006 年德国世界杯上被作为巴西足球队的指定饮品。

Guarana: Guarana is a wild berry from the Amazon region, and it is one of Brazil's well-known and long-documented rainforest medicinal plants, with natural green caffeine and vitamins, as well as alkaloids, tannins, proteins, etc. The drink made by guarana has a unique flavor and is also a health drink. Which became popular in Brazil in 1907, when it was first used drinks to make drinks, and after 1940, it gradually became a symbol of the country. Due to its strong tropical regional flavor, guarana is widely used in the food, beverage and pharmaceutical industries, and has a wide range of consumers. It is known as Brazil's "national drink" and was the official drink of the Brazilian soccer team at the 2006 World Cup in Germany.

卡沙萨酒：卡沙萨酒是巴西的国酒，有 500 多年的酿造历史，年产量为 13 亿升，是世界五大名酒之一。其种类很多，有白色的新酿酒，也有金黄色的陈年酒；有大型酒厂生产的，也有家庭作坊酿制的。巴西全国共有 4 000 多个品牌的卡沙萨酒。

Cachaça: Cachaça is the national wine of Brazil, with more than 500 years' brewing history and an annual production of 1.3 billion liters, making it one of the world's five most famous wines. It is available in many varieties, from white to golden-colored aged wines; it is produced in large wineries and home brewed. There are more than 4 000 brands of cachaça throughout Brazil.

宝石：巴西的宝石世界闻名。全球 80% 的宝石产于巴西，高档的有祖母绿、天然水晶，低档的有红宝石、紫晶洞、紫晶石。

Gemstones: Brazilian gemstones are known worldwide. 80% of the world's gemstones are produced in Brazil, with high-grade emeralds and natural crystals, and low-grade rubies, amethyst caves and amethysts.

皮革：巴西的皮革制品也很有名，如皮鞋、拖鞋、皮包、皮夹等。最上等的皮件来自巴西南部，街头的手工艺集市也可以买到手工皮革制品。另外，还有工艺品，如东北部的陶器、手工蕾丝和刺绣；极富诱惑力的印第安手工艺品多半来自亚马孙平原北部，这些华丽的木器、精美的草编饰物等遍布全国。

Leather: Brazil is also famous for its leather, like shoes, slippers, bags and wallets. Some of the finest leather goods come from the streets of the south of the country, where people can also buy handmade leather products at craft fairs. In addition, there are handicrafts, such as pottery, handmade lace and embroidery from the Northeast. Seductive Indian handicrafts are mostly from the northern part of the Amazon Plain, including ornate woodwork, and beautifully woven grass ornaments found throughout the country.

扫码获取：入境须知及海关规定

本节习题

1. 巴西有哪些风物特产？
2. 请设计一条巴西 7 日游经典线路。
3. 巴西地处南半球，什么时候去巴西旅游最佳？

探戈王国——阿根廷
The Kingdom of Tango—Argentina

导读

　　阿根廷的名胜古迹众多，有五月广场、巴里洛切风景区、伊瓜苏瀑布、罗斯格拉希亚雷斯国家公园等。伊瓜苏瀑布最宽处达 4 000 米，为世界上最宽的瀑布；阿空加瓜山是世界最高的死火山及美洲最高峰；乌斯怀亚是世界最南端的城市，被称为"世界尽头"。阿根廷的旅游业发达，是南美洲的主要旅游国家。在阿根廷及周边国家举办的各种体育赛事、政治会议和文化盛会，也吸引着到阿根廷休闲度假或参加商务活动的游客。阿根廷奉行独立自主的对外政策，坚持不结盟立场和尊重各国人民自主选择发展道路、不干涉别国内政、主权国家一律平等的原则。1972 年 2 月 19 日，中国与阿根廷建交，阿政府坚定奉行一个中国政策，两国在各领域的互利合作日益深化，在国际事务中也保持着良好的合作。近年来，中国成为阿根廷第一大家电进口来源国。

一、地理概览 Geography of Argentina

（一）地理位置 Location

　　阿根廷位于南美洲东南部，东濒大西洋，南与南极洲隔海相望，西邻智利，北与玻利维亚、巴拉圭交界，东北与乌拉圭、巴西接壤。阿根廷国土面积为 278.04 万平方千米（不含马尔维纳斯群岛及阿根廷主张的南极洲领土），居拉丁美洲第二位、世界第八位。海岸线长 4 700 千米。

　　Argentina is located in the southeastern part of South America, bordered by the Atlantic Ocean to the east and separated from Antarctica by the sea to the south. It shares its western border with Chile, its northern borders with Bolivia and Paraguay, and its northeastern borders with Uruguay and Brazil. Argentina covers an area of 2.78 million square kilometers (excluding the Malvinas Islands and the Antarctic territory claimed by Argentina), making it the second-largest country in Latin America and the eighth-largest in the world. The country has a coastline that stretches for 4,700 kilometers.

（二）地形和气候 The Land and Seasons

阿根廷地形复杂多样，地势西高东低，安第斯山脉坐落在西部，阿空加瓜山海拔 6 960 米，为南美洲第一高峰。东部为大片冲积平原，中部和东南部为辽阔富饶的潘帕斯草原，这里土地肥沃，是阿根廷物产最丰富的地区。北部为平原，多为沼泽、森林。南部为巴塔哥尼亚高原。火地岛是南美洲最大的岛屿，高山终年积雪。东北沿岸为平原地区。阿根廷境内主要有两大水系，一为拉普拉塔河流域，这一流域以拉普拉塔河为主干，是仅次于亚马孙河的南美洲第二大河。流域支流繁多，构成了庞大的水系网。另一为河川流域，主要由科罗拉多河、内格罗河、萨拉多河等组成，多发源于安第斯山脉并注入大西洋。阿根廷的气候复杂多样，北部属热带气候，中部属亚热带气候，南部为温带气候。年平均气温北部为 24 ℃，南部为 5.5 ℃。

Argentina's topography is complex and varied, with the terrain high in the west and low in the east, and the Andes lying in the west. Mount Aconcagua, which is 6,960 meters above sea level, is the highest peak in South America. In the east, there are large alluvial plains, and in the center and southeast, there is the vast and rich Pampas grassland, which is fertile and the richest resources' area in Argentina. In the north are plains, mostly swamps and forests. In the south is the Patagonian Plateau. Tierra del Fuego is the largest island in South America, with high mountains covered with snow all year round and plains are along the northeast coast. Argentina's territory has two major water systems, one for the La Plata River Basin. This basin with the La Plata River as the main trunk, is the second largest river in South America after the Amazon River. The basin has a large number of tributaries, forming a huge network of water systems. Another water system is the river basin, mainly composed of the Colorado River, the Negro River, the Salado River and so on, mostly originating in the Andes and injected into the Atlantic Ocean. Argentina's climate is complex and diverse, the northern part of the tropical climate, the central part of the subtropical climate, the southern part of the temperate climate. The average annual temperature is 24 ℃ in the north and 5.5 ℃ in the south.

（三）自然资源 Natural Resources

阿根廷拥有丰富的矿产资源，包括石油、天然气、煤、铁、锌、铜、铅、锡、硫磺等。阿根廷林业资源丰富，森林覆盖率达 45.8%。主要农作物小麦为世界五大出口国之一，玉米为世界第二大出口国，大豆为世界第三大生产和出口国。另外，还种植有大量水果，主要有苹果、柑橘、桃、梨等，葡萄生产居世界第四位。阿根廷也是世界主要的肉类生产国和出口国之一，素有"世界粮仓肉库"之称，阿根廷也是世界主要羊毛出口国。阿根廷渔业发达，产值占国民生产总值的 4.6% 左右。

Argentina boasts abundant mineral resources, including oil, natural gas, coal, iron, zinc, copper, lead, tin, and sulfur. The country is also rich in forestry resources, with forest coverage reaching 45.8%. Major crops such as wheat make Argentina one of the world's top five exporters, while corn ranks second globally in exports, and soybeans are the third-largest producer and exporter. Additionally, a wide variety of fruits are cultivated, including apples, citrus fruits, peaches, and pears. Grape production ranks fourth worldwide. Argentina is also a leading producer and exporter of meat, earning it the nickname "the world's granary and meat locker," and it is a significant exporter of wool. The fishing industry is well-developed, contributing approximately 4.6% to the country's GDP.

二、人文概况 Overview of Argentine Humanities

（一）国情认知 Basic Knowledge of National Conditions

阿根廷全名为"阿根廷共和国"，在西班牙语中是"白银"的意思。阿根廷人口增长迅速，1850 年人口只有 110 万，1930 年增至 1 493.6 万，2000 年为 3 626 万，2022 年已近 4 623.5 万。在阿根廷总人口中，白人和印欧混血儿约占 95%，多属意大利和西班牙后裔，印第安人口约 60 万。阿根廷的官方语言是西班牙语。阿根廷居民中的大多数信奉天主教，其余居民信奉基督教新教及其他宗教。阿根廷的国旗呈长方形，旗面自上而下由浅蓝色、白色、浅蓝色三个平行且相等的横长方形组成，白色长方形中间是一轮"五月的太阳"，象征自由和黎明。国歌为《祖国进行曲》。国花是赛波花，货币名称为"比索"。

Argentina's full name is "Argentine Republic", which means "silver" in Spanish. Argentina's population has grown rapidly, from 1.1 million in 1850 to 14.936 million in 1930, 36.26 million in 2000, and nearly 46.235 million in 2022. Of Argentina's total population, whites and Indo-European mestizos make up about 95%, mostly of which are Italian and Spanish descent, and the Indian population is about 600 000 people. The official language of Argentina is Spanish. The majority of Argentina's inhabitants are Catholic, while the rest follow Protestant Christianity and other religions. The national flag of Argentina is rectangular in shape, consisting of three parallel and equal horizontal rectangles from top to bottom, in light blue, white and light blue, with a "May sun" in the middle of the white rectangle, symbolizing freedom and dawn. The national anthem is the *March of the Fatherland*. The national flower is the Sepoy and the currency is the Peso.

（二）历史简介 History of Argentina

16 世纪中叶，阿根廷沦为西班牙殖民地。1776 年，西班牙设立以布宜诺斯艾利斯为首都的拉普拉塔总督区。1810 年 5 月 25 日，阿根廷爆发反抗西班牙殖民统治的"五月革命"，成立了第一个政府委员会。1812 年，民族英雄圣马丁率领人民抗击西班牙殖民军，并于 1816 年 7 月 9 日宣布阿根廷独立。此后，阿根廷长期处于动乱和分裂状态。1853 年，乌尔基萨将军制定了第一部宪法，建立了联邦共和国，其本人成为阿根廷制宪后的第一任总统。1860 年，阿根廷改为共和国。

Argentina was colonized by Spain in the mid-16th century, and in 1776 the Spanish established the Viceroyalty of La Plata, with Buenos Aires as its capital. On May 25, 1810, the "May Revolution" broke out against Spanish colonial rule, and the first government council was established. In 1812, the national hero San Martín led the people to fight against the Spanish colonial army and on July 9, 1816, declared the independence of Argentina. After a long period of turmoil and division, Argentina was transformed into a republic in 1860 when General Urquiza wrote the

阿根廷高乔人和高乔文化

first constitution and established the Federal Republic, of which he became the first president.

（三）经济状况 The Economy

阿根廷是拉丁美洲地区综合国力较强的国家，农牧业发达，工业门类齐全。阿根廷是世界粮食及肉类的重要生产和出口国，素有"世界粮仓和肉库"之称。阿根廷全国大部分地区土壤肥沃，气候温和，适合发展农牧业。东部和中部的潘帕斯草原是著名的农牧业区。阿根廷还是世界上最大的马黛茶生产国。阿根廷的工业主要有钢铁、电力、汽车、石油化工、纺织、机械、食品等，钢铁产量居拉丁美洲国家前列。阿根廷的渔业资源也很丰富，主要渔产品为鳕鱼、鱿鱼、对虾等。阿根廷的矿产资源主要有石油、天然气、煤炭、铁和银等。

Argentina is one of the strongest countries in Latin America in terms of comprehensive national strength, with a well-developed agriculture and livestock industry and a full range of industrial sectors. Argentina is an important producer and exporter of grain and meat in the world, and is known as the "World's Granary and Meat Bank". Most of the country has fertile soil and mild climate, which is suitable for the development of agriculture and animal husbandry. The eastern and central Pampas grassland is a famous agricultural and pastoral area, Argentina is also the world's largest producer of Mate tea. Argentina's industry is mainly steel, electricity, automobiles, petrochemicals, textiles, machinery, food, etc., iron and steel production ranks first in Latin America. Argentina's fishery resources are also very rich in the main fish for cod, squid, shrimp and so on. Argentina's mineral resources are mainly oil, natural gas, coal, iron and silver.

（四）传统文化 Traditional Culture

阿根廷的礼仪和欧美国家大体相似。人们热情奔放，见面都要热情问候、彼此握手，熟人朋友见面还要拥抱或亲吻。阿根廷人普遍喜欢吃欧式西餐，以牛肉、羊肉、猪肉为喜食之物，烤牛肉是阿根廷的第一名菜和家常菜，各类烤肉店随处可见，年人均消费牛肉高达50多千克。人们喜欢的饮料有红茶、咖啡与葡萄酒。有一种名为"马黛茶"的饮料最具有阿根廷特色。马黛茶有平衡神经、净化体内环境、提升血液质量、促进新陈代谢、增强抗病体质等功效。由于当地人常常以肉食为主食，马黛茶的去脂、利尿的功效正好可以有效地缓解肉食摄入过多之后的油腻感。由于当地人常会以马黛茶和吸管作为最珍贵的礼物赠予远方而来的客人和朋友，将之作为象征友谊的纪念品。

Etiquette in Argentina is generally similar to that of European and American countries. People are warm and passionate, greeting each other enthusiastically with handshakes, and friends or acquaintances often embrace or kiss when they meet. Argentinians have a strong preference for European-style Western cuisine, particularly beef, lamb, and pork. Grilled beef is both the top national dish and a common household meal, with various barbecue restaurants found everywhere. The annual per capita beef consumption is over 50 kilograms. Popular beverages include black tea, coffee, and wine. A unique Argentinian drink is "Mate tea" known for its distinctive qualities. Mate tea is believed to balance nervous system function, purify the body, improve blood quality, boost metabolism, and enhance immunity. The fat-reducing and diuretic properties of mate can help alleviate the heaviness that comes from excessive meat intake. It is customary for locals to gift mate and a straw to visitors and friends from afar as a token of friendship and a cherished souvenir.

阿根廷人热情好动又彬彬有礼，大多喜欢体育项目。足球是深受阿根廷国民喜爱的一项运动，在阿根廷首都就有 180 多个设有足球场的俱乐部，全国共有 9 个可容纳万人以上的大型足球运动场供人们使用，享受足球带给他们的快乐。探戈起源于 19 世纪末的布宜诺斯艾利斯，是集音乐、舞蹈、歌唱、诗歌于一体的综合艺术，探戈作为阿根廷的国粹一直流行至今。

到阿根廷，跳一曲探戈

Argentines are passionate, active and polite, and most of them love sports. Soccer is a popular sport among Argentinians, and there are more than 180 clubs with soccer stadiums in the capital city of Argentina, and 9 large soccer stadiums that each can accommodate more than 10,000 people for people to exercise and enjoy the joy that soccer brings them. Tango originated in Buenos Aires at the end of the 19th century, and is a comprehensive art that combines music, dance, singing and poetry, and has been popularized as the national treasure of Argentina to this day.

（五）礼仪禁忌 Social Etiquettes and Taboos

阿根廷人大多信奉天主教，他们忌讳"13"和"星期五"，认为这是令人沮丧和不吉利的，在商务活动中要注意避开这个数字和日期。阿根廷人忌讳菊花，认为菊花是令人悲伤的花，也不喜欢别人送他们衬衫、领带之类的贴身用品。客人所穿衣服的颜色也要注意，灰色是阿根廷人所忌讳的，他们认为这种颜色阴郁、悲伤，因而要避免穿灰色的服装。人们喜欢谈论足球运动、烹饪技巧或家庭陈设等，不喜欢谈论有争议的宗教和政治问题。

Most Argentinians are Catholics, and they consider the number "13" and "Friday" to be unlucky and depressing. In business, it's important to avoid these numbers and dates. They also avoid chrysanthemums, as they are seen as flowers of sadness, and they do not appreciate receiving intimate items like shirts or ties as gifts. Additionally, guests should be mindful of the colors they wear, as grey is considered a gloomy and sad color by Argentinians, and it's best to avoid wearing it. People enjoy discussing topics like soccer, cooking techniques, and home decor, but they prefer to steer clear of controversial religious and political issues.

带你了解更多阿根廷的礼仪知识

（六）传统节日 Festivals

1. 圣马丁将军不朽纪念日 St.Martin's Day

每年的 8 月 17 日是南美西班牙殖民地独立战争领袖，阿根廷民族英雄何塞·德·圣马丁将军逝世纪念日。这一天是阿根廷法定的假日，全国各地都举行纪念活动。首都的纪念仪式在总统府前的五月广场举行。圣马丁的陵墓就在广场右侧的首府大教堂内，纪念活动之隆重，规模之盛大，不亚于阿根廷的国庆日。

Every year on August 17, Argentina commemorates the death of General San Martin, the national hero and leader of the South American wars of independence from Spanish colonial rule. This day is a public holiday in Argentina, marked by commemorative events across the country. In the capital, the main ceremony takes place at Plaza de Mayo in front of the Presidential Palace. San Martin's mausoleum is located inside the Metropolitan Cathedral on the right side of the square. The solemnity and grandeur of the commemorations rival those of Argentina's Independence Day celebrations.

2. 葡萄节 The Grape Harvest Festival

每年的 2 月 22 日—3 月 9 日为阿根廷的传统节日——葡萄节，每当节日来临之际，人们都身着节日服装载歌载舞，随着彩车游行。葡萄节的最高潮是全国选美比赛，每年都有 6 万名漂亮姑娘参加选美，将从中选出葡萄女王皇冠的获得者。选美结束后还要举行西班牙绘画、雕塑等艺术展览及盛大的探戈舞表演。

Every year from February 22 to March 9, Argentina celebrates its traditional festival—the Grape Harvest Festival. During this festive period, people dress in colorful attire, singing and dancing as they join the parade of floats. The highlight of the festival is the national beauty pageant, where 60,000 beautiful young women compete annually for the coveted title of Grape Harvest Queen. After the pageant, there are exhibitions of Spanish paintings and sculptures, as well as grand tango performances.

3. 牧犊节 Animal Husbandry Festival

阿根廷人对牛、羊等牲畜有特殊的感情，特别在一些牧区，如阿亚库乔区，从 1970 年首创牧犊节到现在，阿亚库乔区一直为全国牧犊节的中心。节日期间，白天要举行传统的赛马和骑术表演，晚上则要由全国最优秀的艺术团体表演传统戏剧和歌舞，还要召开研讨全国农业发展形势的圆桌会议。

Argentinians have a special affection for cattle, sheep, and other livestock, especially in some pastoral areas. Since the founding of the Animal Husbandry Festival in 1970, it has been the center of the national Animal Husbandry Festival. During the festival, traditional horse racing and equestrian performances will be held. In the evening, the country's most outstanding art troupes will perform traditional dramas and dances, and during the festival, a roundtable discussion on the national agricultural development situation will be held.

三、旅游观光 Tourism and Sightseeing

（一）主要旅游城市 Major Tourist Cites

1. 布宜诺斯艾利斯 Buenos Aires

布宜诺斯艾利斯是阿根廷的首都和政治、经济、文化中心，素有"南美巴黎"的美誉。它东临拉普拉塔河入海口，西靠有"世界粮仓"之称的潘帕斯草原，风景秀美、气候宜人。布宜诺斯艾利斯市居民中的 98% 为欧洲移民后裔，城市风格和居民生活方式都深受欧洲文化的影响，充满了浓郁的欧陆风情。其建筑风格也奇异多彩，几乎包罗了欧洲古今建筑的全部风格与造型，市内街心公园、广场绿地、纪念碑和雕塑众多；城市建筑也多受欧洲文化影响，至今仍保留了几个世纪建造的前西班牙和意大利风格的古代建筑。

Buenos Aires, the capital and the political, economic, and cultural hub of Argentina, is often referred to as the "Paris of South America". Situated on the eastern shore at the mouth of the Rio de la Plata and bordered to the west by the Pampas, known as the "World's granary", it boasts beautiful scenery and a pleasant climate. About 98% of Buenos Aires' residents are descendants of European immigrants, and the city's style and way of life are heavily influenced by European culture, exuding a rich continental charm. The architectural style is diverse and colorful, encompassing almost all European architectural styles and forms, both ancient and modern. The city is dotted with numerous parks, squares, monuments, and sculptures, and its buildings are greatly influenced by European culture, with some ancient structures still preserving the Spanish and Italian styles from centuries ago.

2. 科尔多瓦 Cordoba

科尔多瓦是阿根廷第二大城市、科尔多瓦省省会、阿根廷中部经济中心。南美洲最早的大坝——普里梅罗河圣罗克水坝就建在这里。科尔多瓦是阿根廷中部地区铁路和公路的交通枢纽，也是重要的旅游胜地，城内造型各异的欧洲古建筑、郊外山区的瑰丽景色和宜人气候吸引了大批外来游客。

Cordoba is the second largest city in Argentina, the capital of Cordoba Province and the economic center of central Argentina. The San Roque Dam on the Primero River, one of the earliest dams in South America, was built here. Cordoba is the central region of Argentina's railroad and highway transportation hub, and also an important tourist attractions. The city's different shapes of the old European architecture, the outskirts of the mountainous region of the magnificent scenery and pleasant climate attract a large number of foreign tourists.

3. 罗萨里奥 Rosario

罗萨里奥是阿根廷第三大城市、巴拉那河最大河港，位于圣菲省东南部，人口约100万。1852年始建，19世纪末20世纪初由法国投资修建港口后，这里逐渐成为世界上重要的谷物港口。罗萨里奥还是一个重要的工业城市，拥有先进的食品加工、制革、造纸、机械工业。该市有发达的公路及铁路网，将之与阿根廷各地相连。

Rosario is the third largest city in Argentina and the largest river port on the Paraná River, located in the southeast of the province of Santa Fe, with a population of about 1 million people. It was founded in 1852, and after the construction of the port in the late 19th and early 20th centuries with the investment of the French, it has gradually become an important grain port in the world. The city is also an important industrial city with advanced food processing, tanning, paper and machinery industries. The city is well connected by highway and railroad to all parts of Argentina.

（二）著名旅游景点 Famous Tourist Attractions

1. 玫瑰宫（总统府）Casa Rosada

玫瑰宫（图4-6）又称总统府，是一座西班牙风格的玫瑰色建筑，位于五月广场东侧。1873年，萨米恩托总统将总统府漆成粉红色，因为红色是当时联邦党的颜色，而白色是反对党的颜色，两种颜色在一起就成了粉红色。

The Casa Rosada (Figure 4-6), also known as the Presidential Palace, is a rose-colored building in Spanish style located on the east side of Plaza de Mayo. In 1873, President

图 4-6　玫瑰宫
Figure 4-6　Casa Rosada

Sarmiento painted the palace pink, as red was the color of the Federalist Party and white represented the opposition. The combination of these two colors resulted in pink.

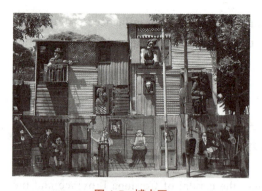

图 4-7 博卡区
Figure 4-7 La Boca

2. 博卡区 La Boca

博卡区（图 4-7）是布宜诺斯艾利斯市的第一个港口。19 世纪中叶，西班牙和意大利移民来到博卡区。由于他们大多从事牛肉加工和运输，因此用建造运输船时留下的船漆粉刷自己的住所，这才有了今天色彩斑斓的景象。博卡区房屋的色彩热情奔放，艺术气息浓厚，非常适合拍照。同时，这里也是伟大的马拉多纳"博卡青年足球队"的诞生地。球队在博卡区的 Bombonera 足球场踢球，距离卡米尼托街有 4 个街区。场内还有一座博物馆，记录了这支球队的光辉历史，喜欢足球的游客一定要去亲身体验一番。此外，这里也是探戈舞的发源地之一。

La Boca (Figure 4-7) is the site of Buenos Aires' first port. In the mid-19th century, Spanish and Italian immigrants settled in La Boca. Many of them worked in beef processing and transportation, and they used leftover paint from shipbuilding to paint their homes, resulting in the vibrant colors seen today. The houses in La Boca are lively and artistic, making it a perfect spot for photography. It is also the birthplace of the legendary Diego Maradona's team, Boca Juniors. The team plays at the Bombonera Stadium, which is just four blocks from Caminito Street. Inside the stadium, there is a museum that chronicles the illustrious history of the team, a must-visit for football enthusiasts. Additionally, La Boca is one of the birthplaces of the tango dance.

图 4-8 马德罗港
Figure 4-8 Puerto Madero

3. 马德罗港 Puerto Madero

马德罗港（图 4-8）是布宜诺斯艾利斯最新开发的市区，这个年轻的市区坐落在市中心和 San Telmo 区的东面，位于古老的海港港区中，在阿根廷的进出口贸易和海运中起着不可估量的作用。自 20 世纪 90 年代开始，这里的房地产开始增值，目前是布宜诺斯艾利斯市最繁荣、游客数量最多的观光区。在这里，你可以看到许多用旧砖砌成的仓库被巧妙地改造成现代化公寓、办公室、酒店和餐馆。现代与传统建筑风格的交相辉映，吸引着来自世界各地的游客。

Puerto Madero（Figure 4-8）is located in the east of the city center and the SanTelmo district. It is located in the old harbor area. It is a newly developed urban area in Buenos Aires. It plays an immeasurable role in Import and export trade in Argentina and shipping. Since the 1990s, the real estate here has begun to appreciate, and it is now a prosperous tourist area with a large number of tourists. Here you can find many warehouses built with old bricks that have been ingeniously transformed into modern LOFTs, offices, hotels and restaurants. The mordern buildings mixed with the traditional style attract tourists from all over the world.

4. 阿根廷湖 Argentina Lake

阿根廷湖（图 4-9）是南美洲罕见的冰川湖之一。它位于阿根廷南部圣克鲁斯省，面积达

1 414平方千米，以冰雪堆积景观而闻名，有来自周围150多个冰川冰流和冰块。巨大的冰块相互碰撞，缓慢向前移动，有时会形成高达80米的造型奇特的冰墙。冰块最后全部汇入阿根廷湖中，形成一座纯白色的冰山雕塑。湖边白雪皑皑，山下森林郁郁葱葱，景色迷人，是阿根廷最令人神往的旅游胜地。

图4-9 阿根廷湖

Figure 4-9 Argentina Lake

Argentina Lake (Figure 4-9) is one of the rare glacial lakes in South America. It is a glacial lake located in the province of Santa Cruz in southern Argentina, covering an area of 1 414 square kilometers. It is famous for its ice accumulation landscape. The lake receives ice streams and ice from more than 150 surrounding glaciers. Huge blocks of ice collided with each other and moved slowly forward, sometimes forming strangely shaped ice walls up to 80 meters high. Then all of them are accumulated in the Argentine Lake, forming a pure white iceberg sculpture. Surrounded by snow-capped peaks by the lake, there are lush forests under the mountains and charming scenery, it is a fascinating tourist attraction in Argentina.

5. 圣马丁将军公园 Parque General San Martin

圣马丁将军公园（图4-10）位于阿根廷门多萨，是该地区最古老、最主要的公园，占地420公顷。公园内绿树成荫，风景优美，有一个迷人的湖泊和几座博物馆可供参观。公园内的玫瑰园种有许多玫瑰，还有一条法式长廊，非常适合休闲散步。

Parque General San Martin (Figure 4-10) is located in Mendoza, Argentina. It is the oldest and the main park in the area, covering an area of 420 hectares. The park is leafy and scenic, with a stunning lake and several museums to visit.

图4-10 圣马丁将军公园

Figure 4-10 Parque General San Martin

The rose garden in the park has many roses, and there is a French-style promenade, which is very suitable for leisure walks.

6. 火地岛国家公园 Tierra del Fuego National Park

火地岛国家公园（图4-11）是世界最南端的一个国家公园。这里充满了大自然的气息，拥有原始的自然景观、湖泊、溪流、森林和海岸，还有各种野生动物和鸟类。这里雨水充沛，一到秋天，山坡上的落叶就红了。游客可以沿3号公路前往阿拉曼主教露营站，再乘坐小火车前往国家公园。火车站现已改建成博物馆，挂着许多历史照片，展柜里还陈列着一

图4-11 火地岛国家公园

Figure 4-11 Tierra del Fuego National Park

些实物和资料。

Tierra del Fuego National Park (Figure 4-11) is a national park at the southern end of the world. This place is filled with the scent of nature, boasting primitive natural landscapes, lakes, streams, forests, and coasts, as well as a variety of wildlife and birds. It is abundant with rain, and when autumn arrives, the leaves on the hillsides turn red. Tourists can follow Route 3 to the Bishop Alamein Camping Station and take the small train to the National Park. The railway station has now been converted into a museum，where many historical photos are hung，and some objects and materials are also displayed in the showcase.

7. 世界尽头的小邮局 Correo del fin del mundo

图 4-12　世界尽头的小邮局
Figure 4-12　Correo del fin del mundo

这座小邮局建在火地岛国家公园南端的巴黑亚湾边上，距南极较近，可谓世界尽头的邮局（图 4-12）。邮局面积很小，里面挂满了各式各样的明信片和邮票。小邮局里出售印有"世界尽头邮政"字样的明信片，可以现场填写后邮寄到世界各地。整个邮局只有一位老爷爷，为大家盖邮戳寄信件，每天都有无数游客慕名而来。

This small post office is located on the shore of Bahia Ensenada at the southern end of Tierra del Fuego National Park, relatively close to Antarctica, making it truly a post office at the end of the world which is called Correo del fin del mundo（Figure 4-12）in Spanish. The post office is very small, filled with all kinds of postcards and stamps. Inside the small post office, they sell postcards with the words "End of the World Post Office" printed on them, which can be filled out on the spot and sent to various destinations worldwide. There is only one elderly gentleman running the entire post office, stamping letters for visitors, and every day countless tourists come to visit.

（三）旅游购物 Shopping

马黛茶：马黛生长于充满神秘和幻想的南美丛林，在阿根廷等南美国家拥有 400 多年的饮用历史，与足球、探戈、烤肉并称为阿根廷四宝。马黛茶源自魁特查语中的"mati"这个词，意思是"葫芦"。西班牙殖民者称这种茶为"马黛茶"，当地人称之为"caiguá"，意思是"与巴拉圭茶有关的东西"。马黛茶也有其他的名字，如"耶稣会茶""巴拉圭来的茶"，以及"传教士的茶"。

Mate tea: Mate grows in the South American jungle full of mystery and fantasy. In Argentina and other South American countries, it has more than 400 years of drinking history，with soccer, tango，and barbecue known as Argentina's four treasures. Mate tea comes from the word "mati" in the Quetzal language，which means "gourd". The Spanish colonizers called this tea "Mate" and the locals called it "caiguá", which means "something related to Paraguayan tea". It was also known by other names，such as "Jesuit tea" "tea from Paraguay" and "missionary tea".

葡萄酒：阿根廷不仅是世界上的第五大产酒国，同时更是全球第四大葡萄酒消费国。阿根廷的大多数葡萄园都受安第斯山脉的影响，浓郁的马尔贝克（Malbec）和芬芳的特浓情（Torrontes）葡萄是阿根廷最重要的葡萄品种。世界著名的酒评家帕克（Robert Parker）的《葡萄酒倡导者》杂志称阿根廷是"世界上最令人兴奋的新兴葡萄酒产区之一"。

Grape wine: Argentina is not only the fifth largest producer of wine in the world, but also the fourth largest consumer of wine. The majority of Argentina's vineyards are influenced by the Andes Mountains, and the rich Malbec and fragrant Torrontes grapes are the most important grape varieties in the country. World-renowned wine critic Robert Parker's *Wine Advocate* magazine has called Argentina "one of the world's most exciting new wine regions".

皮革制品：阿根廷皮革制品种类丰富，如皮衣和皮鞋式样好、质量较高；貂、狐、水獭等裘皮服装也较著名，而且价格比欧洲和北美要低不少。

Leather products: Argentina leather products such as leather jackets and shoes in good style, are in high quality; mink, fox, otter and other fur clothing are also more famous, and the price is much lower than in Europe and North America.

红纹石（阿根廷石）：红纹石的学名叫菱锰矿，因为它在形成过程中含有大量的锰离子，所以它的主色调是粉红色。"Rhodochrosite"（红纹石）这个单词源自两个希腊词，分别指玫瑰（rose）和颜色（color），以凸显它特殊的色彩。菱锰矿最早产于阿根廷，因而有"阿根廷石""印加玫瑰"的别名。

Rhodochrosite (Argentine Stone): The scientific name for rhodochrosite is manganese carbonate. Its pink hue results from the high concentration of manganese ions present during its formation. The word "rhodochrosite" is derived from two Greek words, one meaning "rose" and the other meaning "color," emphasizing its unique hue. Rhodochrosite was first discovered in Argentina, which is why it is also known as the "Argentine Stone" or "Inca Rose".

本节习题

1. 简述阿根廷旅游资源与主要旅游景点。
2. 设计一条阿根廷七日游的经典路线。

扫码获取：入境须知及海关规定

学习目标

1. 熟悉非洲旅游区主要客源国和目的地国的国情。

Get familiar with the national conditions of major tourist source and destination countries in Africa tourist region.

2. 能根据各国特点开展有针对性的客源开发策划和旅游产品设计。

Be able to carry out targeted tourist source development planning and product design according to the characteristics of various countries.

3. 能根据不同旅行团的需求，设计出合适的旅游线路。

Be able to design suitable tourist routes according to the clients' needs.

4. 掌握埃及、南非主要城市和著名景点的概况，能运用所学理论知识从事实际接待和服务工作。

Master the general situation of major cities and famous scenic spots in Egypt and South Africa, be able to put theoretic knowledge into real practice such as reception and service work.

第一节　非洲旅游区特征

The General Situation of Africa Tourist region

非洲的全称是阿非利加洲，意思是阳光灼热的地方。非洲位于亚洲的西南面，东濒印度洋，西临大西洋，北隔地中海与欧洲相望，东北角以苏伊士运河为非洲和亚洲的分界。非洲为高原大陆，地势比较平坦。东南部高，西北部低。大陆海岸线平直，缺少海湾和岛屿。非洲沙漠面积约占全洲面积的1/3，为沙漠面积最大的洲。其中，撒哈拉沙漠是世界上最大的沙漠。非洲东部有世界上最大的裂谷带。除了沙漠，非洲大陆还是一片人与自然、人与动物和谐相处的乐土。埃及、南非、肯尼亚、毛里求斯、塞舌尔、坦桑尼亚、突尼斯等旅游业相对成熟的国家和地区都成为中国公民自费出境旅游的目的地，其旅游产品呈现"神秘"和"高端"的特点。本章主要介绍埃及、南非两个非洲国家的概况、民俗风情、主要旅游城市及景点、旅游资讯等。

非洲旅游区特征（英文版）

非洲面积约 3 020 万平方千米（包括附近岛屿），约占世界陆地总面积的 20.4%，仅次于亚洲，为世界第二大洲。非洲目前有 60 个国家和地区。在地理上，习惯将非洲分为北非、东非、西非、中非和南非五个地区。北非包括埃及、苏丹、利比亚、突尼斯、阿尔及利亚、摩洛哥、亚速尔群岛、马德拉群岛。东非包括埃塞俄比亚、厄立特里亚、索马里、吉布提、肯尼亚、坦桑尼亚、乌干达、卢旺达、布隆迪和塞舌尔。西非包括毛里塔尼亚、西撒哈拉、塞内加尔、冈比亚、马里、布基纳法索、几内亚、几内亚比绍、佛得角、塞拉利昂、利比里亚、科特迪瓦、加纳、多哥、贝宁、尼日尔、尼日利亚和加那利群岛。中非包括乍得、中非、喀麦隆、赤道几内亚、加蓬、刚果（布）、刚果（金）、圣多美和普林西比。南非包括赞比亚、安哥拉、津巴布韦、马拉维、莫桑比克、博茨瓦纳、纳米比亚、南非、斯威士兰、莱索托、马达加斯加、科摩罗、毛里求斯、留尼汪、圣赫勒拿等。

非洲大陆海岸线全长 30 500 千米，海岸比较平直，缺少海湾与半岛。非洲是世界各洲中岛屿数量最少的一个洲。除马达加斯加岛外，其余多为小岛。非洲被称为高原大陆，平均海拔为 650 米。地势东南高、西北低。乞力马扎罗山是一座活火山，海拔 5 895 米，为非洲最高峰，山岳景观秀丽。非洲东部的大裂谷是世界上最长的裂谷带，是非洲地震最频繁、最强烈的地区，也是非洲自然旅游资源最丰富的地区。非洲的大河流受到地质构造和其他自然因素的影响，水系较复杂，多急流、瀑布。湖泊多分布在东非裂谷带。赤道横贯非洲的中部，非洲 75% 的土地受到太阳的垂直照射，年平均气温在 20 ℃ 以上的热带占全洲的 95%，其中有一半以上的地区终年炎热，故有"热带大陆"之称。境内降水较少，仅刚果盆地和几内亚湾沿岸平均年降水量在 1 500 毫米以上，平均年降水量在 500 毫米以下的地区占全洲面积的 50%。刚果盆地和几内亚湾沿岸一带属热带雨林气候。地中海沿岸一带夏热干燥、冬暖多雨，属地中海气候。北非撒哈拉沙漠、南非高原西部雨量极少，属热带沙漠气候。其他广大地区夏季多雨、冬季干旱，属热带草原气候。马达加斯加岛东部属热带雨林气候，西部属热带草原气候。

非洲人口总数约 12.86 亿（2019 年），仅次于亚洲，居世界第二位。但非洲人口分布极不均衡，尼罗河沿岸及三角洲地区，每平方千米约 1 000 人；撒哈拉、纳米布、卡拉哈迪等沙漠和一些干旱草原、半沙漠地带每平方千米不到 1 人，还有大片的无人区。非洲是世界上民族成分最复杂的地区。非洲大多数民族属于黑种人，其余属白种人和黄种人。非洲人信仰的宗教主要有三种：传统宗教、伊斯兰教和基督教。历史上，非洲各国的经济曾长期遭受西方发达国家的控制，使非洲成为世界上经济发展水平最低的洲，大多数国家经济落后。农业人口约占全洲总人口的 2/3，许多经济作物的产量在世界上占有重要地位，如咖啡、花生、可可、丁香、棕榈油等。采矿业和轻工业是非洲工业的主要部门。非洲是世界上交通运输业比较落后的一个洲，还没有形成完整的交通运输体系。交通运输以公路为主，海运业占一定地位，航空业发展较快。

非洲大陆幅员辽阔、历史悠久、文化独特，拥有丰富的历史文化遗迹、秀丽的自然风光和奇异的野生动植物，具有发展旅游业的巨大潜力。15 世纪以来，由于长期遭受西方殖民者的侵略与掠夺，非洲大多数国家都属于发展中国家，经济相对比较落后，旅游基础设施不完善。一些国家和地区甚至长期社会动荡、战乱频繁、自然灾害严重，影响着旅游业的发展。

最近 20 年来，非洲许多国家开始重视旅游开发，充分利用本地独有的自然风光和民俗风情，针对游客的猎奇心理，大力开发各种专项旅游活动，如特色风光游、沙漠探险游、历史考古游等，吸引着来自世界各地的游客。近年来旅游业发展较快的国家有埃及、摩洛哥、突尼斯、南非、肯尼亚、乌干达、毛里求斯和塞舌尔等。尽管非洲旅游业发展潜力巨大，但其接待游客数和旅游业收入在全球旅游行业中的所占比重仍然很低。UNWTO 发布报告称，2018 年非洲共接待游客 7 834 万人，同比增长 10.5%，占全球比重仅为 5.6%；创收约 500 亿美元，同比增长 13.1%，占全球比重仅为 3.4%。2018 年，非洲接待游客数量最多的前五名国家分别是摩洛哥、埃及、南非、突尼斯和津巴布韦。非洲旅游业收入最多的国家前五位分别是埃及、南非、摩洛哥、坦桑尼亚和突尼斯。随着中非关系的进一步加强，2018 年共有 20 个非洲国家和地区对中国游客实施免签或落地签政策。埃及、突尼斯、摩洛哥、阿尔及利亚、毛里求斯、肯尼亚、南非等国家都是中国游客青睐的目的地。中青旅遨游网发布的《2018 中国公民非洲旅游报告》显示，中国赴非游客人数再创新高，增长速度持续保持高位，年均增幅超过 40%；中国游客出境游十大首选目的地中非洲国家占比达 30%。当然，中国人在非洲旅游目的地的选择上，具有鲜明的"南北开花、中间突破、海岛添彩"的特点，即北部以埃及为重点，逐渐向摩洛哥、突尼斯等国扩展；南部以南非为重点，逐渐向纳米比亚、博茨瓦纳、津巴布韦等国扩展；中部以肯尼亚、坦桑尼亚、埃塞俄比亚等国为重点。同时，非洲的毛里求斯、塞舌尔等高端精品海岛在中国旅游市场中也颇受欢迎，已成为具有鲜明特点和独特优势的海岛旅游目的地。

第二节 非洲之旅

Travel in Africa

金字塔之国——埃及
The Land of Pyramids—Egypt

导读

埃及历史悠久，名胜古迹很多，主要旅游景点有金字塔、狮身人面像、卢克索神庙、亚历山大灯塔遗址、阿斯旺高坝、沙姆沙伊赫等。红海和地中海是埃及最具潜力的两大旅游资源，红海、沙漠、航海等主题等都会使人产生强烈的旅游欲望。随着阿维纳特山和大贾勒弗地区沙漠山洞越来越多地被考古发现，考古游、尼罗河上漂流游、海上休闲游、生态游、体育游、沙漠徒步游等旅游业务得到较快的发展。目前，旅游业已成为埃及最重要的支柱产业。埃及奉行独立自主、不结盟政策，主张在相互尊重和不干涉内政的基础上建立国际政治和经济新秩序，加强南北对话和南南合作；致力于加强阿拉伯国家团结合作；反对国际恐怖主义；重视大国外交，巩固同美国的特殊战略关系，加强同欧洲联盟俄罗斯等大国关系；积极加强同发展中国家的关系，在阿拉伯国家联盟、非洲联盟、伊斯兰合作组织等国际组织中较为活跃；日益重视经济外交。中国和埃及两国有着传统的友谊，2 000 多年前就有了友好的交往。1956 年 5 月，埃及与中国建交，成为第一个承认中国的阿拉伯、非洲国家。建交以来，中埃两国友好合作关系不断发展。特别是近年来，两国领导人互访频繁，双方在政治、经济、科技和文化等领域的合作日益密切。

一、地理概览 Geography of Egypt

（一）位置 Location

埃及，全称阿拉伯埃及共和国，是欧、亚、非三大洲的交通枢纽。北部经地中海与欧洲相通，西连利比亚，南接苏丹，东临红海并与巴勒斯坦接壤，东南与约旦、沙特阿拉伯相望，海岸线长 2 700 多千米。苏伊士运河沟通了大西洋与印度洋。埃及国土面积约 100 万平方千米，疆域横跨亚、非两洲，大部分位于非洲东北部，只有苏伊士运河以东的西奈半岛位于亚洲西南部，国土略呈不规则的四方形。

Egypt, officially known as the Arab Republic of Egypt, serves as a transportation hub connecting Europe, Asia, and Africa. To the north, it is linked to Europe via the Mediterranean Sea; to the west, it borders Libya; to the south, it shares a border with Sudan; and to the east, it faces the Red Sea and borders Palestine. Southeast of Egypt lie Jordan and Saudi Arabia, with a coastline stretching over 2,700 kilometers. The Suez Canal connects the Atlantic and Indian Oceans. Egypt covers an area of approximately 1 million square kilometers, straddling both Africa and Asia. Most of its territory is located in the northeastern part of Africa, with only the Sinai Peninsula lying to the east of the Suez Canal in the southwestern part of Asia. The country's landmass is roughly in the shape of an irregular quadrilateral.

（二）地形和气候 The Land and Seasons

埃及地形平缓，没有大山，最高峰凯瑟琳山海拔 2 642 米。埃及全国干燥少雨。埃及南部属热带沙漠气候，夏季气温较高，昼夜温差较大；尼罗河三角洲和北部沿海地区属亚热带地中海气候，气候相对温和；其余大部分地区属热带沙漠气候。1 月平均气温为 12 ℃，7 月平均气温为 26 ℃，最高气温可达 40 ℃；年均降水量为 50 ～ 200 毫米。

Egypt's terrain is relatively flat, lacking major mountains, with its highest peak being Mount Catherine at an elevation of 2,642 meters. The country is characterized by its dry climate and scarce rainfall, with hot and arid conditions prevailing. Southern Egypt experiences a tropical desert climate, where summer temperatures are high and there is a significant temperature difference between day and night. The Nile Delta and the northern coastal regions enjoy a subtropical Mediterranean climate, which is relatively mild. The rest of the country predominantly has a tropical desert climate. The average temperature in January is 12 ℃, while in July it is 26 ℃, with maximum temperatures reaching up to 40 ℃. The annual average rainfall ranges from 50 to 200 mm.

（三）自然资源 Natural Resources

埃及主要资源是石油、天然气、磷酸盐、铁等。已探明的储量为：石油 48 亿桶，天然气 3.2 万亿立方米，磷酸盐约 70 亿吨，铁矿 6 000 万吨。此外，还有锰、煤、金、锌、铬、银、钼、铜和滑石等。2015 年，埃及近海海域发现地中海范围内迄今最大的天然气田，潜在天然气蕴藏量为 8 500 亿立方米。埃及的石油和天然气探明储量分别位居非洲国家第五位和第四位。平均原油日产量达 71.15 万桶，天然气日产量达 1.68 亿立方米，国内消耗的天然气数量占天然气总产量的 70%，其余 30% 供出口。埃及电力供应以火电为主，占 86.9%。全国电网覆盖率达 99.3%，世界排名第 28 位。

Egypt's primary resources include oil, natural gas, phosphates, and iron. The proven reserves are as follows: 4.8 billion barrels of oil, 3.2 trillion cubic meters of natural gas, approximately 7 billion tons of phosphates, and 60 million tons of iron ore. Additionally, Egypt has resources such as manganese, coal, gold, zinc, chromium, silver, molybdenum, copper, and talc. In 2015, the largest natural gas field in the Mediterranean to date was discovered in Egypt's offshore waters, with potential reserves of 850 billion cubic meters. Egypt ranks fifth in Africa for proven oil reserves and fourth for natural gas reserves. The average daily crude oil production is 711,500 barrels, and natural gas production is 168 million cubic meters per day. Of the total natural gas production, 70% is consumed domestically, while the remaining 30% is exported. Egypt's electricity supply is predominantly thermal power, accounting for 86.9%. The national power grid coverage rate is 99.3%, ranking 28th in the world.

二、人文概况 Overview of Egyptian Humanities

（一）国情认知 Basic Knowledge of National Conditions

埃及是阿拉伯世界中人口最多的国家，人口达 1.11 亿（2022 年），其中绝大多数生活在尼罗河谷和三角洲，主要是阿拉伯人。埃及的官方语言为阿拉伯语，通用语言为英语和法语。伊斯兰教为埃及国教，信奉伊斯兰教的阿拉伯人约占总人口的 87%，信奉基督教的科普特人约占 1.8%，希腊东正教、天主教等其他基督教派教徒约 25 万人，还有少数犹太教教徒。埃及的国旗呈长方形，自上而下由红色、白色、黑色的平行且相等的横长方形组成，白色部分中间有国徽图案。红色象征革命，白色象征纯洁和光明前途，黑色象征埃及过去的黑暗岁月。埃及的国徽图案为一只金色的鹰，称萨拉丁雄鹰。金鹰昂首挺立，舒展双翼，象征胜利、勇敢和忠诚，它是埃及人民不畏烈日风暴、在高空自由飞翔的化身。国歌为《阿拉伯埃及共和国国歌》，国花为莲花。世界上莲花的品种很多，而埃及莲花首屈一指。国石是橄榄石，橄榄石产于火成岩中，它的形成必须经历"痛苦"的磨难。经过火的锻造，橄榄石呈现耀眼的绿色，具有玻璃光泽，十分美丽。

Egypt is the most populous country in the Arab world, with a population of 111 million（2022）, the vast majority of whom live in the Nile Valley and Delta and are predominantly Arab. The official language of Egypt is Arabic, and English and French are commonly spoken. Islam is the state religion of Egypt, with about 87% of Arabs practicing Islam, about 1.8% of Copts practicing Christianity, about 250 000 Greek Orthodox, Catholics and other Christians, and a small number of Jews. The Egyptian flag is rectangular, consisting of three parallel and equal horizontal rectangles in red, white and black from top to bottom, with the national emblem in the center of the white part. The red color symbolizes the revolution, the white color symbolizes purity and a bright future, and the black color symbolizes the dark years of Egypt's past. Egypt's national emblem design for a golden eagle, called the Saladin eagle. The golden eagle stands tall and spreads its wings, symbolizing victory, bravery and loyalty, and it is the embodiment of the Egyptian people's defiance of the scorching sun and storms and their freedom to fly high in the sky. The national anthem is the *National Anthem of the Arab Republic of Egypt*, and the national flower is the lotus. There are many varieties of lotus flowers in the world, but the Egyptian lotus flower is second to none. The national stone is peridot, which is produced in igneous rock and must undergo "painful" ordeals to form. Forged by fire, peridot takes on a dazzling green color and a glassy luster.

（二）历史简介 History of Egypt

埃及历史悠久，是世界四大文明发祥地之一。埃及在公元前 3200 年就形成了统一的奴隶制国家。公元前 11 世纪至公元前 7 世纪，埃及断断续续被亚述、波斯、马其顿和罗马帝国征服。公元 7 世纪中期，阿拉伯人入侵，建立阿拉伯帝国。1517 年被土耳其人征服，成为奥斯曼帝国的行省。1798—1801 年被拿破仑占领。1882 年被英国军队占领，1914 年成为英国的保护国。1922 年 2 月 28 日，英国被迫承认埃及独立，但仍保留对埃及的国防、外交等权力。1952 年，以纳赛尔为首的"自由军官组织"发动军事政变，推翻法鲁克王朝，成立"革命指导委员会"，埃及获得真正的独立。1953 年 6 月 18 日废除帝制，成立共和国。1954 年，英国被迫同意分批从埃及撤军，1956 年英军全部撤出埃及，但仍然保持对苏伊士运河区的事实治权。1956 年，纳赛尔将苏伊士运河收为国有，引发第二次中东战争，战后，埃及奠定了在中东的领导地位，英国宣布从苏伊士运河以东撤退。1958 年 2 月，埃及与叙利亚合并。1961 年叙利亚独立。1971 年，埃及改名为阿拉伯埃及共和国。

Egypt has a long history and is one of the four great civilizations of the world. Egypt formed a unified slave state in 3200 BC. In the 11th and 7th centuries BC, Egypt was intermittently conquered by the Assyrian, Persian, Macedonian and Roman empires. In the middle of the 7th century AD, the Arabs invaded and established the Arabian Empire. 1517, it was conquered by the Turks and became a province of the Ottoman Empire. From 1798 to 1801, it was occupied by Napoleon. In 1882, it was occupied by the British army, and in 1914, it became a British protectorate. On February 28, 1922, the British were forced to recognize the independence of Egypt, but retained the power of national defense and diplomacy over Egypt. In 1952, the "Free Officers Organization" led by Nasser staged a military coup to overthrow the Farouk dynasty and set up the "Revolutionary Steering Committee", which led to Egypt's real independence. In 1953, the imperial system was abolished and a republic was established on June 18. In 1954, Britain was forced to agree to withdraw its troops from Egypt in stages, and in 1956 all British troops were withdrawn from Egypt, but still maintained de facto rule over the Suez Canal Zone. In 1956, Nasser nationalized the Suez Canal, which triggered the Second Middle East War, after which Egypt established its leadership in the Middle East, and Britain declared its withdrawal from the eastern part of the Suez Canal. In February, 1958, Egypt merged with Syria. In 1961 Syria became independent, and in 1971 Egypt was renamed the Arab Republic of Egypt.

（三）经济状况 The Economy

埃及是非洲第三大经济体，属开放型市场经济，拥有相对完整的工业、农业和服务业体系。服务业约占国内生产总值的 50%。石油资源丰富，工业以纺织、食品加工等轻工业为主。农村人口占总人口的 55%。国民经济以农业为主，盛产棉花、小麦、水稻、花生、甘蔗、椰枣、水果和蔬菜等农产品，长纤维棉驰名世界。农业占 GDP 的 14%。石油和天然气、旅游、侨汇以及苏伊士运河是四大外汇收入来源。

Egypt is the third largest economy in Africa, with an open market economy and a relatively complete system of industry, agriculture and services. The service industry accounts for about 50% of the GDP. It is rich in petroleum resources, and its industry is dominated by light industries such as textiles and food processing. The rural population accounts for 55% of the total population. The economy is based on agriculture, producing agricultural products such as cotton, wheat, rice, peanuts, sugar cane, dates, fruits and vegetables, and long-fiber cotton is world famous. Agriculture accounts for 14% of the GDP. Oil and gas, tourism, overseas remittances and the Suez Canal are the four major sources of foreign exchange earnings.

（四）传统文化 Traditional Culture

埃及人的交往礼仪既延承传统的民族习俗，又通行西方人的做法，上层人士更倾向于欧美礼仪。在埃及，正式场合通常穿西装。女孩一般不穿暴露过多的奇装异服，甚至在一些思想保守的地区，女子还保留着蒙面纱的习俗。珠宝首饰在古埃及人的心中既是生者的装饰品，也是死者的陪葬品，现已成为尼罗河畔男男女女生活社交的必需品，不论贫穷还是富有，人们都很喜爱佩戴首饰，尤其讲究佩戴脚镯。埃及人见面时异常热情，一般是先握手，随后亲吻对方的脸颊。男子之间一般先吻左颊，再吻右颊，亲戚或关系密切者，再吻一下左颊；妇女们一般是先吻一下右颊，再吻一下左颊，亲戚或关系密切者，再吻一下右颊。当地还有一种"吻手礼"，这是对恩人表示感谢的礼节。异性之间只行握手礼，男士不宜主动伸手，握手时也不应交叉相握。男士握手时必须从座位上站起来，女士则不必，可以继续坐在椅子上。

Egyptian social etiquette combines traditional customs with Western practices, with the upper class leaning more towards European and American manners. Egyptians typically wear long garments such as robes, trousers, and skirts. Girls generally avoid wearing short, tight, or overly revealing clothing. In more conservative areas, women may still practice the tradition of wearing veils. Jewelry holds significant cultural importance, regarded by ancient Egyptians as adornments for both the living and the deceased. Today, jewelry is considered an essential part of social life along the Nile, cherished by both men and women regardless of their economic status, with a particular emphasis on wearing anklets. Egyptians are exceptionally warm and friendly when they meet each other, usually starting with a handshake followed by cheek kisses. Among men, it is customary to kiss the left cheek first, then the right, and for relatives or close friends, to kiss the left cheek again. Women typically kiss the right cheek first, then the left, and for relatives or close friends, kiss the right cheek again. There is also a "hand-kissing" gesture used to express gratitude towards benefactors. Between men and women, only handshakes are exchanged, and men should not initiate the handshake. When shaking hands, crossing hands is avoided. Men are expected to stand up from their seats when shaking hands, while women may remain seated.

埃及人不忌讳外国人的拜访，甚至很欢迎外国人的访问，并引以为荣。但异性拜访是禁止的，即使在埃及人之间，男女同学、同事也不能相互拜访。除贫困户外，埃及人家里都有客厅，卧室作为私房是不欢迎外人入内的。拜访时应主动问候老人并与之攀谈，埃及人乐于天南海北地聊天，一般应在聊完一个话题后告辞。到埃及进行商务活动，最好是在 10 月至次年 4 月间前往。另外，当地每周的工作日是从星期六到下星期四，星期五是伊斯兰教的休息日。在埃及从事商务活动，拜访前应先预约，但当地商业界人士不一定守时。埃及人的主食有米饭、面包、小麦饼、玉米饼和奶酪等，荤菜有牛肉、羊肉、骆驼肉、鸡肉、鸭肉等，素菜有洋葱、黄瓜、南瓜、西红柿、扁豆、蚕豆等。一般口味偏浓重，喜麻辣味道，也爱吃甜食，正式宴会最后一道菜都是上甜食。他们对中国的川菜很欣赏。喜欢饮茶和咖啡，忌讳饮酒，还忌吃猪肉、狗肉。请客时菜肴丰盛，气氛热烈。主

埃及风俗：再穷也不能少了金首饰

人总是希望客人多吃点。

Egyptians are not averse to visits from foreigners; in fact, they welcome and take pride in such visits. However, visits between people of the opposite sex are prohibited, even among Egyptians, meaning classmates and colleagues of different genders cannot visit each other. Except in impoverished households, Egyptian homes typically have a living room, while bedrooms are considered private and off-limits to outsiders. When visiting, it is customary to greet and engage in conversation with the elderly. Egyptians enjoy chatting about a wide range of topics, and it is polite to take your leave after a conversation concludes. For business activities, the best time to visit Egypt is from October to April. The local workweek runs from Saturday to Thursday, with Friday being the Islamic day of rest. When doing business in Egypt, it's important to schedule an appointment before visiting. However, local business people may not always be punctual. Egyptian staple foods include rice, bread, wheat and corn cakes, and cheese. Meat dishes feature beef, lamb, camel, chicken, and duck, while vegetable dishes include onions, cucumbers, pumpkins, tomatoes, lentils, and fava beans. The cuisine generally has strong flavors, with a preference for spicy and sweet dishes. Formal banquets typically end with a dessert course, and Egyptians have a particular appreciation for Chinese Sichuan cuisine. They enjoy drinking tea and coffee but avoid alcohol, pork, and dog meat. When hosting, the dishes are abundant, and the atmosphere is lively, with hosts encouraging guests to eat heartily.

（五）礼仪禁忌 Social Etiquettes and Taboos

在人际交往中，埃及人所采用的见面礼节主要是握手礼。同埃及人握手时，忌用左手。除了握手礼，埃及人在某些场合还会使用拥抱或亲吻礼。埃及人所采用的亲吻礼，往往会因为交往对象的不同而采用亲吻不同部位的具体方式。其中最常见的形式有三种：一是吻面礼，一般用于亲友之间，尤其是女性之间；二是吻手礼，是向尊长表示敬意或是向恩人致谢时用的；三是飞吻礼，多见于情侣之间。埃及人非常好客，贵客登门会令其十分愉快。去埃及人家里做客时，应注意三点：其一，事先需预约，并要以主人方便为宜，通常在晚上6点以后及斋月期间不宜进行拜访；其二，按惯例，穆斯林家里的女性，尤其是女主人是不待客的，故切勿向其打听或问候；其三，就座之后，切勿将足底朝外，更不要朝向对方。

In interpersonal communication, the meeting etiquette is used by Egyptians is mainly a handshake. When shaking hands with Egyptians, avoid using your left hand. In addition to the handshake, Egyptians will also use the embrace or kiss in some occasions. The kissing salute adopted by Egyptians usually involves the special ways of kissing different parts of the body depending on the different objects. There are three kinds of the most common form: First, a kiss face, it is generally used between friends and relatives, especially between women; Second, a kiss hand salute, it is to honor the elders to show respect or to the benefactor to thank with; Third, a flying kiss salute, it is more often seen between lovers. Egyptians are very hospitable. Guests at the door will make them very pleasant. To go to the Egyptian home as a guest, people should pay attention to three points: First, make an appointment in advance, for the convenience of the host as appropriate. Do not visit after 6 : 00 p.m. and during the Ramadan; Second, according to the custom, Muslim women in the house, especially the hostess is not hospitality, so do not ask or greetings; Third, after the seat, do not put the soles of the feet outward, not to mention facing each other.

埃及人很喜欢美丽华贵的仙鹤，认为它代表喜庆与长寿。除了猪，外形被认为与猪相近的大熊猫也为埃及人所反感。埃及人最喜爱"吉祥之色"——绿色与"快乐之色"——白色。他们讨厌的色彩也有两种，即黑色和蓝色，两者在埃及人看来均是不祥之色。在埃及，下午3点到5点之间，人们大都忌讳针，商人决不卖针，人们也不买针，即便有人愿意出高价，店主也会婉言谢绝。在数字方面，"5"与"7"深得埃及人的青睐。在他们看来，"5"会带来吉祥好运，"7"则意味着完美。对信奉基督教的埃及人而言，"13"是最晦气的数字。与埃及人交谈时，应注意以下几点：一是男士不要主动与妇女攀谈；二是切勿夸奖埃及妇女身材窈窕，因为埃及人以体态丰腴为美；三是不要称赞埃及人家中的物品，这种做法被人理解为意欲索要此物；四是不要与埃及人谈论宗教纠纷、政党政治、中东政局及男女关系。

Egyptians have a fondness for the beautiful and elegant crane, which they believe symbolizes celebration and longevity. Besides pigs, pandas, which are considered similar in appearance to pigs, are also disliked by Egyptians. Their favorite colors are green, known as the "color of good fortune", and white, the "color of happiness". Conversely, they dislike black and blue, both considered unlucky colors. In Egypt, between 3 p.m. and 5 p.m, people gengerally avoid seeing or talking about needles.; merchants never sell them, and people do not buy them. Even if someone offers a high price, shopkeepers will politely refuse. As for numbers, "5" and "7" are highly favored by Egyptians. They believe that "5" brings good luck and "7" signifies perfection. For Egyptian Christians, "13" is considered the most unlucky number. When conversing with Egyptians, keep the following points in mind: first, men should not initiate conversations with women; second, avoid complimenting Egyptian women on their slender figures, as fuller figures are considered beautiful; third, do not praise items in an Egyptian's home, as this may be interpreted as a request for the item; and fourth, avoid discussing religious conflicts, party politics, the Middle East situation, and gender relations.

埃及人为什么忌讳"针"？

（六）传统节日 Festivals

1. 斋月 Ramadan

斋月是伊斯兰历的第9个月，该月名字意为"禁月"，《古兰经》里明言规定此月符合条件的伊斯兰教信徒必须守斋戒，从日出到日落停止一切饮食等活动，日落后即可进食并恢复正常作息，直到晨礼（也就是日出）前都能吃喝，晨礼后便又进入斋戒状态。为期一个月的斋月期间，肃静的气氛只出现在白天，斋月期间的夜晚是一年中最热闹的，各大城市都会举行音乐会及各种演出。

Ramadan is the ninth month according to Islamic calendar, which means "the Month of Fast". It is required in the *Qu"ran* that the qualified Muslims must fast from sunrise to sunset with no food etc. The fast is broken at sunset and people can drink and have meal until next morning (before the sunrise) when the fast starts again. The fast month is solemn in the daytime, while the nights during the fast month are the most lively and dynamic in the year when concerts and other performances are held in the big cities.

2. 尼罗河泛滥节 Nile Flood Festival

尼罗河泛滥节是埃及最古老的节日，一般是在每年的8月。数千年来，埃及人一直对尼罗河顶礼膜拜，把它看作是"天赐圣泉"，因而关于尼罗河的传说也数不胜数。每年在洪水泛滥时，人们都要选一个美丽的少女奉献给河神，祈求河神不要让洪水肆虐成灾。自从 1960 年阿斯旺水坝建成发电之后，农业灌溉系统日趋完善，尼罗河不再泛滥，但在一年一度的尼罗河涨水时，埃及人仍然举行祈祷活动，往尼罗河里扔五颜六色的玩具娃娃，还有划船比赛以及放烟火等活动。

The Nile Flood Festival is Egypt's oldest festival, typically celebrated in August each year. For thousands of years, Egyptians have revered the Nile as a "heavenly sacred spring," leading to countless legends about it. In ancient times, during the annual flood, a beautiful maiden was chosen and offered to the river god to pray for protection against destructive floods. Since the completion of the Aswan Dam in 1960, which brought improved agricultural irrigation systems and prevented the Nile from flooding, the tradition has evolved. Today, during the annual rise of the Nile, Egyptians still hold prayer ceremonies, throwing colorful toy dolls into the river, organizing boat races, and setting off fireworks.

3. 闻风节 Sham el-Nessim

每年的 4 月 15 日是埃及的"闻风节"，是埃及最古老的全国性节日之一。庆祝闻风节是为了祈祷和平与繁荣的未来。"闻风节"又称春节、踏青节，意味着可以闻到春天的气息。其历史可追溯到公元前 2700 年甚至更早。传说这天，慈善神战胜了凶恶神。经过约 5 000 年的历史演变，人们就在"闻风节"里祈求人间祥和、太平、春光永驻，这个习俗经久不衰。每年春天，埃及人会在"闻风节"这天举家外出踏青，品尝彩蛋、咸鱼等各种象征吉祥的食品。

Sham el-Nessim is one of the oldest national festivals in Egypt, it is celebrated on April 15th to pray for peace and prosperous future. It is also called Spring Festival when people can go for a walk in the country to "smell" its coming. The tradition can be dated back to 2700 BC or earlier and it is said that Ormazd (the God of All Goodness) defeated Ahriman (the God of Evil). Lasting for about 5 000 years, it now becomes a day for people to pray for happiness as well as everlasting spring in the world. As the most ancient festival in Egypt, the tradition is still observed and in every spring, the family members will go out for a walk on Sham el-Nessim when the grass has just turned green, and they will not forget to bring the lucky food with them, that is, colored eggs and salted fish.

三、旅游观光 Tourism and Sightseeing

（一）主要旅游城市 Major Tourist Cities

1. 开罗 Cairo

开罗是埃及的首都，位于尼罗河三角洲的入口，由开罗省、吉萨省和盖勒尤卜省组成，通称大开罗，被誉为"尼罗河上的明珠"，是整个中东地区的政治、经济和商业中心。开罗西南约 30 千米的孟菲斯是埃及的古都，其历史可以追溯到公元前 3100 年的首位法老美尼斯，古埃及许多王朝都在此定都，并在附近修建金字塔和陵墓。现代的开罗建于公元 973 年，被喻为"胜利之城"。如今，开罗城的西部以现代化的高楼建筑为主，东部则是以古老的阿拉伯建筑为主，250 多座清真寺集中于此。开罗城内清真寺随处可见，有"千塔之城"的美誉。开罗著名的景点有吉萨金字塔群、狮身人面像、埃及博物馆等。

Cairo, capital of Egypt, at the top of the Nile Delta, consisting of Cairo, Giza and Ghayyub governorates, commonly known as Greater Cairo, known as the "Pearl of the Nile", is the political, economic and commercial center of the entire Middle East. Memphis, the ancient capital of Egypt, lies about 30 kilometers southwest of Cairo. It can be dated back to the first Pharaoh Menes in 3100

BC, and afterwards, many dynasties had chosen it for the capital and founded the pyramids and royal tombs nearby. Modern Cairo, literally the "Vanquisher" or the "Conqueror", was built in 973 AD. Now the west of the city is occupied by modern high-rise buildings, while the east is still the world of ancient Arab buildings, including over 250 mosques. There are mosques everywhere in Cairo to win it the name "City of A Thousand Minarets". The famous attractions in Cairo include Giza Necropolis, Great Sphinx of Giza, Egyptian Museum, etc.

2. 亚历山大 Alexandria

亚历山大是埃及的最大海港和全国第二大城市，是历史名城、地中海沿岸的避暑胜地，也是埃及最具有欧洲风格的城市和开放度最高的城市。亚历山大的名字来源于马其顿亚历山大大帝，约建于公元前 331 年，曾经是古埃及的文化中心。亚历山大死后被他的将军引渡葬在亚历山大。亚历山大见证了古罗马帝国的安东尼和埃及王后克里奥佩特拉之间的爱情。之后，阿拉伯人、土耳其人先后在此登陆。拿破仑到来时，亚历山大已成为只有 8 000 人的小镇。英国统治埃及后，亚历山大成为重要的军港。今天的亚历山大被称为"地中海的新娘"，干净整洁，有浓厚的地中海气息。

Alexandria, the largest harbor and the second largest city of the country, is a famous historical city as well as the summer resort in the Mediterranean Sea. It is the most westernized and liberal city in Egypt. The name "Alexandria" derives from Alexander the Great, emperor of Macedonia. Built in about 331 BC, it used to be the cultural center of ancient Egypt. After his death, Alexander was buried by his general in the town across the Mediterranean Sea which witnessed the love story between Cleopatra, queen of Egypt and Antony of ancient Rome. Since then, Arabs and Turks landed on it one after another. When Napoleon came, it was already a town of 8 000 people. During the rule of Britain, Alexandria became an important military harbor. Now it is called "the Bride of the Mediterranean", which is clean and tidy with the strong Mediterranean flavor.

3. 卢克索 Luxor

代表古埃及文明最繁盛时期的卢克索位于开罗以南 675 千米（属于上埃及）。古称底比斯，因埃及古都底比斯遗址在此而闻名，距今已有 4 000 年的历史，是底比斯文物的集中地。底比斯鼎盛时期跨尼罗河两岸，《荷马史诗》把这里称为"百门之都"，有"100 个城门的底比斯"的描述。后被毁于公元前 88 年。沿尼罗河南下，这里是游客必游之地、埃及文化古迹集中的旅游胜地。卢克索古迹中最引人注目的是尼罗河东岸的卡纳克神庙和卢克索神庙。如今的卢克索是世界上最大的露天博物馆，享有"宫殿之城"的美誉。每年都有几十万名游客从世界各地慕名而来。埃及人常说："没有到过卢克索，就不算到过埃及。"

Luxor, lied 675 kilometers south of Cairo (in Upper Egypt), represents the most prosperous period of Ancient Egypt. Originally called Thebes, it is known for the site of the ancient capital Thebes, which started 4,000 years ago to leave numerous cultural and historical relics there. In its heyday, Thebes strode across the Nile to be the "Capital of a Hundred Gates" that was described in *Homers Epic* as "Thebes of a Hundred Gates". It was destroyed in 88 BC. Going down the Nile to the south, it is the must-see for the tourists where the relics of ancient Egypt can be found everywhere. Among them, the Karnak Temple Complex and Luxor Temple are the most attractive. Nowadays, Luxor has become the biggest open-air museum in the world to win the reputation of "City of Palace" that has attracted hundreds of thousands visitors from all around the world to admire it every year. The Egyptians always say："He who has not been to Luxor has not been to Egypt."

4. 阿斯旺 Aswan

阿斯旺是埃及南部的一个重要城市，位于首都开罗以南 900 千米的尼罗河东岸，是埃及的南大门，也是非洲的门户和唯一一条由海上进入非洲腹地的通道。阿斯旺是埃及阳光最充足的南部城市，具有非洲的气候特征，是埃及最热、最干燥的城市之一。阿斯旺的气候冬季温和、阳光明媚，世界闻名；夏季炎热、干燥，全年几乎没有任何降水。阿斯旺是埃及自然风光最优美的地方、南部观光的起点站。阿斯旺的氛围比卢克索或开罗更为轻松惬意，是尼罗河帆船观光及纳赛尔湖巡航游的中心。在这里，既有古代的遗迹，又有现代文明的成果，世界第七大水坝——阿斯旺大坝就建在附近的尼罗河上。

Aswan is an important city in southern Egypt, located on the east bank of the Nile 900 kilometers south of the capital, Cairo, and is the southern gateway to Egypt, the gateway to Africa and the only route by sea into the African hinterland. Aswan is the most sunny city in southern Egypt, and one of the hottest and driest cities with typical African climate. In winter, it is sunny and warm to be world-famous, while in summer, it is too hot and dry with scarcely any rain. With the most beautiful landscape in Egypt, Aswan is the first stop of the sightseeing tour around southern Egypt. More relaxing than Luxor or Cairo, it attracts flocks of sailing boats along the Nile and the cruises on the Lake Nasser. There are both ancient relics and modern civilization, including the Aswan Dam, the world's seventh-largest dam, is built on the nearby Nile River.

（二）著名旅游景点 Famous Tourist Attractions

1. 金字塔 Pyramids

金字塔（图 5-1）是古埃及法老为自己修建的陵墓。埃及共发现金字塔 96 座，最大、最有名的是位于开罗西南面吉萨高地上的金字塔。它们是祖孙三代法老（包括胡夫、哈夫拉、门卡乌拉）的金字塔。大金字塔是法老胡夫的陵墓，建于公元前 2690 年左右，据说，10 万人用了 20 年时间才得以建成。大金字塔是埃及现存规模最大的金字塔，被誉为"世界古代七大奇观之一"。第二座金字塔是胡夫的儿子法老哈夫拉的陵墓，建于公元前 2650 年，

图 5-1　金字塔
Figure 5-1　Pyramids

建筑形式更加完美、壮观，塔前建有庙宇等附属建筑和著名的狮身人面像。第三座金字塔是胡夫的孙子法老门卡乌拉的陵墓，建于公元前 2600 年左右。而著名的阶梯金字塔位于开罗南郊 30 千米的萨卡拉，为古埃及第三王朝法老左塞尔的陵墓，约建于公元前 2700 年。该金字塔是埃及现有金字塔中年代最早的，也是世界上最早用石块修建的陵墓。

Pyramids (Figure 5-1) are the tombs built by the pharaohs of ancient Egypt for themselves. There are altogether 96 Pyramids discovered in Egypt, of which the biggest and most famous lies in Giza, a highland in the southwest of Cairo. They are the pyramids for three generations of pharaohs, that is, Khufu, Khafre, and Menkaure. The Great Pyramid of Khufu was set up in about 2690 BC and it is said to spend 100,000 people 20 years building it. It is the biggest Pyramid existent in Egypt, one of the "Seven Wonders of the Ancient World". The second Pyramid is for Khafre, son of Khufu. Built in 2650 BC, the architecture form is more perfect and magnificent, with the auxiliary buildings like temple, as well as the famous Sphinx in front of it. The third one is built in 2600 BC for Menkaure, Khufu's grandson. The famous Step Pyramid, or Stepped Pyramid, is located in Saqqara, 30 kilometers of southern suburb of Cairo, which was built in about 2700 BC for Zoser, pharaoh of the Third Dynasty. It is the oldest pyramid now in Egypt and the earliest stone-made tomb in the world.

2. 亚历山大港灯塔 The Lighthouse of Alexandria

图 5-2　亚历山大港灯塔
Figure 5-2　The Lighthouse of Alexandria

亚历山大港灯塔（图 5-2）的火焰从公元前 281 年建成点燃起，直到公元 641 年阿拉伯伊斯兰大军征服埃及才熄灭，这座高 135 米的巨型灯塔屹立了 922 年之久才被地震所毁。它日夜不熄地燃烧了近千年，也是人类历史上火焰灯塔所未有过的奇迹。现在，亚历山大港灯塔的遗址位于埃及亚历山大城边的法洛斯岛上，被誉为"世界七大奇迹之一"。它不带有任何宗教色彩，纯粹为人民实际生活而建。亚历山大港灯塔的烛光在晚上照耀着整个亚历山大港，保护海上的船只；另外，它亦是当时世上最高的建筑物。庞贝柱是亚历山大灯塔遗留下来的仅有的古迹，附近有阿匹斯神庙遗址。

世界七大奇迹

The Lighthouse of Alexandria(Figure5-2) was built and lit in 281 BC and remained illuminated until 641 AD when the Arab Islamic army conquered Egypt, extinguishing its flame. This colossal lighthouse, standing 135 meters tall, endured for 922 years before being destroyed by an earthquake. It burned continuously for nearly a millennium, an unprecedented feat for a flame-bearing lighthouse in human history. Now, the site of Alexandria lighthouse is located in Egypt Alexandria city side of the island of Pharos, known as one of the "Seven Wonders of the World", it does not have any religious color, purely for the people's practical life and built, Alexandria lighthouse candlelight in the night shines throughout the port of Alexandria, to protect the ships on the sea. Additionally, it was the tallest building in the world at the time. Pompey's Pillar is the only ancient relic remaining from the Lighthouse of Alexandria, and nearby are the ruins of the Apis temple.

3. 埃及博物馆 Egyptian Museum

图 5-3　埃及博物馆
Figure 5-3　Egyptian Museum

埃及博物馆（图 5-3）坐落在开罗市中心的解放广场，1902 年建成开馆，是世界上最著名、规模最大的古埃及文物博物馆。该馆收藏了 5 000 年前古埃及法老时代至公元 6 世纪的历史文物 25 万件，其中大多数展品的历史超过 3 000 年。博物馆分为二层，展品按年代顺序分别陈列在几十间展室中。该馆中的许多文物，如巨大的法老王石像、纯金制作的宫廷御用珍品、大量的木乃伊及重 242 磅（约 109.77 千克）的图坦卡蒙纯金面具和棺椁，其做工之精细令人赞叹。

The Egyptian Museum (Figure 5-3), located in Tahrir Extensive in downtown Cairo, was opened in 1902 and is the most famous and largest museum of ancient Egyptian artifacts in the world. The museum has a collection of 250,000 historical artifacts from the Pharaonic era of Ancient Egypt 5,000 years ago to the 6th century AD, with most of the exhibits dating back more than 3,000 years. The museum is divided into two floors, with exhibits displayed chronologically in dozens of rooms. Many of the artifacts in the museum, such as the huge stone statue of the Pharaoh, the imperial treasures of the court made of pure gold, a large number of mummies, and the 242-pound (about 109.77 kilograms) pure gold mask and coffin of Tutankhamun, are admired for their fine workmanship.

 讨论题

阅读材料"开罗埃及博物馆"。
我们应该如何做好大型古文物的保护工作？

开罗埃及博物馆

4. 尼罗河 The Nile River

尼罗河（图5-4）发源于东非高原，流经布隆迪、卢旺达、坦桑尼亚、乌干达、苏丹和埃及等国，全长6 600多千米，为世界第一长河，可航行水道长约3 000千米。尼罗河谷和三角洲是埃及文化的摇篮，也是世界文化的发祥地之一，是埃及人口最稠密、最富饶的地区。尼罗河上有许多游船，其中还有仿古式"法老船"。夜晚泛舟河上，可游览两岸旖旎风光，也可观赏船上著名的东方舞表演。

图5-4 尼罗河
Figure 5-4 The Nile River

The Nile River (Figure 5-4) originates from the East African plateau and flows through Burundi, Rwanda, Tanzania, Uganda, Sudan and Egypt, with a total length of more than 6,600 kilometers, which is the first longest river in the world, and the navigable waterway is about 3,000 kilometers long. The Nile Valley and the delta are the cradle of Egyptian culture and one of the birthplaces of the world's cultures, which is the most densely populated and the most fertile area in Egypt. There are many cruise ships on the Nile River, including replicas of the Pharaoh's ships. Boating on the river at night, people can visit the exquisite scenery on both sides of the river and

图5-5 卢克索神庙
Figure 5-5 Luxor Temple

watch the famous oriental dance performance on board.

5. 卢克索神庙 Luxor Temple

卢克索神庙（图 5-5）是主神阿蒙的妻子穆特的神庙，约于公元前 14 世纪修建，规模仅次于卡纳克神庙。它具有令人惊叹的雄伟气势，每一根柱子都代表了法老的威严，置身其中会使人暂时忘却时间的流逝，神思万千。这里的大部分工程是由第 18 王朝法老阿蒙诺菲斯三世完成的，后来的拉美西斯二世又增建了大门和庭院，并在门口竖立了 6 尊他的塑像，现存 3 尊。庙内原来有两座尖方碑，其中一座被穆罕默德·阿里送给了法国，现在巴黎协和广场。

The Luxor Temple(Figure5-5), dedicated to Mut, the wife of Amun, the chief deity of Thebes, was constructed around the 14th century BC. It is second in size only to the Karnak Temple. The temple boasts an astonishing grandeur, with each column symbolizing the pharaohs' majesty, allowing visitors to momentarily forget the passage of time and become lost in thought. Most of the construction was completed by Pharaoh Amenhotep III of the 18th Dynasty. Later, Ramses II expanded the temple by adding the entrance and courtyard, and erected six statues of himself at the entrance, three of which remain today. Originally, the temple had two obelisks, one of which was gifted by Muhammad Ali to France and now stands at the Place de la Concorde in Paris.

图 5-6　卡纳克神庙
Figure 5-6　The Temple of Karnak

6. 卡纳克神庙 The Temple of Karnak

卡纳克神庙（图 5-6）又称阿蒙神庙，位于卢克索以北 5 千米处。始建于约 3 000 年前，是法老们献给太阳神、自然神和月亮神的庙宇建筑群，包括大、小神庙 20 余座。每一个宗教季节的仪式都从卡纳克神庙开始，到卢克索神庙结束。两者之间有一条 1 千米长的石板大道，两侧排列着狮身羊面或牛面的石雕。卡纳克神庙因为其浩大的规模而扬名世界，它是世界上最大的用柱子支撑的寺庙，是世界上最壮观的古建筑物之一，也是埃及最大的神庙。神庙的大柱厅，庙门巍峨，高达 38 米，蔚为壮观；主殿雄伟凝重，面积约 5 000 平方米，分 16 行排列，共 134 根巨石圆柱，其中两排 12 根特别粗大，每根高达 21 米，直径 3.57 米，可容纳百人在上面站立。柱上残留有描述太阳神故事的彩绘。庙内尖顶石碑如林，巨石雕像随处可见。在神庙的石壁上，可见到古埃及人用象形文字刻写的他们的光辉史迹。

The Temple of Karnak (Figure 5-6), also known as the Temple of Amun, is located 5 kilometers north of Luxor. Built about 3,000 years ago, it is a complex of temples dedicated by the pharaohs to the gods of the sun, nature and the moon, including more than 20 large and small temples. Each religious season ceremony starts at the Karnak Temple and ends at the Luxor Temple. Between the two is a 1 kilometer-long stone avenue lined with stone carvings of lions with sheep or bull faces. The Temple of Karnak is world famous for its vastness, it is the largest temple in the world supported by pillars, one of the most spectacular ancient structures in the world and the largest temple in Egypt. The temple of the great column hall, with the lofty temple door, up to 38 meters, which is spectacular. The main hall is majestic and heavy, and has an area of about 5,000 square kilometers. There are a total of 134 giant stone columns, arranged in 16 rows including two rows of 12 particularly thick, each as high as 21 meters, a diameter of 3.57 meters, which can accommodate a hundred people standing on it. There are colorful paintings describing the story of the Sun God remaining on the columns. The temple has a forest of spires and monolithic statues can be seen everywhere. On the stone walls of the temple, one can see their glorious history inscribed in hieroglyphics by the ancient Egyptians.

（三）旅游购物 Shopping

香水：埃及是法国许多著名香水的原产地，也是香料的生产大国。1 000多年以前，开罗就已经是世界上最大的香料贸易中心了。埃及香料的品种繁多、功能各异，像麝香、玫瑰、荷花、香精等是专门用来制作香水的，而枯茗、红番花、樟脑可用于治疗疾病。

Perfume: Egypt is the origin of many famous French perfumes and is also a major producer of spices. Over a thousand years ago, Cairo had already become the biggest trade center of spice in the world. There are a large variety of perfume and spice produced in Egypt for various purposes, for example, musk, rose, lotus essence that are used for fragrance, and cuminum, crocus, camphor that are used for treatment of diseases.

纸莎草：纸莎草是尼罗河三角洲生长的一种类似芦苇的水生植物，可以用来造纸。纸莎草是古埃及文明的一个重要组成部分，纸莎草纸画是埃及文化瑰宝、世界上最早的纸画。纵使过去了几千年，在埃及，制作纸莎草纸画的每一个步骤都不曾变过，目前有许多以纸莎草创作的彩绘作品，题材多取自古埃及神庙和宫殿的壁画。

Papyrus: Papyrus is a weed-like water plant that grows in the Nile Delta, which can be used as raw material for paper-making. It's an important part of ancient Egyptian civilization to contribute papyrus painting, the earliest paper painting in the world. Although thousands of years have passed, the process of making papyrus painting is still there with every step unchanged. You can see many papyrus color paintings whose subject matters are mainly drawn from the wall paintings of ancient temples and palaces in Egypt.

地毯：埃及的地毯在大街上随处可见，是埃及的著名特产，西奈半岛的达哈布有许多商店出售贝都因人制作的既便宜又色彩缤纷的棉制地毯。

Carpet: As a famous local specialty, carpet can be seen everywhere in Egypt. There are many stores in Dahab, Sinai Peninsula to sell inexpensive, colorful cotton carpets made by the Bedouins.

水烟袋：水烟袋在阿拉伯语中称为"nargileh"，是埃及人抽烟用的器具。制作得较精致的水烟袋是一种很有意思的纪念品，以玻璃制品为贵，黄铜次之。

Hubble-bubble: Hubble-bubble is called "nargileh" in Arabic, it is the tool for people to smoke with. Now the delicately made nargilehs have become interesting souvenir for the visitors, of which the glass ones are more expensive than the brass ones.

扫码获取：入境须知及海关规定

本节习题

1. 埃及的主要城市和主要景点有哪些？
2. 旅游业是埃及的经济支柱和外汇的主要来源之一，请分析旅游业对国家经济发展的意义以及如何在发展旅游业和传播文化之间形成和谐发展的有效途径。

黄金之国——南非
The Land of Gold—South Africa

导读

　　南非自然风光绮丽多姿，人文景观丰富灿烂，素有"游览一国如同环游世界"的美誉，这里既有现代化的基础设施、世界一流的酒店和豪华的花园别墅，又有最原始的部落风情。南非通常被称作"彩虹之国"，比喻南非在结束了种族隔离主义后所呈现出的文化多样性。南非的旅游景点主要集中在东北部和东南沿海地区，如开普敦海岸的水上世界、好望角，西开普省的葡萄酒园、克鲁格国家公园、德班海滩等。此外，南非还有一些举世闻名的城市和景观，如南非早期的黄金开采地约翰内斯堡、南半球最大的娱乐中心太阳城、非洲大陆最西南端的"天涯海角"开普敦、南非的革命圣地索韦托、世界钻石之都金伯利等。南非奉行独立自主的全方位外交政策，主张在尊重主权、平等互利和互不干涉内政的基础上同一切国家保持和平发展的双边友好关系。中国与南非于1998年1月1日建立外交关系。建交以来，两国关系全面、快速发展。

一、地理概览 Geography of South Africa

（一）位置 Location

　　南非共和国简称南非，地处南半球，有"彩虹之国"的美誉，位于非洲大陆的最南端，陆地面积为121.9万平方公里，其东、南、西三面被印度洋和大西洋环抱。陆地上与纳米比亚、博茨瓦纳、莱索托、津巴布韦、莫桑比克和斯威士兰接壤，东面隔印度洋和澳大利亚相望，西面隔大西洋和巴西、阿根廷相望。南非西南端有好望角，好望角航线历来是世界上最繁忙的海上通道之一，世界上重要的石油运输线多经过此地，故有"西方海上生命线"之称。

　　The Republic of South Africa, commonly referred to as South Africa, is located in the Southern Hemisphere and is known as the "Rainbow Nation". It lies at the southernmost tip of the African continent, covering a land area of 1.219 million square kilometers. The country is surrounded by the Indian Ocean and the Atlantic Ocean on the east, south, and west. It shares land borders with Namibia, Botswana, Lesotho, Zimbabwe, Mozambique, and Eswatini. To the east, across the Indian Ocean, lies Australia, and to the west, across the Atlantic Ocean, are Brazil and Argentina. The southwestern tip of South Africa is home to the Cape of Good Hope, which has historically been one of the world's busiest maritime routes. It is a crucial passageway for many of the world's major oil transport routes, earning it the nickname "Western Sea Lifeline".

（二）地形和气候 The Land and Seasons

　　南非地处非洲高原的最南端，南、东、西三面之边缘地区为沿海低地，北面则有重山环抱。北部内陆区属喀拉哈里沙漠，多为灌丛草地或干旱沙漠，此区域海拔650～1 250米。周围的高地海拔超过1 200米。南非最高点为东部大陆崖的塔巴纳山，海拔3 482米。东部则是龙山山脉纵贯。

South Africa is situated at the southernmost part of the African plateau. The southern, eastern, and western edges are characterized by coastal lowlands, while the northern part is surrounded by rugged mountains. The northern inland region is part of the Kalahari Desert, predominantly consisting of shrubland and arid desert, with elevations ranging from approximately 650 to 1,250 meters. The surrounding highlands have elevations exceeding 1,200 meters. The highest point in South Africa is Thabana Ntlenyana, located in the eastern Great Escarpment, with an elevation of 3,482 meters. The eastern part of the country is traversed by the Drakensberg Mountains.

奥兰治河和林波波河为两大主要河流。大部分地区属热带草原气候，东部沿海为热带季风气候，南部沿海为地中海气候。全境气候分为春、夏、秋、冬4季。12月至次年2月为夏季，最高气温可达32 ℃～38 ℃；6—8月是冬季，最低气温为 –12 ℃～ –10 ℃。全年降水量由东部的1 000毫米逐渐减少到西部的100毫米以下。首都比勒陀利亚年平均气温为17 ℃。

The Orange and Limpopo Rivers are the two main rivers. Most of the area has a tropical grassland climate，with a tropical monsoon climate on the eastern coast and a Mediterranean climate on the southern coast. The climate of the whole territory is divided into four seasons: spring，summer，fall and winter. From December to February is summer，the highest temperature can reach 32 ℃ –38 ℃；from June to August is winter，the lowest temperature is −12 ℃ − −10 ℃ . The annual precipitation gradually decreases from 1,000 mm in the east to less than 100 mm in the west. The average annual temperature in Pretoria，the capital，is 17 ℃ .

（三）自然资源 Natural Resources

南非矿产资源丰富，是世界五大矿产国之一。黄金、铂族金属、锰、钒、铬和铝硅酸盐的储量均居世界第一位，蛭石、锑、钛、锆居世界第二位，氟石、磷酸盐居世界第三位，锑、铀居世界第四位，煤、钻石、铅居世界第五位。南非是世界上最大的黄金生产国和出口国，黄金出口额占全部对外出口额的1/3，因此又被誉为"黄金之国"。南非以其丰富、珍稀的野生动植物和美丽的自然风光著称。南非有五大国宝动物，分别为狮子、豹子、大象、水牛和犀牛。南非于1994年6月4日签署了《生物多样性公约》，并在1995年11月2日成为该公约的缔约国。在全球17个超级生物多样性国家同盟的成员中，南非排名第六位。

South Africa is rich in mineral resources and is one of the world's top five mineral countries. Gold，platinum group metals，manganese，vanadium，chromium and aluminosilicate reserves ranke first in the world; vermiculite，antimony，titanium，zirconium rank second in the world; fluorite，phosphate rank third in the world; antimony，uranium rank fourth in the world; and coal，diamonds，lead rank fifth in the world. South Africa is the world's largest gold producer and exporter，gold exports accounting for 1/3 of all foreign exports，so it is also known as the

一个被誉为
"黄金之国"
的国度

"Country of Gold". South Africa is renowned for its rich and rare wildlife, as well as its stunning natural landscapes. The country is home to the five national treasures: lions, leopards, elephants, buffalo, and rhinos. On June 4, 1994, South Africa signed the *Convention on Biological Diversity* and became a party to the convention on November 2, 1995. Among the world's 17 mega diverse countries, South Africa ranks sixth.

二、人文概况 Overview of South Africa's Humanities

（一）国情认知 Basic Knowledge of National Conditions

南非人口有 5 989.4 万（2022 年），包括 79％的黑人，9.6％的白人，8.9％的有色人种和 2.5％的亚裔（主要为印度人和华人）。在非洲，南非是拥有最多欧洲人后裔、最多印度人后裔，以及最多白人、马来人和黑人混血儿的国家，也是非洲大陆上种族最多元化的国家之一。

South Africa has an estimated population of 59.894 million（2022）. The ethnic groups include Black 79%, White 9.6%, Coloured 8.9%, Asians 2.5%（predominantly Indian and Chinese）. South Africa has the largest population of people of European descent in Africa, the largest Indian population in Africa, the largest mixed White, Malay, and Black population community in Africa, making it one of the most ethnically diverse countries on the continent.

南非有 11 种官方语言，主要以班图语，英语和阿非利卡语（南非荷兰语）作为通用语言。居民主要信奉基督教新教、天主教、伊斯兰教和原始宗教。南非的国旗呈长方形，由红色、绿色、蓝色、白色、黑色、黄色六种颜色组成，呈 V 形。南非的国歌为《上帝保佑非洲》和《南非的呐喊》合编曲。国花是帝王花，又名菩提花，俗称"木百合花"或"龙眼花"。

There are 11 official languages in South Africa, with Bantu being the main language spoken, and English and Afrikaans being the lingua franca. The inhabitants mainly follow Protestant Christianity, Catholicism, Islam and primitive religions. The national flag of South Africa is rectangular in shape and consists of six colors: red, green, blue, white, black and yellow in a V-shape. The national anthem of South Africa is a compilation of *God Bless Africa* and *The Cry of South Africa*. The national flower is the monarch, also known as the linden flower, commonly known as the "wood lily" or "longan flower".

（二）历史简介 History of South Africa

南非最早的土著居民是桑人、科伊人和后来南迁的班图人。17 世纪之后，荷兰、英国相继入侵南非。20 世纪初，南非曾一度成为英国的自治领地。1961 年 5 月 31 日，南非退出英联邦，成立南非共和国。由于南非白人当局在国内推行种族歧视和种族隔离政策，南非人民在以纳尔逊·曼德拉为首的非洲人国民大会（ANC）的领导下，为推翻种族隔离制度进行了英勇的斗争，并最终取得胜利。1994 年 4 月，南非举行首次由各种族参加的大选，纳尔逊·曼德拉当选为南非首任黑人总统。

The earliest indigenous inhabitants of South Africa were the San, the Khoi and the Bantu, who later migrated southward, and were invaded by the Dutch and the British after the 17th century; at the beginning of the 20th century, South Africa was once a British self-governing territory, and on May 31, 1961, South Africa withdrew from the British Commonwealth and established the Republic of South Africa. As the white authorities of South Africa implemented racial discrimination and apartheid policies in the country, the people of South Africa, under the leadership of the African National Congress（ANC）headed by Nelson Mandela, fought valiantly to overthrow the apartheid system and eventually won the victory. In April, 1994, South Africa held its first general election in which all races participated, and Nelson Mandela was elected as the first black President of South Africa.

讨论题

　　南非因多种族和多元文化而有"彩虹之国"的美称，而南非前总统曼德拉更是一个时代的标志，尤其对于南非的人民而言，曼德拉的角色无人可以替代，请欣赏曼德拉的原声演讲"我愿为梦想而死"（*I am Prepared to Die for An Idea*），并讨论曼德拉的理想和追求是什么。

我愿为梦想而死——曼德拉

（三）经济状况 The Economy

　　南非属于中等收入的发展中国家，是非洲经济最发达的国家。采矿业、制造业、建筑业和能源工业为四大经济支柱，深矿开采技术在世界处于领先地位。南非的制造业门类齐全、技术先进，主要包括钢铁、金属制品、化工、运输设备、食品加工、纺织、服装等。制造业产值占国内生产总值的近 1/5。南非的电力工业较发达，拥有世界上最大的干冷发电站，发电量占全非洲的 3/5。各类罐头食品、烟、酒、咖啡和饮料畅销海外。主要农作物有玉米、小麦和高粱，盛产花卉、水果，葡萄酒享有盛誉。羊毛产量居世界前列。

　　South Africa is a middle-income developing country and the most economically advanced country in Africa. Mining, manufacturing, construction and energy industries are the four major economic pillars, and the deep mining technology is in a leading position in the world. South Africa's manufacturing industry is complete and technologically advanced, mainly including iron and steel, metal products, chemicals, transportation equipment, food processing, textiles, clothing and so on. The output value of the manufacturing industry accounts for nearly 1/5 of the GDP. South Africa's electric power industry is more developed, with the world's largest dry-cooled power station, power generation accounting for 3/5 of the whole of Africa. Various types of canned food, cigarettes, alcohol, coffee and beverages sell well overseas. The main crops are corn, wheat and sorghum. Flowers and fruits are abundant in South Africa, and wine has a good reputation. Wool production is among the highest in the world.

（四）传统文化 Traditional Culture

　　在社交场合，南非人所采用的普遍见面礼节是握手。南非流行的打招呼方式是举起右手，手掌朝向对方，目的是表示"我没带武器"，象征友好和平。南非人为人处事非常大胆、直爽。与对方进行交谈时，过分地委婉或兜圈子都是不受欢迎的。在南非，正式场合讲究穿着端庄、严谨。进行官方交往或商务交往时，最好穿样式保守、色彩偏深的套装或裙装，不然会被对方视为失礼。黑人受到西方文化的影响经常身着西装，但在日常生活中，大多爱穿休闲装，白衬衣、牛仔装、西装短裤均受其喜爱。大部分黑人，特别是妇女仍保持着本民族传统的服饰风格。不同部落的黑人在着装上往往会有不同的特色，例如，有的部族的黑人喜欢用兽皮做成斗篷，将自己从头到脚遮在里面；有的部族的黑人则喜欢上身赤裸，仅在腰间围上一块腰布。

　　In social occasions, the common greeting among South Africans is a handshake. A popular way to say hello is by raising the right hand with the palm facing the other person, symbolizing "no weapon" and representing friendliness and peace. South Africans are very bold and straightforward. When talking to each other, excessive euphemisms or beating around the bush are not welcome. In formal occasions, there is an emphasis on dressing appropriately and conservatively. For official or business interactions, it is best to wear conservative, dark-colored suits or dresses, as anything else may be considered disrespectful. While influenced by Western culture, many Black South Africans often wear suits, but in daily life, most South Africans prefer casual attire, such as white shirts, denim, and shorts. Many Black South Africans, especially women, still maintain their traditional clothing styles. Different tribes often have distinctive dress features; for example, some tribes wear animal skin cloaks that cover them from head to toe, while others may prefer to go bare-chested with just a loincloth around the waist.

饮食方面，南非黑人的主食是玉米、薯类、豆类。在肉食方面，南非人爱吃牛肉、羊肉，一般不吃猪肉和鱼类。饮料主要是牛奶、羊奶和自制的啤酒。与其他许多国家的黑人不同的是，南非的黑人不喜欢生食，而是爱吃熟食。前往南非黑人家中做客时，十分好客的主人一般都要送上刚刚挤出来的新鲜牛奶或羊奶，诚心诚意地请客人品尝。有的时候，他们则会献上以高粱自制而成的、风味独特的啤酒。遇到这种情况，不论自己渴不渴、爱不爱喝，都一定要大大方方地"来者不拒"，尽量多喝一些，并且最好一饮而尽。若是百般推辞，坚决不喝一口，主人必定会很不高兴。

In terms of diet, the staple foods of South African Blacks are corn, potatoes and beans. In terms of meat, South Africans love to eat beef and mutton, and generally do not eat pork and fish. Drinks are mainly cow and sheep milk and home-made beer. Unlike Blacks in many other countries, Blacks in South Africa do not like raw food, but love cooked food. When you go to the South African Blacks' home as a guest, the very hospitable hosts usually send fresh milk, and sincerely invite the guests to taste it. Sometimes, they will offer a unique flavor of beer made from sorghum. Encountered this situation, regardless of your own thirst, love to drink, must be generous to "come to those who do not refuse", try to drink some, and it is best to drink it all. If you are all excuses, determined not to drink a mouthful, the host will be very unhappy.

（五）礼仪禁忌 Social Etiquettes and Taboos

信仰基督教的南非人，最为忌讳数字"13"和"星期五"，特别是与 13 日同为一天的星期五，更是讳言忌提，并且尽量避免外出。一般来说，南非的黑人都非常敬仰自己的祖先，认为祖先不仅有消除灾祸的能力，还有惩罚子孙的力量，所以特别忌讳外人对自己的祖先言行失敬。交谈时，不要称南非人为"African"，而应该是"South African"。在非洲，所谓"African"，并非泛指所有非洲人，而是指特定的一群人，那就是南非共和国的荷兰裔白人。

South Africans who practice Christianity are particularly superstitious about the number "13" and "Friday". They are especially wary of Friday the 13th, often avoiding mentioning it and trying to stay indoors. Generally speaking, the South African Blacks are very much respect for their ancestors, that the ancestors not only have the ability to eliminate disasters, but also the power to punish their descendants, so it is improper for others to show disrespect toward one's ancestors. When talking, do not call South Africans "African", it should be "South African". In Africa, the term "African" does not refer to all Africans, but to a specific group of people, namely the white Dutch of the Republic of South Africa.

在南非不要随便拍照，南非人普遍认为用相机对准某物进行拍摄，某物的"精气"就会全被吸走，因此当地人痛恨拍照，人、房屋、家畜一律不准拍摄，如想拍摄，一定要事先征得对方同意。

In South Africa, you should be cautious about taking photographs. Many South Africans believe that when a camera is pointed at something and a picture is taken, the soul will be sucken away. As a result, locals generally dislike having photos taken of them, their homes, or their livestock. If you wish to take a photograph, it is essential to obtain permission beforehand.

交谈时应避免四个方面的话题：一不要为白人评功摆好；二不要非议黑人的古老习俗；三不要评论不同黑人部族或派别之间的关系及矛盾；四不要为对方生了男孩而表示祝贺，在许多部族中，这件事并不令人欣喜。

When engaging in conversation, it's important to avoid four specific topics: First, refrain from praising or glorifying white people. Second, do not criticize the ancient customs of Black people. Third, avoid commenting on the relationships or conflicts between different Black tribes or factions. Fourth, do not congratulate someone on the birth of a baby boy, as in many tribes, this is not necessarily considered a cause for celebration.

（六）传统节日 Festivals

1. 人权日 Human Rights Day

1960 年 3 月 21 日，沙佩维尔镇黑人举行和平游行，抗议《通行证法》实施。这部法律要求黑人外出必须携带通行证，否则将会被逮捕。种族主义政府武力镇压游行，导致 69 人死亡、180 人受伤。后来，3 月 21 日被定为"人权日"，也叫"国际消除种族歧视日"。

On March 21, 1960, the Blacks in the town of Sharpeville held a peaceful march to protest the implementation of the *Pass Act*. This law required blacks to carry passes when they went out or they would be arrested. The racist government suppressed the march with force, resulting in 69 deaths and 180 injuries. March 21 was later designated as Human Rights Day, also known as the International Day for the Elimination of Racial Discrimination.

2. 自由日 Freedom Day

定于 4 月 27 日的自由日是新南非首次不分种族的大选日，也是南非国庆日。1994 年废除种族隔离制度之后，南非进行了历史上第一次不分种族的全民大选。这次大选，凡是年满 18 岁的南非国民，不分种族，都有投票权。而在此之前，在种族隔离制度下，南非有色人种在大选中只有有限的投票权。

Freedom Day, the National Day, falls on April 27, which was the first election day of all races in South African history. In 1994 when social segregation was abolished, the first national election in South African history was held among people of all races. All citizens aged above 18, irrespective of the race, have the right to vote. Whereas during the period of racial segregation, the colored people in South Africa had only limited right to vote in the election.

3. 青年日 Youth Day

6 月 16 日是青年日。1976 年 6 月 16 日，约翰内斯堡市郊黑人聚居区索韦托的黑人学生举行示威，抗议强迫黑人学习非洲语言的《班图教育法》实施。示威遭到镇压，170 多人被打死，1 000 多人受伤。联合国安理会强烈谴责这次暴行，非洲统一组织将这一天定为"索韦托烈士纪念日"，后来被定为南非青年日。

June 16 is the Youth day. On June 16, 1976, Black students in Soweto, a Black ghetto on the outskirts of Johannesburg, demonstrated against the implementation of the *Bantu Education Act*, which forced Blacks to learn African languages. The demonstration was suppressed and more than 170 people were killed and more than 1,000 injured. The United Nations Security Council strongly condemned the atrocity, and the Organization of African Unity designated the day as "Soweto Martyrs' Day", which was later designated as South African Youth Day.

4. 曼德拉国际日 Mandela Day

7月18日是纳尔逊·曼德拉的生日。2009年11月，为表彰南非前总统对和平文化与自由的贡献，联合国大会宣布从2010年开始，每年的7月18日为"纳尔逊·曼德拉国际日"。作为人权律师、国际和平的缔造者以及自由南非的第一位民选总统，纳尔逊·曼德拉将自己一生中的67年时光贡献于服务人类。每年的纳尔逊·曼德拉国际日，联合国都会号召人们至少花67分钟用于公益服务，以纪念曼德拉为反种族隔离事业而奋斗的67年。

July 18th is Nelson Mandela's birthday. In November, 2009, the United Nations General Assembly declared that starting from 2010, July 18 would be observed annually as "Nelson Mandela International Day" in recognition of the former South African President's contributions to a culture of peace and freedom. Nelson Mandela, as a human rights lawyer, international peacemaker, and the first democratically elected President of a free South Africa, dedicated 67 years of his life to serving humanity. Each year on Nelson Mandela International Day, the United Nations encourages people to spend at least 67 minutes engaging in community service, honoring Mandela's 67 years of struggle against apartheid.

5. 全国妇女节 National Women's Day

全国妇女节是8月9日。1956年8月9日，数百名黑人妇女在比勒陀利亚举行示威游行，抗议当局推行《通行证法》。新政府将这一天定为南非的妇女节，以纪念南非妇女在争取种族平等的斗争中所做的贡献。

National Women's Day is on August 9. On August 9, 1956, hundreds of Black women demonstrated in Pretoria to protest the introduction of the *Pass Act* by the authorities. The new government designated this day as Women's Day in South Africa to commemorate the contribution of South African women in the struggle for racial equality.

6. 和解日 Reconciliation Day

12月16日是南非政府法定的"种族和解日"，原称"誓言日"，是为了纪念1838年荷兰裔非洲人逃离英国殖民者的统治向北方迁移的历史。1994年新南非政府成立后，这一天被改名为"和解日"，是希望南非各种族实现和解，和平共处。

December 16th of each year is officially recognized as "Reconciliation Day" by the South African government. Originally called "Day of the Vow", it commemorated the historical migration of Dutch-speaking Africans who fled the rule of British colonizers in 1838. After the establishment of the new South African government in 1994, this day was renamed "Reconciliation Day", symbolizing the hope for reconciliation and peaceful coexistence among the various ethnic groups in South Africa.

三、旅游观光 Tourism and Sightseeing

（一）主要旅游城市 Major Tourist Cities

1. 开普敦 Cape Town

开普敦位于南非西南端，又名角城，是南非最古老的城市，被誉为"非洲明珠""南半球花园"，为游客带来了无穷的乐趣和丰富多彩的生活。开普敦因其天然良港和靠近好望角而闻名。该地区还以其独特的植物和优质葡萄酒而闻名。开普敦气候温暖、景色宜人，每年 10 月至次年的 3 月是最佳旅游季节。城区内，多种风格的欧洲古老建筑围绕着桌山而建。桌山因山顶平整如桌而得名，是开普敦的地标，在此可以观赏大西洋和印度洋的不同风光。

Cape Town, located at the southwestern tip of South Africa and also known as the "Cape City", is the oldest city in the country, often referred to as the "Pearl of Africa" and the "Garden of the Southern Hemisphere". It offers endless enjoyment and a vibrant lifestyle for visitors. Cape Town is famous for its natural harbor and proximity to the Cape of Good Hope. The region is also renowned for its unique flora and high-quality wines. With a warm climate and picturesque scenery, the best time to visit is from October to March each year. The city features various styles of historic European architecture built around Table Mountain. Named for its flat-topped summit, Table Mountain is a landmark of Cape Town, where one can enjoy views of the Atlantic and Indian Oceans.

2. 约翰内斯堡 Johannesburg

约翰内斯堡是南非最大的城市和经济中心，是世界最大的产金中心，素有"黄金之城"之称。今天的约翰内斯堡已发展成为繁华的现代化大都市，融合了东方、西方、非洲三种文化色彩。主要旅游景点有黄金城、人类摇篮遗址等。黄金城是建立在旧金矿遗址上的主题公园，园内逼真地重现了 18 世纪后期到 19 世纪初期淘金热潮时黄金城的建筑。人类摇篮遗址有占全世界一半的人类祖先化石，1999 年被列入《世界遗产名录》。

Johannesburg is the biggest city of South Africa. It is the biggest gold production center in the world to be known as "City of Gold". Now it has become a prosperous modern metropolis to fuse the cultural elements of the East, West and Africa. The main tourist attractions include Gold Reef City, Cradle of Humankind, etc. Gold Reef City is a theme park built on the site of an old gold mine, where the architecture of the gold rush era from the late 18th century to the early 19th century is vividly recreated. The Cradle of Humankind, which contains half of the world's hominin fossils, was inscribed by UNESCO on the World Heritage List in 1999.

3. 比勒陀利亚 Pretoria

比勒陀利亚位于约翰内斯堡以北 50 千米处，是南非的行政首都（南非是世界上唯一一个同时存在三个首都的国家）。这里是南非的交通枢纽、南半球空中交通的必经之路。比勒陀利亚建于 1855 年，以布尔人首领比勒陀利乌斯的名字命名，市内立有父子的塑像。比勒陀利亚是一个矿业城市，近郊为金刚石、白金、黄金、锡、铁、铬、煤等矿物开采中心。全球已知最大的天然钻石库利南就是在比勒陀利亚附近的矿坑发现的。

Located 50 kilometers north of Johannesburg, Pretoria is the administrative capital of South Africa (South Africa is the only country in the world to have three capitals at the same time). It is the transportation hub of South Africa and a must for air traffic in the southern hemisphere. Pretoria was founded in 1855 in honor of the first president of Boer Republics, Pretorius, and a statue of the father and son stands in the city. Pretoria is a mining city, and the suburbs are for diamond, platinum, gold, tin, iron, chromium, coal and other mineral mining centers. The world's largest known natural diamond, the Cullinan, was discovered in a pit near Pretoria.

4. 彼得马里茨堡 Pietermaritzburg

彼得马里茨堡是夸祖鲁 - 纳塔尔省（KwaZulu-Natal）的首府。彼得马里茨堡的主要产业有食品、金属和木材加工、制革、制鞋、橡胶、毛毯等工业。有纳塔尔大学、纳塔尔博物馆、艺术馆和植物园。纳塔尔大学始建于 1909 年。它在反对种族隔离的斗争中发挥了重要作用，是该国最早向黑人学生提供教育的大学之一。彼得马里茨堡有世界上最大的马雕像，矗立在最近建成的金马赌场外。

Pietermaritzburg is the capital of KwaZulu-Natal Province. The main industries in Pietermaritzburg include food processing, metal and wood working, tanning, shoemaking, rubber, and blanket manufacturing. It is home to the University of Natal, Natal Museum, art galleries, and botanical gardens. The University of Natal was established in 1909 and played a significant role in the fight against apartheid, being one of the first universities in the country to offer education to black students. Pietermaritzburg is also home to the world's largest horse statue, which stands outside the recently built Golden Horse Casino.

5. 德班 Durban

德班被誉为"南非的游乐场"，是夸祖鲁 - 纳塔尔省一个充满活力的亚热带国际化大都市。德班是南非最繁忙的集装箱港口，拥有发达的工业体系。该港口是世界上最大的天然深水港之一。城市海滨的酒店鳞次栉比，被称为德班的"金色一英里"。这里全年气候温暖，吸引了众多游客前往德班的冲浪海滩。罗马旋转餐厅是港口的一座著名建筑，它的圆形餐厅可以 360 度环视整个城市。市政厅内有一个收藏了大量南非当代艺术作品的画廊和一个自然科学博物馆。

Durban, being marketed as "South Africa's Playground", is a vibrant subtropical cosmopolitan city in KwaZulu-Natal Province. Durban is South Africa's busiest container port and has a substantial industrial sector. The port is one of the world's largest natural deep water ports. The long continuous stretch of hotels that line the city's beachfront is known as Durban's "One Golden Mile". The weather stays warm year-round drawing the crowds to Durban's surf beaches. Roma Revolving Restaurant, is a prominent building from the port with a rotating circular restaurant room that provides 360-degree views of the city. The city hall houses a gallery with a good collection of contemporary South African art and a natural science museum.

（二）著名旅游景点 Famous Tourist Attractions

1. 桌山 Mountain Table

桌山（图 5-7）其实是一组群山的总称，位于开普敦城区西部，有狮子头、信号山、魔鬼峰等，千姿百态、气势磅礴、郁郁葱葱。令人感到惊奇的是，桌山主峰海拔 1 067 米，山顶却平展得好似一个巨大的桌面。由于地处两洋交汇的特殊地理位置，加上地中海的奇特气候环境，山顶终年云雾缭绕，充满神秘莫测的气氛。有时云雾也会偶然散去，但这样的日子在一年中屈指可数，而且每次也就持续数个小时。桌山自然保护区拥有 2 000 多种濒临灭绝的原生花卉、植物、

图 5-7　桌山

Figure 5-7　Table Mountain

约 150 种鸟类以及岩兔、狒狒、狸猫等小型野生动物。人们可以通过缆车抵达桌山山顶，此处已被当地市政府评选为"南非之美"的宣传路标。

Table Mountain (Figure 5-7) is actually a group of mountains, located in the western part of Cape Town, Lion's Head, Signal Hill, Devi's Peak, etc., in a variety of forms, which are magnificent and lush. Surprisingly, the main peak of Table Mountain is 1,067 meters above sea level, but the top of the mountain is spreading just like a huge desktop, because it is located in the special geographic location of the confluence of the two oceans, coupled with the Mediterranean's peculiar climatic environment, the top of the mountain year-round clouds, full of magical and unpredictable atmosphere, and sometimes the clouds will be scattered by chance, but only a handful of days a year, and each time it lasts only a few hours. Table Mountain Nature Reserve is home to more than 2,000 species of endangered native flowers and plants, about 150 species of birds and small wildlife including rock rabbits, baboons and civets. The top of Table Mountain can be reached by cable car and has been chosen by the local municipality as a signpost for the "Beauty of South Africa".

2. 太阳城 Sun City

太阳城（图5-8）位于南非第一大城约翰内斯堡的西北方187千米处。太阳城是集娱乐、体育、休闲、博彩和观光为一体的豪华度假村，有"世外桃源""非洲的拉斯维加斯"的美誉，也是世界小姐大赛的举办地。城内有令人痴迷的人造森林和动感十足的人工海浪游泳池，还有每小时发生一次"地震"的地震桥，能满足人们的好奇心。游览太阳城已成为南非之旅的一大亮点，每年有300多万名游客前来观光休闲。

图5-8 太阳城
Figure 5-8 Sun City

The famous tourist attraction, Sun City (Figure 5-8), is located 187 kilometers northwest of Johannesburg. It is a collection of entertainment, sports, leisure, gaming and sightseeing as one of the luxury resorts, to be called "an Arcadia", or "Las Vegas of Africa". It is also a famous host city of the Miss World Pageant. There is a fascinating artificial forest, a swimming pool with dynamic artificial waves, and the Earthquake Bridge, where "earthquakes" occur once an hour, to satisfy the curiosity of the people. Visiting Sun City has become a highlight of South African tour and has attracted about 3 million tourists yearly to come for sightseeing or entertainment.

3. 金矿游乐场 Goldmine Playground

金矿游乐场（图5-9）位于约翰内斯堡以南6千米处，曾为世界上最大的金矿区，现已开辟为旅游区，并按当年淘金时代旧约翰内斯堡的面貌建成街市。南非的黄金储量居世界第一。1880年，这一片土地还只是价值两头牛的农场，而如今，随着南非成为世界上最大的黄金生产国（2007年被中国赶超，至今中国一直占据榜首，但从中长期发展来看南非有着绝对的优势），约翰内斯堡也成为世界最大的产金中心，获得了"黄金之城"的称号。黄金城，自然就有黄金梦，而金矿游

图5-9 金矿游乐场
Figure 5-9 Goldmine Playground

乐场（又称金矿城、金矿主题公园）给了所有人一次圆梦的机会。在游乐场内，最吸引人之处是在地下 300 米的矿洞体验一回矿工的工作。这只是让游客体验的深度，该矿在开采期间，矿洞最深可达几千米。

Goldmine Playground(Figure 5-9) is located 6 kilometers south of Johannesburg and is part of the world's largest gold mining area, now developed into a tourist attraction. It features a marketplace built to resemble old Johannesburg during the gold rush era. South Africa holds the world's largest gold reserves. In 1880, this piece of land was still just a piece of farms worth two cows, and now, as South Africa has become the world's largest gold-producing countries（2007 was overtaken by China, so far, China has been occupying the top of the list, but in the medium and long term, South Africa has an absolute advantage）, Johannesburg has also become the world's largest gold-producing centers, known as the "City of Gold". City of gold, naturally, there is a dream of gold, and gold mine amusement park（also known as gold mine city, gold mine theme park）, gives everyone a chance to fulfill their dreams. In the playground, the most attractive thing is to go deep into the 300 meters mine to experience a miner's work. This depth is only for visitors to experience. The mine could be up to several thousand meters deep during mining.

4. 约翰内斯堡动物园 The Johannesburg Zoo

图 5-10　约翰内斯堡动物园
Figure 5-10　The Johannesburg Zoo

约翰内斯堡动物园（图 5-10）拥有 3 000 种以上的哺乳类、鸟类和爬虫类动物。狮子、大象、长颈鹿，以及大型猿类的围场四周只用壕沟隔开，完全没有铁栏杆，因此大受游客欢迎。另外，新设计的北极熊栖息地，以及可供游客来回走动的大鸟笼也同样受到游客的青睐。在位于约翰内斯堡的米德兰德有座特兰斯瓦蛇园，园里展出各式各样的非洲蛇，布景相当吸引人。蛇园还一天两次专为游客表演如何抽取世上最毒之蛇的毒液。

The Johannesburg Zoo (Figure 5-10) is home to over 3,000 species of mammals, birds and reptiles. The lions, elephants, giraffes, and great apes are very popular with visitors as their enclosures are surrounded only by trenches and have no railings at all. Newly designed polar bear habitats and large aviaries that allow visitors to walk back and forth are also popular. The Transvaal Snake Park in Midrand, Johannesburg, features a variety of African snakes in an attractive setting. Twice a day, visitors are shown how to extract the venom of the world's most poisonous snakes.

（三）旅游购物 Shopping

南非有"购物天堂"的美名，各种商品物美价廉。南非的传统工艺品很有纪念价值，如碗、泥罐、珠饰、木雕、挂毯（动物毛皮）等，鸵鸟蛋和木雕是最有南非特色的旅游纪念品。在南非通用的货币是兰特（Rand），兰特的标记符号为 R，100 分为 1 兰特。外国的游客可以去当地的银行或外币兑换处兑换货币。一些主要的国际性信用卡，如美国运通卡（American Express）、大来卡（Diners Club）、万事达卡（MasterCard）、Visa 卡和他们的加盟信用卡都能在南非使用。

South Africa is known as a "Shopping Paradise" with quality goods at affordable prices. Traditional crafts in South Africa hold significant commemorative value, such as bowls, clay pots, beadwork, wood carvings, tapestries (made from animal hides), ostrich eggs, and wood carvings, which are the most distinctive souvenirs of South Africa. The currency commonly used in South Africa is the Rand, symbolized as R, with 100 cents equaling 1 Rand. Foreign visitors can exchange currency at local banks or foreign exchange outlets. Major international credit cards like American Express, Diners Club, MasterCard, Visa, and their affiliated cards are widely accepted in South Africa.

钻石：钻石号称"宝石之王"。南非是世界重要的钻石生产国，而且以生产名钻闻名于世。南非生产的钻石大多属于珍品级，在国际市场上有很高的声誉。

Diamond: Diamond is known as the "King of Precious Stones". South Africa is the most important producer of diamond and is known to the world for the famous diamonds it has produced. They are for the most part rarities and enjoy very high reputation in the international market.

非洲木雕：在非洲的黑土地上，最有民族特色的东西莫过于木雕艺术品。非洲木雕大都具有宗教神圣性，被认为放在家里能镇宅驱邪。从民间的收藏家到普通的老百姓，越来越多的人爱好收藏非洲木雕艺术品。

African wood carvings: In the black soil of Africa, one of the most distinctive things is the art of wood carvings. African wood carvings are mostly imbued with religious sanctity, believed to protect homes and ward off evil spirits. From folk collectors to ordinary citizens, an increasing number of people have developed a love for collecting African wood carvings.

南非葡萄酒：南非是目前世界上六大知名的葡萄酒产区之一，产量约占世界的 3%，是非洲的葡萄酒王国。南非的葡萄酒价廉物美。

South African wine: South Africa is currently one of the six most renowned wine-producing regions in the world, accounting for approximately 3% of global wine production. It is often referred to as the "Wine Kingdom of Africa". South African wines are known for their excellent quality and affordability.

路依保斯茶：路依保斯茶富含矿物质，非常有益健康。它不含色素、防腐剂和咖啡因，丹宁酸的含量也非常低，还不含草酸，因而对易患肾结石的人来说，是一种非常好的饮料。

扫码获取：入境须知及海关规定

Rooibos tea: Rooibos tea is rich in minerals and highly beneficial for health. It contains no colorants, preservatives, or caffeine, and has very low tannin levels. Additionally, it is free of oxalic acid, making it an excellent beverage choice for those prone to kidney stones.

本节习题

1. 南非的旅游景点主要集中在哪个区？主要景点有哪些？

2. 北京某旅行社接待了南非某旅行社一旅游团队，在团队抵达酒店后，地陪协助办理住店手续，介绍完饭店设施后，带领旅游团用第一餐。酒店为欢迎南非客人，特意安排了以下菜品：卤水豆腐、蜜汁叉烧、五香牛肉、蔬菜沙拉、北京烤鸭、京酱肉丝、东坡肉、烤羊腿、蛋羹、松鼠鳜鱼、扒香菇油菜、九重茄子、清汤三鲜。请问：地陪和酒店在接待南非客人时有哪些不妥之处？

学习目标

1. 熟悉大洋洲旅游区主要客源国和目的地国的国情。

Get familiar with the national conditions of major tourist source and destination countries in the Oceania tourist region.

2. 能根据各国特点开展有针对性的客源开发策划和旅游产品设计。

Be able to carry out targeted tourist source development planning and product design according to the characteristics of various countries.

3. 能根据不同旅行团的需求，设计出合适的旅游线路。

Be able to design suitable tourist routes according to the clients' needs.

4. 掌握澳大利亚和新西兰两个国家主要城市和著名景点的概况，能运用所学理论知识从事实际接待和服务工作。

Master the general situation of major cities and famous scenic spots in Australia and New Zealand, be able to put theoretic knowledge into real practice such as reception and service work.

第一节　大洋洲旅游区特征

The General Situation of Oceania Tourist Region

大洋洲旅游区位于太平洋西南部，介于亚洲旅游区和南极洲之间，西临印度洋，东濒太平洋。大洋洲旅游区包括澳大利亚大陆、塔斯马尼亚岛、新西兰南北二岛、新几内亚岛及太平洋上的三大岛群（即波利尼西亚、密克罗尼西亚和美拉尼西亚三大岛群）等1万多个岛屿。陆地总面积约为897万平方千米，约占世界陆地总面积的6%。

大洋洲旅游区
特征
（英文版）

大洋洲旅游区地形分为大陆和岛屿两部分，大陆海岸线长约1 900千米，澳大利亚独占整个大陆。岛的面积约为133万平方千米，其中新几内亚岛最大，是世界第二大岛。大洋洲有活火山60多座（不包括海底火山），火山旅游资源丰富。大洋洲旅游区大部分处在南、北回归线之间，绝大部分地区属热带和亚热带，除澳大利亚的内陆地区属大陆性气候外，其余地区属海洋性气候。

　　大洋洲旅游区总人口约 4 126 万，约占世界总人口的 0.5%。其中，欧洲人后裔约占 70% 以上，集中在澳大利亚和新西兰两国。各岛国人口密度差异显著，大部分居民通用英语。20 世纪 50 年代以来，大洋洲以其丰富的自然旅游资源和独特的毛利文化成为全世界发展较快的旅游区。澳大利亚和新西兰旅游基础接待设施良好，入境游客多来自欧美国家和亚洲的中、日等经济实力较强的国家。澳、新两国的出境旅游势头也很强劲，两国到中国来的游客数量占中国海外游客总人数的 5% 左右，成为中国主要的客源国。

　　本章选取大洋洲旅游区的澳大利亚和新西兰这两个富有代表性特色的国家，主要从国家地理概览、自然资源、传统节日、主要旅游城市及景点、旅游购物等几个方面展开叙述。

第二节　大洋洲之旅

Tvavel in Oceania

袋鼠之国——澳大利亚
The Land of Kangaroos—Australia

导读

　　澳大利亚是世界上唯一一个独占一整个大陆的国家，70% 的国土属于干旱或半干旱地带，是世界上最平坦、最干燥的大陆。澳大利亚是典型的移民国家，被社会学家喻为"民族的大拼盘"。多民族形成的多元文化是澳大利亚社会的最显著特征，中国和澳大利亚的外交关系可追溯到清代，1901 年，澳大利亚宣布在英联邦内部自治，减少中澳建交的障碍，1907 年光绪三十三年，双方达成建交协议。中华人民共和国成立后，中澳于 1972 年建交，双边关系发展顺利，两国领导人保持经常性接触和互访。中国已成为澳大利亚最大的贸易伙伴和主要的投资来源国，澳大利亚对中国的经济发展也十分重要，中澳双方的经济增长相互促进，形成了相互依赖的良性战略伙伴关系。旅游业是澳大利亚近年来发展最快的行业之一，在澳大利亚的经济中占有重要地位。澳大利亚的旅游资源丰富，大堡礁、黄金海岸等都是国际著名海岛海滩旅游胜地，特有的古老动物和独特的艺术建筑也深受游客喜爱。

一、地理概览 Geography of Australia

（一）位置 Location

　　澳大利亚，全称澳大利亚联邦，位于横跨南半球和东半球的大洋洲。澳大利亚国土面积为 769 万平方千米，位列全球第 6，是大洋洲最大的国家，东南邻近新西兰，西北邻近印度尼西亚，北边邻巴布亚新几内亚及东帝汶。

Australia, officially the Commonwealth of Australia, is part of Oceania in the south and the east hemisphere. Covering an area of 7.69 million square kilometers, it is by area the 6th largest country in the world and the largest in Oceania. Across the sea, Australia is neighbored by New Zealand to the southeast, Indonesia to the northwest, Papua New Guinea and East Timor to the north.

（二）地形和气候 The Land and Seasons

澳大利亚四面环海，占有大洋洲的大部分土地。澳大利亚所处的位置又称为澳大利亚大陆，是地球上最小的大陆板块。澳大利亚境内多沙漠和半沙漠（约占 70%），平均海拔为300 米。澳大利亚自东向西可分为三大地形区：东部和东南部为地势较高的山地，西部为沙漠广布的高原，中部为盆地和平原。东北部的大堡礁是世界上最大的珊瑚礁群。

Australia is surrounded by sea and occupies most of the land in Oceania. The location of Australia is known as Australian continent. It is the smallest continental plate on the earth. Most of the Australia land is covered by desert or semi-desert (70%) with an average altitude of 300 meters above the sea level. The eastern and southeastern part of the terrain is higher. The west is highland and the central is plain. The Great Barrier Reef in the northeast is the largest coral reefs in the world.

澳大利亚全国大部分地区雨水稀少，年平均降水量为 470 毫米，是全球最干燥的地区之一，西部和内陆沙漠为热带沙漠气候，北部属热带草原气候，少数地区为亚热带气候。年平均气温北部为 27 ℃，南部为 14 ℃。

Most of Australia experiences low rainfall, with an average annual precipitation of just 470 millimeters, making it one of the driest places on Earth. The western and inland desert regions have a tropical desert climate, while the northern part of the country has a tropical savanna climate. A few areas in Australia also fall under a subtropical climate. The average annual temperature in the north is around 27℃, while in the south it is approximately 14℃.

（三）自然资源 Natural Resources

澳大利亚矿产资源丰富，铁、铝、镍、铀等矿藏均居世界前列。澳大利亚特产包括欧泊（也叫作"澳宝"，一种珍贵的彩色宝石）、羊皮、牛皮、绵羊油、葡萄酒、红酒、白酒，以及代表土著文化的手工艺品和艺术品等。

Australia is rich in mineral resources, with deposits of iron, aluminum, nickel, and uranium ranking among the top in the world. Australian specialties include opal (also known as " Aussie Gem ", a precious colorful gemstone), sheepskin, cowhide, lanolin, wine, red and white wines, as well as indigenous cultural handicrafts and artworks.

澳大利亚坚果又名澳大利亚胡桃、昆士兰栗，在中国香港称为"夏威夷果"。澳大利亚坚果含油量达 60% ～ 80%，蛋白质和糖的含量各约 9%，并含有相当丰富的钙、磷、铁、氨基酸和维生素 B，经炒制后风味独特、质地细腻、清脆可口、香气浓郁。近年来澳大利亚坚果风靡全球，身价日增，成为国际市场上最受欢迎的高级坚果之一。

Macadamia nuts, also known as Australian walnuts or Queensland chestnuts, known as " macadamia nuts " in Hong Kong, China. Macadamia nuts contain 60%-80% oil, about 9% of protein and sugar, and contains a considerable amount of calcium, phosphorus, iron, amino acids

6

and vitamin B. After frying, macadamia nuts have the unique flavor, delicate texture, and they are crisp and tasty, riching in aroma. In recent years, macadamia nuts have become popular all over the world, and their value has increased day by day, becoming one of the most popular high-level nuts in the international market.

澳大利亚出产的羊毛质量远近驰名，其中美丽诺羊毛的纤维是世界最长的。澳大利亚设计师巧用这种优质的羊毛制成各种精美的服装。除了服装，还有羊毛被褥等羊毛制品。由于高超的处理工艺和优良的品质，羊毛制品冬暖夏凉、柔软、不易生蛀虫。

The wool produced in Australia enjoys great reputation for its superior quality. Merino Wool has the longest fiber in the world, with which Australian designers make fine featured clothes. Apart from the clothing, there are other woolen products such as woolen blanket. Due to its super workmanship and quality, woolen products are cool in summer and warm in winter, soft and resistant to moths.

澳大利亚具有优越的自然环境，是世界上空气污染最少的地区之一。澳大利亚还有近乎苛刻的药检标准及保健品管理制度，因此这里出产的健康食品早已享誉全球，如鱼油、蜂胶等。

Australia has superior natural environment and is one of the least air-polluted regions in the world. Moreover, with its stringent pharmaceutical testing standards and rigorous regulations for health products, Australia has gained a global reputation for producing high-quality health foods such as fish oil, propolis, and so on.

澳大利亚独特
的动物

二、人文概况 Overview of Australian Humanities

（一）国情认知 Basic Knowledge of National Conditions

国家整体为联邦议会制，英国女王是澳大利亚的国家元首，由女王任命的总督为法定的最高行政长官。澳大利亚全国人口约 2 600 万（2022 年），居民中约有 75% 是英国及爱尔兰后裔，18% 为其他民族，亚裔占 5%，土著居民约占 3%。自英国移民踏上这片土地后，已经先后有 120 个国家、140 个民族的移民来到澳大利亚谋生与发展。澳大利亚的通用语言是英语，其次是意大利语、汉语（粤语、普通话）、希腊语、阿拉伯语和越南语。澳大利亚是一个宗教自由的国家，居民中约 65% 信奉基督教，5% 信奉佛教、伊斯兰教、印度教等其他宗教，非宗教信仰人口约占 30%。澳大利亚首都是堪培拉，国花为金合欢，货币为澳大利亚元。澳大利亚是全球经济最发达、国民生活水平最高的国家之一。

Australia has a federal parliamentary system of government. The queen of the United Kingdom is the head of state of Australia, and the governor appointed by the queen is the statutory chief executive. Australia's national population is about 26 million (2022), about 75% of the residents are of British and Irish descent, 18% are of other ethnicities, 5% are Asian, and about 3% are Aboriginal. Ever since British immigrants disembarked on this land, immigrants from 120 countries and 140 nationalities have come to Australia to seek a livelihood. English is the most commonly-used language in Australia, followed by other languages like Italian, Chinese (Cantonese and Mandarin), Greek, Arabic and Vietnamese. Australia is a country of religious freedom, with about 65% of the population practicing Christianity, 5% practicing other religions such as Buddhism, Islam, and Hinduism, and about 30% of the population being non-religious. The capital of Australia is Canberra, the national flower is Acacia, and the currency is Australian dollar. Australia is one of the most economically developed and the highest living standard countries in the world.

澳大利亚国旗是蓝色背景，呈横长方形，长与宽之比为2∶1，由英国国旗（米字旗）、英联邦之星和南十字星座三个元素组成。澳大利亚国徽左边是一只袋鼠，右边是一只鸸鹋，这两种动物均为澳大利亚特有，一般只会向前走，不轻易后退，象征澳大利亚是一个永远迈步向前的国家。澳大利亚国歌为《澳大利亚，前进》。

Australian flag has a blue background, is horizontally rectangular with a length to width ratio of 2∶1, and has three elements, including the British flag (the beige flag), the Commonwealth star and the Southern Cross constellation. The national emblem of Australia features a kangaroo on the left and an emu on the right, both of which are endemic to Australia and generally only move forward, not easily backward, symbolizing a country that always moves forward. The national anthem of Australia is *Advance Australia Fair*.

（二）历史简介 History of Australia

澳大利亚原为土著人居住。1770年，英国航海家库克发现这块大陆并将其命名为"新南威尔士"，宣布其为英国领土。美国独立战争后，英国需要一块地方安置犯人，1788年1月26日，阿瑟·菲利普船长带着第一批犯人登陆澳大利亚，并建立了第一个英国殖民区。1月26日也被定为澳大利亚的国庆日。此后很长一段时间，澳大利亚成为英国的犯人流放地。由于需要技术人员来生产粮食、建造房屋，英国又陆续迁移了许多民众，悉尼成为第一座城市。1797年，英国军官约翰·麦克阿瑟由好望角引进一批西班牙美丽诺羊，澳大利亚畜牧业迅速发展起来。19世纪50年代，在新南威尔士和维多利亚两州发现金矿，大批来自欧洲、美洲的淘金者蜂拥而至，澳大利亚人口迅速增长。1901年1月1日，6个殖民区组成联邦，建立澳大利亚联邦，成为大英帝国的自治领，实际是一个独立国家。1931年，取得内政和外交权。第二次世界大战以后，澳大利亚政府启动移民计划，该计划已为澳大利亚带来600多万移民。1986年，英国女王签署《与澳大利亚关系法》，英国法律在澳大利亚失效，澳大利亚正式脱离英国成为真正意义上的独立国家。

The Continent of Australia had long been inhabited by indigenous Australians. In 1770, Captain Cook, the great navigator, found this continent and named it New South Wales and claimed it a British territory. After the American Revolutionary War, Britain needed a location for the prisoners. On January 26, 1788, Captain Arthur Philip and the first British fleet arrived here, and later the first British colony was established. The date January 26 was later designated as the National Day of Australia. Australia had since served as the penal colony for a long time. Meanwhile, due to the need of labors for farming and house building, many British free men emigrated to Australia and Sydney was established as the first city. In 1797, John MacArthur, a British army officer, purchased a portion of a small flock of Spanish merinos imported from the Cape Colony, contributing them to the fast development of animal husbandry in Australia. In the 1850s, gold mines were discovered in New South Wales and Victoria, attracting a great many gold diggers from Europe and America, which accelerated the growth of population in Australia. On January 1, 1901, the six crown colonies federated, forming the Commonwealth of Australia, as a dominion of the British Empire, but actually it was already an independent country. In 1931, it obtained the right to deal with its domestic and foreign affairs. After the Second World War, Australian government launched a migration program, as a result of which more than 6 million people have come to Australia as new settlers.

In 1986, the British Queen signed the *Australia Act* that ended all power of the UK Parliament for effective legislation in Australia, and Australia has since become a truly independent country.

（三）经济状况 The Economy

农业、采矿业、制造业和服务业是澳大利亚的支柱产业。澳大利亚是世界上最大的羊毛生产地，享有"骑在羊背上的国家""坐在矿车上的国家""手持麦穗的国家""南半球的聚宝盆""野生动物的世外桃源""珍奇植物的王国"等美称。澳大利亚的渔业资源也十分丰富，是世界上第三大捕鱼区，主要产品有对虾、龙虾、鲍鱼、金枪鱼、扇贝和牡蛎等。澳大利亚凭借其得天独厚的自然条件和地理优势大力发展服务业，特别是旅游业和教育业。

Agriculture, mining, manufacturing and service are the pillar industries in Australia. Australia is the largest wool producer in the world. It is reputed as the " Country Riding on Sheep's Back ", the " Country on A Mine Car ", the " Country Holding Wheat Ears ", the " Cornucopia of the South Hemisphere ", the " Paradise for Wild Animals " and the " Kingdom of Rare Plants ". Australia is also rich in fisheries resources, the main products are shrimp, lobster, abalone, tuna, scallops and oysters. The natural blessings and geographical advantages combined greatly promoted the development of service industry, especially tourism and education.

（四）传统文化 Traditional Culture

澳大利亚民众的生活方式与西欧和北美相似，澳大利亚的生活轻松、舒适且充满各种可能。来自世界各地的移民大都喜欢这里的生活。澳大利亚人既有西方人的爽朗，又有东方人的矜持。澳大利亚人的风俗礼仪在许多方面同英国人十分相似。澳大利亚人在公共场合不会喧哗，讲究礼貌，待人谦恭有礼。人们相见总是热情打招呼，握手致意，彼此称呼对方的名字，男女老幼均是如此。

The mainstream of Australian culture essentially belongs to the western culture. The lifestyle is similar to that of Western Europe and North America. The life here is slow-paced, comfortable and full of possibilities. Those immigrants from all corners of the world enjoy living here. Australians have both the candidness of the western people and the reservedness of the oriental people. The Australian customs are quite similar to the British in many aspects. Australians usually do not talk aloud in public, and are polite and courteous. They greet each other warmly with handshakes. They tend to call each other's names, regardless of gender and age.

澳大利亚人的时间观念很强，约会要提前联系并准时赴约。如果被邀请到澳大利亚人家中做客，最合适的礼物是给女主人带上一束鲜花，澳大利亚人喜欢喝酒，也可以给男主人送一瓶葡萄酒。告别时，客人需对主人的款待表示感谢。澳大利亚人好流动，频频变换居住之地，很少固定在一个地方终其一生。澳大利亚人也爱旅游，并乐在其中。他们兴趣广泛，喜欢体育运动，如冲浪、帆板、赛马、钓鱼、澳式橄榄球及游泳等。

Australians have a strong sense of punctuality, and it's important to schedule appointments in advance and arrive on time. If invited to an Australian's home, the most appropriate gift is a bouquet of flowers for the hostess. Australians enjoy drinking, so a bottle of wine for the host is also a good choice. When leaving, guests should thank their hosts for their hospitality. Australians tend to be mobile, frequently changing their place of residence and rarely staying in one location for their entire lives. They also love to travel and find joy in it. They have a wide range of interests and enjoy sports such as surfing, windsurfing, horse racing, fishing, Australian rugby and swimming,etc.

居住在澳大利亚的土著人仍然保留着自己的风俗习惯。他们以狩猎为生，"飞去来器"是他们独特的狩猎武器。很多土著人仍居住在用树枝和泥土搭成的窝棚里，围一块布或用袋鼠皮蔽体。他们喜欢文身并在身上涂抹各种颜色，一些土著人会佩戴臂环、项圈、前额箍和骨制鼻针。随着时代的变迁，一些土著人渐渐离开部落，搬迁到城市居住。在旅游区，土著人的艺术品和手工艺品深受游客的喜爱，这也是土著人的主要收入来源。

Australian aborigines or indigenous people still hold onto their traditional customs and habits. They make a living by hunting with their characteristic hunting weapon "Boomerang". Many of them live in shacks made by tree branches and mud, their bodies covered by a piece of cloth or kangaroo fur. They like tattoos and painting all kinds of colors on their bodies. Some wear arms band, collar, forehead hoop and nose piercing bone needles. With the passage of time, some aborigines have left their tribes and settled down in city. In tourist areas, the aboriginal works of art and handicrafts are favored by tourists, and it becomes the main source of income for the aborigines.

带你认识"飞去来器"

（五）礼仪禁忌 Social Etiquettes and Taboos

在社交场合，澳大利亚人显得非常随和，喜爱同陌生人交往，对待客人也是如此。同英国人一样，澳大利亚人同样遵循女士优先的原则。在社交场合打哈欠、伸懒腰是不礼貌的行为。澳大利亚的基督教徒有周日做礼拜的习惯，因此要避免在这一天和他们邀约。应邀到澳大利亚人家做客，最合适的礼物是给女主人带上一束鲜花，也可以给男主人送瓶葡萄酒。

On social occasions, Australians are very easygoing and like to make contact with strangers, so is it with stranger, so is it with guests. Like Britain, Australia advocates the practice of "lady first". It is considered rude to yawn or stretch oneself on social situations. Australian Christians are in the habit of worshiping on Sundays, so avoid inviting them on this day. When invited to an Australian home, the most appropriate gift is to bring a bouquet of flowers for the hostess and a bottle of wine for the hostess.

澳大利亚人忌讳兔子及兔子图案，认为兔子是一种不吉利的动物，看到它会倒霉。澳大利亚人喜爱袋鼠、琴鸟和金合欢图案。忌送澳大利亚人菊花、杜鹃花、石竹花和黄颜色的花。切忌对其国内事务发表议论，与当地人交谈时，应多谈旅行、体育运动及在澳大利亚的有趣见闻。

Australians generally avoid rabbits and rabbit motifs, as they consider rabbits to be symbols of bad luck and believe that seeing one may bring misfortune. On the other hand, Australians are fond of kangaroos, lyrebirds, and golden wattle designs. It is best to avoid gifting Australians chrysanthemums, azaleas, carnations, or yellow flowers. Additionally, one should refrain from commenting on their domestic affairs. When engaging in conversation with locals, it's better to talk about topics like travel, sports, or interesting experiences in Australia.

（六）传统节日 Festivals

1. 澳大利亚国庆日 Australia Day

1788 年 1 月 26 日，阿瑟·菲利普船长和他的第一舰队携带 1 350 人（其中多数是囚犯）抵达悉尼港，英国殖民者开始在澳大利亚定居。后来，这一天被定为澳大利亚国庆日，即澳大利亚日。每年 1 月 26 日这天，澳大利亚各大城市都会举行各种大型的庆祝活动。

On January 26, 1788, Captain Arthur Phillip and his First Fleet arrived at Sydney harbour with more than 1,350 people, among whom most were prisoners, and it marked the day when British colonists started settling in Australia. Later this special day was designated the National Day of Australia or known as Australia Day. On this day, all kinds of celebrations will be launched in the big cities all over the country.

2. 复活节 Easter

复活节是西方的一个重要节日，通常是 3 月末或 4 月初的某个星期日。复活节是基督教纪念耶稣复活的节日，象征着重生与希望。复活节的庆祝活动丰富多样，有宗教信仰的人们会去教堂做礼拜、孩子们互换彩蛋；全国性的民间艺术节、园艺竞赛、娱乐节目表演等也会在复活节期间举办。

Easter is an important holiday in the West, usually celebrated on a Sunday in late March or early April. Easter is a Christian holiday commemorating the resurrection of Jesus, symbolizing rebirth and hope. Easter celebrations are rich and varied, for example: religious people will go to church to worship, children exchange colored eggs; national folk art festivals, horticultural competitions, entertainment programs and other performances held annually during the Easter season.

3. 澳新军团日 Anzac Day

澳新军团日又称“澳纽军团日”，是纪念 1915 年 4 月 25 日在“加里波利之战”中牺牲的澳大利亚和新西兰军团（简称澳新军团）将士的日子。澳新军团日在澳大利亚和新西兰均被定为公众假日，以缅怀为国牺牲的将士。

Anzac Day, also known as “Australian and New Zealand Army Day”, commemorates the men of the Australian and New Zealand Army Corps (ANZAC) who lost their lives on April 25, 1915, at the Battle of Gallipoli. Anzac Day is recognized as a public holiday in both Australia and New Zealand in order to honour the memory of those who died in the service of their country.

4. 女王诞生日 Queen's Birthday

女王诞生日设在 6 月的第二个星期一，此节日是庆祝伊丽莎白二世的生日，也是一个公众假日。

The Queen's Birthday falls on the second Monday of June. This holiday celebrates the birthday of Queen Elizabeth II and is also recognized as a public holiday.

5. 墨尔本赛马节 Melbourne Cup

始于 1861 年的墨尔本赛马节是澳大利亚最重要的盛事，已有 150 年的历史。每年 11 月的第一个星期二为全国公假，家家户户都穿着节日盛装，兴致勃勃地参加这一盛典。全球的澳大利亚人无论身在世界何处，都会驻足观看这场赛事并为他们喜爱的赛马冲线而兴奋喝彩。墨尔本赛马节深深地嵌入了澳大利亚的文化，成为这个国家的一个符号。

The Melbourne Cup, which began in 1861, is Australia's most significant event and has a history spanning over 150 years. The first Tuesday of November is a national public holiday, during which families dress in their finest attire and enthusiastically participate in the celebration. Australians around the world, no matter where they are, pause to watch the race and cheer excitedly for their favorite horses as they cross the finish line. The Melbourne Cup is deeply embedded in Australian culture and has become a symbol of the nation.

三、旅游观光 Tourism and Sightseeing

（一）主要旅游城市 Major Tourist Cities

1. 悉尼 Sydney

悉尼位于澳大利亚东南部，是新南威尔士州的首府，它是澳大利亚最古老、最大和最多样化的城市之一。悉尼是澳大利亚的经济与文化中心、澳大利亚第一大城市，也是著名的旅游城市。同时，悉尼是澳大利亚最繁华的现代化、国际化城市，有"南半球的纽约"之称。悉尼拥有众多的名胜古迹，其中以悉尼歌剧院、海港大桥、悉尼塔、达令港、中城、岩石区、维多利亚女王大厦、邦迪海滩等最为著名。

Sydney, located in the southeastern part of Australia, is the capital of New South Wales and is one of the oldest, largest, and most diverse cities in Australia. It serves as the economic and cultural center of the country, being the largest city in Australia and a renowned tourist destination. Sydney is also considered the most vibrant, modern, and international city in Australia, often referred to as the "New York of the Southern Hemisphere". The city boasts numerous landmarks, with the Sydney Opera House, Sydney Harbour Bridge, Sydney Tower, Darling Harbour, the Central Business District, The Rocks, the Queen Victoria Building, and Bondi Beach being among the most famous.

2. 墨尔本 Melbourne

墨尔本是澳大利亚第二大城市，是有"花园之州"之称的维多利亚州的首府、知名的国际大都市。1901年至1927年，墨尔本曾是澳大利亚的首都。墨尔本也是澳大利亚的文化重镇和体育之都，具有深厚的文化底蕴，被称为"澳大利亚的文化首都"，曾主办1956年夏季奥运会，也是一年一度的澳大利亚网球公开赛、一级方程式赛车澳大利亚分站比赛的常年主办城市。全澳大利亚乃至全球都很有影响力的墨尔本赛马节每年都会在此举行。墨尔本是在19世纪中期淘金热潮中迅速发展起来的城市，目前仍保留着许多19世纪华丽的维多利亚式建筑，是澳大利亚最具有欧洲韵味的城市，被称为"澳大利亚的伦敦"。

Melbourne, a famous metropolis and the second largest city in Australia, is the capital city of the state of Victoria renowned as the "State of Gardens". From 1901 to 1927, it served as the capital of the country. Often referred to as the "Cultural Capital of Australia", the city is the hub of culture and sports, boasting profound cultural implications. It was the host city of the Olympic Games in 1956 and is the perennial host city for annual Australian Open and Formula 1 Australian Grand Prix. The Melbourne Cup, a world famous horse racing event, is held in Melbourne every year. Melbourne is the city bred by the gold rush in mid-19th century. At present, it still retains many splendid Victorian style buildings dating from the 19th century, making it a distinctive city with strong European flavor and thus gaining itself a nickname "London in Australia".

图 6-1　布里斯班
Figure 6-1　Brisbane

3. 布里斯班 Brisbane

布里斯班（图6-1）是有"阳光之州"美誉的昆士兰州的首府，因此被称为"阳光之城"，是澳大利亚的第三大城市，有"考拉之都"的美誉。整个城市由布里斯班河环绕，拥有美丽的自然风景和四季如春的气候，有女王花园、维多利亚公园、考拉动物园等观光游览胜地。布里斯班是澳大利亚东部前往热带地区的中转站，搭乘火车可以直达凯恩斯、黄金海岸、阳光海岸等旅游胜地。

Brisbane (Figure 6-1), the third largest city in Australia, is the capital of the "Sunshine State" Queensland. Thus it is proclaimed as the "Sunshine City" and also as the "Koala Capital". The whole city is encircled by the Brisbane River, boasting beautiful natural scenery and pleasantly mild climate. It has the attractions such as Queen's Garden, Victoria Park, Koala Zoo, etc. Brisbane is the junction to the tropical area on the east coast of Australia, linking directly to tourist resorts such as Cairns, Gold Coast and Sunshine Coast by railway.

4. 凯恩斯 Cairns

凯恩斯是地处热带的昆士兰州北部的旅游城市，位于澳大利亚大陆东海岸最北端，是最接近"世界七大自然景观"之一的大堡礁的观光城市。靠近赤道的凯恩斯被称为"热带之都"，保有大片原始热带雨林。凯恩斯是前往大堡礁和热带雨林的必经大门。

A tourist city of tropical North Queensland, Cairns is at the north tip of east coast of Australia, closest to the Great Barrier Reef, one of the "Seven Natural Wonders of the World". As it is close to the Equator and home to vast pristine tropical rain forest, Cairns is often referred to the "Tropical Capital". It serves as a gateway for people to visit the Great Barrier Reef and tropical rain forest.

（二）著名旅游景点 Famous Tourist Attractions

1. 悉尼歌剧院 Sydney Opera House

悉尼歌剧院（图 6-2）是 20 世纪最具特色的建筑之一，是世界著名的艺术表演中心之一。在现代建筑史上，它被认为是巨型雕塑式风格的典型作品，是悉尼的标志性建筑。悉尼歌剧院于 1959 年开始修建，1973 年建成，外形犹如即将乘风出海的白色风帆，与周围景色相映成趣，其特有的风帆造型每年吸引着无数的游客。悉尼歌剧院是公认的"20 世纪世界十大奇迹"之一，该剧院的设计者为丹麦设计师约恩·乌松。2007 年 6 月 28 日，悉尼歌剧院被联合国教科文组织评为世界文化遗产。

图 6-2　悉尼歌剧院
Figure 6-2　Sydney Opera House

Sydney Opera House (Figure 6-2) is one of the 20th century's most distinctive buildings and one of the most famous performing arts centers in the world. It is recognized as a typical work of giant statue style in modern architecture history and the landmark of Sydney. Sydney Opera House was commenced in 1959 and finished in 1973, designed in the shape of a white swollen sail, forming a nice contrast with its neighbors. Every year, millions of tourists are attracted by its unique design. Sydney Opera House was designed by a famous Danish architect Jom Utzon,

澳洲的国家级地标建筑——悉尼歌剧院

it is reputed as one of "Ten Wonders of the 20th Century". On June 28, 2007, it was elected by UNESCO as one of the World Cultural Heritage.

图 6-3　悉尼海港大桥
Figure 6-3　Sydney Harbor Bridge

2. 悉尼海港大桥 Sydney Harbor Bridge

悉尼海港大桥（图 6-3）号称世界第一单孔拱桥，是早期悉尼的代表性建筑，与举世闻名的悉尼歌剧院隔海相望。大桥于 1857 年开始设计，1924 年建造桥基，直到 1932 年才竣工。它的拱架跨度为 503 米，桥身长 1 149 米，桥面宽 49 米，中间铺有双轨铁路，两侧人行道各宽 3 米。澳大利亚人形容悉尼海港大桥的造型像一个巨型衣架，并把它视为悉尼的象征。

The Sydney Harbour Bridge (Figure 6-3), known as the world's first single-arch bridge, is a representative structure of early Sydney, across the sea from the world-famous Sydney Opera House. Design of the bridge began in 1857, the bridge foundation was built in 1924, and it was not completed until 1932. Its arch span is 503 meters, the bridge body is 1,149 meters long, the bridge deck is 49 meters wide, the middle is paved with a double-track railroad, and the sidewalks on each side are 3 meters wide. Nicknamed "the coat-hanger" by Australians, it is an iconic symbol of Sydney.

图 6-4　悉尼塔
Figure6-4　Sydney Tower

3. 悉尼塔 Sydney Tower

悉尼塔（图 6-4）是悉尼的另一大地标，它与悉尼歌剧院、海港大桥并列为悉尼三大标志性建筑。塔高 309 米，为南半球第二高的建筑物，其金黄色的外观闪耀夺目。游客登上圆锥形塔楼，纵目四望，悉尼市容一览无余。

Sydney Tower (Figure 6-4) is another landmark of Sydney. Together with Sydney Opera House and Harbor Bridge, they are known as three landmarks of Sydney. It has a dazzling golden exterior, with a height of 309 meters, making it the second tallest observation tower in the Southern Hemisphere. On the top of its cone-shaped tower, tourists may have a panoramic view of the whole Sydney city.

4. 邦迪海滩 Bondi Beach

邦迪海滩（图 6-5）是一个非常受欢迎的海滩，位于悉尼中央商务区以东 7 千米处，是澳大利亚游客最多的景点之一。邦迪海滩迷人的海岸线、明亮的蓝天、白色的海浪、柔软和粉状的沙子对游客具有巨大的吸引力，是适合冲浪、游泳和晒日光浴的绝佳胜地。

Bondi Beach (Figure 6-5) is a popular beach, located 7 kilometers east of Sydney CBD, and is one of the most attractive spots in Australia. Bondi Beach's amazing shoreline with bright blue sky, white waves, soft and powdery sand are great attractions for tourists. It is a great place for surfing, swimming and sunbathing.

图 6-5　邦迪海滩

Figure 6-5　Bondi Beach

5. 曼利海滩 Manly Beach

曼利海滩（图 6-6）位于悉尼北部，是悉尼顶级海滩之一，有三个独立的部分：南斯泰因、北斯泰因和昆斯克利夫。曼利海滩是有孩子的家庭的最佳去处，因为这里的水干净而平静，到处都是草地。要到达海滩，必须使用渡轮服务通过悉尼港，这需要 30 分钟。曼利海滩拥有众多的商店、餐厅、活动和娱乐项目。曼利海滩最迷人之处是黄金海岸，海岸线很长，是悉尼最漂亮的海滩之一。沙滩沿海岸线延伸约 3 千米，游客们可以在出租的椅子上和遮阳伞下享受阳光。

图 6-6　曼利海滩

Figure 6-6　Manly Beach

Located north of Sydney, Manly Beach (Figure 6-6) is one of Sydney's top beaches and has three separate sections: South Staines, North Staines and Queens cliff. Manly Beach is the perfect place for families with children, as the water is clean and calm, and there are grassy areas everywhere. To get to the beach, you have to use the ferry service through Sydney Harbor, which takes 30 minutes. Manly Beach has an abundance of stores, restaurants, activities and entertainment options. Manly Beach is charmingly Gold Coast with a long coastline and is one of the prettiest beaches in Sydney. The beach stretches for about 3 kilometers along the coastline and visitors can soak up the sun in rented chairs and umbrellas.

6. 蓝山三姐妹峰 The Three sisters of Blue Mountains

蓝山国家公园坐落在新南威尔士州境内，该州共有 7 座澳大利亚国家公园。蓝山曾被英国伊丽莎白女王二世誉为"世界上最美丽的地方"，在 2000 年被列入世界自然遗产名录。蓝山的得名源于满山的油性桉树。由于桉叶散发出浓郁芬芳的油滴，与尘埃颗粒和水蒸气一起在阳光的折射下散射出以蓝色为主的短波光线，使山峰笼罩在蓝色的氤氲中。蓝山的标志是著名的"三姐妹峰"（图 6-7）。

图 6-7　蓝山三姐妹峰

Figure 6-7　The Three Sisters of Blue Mountains

Blue Mountains National Park is situated in

New South Wales in which there are altogether 7 national parks. Described as the "Most Beautiful Place in the World" by Queen Elizabeth Ⅱ, it was later inscribed on the World Heritage List in 2000. Blue Mountains derive its name from eucalyptus all over the mountains. It is based on the fact that the constant fragrance emitted by the eucalyptus forest becomes evaporated and dispersed under the refraction of the sunlight, thus making the mountain shrouded in the blue veil of mist. The Blue Mountains are marked by the famous "Three Sisters" (Figure 6-7).

图 6-8　大洋路
Figure 6-8　The Great Ocean Road

7. 大洋路 The Great Ocean Road

大洋路（图6-8）位于墨尔本西南，是一条连接王子镇与菲利普海港的全长达320千米的海滨公路。1980年，大洋路被确定为国家自然公园，对游客开放，是世界著名的观光景点之一。大洋路是为纪念参加第一次世界大战的士兵修建的，共有3 000余名工人参与建造，其中包括参战老兵。大洋路沿着维多利亚州西海岸蜿蜒伸展，带给游客壮丽的海洋风光，游客可体验各种海滩活动。十二门徒的断崖奇景（图6-9）是大洋路上的一绝。

图 6-9　十二门徒
Figure 6-9　The Twelve Apostles Cliff

Located in the southwest of Melbourne, the Great Ocean Road (Figure 6-8) is a 320 kilometers stretch of road along the coast. In 1980, the Great Ocean Road was open to public as a national nature park. It is a world famous tourist attraction. Dedicated to the veterans of the First World War, the road was built by over 3,000 laborers, including many retired servicemen from the First World War. The road winds alongside the west coast of Victoria, providing tourists with splendid ocean view and beach amusements. The Twelve Apostles Cliff (Figure 6-9) is a unique sight on the Great Ocean Road.

图 6-10　大堡礁
Figure 6-10　The Great Barrier Reef

8. 大堡礁 The Great Barrier Reef

大堡礁（图6-10）是世界上最长、最大的珊瑚礁群。它纵贯蜿蜒于澳大利亚的东海岸，全长2 011千米，最宽处为161千米，南端离海岸241千米，北端离海岸仅16千米。礁群由珊瑚虫以及单细胞藻类残骸堆积而成，历经沧桑演变形成巨大的珊瑚礁群，在落潮时，部分珊瑚礁露出水面形成珊瑚岛，像一座座堡垒护卫海岸，所以称为堡礁。大堡礁有400余种不同类型的珊瑚，颜色有赤、橙、黄、绿、青、蓝、紫，深浅各异，造型千姿百态。1981年，大堡礁被联合国教科文组织列入《世界遗产名录》。

The Great Barrier Reef (Figure 6-10) has the world's longest and largest coral reef system. It winds along the Australia's east coast, with overall length of 2,011 kilometers and maximum width as large as 161 kilometers. Furthermost in the south is 241 kilometers off the coast, whereas in the north is just 16 kilometers off the coast. The reef is formed by the accumulation of coral polyps and the remains of single-celled algae, evolving over time into a vast coral reef system. During low tide, parts of the reef emerge above the water, creating coral islands that act like fortresses guarding the coast, hence the name "barrier reef". The Great Barrier Reef is home to over 400 different types of coral, displaying a range of colors including red, orange, yellow, green, indigo blue, and purple, with varying depths and diverse shapes. In 1981, the Great Barrier Reef was inscribed on the UNESCO World Heritage List by UNESCO.

自然奇观——
大堡礁

9. 艾尔斯岩石 Ayers Rock

澳大利亚北方领土地区是古代土著文化的发源地，以自然景观和文化特色著称，特别是著名的红土中心及世界上最大的独立巨石艾尔斯岩石（图6-11）。艾尔斯岩石底面呈椭圆形，形状有些像两端略圆的长面包，长为3 600米，宽约2 000米，高为348米，基围周长约9 400米。该岩石主要成分为砾石，含铁量高，其表面因被氧化而发红，整体呈红色，因此又被称作红石。艾尔斯岩石的俗称为"人类地球上的肚脐"，号称"世界七大奇景"之一。如今这里成为国家公园，每年有数百万人从世界各地纷纷慕名前来观赏巨石风采。这块独体岩石随着太阳高度的不同而变色，因此被土著人作为圣石来膜拜。1987年，艾尔斯岩石及其所处的国家公园被列入《世界遗产名录》。

图6-11　艾尔斯岩石
Figure 6-11　Ayers Rock

Northern Territory is the origin place of ancient aboriginal culture, renowned for its natural landscape and cultural features, especially the famous Red Center and Uluru (Ayers Rock) (Figure 6-11), the biggest free standing monolith in the world. Ayers Rock is oval at the bottom, resembling a long loaf of bread with two round ends. It is 3.6 kilometers long, 2 kilometers wide, 348 meters high with a total circumference of 9.4 kilometers. The rock is mainly composed of gravel containing high level of iron. Weathering of iron-bearing minerals by the process of oxidation gives the surface layer of rock a red-brown rusty color, thus, it is also called Red Rock. Nicknamed the "Belly Button of the Earth", it is one of the "Seven Natural Wonders of the World". It is now a national park, receiving millions of visitors from different parts of the world. It was worshiped by the aboriginal as the sacred rock as its color changes with the height of sun. In 1987, Ayers Rock and the surrounding National Park were inscribed on the World Heritage List.

（三）旅游购物 Shopping

袋鼠肉：袋鼠肉的味道和牛肉很接近，但没有牛肉嫩，袋鼠肉在澳大利亚的大部分州允许销售，一些肉店有鲜肉供应。一些餐馆有用袋鼠肉制成的美食，价格与牛肉差不多。吃烤袋鼠肉时候要使用椒盐、柠檬和胡椒等作料，最好再来点辣椒压住原本的酸味。

Kangaroo meat: Kangaroo meat is very close in flavor to beef, but not as tender as beef. Kangaroo meat is allowed to be sold in most states in Australia, and some butchers have fresh meat available. Some restaurants serve kangaroo meat for about the same price as beef. Roasted kangaroo should be eaten with salt, lemon and pepper, and preferably a bit of cayenne pepper to suppress the original sour flavor.

皇帝蟹：龙虾、皇帝蟹、白牡蛎是澳大利亚的三宝。澳大利亚出产的皇帝蟹品种肥大，一般可以长到 8～10 千克。一只皇帝蟹差不多要 2 000 元人民币。皇帝蟹的吃法多种多样，如 XO 蟹块、葱姜焗蟹、椒盐蟹腿、蟹黄面和蟹黄酸辣汤。

King crab: Lobster, king crab, and white oysters are considered Australia's top three treasures. Among them, Australian king crabs are particularly large, typically weighing between 8 to 10 kilograms. A single king crab can cost around 2,000 RMB. There are various ways to prepare and enjoy king crab, including XO-style crab pieces, crab baked with scallions and ginger, salt and pepper crab legs, crab roe noodles, and crab roe hot and sour soup.

鳄鱼肉：如果想品尝一下鳄鱼肉，就一定要去爱丽斯泉的"陆上牛排屋"。除了鳄鱼肉，还可以在那里尽情享用鸸鹋肉、袋鼠肉和其他本土美食。

Crocodile meat: If you want to try crocodile meat, you must visit the "Overland Steakhouse" in Alice Springs. In addition to that, you can also enjoy emu meat, kangaroo meat, and other local delicacies there.

牡蛎：澳大利亚的牡蛎又大又干净，且价格低。牡蛎可以生吃，也可以蒸着吃。牡蛎有细腻肌肤、美容养颜、降血压、滋阴养血、强身健体等多种功效。

Oysters: Australia oysters are large, clean, and affordable. They can be eaten raw or steamed. Oysters offer various benefits, including improving skin texture, enhancing beauty, lowering blood pressure, nourishing the body, and promoting overall health.

大马哈鱼：大马哈鱼现在已经成为澳大利亚价格最高的一种鱼。这种鱼不仅大，而且肉质鲜美。

扫码获取：入境须知及海关规定

Salmon: Salmon is now one of the most expensive fish in Australia. This fish is not only big, but also has delicious meat.

本节习题

1. 澳大利亚的旅游宣传口号"Australia is different"（澳大利亚，尽是不同）体现在哪些方面？

2. 以小组为单位，制作一份澳大利亚旅游宣传册。

3. 请结合澳大利亚的旅游资源特色，设计一条适合中国游客的 8 日自助游线路。

绵羊之国——新西兰
The Land of Sheep—New Zealand

导读

新西兰是全球最美丽的国家之一，约有 30% 的国土为保护区，拥有 3 项世界遗产、

14 个国家公园、3 座海洋公园、数百个自然保护区和生态区。优美的沙滩、幽静的峡湾、葱茏的山峰、秀丽的湖泊、多样的人文风情、传统的乡村农庄、珍稀的动物，无不散发着诱人的魅力，吸引着世界各地的旅游者慕名而来。新西兰每年入境旅游人数有 200 万左右，纯旅游观光的人数约占总数的 60%。随着《指环王》《垂直极限》等一系列国际知名影片在新西兰的成功拍摄，新西兰已成为广大游客心目中神圣的中土世界。新西兰将亚太地区作为对外关系的优先领域，积极支持和参与联合国的维和行动、人道主义援助和国际反恐合作，重视参与地区经济合作。在全球整体入境旅游不景气的背景下，新西兰的入境旅游维持在稳定的水平，主要客源市场为澳大利亚、中国、美国、韩国等。新西兰出境旅游市场占比较多的地区依次为大洋洲（83%）、亚洲（10%）、欧洲（4%）和美洲（3%）。

一、地理概览 Geography of New Zealand

（一）位置 Location

新西兰是个岛屿国家，位于太平洋西南部，介于赤道和南极洲之间。新西兰西隔塔斯曼海与澳大利亚相望，两国相距 1 600 千米；北邻新喀里多尼亚、斐济、汤加。作为一个由海洋孕育的国家，新西兰的陆地面积约 27 万平方千米，在世界各国中仅居第 75 位，海域面积超过 41 万平方千米，居世界第 4 位。

New Zealand is an island country located between the Equator and the Antarctica, in the southwest of Pacific Ocean, with Australia 1,600 kilometers to its west across the Tasman Sea, New Caledonia, Fiji and Tonga to its north. As a nation born and bred in ocean, it occupies a land area of 270,000 square kilometers, ranking the 75th in the world, and a sea area of over 410,000 square kilometers, ranking the 4th around the world.

（二）地形和气候 The Land and Seasons

新西兰由南岛、北岛及附近的一些小岛组成。境内多山，75% 以上的面积为山地和丘陵，森林覆盖率超过 31%，天然牧场或农场占国土面积的一半。北岛多火山和温泉，南岛多冰河和湖泊。新西兰属于温带海洋性气候，夏季从 12 月开始到次年 2 月，冬季从 6 月开始到 8 月，夏季平均气温在 20 ℃左右，冬季在 10 ℃左右，全年适合旅游。

New Zealand consists of South Island, North Island and a number of smaller islands. Its territory is predominantly mountainous, of which above 75% are mountains and hills. 31% of the land is covered by forest and half of its land are natural pastures or farms. There are lots of volcanoes and thermal springs on the North Island, glacial and lakes on the South Island. New Zealand has a mild and equable temperate maritime climate. Summer begins from December to next February and winter begins from June to August, with the summer average temperature of 20 ℃ and winter 10 ℃. It is suitable for traveling all year round.

（三）自然资源 Natural Resources

新西兰的矿藏主要有煤、金、铁矿、天然气，还有银、锰、钨、磷酸盐、石油等，但储量不大。石油储量为 3 000 万吨，天然气储量为 1 700 亿立方米。新西兰是罕见鸟类的天堂。最著名的是不会飞的奇异鸟，它是新西兰的非正式国家标志。其他不会飞的鸟还有威卡秧鸡及濒临灭绝的鸮鹦鹉。新西兰的森林资源丰富，森林面积为 810 万公顷，占全国土地面积的 30%，其中 630 万公顷为天然林，180 万公顷为人造林，主要森林产品有原木、圆木、木浆、纸及木板等。渔产丰富。

New Zealand's mineral deposits are mainly coal, gold, iron ore and natural gas, as well as silver, manganese, tungsten, phosphates and petroleum, but the reserves are small. Oil reserves are 30 million tons and natural gas reserves are 170 billion cubic meters. New Zealand is a paradise for rare birds. The most famous is the flightless kiwi, New Zealand's unofficial national symbol. Other flightless birds include the weka and the endangered owl parrot. New Zealand is rich in forest resources, with a forest area of 8.1 million hectares, accounting for 30% of the country's land area, of which 6.3 million hectares are natural forests and 1.8 million hectares are planted forests, with the main products being logs, round logs, wood pulp, paper, and wood panels. The fishery resources of New Zealand is abundant.

二、人文概况 Overview of the New Zealand's Humanities

（一）国情认知 Basic Knowledge of National Conditions

新西兰人口约 512.4 万（2022 年），其中欧洲移民后裔约占 67.6%，毛利人占 14.6%，亚裔占 9.2%（华人约 20 万），太平洋岛国裔占 6.9%。新西兰官方语言为英语、毛利语。新西兰有近一半的居民信奉基督教新教和天主教。新西兰的国旗呈横长方形，旗底色为深蓝色，左上方为同英国国旗一样的由红色、白色组成的米字图案，右边有四颗镶白边的红色五角星。新西兰是英联邦成员国，红色、白色米字图案表明同英国的传统关系。新西兰国歌为《天佑新西兰》，国花是银蕨，国鸟是几维鸟，货币名称为新西兰元。

New Zealand has a population of approximately 5.124 million (2022), of which approximately 67.6% are of European immigrant descent, 14.6% are Maori, 9.2% are Asian (approximately 200 000 are Chinese), and 6.9% are Pacific Islander. The official languages of New Zealand are English and Maori. Nearly half of New Zealand's inhabitants are Protestant and Catholic Christians. The flag of New Zealand is a horizontal rectangle, with a dark blue background, the red and white "✳" design of the British flag in the upper left, and four red five-pointed stars with a white border on the right. New Zealand is a member of the Commonwealth of Nations, and the red and white "✳" design indicates the traditional relationship with the United Kingdom. The national anthem is *God Bless New Zealand*, the national flower is the silver fern, the national bird is the guinea fowl, and the currency is the New Zealand dollar.

新西兰的国鸟——奇异鸟

（二）历史简介 History of New Zealand

新西兰的历史较短，是世上最年轻的移民国家之一。最早的土著人是 14 世纪从波利尼西亚移民来此的毛利人。荷兰人埃布尔·杨森·塔斯曼所带领的船队在 1642 年抵达这里，并将其命名为"Nieuw Zealand"。1769 年至 1777 年，英国人库克先后 5 次到这里，并绘制地图。随后，英国向新西兰大批移民并宣布占领新西兰，把名字改为"新西兰"。1840 年，英国迫使毛利人族长签署《威坦哲条约》，将新西兰纳入英帝国版图。1907 年，新西兰独立，但仍为英国自治领。1947 年，新西兰成为主权国家，同时也是英联邦成员。

As one of the youngest immigrant countries in the world, New Zealand has a very short history. The earliest settlers were a group of Maori who migrated from Polynesia in 14th century and settled in New Zealand. A Dutch man named Abel Janszoon Tasman arrived here with his fleet in 1642 and named the place "Nieuw Zealand". During the year of 1769 to 1777, Captain Cook had come here for five times and mapped the coastlines. The migrants from UK came, occupied this land and named the land "New Zealand". New Zealand was annexed as part of the British Empire after the *Treaty of Waitangi* signed with Maori cacique in 1840. It declared independence in 1907 but still remained a dominion of the United Kingdom. In 1947, New Zealand became a completely independent country and joined the Commonwealth of Nations.

（三）经济状况 The Economy

新西兰是一个经济发达国家。畜牧业是新西兰的经济基础，羊肉、乳制品出口量居世界第一，羊毛出口量居世界第二位。新西兰是全球最大的鹿茸生产国和出口国，出口量约占全球的 30%。新西兰森林资源丰富，工业以农林牧产品加工、造纸和木材加工为主。新西兰渔产丰富，拥有世界第四大专属经济区，200 海里专属经济区内的捕鱼潜力每年可达 500 000 吨。新西兰气候宜人、环境清新、风景优美，旅游胜地遍布全境，地表景观富于变化，旅游业发达，旅游业收入约占新西兰国内生产总值的 10%，是仅次于乳制品业的第二大创汇产业。

New Zealand has an advanced economy and is one of the developed countries. Animal husbandry is the foundation of New Zealand's economy. The value of exporting mutton, dairy products ranks the first in the world and raw wool ranks the second in the world. New Zealand is the largest country of producing and exporting pilose antler, making up 30% of the total global exporting amount. It has rich forest resources. Its main industries are farming, forestry and animal products processing, paper making and timber processing industry. New Zealand boasts the world's fourth largest exclusive economic zone on its abundant aquatic products. In this 200 miles long exclusive economic zone, 500,000 tons of fishes are captured every year. Blessed with pleasant climate, tranquil environment, beautiful landscapes, varied land forms and resources, Tourism in New Zealand is highly developed. The total revenue from the tourist industry takes up 10% of the GDP, making tourism the second largest industry to earn foreign exchange, next to the dairy industry.

（四）传统文化 Traditional Culture

新西兰的大部分国民是欧洲移民的后裔，特别是英国移民的后裔，故一直保持着早期白人殖民者所带来的纯英国式的生活方式，享受生活。社会上流行的礼仪也主要是英国式的，握手是新西兰人见面和告别时的常用礼仪。新西兰人的时间观念很强，约会要提前联系并准时赴约。拜访时，客人最好带上一束鲜花、一瓶威士忌酒或巧克力等。新西兰人的生活悠闲、节奏较慢，除了正餐以外，新西兰人每天要喝六次茶，而且他们很喜欢喝酒，几乎每家都有自己的酒窖。

Most citizens of New Zealand are descendants of European immigrants, especially the British. Therefore, like those white settlers in the early days, they have held onto pure British life style, enjoying life. The prevailing social etiquette is also British style. A handshake is commonly used when people meet and bid farewell. New Zealand people have strong time concept. You should make an appointment in advance for your visit and arrive on time. It is customary to bring a bunch of flowers to the hostess or a bottle of whiskey or a box of chocolate with you. The life of New Zealand people is slow-paced and easy. Besides the regular meals, they drink tea for 6 times one day. They enjoy drinking so much that almost every family has their own cellar.

新西兰人热爱运动，有近一半的人参加至少一种运动或一家健身俱乐部。新西兰最主要的运动是橄榄球，其具有非正式"国民运动"的地位。其他流行的运动有板球、足球、赛车、高尔夫球、游泳和网球等。新西兰的极限运动和探险旅行全球知名，如登山运动在该国就颇为流行。著名的登山家埃德蒙·珀西瓦尔·希拉里爵士，是全球第一位成功攀登珠穆朗玛峰峰顶的人。

Known for being sporty, half of people join at least one sport or fitness club. The major sport in New Zealand is rugby, almost an unofficial "National Sport". Other popular sports include cricket, football, car racing, golf, swimming and tennis, etc. The country enjoys world reputation for its extreme sports and adventure travels, such as the popular mountaineering. Sir Edmund Percival Hillary, a renowned mountaineer, is the first climber in the world to have reached the summit of Mount Everest.

新西兰人的饮食习惯大体上与英国人相同，以西餐为主。但是当地人非常热爱烧烤，各种鱼类、扇贝都是烧烤的食材。新西兰人喜欢饮酒，特别是啤酒和葡萄酒。新西兰的白葡萄酒，特别是夏敦埃酒和塞纳维翁·布兰卡赢得了国际声誉。此外，喝咖啡和红茶也是新西兰人的嗜好。

Generally speaking, the diet habit of New Zealanders is similar with the Britons, mostly dining on Western food. But local people are also enthusiastic about grilled food. All kinds of fishes and scallops are all the good ingredients for grilling. New Zealanders enjoy drinking, especially beer and wine. New Zealand white wines, particularly Chardonnay and Sauvignon Blancs, have won global reputation. New Zealanders are also obsessed with coffee and black tea drinking.

毛利文化是新西兰所独有的。毛利人的雕刻技术非常发达，在新西兰各地随处可见毛利人像木雕。新西兰的毛利人保留了许多传统习俗以及他们自己的语言。毛利人在工艺美术、运动娱乐、歌舞表演方面的才华广受赞誉。毛利人有一种独特的舞蹈，被称为"哈卡"（Haka），这种舞蹈来源于毛利土著武士的战舞，男女舞蹈的具体方式有所不同。新西兰国家橄榄球队在每次开场比赛前会集体表演这种舞蹈，用以鼓舞士气。

毛利人神秘的木雕

Maori culture is unique to New Zealand. Maori carving skills are highly developed and Maori statues can be found throughout New Zealand. New Zealand's Maori people have retained many of their traditional practices as well as their own language. Maori are widely recognized for their talents in arts and crafts, sports and entertainment, and song and dance. The Maori have a distinctive dance known as the Haka, which is derived from the standing dance of the indigenous Maori warriors, and differs in specific ways for men and women. The New Zealand national rugby team performs this dance as a group before each opening game to boost morale.

（五）礼仪禁忌 Social Etiquettes and Taboos

新西兰非常注重动植物保护，即使是公园的花草、野鸭或小鸟都不得随意伤害，违法者将受到严厉的处罚。《休闲捕鱼规定》详细说明了鱼虾、贝类等不同生物的捕捞数量、尺寸、季节及捕捞用具的种类，若违反动植物保护方面的规定，会被罚款甚至判刑。新西兰重视未成年人的保护，法律规定比较严厉。新西兰是禁烟国家，所有的公共场所均不准吸烟，一旦违法将引起不必要的麻烦。

New Zealand attaches great importance to the protection of flora and fauna, and even the flowers and plants in parks, ducks or birds are not allowed to be infringed upon, and offenders will be severely penalized. *The Recreational Fishing Regulations* specify in detail the quantity, size, season and type of fishing gear to be used for catching different species of fish, shrimp, shellfish and other creatures, and violators of animal and plant protection regulations are liable to fines and even imprisonment. New Zealand attaches importance to the protection of minors, and the laws are relatively strict. New Zealand is a no-smoking country, and smoking is not allowed in all public places, which will cause unnecessary trouble if violated.

毛利人是新西兰最早的定居者，仍保留着自己的传统礼仪和文化，散发着独特的魅力。毛利人擅长雕刻和编织，雕刻被视为毛利艺术的精髓。毛利人对传家宝物极为重视，如权杖、翡翠项链等，深信它们蕴藏着祖先的灵气，他们会将这些传家之宝传给子孙们。毛利人相信灵魂不灭，拍照会把灵魂摄走，因此他们非常厌恶游客对着自己拍照、摄像。碰鼻礼是毛利人特有的迎接客人的礼仪。根据毛利人的传统，双方碰鼻的时间越长，表示客人越尊贵。

Maori people were the earliest settlers of New Zealand. They still preserve their own traditional etiquette and culture, representing its unique charm. They are skilled in weaving and carving which is recognized as the essence of Maori culture. Maori people cherish their family treasures such as scepter, emerald necklace, etc., with a firm belief that they bear the spirits of the ancestors and those treasures will be passed down to their descendants. They believe that souls never die and a snapshot can take away one's soul, so they hate to be photographed or recorded in a video by tourists. Maori is a branch of Polynesians and has its characteristic etiquette. According to their tradition, the longer the nose-touching lasts, the deeper respect they have for the guests.

（六）传统节日 Festivals

1. 威坦哲日（又称作"怀唐伊日"）Waitangi Day

2月6日是新西兰一个非常重要的节日——威坦哲日。1840年2月6日，毛利人族长和英国王室的代表签署了《威坦哲条约》，该文件是新西兰的立国奠基文件，明确新西兰成为英国的一个殖民地。每年的2月6日，举国上下共同举办为期四天的庆典活动，包括正式的典礼、由新西兰皇家海军和地方文化团体带来的阅兵式及表演，以及各式各样的体育活动和文化活动。

February 6 is a very important holiday in New Zealand—Waitangi Day. On February 6th, 1840, Maori chiefs and representatives of the British Crown signed the *Treaty of Waitangi*, which is considered the founding document of New Zealand, establishing it as a colony of Britain. Every year on February 6, the country comes together to celebrate with a four-day event including formal ceremonies, parades and performances by the Royal New Zealand Navy and local cultural groups, as well as various sports and cultural activities.

2. 澳新军团日 Anzac Day

每年的 4 月 25 日为澳新军团日，是为了纪念 1915 年在"加里波利之战"中牺牲的澳大利亚和新西兰军团的将士们，缅怀将士们为国牺牲的勇敢精神。

Anzac Day is to commemorate the day of April 25, 1915 when Australian and New Zealand troops suffered heavy casualties and endured great hardships in the "Gallipoli Campaign". It has been declared as a public holiday in memory of the sacrifices those soldiers made for the country.

三、旅游观光 Tourism and Sightseeing

（一）主要旅游城市 Major Tourist Cities

1. 奥克兰 Auckland

奥克兰是新西兰第一大城市，位于新西兰北岛的中北部，依海而建，景色优美，是新西兰的工业、商业和经济、贸易中心，也是新西兰人口最多的城市。奥克兰的气候温和多雨，四季分明，全年气温为 6 ℃～ 28 ℃。奥克兰港风大浪小，非常适合帆船运动。这里每年都会吸引世界各国的帆船爱好者。奥克兰是全球拥有私人船只比例最高的城市，有"千帆之都"的美誉。

Located in the north center of the North Island, Auckland is the largest and most populous city and the industrial, commercial and trade center of the country. It borders the sea and have a beautiful harbour view. Auckland is warm and rainy with four distinct seasons and the temperatures of the year vary from 6 ℃ to 28 ℃ . The strong wind and calm waves make Auckland harbour a wonderful place for sailing, so sailing enthusiasts flock to the harbour every year. Auckland has the biggest number of private yachts worldwide, thus popularly known as the "City of Sails".

2. 惠灵顿 Wellington

惠灵顿位于北岛的最南端，是处于世界最南端的首都，三面环山，一面朝海，是往来南、北二岛的交通枢纽，也是世界最佳深水港之一。整个城市依山而建，地势较高，时常受到海风的侵袭，一年之中大部分日子都会刮风，因而有"风城"之称。

Located at the south tip of the North Island, the capital city Wellington is the pivot of transportation between South Island and North Island, and one of the best deep water ports in the world as well. Wellington is a capital in the world's furthest south, surrounded by mountains on three sides with one side facing the sea. The entire city is built on a hillside, with a relatively high elevation, and is often swept by sea breezes. It experiences windy days for most of the year, earning it the nickname "Windy City".

3. 罗托鲁阿 Rotorua

罗托鲁阿是新西兰北岛中北部著名的地热观光城市，因坐落在火山多发区，被誉为"火山上的城市"。罗托鲁阿距奥克兰市 221 千米，市内的天然温泉、热泉及泥浆池数不胜数。城市空气中硫黄弥漫，热泉泥浆沸腾。除了令人惊讶的火山口、高山和湖泊景观，罗托鲁阿还有美丽的英国哥特式建筑和园林。在新西兰流传着这样一句名言："没到过罗托鲁阿，就不算到过新西兰。"

Rotorua, a geothermal sightseeing city in north-central part of North Island of New Zealand, is popularly known as the "City on the Volcano", as it is located in a volcanic area. 221 kilometers away from Auckland, the city is known for its natural thermal springs, particularly geysers and mud pools. The smell of sulfur permeates in the air, and thermal springs and yellow mud are bubbling. As a tourist city, Rotorua has so much to offer, from the crater, high mountains and lakes, to British style gothic architecture and gardens. A saying in New Zealand goes like this; "No trip to New Zealand is complete without visiting Rotorua."

4. 克赖斯特彻奇 Christchurch

克赖斯特彻奇西临南阿尔卑斯山，东临太平洋海岸，是南岛的第一大城市，新西兰第三大城市，也是仅次于奥克兰的通往世界各地的第二大门户。它同时也是进入南极的门户，还是除奥克兰外的重要港口。这里处处洋溢着英国的气息，是英国本土之外最具有英国色彩的城市，19世纪的建筑比比皆是，公园绿草如茵、花草艳丽、道路洁净，故有"花园城市"的美誉。这里文化艺术气息浓厚，经常举办歌剧、演奏会、芭蕾舞表演。

Christchurch, also known as the Garden City, is located on the South Island of New Zealand. It lies to the west of the Southern Alps and to the east of the Pacific Ocean. It is the largest city on the South Island, the third largest in New Zealand, and the second major gateway to the world after Auckland. It serves as a gateway to Antarctica and is an important port besides Auckland. The city is imbued with a British atmosphere, making it the most British city outside of the UK. It is filled with 19th-century architecture, lush green parks, vibrant flowers, clean roads, earning it the nickname "Garden City". Christchurch has a strong cultural and artistic presence, regularly hosting operas, concerts, and ballet performances.

5. 达尼丁 Dunedin

达尼丁是南岛的第二大城市、全国第四大城市，大约有12万人口。达尼丁是苏格兰人于1848年建立的，城市也承袭了苏格兰丰富多彩的文化遗产，被称为"苏格兰以外最具苏格兰风格的城市"。达尼丁气候宜人，没有严寒和酷暑。达尼丁的旅游业比较发达，拥有众多维多利亚时代与爱德华时代的建筑，并以其珍奇的野生动物而闻名世界。达尼丁也是新西兰的教育中心，享有"大学城"的美誉。

Dunedin is the second largest city in the South Island and the fourth largest in the country, with a population of about 120 000 people. Founded by the Scots in 1848, Dunedin has inherited the rich and colorful cultural heritage of Scotland and has been described as the "Most Scottish City Outside of Scotland". Dunedin has a pleasant climate, with no severe cold or heat. Dunedin has a well-developed tourist industry and is home to many Victorian and Edwardian buildings, and is known worldwide for its rare wildlife. Dunedin is also the educational center of New Zealand and is known as the "City of University".

6. 昆斯敦 Queenstown

昆斯敦位于新西兰南岛中南部，海拔310米，地处南阿尔卑斯山脚下、瓦卡蒂普湖边。昆斯敦是新西兰主要的冰雪运动中心，1947年开设了第一家滑雪场，自此逐步从一座宁静小镇发展成为新西兰的旅游胜地。飞机场、滑雪场、高尔夫球场、餐馆、商店、葡萄园及各种娱乐设施应有尽有，每年吸引游客上百万人。昆斯敦享有"冒险之都"的声誉，喜欢冒险运动的人们可在这里进行蹦极、漂流、冲浪、汽艇等运动。游客还可参观华尔特皮克农场的各种牧场游乐活动，如剪羊毛、牧羊犬表演等。在昆斯敦市郊，可搭乘空中缆车上到400米高的博士峰高山游乐场。昆斯敦曾被多个国际旅游杂志和旅游组织评为"最友好的外国城市"。

Queenstown is located in the south-central part of New Zealand's South Island, at an altitude of 310 meters above sea level, at the foot of the Southern Alps and on the shores of Lake Wakatipu. Queenstown is the main center of snow sports in New Zealand, the first ski resort was opened in 1947, and since then it has gradually developed from a quiet town to a tourist destination in New Zealand. With an airport, ski slopes, golf courses, restaurants, stores, vineyards and a wide range of recreational facilities, it attracts millions of visitors each year. Queenstown has a reputation as the "Adventure Capital", where adventure sports enthusiasts can engage in bungee jumping, rafting, surfing, motor boating and other sports. Tourists can also visit Walter Peek Farm for a variety of ranch rides such as sheep shearing and sheepdog shows. On the outskirts of Queenstown, one can take the aerial gondola up to the 400-meter-high Dr. Peak Alpine Playground. Queenstown has been named the "Friendliest Foreign City" by several international travel magazines and travel organizations.

讨论题

阅读拓展材料"澳大利亚、新西兰休闲农业与观光农业"。请问澳新"互联网＋休闲农业"的成功对中国乡村旅游发展有何启示？

提示：引导学生知农爱农，认识到健康中国战略的重要性，激发学生的使命感和责任感，引导学生投身"三农"，围绕"奋进新时代""助力乡村振兴，投身强国伟业""美丽中国""助力新农村建设"等主题，开展"三下乡"社会实践活动，积极投身乡村振兴建设。

澳大利亚、新西兰休闲农业与观光农业

（二）著名旅游景点 Famous Tourist Attractions

1. 莫尔伯勒 Malborough

莫尔伯勒（图6-12）群山环绕，气候干燥，夏季较长，是新西兰最炎热的地区之一。这里也是新西兰最大的葡萄酿酒区，在著名的酿酒小镇布莱尼姆可以品尝到原汁原味的葡萄酒。莫尔伯勒的海湾曲折而众多，这里盛产各种美味海鲜，最著名的是三文鱼，此外还盛产橘子、草莓、樱桃及果仁等。峡湾遨游、扬帆出海，是一项有趣的旅游活动，从凯库拉乘坐快艇出海，追踪罕见

图6-12 莫尔伯勒
Figure 6-12 Malborough

的抹香巨鲸，是接触大自然生态环境的奇妙旅途，如果幸运，游客可以见到座头鲸及杀人鲸等珍稀鲸类，欣赏巨鲸的各种表演。

Surrounded by mountains, Malborough (Figure 6-12) has a dry climate and long summers, making it one of the hottest regions in New Zealand. It is also New Zealand's largest wine-making region, and you can sample a wide range of original wines in the famous wine-making town of Blenheim. Malborough Bay, with its many twists and turns, produces a variety of delicious seafood, most notably salmon, as well as oranges, strawberries, cherries and nuts. Invitational tours of the fjords and sailing is an interesting tourist activity. Taking a speedboat out of Kaikoura and tracking the rare sperm whale is a wonderful journey to get in touch with nature's ecology, and if lucky, tourists can see rare cetaceans such as humpback and killer whales, and enjoy the various performances of the giant whales.

2. 天空塔 The Sky Tower

天空塔（图6-13）坐落在奥克兰的市中心，始建于1996年，1997年正式开幕，高328米，是奥克兰的标志性建筑，也是南半球的最高建筑。天空塔是观光及电台广播塔，位列全球独立式观光塔第13位。天空塔共用15 000立方米的混凝土和2 660吨的高强度钢建成，地基深达15米。塔上190米处有多层观景台和高倍望远镜，可以方便游客观赏奥克兰的全景。主观景台内设有计算机，用来检索在观景台看到的景点资料，还有多种语言的广播服务和交互式科技设备以及视听展览。

图 6-13　天空塔
Figure 6-13　The Sky Tower

Located in the heart of Auckland, the Sky Tower (Figure 6-13) was built in 1996 and officially opened in 1997. Standing at 328 meters tall, it is an iconic landmark of Auckland and the tallest building in the Southern Hemisphere. The Sky Tower is the 13th tallest freestanding observation tower in the world for sightseeing and radio broadcasting. The Sky Tower was built with a total of 15,000 cubic meters of concrete and 2,660 tons of high-strength steel, with a foundation 15 meters deep. At 190 meters above the tower, there are multi-storey observation decks and high-powered telescopes, allowing visitors to enjoy panoramic views of Auckland. The main observation deck contains computers for retrieving information about the attractions seen from the observation deck, a multilingual radio service and interactive technology equipment, and audio-visual exhibitions.

3. 伊甸山 Mount Eden

伊甸山（图6-14）位于奥克兰市中心以南约5千米处，是一座死火山形成的火山口，形成于大约3万年前，高196米，是奥克兰陆地火山带中最高的火山，也是奥克兰最重要的象征之一。山顶设有瞭望台，视野开阔，可以眺望奥克兰全市的景色。山上有一个标志牌，上面标有世界较大首都距离此地的千米数。伊甸山属温带海洋性气候，四季温差不大，四季皆适宜旅游。

图 6-14　伊甸山
Figure 6-14　Mount Eden

Mount Eden (Figure 6-14) is located about 5 kilometers south of Auckland's city center and is a dormant volcanic crater formed approximately 30,000 years ago. Rising to a height of 196 meters, it is the highest volcano in Auckland's volcanic field and one of the city's most significant landmarks. At the summit, there is a lookout point offering expansive views of Auckland's skyline. A notable sign on the mountain displays the distances to some of the world's major capital cities. Mount Eden enjoys a temperate oceanic climate with minimal seasonal temperature differences, making it a destination suitable for visiting year-round.

4. 新西兰国家博物馆 National Museum of New Zealand

新西兰国家博物馆（图6-15）坐落在惠灵顿皇后湾附近，是新西兰唯一一家由政府直接

图 6-15　新西兰国家博物馆
Figure 6-15　National Museum of New Zealand

管理的博物馆，也是南半球最大的博物馆。博物馆始建于 1933 年，1986 年后进行了搬迁和扩建。1998 年 2 月新馆开馆，终年免费向游客开放。馆内设毛利族陈列大厅、太平洋陈列室、地质史陈列室、动物陈列室等展厅。其中，毛利族陈列大厅展有许多毛利族人的珍贵器物、个人饰品及仪式用武器。这里还陈列着毛利人的特有服装，如夏季的"麻洛"，以及用狗毛皮制成的、象征身份和地位的冬季披风等。

The National Museum of New Zealand (Figure 6-15), located near Queen's Bay in Wellington, is the only museum in New Zealand directly managed by the government and the largest museum in the southern hemisphere. The museum was founded in 1933 and was relocated and expanded in 1986, and in February, 1998, the new museum was opened and is open to visitors free of charge all year round. The museum has a Maori display hall, Pacific display room, geological history display room, animal display room and other exhibition halls. Among them, the Maori display hall has many precious artifacts, personal ornaments and ceremonial weapons of the Maori people. There are also displays of the Maori's unique summer garment, the malo, and a winter cape made of dog fur, which symbolizes status and position.

5. 惠灵顿植物园 Wellington Botanic Gardens

图 6-16　惠灵顿植物园
Figure 6-16　Wellington Botanic Gardens

惠灵顿植物园（图 6-16）是一座自然与人工相结合的大型园林，位于惠灵顿一道"V"形的山岭上，占地 26 公顷。植物园汇聚世界各国的名树名花，是一座国际性的花园，其中有中国的山茶、法国的月季、巴西的珊瑚树、澳大利亚的毛榉、非洲的雪松、荷兰的郁金香及多种颜色的日本樱花。园内数量最多的是新西兰土生土长的松、柏、榆、柳、蕨等。

Wellington Botanic Gardens (Figure 6-16) is a large-scale garden combining nature and artificiality, located on a V-shaped hill in Wellington, covering an area of 26 hectares. The Botanic Gardens is an international garden of famous trees and flowers from all over the world, including Chinese camellias, French rosewood, Brazilian coral trees, Australian beeches, African cedars, Dutch tulips and Japanese cherry blossoms in many colors. The most abundant plants in the garden are New Zealand native pines, cypresses, elms, willows and ferns.

（三）旅游购物 Shopping

麦卢卡蜂蜜：在新西兰有一种叫作麦卢卡的红茶树。每逢初夏，它盛开的花朵会引得成群的蜜蜂来采集花蜜，酿造出独具特色的麦卢卡蜂蜜。麦卢卡蜂蜜中含有一种独特的活性抗菌物质麦卢卡因子（Unique Manuka Factor，UMF），它具有强大而独特的抗菌及抗氧化能力，有摧毁细菌的能力，可以更好地治疗机体创伤、促进伤口自然愈合。在胃肠道调养方面，麦卢卡蜂蜜也有很好的功效。

Manuka honey: In New Zealand there is a black tea tree called Manuka. In early summer, its blooming flowers attract swarms of bees to collect the nectar and produce the distinctive Manuka honey. Manuka honey contains a unique active antimicrobial substance, Unique Manuka Factor (UMF), which has powerful and unique antibacterial and antioxidant properties, with the ability to destroy bacteria, allowing for better healing of organic wounds and promoting natural healing. Manuka honey is also very effective in toning the gastrointestinal tract.

绿贝：绿贝又名"绿壳贻贝"，是新西兰特有的贝类，壳和唇边均为绿色，肉质鲜美、非常多汁，也很易于烹饪。雌性绿贝肉质呈杏黄色，雄性呈奶油色，营养都非常丰富。

Green-lipped Mussel: Green-lipped Mussel, also known as Green Shell Mussel, is a species unique to New Zealand. Its shell and lip edges are distinctly green, and it is renowned for its tender, juicy flesh, making it easy to cook. The meat of the female mussel is apricot-colored, while the male's is cream-colored, and both are highly nutritious.

羊毛制品：新西兰是世界上最大的羊毛出口国，其羊毛质量也备受认可。因此，新西兰出产的羊毛制品非常受欢迎。其中，最具代表性的是新西兰纯羊毛绒毯，柔软舒适且保暖性能出色，在国际市场上备受青睐。

Wool products: New Zealand is the world's largest exporter of wool and the quality of its wool is highly recognized. Therefore, New Zealand wool products are very popular. The most representative of these products is the New Zealand Pure Wool Fleece Blanket, which is soft, cozy and has excellent warmth-keeping properties, and is highly favored in the international market.

佳沛奇异果：佳沛奇异果是一种来自新西兰的水果，也称为猕猴桃。它的产地主要集中在新西兰北岛的东部和南岛的北部地区，这些地方拥有温和的气候和肥沃的土壤，非常适合奇异果的生长。除了含有丰富的维生素 C、A、E 以及钾、镁、纤维素，还含有其他水果比较少见的营养成分——叶酸、胡萝卜素、钙、黄体素、氨基酸、天然肌醇。口感酸甜，有益健康。

Zespri Kiwifruit: Zespri Kiwifruit, also known as kiwi, is a fruit native to New Zealand. It is primarily grown in the eastern regions of New Zealand's North Island and the northern areas of the South Island, where the mild climate and fertile soil provide ideal conditions for its cultivation. Packed with an abundance of Vitamin C, A, and E, as well as potassium, magnesium, and fiber, kiwifruit also contains nutrients that are rare in other fruits, such as folic acid, carotenoids, calcium, lutein, amino acids, and natural inositol. With its sweet and tangy flavor, it is delicious and highly nutritious.

本节习题

1. 请介绍一下新西兰的经济状况和主要物产。
2. 以小组为单位，制作一份新西兰旅游宣传册。
3. 讨论并设计一条新西兰旅游经典线路。
4. 你是如何理解新西兰旅游宣传口号"百分之百纯净保证"（100% Pure New Zealand）的？

扫码获取：入境须知及海关规定

参考文献

Reference

［1］金丽娟.旅游客源国（地区）概况［M］.北京：北京大学出版社，2020.

［2］张金霞，王越.中国主要旅游客源国与目的地国概况［M］.武汉：华中科技大学出版社，2021.

［3］于英.出境旅游目的地概况［M］.北京：中国人民大学出版社，2018.

［4］饶华清.中国出境旅游目的地概况（双语）［M］.北京：中国人民大学出版社，2014.

［5］周凤杰，舒惠芳，宝胜.客源国（地区）概况［M］.2版.北京：机械工业出版社，2017.

［6］杨静达.旅游客源国（地区）概况［M］.2版.大连：大连理工出版社，2014.

［7］https://www.trip.com/blog/musts-for-tourists-in-jakarta/.

［8］https://au.hotels.com/go/indonesia/best-bali-things-to-do.

［9］中国领事服务网 http://cs.mfa.gov.cn/zggmcg/ljmdd/yz.

［10］http://www.australia.cn.

［11］http://newzealand.com/cn/.